PACE

A Practical Guide to the Police
and Criminal Evidence Act 1984

PACE

A Practical Guide to the Police and Criminal Evidence Act 1984

Third Edition

Paul Ozin

HHJ Heather Norton

and

Perry Spivey

OXFORD
UNIVERSITY PRESS

OXFORD
UNIVERSITY PRESS

Great Clarendon Street, Oxford, OX2 6DP,
United Kingdom

Oxford University Press is a department of the University of Oxford.
It furthers the University's objective of excellence in research, scholarship,
and education by publishing worldwide. Oxford is a registered trade mark of
Oxford University Press in the UK and in certain other countries

First Edition published in 2006
Third Edition published in 2013
Impression: 1

Cover photos: © ImageSource / Punchstock; Jorge Delgado / iStockphoto.com;
dra_schwartz / iStockphoto.com; loopa / iStockphoto.com; Up The Resolution
(uptheres) / Alamy; Brand X Pictures / Punchstock; Giacoff / iStockphoto.com;
Dominicg Harrison / Alamy; Jasc / iStockphoto.com; Chris George / Alamy;
photodisc / Punchstock; Simon Bradfield / iStockphoto.com

Published in the United States of America by Oxford University Press
198 Madison Avenue, New York, NY 10016, United States of America

British Library Cataloguing in Publication Data
Data available

Library of Congress Control Number: 2013942363

ISBN 978-0-19-968185-3

Printed in Great Britain by
Clays Ltd, St Ives plc

Foreword

The Police and Criminal Evidence Act 1984 was introduced at a time when public confidence in the police was at an all-time low due to high-profile miscarriages of justice. It was a time when police officers, particularly detectives, were under great pressure to achieve convictions and the ends justified the means. It was a criminal justice system which turned a blind eye to some of the practices or, indeed, often connived in them; a time when there was still a notion that it was the job of the police to control the public.

The Act and its associated Codes of Practice brought accountability and transparency to the criminal justice system, directed how evidence should be lawfully obtained and, more importantly, ensured that suspects and detainees were treated justly and appropriately.

In the 27 years since its introduction, the Act and Codes have seen many changes driven by further legislation, reviews and interpretations. The latest consultation on changes to Codes of Practice A, B, E and F concluded earlier in 2013. The rate of change is difficult to keep up with for any criminal justice professional, but this pragmatic and practical book featuring guidance and examples of the application of the Act and Codes will help all those working in this important area of business to stay current. It will also help to preserve the transparency and accountability delivered by PACE that has brought about an improved public confidence. I hope that the book is a huge success.

Sir Peter Fahy MA QPM
Chief Constable Greater Manchester Police

Preface

Is this, the 3rd edition of *A Practical Guide to PACE*, overdue or premature? In the preface to the 2nd edition, written shortly after the 2010 general election, we queried whether the coalition government would undertake a wholesale reform of PACE (something which had been hinted at by the previous government) or whether there would be further piecemeal amendments.

We now know that, at least for the time being, it is the latter course that is to be followed.

Amended Codes A and D came into effect in March 2011, and following the last consultation published in November 2011, revised versions of Codes C and H came into effect in July 2012; they were followed by a revised Code G in November 2012. Further changes have been made to the Act itself as other legislation has been repealed or brought into effect; sometimes with what might appear to be unseemly haste. A prime example is s63 and s64 of the Act which deal with the retention of DNA samples. Following the ruling of the European Court in *S and Marper v UK* [2008] ECHR 1581, which held that it was a breach of Article 8 to retain fingerprints and DNA samples from those suspected (but not convicted) of offences, a new s64 was provided for by section 14 of the Crime and Security Act 2010. In the event, that section was repealed before it was brought into force and instead, the new regime for the retention of samples will be set out in an amended s63 provided for in the Protection of Freedoms Act 2012 due to come into force in October 2013. We have set out the details of the intended amendments in Chapter 6 in the hope and expectation that the relevant sections of the Protection of Freedoms Act 2012 will come into force as promised rather than be overtaken by a third piece of legislation.

The continually evolving character of PACE, and the Codes in particular, is demonstrated by the use of stop and search powers under s44 of the Terrorism Act. In *Gillan and Quinton v United Kingdom* [2010] ECHR 28, it was held that the safeguards provided by Code A of PACE did not provide adequate protection against the interference with a person's Article 8 rights when a s44 TACT search was carried out. In response, the Home Secretary issued interim guidance on the use of such powers which was subsequently incorporated into the amended Code A issued in March 2011. Since that time, a new Code of Practice has been issued under TACT to which the powers of stop and search when carried out under that Act will be subject; as a result, Code A will no longer apply to such stops and further amendments to Code A are proposed to remove references to TACT stop and search powers altogether.

Where a stop and search is carried out under PACE, as foreshadowed in the preface to the previous edition of this book, changes have been made to reduce the burden of record keeping: there is no longer any requirement to make a record if a person is stopped under s1 but where no search in fact takes place at all; neither is any record required for a 'stop and account'. Where a record is required, far fewer details now need to be recorded, and if the stop and search has resulted in an arrest, the record required is made on the detainee's custody record rather than in a separate document. At the time of writing, the Home Secretary has announced a further consultation to reduce the requirement to keep records still further.

Other important changes can be found in the chapters dealing with entry, search and seizure (chapter 2), arrest (chapter 3), and identification (chapter 6). Chapter 2 contains expanded sections on the high duty of candour in making *ex parte* applications for search warrants, taking account of recent developments in case law, in particular, *R (Tchenguiz) v Director of Serious Fraud Office* [2012] EWHC 2254 (Admin). Chapter 3 has been substantially amended to take account of the extensive revisions to Code G and recent case law, in particular *Hayes v Chief Constable of Merseyside* [2011] EWCA Civ 911, clarifying the meaning and effect of the 'necessity criteria' for making arrests. Code D now distinguishes between the approach to be taken where identification is made by an eyewitness, and where it is evidence of recognition from a film, photo or other image. Given the increasing number of cases (and associated problems caused) where identification is purportedly made via Facebook, it would be unsurprising if Code D was further amended in due course to increase the safeguards in such circumstances. In the meantime, the guidance given in *R v Alexander and McGill* [2012] 177 JP 73 is likely to prove helpful.

To some extent therefore, this new edition may seem overdue; but, as will already be clear from the changes detailed above, PACE does not stand still and more revisions are already on the horizon, particularly as regards the Codes for which the most recent consultation setting out proposed changes to Codes A, B, E, and F, concluded in May 2013. We have, where appropriate, indicated in the course of the book what effect these proposed changes—if they come into effect—will have; but they are not substantial and are largely concerned with terrorism cases. There will no doubt be other changes before the 4th edition is written, some the inevitable result of case law—particularly European. One change that we can confidently assert will take place in the near future is the extension to 17-year-old detainees of the safeguards that apply to juveniles; the result of the ruling in *R (HC) v Secretary of State for the Home Department* that to treat a 17-year-old as an adult is to breach Article 8 and the UN Convention on the Rights of the Child.

What else may or may not change, we shall have to wait and see. Change there will be as governments come and go, and priorities, needs (and budgets) change; but PACE and its Codes of Practice looks likely to continue to hold its place as one of the most significant and influential pieces of legislation for some time yet.

We would like to thank Sir Peter Fahy, MA QPM, for his generous Foreword. In addition, we extend our thanks to Kabir Sondhi, pupil barrister at 23 Essex Street, for his invaluable assistance in researching and updating changes to the Act; and we are, as ever, grateful to Lucy Alexander and her colleagues in the Police Law and Criminology team at Oxford University Press; their tolerance of our continually missed deadlines has been remarkable, as has been their encouragement and confidence that we would ultimately produce a manuscript in time (just) to meet the publication date.

We have endeavoured to state the law as at July 2013; the mistakes are, of course, ours.

Heather Norton
Paul Ozin

24 July 2013

Contents

Contents

Contents

Table of Cases

Table of Legislation

Table of Statutory Instruments

Table of International Conventions

Powers to Stop and Search: Part I

Law and Commentary

Practical Guidance

Law and Commentary

1.1 Introduction

Part I provides the police with powers to stop and search persons and vehicles for stolen or prohibited articles without first exercising their powers of arrest. The Act provides safeguards for those who have been detained for the purposes of a search and imposes duties upon the searching officer, although the recording requirements have been considerably reduced from those that were hitherto in place.

Part I must be read in conjunction with Code A, updated as of 6 March 2011, which expands and explains the main provisions. Of particular importance in Code A are paragraphs 2.2–2.11, which provide important guidance about what can, and more importantly, cannot amount to reasonable grounds for suspicion justifying the use of these powers. As in previous versions of Code A, paragraph A 1.1 emphasizes that the powers must be used 'fairly, responsibly, with respect for people being searched and without unlawful discrimination', however all Codes of Practice now make specific reference to the terms of the Equality Act 2010, and to the duty incumbent upon the police to 'have regard to the need to eliminate unlawful discrimination, harassment and victimization and to take steps to foster good relations'.

Code A also covers searches carried out under a large number of other statutory provisions, principal among which are s 60 of the Criminal Justice and Public Order Act 1994 (now expanded to enable authority to be given to search for any dangerous instrument or offensive weapon used in an incident of serious violence where it is 'expedient' to do so), s 23 of the Misuse of Drugs Act, and s 139B of the Criminal Justice Act (searches carried out on school premises for offensive weapons).

At the time of writing, Code A also applied to searches of vehicles under s 44(1) and persons reasonably suspected to be terrorists under s 43 of the Terrorism Act 2000 (TACT). The Protection of Freedoms Act 2012 will, however, repeal the existing stop and search powers in TACT and replace them with a new s 43A and s 47A, which will be subject not to Code A of PACE but a new Code of Practice for terrorism stop and search powers. References to s 44 and s 43 TACT searches are highly likely therefore to be deleted in the next revision of Code A. Conversely, consultation is ongoing to extend the applicability of Code A to searches of those who are subject to or on whom is served a notice under the Terrorism Prevention and Investigation Measures Act 2011.

1.2 Powers to Stop and Search (Section 1)

1.2.1 Who may be stopped?

Under s 1(2), a constable may detain and search any person or vehicle, or anything which is in or on a vehicle for:

- stolen or prohibited articles (as defined in s 1(7)–(8));
- a bladed article to which s 139 of the Criminal Justice Act relates (s 1(8A)); or
- any firework which a person possesses in contravention of a prohibition imposed by fireworks regulations (s 1(8B)–(8C)).

However, the power to detain and search can only be exercised where the constable has reasonable grounds for suspecting that he will find such articles (s 1(3)). In *Howarth v Commr of Police of the Metropolis* [2012] ACD 119(41) DC, it was held that the test of lawfulness of a search by a police officer under s 1 of PACE was that (i) the constable suspects that he will find stolen or prohibited articles; (ii) the constable must have reasonable grounds for so suspecting; and (iii) he must exercise his discretion to search reasonably.

1.2.2 Who may carry out the stop?

Only a 'constable', that is, a police officer, may carry out a stop and search. There is no requirement for the constable to be in uniform, save where the stop and search is carried out under the provisions of s 60 of the Criminal Justice and Public Order Act 1994, or under s 44 of the Terrorism Act 2000.

It follows from this that a Police Community Support Officer (PCSO) cannot carry out a stop and search under PACE, although they may carry out a 'stop and account'.

1.2.3 Where may the power be exercised?

The power to stop and search is one which can only be exercised in a public place. What is capable of constituting a public place has, in the context of other Acts such as the Road Traffic Act or the Prevention of Crime Act 1953, given rise to a substantial amount of case law with the courts' conclusions influenced by the purposes for which a person sought or was granted permission to enter a particular place and whether a place was open to the general public or restricted to a specified class of people. Section 1(1) does away with the need to make judgments on such considerations insofar as s 1 stop and search powers are concerned, as it specifies that a constable may exercise the power:

(a) in any place to which at the time when he proposes to exercise the power the public, or any section of the public has access on payment or otherwise, as of right or by virtue of express or implied permission; or,

(b) in any place to which people have ready access at the time when he proposes to exercise the power but which is not a dwelling.

'Dwelling' extends to land occupied with and used for the purpose of a dwelling. Accordingly, a constable could not carry out a search, whether of a person or a vehicle, in the garden or driveway of a private house. There is an exception to this prohibition, however, and that is where the officer has reasonable grounds to believe that the person or (in the case of a proposed search of a vehicle) the person in charge of the vehicle, does not reside in the dwelling, and that the person or vehicle is not on the land with the express or implied permission of the person who does (s 1(4)–(5)).

1.2.4 **What are 'stolen or prohibited articles'?**

These are set out in s 1(7)–(9). They are:

- an offensive weapon—ie any article made or adapted for use for causing injury to persons, or intended by the person having it with him for such use by him or by some other person;
- an article made or adapted for use or intended to be used in the course of:
  - burglary,
  - theft,
  - taking a motor vehicle or other conveyance without authority,
  - fraud,
  - destroying or damaging property.

Under s 1(8A) an officer may also search for an article to which s 139 of the Criminal Justice Act 1988 applies, that is:

- a bladed article.

And under s 1(8B) and (8C):

- a firework (where possessed in contravention of a prohibition imposed by firework regulations).

1.2.5 **What are 'reasonable grounds' for suspicion?**

Whether reasonable grounds for suspicion exist depends on the circumstances in each situation. There must be an objective basis for the suspicion although in each case, both objective and subjective factors are likely to be relevant. The officer must in fact himself suspect that stolen or prohibited articles will be found on the person or in the vehicle; simply being told by a superior officer to stop and search an individual will not of itself suffice—see *O'Hara v Chief Constable of the RUC* [1997] AC 286 (applied in *Metropolitan Police Commr v Raissi* [2008] EWCA Civ 1237)—but there must also be an objective reason or reasons upon which that suspicion is based which can arise from information supplied by another, even when that information proves to be false. In *Samuels v Metropolitan Police Commr* CCRTF 98/0410/2, 3 March 1999, CA, the court held that whether a suspicion is reasonable, 'has to be determined as an objective matter from the information available to the officer'. The officer will need to be clear about the reasons for the stop and able to justify it; he must tell the individual at the time of the stop and prior to the search the grounds for the exercise of the power, and in circumstances in which a record is required to be made of the search, will have to detail the grounds in writing.

Code A 2.2–2.6 provides comprehensive guidance on what would or would not suffice to constitute an objective basis. Under the Code 'objective' means based on relevant facts, information, or intelligence. 'Relevant facts' could include a person's behaviour and/or the locality in which that behaviour is witnessed, for example a person seen late at night close to an area where a burglary has taken place apparently trying to conceal an item similar in size or general description to the type of item stolen in that burglary. Information or intelligence may be specific to an individual or to a specified group; Code A 2.6 provides the example of a gang known to habitually carry knives or other unlawful weapons. Code A 2.2, however, states that: '[r]easonable suspicion cannot be based on generalizations or stereotypical images of certain groups or categories of people as more likely to be involved in criminal activity'. A person's race, age, gender, appearance, antecedent history, or religion cannot therefore provide an objective basis for reasonable suspicion, whether alone or in combination with any other factor unless linked to other reliable information or intelligence—for example, where the appearance of the person stopped matches the description of a suspected offender.

In the context of a group, where intelligence, past experience, or other factors give rise to a reasonable suspicion that stolen or prohibited articles will be found on one or more group members, it is not essential for the searching officer to suspect that each and every individual member of the group is carrying such items for a search of all the group members to be lawful (*Howarth v Commissioner of Police of the Metropolis* [2012] ACD 119(41) DC; *Tuthill v DPP* [2012] ACD 77(26) DC).

1.2.6 **Can reasonable grounds be established through questioning?**

All officers routinely have contact with and speak to members of the public in the normal exercise of their duties. The Act is not intended to prevent what is a desirable and useful everyday occurrence. If, in the course of such contact, reasonable grounds for suspicion emerge, even though none had existed before, the officer may exercise his powers to detain and search that person under this part of the Act. Moreover, an officer who has reasonable grounds for suspicion to stop and search an individual may, prior to carrying out that search, ask questions about that person's behaviour, presence, or other factors that gave rise to the grounds for suspicion. What is not permitted, however, is the questioning of a person in order to find reasonable grounds. The power conferred on officers is one of stop and search, not stop and question. Accordingly, there is no power to detain a person for questioning under this part of the Act if no reasonable grounds exist to suspect that he is in possession of a stolen or prohibited article, and the person must be allowed to leave at will. Neither can reasonable grounds be provided retrospectively by a person's subsequent behaviour. In *Samuels v Metropolitan Police Commr* CCRTF 98/0410/2, March 3 1999, CA, the police wanted to stop and search Samuels, a black man in a high-risk burglary area who looked suspicious. Samuels was asked where he was going but he refused to tell them (although he was in fact on his way home). The police then asked to see his hands, but he refused and walked away. The police then tried to forcibly detain and search him. Finding that no reasonable grounds for suspicion existed prior to the stop, the court held that the fact that Samuels had then walked away could not turn an unreasonable suspicion into a reasonable one.

1.2.7 **Can a person voluntarily consent to a search?**

Code A 1.5 makes it clear that even where a person is prepared to submit to a search, an officer must not carry out a search unless there is a legal power to do so; therefore, if no reasonable grounds exist to carry out a search of a person under this part of the Act then no search may be carried out. Moreover, where a legal power does exist, the person may only be searched in accordance with the relevant provisions and the Code; a person cannot 'volunteer' to circumvent the Act or Codes. The only exception, set out in this part of the code, applies to persons entering sports grounds or other premises where it is a condition of entry that they should agree to a search being carried out.

1.3 **Search Safeguards (Section 2)**

1.3.1 **Does an officer *have* to search a person or vehicle stopped under section 1?**

An officer who detains a person or vehicle, whether under s 1 of Part 1 of the Act, or in pursuance of any other power to search a person or vehicle without first making an arrest, need not carry out such a search if it appears that a search is no longer required or is impracticable (s 2(1)).

A person who has been lawfully detained may be asked questions by the officer about the circumstances which have given rise to the reasonable suspicion that he may be in possession of a stolen or prohibited article. If, as a result of that questioning, or for any other reason, there cease to be reasonable grounds for such suspicion then the legal basis for the search has been lost. The original detention is not thereby rendered unlawful in such circumstances (Code A, Note 3), but no search can take place and the person detained must be informed that he is free to leave (Code A 2.10). In these circumstances, there is no longer any requirement to make a record of the stop (Code A 4.7).

1.3.2 **What are the officer's duties prior to undertaking a search?**

Under s 2(2), if the officer is not in uniform, he must produce documentary evidence to show that he is a constable, and, whether in uniform or not, must inform the person that he is being detained for the purpose of a search and notify the appropriate person of:

- the officer's name (or warrant number if the officer reasonably believes that giving his name might put him in danger), and the name of the police station to which he is attached;
- the object of the proposed search;
- the grounds for the proposed search;
- his entitlement to a copy of the record of the search, unless it appears to the officer that it will not be practicable for such a record to be made, and how he can obtain such a copy (s 2(3); s 3(7), (8)).

In giving this information, the appropriate person must be given a clear explanation of the powers that are being exercised, the object of the search in terms of the article(s) for which there is a power to search, and the grounds for the reasonable suspicion that has given rise to the stop and search (Code A 3.8).

Section 2(2)(b) makes it clear that the officer 'shall not' commence a search (other than that of an unattended vehicle) before such information has been given. Failure to comply with the requirements of s 2(2) and (3) may lead to evidence obtained as a result of the search being excluded: see *R v Bristol* [2007] EWCA Crim 3214 (searching officer, who was known to the person stopped, failed to identify himself or his station. The Court of Appeal held that however technical the error, a failure to comply with the requirements of s 2(3) rendered a subsequent search unlawful.) Applied in *Michaels v Highbury Corner Magistrates Court* [2009] EWHC 2928 (Admin).

If it appears that the appropriate person may not understand what is being said, for example, because of a language barrier or through disability, the officer must take reasonable steps to bring to his attention information about his rights and the powers to be exercised (Code A 3.11). This may include seeking the help of a person able to act as an interpreter.

The 'appropriate person' referred to here is the person to be searched, or in the case of a search of a vehicle, the person in charge of that vehicle (s 2(5)).

Only an officer in uniform may stop a vehicle (Code A 3.9).

1.3.3 Does an officer have any duties in respect of a search of an unattended vehicle?

Where the search is of an unattended vehicle, the officer must leave a notice:

- stating that he has searched it;
- giving the name of the police station to which he is attached;
- stating that any application for compensation for any damage caused may be made to that police station;
- detailing the entitlement to a copy of the search record (if any was made) (s 2(6)).

The notice should be left inside the vehicle unless it is not reasonably practical to do so without damaging the vehicle (s 2(7)).

1.3.4 **For how long may a person or vehicle be detained for the purposes of a search?**

A person or vehicle may only be detained for the minimum amount of time reasonably necessary for the search to be carried out (s 2(8)). What is reasonable will depend on the circumstances pertaining to that particular stop and search and the extent and degree of thoroughness required. For example, where a person has been seen trying to conceal an item in a coat pocket, then in the absence of any reasonable grounds for suspicion that there are other items concealed elsewhere, the search should be confined to that pocket (Code A 3.3) and would (in those particular circumstances) be very brief indeed.

1.3.5 **Where should the search be conducted?**

The search must be carried out at or near the place where the person or vehicle was first detained (Code A 3.4). Code A 3.1 states that any search must be carried out 'with courtesy, consideration and respect' with every reasonable effort made to minimize embarrassment for the person being searched. Depending upon the nature and degree of the search, this may necessitate moving to a different area from that in which the person was originally detained—for example, somewhere quieter or more private. Such a place, whether a police station or otherwise, must be located nearby and within a reasonable travelling distance (whether by car or on foot) (Note 6).

1.3.6 **Can the officer require the removal of clothing to facilitate the search?**

Under s 2(9) an officer exercising powers under ss 1 and 2 can only require the person detained to remove an outer coat, jacket, or gloves in public, although a person may be asked to voluntarily remove other items of clothing. A search in public of clothing which has not been removed must be restricted to a superficial examination of the person's outer clothing (Code A 3.5). Where a more thorough search extending beyond that of the outer clothing is required, that search must be conducted out of public view (Note 6). 'Public view' means both actual and potential public view; therefore a street, albeit deserted, would nevertheless be classed as a place within the public view. A search involving the removal of more than the outer clothing can only be conducted by an officer of the same sex as the person being searched and may not take place in the presence of anyone of the opposite sex unless the person specifically requests it (Code A 3.6). A new Annex F to Code C deals with the approach to be taken towards transsexual or transvestite persons. Annex F 3 sets out the legal position: a person's gender is that registered at birth or, if the person possesses a gender recognition certificate issued under the Gender Recognition Act 2004, the acquired gender. In the absence of a gender recognition certificate, and where there is doubt as to the person's gender, the person should be asked what gender they consider themselves to be and, if they express a preference to be dealt with as a particular gender, dealt with in that way if it is appropriate to do so.

Searches involving the exposure of intimate parts of the body may only be carried out at a nearby police station or other place out of public view, but not in a police van (Code A 3.7). It should be noted, however, that an intimate search (that is a search of the body orifices other than the mouth) cannot be carried out under the stop and search provisions, and that any search involving the removal of more than outer clothing (including shoes and socks) is regarded as a strip search and must therefore be carried out in accordance with the provisions of paragraph 11 of Annex A to Code C.

1.4 Search Records (Section 3)

1.4.1 When must a record of a search be made?

The recording requirements have substantially altered in recent years with different requirements depending upon whether or not the search has resulted in an arrest or not.

Where a search has been carried out of a person or a vehicle under s 2(1) of the Act, the searching officer must make a written record of the search unless it is not practicable to do so. Where and when that record has to be made depends upon whether or not the search resulted in an arrest. Where the search has resulted in an arrest, the search record should be made as part of the person's custody record and it is the responsibility of the officer who has conducted the search to ensure that this is done (Code A 4.2B). In any other case, the record must be made on the spot, or if that is not practicable, as soon as is practicable after the search. The emphasis is, however, firmly on contemporaneity; Code A 4.1 makes it clear that the record must be completed at the time of the search 'unless there are exceptional circumstances that would make this wholly impracticable'; examples provided by the Code are where there is a public disorder at the time, or the officer's presence is urgently needed elsewhere.

1.4.2 What must the search record contain?

The information required to be included within the search record is set out at s 3(6) and Code A 4.3. The record must contain the following information:

- the object of the search—s 3(6)(a)(i);
- the grounds for making it—s 3(6)(a)(ii);
- the date and time when it was made—s 3(6)(a)(iii);
- the place where it was made—s 3(6)(a)(iv);
- except in the case of a search of an unattended vehicle, the ethnic origins of the person searched or the person in charge of the vehicle searched (as the case may be)—s 3(6)(a)(v). Ethnic origin can be self-defined or, if different, that perceived by the officer;
- the identity of the constable who carried out the search—s 3(6)(a)(vi).

Somewhat oddly, it may be thought, there is no longer any requirement to record whether anything (and if so what) was found, or whether any injury to a person or damage to property resulted from the search. Neither is there any longer a requirement to record the name, address, and date of birth of the person searched or in charge of a vehicle which is searched and the person is under no obligation to provide such information (Code A 4.3A).

Code A 4.3(b) makes clear that the recording requirements of date, time, and place relate to the date, time, and place of the search.

As previously stated, where a person is detained for the purposes of a search but where in the event no search is in fact carried out, a record is no longer required (Code A 4.7).

Where the search is of an unattended vehicle (or anything in or on it), an officer must leave a notice recording that it has been searched and including the name of the police station to which the searching officer is attached, and explaining where a copy of the search record may be obtained or electronic copy accessed, and any application for compensation directed. Where practicable, the vehicle must be left secure (Code A 4.8–4.10).

1.4.3 When must a record be provided?

Where a search record has been made, the person searched or owner of or person in charge of a vehicle that has been searched is entitled on request to a copy of that record within three months of the date of search.

Where a record has been made at the time, Code A 4.2 specifies that the person must be asked if they want a copy and, if they do, either a copy of the record or a receipt explaining in sufficient detail how they can obtain a copy or access to an electronic copy of the record must be provided immediately unless the officer is called to an incident of higher priority.

When the search is of an unattended vehicle (or anything in or on it), an officer must leave a notice recording that it has been searched, including the name of the police station to which the searching officer is attached, and explaining where a copy of the search record may be obtained, or an electronic copy accessed, and where any application for compensation should be directed. Where practicable, the vehicle must be left secure (Code A 4.8–4.10).

1.5 **Stop and Account**

Although the only power (short of arrest) to detain a person is provided where the requirements for a stop and search are fulfilled, as already noted there may be other circumstances where the police and/or police community support officers (PCSOS) do have occasion to stop a person and ask them to account for their presence in a particular place, their behaviour, or the objects in their possession.

1.5.1 **What record must be made of a Stop and Account?**

Prior to 1 January 2009, records were required to be kept of all encounters in which a person was requested to account for their actions, behaviour, presence, or possession of anything with a similar level of detail to that required in a stop and search record. Since that time, the burden has been reduced. Initially, fewer details were required and now under the latest version of Code A, the national requirement to make a record of an encounter has been removed altogether, although any person who is asked to account for themselves should on request be given information about how they can report any dissatisfaction about how they have been treated (Note 22A).

Notwithstanding the removal of any requirement to record encounters, forces have a discretion whether to direct officers to record the self-defined ethnicity of persons stopped but who are not searched where local concerns make it necessary to monitor any disproportionality (Note 22B).

1.6 **Road Checks (Section 4)**

1.6.1 **What is the purpose of a road check?**

For the period of a road check, all vehicles or classes of vehicles selected by any criteria may be stopped in the locality in which the road check is being conducted, in order to ascertain whether the vehicle is carrying:

- a person who has committed an offence (other than a road traffic or vehicle excise offence), where the authorizing officer has reasonable grounds to believe that the offence is an indictable offence, and that the person is, or is about to be, in the locality of the proposed road check (s 4(1)(a), s 4(4)(a));
- a person who is witness to such an offence (s 4(1)(b), s 4(4)(b));
- a person who is intending to commit such an offence where the authorizing officer has reasonable grounds for suspecting that that person is in or about to be in the locality of the proposed road check (s 4(1)(c), s 4(4)(c));
- a person who is unlawfully at large where the authorizing officer has reasonable grounds for suspecting that that person is, or is about to be, in the locality of the road check (s 4(1)(d), s 4(4)(d)).

11

1.6.2 **Who can authorize a road check?**

Subject to one exception, a road check can only be carried out if it is authorized in writing by an officer of the rank of superintendent or above. The exception is where a road check is required as a matter of urgency for one of the reasons previously set out (s 4(5)). Then, an officer below the rank of superintendent may authorize a road check provided that, as soon as it is practicable to do so, he makes a written record of the time at which he has given the authorization and causes an officer of the rank of superintendent or above to be informed that it has been given (s 4(6), (7)). The officer so informed may either:

- authorize the road check to continue in writing, or if he does not so authorize it,
- record in writing the fact that the road check took place and the purpose for which it took place (s 4(8), (9)).

1.6.3 **What must the authorization contain?**

The authorization must detail:

- the name of the officer giving the authorization (s 4(13)(a));
- the purpose of the road check, including specifying the relevant indictable offence (s 4(13)(b), s 4(14));
- the locality in which vehicles are to be stopped—(s 4(10), s 4(13)(c)).

Where the authorization is given by an officer of the rank of superintendent or above, the authorization shall in addition:

- specify the duration of the road check (not to exceed 7 days) (s 4(11)(a));
- direct whether the road check is to be continuous or to be conducted at specified times (s 4(11)(b)).

1.6.4 **Can the period of authorization be extended or renewed?**

Where it appears to an officer of the rank of superintendent or above that the period of the road check ought to extend beyond that originally authorized, he may in writing specify further periods not exceeding seven days during which it may continue (s 4(12)).

1.6.5 **What are the safeguards?**

The person in charge of a vehicle at the time it was stopped is entitled to obtain a written statement of the purposes of the road check on request where that request is made within 12 months of the day upon which the vehicle was stopped (s 4(15)).

1.7 **Additional Powers of Stop and Search**

Stop and search powers can be found in numerous other pieces of legislation, however under Code A 2.1, Code A specifically applies to powers of stop and search which:

- require reasonable grounds for suspicion before they can be exercised; that articles unlawfully obtained or possessed are being carried, or (under s 43 of the Terrorism Act 2000), that a person is a terrorist;
- are authorized under s 60 of the Criminal Justice and Public Order Act 1994;
- are authorized under s 44(1) of the Terrorism Act 2000 (these searches will be covered by a new Code of Practice issued under TACT when the Protection of Freedoms Act 2012 is fully in force);
- enable the search of a person who has not been arrested in the exercise of a power to search premises.

Code A 2.27 also extends the provisions of Code A to searches conducted in school premises under s 139B of the Criminal Justice Act 1998 for bladed or pointed articles or offensive weapons, and to searches of persons found on premises being searched under a warrant issued under the Misuse of Drugs Act 1971 where the warrant so provides.

Section 6(1) provides constables employed by statutory undertakers with powers to stop and search.

1.7.1 **Powers attaching to statutory undertakers**

By s 6(1) a constable employed by statutory undertakers (persons authorized by any enactment to carry on any railway, light railway, road transport, water transport, canal, inland navigation, dock, or harbour undertakings) is empowered to stop, detain, and search any vehicle before it leaves a goods area (area used wholly or mainly for the storage or handling of goods) included in the premises of the statutory undertakers. By definition, the power can be exercised in places to which the public do not normally have access and no grounds for reasonable suspicion are required. This extension of powers applies only to vehicles and not to persons.

1.7.2 **Powers under section 60 of the Criminal Justice and Public Order Act 1994**

An officer of the rank of inspector or above may give written authorization for a constable in uniform to stop and search where the authorizing officer reasonably believes:

- that incidents involving serious violence may take place in any locality in the officer's police area, and it is expedient to use these powers to prevent their occurrence;

- that persons are carrying dangerous instruments or offensive weapons without good reason in any locality in the officer's police area; or
- that an incident involving serious violence has taken place in the officer's police area, a dangerous instrument or offensive weapon used in the incident is being carried by a person in any locality in that area, and it is expedient to use these powers to find that instrument or weapon (Code A 2.12).

Where the authorization has been given by an inspector, he must inform an officer of or above the rank of superintendent as soon as practicable (Code A 2.14).

These powers, which are separate from and additional to the normal powers that exist under the stop and search provisions, exist to prevent serious violence or the carrying of weapons which might lead to serious injury. They are not intended to be used to deal with routine crime problems. Code A 2.14A emphasizes the need for an objective basis for the exercise of these powers, which must not be used as a means of stopping and searching persons or vehicles for reasons unconnected with the purpose of the authorization.

The authorization must specify the grounds upon which it was given, the locality in which the powers may be exercised, and the period of time for which they are in force. That period shall be no longer than appears reasonably necessary to prevent or deal with the risk of violence or carrying of weapons, or to find a dangerous instrument or offensive weapon that has been used, and shall in any event not exceed 24 hours (Code A 2.13). An officer of the rank of superintendent or above may, in writing, extend the period of authorization by a further 24 hours but may do so only once. Further periods will require a separate authorization (Code A, Note 12).

The locality specified in the authorization must similarly be restricted to an area no wider than that believed necessary for the proper exercise of the powers. If the area straddles different police force areas, an authorization must be obtained from an officer in each one (Code A, Note 13).

Under Code A 2.14B, the driver of a vehicle stopped or a person searched under s 60 is entitled to a written statement to that effect if they apply within 12 months from the day of the stop or search; such a statement may form part of a search record or be supplied as a separate record. Note the differing timescale within which such an application may be made from the much narrower window of three months that applies to stop and search records.

1.7.3 Powers under section 60AA of the Criminal Justice and Public Order Act 1994

An officer of the rank of inspector or above may in writing authorize the removal and seizure of face coverings worn or intended to be worn wholly or mainly to conceal someone's identity, where the authorizing officer has reasonable grounds to believe that activities may occur in the officer's police area that are likely to involve the commission of offences, and it is expedient to use these powers to prevent or control such activities. The authorization must specify the grounds upon which it has been made, the locality in which the powers may be exercised, and the period of time for which they are in force. The period specified must be for no longer than reasonably necessary to prevent the commission of offences and may in any event not exceed 24 hours. An officer of the rank of superintendent or above may in writing extend the period by a further 24 hours.

There is no power to stop and search for disguises, although if an authorization under this section or s 60 is in force, and an item is found when exercising a search for something else (eg a weapon), the officer may seize it if he reasonably believes it is intended to be used to conceal someone's identity.

Note 4 reminds of the need for caution to be applied where the head or face covering may be worn for religious reasons. Such an item should be removed out of public view and, where practicable, out of the sight of anyone of the opposite sex. Even so, an officer cannot order the removal of the item unless there is reason to believe that the item is being worn wholly or in part in order to disguise identity and not merely because it in fact does so.

Code A applies to searches under this power. See especially Code A 2.15–2.18.

1.7.4 Searches under s 44 of the Terrorism Act 2000

As previously noted, s 59 of the Protection of Freedoms Act 2012 will, when in force, repeal the stop and search powers in ss 44 to 47 TACT and replace them with a new s 47A; a new s 43A will cater for the stop and search of vehicles. The new powers under s 47A, s 43A, as well as the existing s 43 power, will be subject not to Code A but to a new Code of Practice for terrorism stop and search powers. Pending these changes the law is as now set out:

Section 44 TACT provides that where expedient for the prevention of terrorism, an officer of the rank of assistant chief constable or above may give authority providing powers for a constable or Community Support Officer in uniform to:

• stop and search any vehicle, its driver, any passenger, and anything in or on the vehicle or carried by the driver or any passenger; and/or
• stop and search any pedestrian and anything carried by the pedestrian (Code A 19)

for the purpose of searching for articles that could be used in connection with terrorism.

The primary distinction between stop and search powers exercised under s 44 TACT, and those carried out under s 1 PACE, is that there is no requirement, for reasonable grounds for suspicion (whether about the individual stopped or articles that he might be carrying) prior to the search. Consequently, s 44 presented what has been described as 'an extremely wide power to intrude on the privacy of members of the public' and amounts to an interference with the person's Art 8 rights of privacy.

The lawfulness of s 44 was considered by the European Court of Human Rights in *Gillan and Quinton v United Kingdom* [2010] ECHR 28. Gillan and Quinton, who were a photographer and journalist, had been searched under s 44 TACT when attending an arms fair. The European Court found that the use of s 44 was a clear interference with a person's Art 8 rights, and that the safeguards contained within Code A of PACE did not provide adequate protection against that interference being applied in an arbitrary manner as they only governed the *manner* in which the search was carried out and did not restrict the officer's decision to stop and search. The broad discretion afforded to an officer who required neither objective nor subjective grounds for suspicion before carrying out a stop and search led to a clear risk of arbitrariness. Accordingly, they found that the powers of authorization, and confirmation as well as those of stop and search under s 44 TACT were neither sufficiently circumscribed nor subject to adequate legal safeguards against abuse, were not in accordance with the law and violated Art 8.

As a result of this ruling, interim guidelines were introduced by the Home Secretary on 8 July 2010. These interim guidelines have been incorporated into Code A and are set out at Code A 2.18A. Authorizations under s 44(1) TACT may now only be given and confirmed in respect of searches of vehicles and anything in or on vehicles, but not searches of drivers, passengers, or anything being carried by a driver or passenger, and where such searches are considered to be necessary (taking account of all the circumstances) for the prevention of acts of terrorism.

A number of points should be noted. Firstly, authorizations to search individuals or anything carried by a driver or passenger in a vehicle can no longer be given under either s 44(1) or (2) of TACT; the police can only carry out such a search under s 43 where a person is reasonably suspected of being a terrorist. Secondly, although under s 44(3) of TACT an authorization can be given where the authorizing officer considers it expedient to do so, this is superseded by Code A 2.18A(i) which imports a (stricter) test of necessity. Code A 2.18A(ii) also supersedes s 45(1)(b) TACT by importing a reasonable suspicion test prior to the search of a vehicle under s 44(1) (see Code A 2.24(b)).

An authority under s 44(1) TACT may only be given by an officer of at least the rank of assistant chief constable to a constable in uniform or by a Chief Officer to a Community Support Officer on duty and in uniform.

Code A 2.2 to 2.11 apply to the stop and search of vehicles under s 44(1) TACT.

Note that although ss 43 and 44(1) of TACT only confer powers to search for articles which could be used for terrorist purposes, this would not prevent an officer from carrying out a search under other stop and search powers (eg under ss 1 and 2 PACE) if in the course of exercising those powers the officer had reasonable grounds for suspicion to justify such a search.

1.7.5 **Powers to search in the exercise of a power to search premises**

A person not under arrest may be searched in the course of:

- a search of school premises under s 139B of the Criminal Justice Act 1988 for any bladed or pointed articles or offensive weapons (Code A 2.27(a)); or
- a search authorized by a warrant issued under s 23(3) of the Misuse of Drugs Act 1971 to search premises and persons found on those premises for drugs or documents (Code A 2.27(b)); or
- a search authorized by warrant or order under paragraph 1, 3, or 11 of Schedule 5 to the Terrorism Act 2000 to search premises and any person found there for material likely to be of substantial value to a terrorist investigation (Code A 2.27(c)).

There is no requirement in any of these cases for specific grounds to suspect that the person to be searched is in possession of an item for which there is an existing power to search (Code A 2.29), but before exercising a power under s 139B of the Criminal Justice Act 1988, the constable must have reasonable grounds to believe (likely to be amended from a test of reasonable belief to reasonable suspicion when Code A is next revised) that an offence under s 139A of the same Act (having a bladed or pointed article or an offensive weapon on school premises) has been or is being committed; and a warrant to search premises and persons under s 23(3) of the Misuse of Drugs Act 1971 can only be issued if there are reasonable grounds to suspect that controlled drugs (or other specified items) are in the possession of a person on the premises.

Practical Guidance

1.8 **Case Study 1 (Section 1)**

PC Brown is on foot patrol at 3am in a suburban street. He sees a black youth wearing a hoodie with the hood up, carrying what appears to be an electrical item that is partially hidden under the youth's jacket. PC Brown asks the youth to stop, but he ignores him and quickens his step. PC Brown follows, but before he can reach him the youth turns into the garden of a private house.

Did PC Brown have the power to carry out a search under section 1 of PACE when he first saw the youth in the street?

In accordance with s 1 PACE, PC Brown has the power to detain and search a person for stolen or prohibited articles provided:

(a) he is in a place to which the public have access, or to which people have ready access at the time he proposes to exercise the power, and

(b) he has reasonable grounds for suspecting that he will find such items.

When PC Brown first saw the youth, on the street he was clearly in a place to which the public had access. Considering Code A 2.3, an objective assessment of the circumstances in which PC Brown sees the youth—during the early hours of the morning; carrying what appears to be an electrical item under his jacket—would give rise to a reasonable suspicion that that item was stolen. A search under section 1 of PACE at this point would therefore have been justifiable.

Suppose the circumstances were the same save that the youth was not obviously carrying or concealing anything; would PC Brown have had reasonable grounds for suspicion to justify a stop and search?

The stop and search powers are ones that must be used, 'fairly, responsibly, with respect for people being searched and without unlawful discrimination'. Code A 2.2 makes it absolutely clear that reasonable grounds for suspicion must be founded on an objective basis and can never be based simply on personal factors, generalizations, or stereotypical images of certain people as more likely to be involved in criminal activity. In this case, the fact that the person is young, black, and wearing a hoodie is clearly wholly insufficient to found an objective basis for reasonable suspicion. The mere fact that the youth is out on the streets at 3am is highly unlikely in itself to allow the officer to form reasonable grounds to detain him. Had he attempted to do so, the youth would have been entitled to refuse to stay and to walk away. That being so, his actions of ignoring the officer and quickening his step cannot provide retrospective grounds for a search—see *Samuels v Metropolitan Police Commissioner*.

Assuming that reasonable grounds for suspicion do exist, if PC Brown had caught up with the youth in the driveway before he reached the house, would there be a power to search under section 1 of PACE?

Although at this point the youth is not in a place where the public have access as of right, he is in a place where there is ready access. The garden and driveway are, however, occupied by or used for the purposes of a dwelling. In accordance with s 1(4) PACE, PC Brown only has a power to search in this situation if he has reasonable grounds to believe the person does not reside in the house and is not there with the express or implied permission of the occupier. PC Brown would need to make enquires to ensure that he can justify a belief that the youth does not reside at the premises and is there without the occupier's consent; the simplest way of dealing with that question in the scenario presented would be to ask the youth questions, and/or check with the occupant of the house. Other means of enquiry could be via a PNC check, local systems check, or voters check.

Clearly, if the youth does reside at the house this could no doubt be readily established. Once the youth reaches the sanctuary of his own front garden he is no longer susceptible to a search under s 1. Had this been a case where the youth had simply walked into the garden of a stranger's house then the ready access condition of s 1(b) would have applied and would have enabled PC Brown lawfully to carry out a search.

PC Brown is able to establish that the youth has no connection with the dwelling house. To what extent is he able to search the youth?

Code A 3.3 makes it clear that the length of time for which a person can be detained must be reasonable and kept to a minimum and that the extent of the search depends upon what is suspected of being carried. At this stage, PC Brown's suspicions are limited to one item that he has seen, apparently concealed, beneath the youth's hoodie. Having given the youth the information about the reasons for the search as set out in Code A 3.8, the search should in this case be limited to that item of clothing.

What record must PC Brown make of the search?

The type of record to be made will depend upon whether the youth is arrested or not. If he is not arrested, a record of the search should be made on the spot unless this is not practicable. If he is arrested, the record should form part of the custody record. In either case, the record must comply with s 3(6) and Code A 4.3. Had PC Brown's suspicions been allayed by questioning the youth such that the need to search was eliminated, no record would have been required.

1.9 Case Study 2 (Section 1)

PC Brown, a male officer, is on patrol in a busy high street when he receives information over his personal radio that a female is attempting to use a stolen credit card. He is given a full description of the suspect. PC Brown begins to make his way to the store and is then further informed that the female had become suspicious and has now left with the credit card. As PC Brown approaches the location he sees a female who exactly matches the description of the suspect walk out of the store in question.

Does PC Brown have reasonable grounds to search the female suspect under section 1 of PACE?

In this scenario, the officer has a full description of the suspect and the female seen leaving the store exactly matches that description. The offence occurred only a few minutes before and it is known that the suspect retained possession of the credit card. An objective assessment can only lead to the conclusion that there are reasonable grounds to suspect that the female may be carrying a stolen credit card. The female suspect is in a public place and PC Brown would therefore be able to exercise the power under s 1.

Who should carry out the search?

In this case the suspected stolen article could easily be concealed and a more thorough search would be justified. As such a search would invariably involve the removal of more than outer jacket, coat, gloves, and footwear, the search should be carried out by an officer of the same sex as the suspect—Code A 3.6. Whilst not required for less intrusive searches, it is good practice whenever possible to use an officer of the same sex to carry out the search.

Where should the search be carried out?

The search must be carried out where the suspect was first detained or 'nearby'. As this case will involve the removal of more than the outer clothing, the search must be carried out away from public view. Note 6 to Code A states that the place of search should be located within a reasonable travelling distance. Moving a person a few yards to a more private place such as the police van, or, in the circumstances of this example, a private office in the store, would not be unreasonable.

How should the search be conducted?

The nature of the circumstances and the item sought will determine the extent to which the search should be carried out. In this case, a credit card can be easily concealed and a much more thorough search would be justified.

1.10 Case Study 3 (Section 1)

Derek snatches the handbag of an elderly victim and runs off down the High Street. An accurate description of Derek and the property stolen is quickly circulated and John, a recently recruited PCSO who is nearby, receives the information on his personal radio. Moments later, John sees Derek running towards him and notices that he fits the description of the suspect of a recent theft. John stops Derek and requires him to submit to a search; under his jacket he finds a lady's purse containing cash and credit cards. John then asks Derek for his name and address and is informed by Derek that he lives rough, and has no permanent home. Although Derek is compliant and makes no effort to leave, John informs him that he is being arrested for theft and requests transport to take him and his prisoner to the police station. John is informed by radio that an officer will be with him shortly and a few moments later PC Cobo arrives at the scene. PC Cobo is unsure of the powers held by PCSOs and decides to simply take John and Derek to the station where he explains the circumstances to the custody officer, PS Jones. PS Jones is also unsure of the powers of PCSOs and seeks advice from Inspector Orton.

Was John entitled to carry out a stop and search?

Inspector Orton should advise PS Jones that PCSOs have limited powers and that these do not extend to the power to search under s 1 PACE; this power is limited to constables. Had John been a constable then the circumstances were such that a search under s 1 could be justified. As a PCSO, however, John had no power to require Derek to submit to a search.

Because John had reasonable grounds to believe that Derek had committed a relevant offence (loss of property), he had good reason to carry out a 'stop and account' and was entitled to ask Derek to provide his name and address.

Was John entitled to arrest Derek?

As John had grounds to suspect that Derek had committed a relevant offence, and as Derek had failed to comply with the requirement to provide details of his name and address, John could have required Derek to remain with him for a period of up to 30 minutes pending the arrival of a police officer and could have used reasonable force to detain Derek for this purpose if necessary. John had no power, however, to arrest Derek. Neither is it likely that John would be able to rely on the 'citizen's power' of arrest provided for by s 24A PACE; whilst theft is an indictable offence and therefore the first condition of s 24A is met, John would also have to show that it appeared to him that it was not reasonably practicable for a constable to make the arrest instead. In view of the compliant nature of Derek and the imminent arrival of PC Cobo it is unlikely that this pre-condition could be made out. The arrest of Derek by John was therefore unlawful.

What action should PC Cobo have carried out?

When PC Cobo arrived, John should have outlined the facts to him. PC Cobo would then have the responsibility of deciding on any further action. One option would be to carry out a s 1 search. PC Cobo must decide for himself whether there are reasonable grounds to justify a search, but it is likely in this case that the information provided by John together with the original information provided over the radio about the suspect would afford reasonable grounds for suspicion. PC Cobo could then have carried out the search and arrested Derek on suspicion of theft.

What are likely to be the effects of an unlawful search and arrest?

Inspector Orton should advise PS Jones that PC Cobo should arrest Derek for theft and caution him without delay. The full circumstances should be recorded in the custody record. The purse seized by John in what was in fact an unlawful search is still evidence and could be used as such although the circumstances in which it was found may give rise to an application to exclude the admission of that evidence under s 78 PACE.

The period of detention between the 'arrest' by John and the arrest by PC Cobo is likely to be held to be unlawful; however, it is likely that this would give rise to a potential civil action, rather than have any material effect upon any criminal trial.

Powers of Entry, Search, and Seizure: Part II

Law and Commentary

Law and Commentary

2.1 Introduction

Part II of the Act has the title 'Powers of Entry, Search, and Seizure'. The powers and duties covered by the Part are:

(i) Search warrants and access to material (ss 8–16).

The Act gives power to issue search warrants both to magistrates (s 8) and to judges (the 'special procedure' under s 9 and Sch 1), reserving to the latter the more complex and sensitive applications. It separates the two by creating special categories of material (ss 11–14) which are used to describe the type of items which can only be obtained by an application to a judge. Under the special procedure, an alternative to a search warrant is provided by Sch 1, para 4 which provides a procedure for compelling a person, by notice, to provide access to material (production orders). Legally privileged material (s 10) cannot be obtained by any application. Section 15 provides safeguards, common to both s 8 applications and Sch 1, para 12 applications, as to the form of the application and the form of the warrant. Section 16 sets out the requirements and procedure, common to both s 8 applications and Sch 1, para 12 applications, for the execution of warrants. Extensive guidance is contained in Code B.

(ii) Entry for particular purposes, including arrest (s 17); and entry and search after arrest (s 18).

(iii) General provisions relating to seizure, retention, and rights and duties with respect to seized things (ss 19–22).

2.2 The Two Types of Warrants: 'Specific Premises Warrants' and 'All Premises Warrants'

The Serious Organised Crime and Police Act 2005 introduced a significant modification to the requirement that the premises should be specified (s 8(1A), s 8(1B); amendment of s 8(1)(b)). The s 9, Sch 1 procedure was similarly modified: see the discussion subsequently in the chapter. There are two different types of warrant:

(i) a 'specific premises warrant'.

This permits the search of specified premises, including multiple premises.

(ii) an 'all premises warrant'.

This permits the search of all the premises under the control of a specified person, including, where it is not reasonably practicable to specify all of them, unspecified premises. The effect is that those premises which can be specified, should be.

Under both types of warrants, authorization may be given for multiple entries, either limited in number or unlimited (ss 8(1C) and 8(1D)).

2.3 Power of Magistrates to Issue Warrants to Enter and Search Premises (Section 8)

2.3.1 Who may hear the application and issue a warrant under section 8?

Section 8 confers the power to issue search warrants on 'a justice of the peace'. This includes both 'lay' magistrates (non-professional civilian appointees) and 'District Judges (Magistrates' Courts)' (formerly known as 'stipendiary magistrates', legally qualified professional appointees) (Courts Act 2003, Part 2).

2.3.2 Who may apply for a warrant under section 8 and to whom may it be issued?

The application must be made by a constable (s 8(1)) or by a civilian designated as an 'investigating officer' under s 38 of the Police Reform Act 2002 (Sch 4, Pt 2, para 16(a)) and the warrant may be issued to both (s 8(1); Police Reform Act 2002, Sch 4, Pt 2, para 16(b)).

2.3.3 What are the preconditions to the granting of an application under section 8?

magistrate has reasonable grounds for believing...

Before granting the application, the magistrate must have reasonable grounds for believing that all five of the preconditions set out in s 8(1)(a)–(e) are established. For this test, belief is what is required; mere suspicion will not suffice: *R (Malik) v Manchester Crown Court* [2008] EWHC 1362 (Admin) at para 34. The magistrate must satisfy himself that there are reasonable grounds for believing the various matters set out; the fact that a police officer, who has been investigating the matter, states in the information that he considers that there are reasonable grounds is not enough: *R v Guildhall Magistrates' Court, ex p Primlaks Holdings Co (Panama) Inc* [1990] 1 QB 261, DC at 272; *R (Rawlinson and Hunter Trustees) v Central Criminal Court, R (Tchenguiz) v Director of Serious Fraud Office* [2012] EWHC 2254 (Admin) at para 84.

(i) An indictable offence has been committed: s 8(1)(a). The Serious Organised Crime and Police Act 2005 replaced the phrase 'serious arrestable offence' with the phrase 'indictable offence' which represents a loosening of this requirement: an extension from the most serious offences to a wider class of more serious offences. An indictable offence is defined in the Interpretation Act 1978, Sch 1: it includes both 'indictable only' and 'triable either way' offences, ie both offences which are only triable in the Crown Court and offences which are triable in both the Magistrates' Court and in the Crown Court. Where there is a request for assistance from an overseas authority, the definition of an indictable offence in Part 2 of PACE is extended by s 16 of the Crime (International Co-operation) Act 2003 to conduct which (a) constitutes an offence under the law of a country outside the United Kingdom, and (b) would, if it occurred in England and Wales, constitute an indictable offence.

(ii) There is material on the premises mentioned which is likely to be of substantial value (either by itself or together with other material) to the investigation of the offence: s 8(1)(b). The magistrate does not have to be satisfied that the material is in fact likely to be of substantial value; merely that there are reasonable grounds for believing that it is likely to be: see by analogy *R (Malik) v Manchester Crown Court*, cited previously. The word 'material' has a wide meaning and is capable of covering a computer and its hard disk: *R (Faisaltex Ltd) v Preston Crown Court* [2008] EWHC 2832 (Admin).

(iii) The material is likely to be relevant evidence: s 8(1)(c). 'Relevant evidence' is anything which would be admissible at a trial for the offence (s 8(4)).

(iv) The material does not consist of or include 'items subject to legal privilege', 'excluded material' or 'special procedure material': s 8(1)(d). These terms are defined in ss 10–14 (discussed subsequently in the chapter). This condition is likely to be the key consideration in deciding whether to apply to a magistrate or a judge for a warrant. It requires the applicant to make a realistic and fact-specific assessment of whether what is sought is free of the specified categories. A warrant was quashed where the magistrates could not have been satisfied that there were reasonable grounds for believing that computers belonging to B, a forensic expert, would not contain material subject to legal privilege or special procedure material: *Bates v Chief Constable of Avon and Somerset* [2009] EWHC 942 (Admin). As the discussion in *Bates* illustrates, the existence of the seize and sift powers (discussed subsequently in the chapter) complicate the assessment in that they provide a lawful basis for the seizure of the specified categories. However, in order to justify a s 8 warrant, the courts are likely to expect that there are reasonable grounds for believing that at least some of the material targeted in the application is free of the specified categories. The words 'prima facie' should be read into s 8(1)(d) so that a magistrate faced with a case where he cannot be satisfied that there are reasonable grounds for believing that the material sought does not include any items which are, *prima facie*, subject to legal privilege, or any material which is, *prima facie*, special procedure material, should refuse the application under s 8 and leave the applicant to proceed under s 9: *R v Guildhall Magistrates' Court, ex p Primlaks Holdings Co (Panama) Inc,* cited previously, at 272.

(v) It is not practicable to communicate with a person entitled to grant entry and access to the material; or such access would not be granted without a warrant; or the purpose of the search may be frustrated or seriously prejudiced unless immediate access is secured: s 8(1)(e) and s 8(3).

What is contemplated by the last of these is the situation where there are reasonable grounds for believing that evidence would be destroyed should the occupier be asked to grant entry.

2.3.4 What is the procedure for making an application under section 8?

(i) *ex parte* application

The application is made *ex parte* and supported by an information in writing s 15(3). Section 15 provides safeguards, common to both s 8 applications and Sch 1, para 12 applications, as to the form of the application and the form of the warrant (discussed subsequently in the chapter).

(ii) duty of assistance, disclosure, and candour

There is a strong positive duty on the applicant in an *ex parte* application of this kind to assist the court by making full disclosure of relevant matters and, in particular, matters that might weigh against the issuing of the warrant. It requires full disclosure of relevant matters: *R v Zinga* [2012] EWCA Crim 2357. The duty was described by Hughes LJ in *Serious Fraud Office v Wastell* [2010] EWCA Civ 137 at para 159: 'In effect a prosecutor seeking an ex parte order must put on his defence hat and ask himself what, if he were representing the defendant or a third party with a relevant interest, he would be saying to the judge, and, having answered that question, that is what he must tell the judge.' The applicant has a duty to give full assistance to the court, and that includes drawing to its attention anything that militates against the issuing of a warrant: *R (Energy Financing Ltd) v Bow Street Court* (DC) [2005] EWHC 1626 (Admin) at para 24(3). See also the *Tchenguiz* case, cited previously, at paras 81–82.

Information demanding disclosure will include: whether there has been an earlier search of the premises (since this will have a bearing on whether material of substantial value to the investigation is presently on the premises); whether there was cooperation during an earlier search (since this will have a bearing on whether the purposes of a search would be frustrated or seriously prejudiced if advance warning were to be given). (See *R (Wood) v North Avon Magistrates' Court* [2009] EWHC 3614 (Admin).)

(iii) content of information; recording extraneous information

All the material necessary to justify the grant of a warrant should be contained in the written information provided. If the magistrate (or the judge in the case of an application under section 9) requires any further information in order to satisfy himself that the warrant is justified, a note should be made of the additional information so that there is a proper record of the full basis upon which the warrant has been granted: *Redknapp v Commissioner of Police of the Metropolis* [2008] EWHC 1177 (Admin) at para 13.

It follows that it is prudent, in the light of recent case law emphasizing the applicant's duty of candour and the need to record all material information placed before the magistrate, to record in the information points that are made by the applicant 'putting on his defence hat'.

(iv) fact-sensitive duty of judge to give reasons where needed

The magistrate has no statutory duty to give reasons why he is satisfied that the requirements of s 8(1)(a)–(d) are fulfilled. In a case where the written information is compelling and addresses the statutory requirements, there will be no need to state reasons: *R (Cronin) v Sheffield Justices* [2002] EWHC 2568 (Admin); *R (Glenn & Co) v HM Commissioners for Revenue and Customs* [2011] EWHC 2998 (Admin) at para 29. However, in most cases, and particularly where the information is given or supplemented orally, magistrates should give reasons for their decisions: the *Glenn & Co* case, cited previously, at para 29. This line of cases is somewhat at odds with other recent cases which emphasize the need to give reasons: see para 2.5.5(ii) and (iii). Accordingly, it is prudent for a magistrate to give reasons in all cases sufficient to demonstrate that he has applied the statutory criteria to the particular facts. Proportionality should be the guiding principle in determining the extent of the reasons necessary, taking into account such matters as the complexity of the case, the extent of the interference contemplated, the quality of the written information, and the extent of oral supplementation of the written information. As a matter of practicality if not principle, what passes muster on a s 8 application may not suffice on a s 9 Sch 1 application.

2.3.5 Who may seize and retain things under section 8?

Things may be seized and retained by a constable (s 8(2)) or a civilian designated as an 'investigating officer' under s 38 of the Police Reform Act 2002 (Sch 4, Pt 2, para 16(c)).

2.3.6 What may be seized and retained under section 8?

Anything for which the search is authorized under the warrant may be seized and retained (s 8(2)). There is an extension of the power to require electronic data to be produced in a form in which it is or may readily become intelligible (see s 20 discussed subsequently in the chapter). Rights to access and copies of things seized are provided (see s 21 discussed subsequently in the chapter). The length of time that seized things may be retained is set out in s 22 (discussed subsequently in the chapter).

2.3.7 **Execution of warrant under section 8 and conduct of search**

Section 16 provides safeguards, common to both s 8 applications and Sch 1, para 12 applications, as to the execution of a warrant and the conduct of the search (see subsequently in the chapter).

2.4 **Items Subject to Legal Privilege (Section 10), Excluded Material (Section 11), and Special Procedure Material (Section 14)**

2.4.1 **The significance of the categories under sections 10, 11, and 14**

These categories are referred to throughout this Part of the Act. Their significance is:

- any item which falls within these categories cannot be the subject of a search warrant issued by a magistrate under s 8 (see s 8(1)(d));
- 'excluded material' (s 11) and certain types of 'special procedure material' (s 14) can, however, be the subject of a warrant issued by a judge under s 9 and Sch 1;
- 'items subject to legal privilege' (s 10) cannot be the subject of a warrant by either a magistrate or a judge; nor can they be the object of entry and search after arrest (s 18(1)); nor can they be seized by a constable exercising his general power of seizure under s 19 or under any statutory power of seizure (s 19(6)); nor can they be the subject of an order under the Terrorism Act 2000, Sch 5, Pt I.

However, this basic position is now subject to an important qualification introduced by the Criminal Justice and Police Act 2001, Pt 2. Items which an officer has no power to seize, including items subject to legal privilege, excluded material, and special procedure material, may now be removed in accordance with the 'seize and sift powers' contained in that Part (discussed subsequently in the chapter).

2.4.2 **Items subject to legal privilege (section 10)**

Subject to the exception set out subsequently, 'items subject to legal privilege' are:

(i) (by s 10(1)(a)) communications which are *made in connection with the giving of legal advice to a client* between:

- a lawyer and client; or
- a lawyer and a person representing the client; and

(ii) (by s 10(1)(b)) communications which are *made in connection with or in contemplation of legal proceedings and for the purpose of such proceedings* between:

- a lawyer and client; or
- a lawyer and a person representing the client; and
- a lawyer and any other person; and
- the client and any other person (which, as a matter of principle, would include a person representing the client, although this is not stated); and
- the person representing the client and any other person.

The privilege in s 10(1)(b) extends to what occurs in a psychiatrist's examination and the resulting opinion of the psychiatrist where the predominant purpose of the examination was to report on a person's mental state to his solicitors: *R v Davies (Keith)* [2002] EWCA Crim 85 (where the court rejected the submission that the privileged report was divisible from the expert's opinion).

(iii) (by s 10(1)(c)) items enclosed with or referred to in such communications (ie those in (i) and (ii)), which are made in connection with either of the two purposes in (i) or (ii) 'when they are in the possession of a person who is entitled to possession of them'.

The word 'made' in s 10(c) applies to the items enclosed or referred to in the communication. It is used in a general sense, wide enough to include 'brought into existence' but does not extend to objects which do not come into existence for the purpose of obtaining legal advice, etc: *R v R* [1994] 1 WLR 758, where it was held that a blood sample obtained for the purpose of a defence report in criminal proceedings was privileged as an item within s 10(1)(c). The corollary would be that a pre-existing blood sample brought into existence for some other purpose would not be a privileged item.

There is no case interpreting the phrase 'when they are in the possession of a person who is entitled to possession of them' in s 10(1)(c). It would plainly exclude such items being privileged when in possession of a thief. It probably reflects the common law principle that privilege prevents the production of evidence and is not concerned with its admissibility once it is in the possession of another party: *Calcraft v Guest* [1898] 1 QB 759.

The communications covered by (i) and (ii) are represented in the following diagrams

(I) Communications made in connection with the giving of legal advice to a client, protected by legal privilege

(II) Communications made in connection with or in contemplation of legal proceedings and for the purpose of such proceedings, protected by legal privilege

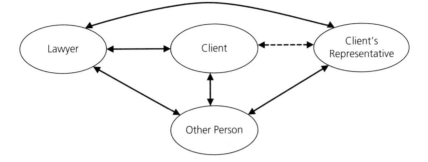

The stated exception in s 10 is with respect to items held with the intention of furthering a criminal purpose (s 10(2)).

The phrase 'held with the intention of furthering a criminal purpose' contained in s 10(2) should be given a purposive rather than a literal construction so as to include not just the intentions of the person holding the item but also the intentions of any other person (regardless of whether the holder was aware of such intention): *R v Central Criminal Court, ex p Francis and Francis (a Firm)* [1989] AC 346. In that case, documents held innocently by a solicitor on behalf of an innocent client did not attract privilege because of the intentions of a third party to which the documents related.

The types of items not covered by legal privilege include:

- documents sent by a client to a lawyer, for the purpose of obtaining advice, if they were pre-existing documents which do not themselves fall within the definition of privileged material: *R v Guildhall Magistrates' Court, ex p Primlaks Holdings Co (Panama) Inc* cited previously, at 273. (The enclosures do not fall within s 10(1)(c). They would, however, be, *prima facie*, 'special procedure material'. Technically, the covering letter would be privileged as falling within s 10(1)(a));
- documents created by a lawyer which are formal instruments or administrative records such as conveyancing and financing documents (*R v Inner London Crown Court, ex p Baines and Baines (a Firm)* (1988) 87 Cr App R 111, CA) or a solicitor's attendance note or other record of time devoted to a case (*R v Manchester Crown Court, ex p Rogers* [1999] 2 Cr App R 267, DC);
- forgeries made to support a civil claim since the phrase 'made in connection with or in contemplation of legal proceedings' in s 10(1)(b) should be read as meaning 'lawfully made': *R v Leeds Magistrates' Court, ex p Dumbleton* [1993] Crim LR 866, DC.

2.4.3 **Excluded material (section 11)**

'Excluded material' is material held by a 'person' (ie either an individual or an organization: Sch 1, Interpretation Act 1978) in confidence owed to a third party.

It takes three forms and the nature of the confidence required differs as between the first two, on the one hand, and the last, on the other.

(i) personal records.

Essentially, they are the most private records. They consist of records which:

(a) are acquired or created by a person in the course of any trade, business, profession, or other occupation, or for the purposes of any paid or unpaid office (s 11(1)(a)); and

(b) are held by that person in confidence in the sense that they are held either (1) subject to an express or implied undertaking to hold them in confidence or (2) subject to a statutory obligation imposing a restriction on disclosure or an obligation of secrecy (s 11(1)(a) and s 11(2)); and

(c) concern identifiable individuals (living or dead); and are either: (1) records relating to an individual's physical or mental health, or spiritual counselling or assistance (whether given or to be given); or (2) records relating to counselling or assistance for the purposes of an individual's personal welfare (whether given or to be given) by a voluntary organization or individual who, by reason of his office or occupation, or an order of a court, has responsibilities for the first individual's personal welfare (s 12).

The result is that all records relating to the core private categories of an individual's physical, mental, or spiritual welfare are within the definition whereas records relating to counselling or assistance for 'personal welfare' (a wider but undefined term) will only be within the definition if the person giving the counselling or assistance has some special responsibility for such counselling or assistance. Counselling or assistance by priests and probation officers would fall within the definition whereas counselling or assistance by obliging accountants or mortgage brokers would not.

(ii) human tissue or tissue fluid, taken for the purposes of diagnosis or medical treatment and held in confidence in the sense that they are held either (1) subject to an express or implied undertaking to hold it in confidence, or (2) subject to a statutory obligation imposing a restriction on disclosure or an obligation of secrecy (s 11(1)(b) and s 11(2)).

(iii) journalistic material held in confidence, consisting of documents or records other than documents.

This is material which:

(a) consists of documents or records other than documents (s 11(1)(c)); and

(b) is held in confidence in the sense of being subject to an undertaking, restriction, or obligation, and it must have been continuously so held by one or more persons since first acquired or created for the purposes of journalism (s 11(1)(c) and s 11(3)); and

(c) is 'journalistic material', ie material in the possession of a person who acquired or created it for the purposes of journalism (and a person who receives material from someone who intends that the recipient shall use it for the purposes of journalism shall be taken to have acquired it for the purposes of journalism) (s 13).

The result of (b) is that material which initially falls within the definition of journalistic material will cease to do so if there is any time during which nobody holds it in confidence. The result of (c) is that material will remain journalistic material only when in the possession of someone who acquires or creates it for the purposes of journalism (in effect, someone who is a journalist); but if he acquires it without that purpose (for example, if it is dropped through his letter-box) it may nonetheless be regarded as journalistic material (if the provider of the material intended that the recipient should use it for the purposes of journalism). The effect of the two is that, in order for such material to remain excluded material, there must be a continuous chain, from the creation or acquisition of the material for the purposes of journalism, of journalists holding it in confidence, although they can pass it from one to another.

2.4.4 Special procedure material (section 14)

This is a sweeping-up category of material meriting special protection but falling outside of the categories of 'items subject to legal privilege' (s 10) and 'excluded material' (s 11). It is broken up into two categories.

(i) material created or acquired by a person in their work and held by them in confidence.

This is material which:

(a) is other than items subject to legal privilege and excluded material (s 14(2)); and
(b) is in the possession of a person who acquired or created it in the course of any trade, business, profession, or other occupation, or for the purpose of any paid or unpaid office (s 14(2) and s 14(2)(a)); and
(c) is held by that person subject either (1) to an express or implied undertaking to hold it in confidence, or (2) subject to a statutory obligation imposing a restriction on disclosure or an obligation of secrecy (s 14(2)(b)).

(ii) 'journalistic material' other than 'excluded material' (s 14(1)(b)).

This is material which:

(a) is 'journalistic material', ie material in the possession of a person who acquired or created it for the purposes of journalism (and a person who receives material from someone who intends that the recipient shall use it for the purposes of journalism shall be taken to have acquired it for the purposes of journalism) (s 13); and
(b) is not 'excluded material' within s 11.

What remains for category (ii), given the scope of journalistic material falling within s 11, is either (1) journalistic material which consists of material which is not in the form of either 'documents' or 'records other than documents', and (2) journalistic material which is not held 'in confidence' (as defined in s 11(3)). The former might include items of real evidence created or acquired for the purposes of journalism.

The section extends to 'material' generally and is not confined to documents.

The remaining parts of the section, s 14(3)–(6), have the effect of preventing an employer or group of companies artificially creating a duty of confidence internally within the business or group for the purposes of the section and thereby gaining the protection of a special procedure material classification: the duty of confidence only arises with respect to a true third party individual or company. The obvious application of these subsections is to the first rather than the second (journalistic material) category of special procedure material; and the wording of s 14(1) and s 14(2) suggest that it is only the first category which is qualified by s 14(3) to s 14(6).

2.5 Search Warrant and Other Orders Issued by Judge under the 'Special Procedure' (Section 9 and Schedule 1)

Section 9(1) provides that a constable may, for the purposes of a criminal investigation, obtain access to 'excluded material' and 'special procedure material' (but not 'items subject to legal privilege') by making an application under and in accordance with Sch 1. The Schedule provides for two forms of access: (1) an order requiring a person to surrender or grant access to material (para 4); and (2) a warrant authorizing a constable to enter and search premises (para 12), and to seize and retain things (para 13). In contrast to applications for warrants to search for evidence outside of these categories of material, which can be made to a magistrate (s 8), Sch 1 provides that the application must be made to a judge, reflecting the added seriousness, sensitivity, and complexity of such applications.

2.5.1 Who may hear the special procedure application and make the production order or issue the warrant?

The provisions presently state that a 'circuit judge' may make the production order or issue the warrant. Recorders have no jurisdiction (*R v Central Criminal Court, ex p Francis and Francis (a Firm)* [1989] AC 346, HL, at 368 and 382).

Prospective amendments provided for under the Courts Act 2003, the Serious Organised Crime and Police Act 2005, and the Armed Forces Act 2011, which would add a new para 17 to Sch 1 of the Act and extend jurisdiction, in addition, to a High Court Judge, Recorder, and District Judge, have not yet been brought into force.

2.5.2 Who may apply for a special procedure warrant or order; and with respect to whom may an order be made; and to whom may a warrant be issued?

The application must be made by a constable (s 9(1)) or by a civilian designated as an 'investigating officer' under s 38 of the Police Reform Act 2002 (Sch 4, Pt 2, para 17(a) and (b)); and the order may be made with respect to both; and the warrant may be issued to both.

2.5.3 Understanding the preconditions to the granting of special procedure applications: the 'access conditions' of Schedule 1

The scheme of the schedule is to employ, for the purposes of describing the preconditions to both applications, sets of requirements described as 'access conditions'.

(i) The first set of access conditions. This is the wider gateway but to a narrower class of material: it permits access to important evidence relating to serious offences but cannot include 'excluded material' (as defined in s 11). It requires the judge to be satisfied as to all of the following (Sch 1, para 2):

(a) that there are reasonable grounds for believing that (1) an indictable offence has been committed; and (2) that there is material on any premises specified in the application or, in the case of an 'all premises' warrant, premises occupied or controlled by the person specified, which consists of or includes 'special procedure material' and does not also include 'excluded material'; and (3) that the material is likely to be of 'substantial value' (which is further defined) to the investigation; and (4) that the material is likely to be relevant evidence; and

(b) other methods of obtaining the material have been tried without success or have not been tried because it appeared that they were bound to fail; and

(c) it is in the public interest, having regard to the likely benefit to the investigation and the circumstances under which the person holds the material, that it should be produced or that access should be granted.

(ii) The second set of access conditions. This is the narrower gateway but to a wider class of material. It permits access to both 'excluded material' (as defined in s 11) and 'special procedure material' (as defined in s 14) in circumstances in which historically a search warrant could have been issued. Such historical powers cease to have effect, by virtue of s 9(2), in so far as they relate to the authorization of searches for 'items subject to legal privilege', 'excluded material', or, with respect to documents or other records, 'special procedure material'. This set requires the judge to be satisfied as to all of the following (Sch 1, para 3):

(a) that there are reasonable grounds for believing that there is material which consists of or includes 'excluded material' or 'special procedure material' on any premises specified in the application, or, in the case of an 'all premises' warrant, premises occupied or controlled by the person specified; and

(b) that such a warrant could have been issued under one of the historical statutory provisions; and

(c) that the issue of such a warrant would have been appropriate.

2.5.4 What are the preconditions to the granting of a special procedure application requiring a person to surrender or grant access to material, i.e. a production order (Schedule 1, paragraph 4)?

If the judge is satisfied that one or other of the sets of access conditions is fulfilled (see para 2.5.3), he may make an order (Sch 1, para 1).

2.5.5 What is the procedure for special procedure applications under Schedule 1, paragraph 4 (production order) or 12 (warrant)?

(i) General: para 12 (warrant) applications to be made exceptionally; presumption in favour of para 4 (production order) applications. Recognizing that para 12 applications, which are made *ex parte*, are a serious inroad into the liberty of the subject, the courts have emphasized that applications should normally be made *inter partes* (ie by way of a para 4 application) unless to do so would frustrate the purpose of the application. All the circumstances had to be considered, including the seriousness of the matter being investigated, evidence already available to the police, and the extent to which the person in possession already knew of the interest in his affairs such as might have caused him to destroy or interfere with documents: *R v Southampton Crown Court, ex p J and P* [1993] Crim LR 961, DC. See also *R v Central Criminal Court, ex p A J D Holdings Limited* [1992] Crim LR 669.

(ii) applications for order to surrender or grant access to material (production order; Sch 1, para 4):

• *Applications made on notice,* inter partes. The application is made *inter partes* (with notice to the affected party and that party's ability to appear) by the service of a notice on the person believed to be in possession of the material (Sch 1, paras 7–10). The person served is under an obligation to preserve the material until the application is determined (subject to certain exceptions) (Sch 1, para 11).

• *No notice to suspect.* There is no requirement to give notice, in addition, to any accused person or suspected party since the purpose of the Act is to permit the police to seek access to special procedure material before they had identified anyone as a likely perpetrator of the crime being investigated: *R v Leicester Crown Court, ex p DPP* [1988] 86 Cr App R 254.

• *In chambers or open court.* The application may be made, at the judge's discretion and in the light of submissions made, in chambers or in open court: *R v Central Criminal Court, ex p DPP*, DC (1988) The Times, 1 April.

- *Application particularized in writing*. The police should set out in writing in the application or in a supporting document what is sought and must bear the risk that the provision of such detail to the person who is the subject of the application will lead to the destruction of evidence: *R v Central Criminal Court ex p Adegbesan* (1987) 84 Cr App R 219, CA, at 224 and 226. However, a failure to do so is not fatal where the information was given orally before the notice was given and the recipient of the notice was specifically referred to the officer to whom that information was given orally (*R v Crown Court at Manchester ex p Taylor* (1988) 87 Cr App R 358 at 370). The notice should set out the general nature of the offence (*Taylor*). Anything served on the court must be served on the person against whom the application is made: *R v Inner London Crown Court ex p Baines and Baines (a firm)* (1988) 87 Cr App R 111, DC at 117. However, it is a matter for the judgment of the police, having regard to any special features of the investigation, whether to disclose evidence relied upon in advance of the hearing, although the omission to do so may justify the granting of an adjournment (*Baines*).
- *Duty of openness on the police*. The police have a duty to be open handed and to set out all the material in their hands, whether it assisted the applications or militated against them; and the Crown has a duty to make a clear revelation to the Court of all appropriate material in their possession so the judge could safely decide whether the access conditions were fulfilled: *R v Acton Crown Court, ex p Layton* [1993] Crim LR 459. However, where on an *inter partes* application, the respondent had the material in question, a failure by the applicant to reveal the material to the judge was not fatal to the legality of the order. However, as previously stated, there is a discretion in the police as to when to disclose evidence relied upon in support.

(iii) warrant issued by a judge (Sch 1, para 12):

- Safeguards are provided as to the form of the application and the form of the warrant, common to both s 8 applications and Sch 1, para 12 applications. See s 15 discussed subsequently in the chapter.
- *Application made* ex parte. Although Sch 1 is silent as to the form of the application, s 15(3) states that the application shall be made *ex parte* (without notice to or argument from the affected person).
- *Duty of assistance, disclosure, and candour*. See the discussion at para 2.3.4 An officer making an application should draw the judge's attention to material arguably subject to legal privilege and provide him with sufficient information to reach a decision on the question of privilege. Where there is doubt, legal advice should be obtained to assist the judge (*R v Southampton Crown Court ex p J and P* [1993] Crim LR 962, DC).
- *Judge should give reasons; although they may in some instances be inferred if not stated*. If it is apparent from the record that the judge had given the matter cursory consideration and allowed the application to go through on the nod, the warrant is liable to be quashed (*R v Southwark Crown Court, ex p Sorsky*

Defries [1996] Crim LR 195). Whether reasons should be given, or the consequence of not giving reasons, is fact-sensitive. A judge's reasons for issuing a warrant may, in appropriate circumstances, be inferred to be adequately stated from the contents of documents placed before him: *R (Burgin & Purcell) v Commissioner of Police for the Metropolis & Chief Constable for Leicestershire Police Defendants* [2011] EWHC 1835 (Admin) at para 33. Realistically, this will require the reasons to be stated persuasively, comprehensively, and fairly in the material placed before the judge and for the surrounding evidence to demonstrate that the judge has considered the application properly and adopted those reasons. (See para 2.3.4(iv) and the discussion of *R (Glenn & Co) v HM Commissioners for Revenue and Customs* [2011] EWHC 2998 (Admin).) There is an increasing trend to challenge the issuing of warrants by judicial review on the ground of inadequacy of reasons (in addition to other grounds including the width of the warrant and the failure of the applicant to disclose relevant matters). Transcripts of the application and copies of the written information, suitably redacted where necessary, are routinely provided for the purposes of those proceedings. Given the emphasis in recent case law on the high duty to give reasons (see *Burgin & Purcell*, at paras 30–37, and the *Tchenguiz* case, at para 207, both cited previously) it is prudent for a judge to give reasons in all cases sufficient to demonstrate that he has applied the statutory criteria to the particular facts.

• *Content of information; recording extraneous information.* See the discussion at para 2.3.4.

2.5.6 What order may be made on a special procedure application requiring a person to surrender or grant access to material (production order; Schedule 1, paragraph 4)?

The order is for the person who appears to the judge to be in possession of the material, within seven days or such longer period as may be specified, either to (a) produce it to a constable for him to take it away or (b) give a constable access to it (Sch 1, para 4). Specific provision is made for the viewing and printing out of electronic data (Sch 1, para 5).

2.5.7 What are the consequences of failing to comply with a special procedure order requiring a person to surrender or grant access to material (production order; Schedule 1, paragraph 4)?

If a person fails to comply with such an order, the judge may deal with him as if he had committed a contempt of the Crown Court (Sch 1, para 15). In addition, such a failure leads naturally to an application under para 12 for a warrant since it is one of the conditions for one of the routes to the granting of a warrant (para 12(b)(ii)).

2.5.8 What are the preconditions for the issue of a warrant by a judge under the special procedure (Schedule 1, paragraph 12)?

There are two alternative routes:

(i) *The first route.* The judge must be satisfied (Sch 1, para 12, 14) that:
   (a) either set of access conditions is fulfilled; and
   (b) any of the following apply: (1) access could not practicably be granted by a person entitled to grant entry to the premises or access to the material; or (2) the material contains information which is likely to be disclosed in breach of a statutory restriction on disclosure or obligation of secrecy if a warrant is not issued; or (3) the service of notice of an application under Sch 1, para 4 may seriously prejudice the investigation.
(ii) *The second route.* The judge must be satisfied (Sch 1, para 12, 14) that:
   (a) the second set of access conditions is fulfilled; and
   (b) an order under Sch 1, para 4 has not been complied with.

2.5.9 What may be seized under a warrant issued by a judge under the special procedure (Schedule 1, paragraph 12)?

A constable may seize and retain anything for which a search has been authorized by the judge (Sch 1, para 13). There is an extension of the power to require electronic data to be produced in a form in which it is or may readily become intelligible (see s 20 discussed subsequently in the chapter). Rights to access and copies of things seized are provided (see s 21 discussed subsequently in the chapter). The length of time that seized things may be retained is set out in s 22 (discussed subsequently in the chapter).

2.5.10 Execution of warrant under the special procedure and conduct of search

Section 16 provides safeguards, common to both s 8 applications and Sch 1, para 12 applications, as to the execution of a warrant and the conduct of the search (discussed subsequently in the chapter).

2.6 Search Warrant Safeguards (Section 15)

Section 15 provides safeguards, common to both s 8 applications and Sch 1, para 12 applications, as to the form of the application and the form of the warrant. Its reach, together with that of s 16, goes beyond the Act and extends to any statutory power to issue warrants to enter and search premises (s 15(1)). Further guidance as to the specific statutory powers covered is contained in Code B, Note 2A.

It is now settled that, despite a lack of clarity in the wording of s 15(1), in order for a search to be lawful, both s 15 and s 16 must be satisfied (*R v Longman* (1989) 88 Cr App R 148, CA; *R v Central Criminal Court, ex p AJD Holdings Limited* [1992] Crim LR 669; *R v Chief Constable of Lancashire, ex p Parker and Another* (1993) 97 Cr App R 90, DC, at 95; *R v Chesterfield Justices, ex p Bramley,* [2000] 1 Cr App R 486 at 499).

2.6.1 What are the duties of the officer applicant?

(i) preliminary enquiries

Requirements in Code B 3 include the following:

- When information appears to justify an application, the officer must take reasonable steps to check the information is accurate, recent, and not provided maliciously or irresponsibly; and an application may not be made on the basis of information from an anonymous source if corroboration has not been sought.
- The officer shall ascertain as specifically as possible the nature of the articles concerned and their location.
- The officer shall make reasonable enquiries to establish: whether anything is known about the likely occupier of the premises and the nature of the premises themselves; whether the premises have been searched previously and how recently; and to obtain any other relevant information.
- Consultation with the local police/community liaison officer should be made if there is reason to believe that a search might have an adverse effect on relations between the police and the community, save in urgent cases when the consultation should be as soon as possible after the search.

(ii) matters to be stated in the application

It is the duty of the officer (s 15(1)–(3)), who must answer under oath any question asked by the magistrate or judge (s 15(4)), to state:

- the ground of the application (however the identity of informants need not be disclosed, although answers may be given as to the reliability of the source: Code B, Note 3A);
- the enactment under which the warrant would be issued (including the Act itself);
- where the application is for multiple entries, the grounds for such application; whether he seeks a warrant authorizing an unlimited number of entries, or, if not, the maximum number sought;
- where the application is for a 'specific premises warrant' (under s 8(1A)(a) or Sch 1, para 12), the premises;
- where the application is for an 'all premises warrant' (under s 8(1A)(b) or Sch 1, para 12), as many premises as it is reasonably practicable to specify; why it is necessary to search more than may be specified, and why it is not reasonably

practicable to specify them all; the person/s in occupation or control of the premises;

- so far as practicable, the identity of the articles or person sought.

This is supplemented by guidance and requirements in the Code. Additional matters which should be specified in writing, by virtue of Code B 3.6 are:

- how the evidence relates to any investigation;
- the object of the search;
- that there are no reasonable grounds to believe that the material sought (a) in the case of an application to a judge (s 9 and Sch 1), consists of or includes items subject to legal privilege (s 10); and (b) in the case of an application to a magistrate (s 8), consists of or includes excluded material (s 10) or special procedure material (s 14).

Code B, Note 3B states that the information supporting a search warrant application should be as specific as possible, particularly in relation to the articles or persons being sought and where in the premises it is suspected they may be found.

(iii) signed written authority required in application

Code B 3.4 requires any application to a magistrate (s 8) or to a judge (Sch 1) to be supported by a signed written authority from an officer of at least the rank of inspector; although, in an urgent application, the next most senior officer on duty can give such authority. (In addition, the principle in s 107 and Code B 2.7 applies: sergeants authorized to act as inspectors have a like power.)

2.6.2 Formalities and form of a warrant

The warrant must specify (s 15(4)–(6)):

- if it specifies multiple entries, whether they are limited (and, if so, the number) or unlimited;
- the name of the applicant;
- the date issued;
- the enactment under which it is issued;
- the premises to be searched or, in the case of an 'all premises warrant', the person in occupation or control and any premises which can be specified;
- so far as practicable, the identity of the articles or person sought.

Provision is made for the number of copies required (s 15(7)).

An increasingly popular ground of challenge to warrants in judicial review claims is that they are drafted too widely. The permissible width is to be decided by reference to the particular facts of the case. As a generality, wider categories of material are more likely to be permissible in complex cases and cases in their early stages: R (Energy Financing Ltd) v Bow Street Court (DC); R (Glenn & Co) v HM Commissioners for Revenue and Customs, at paras 59–65, both cited previously.

2.7 **Execution of Search Warrants (Section 16)**

2.7.1 **Who may execute a warrant or accompany persons executing warrants?**

(i) constables or designated persons

The warrant may be executed by 'any constable' (s 16(1)) or by a civilian designated as an 'investigating officer' under s 38 of the Police Reform Act 2002 (Sch 4, Pt 2, para 16(e)). The effect of s 16(1) was to remove the requirement in certain statutes of limiting the execution of warrants to a constable named in the warrant.

(ii) persons accompanying

However, a person authorized by the warrant may accompany any person executing the warrant (s 16(2)) and, so long as he is in the company of and under the supervision of the latter, he has the same powers as the latter with respect to (a) the execution of the warrant, and (b) the seizure of anything to which the warrant relates (s 16(2A) and (2B); Code B 2.11; and Police Reform Act 2002, Sch 4, Pt 2, para 16(e)). Code B, Note 3C states that this includes any suitably qualified or skilled person or an expert in a particular field whose presence is needed to help accurately identify the material sought or to advise where certain evidence is most likely to be found and how it should be dealt with. The obvious application is to forensic experts of all types, eg those concerned in the retrieval and preservation of electronic data.

2.7.2 **Who is in charge of the execution of a warrant?**

Code B 2.10 requires that whenever there is a search of premises to which the Code applies, one officer must act as the officer in charge of the search. This should normally be the most senior officer present; but a supervising officer may appoint a person of lower rank; or select an officer where all are of the same rank; otherwise, the officers themselves should nominate one of their number to be in charge (Code B, Note 2F).

2.7.3 **How long does a warrant remain valid?**

Any entry and search under a warrant must be within three months from the date of its issue (s 16(3)). (An amendment effected by the Serious Organised Crime and Police Act 2005 extended the period from one month to three months.)

2.7.4 **What are the conditions for entry and search on more than one occasion?**

Multiple entries are now permitted under the two types of warrants introduced by the Serious Organised Crime and Police Act 2005, the 'specific premises warrant' and the 'all premises warrant' (see the discussion at para 2.2 as to the meaning of these terms). Amendments to s 16 are made by the Serious Organised Crime and Police Act 2005 to introduce additional safeguards into the execution of warrants where either multiple entries are to be made or entry is to be made to premises not specified in an 'all premises warrant'.

Written authorization by a police officer of at least the rank of inspector is required for:

(i) entry and search of premises not specified in an 'all premises warrant' (s 16(3A); Code B 6.3B); or

(ii) entry and search of premises entered on a second or any subsequent time under a warrant authorizing multiple searches (s 16(3B); Code B 6.3A).

There is provision for sergeants to perform the role of the authorizing inspector, if so authorized by an officer of at least the rank of superintendent (s 107; Code B 2.7). (In addition, as previously stated, there is a requirement in Code B 3.4—although not the Act—for all applications to magistrates or judges to be authorized in writing by a senior officer.)

2.7.5 Are there restrictions on when in the day a warrant may be executed?

Entry and search under a warrant must be at a reasonable hour unless it appears to the constable executing it that the purpose of a search may be frustrated on an entry at that time (s 16(4); Code B 6.3).

2.7.6 What is meant by 'premises'?

Section 23 defines 'premises' as 'any place', including:

(a) any vehicle, vessel, aircraft or hovercraft;
(b) any offshore installation;
(ba) any renewable energy installation;
(c) any tent or movable structure.

The entire premises may be seized where it is necessary and physically possible to do so—for example, where the premises is a vehicle, tent or caravan (Code B, Note 7B).

Despite the wide definition that can be attached to the word 'premises', the powers of entry search and seizure conferred by a warrant are strictly limited to those premises that are identified within that warrant. In *Wood v North Avon Magistrates Court* [2009] EWHCA 3614 (Admin), the seizure of a Mercedes car from a car park to a block of flats was held to be unlawful where the warrant was limited to one of the flats in the block. The 'premises' was the flat and any common parts necessary to gain access to those premises. The court found that the terms and scope of the warrant are so important that it would be wrong and dangerous to assume that the warrant covered the car park to the flat.

43

2.7.7 **What are the formalities at entry and search and when is the use of force permissible?**

(i) where premises are occupied or person entitled to grant access is present:

(a) The statutory requirements are stated in s 16(5) and s 16(6), which do not, however, state anything about timing. The constable must:

- identify himself to the occupier or other person entitled to grant access and, if not in uniform, produce to him documentary evidence that he is a constable;
- produce the warrant to him; and
- supply him with a copy of it.

(b) Code B sets out the timing of the formalities of introduction.

- Prior to entry, an attempt should ordinarily be made to secure entry by agreement. The officer in charge should first attempt to communicate with the occupier or any other person entitled to grant access to the premises and explain the authority under which he seeks entry to the premises and ask the occupier to allow him to enter. However, this is unnecessary where there are reasonable grounds for believing that to alert the occupier or any other person entitled to grant access by attempting to communicate with him would frustrate the object of the search or endanger the officers concerned or other people (Code B 6.4). An example of this proviso is where there is a search for small disposable items, such as drugs, which could readily be flushed down the lavatory.
- Prior to search, the officer should: identify himself and, if not in uniform, show his warrant card; state the purpose of and grounds for the search; and identify any person accompanying the officer and describe their role in the process (Code B 6.5). However, in terrorism cases or where officers reasonably believe that recording or disclosing their names might put them in danger, warrant and identification numbers and the name of their police station may be used for identification (Code B 2.9). The names of persons accompanying the officers may be withheld in like cases (Code B 2.9).

(c) Search with consent. A distinction is drawn in Code B between searches made in exercise of a police power (under authority of a warrant or a power of entry and searches) and those made solely with consent. Where the search is made solely with consent of the person entitled to grant entry, Code B.5 imposes particular requirements: before seeking consent, the officer in charge should state as specifically as possible the purpose of the proposed search and its extent and, if the person concerned is not presently suspected of an offence, that fact; the person concerned must be informed that they are not obliged to consent and may withdraw consent at any time; consent must, if practicable be given in writing on the Notice of Powers and Rights before the search. However, where the search is made in exercise of a police power, although there is a duty to seek the cooperation of the occupier or other person entitled to grant entry (Code B 6.4), there is no need to obtain written consent from that person (Code B, Note para 5B).

(d) Search with assumed consent. Code B, para 5.4 and Note para 5C allow for the search of premises without obtaining consent where it is necessary and reasonable to assume that consent would be given. Para 5.4 relieves the officer of the duty of obtaining consent where 'this would cause disproportionate inconvenience to the person concerned'. However, the examples given in Note para 5C are instances of hot pursuit where the justification arises more from the impracticability in the circumstances of obtaining express consent than the inconvenience that would be caused.

(e) Search of communal accommodation. In a lodging house, hostel or similar accommodation, every reasonable effort should be made to obtain the consent of the tenant, lodger, or occupier; and a search should not be made solely on the basis of the landlord's consent (Code B, Note para 5A).

(f) Use of force. Reasonable and proportionate force may be used to effect entry where the occupier or other person entitled to grant access has refused entry or it is impossible to communicate with such persons (Code B 6.6).

(ii) where premises are unoccupied and no one entitled to grant access is present.

The officer is relieved of the formalities of introduction (Code B 6.4) and reasonable and proportionate force may be used to effect entry (Code B 6.6). In addition, the circumstances may permit consent to be assumed: see Code B, para 5.4 and Note para 5C, previously discussed.

2.7.8 How should a search be conducted?

(i) the extent of the search permitted by a warrant.

The search may only be to the extent required for the purpose for which the warrant was issued (s 16(5)). Further guidance is provided by Code B 6.9, 6.9A, and 6.9B: regard is to be had to the size and nature of whatever is sought; a search may not continue once everything specified in the warrant is found or the officer in charge is satisfied that whatever is being sought is not on the premises.

(ii) Guidance as to the conduct of the search.

Guidance in Code B includes these important points:

• A general reminder to the police regarding the impact of racial and disability legislation on the exercise of the powers to search and seize was added by new para 1.3A of the 2011 Revised Code B which states:

Powers to search and seize must be used fairly, responsibly, with respect for people who occupy premises being searched or are in charge of property being seized and without unlawful discrimination. The Equality Act 2010 makes it unlawful for police officers to discriminate against, harass or victimise any person on the grounds of the 'protected characteristics' of age, disability, gender reassignment, race, religion or belief, sex and sexual orientation, marriage and civil partnership, pregnancy and maternity when using their powers. When police forces are carrying out their functions they also have a duty to have regard to the need to eliminate unlawful discrimination, harassment and victimisation and to take steps to foster good relations.

- Searches must be conducted with due consideration for the property and privacy of the occupier and with no more disturbance than necessary; and reasonable force may be used only when necessary and proportionate because the cooperation of the occupier cannot be obtained or is insufficient for the purpose (Code B 6.10).
- If the occupier wishes, a friend or neighbour of the occupier may witness the search, subject to certain exceptions (Code B 6.11).
- Questions solely necessary for the purpose of furthering the effective and proper conduct of the search may be asked of a person without first cautioning them; but questioning which goes beyond that, is likely to constitute an interview within Code C (Code B 6.12 and 12A).

2.7.9 Documents used in a search or recording a search

(i) Notice of powers and rights

Unless impracticable, such a notice should be provided to the occupier (Code B 6.7). It should ordinarily be provided before the search begins (Code B 6.8).

(ii) The warrant

A copy should ordinarily be provided to the occupier before the search begins (Code B 6.8). Where there is no occupier present or other person in charge of the premises, the warrant should be left in a prominent place on the premises and endorsed with certain details (s 16(7); Code B 6.8). The original of the warrant must be endorsed with a record of what was found and seized (s 16(9); Code B 8.2). It must be returned to the appropriate person at the issuing court when it has been executed or within three months of the date of its issue (s 16(10) and (10A); and Code B 8.3) where it must be retained for 12 months (s 16(11)) during which the occupier has the right to inspect it (s 16(12)).

(iii) Search records and search registers

A detailed record must be made by the officer in charge of the search of specified details relating to the execution of the warrant (Code B 8.1). A search register, in which all search records for the area are made, copied, or referred to must be maintained at specified police stations (Code B 9.1).

2.7.10 **How should premises entered by force be left?**

Before leaving, the officer in charge of the search must make sure they are secure by arranging for the occupier or their agent to be present or by any other appropriate means (Code B 6.13).

2.8 **Alternative Powers of Search and Seizure, Supplementary to PACE**

2.8.1 **Powers of seize and sift under Criminal Justice and Police Act 2001, Part 2 (Code B 7)**

These provisions apply to all the powers of seizure in Part II of the Act.

Where it is not reasonably practicable to determine whether things on premises fall, in whole or part, within the class of things which a person is entitled to seize, or where it is not reasonably practicable to separate seizable things from things that the person has no power to seize, he may nonetheless remove the whole of it. It thus permits the removal of items subject to legal privilege, excluded material, special procedure material, and material that is irrelevant to the investigation. It is intended to allow for the bulk seizure of property where necessary: *R v Chesterfield Justices, ex parte Bramley*, cited previously; the Explanatory Notes to the 2001 Act at para 159; Code B, para 7.7 (cited subsequently in the chapter).

The power is conferred on a person lawfully on any premises and extends to a constable, a civilian designated as a 'community support officer' under s 38 of the Police Reform Act 2002 (Sch 4, Pt 1, para 24), and a person authorized to accompany them under s 16.

Provision is made, amongst other things, for the service of notices, access to the material, and the return of things which the person has no power to seize following the sift process. Section 59 of the 2001 Act allows for applications to a judicial authority for the return of property and imposes a duty on the part of the police to 'secure' property subject to such an application preventing the material from being examined or copied or put to any use except with the consent of the applicant or in accordance with directions of the court (ss 60 and 61).

Extensive guidance on the use of the powers is contained in Code B para 7. In particular, para 7.7 states:

> ...Officers must be careful they only exercise these powers when it is essential and they do not remove any more material than necessary. The removal of large volumes of material, much of which may not ultimately be retainable, may have serious implications for the owners, particularly when they are involved in business or activities such as journalism or the provision of medical services...

2.8.2 Modified powers of access, search, and seizure in terrorist cases

(i) Terrorism Act 2000, Schedule 5; Code B 6.14 and 6.15

A modified version of PACE, s 8 and Sch 1 procedures, applicable to terrorist investigations, is provided in the Terrorism Act 2000, Sch 5. Specific guidance is given in Code B 6.14 and 6.15. Applications may be made to a magistrate for a search warrant with respect to material that does not include material subject to legal privilege, excluded material, or special procedure material (PACE, ss 10, 11, and 14). Applications may be made to a Crown Court judge for orders requiring production of or access to, or for a search warrant with respect to, material that includes excluded material or special procedure material. There are additional exceptional powers such as: the power to require a person to state the location of material to which a production order relates; the power to require a person to provide an explanation for material seized or produced; and the power, in urgent cases, of an officer of at least the rank of superintendent to give written authorization for the (aforementioned) powers normally granted only by magistrates and judges.

PACE, ss 15 and 16 apply to search warrants issued to and executed under Sch 5: Code B, Note 2A; and guidance is contained in the Code at B 6.14 and 6.15. The powers in question are exercisable by a constable.

(ii) entry, search, and seizure in connection with terrorism prevention and investigation measures

The current version of Code B makes modifications to the Code with respect to searches made under the Prevention of Terrorism Act 2005 in connection with control orders: Code B 10 and Note 2A. That Act has now been repealed. The tortuous history leading to the current legislative position is helpfully set out in the Explanatory Notes to the Terrorism Prevention and Investigation Measures Act 2011. Section 24 and Sch 5 of that Act provide powers of entry and search for the purpose of serving a relevant notice on an individual and for notice compliance and public safety purposes. In due course, Code B will need to be updated to keep pace with these changes.

2.9 Power of Entry for Specified Purposes, Including Arrest (Section 17)

As the Code states, s 17 does not create or confer any powers of arrest (Code B 4.1). It abolishes some powers and imposes conditions on the exercise of others. It abolishes all common law powers of a constable to enter premises without a warrant, save the power of entry to deal with or prevent a breach of the peace (s 17(5) and (6)). (A breach of the peace is an act done or threatened to be done which either actually harms a person, or, in his presence, his property, or is likely to cause such harm or which puts someone in fear of such harm being done.) It does not affect statutory powers, save those expressly mentioned. Nor does it apply to an officer invited into premises (*Hobson v Chief Constable of Cheshire* [2003] EWHC 3011).

2.9.1 Who may exercise the power under section 17?

The full extent of the power may be exercised by a constable (s 17(1)). A civilian designated as a 'community support officer' under s 38 of the Police Reform Act 2002 may exercise one limited component of the full power: the power to enter and search any premises in the relevant police area for the purpose of saving life or limb or preventing serious damage to property, ie that contained in s 17(1)(e) (Sch 4, Pt 1, para 8).

2.9.2 What are the preconditions to the exercise of the power under section 17?

Entry and search of premises is permitted by s 17 for the following purposes and subject to the following conditions:

(i) executing specified powers of arrest or recapture, where the constable has reasonable grounds for believing that the person whom he is seeking is on the premises

Section 17(1) lists a wide range of powers of arrest or recapture for which purpose a constable may enter and search premises. They fall within the following categories:

- the execution of a warrant of arrest in criminal proceedings or a 'warrant of commitment' (relating to the failure to pay a sum arising from conviction or order in a Magistrates' Court);
- the arrest of a person for an 'indictable offence';
- the arrest of a person for a wide range of specified particular offences (three of which offences—such as trespassing and squatting—connected to the entering or occupation of premises, are stated to be exercisable only by an officer in uniform (s 17(3)));
- the arrest of a child or young person remanded or committed to local authority accommodation;
- the recapturing of a person unlawfully at large, consisting either of (1) persons 'unlawfully at large' whom the officer is 'pursuing' (s 17(1)(d)), or (2) persons who have escaped from a specified category of places of detention, ie prisons etc, whether or not they are being pursued (s 17(1)(cb)). The phrase 'unlawfully at large' is used in many statutes. It denotes that a person is subject to lawful detention of any kind and has either absconded or escaped or failed to surrender.

49

(ii) for the purpose of saving life or limb or preventing serious damage to property (s 17(1)(e))

For this purpose, it is not necessary for the person exercising the power to have reasonable grounds for believing that the person whom he is seeking is on the premises (s 17(2)).

There is no express requirement that the dangers giving rise to the power should relate to the property entered. However, in view of the need to protect a person's rights under Article 8 of the European Convention on Human Rights (right to respect for private and family life, home, and correspondence) it must be demonstrated that the purpose requirement stated in s 17(1)(e) is strictly satisfied. In *R v Veneroso* [2002] Crim LR 306 (Crown Ct (Inner London)), a search of the home of a seriously injured person to ascertain his identity and next of kin, which resulted in the discovery of drugs, was held by the trial judge to be outside of the purpose in s 17(1)(e) and in breach of Article 8, with the result that the evidence was excluded under s 78.

In *Baker v Crown Prosecution Service* [2009] EWHC 299 (Admin) at para 20, the following propositions as to the scope of the power were accepted:

- A constable entering and searching premises for the purpose of saving life or limb does not need the permission of the occupant.
- The words 'saving life or limb' are wide enough to cover saving a person from seriously harming himself or herself, as well as from seriously harming third parties.
- Although it may be desirable in many cases for the officer exercising his power under s 17(1) to enter premises to give the occupant present the reason for his exercising that power, there is no hard and fast rule to that effect. There is no need for the officer to give the occupant any such explanation where it is impossible, impractical, or undesirable to do so, such as when an emergency required the officers to enter the premises in question.

2.9.3 What is the extent of the search permitted by the power under section 17?

The power of search conferred by the section is limited to the extent that is reasonably required for the purpose for which the power of entry is exercised (s 17(4)).

Except for searches under s 17(1)(e) (ie the second of the two categories previously described), where the premises consist of two or more separate dwellings, the search is limited to common parts and any dwelling in which the constable has reasonable grounds for believing that the person whom he is seeking is on (s 17(2)). Where a flat was a single premises with three bedrooms separately occupied, which were individually numbered, and each could be locked by its occupant, there was a sufficient degree of exclusive occupancy and privacy provided by the allocation of a separate bedroom, as to create separate dwellings for the purposes of s 17 PACE: *Thomas v DPP* [2009] EWHC 3906 (Admin), where it was said (para 5) that 'homeless people living in rooms in local authority hostels are as much entitled to the protection of the law as those living a more settled and conventional life'.

2.9.4 In what circumstances may force be used under section 17?

The constable may use reasonable force, if necessary, in the exercise of the power (s 117). However, before doing so, he should, unless it was impossible, impracticable, or undesirable to do so, give the occupant of the property reasons for his seeking to gain access. This is because Parliament clearly had that common law obligation in mind when conferring the power of entry on the police under the Act: *O'Loughlin v Chief Constable of Essex* [1998] 1 WLR 374, CA (Civ Div).

2.10 Entry and Search after Arrest (Section 18)

2.10.1 Who may exercise the power under section 18?

The power may be exercised by a constable (s 18(1)) or by a civilian designated as an 'investigating officer' under s 38 of the Police Reform Act 2002 (Sch 4, Pt 2, para 18(a)).

2.10.2 What are the preconditions to the exercise of the power under section 18?

A constable may enter and search premises under s 18 if the following conditions are satisfied:

(i) the premises are occupied or controlled by a person under arrest for indictable offence (s 18(1)); and...

Actual occupation or control is a strict factual requirement and where there is uncertainty other powers should be preferred. A reasonable belief as to the facts is not enough to make the search lawful: *Khan v Commissioner of Police of the Metropolis* [2008] EWCA Civ 723. As the court noted in that case, other powers of entry, for which 'reasonable belief' will suffice, were available to the police under s 32 PACE, or by obtaining a search warrant under s 8 of PACE. 'Controlled' is a wider notion than 'occupied': it will embrace premises which the person manages in the sense that he runs them or organizes their occupation, even if he has no legal right to be in them.

(ii) the constable has reasonable grounds for suspecting that there is on the premises evidence, other than items subject to legal privilege (as defined in s 10), that relates either (1) to the offence for which the person was arrested

or (2) to some other indictable offence, connected with or similar to that offence (s 18(1)); and ...

The word 'offence' means a domestic (rather than foreign) offence, although there is a surviving common law power of search and seizure with respect to the investigation of foreign offences: *R (Rottman) v Metropolitan Police Comr* [2002] 2 WLR 1315 (HL).

(iii) either the search has been authorized in writing by an officer of the rank of inspector or above (or a sergeant authorized to exercise that power under s 107) or that, before the arrested person has been taken to a police station or released on bail, his presence at a place other than a police station is necessary for the effective investigation of the offence (in which case no written authorization is required) (s 18(4)–(5A))

Where a search is conducted in the circumstances which permit a search without authorization, an officer of the rank of inspector or above (or a sergeant authorized to exercise that power under s 107) must be informed of the search as soon as practicable after it has been made. Authority should only be given if the authorizing officer is satisfied that the necessary grounds exist (Code B 4.3). If possible the authorizing officer should record the authority on the Notice of Powers and Rights and, unless revealing his identity would put him in danger, sign the Notice (Code B 4.3). The record of the grounds for the search and the nature of the evidence sought as required by s 18(7) of the Act should be made in the custody record if there is one; otherwise the officer's pocket book, or the search record (Code B 4.3).

2.10.3 What is the extent of the search permitted by the power under section 18?

The power of search conferred by the section is limited to the extent that is reasonably required for the purpose of discovering such evidence (s 18(3). Unlike s 17(2), there is no express limitation with respect to premises consisting of multiple dwellings. However, the limitation in s 18(1) achieves a similar effect because only premises occupied and controlled by the person under arrest may be searched and, where the premises consist of multiple dwellings, that will limit the search to those parts actually occupied or controlled by the person. Code B 6.9 confines the extent of a search to that which is necessary to achieve the purpose of the search, having regard to the size and nature of whatever is sought. Code B 6.9A requires the search to stop once the object of that search has been achieved.

2.10.4 In what circumstances may force be used under section 18?

The constable may use reasonable force, if necessary, in the exercise of the power (s 117). However, before doing so, he should, unless it was impossible, impracticable, or undesirable to do so, give the occupant of the property reasons for his seeking to gain access. This is because Parliament clearly had that common law obligation in mind when conferring the power of entry on the police under the Act (*O'Loughlin v Chief Constable of Essex* [1998] 1 WLR 374, CA (Civ Div)) and because of the mandatory language in Code B (*Linehan v DPP* [2000] Crim LR 861, DC).

2.10.5 **What may be seized and retained under section 18?**

'Anything' for which he may search under the section may be seized and retained, (ie, evidence, other than items subject to legal privilege (as defined in s 10), that relates either (1) to the offence for which the person was arrested, or (2) to some other indictable offence, connected with or similar to that offence (s 18(1)); s 18(2)).

A movable vehicle may be seized as 'anything' within the section, notwithstanding that the vehicle itself amounts to 'premises' within the meaning of the Act (s 23) since 'anything' includes 'everything' (*Cowan v Condon* [2000] 1 WLR 254, CA (Civ Div)). See Code B, Note 7B: the principle extends to tents and caravans.

There is an extension of the power to require electronic data to be produced in a form in which it is or may readily become intelligible (see s 20 discussed subsequently in the chapter). Rights to access and copies of things seized are provided (see s 21 discussed subsequently in the chapter). The length of time that seized things may be retained is set out in s 22 (discussed subsequently in the chapter).

2.10.6 **What records must be kept of the search under section 18?**

The authorizing officer, or the officer informed of the search, must make a record in writing of the grounds for the search and the nature of the evidence sought (s 18(7)); and, where the arrested person is in police detention at the time of the making of the record, it should be made in that person's custody record (s 18(8)). If there is no custody record, it should be made in the authorizing officer's pocket book or the search record (Code B 4.3).

2.11 **General Power of Seizure (Section 19)**

2.11.1 **Who may exercise the power under section 19?**

The power may be exercised by a constable (s 19(1)) or by a civilian designated as an 'investigating officer' under s 38 of the Police Reform Act 2002 (Sch 4, Pt 2, para 19(a)).

2.11.2 **What are the preconditions to the exercise of the power under section 19?**

The officer may seize items in premises under s 19 if the following conditions are satisfied.

(i) he is lawfully on the premises (s 19(1)); and...

In *R (Cook) v Serious Organised Crime Agency* [2010] EWHC 2119 (Admin), the court rejected the proposition that however unlawful the seizure of property, provided it ends up on premises at which the presence of a police officer is lawful (such as a police station), that officer can then convert what is unlawful possession into lawful possession by seizing it a second time. The issue was decided on the basis that the alternative construction failed to have regard to the structure of the legislation and the seriousness of the interference with rights that would result. The position may be different where what precedes the later seizure in premises is a taking into possession otherwise than by unlawful seizure, eg the taking of samples in a post mortem examination where a body has previously been taken by police from an open space.

(ii) he has reasonable grounds for believing:

(a) that the item seized is either (1) a thing which has been obtained in consequence of the commission of an offence (s 19(2): eg stolen items or the proceeds of crime) or (2) that it is evidence in relation to an offence he is investigating or any other offence (s 19(3)); and

(b) that it is necessary to seize it in order to prevent it being concealed, lost, damaged, altered or destroyed (s 19(2)(b) and s 19(3)(b)); and...

In fact, the word 'damaged' is omitted from s 19(3)(b) (which is otherwise in identical form to s 19(2)(b)) but this is probably an inadvertent drafting error. It would appear that, unlike the use of the phrase 'relevant evidence' in s 8, 'evidence' may here include material which would be inadmissible at trial. The word 'offence' means a domestic (rather than foreign) offence, although there is a surviving common law power of search and seizure with respect to the investigation of foreign offences (*R (Rottman) v Metropolitan Police Comr* [2002] 2 WLR 1315 (HL)). The section supplements without repealing existing powers of seizure (s 19(5)). (An example of such a power in a different statute is s 26(3) of the Theft Act 1968.)

(iii) the item is not one which he has reasonable grounds for believing to be subject to legal privilege (as defined in s 10) (s 19(6)).

2.11.3 How may an officer seize electronic data under the general section 19 power?

There is a special rule for electronic data in s 19(4). The officer may require it to be produced in a form in which it can be taken away and is either a form (1) in which it is visible or legible, or (2) from which it can readily be produced in a visible and legible form. This would include print-outs and copies of data processed so as to be intelligible. It may include a whole computer.

The conditions are similar to the general seizure conditions but tailored to deal with electronic data. In that respect, they are narrower than the extension of specific powers of seizure to electronic data effected by s 20. The conditions are:

(i) he is lawfully on the premises (s 19(1)); and

(ii) electronic information is accessible from the premises; and...

This would include electronic information which is stored off the premises but is accessible, for example, through a network.

(iii) he has reasonable grounds for believing:

> **(a)** that the electronic information either (1) has been obtained in consequence of the commission of an offence or (2) is evidence in relation to an offence he is investigating or any other offence; and

> **(b)** that it is necessary to seize it in order to prevent it being concealed, lost, tampered with or destroyed; and

(iv) the information is not information which he has reasonable grounds for believing to be subject to legal privilege (as defined in s 10) (s 19(6)).

Section 19(6) speaks of an 'item' but, from the context, this must include electronic data.

2.11.4 How long may seized things be retained?

See s 22 discussed subsequently in the chapter.

2.12 Extension of Powers of Seizure to Computerized Information (Section 20)

2.12.1 Who may exercise the power under section 20?

The power may be exercised by a constable (s 20(1)) or by a civilian designated as an 'investigating officer' under s 38 of the Police Reform Act 2002 (Sch 4, Pt 2, para 16(g)).

2.12.2 How may an officer seize electronic data under the extension in section 20?

The power is framed in similar terms to that in s 19 but without the requirement that the officer must fear the destruction, etc of the electronic data. Under s 20, the officer may require it to be produced in a form in which it can be taken away and is either a form (1) in which it is visible or legible, or (2) from which it can readily be produced in a visible and legible form. This would include print-outs and copies of data processed so as to be intelligible. It may include a whole computer.

The officer may seize items in premises under s 20 if the following conditions are satisfied.

(i) he has entered premises under any statutory power; and

(ii) he is exercising a statutory power of seizure in any Act (whether passed before or after PACE) or the powers of seizure contained in PACE in (1) s 8 (magistrates' search warrant) or (2) Sch 1 (judge's search warrant) or (3) s 18 (entry and search after arrest).

2.12.3 How long may seized things be retained?

See s 22 discussed subsequently in the chapter.

2.13 Rights to Access and Copies or Photographs of Seized Material (Section 21)

Rights are extended to persons with respect to seized material. In the case of companies, the person possessing the statutory right is the company itself and not its directors (*Re DPR Futures Limited* [1989] 1 WLR 778, Ch D).

2.13.1 Record of seizure (Section 21(1), (2), and (9); Code B 7.16)

The occupier of premises or person having custody or control of them immediately before seizure has a right, upon request, to a record of what is seized, which must be provided within a reasonable time of the request, in the following circumstances:

- a thing is seized by a constable or by a civilian designated as an 'investigating officer' under s 38 of the Police Reform Act 2002 (Sch 4, Pt 2, para 16(h)) or by a person authorized (under s 16(2)) to accompany a person executing a warrant;
- the constable etc is acting under any statutory power.
- Code B 7.16 describes what must be provided as a 'list or description of the property'.

2.14 Access to Seized Material (Section 21(3), (8), and (9); Code B 7.17)

Access, on request, to seized and retained things must be allowed to a person having custody or control of the thing immediately before seizure (or someone acting on their behalf) in the following circumstances and subject to the following conditions (s 21(3)):

- the thing is seized and retained for the purpose of investigating an offence by a constable or by a civilian designated as an 'investigating officer' under s 38 of the Police Reform Act 2002 (Sch 4, Pt 2, para 16(i)) or by a person authorized (under s 16(2)) to accompany a person executing a warrant;

- access is under the supervision of a constable or by a civilian designated as an 'investigating officer' under s 38 of the Police Reform Act 2002 (Sch 4, Pt 2, para 16(i)).

There are two important provisos permitting the denial of such access, one statutory, the other derived from Code B:

- Where the officer in charge of the investigation for the purposes of which it was seized has reasonable grounds for believing that granting access would prejudice that investigation or the investigation of another offence or the criminal investigations into those offences (s 21(8)).
- When such access might lead to the commission of an offence by providing access to unlawful material such as pornography (Code B 7.17).

The affected persons are to be provided, on request, with photographs or copies 'at their own expense' (Code B 7.17) and within a reasonable time from the making of the request (s 21(4)–(7)). Oddly, there is no requirement that access should be provided within a reasonable time. Given the general scheme of the section, this is probably an oversight and should be read into the section. Code B 7.17 preserves the ambiguity but tends to suggest that the reasonable time requirement should apply to providing access on request.

2.15 Photographs or Copies (Section 21(3)–(9))

Photographs and copies of things should be provided, on request, in the same circumstances and subject to the same conditions and provisos as set out in para 2.14 in relation to access, with these differences:

- Photographs or copies, made on request, must be provided within a reasonable time of a request (s 21(7)).
- The constable etc has the option, where there is a request for a photograph or copy (and the provisos don't apply) of either obtaining such copies himself or of permitting access under supervision to the person affected for the purpose of photographing it (s 21(4)).
- In addition, a photograph or copy may be made without such a request (s 21 (5)). There is nothing in the section to require (or to prevent) the provision of a copy to the affected person in those circumstances.

2.16 The Duration of Retention of Seized Items (Section 22)

Anything seized by a constable or by a civilian designated as an 'investigating officer' under s 38 of the Police Reform Act 2002 (Sch 4, Pt 2, para 16(i)) or by a person authorized (under s 16(2)) to accompany a person executing a warrant may be retained for the following periods:

(i) in the case of (1) anything lawfully seized, whether justified by statute or common law, or (2) electronic data taken following a requirement under s 19 (general power of seizure) or s 20 (extension to electronic data), for so long as is necessary in all the circumstances (s 22(1); Code B 7.14 and 7.15).

See *R v Chief Constable of Lancashire, ex p Parker* 97 Cr App R 90, DC at 98 (discussed subsequently).

Section 22 requires a fact-sensitive judgement as to what is necessary in terms of the retention of material in order to carry out the purposes of the powers in ss 19 and 20; and one which balances all the factors relevant to those purposes. On that basis, the police could lawfully retain property seized under ss 19 and 20 PACE, after the CPS had decided not to prosecute, for the purpose of facilitating a private prosecution by the Federation Against Copyright Theft Ltd: *Scopelight Ltd and others v Chief Constable of Northumbria Police Force and another* [2009] EWCA Civ 1156.

(ii) in the case of anything falling within (i) but seized for the purpose of a criminal investigation, unless a photograph or copy would suffice, for the time required for its use either (1) as evidence at a trial or (2) for forensic examination in connection with an offence or (3) for investigation in connection with an offence (s 22(2)(a) and (4); Code B 7.14 and 7.15).

The wording of this section was wrestled with by the Court of Appeal in *R v Chief Constable of Lancashire, ex p Parker*, cited previously, at 98. In rejecting the suggestion that s 22(2)(a) permitted the retention of unlawfully obtained items, the Court held that s 22(2)(a) gave specific examples of matters falling within s 22(1).

(iii) in the case of anything for which there are reasonable grounds for believing that it has been obtained in consequence of the commission of an offence, unless a photograph or copy would suffice, for the time required to establish its lawful owner (s 22(2)(b) and (4)).

(iv) in the case of an item seized on the ground that it may be used to cause physical injury or to damage property or to interfere with evidence or to assist in the escape of a person lawfully detained, until the person from whom it was seized is released from the custody of the police or the court on bail or otherwise (s 22(3)).

Practical Guidance

2.17 Case Study 1 (Sections 18 and 19)

Smith, a well-known thief, is arrested for stealing a car radio from an unattended vehicle in an area where numerous other thefts from vehicles have recently taken place. Smith occupies a bed sit in a large house that is separated into several rooms where residents share a communal kitchen. At the station, the arresting officer applies to his inspector for written authority to search Smith's room under s 18 of PACE. This is granted and officers attend the address to carry out the search. At the house, other residents have no objection to Smith's room being searched but refuse access to the communal kitchen. A search of Smith's room by PC Gordon reveals no stolen property but a substance is discovered hidden under a mattress believed to be a controlled drug. PC Gordon considers that other rooms within the house may also have drugs in them.

Was the inspector correct to authorize a search of Smith's house?

Smith is under arrest for an indictable offence and his address is known. He is a well-known thief and there have been other thefts from vehicles in the same area. Therefore, there are reasonable grounds to suspect that stolen property from other vehicle thefts may be found at his address and the authority was fully justified.

What parts of the house can be searched?

The officers have the right to search those parts of the premises occupied or controlled by Smith (s 18(1) and s 18(3); Code B 6.9 and 6.9A). In addition to his own room, this includes those communal areas to which Smith has access such as the kitchen. It does not include those parts that are occupied as separate dwellings by other persons. PC Gordon's suspicion is not enough to empower him to search under s 18 in the other separate dwellings in the premises. If he really has reasonable grounds to believe that such substances will be found, he should obtain a search warrant.

Do the searching officers have any power to seize the substance suspected of being a controlled drug?

Although the substance is not directly connected with or similar to the offence for which Smith was arrested, the general power of seizure under s 19 is relevant. The officers are lawfully on the premises and may seize anything if there are reasonable grounds to believe the item in question has been obtained in consequence of the commission of an offence (and that it is necessary to seize it in order to prevent it being destroyed etc).

2.18 Case Study 2 (Sections 17, 18, and 19 [and Section 32])

PC Brown lawfully arrests Jones for interfering with a motor vehicle. Whilst waiting for the police van and before being searched, Jones breaks away and runs to his house, closely pursued by the officer, and goes inside. Having received no response to repeated knocking, PC Brown forces the door open, searches the premises, and finds Jones hiding in the loft.

Did PC Brown have lawful authority to use force to enter the premises?

Although Jones was not under arrest for an indictable offence he was unlawfully at large and was being pursued by police. In these circumstances PC Brown had a right to enter the premises by virtue of s 17(1)(d) of PACE. He was entitled to use reasonable force in the exercise of the power by virtue of s 117.

Could PC Brown have carried out a search under section 18 or section 32 PACE whilst on the premises?

In this case, the offence for which Jones was arrested is 'summary only'. Under s 18, PC Brown can only search premises occupied or controlled by a person under arrest for an indictable offence. Under s 32, a search of premises is only permitted where the person is arrested for an indictable offence and was in premises when arrested, or immediately before being arrested (s 32(1)(b)). Accordingly, PC Brown had no power, in these circumstances, to search under either s 18 or s 32. However, if while searching for Jones, PC Brown found any item that he reasonably suspected had been obtained as a result of a criminal offence (and that it was necessary to seize it to prevent it being concealed etc) then the officer could seize this as well by virtue of s 19.

2.19 Case Study 3 (Search Warrants)

DC Potts has received information from an informant that stolen goods are hidden in the house of a man known to the officer to have previous convictions for burglary. DC Potts is unsure about the best way to respond to this information. What advice should DC Potts be given?

DC Potts should be advised that obtaining a search warrant may be the best way forward but he must first take reasonable steps to check the information is correct. The credibility of the informant is very important and it would be relevant that the person has on a number of previous occasions provided accurate information. Even if the informant is tried and tested, DC Potts should still take steps to verify the accuracy of the information, for example, by obtaining a description of the stolen goods and their location in the house. This may connect the goods to a recent theft or burglary in the area and add more credence to the information. In addition, DC Potts should make reasonable enquiries to establish if anything is known about the premises and the occupier and obtain any other information that may be relevant (Code B 3.1 to 3.3(i)–(ii)). Having taken steps to verify the information, DC Potts should then seek the written authority of an officer of at least Inspector rank to proceed with the application.

Inspector North is approached by DC Potts and requested to provide written authority for him to apply for a search warrant. What should Inspector North establish before complying with this request?

Inspector North should establish that DC Potts has indeed taken reasonable steps to check the accuracy of the information and properly carried out the steps as listed in the Code of Practice. He should also satisfy himself that the criteria under s 8 are present. The execution of a search warrant is a serious infringement of an individual's liberty and the role of the inspector is vital to ensure that applications for search warrants are both necessary and reasonable.

DS Cooper has obtained an 'all premises' search warrant under s 8(1A)(b). He has identified a house that is controlled by a suspect who was specified in the application. DS Cooper is unsure how to proceed and asks Inspector North for advice.

Inspector North should advise DS Cooper that if the identified premises are not specified on the search warrant then they may not be searched unless the prior written authority of an officer of at least inspector rank is obtained. Providing Inspector North is not involved in the investigation himself he may give the necessary authorization. Inspector North should ensure the search warrant is with respect to 'all premises' and that there are reasonable grounds to believe that a person who was specified in the application controls the premises DS Cooper wishes to search. If so satisfied, Inspector North should prepare a written authorization (s 16(3A); Code B 6.3B).

DS Cooper informs Inspector North that there is likely to be a considerable quantity of documentary material at the premises, only a small part of which will be of substantial value to the investigation. He suggests that the most efficient method would be to seize all the documents and bring them to the station for examination. Any not connected with the investigation can then be returned to the owner. What advice should Inspector North give DS Cooper?

Inspector North should advice DS Cooper that before any item is seized there must be reasonable grounds for believing the item in question is likely to be relevant evidence, of substantial value to the investigation, and not subject to legal privilege or excluded or special procedure material. Therefore, the wholesale seizure of large amounts of documents to be sifted through later is not allowed under the Act. DS Cooper should be advised that he has two alternatives: either the documents should be examined at the premises and only those that come within the previously stated criteria seized; or the material may now be removed in accordance with the 'seize and sift powers' contained in Criminal Justice and Police Act 2001, Pt 2.

DS Cooper carries out the search and subsequently discovers that a letter from the suspect's solicitor, addressed to the suspect and giving legitimate legal advice was inadvertently seized. Having examined the document he considers that it may provide some evidence of the offence he is investigating. DS

Cooper asks Inspector North if he can use the document as evidence against the suspect.

Inspector North should advise DS Cooper that the letter is subject to legal privilege and despite being seized in good faith cannot be used as evidence against the suspect. DS Cooper should be advised to destroy any copies made of the letter and return it to the suspect.

2.20 Case Study 4 (Search Warrants)

DC Brown is the investigating officer in a case where a male suspect, Burton, is believed to have used his laptop computer to access sites containing indecent images of children and to download them. Intelligence indicated that the suspect had been tipped off about the enquiry and DC Brown therefore swiftly obtained a warrant under s 8 PACE to search the suspect's home address for the computer. No computer was found; however DC Brown was in possession of sufficient other evidence to provide reasonable grounds to arrest Burton who, on arrival at the station, requested the attendance of a local solicitor.

In the course of the interview, Burton submitted a pre-prepared statement in which he admitted that he did get wind of the fact that the police suspected him of downloading images. Although maintaining innocence, he further states that he did not trust the police to carry out a fair examination of his computer and so took the laptop to the office of his solicitor, Mr Green, for safe-keeping.

Mr Green confirms to DC Brown that he does have the computer in his possession and is arranging for its examination. Further, Mr Green informs DC Brown that he cannot hand over the laptop to the police without his client's permission, but is willing to confirm in writing that his firm has the laptop, that arrangements are being made expeditiously to have it examined by an independent expert, and that all relevant content, including any that is adverse to his client will be passed to the police. Mr Green adds that in view of his client's mistrust of the police this would be the most appropriate way forward, and one that would ensure his client maintained confidence in the integrity of the investigative process.

DC Brown, however, is keen to obtain a search warrant to search Mr Green's office for the laptop and believes that it would be appropriate to make an application under the Special Procedure provisions of Sch 1 PACE. In accordance with Code B, para 3.4, DC Brown seeks written authority from an inspector to apply to a circuit judge for a search warrant and approaches Inspector Orton with this request.

Into which category does the laptop fall?

Inspector Orton should consider whether the laptop can be placed in the category of excluded material under s 11(1) (personal records, human tissue or journalistic material), or special procedure material under s 14(1), (2) (material acquired by a trade, business or profession and held in confidence subject to an express or implied undertaking to that effect). Under these circumstances the laptop is unlikely to fit into the former category but is very likely to come within the latter. Indeed, it is difficult to conceive of circumstances where material passed by a client to a solicitor would not constitute special procedure material, and it would be sensible to apply a generous interpretation and err on the side of caution.

What factors should be considered by Inspector Orton in deciding whether to authorize an application and by the judge in deciding whether to issue a search warrant?

As only special procedure material is sought, it is only necessary to pass through the first set of access conditions (Sch 1, para 2). Inspector Orton should therefore consider whether there are reasonable grounds to believe that:

- an indictable offence has been committed (possession of indecent images of a person under 18 is an indictable offence);
- there is material consisting of special procedure material on the relevant premises (the laptop is such material and Mr Green has stated that the laptop is in his possession);
- the material is likely to be of substantial value to the matter under investigation and relevant evidence (any indecent images found on the laptop would be primary evidence);
- other methods of obtaining the laptop have been tried without success, or would be bound to fail if tried (Mr Green has been asked to hand over the laptop and has refused);
- it is in the public interest that access to the laptop is granted (possession of indecent images of children is a serious offence, which it is in the public interest to investigate).

Inspector Orton could be satisfied that he should authorize DC Brown to apply to a circuit judge for an order compelling Mr Green to produce the laptop to him within seven days from the date the order was made. However, to obtain a search warrant it would be necessary to satisfy the judge of one or more further conditions.

What further conditions must the judge be satisfied of?

Under Sch 1, para 14, it would be necessary to satisfy the judge of one or more of the following:

- It was not practicable to communicate with Mr Green or other persons regarding access to the premises or the material ('practicable' bears a wider meaning than 'feasible' or 'physically possible'; nevertheless, in this case it would be difficult to suggest that this condition applies).
- Material subject to a statutory restriction on disclosure is likely to be disclosed unless a search warrant is issued (not applicable here).

- The service of a notice of application of an order would seriously prejudice the investigation (because, eg, the laptop, or any evidence on it, would be removed or destroyed).

If none of the further conditions are satisfied, what alternative options are available?

It is unlikely in the circumstances of this case that any of the further conditions would be made out. As previously indicated, the appropriate course of action in such circumstances would be to apply to the judge for a production order directing Mr Green to hand over the laptop to the police.

What if it is believed that the solicitor will not comply with such an order?

The application for a production order should take place *inter partes* and on notice; once notice has been served on Mr Green then no steps can be taken to conceal, destroy, alter or dispose of the material without the leave of the judge or written authority from the police. Failure to comply with the order can be dealt with as a contempt of court (Sch 1, para 15). A solicitor is not to be regarded as somehow tainted or unreliable simply because he has acted for someone charged or convicted of a criminal offence; however it may be appropriate to obtain a search warrant where the solicitor's firm itself is being investigated— *R (Faisaltex Ltd) v Preston Crown Court* [2008] EWHC 2832 (Admin). In addition, a subsequent application for a search warrant could of course be made on the grounds that the production order has not been complied with—Sch 1, para 12(b)(i), (ii).

2.21 **Decision-making Chart for Obtaining Material on Premises by Warrant etc**

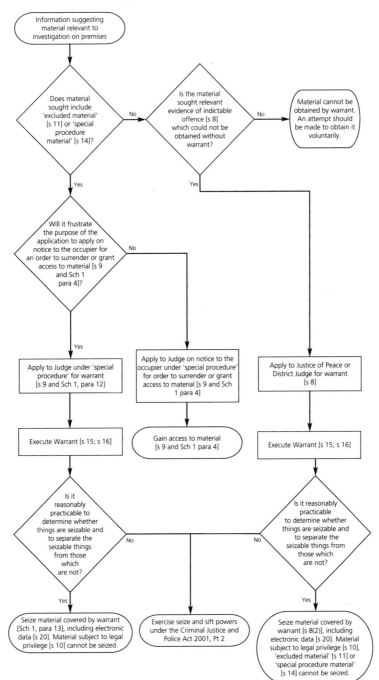

3

Arrest: Part III

Law and Commentary

3.1 Introduction

Part III of the Act has the title 'Arrest'. The principal provisions in this Part provide the following powers and duties:

(i) Arrest without warrant by constables (s 24) and other persons (s 24A)

(ii) Information to be given on arrest (s 28)

(iii) Powers and procedures with respect to persons arrested elsewhere than at police station (s 30)

(iv) The bail of persons arrested elsewhere than at police station ('street bail') (ss 30A–D)

(v) The arrest of persons at police stations, attending voluntarily (s 29) or by arrest for further offence (s 31)

(vi) Search of persons and search and entry of premises upon arrest at a place other than a police station (s 32)

A revised Code G, effective from 12 November 2012, substantially increases the guidance on the statutory power of arrest by police officers.

3.2 Arrest without Warrant by Constables (Section 24) and Other Persons (Section 24A)

3.2.1 The SOCPA reforms; powers of constable and civilians compared

The SOCPA reforms

The Serious Organised Crime and Police Act 2005 reformed this general power, splitting it into two sections which cover separately, first, arrests effected by constables and, secondly, those effected by other persons.

The new sections retain the division that existed in the old s 24 between arrests for which 'reasonable grounds to suspect' are necessary and arrests for which such grounds are not necessary. Essentially, if it is established that the right person has been arrested, the arrest is regarded as lawful without more; otherwise, its lawfulness will depend upon the arresting person having such grounds. This distinction is more relevant to the assessment after the event of whether an arrest is lawful than to the assessment by an officer of whether he may arrest. (No sensible officer is going to set out to arrest the right person for the wrong reason.) Accordingly, we suggest below both a practical test for arrests and a test for determining after the event whether the arrest is in fact lawful. (Further, it is arguable that, notwithstanding the terms of ss 24 and 24A where an arrest is made without reasonable suspicion of the person having committed an offence, the arrest is in breach of Art 5 of the European Convention on Human Rights: see *Blackstone's Criminal Practice 2013* para D1.24.)

Under both sections, the arresting person must have reasonable grounds for believing that a power of summary arrest is necessary for one of a number of specified reasons (the 'necessity criteria'): s 24(4) and (5) and s 24A(3)(a) and (4). (The meaning of the phrases 'reasonable grounds to suspect' and 'reasonable grounds for believing' is different: see subsequently in the chapter.) The introduction of the necessity criteria was part of the most radical reform: the extension of a constable's power of summary arrest from being limited to more serious offences (the old 'arrestable offence' now gone from s 24(1)) to extending now to all offences. The trade-off involved is described in Code G 2.6:

> Extending the power of arrest to all offences provides a constable with the ability to use that power to deal with any situation. However applying the necessity criteria requires the constable to examine and justify the reason or reasons why a person needs to be arrested...

In the case of constables, the necessity criteria in s 24(5) are in substance the same as the old 'general arrest conditions' contained in s 25, now repealed, but with one important addition: the additional ground in s 25(5)(e) 'to allow the prompt and effective investigation of the offence or of the conduct of the person in question'.

Indictable offence

The terms 'indictable offence', 'summary offence', and 'offence triable either way' are defined in the Interpretation Act 1978 Sch 1. The term 'offence' is not further defined but plainly consists of all three. Code G, Note 1 states that, for the purposes of the Code (which are, in this instance, the same as the Act) '"offence" means any statutory or common law offence for which a person may be tried by a magistrates' court or the Crown court and punished if convicted'. It goes on to give examples of statutory and common law offences. An indictable offence includes both 'indictable only' and 'triable either way', ie both offences which are (a) only triable in the Crown Court and (b) triable in both the Magistrates' Court and in the Crown Court.

Comparison of powers of arrest without warrant by constables and civilians

As one would expect, the constable's powers are wider than those of civilians in a number of respects:

- the constable's powers extend to arrest for *any offence* whereas the powers of other persons are confined to arrest for the more serious category of *indictable offences*;

- even then, the other person may only make the arrest where it is not reasonably practicable for a constable to make it;
- the constable has a broader list of reasons which can make out the necessity for the arrest (extending to such matters as highway obstruction, public decency, and child protection, in addition to the ascertaining of the person's identity);
- the constable may arrest persons for future offences (which are about to occur) whereas other persons can only arrest for present offences (which are occurring) or past offences (which have occurred).

There is, of course, logic to allowing civilians more limited powers than those given to constables to arrest persons, which is likely to tie in with an ordinary person's intuitive sense of when, exceptionally, a civilian arrest is justified. Other persons should never contemplate making an arrest for less serious offences or where an officer might otherwise be expected to deal with the matter. They cannot arrest in anticipation of future offending of any kind. They can only ever make an arrest where it is necessary to prevent injury, damage, or the suspect getting away. They should be very cautious about making an arrest for a completed serious offence. If nobody has committed the offence, the arrest by them will be unlawful even if they had reasonable grounds for suspecting the person arrested was guilty. (There is, however, a power given to civilians by s 3 of the Criminal Law Act 1967 to 'use such force as is reasonable in the circumstances in the prevention of crime, or in effecting or assisting in the lawful arrest of offenders or suspected offenders or of persons unlawfully at large'. It follows that a civilian may assist a constable making a lawful arrest in circumstances in which it would not be lawful for the civilian to make an arrest were the constable not present.)

The different powers of constables and other persons are represented in Table 3.1.

3.2.2 The meaning of 'reasonable grounds to suspect' and 'reasonable grounds for believing' in sections 24 and 24A

'reasonable grounds to suspect'

The classic statement of the meaning of the word suspicion in the context of the phrase 'reasonable suspicion' is that of Lord Devlin in *Hussein v Chong Fook Kam* [1970] AC 942, (PC) at p 948:

> Suspicion in its ordinary meaning is a state of conjecture or surmise where proof is lacking: 'I suspect but I cannot prove'. Suspicion arises at or near the starting-point of an investigation of which the obtaining of prima facie proof is the end. When such proof has been obtained, the police case is complete; it is ready for trial and passes on to its next stage. It is indeed desirable as a general rule that an arrest should not be made until the case is complete. But if arrest before that were forbidden, it could seriously hamper the police. To give power to arrest on reasonable suspicion does not mean that it is always or even ordinarily to be exercised. It means that there is an executive discretion. In the exercise of it many factors have to be considered besides the strength of the case.

Table 3.1

	about to commit offence		in the act of committing offence		committed an offence	
	Constable [subject to necessity criteria in 24(5)&(6)]	Other Persons	Constable [subject to necessity criteria in 24(5)&(6)]	Other Persons [subject to necessity criteria in 24A(4) AND perception of non-practicability of constable arresting 24A(3)(b)]	Constable [subject to necessity criteria in 24(5)&(6)]	Other Persons [subject to necessity criteria in 24A(4) AND perception of non-practicability of constable arresting 24A(3)(b)]
suspect actually is/ has	24(1)(a)	No power	24(1)(b)	Power limited to indictable offence 24A(1)(a)	24(3)(a)	Power limited to indictable offence 24A(2)(a)
Arresting person has reasonable grounds to suspect that suspect is/ has [even if suspect not guilty]	24(1)(c)	No power	24(1)(d)	Power limited to indictable offence 24A(1)(a)	24(2); 24(3)(b) Where no offence has been committed by anyone, power limited to where constable reasonably suspects an offence has been committed: 24(3)(b)	Power limited (a) to indictable offence & (b) only where an indictable offence has been committed by someone (even if not the suspect) 24A(2)(b)

The threshold for the existence of reasonable grounds for suspicion has been described as 'low': *Metropolitan Police Commissioner v Raissi* [2008] EWCA Civ 1237 at para 20; *Alford v Chief Constable of Cambridgeshire Police* [2009] EWCA Civ 100 at para 34.

Code G, 2.3A states: 'There must be some reasonable, objective grounds for the suspicion, based on known facts and information which are relevant to the likelihood the offence has been committed and the person liable to arrest committed it.' (See also Code C, Note 10A and the parallel terrorism provision at Code H, Note 10A; both in similar form to Code G, Note 2.3A but relating to cautions.)

'reasonable grounds for believing'

The phrase 'reasonable grounds for believing' imposes a test that is more stringent than the test of 'reasonable grounds to suspect'. Mere suspicion is insufficient: *R (Malik) v Manchester Crown Court* [2008] EWHC 1362 (Admin) at para 34.

3.2.3 Arrest without warrant by constables (section 24)

The practical test for a lawful arrest by constables

From the perspective of a constable contemplating making an arrest, practically speaking, there is a simple two-part test. The constable must have in his contemplation:

(1) reasonable grounds for suspecting that someone is about to commit/in the act of committing/has committed an offence; *and*
(2) reasonable grounds for believing that it is necessary to arrest the person for any one or more of a number of specified grounds ('the necessity criteria'):
  • to ascertain the person's name or address (including where he has reasonable grounds for doubting that he has been provided with real details);
  • to prevent the person causing physical injury to himself or another or suffering it;
  • to prevent the person causing loss or damage to property;
  • to prevent the person committing an offence against public decency (although this is confined to cases where members of the public going about their normal business cannot reasonably be expected to avoid the person);
  • to protect a child or vulnerable person from the person in question;
  • to allow the prompt and effective investigation of the offence or conduct of the person;
  • to prevent any prosecution for the offence being hindered by the disappearance of the person.

This is reflected in Code B, para 2.1 which states:

A lawful arrest requires two elements:

A person's involvement or suspected involvement or attempted involvement in the commission of a criminal offence;

AND

Reasonable grounds for believing that the person's arrest is necessary.
  • both elements must be satisfied, and
  • it can never be necessary to arrest a person unless there are reasonable grounds to suspect them of committing an offence.

The assessment of the lawfulness of an arrest by a constable

The arrest by a constable without warrant of a person for any offence will be lawful where:

(i) the constable has in his contemplation reasonable grounds for believing that it is necessary to arrest the person for any one or more of the necessity criteria (as previously discussed); *and*

(ii) the person is, in fact, about to commit an offence, or is in the act of committing an offence, or has committed an offence (whether or not the constable has reasonable grounds to suspect those matters); or

(iii) the constable has in his contemplation reasonable grounds for suspecting that the person is about to commit an offence, or is in the act of committing an offence, or has committed an offence (whether or not the person, in fact, is guilty of such misconduct). Where no offence has been committed by anyone, the power is limited to cases where the constable reasonably suspects that an offence has been committed: s 24(3)(b).

The necessity criteria

The necessity criteria in s 24(4)–(6) require that:

(1) the officer honestly believes that arrest is necessary, for one or more identified s 24(5) reasons; and

(2) his decision is one which, objectively reviewed afterwards according to the information known to the officer at the time, is held to have been made on reasonable grounds.

This test was authoritatively decided by the Court of Appeal in *Hayes v Chief Constable of Merseyside* [2011] EWCA Civ 911 esp at paras 39–41. (Permission to appeal to the Supreme Court was refused: [2012] 1 WLR 531.) The old case law suggesting that there was a third stage in the test for a lawful arrest, requiring a constable to exercise the discretion to arrest reasonably (in the public law sense) no longer applies. It has, as the court held in *Hayes*, effectively been replaced by the requirement of necessity in the necessity criteria: *Hayes*, para 15(c); *Shields v Chief Constable of Merseyside* [2010] EWCA Civ 1281, para 13; *Fitzpatrick v Commissioner of Police of the Metropolis* [2012] EWHC 12 (Admin) paras 123–129. That does not mean that there is no discretion to be exercised in deciding whether to make an arrest, but rather, that the discretion has been subsumed within the necessity criteria.

In practical terms, the difference has little impact on the way in which officers should go about deciding whether to make an arrest. The real impact, if any, is on how the courts determine the lawfulness of the arrest after the event. Constables should still act reasonably in exercising their discretion to arrest and consider what else might be done to avoid an arrest, including making other enquiries and adopting alternatives short of arrest. (These alternatives are discussed further subsequently in the chapter.)

However, as the *Hayes* case makes clear, a sense of reality and proportionality is required. It is not necessary for the constable actively to have considered every possible alternative to arrest, or to have considered every factor that is relevant and to have disregarded every factor that is irrelevant to the issue. However, an officer ought to apply his mind to alternatives short of arrest and, if he does not do so, he is exposed to the plain risk of being found by a court to have had, objectively, no reasonable grounds for his belief that arrest was necessary: *Hayes* at paras 34 and 39; *R (Hicks) v Commissioner of Police of the Metropolis* [2012] EWHC 1947 (Admin) at para 206. This is reflected in Code G, Note 2C, which states: 'For a constable to have reasonable grounds for believing it necessary to arrest, he or she is not required to be satisfied that there is no viable alternative to arrest. However, it does mean that in all cases, the officer should consider that arrest is the practical, sensible and proportionate option in all the circumstances at the time the decision is made.'

The fact that exhaustive enquiries are not needed is nothing new. The old third stage in the test for a lawful arrest, requiring a constable to exercise the discretion to arrest reasonably in the public law sense, did not require a constable to make exhaustive enquiries but merely to have reasonably considered alternative courses where, exceptionally, they were an obvious alternative to an arrest: see *Castorina v Chief Constable of Surrey* (CA), per Purchas LJ, The Times, 15 June 1988.

There are indications in the *Hayes* case as to where courts are likely to draw the line. The court referred with apparent approval (at para 34) to an Irish case in which an officer was shown to have wrongly adopted an invariable practice to arrest where he considered that a voluntary attender would have to be arrested if he sought to leave a police station. The Divisional Court in Northern Ireland observed that the constable's policy precluded him from considering whether voluntary attendance would suffice and the court concluded that, in those circumstances, the arrest could not be said to have been based on reasonable grounds for believing that it was necessary. This is plainly a stark and unusual example. A policy precluding the consideration of alternatives cannot meet the necessity criteria. On the other hand, in a case lacking that feature, the court is likely to focus on whether there were reasonable grounds for believing that the arrest was necessary for the s 24(5) reason relied upon by the arresting constable, without being unduly distracted by consideration of possible alternatives or whether the constable had considered them. The exceptions are likely to be rare and confined to cases where it is demonstrable that the officer has shut his mind to an obvious and readily achievable alternative to arrest.

Code G guidance on the 'necessity criteria' grounds

The 2012 revised Code G puts flesh on the bones of the necessity criteria, with a greatly expanded para 2.9. Notable features include these:

- reluctance or hesitance in providing an address may indicate that a person's name cannot readily be identified;

- the fact that a person has already used or threatened violence may indicate a necessity to prevent injury;
- the fact that a suspect is a known persistent offender with a history of serial offending against property may indicate a necessity to prevent damage to property.

Valuable additions (para 2.9(e)) address the investigative necessity criteria (s 24(5)(f)) and, in particular, the circumstances in which arresting in order to interview a suspect may be justified, which include where special warnings need to be given and where it is necessary to interview suspects about other investigative action for which their arrest is necessary, such as the search of premises. (Consideration should always be given to whether voluntary attendance at an interview is a practicable alternative: Code G, Note 2F.) Code G, Note 2E states 'The meaning of "prompt" should be considered on a case by case basis taking account of all the circumstances. It indicates that the progress of the investigation should not be delayed to the extent that it would adversely affect the effectiveness of the investigation.'

Code G guidance on the requirements of proportionality and non-discriminatory behaviour

Important overriding principles are set out in the introductory paragraphs of Code G, including:

- Paragraph 1.1 states that '...[T]he power of arrest must be used fairly, responsibly, with respect for people suspected of committing offences and without unlawful discrimination. The Equality Act 2010 makes it unlawful for police officers to discriminate against, harass or victimise any person on the grounds of the "protected characteristics" of age, disability, gender reassignment, race, religion or belief, sex and sexual orientation, marriage and civil partnership, pregnancy and maternity when using their powers. When police forces are carrying out their functions they also have a duty to have regard to the need to eliminate unlawful discrimination, harassment and victimisation and to take steps to foster good relations.'
- Paragraph 1.2 states that '[T]he exercise of the power of arrest represents an obvious and significant interference with the Right to Liberty and Security under Article 5 of the European Convention on Human Rights set out in Part I of Schedule 1 to the Human Rights Act 1998'. (Art 5.1.c. of the Convention states '1. Everyone has the right to liberty and security of person. No one shall be deprived of his liberty save in the following cases and in accordance with a procedure prescribed by law:...c. the lawful arrest or detention of a person effected for the purpose of bringing him before the competent legal authority on reasonable suspicion of having committed an offence or when it is reasonably considered necessary to prevent his committing an offence or fleeing after having done so.')

- Paragraph 1.3: 'When the power of arrest is exercised it is essential that it is exercised in a non-discriminatory and proportionate manner which is compatible with the Right to Liberty under Article 5.'

The duty to consider alternatives to arrest

The old case law suggesting that such a duty exists as a feature of the duty to exercise the discretion to arrest reasonably in the public law sense (see eg *Castorina v Chief Constable of Surrey*, cited previously) requires reappraisal. The law is now that previously stated in relation to the two-part necessity criteria test: failure to consider alternatives does not of itself invalidate the arrest but does expose an officer to the risk of being found to have had, objectively, no reasonable grounds for his belief that arrest was necessary. As previously stated, in practical terms, the difference has little impact on the way in which officers should go about deciding whether to make an arrest.

Code G gives helpful guidance on the exercise of the discretion:

- Code G, para 1.3 states: 'The use of the power [of arrest] must be fully justified and officers exercising the power should consider if the necessary objectives can be met by other, less intrusive means.'
- Code G, Note para 2 states: '...Before making a decision to arrest, a constable should take account of any facts and information that are available, including claims of innocence made by the person, that might dispel the suspicion.'
- Code G, Note para 2A gives particular examples of facts and information which might point to a person's innocence and may tend to dispel suspicion. Examples given are the permissible use of force provided by common law and statute to civilians in relation to the prevention of crime, arrest, self-defence and, in particular, by school staff in certain circumstances.

Reliance on information or instructions provided by another

The case law establishes that constables need to have sufficient information to form their own independent view of the reasonableness of an arrest. That is because s 24 is within the class of statutes in which Parliament has proceeded on the longstanding constitutional theory of the independence and accountability of the individual constable. (See *O'Hara v Chief Constable of RUC* (HL (NI)) [1997] AC 286 at p 293.) The important distinction is between information upon which an independent judgement can be made (which will suffice if it affords reasonable grounds) and a mere instruction to arrest (which will not). Quite where one draws the line will depend upon the facts of the case. Self-evidently inadequate reasons will never be enough even if they come from a senior officer. In *O'Hara*, the House of Lords rejected the suggestion that reliance upon the mere orders of a senior officer was sufficient. On the other hand, an officer's reasonable grounds to suspect did not have to be based on the officer's own observations but could arise from information he had received. Information that is anonymous or from an informant, or which turns out subsequently to be wrong, may be enough. The question whether it provided reasonable grounds for the suspicion depends on the source of the information and its context, seen in the light of the whole surrounding circumstances. (See *O'Hara* at p 298.)

In *Hayes*, cited previously, it was held (at para 41) that the *O'Hara* principle was readily incorporated in to the new statutory test in s 24 in that information provided by others can be, and usually will be, part of the information which goes to an arresting officer's grounds for belief that the suspect has committed an offence and for believing that it is necessary, for a s 24(5) reason or reasons, to arrest him, and thus to the reasonableness of the beliefs.

The application of the principle was illustrated in *Raissi*, cited previously: where an officer arrested a person on instructions indicating that he was a close brother of a major suspect, that the two of them lived fairly close to each other, and that each had access to the other's homes, that was insufficient to amount to reasonable suspicion to justify the arrest; and it did not avail the officer to say that his superior probably had other information justifying arrest but had not told him what it was. In contrast, a genuine suspicion derived from a briefing by another officer could provide reasonable grounds for that suspicion even if relevant material has been omitted from the briefing: *Alford v Chief Constable of Cambridgeshire*, cited previously.

An entry in the police national computer was capable of constituting sufficient objective justification for an arrest since an officer was clearly entitled to base the grounds for his suspicion upon information received via a police informer or from the public; although, in certain other circumstances, such as where the situation was not so urgent, the arresting officer was likely to be subject to a duty to make additional enquiries before a reasonable suspicion could be founded (*Hough v Chief Constable of Staffordshire* (CA (Civ Div)) [2001] EWCA Civ 39).

In the case of information provided by others such as informants or members of the public, the reasonableness of a suspicion founded solely on such information will depend upon the reputation and reliability of the source (*Lister v Perryman* (1870) LR 4 HL 521 (HL) where it was said that 'information given by one person of whom the party knows nothing, would be regarded very differently from information given by one whom he knows to be a sensible and trustworthy person').

Assisting another officer in detaining a suspect

Under the old law, in a 'hot pursuit' or public order situation, an officer could form reasonable grounds to suspect as an inference derived from the conduct of a fellow officer: see the unreported cases referred to in R Clayton and H Tomlinson, *Civil Actions Against the Police* (3rd edn, 2003), para 5-082. The position is bound to be the same under the current statutory test. However, it must now be viewed through the lens of the two-part necessity criteria test (discussed previously in the chapter): the fact that the circumstances permit only the scantiest of facts to be inferred will support the reasonableness of forming the suspicion of the commission of an offence and the belief that the arrest is necessary on those limited facts.

Records

Records are to be made of arrest in the arresting officer's pocket book or by other methods (Code G 4).

3.2.4 **Arrest without warrant by civilians (section 24A)**

The practical test for a lawful arrest by civilians

From the perspective of a civilian contemplating making an arrest, practically speaking, there is a simple three-part test. The civilian must have:

(1) reasonable grounds in his contemplation for suspecting that someone is in the act of committing/has committed an indictable offence; *and*
(2) reasonable grounds in his contemplation for believing that it is necessary to arrest the person for any one or more of a number of specified grounds ('the civilian necessity criteria'):

- to prevent the person causing physical injury to himself or another or suffering it;
- to prevent the person causing loss or damage to property;
- to prevent the person making off before a constable can assume responsibility for him;

and
(3) it appears to the person making the arrest that it is not reasonably practicable for a constable to make it instead.

The term indictable offence is explained at para 3.2.1.

The assessment of the lawfulness of an arrest by a civilian

The arrest by a civilian of another person will be lawful where:

(i) he has in his contemplation reasonable grounds for believing that it is necessary to arrest the person for any one or more of 'the civilian necessity criteria' (as discussed previously); *and*
(ii) it appears to the person making the arrest that it is not reasonably practicable for a constable to make it instead; *and*
(iii) that the other person is in the act of committing an indictable offence or has committed an indictable offence (whether or not the arresting person has reasonable grounds to suspect these matters); *or*

(iv) the arresting person has in his contemplation reasonable grounds for suspecting that the other person is in the act of committing an indictable
offence, or has committed an indictable offence (whether or not that other
person, in fact, is guilty of such misconduct).

The requirement that it should 'appear' to the person making the arrest that it
is not reasonably practicable for a constable to make it instead (s 24A(3)(b))
does not expressly include a requirement that the person should be reasonable
in having that perception. Indeed, the use of the word 'appear' suggests that a
degree of latitude should be allowed to the person concerned, provided that
they genuinely hold the perception.

3.2.5 What act constitutes an arrest?

Neither the Act nor the Codes state what act constitutes an arrest. The case law
indicates the following:

- PACE did not change the law in relation to the question of what is an arrest.
  That question continues to be governed by the common law developed both
  before and after the enactment of PACE. (See *Lewis v Chief Constable of South
  Wales* [1991] 1 All ER 206 (CA).)
- 'Arrest' is an ordinary English word. Whether or not a person has been
  arrested depends not on the legality of the arrest but on whether he has been
  deprived of his liberty to go where he pleases. (*Lewis v Chief Constable of South
  Wales*, cited previously; *Spicer v Holt* [1977] AC 987 (HL).)
- Arrest is a continuing act; it starts with the arrester taking a person into his
  custody, (by action or words restraining him from moving anywhere beyond
  the arrester's control), and it continues until the person so restrained is either
  released from custody or, having been brought before a magistrate, is
  remanded in custody by the magistrate's judicial act. (*Mohammed-Holgate v
  Duke* [1984] AC 437 (HL) at 441.)
- Physical restraint is not required. Mere words sufficient to convey a power of
  compulsion to the arrested person will be enough: *Alderson v Booth* [1969] 2
  QB 216 (DC).
- A more nuanced analysis is required where what is in issue is confinement for
  a legitimate policing purpose: see *Austin v Commissioner of Police of the
  Metropolis* [2009] UKHL 5, which concerned the use of a cordon by police
  engaged in an unusually difficult exercise in crowd control, in order to avoid
  personal injuries and damage to property.

3.2.6 What degree of force may be used in making an arrest?

A constable may use reasonable force, if necessary, in the exercise of the power
of arrest: s 117. Similarly, a civilian may use such force as is reasonable in the
circumstances in making a lawful arrest: s 3 of the Criminal Law Act 1967.

3.3 **Repeal of Earlier Statutory Powers of Arrest Without Warrant or Order of Court (Section 26)**

Any statutory powers of arrest without warrant or order of court contained in Acts preceding the passing of the Act are repealed except for preserved powers specified in Sch 2 (those in particular Acts concerned with such matters as the Armed Forces).

3.4 **Regulations Relating to Recordable Offences (Section 27)**

Prior to their repeal by the Crime and Security Act 2010, s 27(1)–(3) consisted of provisions relating to the fingerprinting of persons in connection with recordable offences. Those provisions are now to be found in s 63A(4) and Sch 2A. See Chapter 5.

There is now little of the original s 27 left. What remains is there to maintain the framework for the creation of recordable offences. Section 118(1) states that '"recordable offence" means any offence to which regulations under section 27 above apply'. Section 27(4) and the new s 27(4A) empower the Secretary of State to make regulations providing for recording in national police records convictions etc for such offences as are specified in the regulations. (Section 27(4A), inserted by the Protection of Freedoms Act 2010, adds to the definition of convictions, cautions under Part V of the Police Act 1997, and a reprimand and warning under s 65 of the Crime and Disorder Act 1998.) The National Police Records (Recordable Offences) Regulations 2000/1139, and a number of subsequent amending Statutory Instruments, specifying offences, are currently made under s 27(4).

3.5 **Information to be Given on Arrest (Section 28)**

3.5.1 **Information needs to be given as to (a) that a person is arrested and (b) why**

Regardless of whether the fact of the purported arrest or the grounds for the arrest is obvious, the arrest of a person is not lawful unless, either at the time of the arrest or as soon as is practicable thereafter, the person is informed (s 28(1)–(4)):

(i)   that he is under arrest, and
(ii) the grounds of the arrest.

It follows that the failure to comply with this section, even when such failure appears to be inconsequential, has highly significant consequences in law. The arrest is rendered unlawful. However, if the information is given subsequently, then from that moment onwards the arrest is lawful: *R v Kulynycz* [1971] 1 QB 367 (CA); *Lewis v Chief Constable of South Wales*, cited previously.

The allegation of failure to comply with this requirement is often a feature of civil actions for false imprisonment.

Section 28(5) makes it explicit that if a person escapes before it is reasonably practicable for him to be informed of these matters, there is no requirement for the information to be given. (Presumably, the purpose is to relieve the constable of the obligation which might otherwise arise of tracking down apprehended absconders in order to render the original incomplete apprehension a lawful arrest.)

3.5.2 The gist of the legal and factual reasons why the person is arrested is enough

Guidance is contained in Code G as to information to be given on arrest. (Guidance in the same form, but specific to cautions, may be found in both Code C and Code H. See Code C 10.3; Code C, Note 10B; Code H 10.2; Code H, Note 3G and 10B.)

- Code G 3.3 states the requirements of s 28. (G 3 is mostly concerned with the interrelated requirement to caution.) It states that the arrested person should be told of 'the grounds and reasons for their arrest', which is wider than the statutory words ('grounds for') and echoes Note 3 (see the discussion subsequently in the chapter) in suggesting that a person should be told in non-technical language *why* they have been arrested.
- Code G, Note 3 states: 'An arrested person must be given sufficient information to enable them to understand they have been deprived of their liberty and the reason they have been arrested, as soon as practicable after the arrest, eg when a person is arrested on suspicion of committing an offence they must be informed of the nature of the suspected offence and when and where it was committed. The suspect must also be informed of the reason or reasons why arrest is considered necessary. Vague or technical language should be avoided.'
- A further part of Code G, Note 3 makes it clear that information on arrest should not be given to the extent that it might prejudice the investigation. 'When explaining why one or more of the arrest criteria apply, it is not necessary to disclose any specific details that might undermine or otherwise adversely affect any investigative processes. An example might be the conduct of a formal interview when prior disclosure of such details might give the suspect an opportunity to fabricate an innocent explanation or to otherwise conceal lies from the interviewer.'

The courts have provided guidance, which similarly emphasizes that, provided that the gist of the important matters is conveyed, that will suffice.

- *Christie v Leachinsky* [1947] AC 573 (HL) (the case establishing the common law principle from which s 28 was derived) at p 587: 'technical or precise language' need not be used, 'the matter is a matter of substance'.
- *Chapman v DPP* (1989) 89 Cr App R 190 (DC) at p 197: 'It is not of course to be expected that a police constable in the heat of an emergency, or while in hot pursuit of a suspected criminal, should always have in mind specific statutory provisions, or that he should mentally identify specific offences with technicality or precision. He must, in my judgment, reasonably suspect the existence of facts amounting to an arrestable offence of a kind which he has in mind. Unless he can do that he cannot comply with s 28(3) of the Act by informing the suspect of grounds which justify the arrest.'
- The arrested person must be told both the essential legal and the essential factual grounds for the arrest. The words spoken must therefore include some statement of the factual as well as some statement of the legal basis of the arrest. (*Taylor v Chief Constable of Thames Valley* [2004] EWCA Civ 858 at para 27, commending para 40 of *Fox, Campbell and Hartley v United Kingdom* (1990) 13 EHRR 157, 170 as representing the modern test. See the discussion subsequently in the chapter.)

3.5.3 Information may, where the circumstances justify it, be given in stages provided that adequate information is given promptly

In *Taylor v Chief Constable of Thames Valley*, cited previously, the Court of Appeal said (at paras 23, 26, and 57) that the best statement of the relevant principles in recent times was in para 40 of the decision of the European Court of Human Rights (ECHR) in *Fox, Campbell and Hartley v United Kingdom*, cited previously. (*Fox* was concerned with Art 5(2) of the Convention for the Protection of Human Rights and Fundamental Freedoms, which provides: 'Everyone who is arrested shall be informed promptly, in a language which he understands, of the reasons for his arrest and of any charge against him.') In *Fox*, the ECHR said at para 40:

> any person arrested must be told, in simple, non-technical language that he can understand, the essential legal and factual grounds for his arrest, so as to be able, if he sees fit, to apply to a court to challenge its lawfulness... Whilst this information must be conveyed 'promptly'... it need not be related in its entirety by the arresting officer at the very moment of the arrest. Whether the content and promptness of the information conveyed were sufficient is to be assessed in each case according to its special features.

In *Fox* itself, the ECHR held that there was no breach of Art 5(2) of the Convention where persons were initially told on arrest that they were arrested on the basis that they were 'terrorists' but were informed in the course of questioning three to four hours later sufficient detail of the specific allegations against them. Similarly, in *Taylor*, the court concluded that on an arrest (some time after the event) for violent disorder it was sufficient to tell the person arrested the date and place when it was suspected he had committed 'violent disorder'. The approach of the court in *Taylor* suggests that the statutory requirement in s 28 of providing information 'as soon as is practicable' is equivalent to the requirement of 'promptness' in Art 5(2) of the Convention.

3.6 Powers and Procedures with Respect to Persons Arrested Elsewhere than at Police Station (Section 30)

3.6.1 What are the powers and procedures?

A 'designated police station' is one which, by virtue of s 35, the chief officer designates in that area to be used for the purpose of detaining arrested persons. The effect of s 30 is that there is a presumption in favour of bringing the person to a designated police station speedily but that it can be displaced either where the person can properly be released or bailed, or where the circumstances justify taking him, in the alternative, to any police station or to some other place to carry out immediate investigations. If displaced, he must be taken to a designated police station soon thereafter unless released or bailed.

The effect of s 30 may be summarized as follows.

(i) Where, at any place other than a police station, a person is arrested by a constable or taken into custody by a constable after being arrested by a person other than a constable, the person must be taken by a constable to a police station as soon as practicable after arrest (s 30(1) and (1A)) unless (a) the person is released on bail under s 30A, or (b) released without bail under s 30(7) and (7A) (ie where there are no grounds for keeping him under arrest or releasing him on bail under s 30A), or (c) a delay is necessary in order to carry out such investigations as it is reasonable to carry out immediately (s 30(10) and s 30(10A)).

(ii) The police station to which he must be taken must be a designated police station (s 30(2)) unless the following conditions apply, in which case he may be taken to any police station:

   (a) the arresting constable works in a locality covered by a police station which is not a designated police station or the constable is maintained by an authority other than a police authority, unless it appears to the constable that it may be necessary to keep the person in police detention for more than six hours (s 30(3) and (4));

   (b) in the case of any lone constable (who has arrested or taken the person into custody without assistance and who thereafter has no assistance available), where it appears to the constable that he will be unable to take the person to a designated police station without the person injuring either himself, the constable, or some other person (s 30(5)).

(iii) Where (in accordance with the foregoing) the person is taken to a police station which is not designated, he must be taken to a designated police station within six hours unless he is first released (s 30(6)).

(iv) The release of a person or any delay in releasing him or taking him to a police station must be recorded (s 30(8) and (11)).

(v) Exceptions to the application of the procedures are specified in s 30(12) and (13). They include certain immigration and terrorism cases.

3.6.2 **To whom do the provisions apply?**

The provisions of s 30 apply to a constable and, subject to certain exceptions (eg the 'lone constable' provisions and the release without bail provisions) by a civilian designated as an 'escort officer' under s 38 of the Police Reform Act 2002 (Sch 4, Pt 4, para 34).

3.7 **The Bail of Persons Arrested Elsewhere than at Police Station ('Street Bail') (Sections 30A, 30B, and 30C)**

The Criminal Justice Act 2003 introduced a new power to release arrested persons elsewhere than at police stations, referred to in Code C as 'street bail'.

The power is free of the normal bail framework contained in the Bail Act 1976 (s 30C(3)). A person released on street bail may nonetheless be re-arrested without a warrant 'if new evidence justifying a further arrest has come to light since his release' (s 30C(4)).

Originally the only condition of bail that could be imposed when granting street bail was the requirement to attend at a police station. There is now an elaborate structure for the imposition and subsequent variation of conditions attached to street bail.

Street bail is referred to in Code G at 2.4, 2.9(e) and (f) and at Notes 2E and 2J. The latter suggests how street bail fits in with the necessity criteria:

> 2J Having determined that the necessity criteria have been met and having made the arrest, the officer can then consider the use of street bail on the basis of the effective and efficient progress of the investigation of the offence in question. It gives the officer discretion to compel the person to attend a police station at a date/time that best suits the overall needs of the particular investigation. Its use is not confined to dealing with child care issues or allowing officers to attend to more urgent operational duties and granting street bail does not retrospectively negate the need to arrest.

3.7.1 **What are the terms and conditions of the power?**

(i)   The power applies to persons who, at any place other than a police station, are arrested by a constable or taken into custody by a constable after being arrested by a person other than a constable (s 30A(1) and s 30(1)).
(ii) Such a person may be released on bail at any time before he arrives at a police station (s 30A(2)).
(iii) A person released on bail must be subject to a requirement to attend a police station (whether designated or not) (s 30A(3), (5)).
(iv) A person released on bail may be made subject to such conditions as the constable who releases that person on bail deems necessary (s 30A(3B)):
   (a) to secure that the person surrenders to custody;
   (b) to secure that the person does not commit an offence on bail;
   (c) to secure that the person does not interfere with witnesses or obstruct justice;
   (d) for the person's own protection or interests, or, if under 17, for the person's own welfare.
(v)   Bail conditions can be imposed but cannot include a requirement of a surety, security, or recognizance; neither can a requirement be made that the person reside in a bail hostel (s 30A(3A)).
(vi) The person must be given a notice in writing before he is released stating (s 30B):
   (a) the offence for which he is arrested;
   (b) the ground on which he is arrested;
   (c) that he is required to attend a police station;
   (d) any requirements imposed by any conditions of bail;
   (e) the opportunities to vary the conditions of bail.
(vii) the police station and the time he is required to attend must be specified either (s 30B):
   (a) in the original notice in writing; or, if it is not,
   (b) in a further notice in writing; or, if those requirements are altered,
   (c) in a further notice or notices in writing of any changes in the requirements.

3.7.2 **Who may exercise the power?**

The power may be exercised by a constable (s 30A and s 30B).

3.7.3 **What are the possible ultimate outcomes of street bail?**

The possibilities are (s 30C):

(i)   that the person is given further notice in writing that he is no longer required to attend a police station; or

(ii) in the case of a person who is bailed to a non-designated police station, that he is, within six hours, either released or taken to a designated police station; or

(iii) in the case of a person who is bailed to a designated police station, there are no further restrictions as to the way in which he is dealt with.

3.7.4 How may conditions of bail be varied?

Variation by police

A person who has been released on bail subject to conditions may (s 30CA) make a request to vary those conditions to a relevant officer at the police station at which he is required to attend (the custody officer) or, where no notice specifying that police station has been given, to a relevant officer at the police station specified in the notice as that to which he may apply for the variation of those conditions (an officer not involved in the investigation unless such an officer is not readily available, in which case an officer other than the officer who granted bail unless such an officer is not readily available).

There is no restriction on the number of requests to vary conditions that may be made; however, any subsequent request must be based on new information. The restrictions on the types of conditions that may be attached, and the purpose of conditions attached are as before.

Variation by Magistrates' Court

Conditions may also be varied, on application by or on behalf of the arrested person, by a Magistrates' Court (s 30CB). The conditions for such an application are:

- Street bail must first have either been varied by police or an application made to police to vary must either have been refused or ignored for 48 hours.
- It must be based on grounds relied upon in an application to vary (although the court can take account of different grounds where they arise from a change in circumstances).

In imposing conditions, the court is limited in the same way as to the type of conditions that may be imposed and is bound by the same necessity requirements.

3.7.5 What are the powers to deal with a person for breach of street bail?

A person released on street bail may be arrested without warrant by a constable (s 30B):

(a) where the bailed person fails to attend at a police station at the specified time (ie specified in a street bail notice); or

(b) where the constable has reasonable grounds for suspecting that the person has broken any of the conditions of bail.

Where the person released on street bail is arrested under the latter power, he must be taken to a police station (which may be any police station) as soon as practicable after arrest.

3.8 The Arrest of Persons at Police Stations, Attending Voluntarily (Section 29) or by Arrest for Further Offence (Section 31)

These sections deal with two situations in which a person already at a police station may come to be arrested:

(i) A person who has attended voluntarily at a police station without having been arrested is entitled to leave unless he is arrested; and, if a decision has been taken to prevent him from leaving at will, he must be informed 'at once' that he is under arrest (s 29).
(ii) A person at a police station as a result of being arrested must be further arrested at the police station for any other offence for which he would be liable for arrest if released (s 31).

The safeguards afforded to persons at police stations by these provisions are limited in important respects.

3.8.1 Persons attending voluntarily (section 29)

The right to be informed of an arrest under s 29 is only triggered by the decision of an officer to stop the person from leaving the police station or, in practical terms, by a determination on the part of the person to leave. (See also Code C 3.21 which supports this view.) Up until that time, the converse does not apply: he is not entitled to be told that he is not under arrest and is entitled to leave.

However, if he is cautioned whilst not under arrest, he must at the same time be told that he is not under arrest and is free to leave (Code C 10.2).

Code C does not apply to persons attending a police station voluntarily unless they are arrested (Code C 1.10); although guidance is provided in that Code as to how they should be dealt with and their rights to legal advice and communication (Code C, Note 1A; C 3.21). Code H treats persons attending police stations voluntarily in connection with terrorism cases in the same way (Code H, Note 1A).

Particular guidance is provided in relation to the circumstances in which it is appropriate to arrest a person attending voluntarily for interview: Code C 3.21; Code G, Notes 2F and 2G. The latter makes it clear that a pre-emptive arrest in anticipation of a voluntary attender deciding to leave would not be justified because where 'a person who attends the police station voluntarily to be interviewed decides to leave before the interview is complete, the police would at that point be entitled to consider whether their arrest was necessary to carry out the interview'.

When a person attending voluntarily at a police station is arrested, the rights and obligations contained in Code C (with respect to the custody officer, a custody record, legal rights, and legal advice) become engaged (C 2.1A, 2.1, 3.1, 3.21, 3.22). Parallel provisions apply to persons attending police stations voluntarily in connection with terrorism cases under Code H (Code H 2.1, 2.2, 3.1).

3.8.2 Arrest at police station for further offences (section 31)

Section 31 imposes a duty to arrest for further offences where 'it appears to a constable that, if [the arrested person already at a police station] were released from the arrest, he would be liable to arrest for [some] other offence'. The purpose and limitations of the duty were described in *R v Samuel* [1988] QB 615 (CA) at p 622:

> It seems to this court that the obvious purpose of that section is to prevent the release and immediate re-arrest of an alleged offender. Nor does the section impose any duty on the constable to arrest immediately. We see nothing in the section which would prevent the constable delaying arresting him until the time (if it ever arrived) when his release was imminent.

A person further arrested must be informed at the time, or as soon as practicable thereafter, that they are under arrest and the grounds for their arrest (Code C 10.3); and, unless they have already been cautioned immediately prior to arrest, they must be cautioned on being arrested unless it is impracticable to do so by reason of their condition or behaviour (Code C 10.4). Parallel provisions appear in Code H with respect to persons further arrested in terrorism cases (Code H 10.2 and 10.3).

3.9 Search of Persons and Search and Entry of Premises Upon Arrest at a Place Other than a Police Station (Section 32)

This is one of the most important and frequently employed provisions permitting the search of persons or premises.

3.9.1 Who may exercise the powers under section 32?

The powers may be exercised:

(i) in their entirety, by a constable; or

(ii) by a civilian designated as a 'Community Support Officer' under s 38 of the Police Reform Act 2002 (Sch 4, Pt 1, para 2A) but only with respect to the power to search the person and only with respect to a person upon whom the Community Support Officer has imposed a 'requirement to wait' under that schedule.

3.9.2 What power is there to search a person on arrest at a place other than a police station?

A person arrested at a place other than a police station may be searched:

(i) if the constable has reasonable grounds for believing that the arrested person may present a danger to himself or others (s 32(1)); or

(ii) if the constable has reasonable grounds for believing that the person may have concealed on him anything (a) which the person might use to assist him to escape from lawful custody, or (b) which might be evidence relating to an offence, to the extent which is reasonably required for the purpose of discovering those things (s 32(2)(a), (3), and (5)).

Code A 2.2 to 2.11 contains extensive guidance on powers of search of the person requiring reasonable grounds for suspicion. Code A 3.8 to 3.11 and 4 sets out requirements in relation to steps to be taken prior to a search (including information to be given) and recording of searches.

3.9.3 What is the extent of the search of the person permitted under section 32?

In the course of the search (s 32(4)):

(i) the person may be required to remove in public only the following items of clothing: an outer coat, jacket, or gloves; and

(ii) the constable is authorized to search the person's mouth.

Code A 3.5 states:

> ...A search in public of a person's clothing which has not been removed must be restricted to superficial examination of outer garments. This does not, however, prevent an officer from placing his or her hand inside the pockets of the outer clothing, or feeling round the inside of collars, socks and shoes if this is reasonably necessary in the circumstances to look for the object of the search or to remove and examine any item reasonably suspected to be the object of the search. For the same reasons, subject to the restrictions on the removal of headgear, a person's hair may also be searched in public...

The power is limited to the extent which is reasonably required for the purpose of discovering those things (s 32(3)).

The words 'in public' may imply a corollary: that if taken to a place out of the public eye, the person can be required to remove items of clothing other than those specified in s 32(4).

Reasonable force may be used, if necessary, in the exercise of the power (s 117).

3.9.4 What may be seized or retained in the course of a search of the person under section 32?

(i) An item found following a search of the person (under s 32(1)) on the ground that the person may present a danger to himself or others may be seized and retained if the constable has reasonable grounds for believing that the person may use it to cause physical injury to himself or to any other person (s 32(8)).

(ii) An item found, other than an item subject to legal privilege (see s 10), following a search of the person (under s 32(2)(a), ie on the ground that that the person may have concealed on him anything (a) which the person might use to assist him to escape from lawful custody, or (b) which might be evidence relating to an offence), may be seized and retained if the constable has reasonable grounds for believing (a) that the person might use it to assist him to escape from lawful custody, or (b) that it is evidence of an offence or has been obtained in consequence of an offence (s 32(9)).

3.9.5 What power is there to enter and search premises under section 32?

Where a person is arrested at a place other than a police station for an indictable offence, any premises in which he was when arrested or immediately before he was arrested may be searched for evidence relating to the offence if the constable has reasonable grounds for believing that such evidence is in the premises (s 32(2)(b) and s 32(6)).

An indictable offence is defined in the Interpretation Act 1978, Sch 1: it includes both 'indictable only' and 'triable either way', ie both offences (a) which are only triable in the Crown Court, and (b) offences which are triable in both the Magistrates' Court and in the Crown Court.

Code B applies to searches under s 32 (see Code B 2.3(b)). In particular, the guidance contained in Code B 6 'searching premises—general considerations' is of importance. The procedural and record-keeping requirements of Code B in relation to searches (considered in greater detail in relation to Part II of the Act) apply.

3.9.6 What is the extent of the search of the premises permitted under section 32?

The power is limited to:

(i) in all cases, the extent which is reasonably required for the purpose of discovering any evidence relating to the indictable offence for which the
person was arrested (s 32(2) and (3)); and

(ii) in the case of multi-occupational dwellings, to the search of the premises in
which the arrest took place or in which the person arrested was immediately before his arrest and the common parts of the premises used by the
occupier of that dwelling (whether or not the occupier is the person arrested)
(s 32(7)).

Reasonable force may be used, if necessary, in the exercise of the power
(s 117).

   The case law establishes that s 32 confers a power which is immediately exercisable. Whilst a certain degree of latitude is allowable, it will not permit a
search hours later: *Hewitson v Chief Constable of Dorset Police* [2003] EWHC 3296
(Admin) (a gap of 2 hours 10 minutes); *Badham* [1987] Crim LR 202 (a decision
of a Crown Court judge that a gap of several hours was too long).

Practical Guidance

3.10 Case Study 1 (Section 24 [and Section 1])

PC Smith has reasonable grounds to carry out a search under s 1 of PACE on
Jones. His attempts to gain Jones' cooperation fail and PC Smith uses reasonable
force to carry out the search. Jones resists and punches PC Smith in the lip causing minor bleeding. Jones finally calms down and the subsequent search reveals
no unlawful or prohibited articles. PC Smith asks Jones for his name and address.
Jones initially refuses and then points to a few business cards in his wallet for a
'DJ Jonesey'. The wallet also contains credit cards for a J Jones. Jones says that
he does not drive and has no other identification on him. PC Smith has his
doubts about the business card.

How should PC Smith deal with the assault on him?

Prior to 1 January 2006 the arrest of Jones would have been virtually automatic
and detention authorized merely for the purpose of charging. How PC Smith
will have to deal with the above scenario demonstrates the profound changes
introduced by the Serious Organised Crime and Police Act 2005. Whatever the
offence, the power to arrest is underpinned by necessity. Under s 24, PC Smith
must have reasonable grounds to believe that the arrest is necessary for any
one or more of the reasons specified in s 24(5). In many instances the necessity
criteria will be obvious, for example where it is not possible to establish the

suspect's identity or where it is clear that the suspect will have to be interviewed at the station. In this scenario, if Jones convincingly confirms his identity and is no longer violent then the most obvious necessity criteria are not present.

It may be that Jones' arrest is necessary to ascertain Jones' real name and address. Section 24(5)(a) specifically gives 'reasonable grounds for doubting whether a name given by the person as his name is his real name' as a reason why arrest may be necessary. Code G 2.9(a) suggests that reluctance or hesitance in giving a name is relevant to the assessment. The assessment must be based on reasonable objective grounds rather than a stereotypical assessment of the habits and reliability of DJs. The fact that there are a number of business cards and that the name matches the credit cards is plainly of significance.

In addition, it may be that Jones' arrest is necessary to allow the prompt and effective investigation of the offence. Jones may have injured his own hand or have traces of PC Smith's blood on his clothing. His arrest for the purposes of having his hand examined by a Forensic Medical Examiner and the taking of photographs and or swabs may provide PC Smith with reasonable grounds to believe arrest is necessary. The Code of Practice provides useful examples of when arrest may be necessary to allow the prompt and effective investigation of an offence (Code G 2.9(e)).

3.11 Case Study 2 (Section 24)

PC Smith is on mobile patrol and sees White driving a car along the High Street.

PC Smith was present in court three months before when White, a youth well known to local police, was disqualified for a period of 12 months for a drink-drive offence. PC Smith stops the vehicle and questions White, who adopts an aggressive and rude manner, refusing to answer questions and shouting out that he is not disqualified, his name is Clark, and he is being harassed by police.

Can PC Smith arrest White for driving whilst disqualified?

PC Smith must first have reasonable grounds to suspect White is committing an offence and additionally must have reasonable grounds to believe that arrest is necessary for any of the reasons mentioned in s 24(5).

In this case, it is three months since the conviction and PC Smith should carry out checks on the Police National Computer to ensure the disqualification is still current. White may have successfully appealed against conviction or had the disqualification period reduced. Once satisfied the disqualification is current, PC Smith has reasonable grounds to suspect White of committing an offence but now, in addition, must be able to show at least one of the reasons to arrest is present. As White is known to local police, the name and address

4

Detention: Part IV

Law and Commentary

Practical Guidance

Law and Commentary

4.1 Introduction

Sections 34 to 51, which make up Part IV of the Act, set out the conditions under which a person can be held in police detention and when they must be released, the role and responsibilities of the custody officer, and importantly sets out a timetable within which decisions relating to detention and charge must be made.

Code of Practice C applies to this Part.

4.2 Police Detention

4.2.1 What is police detention?

Section 118(2) states that a person is in police detention for the purposes of the Act if he has been taken to a police station following arrest, or is arrested at the police station after attending there voluntarily and is detained there or elsewhere (other than at court following charge) in the charge of a constable.

A person is in addition to be treated as under arrest for an offence (and therefore in police detention) where he returns to a police station to answer bail (save where that bail is live link bail (s 46ZA(2)) or is arrested for failing to answer bail (s 34(7)).

Under the Police Reform Act 2002, paragraphs 22 and 34(1) and 35(3) of Sch 4 to that Act, a person is also in police detention where they have been transferred into the lawful custody of an investigating officer, or are being escorted to a police station or to any other place authorized by the custody officer.

Once in police detention, a person cannot be released except on the authority of a custody officer at the station where his detention was last authorized (s 34(3)). That custody officer must, however, release a detainee (other than one who was unlawfully at large on arrest) once he is aware that the grounds for detention have ceased to apply and that there are no other grounds on which continued detention could be justified (s 34(2)).

Section 34(1) specifies that a person arrested for an offence shall not be kept in police detention except in accordance with the provisions of the Act. The relevant provisions must be read together with Code C of the Codes of Practice. With the exception of identified classes of people set out in Code C 1.12, and those detained under the Terrorism Act (to whom Code H of the Codes of Practice or the Code issued under paragraph 6 of Sch 14 to the Terrorism Act apply), Code C 1.10 makes it clear that the Code applies to people in custody at police stations in England and Wales *whether or not they have been arrested*, as well as to those who have been removed to a police station as a place of safety under ss 135 and 136 of the Mental Health Act 1983.

Code C, Note 1A states:

> Although certain sections of this Code apply specifically to people in custody
> at police stations, those there voluntarily to assist with an investigation should
> be treated with no less consideration, eg offered refreshments at appropriate
> times, and enjoy an absolute right to obtain legal advice or communicate with
> anyone outside the police station.

It should be noted that even for the excepted classes under Code 1.12 there are
minimum standards of treatment to be applied which are set out at ss 8 and 9
of Code C.

4.2.2 Where can a person be detained?

The primary rule is that a detained person should be held at a 'designated police
station', that is, a station designated by the chief officer of police for each police
area as one that appears to him to provide sufficient accommodation for the
purpose of detaining arrested persons in that area (s 35(1)–(2)).

In certain circumstances, set out in s 30(3)–(5), an arrested person can be
taken to and detained at a police station that is not a designated police station;
however, where that occurs, the detainee must be transferred to a station that
is a designated police station not more than six hours after his first arrival at
a police station unless he is earlier released (s 30(6)).

All police stations are designated for the purposes of detention of a person
arrested under s 41 of the Terrorism Act 2000, however such a detainee must be
taken to the police station considered by the arresting officer to be 'most appropriate' (Code H Note 1M).

4.3 The Custody Officer (Sections 36–40A)

4.3.1 Who may perform the functions of the Custody Officer?

The chief officer (or such other officer as the chief officer may direct) for the
area in which the designated police station is situated must appoint one or
more custody officers for each designated police station (s 36(1)–(2)). Following
the implementation of the Policing and Crime Act 2009, the custody officer
must be a police officer of at least the rank of sergeant; a return to the position
that existed before the Serious Organised Crime and Police Act came into force,
which allowed for civilians to take on this important role. Even so, circumstances may arise where an officer of any rank may have to take on the functions of the custody officer. In *Vince v Chief Constable of Dorset Police* [1993]
1 WLR 415 it was held that there was no duty to ensure that an appointed custody officer was on duty at all times. If therefore the circumstances are such that
a custody officer at a designated police station cannot be readily available without undue delay, an officer of any rank may perform the functions of a custody

officer (s 36(4)). However, as it is the clear intention of the Act that the roles of the custody officer and the investigating officer should be kept separate, whoever takes on the role of the custody officer should not be involved in the investigation of the offence for which the person is in police detention (s 36(5)).

Another situation that might arise is where the arrested person has been taken to a police station that is not a designated police station. There any officer who is not involved in the investigation of the offence for which he is in police detention can carry out the functions of a custody officer. If no such officer is readily available, then the officer who took the arrested person to the station or any other officer (including an investigating officer) can act as the custody officer (s 36(7)). This would clearly be a matter of last resort, however, and where this is going to occur an officer of at least the rank of inspector and who is attached to a designated police station must be informed as soon as practicable (s 36(9), (10)).

Even where a custody officer is available and on duty, some procedures such as fingerprinting or searches may be delegated to other 'designated persons', that is, a person other than a police officer designated under the Police Reform Act 2002 who has specified powers and duties of police officers conferred or imposed on them. Indeed, under Code C 1.15, an acting custody officer may allow certain other police staff who are not designated persons to carry out individual procedures or tasks (Code C 1.15) provided that he is satisfied that that other is suitable, trained, and competent to carry out the task or action in question (Note 3F). Whoever in fact carries out the procedures, the responsibility for ensuring that all procedures are carried out correctly and in accordance with the Codes of Practice rests with the custody officer (Code C 1.13–1.16).

4.3.2 What are the duties of the custody officer before charge?

Whenever a person is brought to a police station under arrest, is arrested at the police station, or attends a police station to answer bail, they must be brought before the custody officer as soon as practicable (Code C 2.1A).

Code C 1.1 states that:

> All persons in custody must be dealt with expeditiously, and released as soon as the need for detention no longer arises.

The task of dealing with all such persons is that of the custody officer who must perform the functions attributed to him by the Act and Code C as soon as practical. Should delays occur, a note should be made in the custody record detailing the fact of the delay and the reason for it. Provided that all reasonable steps are taken to prevent unnecessary delays, and provided that any delay that does occur can be justified, then there will not be a breach of the Code.

In respect of each person in police detention, the custody officer must:

- open a custody record;
- ensure that the detainee is given his rights;

- assess whether the detainee may be a juvenile, suffer from a mental disorder, or have difficulties in communication;
- determine whether there is sufficient evidence to charge or whether the detainee needs to be kept in custody in order to secure, preserve, or obtain such evidence;
- make decisions on charging and on bail;
- ensure that the detainee is treated in accordance with the Act and the Codes.

Each of these duties is dealt with in turn below.

4.3.3 The custody record

A custody record must be opened for each person in police detention. This is an extremely important document. All information that must be recorded in accordance with the provisions of the Act and Code must be recorded as soon as practicable within it (Code C 2.1).

It should be borne in mind that the custody record is an 'open' document that must be made available to the defence. A solicitor is entitled to consult a detainee's custody record as soon as practicable after his arrival at the police station (Code C 2.4), the detainee and his legal representative must be given a copy of the record on request at any time within 12 months after he has left police detention or has been taken before a court (Code C 2.4A), and shall in addition be permitted to inspect the original custody record on giving reasonable notice (Code C 2.5).

All entries in the custody record must be timed and signed by the maker unless he reasonably believes that to disclose a name might put him in danger (Code C 2.6, 2.6A), or the case is linked to the investigation of terrorism (Code H 2.8). In either case it is sufficient for the maker to use a warrant or other identification number.

Where the detainee has been arrested and taken to a police station as a result of a search under any stop and search power to which Code A or the search powers code under the Terrorism Act applies, then the record of that search must form part of the custody record. The detainee is entitled to a copy of the search record in addition to the copy of the custody record. Although it is the responsibility of the officer who carried out the search to ensure that the record of that search is made as part of the custody record (Code 2.3A) it is the custody officer's responsibility to ensure that the custody record as a whole is accurate and complete (Code C 2.3).

4.3.4 Rights of detainees

All detainees have three basic rights under Code C which can be exercised at any time. They are:

- the right to have someone informed of their arrest;
- the right to consult privately with a solicitor and the provision of free legal advice;
- the right to consult the Codes of Practice.

The detainee must be told about these rights in clear terms at the outset of their detention, and must also be served with a written notice setting out in addition to those rights the arrangements for obtaining legal advice, their right to a copy of the custody record, and the caution (Code C 3.2). A further written notice setting out the detainee's 'entitlements whilst in custody' should also be served. Those entitlements are detailed in the Notes for Guidance at 3A and B.

In certain circumstances, set out in Annex B to Code C and considered in more detail in Chapter 5, a detainee's right to have someone informed of their arrest and the right to obtain free legal advice may be delayed for up to 36 hours.

Where a person has attended the police station voluntarily to assist the police they are entitled to leave at will unless subsequently arrested. If they are not arrested but are cautioned, they must at the same time be told that they are not under arrest and are not obliged to remain at the police station, but that if they do so then they are entitled to free and independent legal advice (Code C 3.21). If legal advice is requested, the interviewer must ensure that such advice is provided, and that Codes E and F are followed.

4.3.5 Assessment of the detainee

The first task of the custody officer is to assess the arrested person. The custody officer is required to carry out an assessment of any potential risks that the detainee may pose, whether to himself, the custody staff, or any person acting on behalf of the detainee. In order to discharge this function properly the custody officer may need to consult with others, for example the arresting officer or a healthcare professional, should carry out a check on the Police National Computer, and should consult the publications referred to in Note 3E, which provide detailed guidance on the conduct of a risk assessment. The custody officer is responsible not only for initiating the assessment, but also for implementing any measures required as a consequence (Code C 3.6–3.10).

Persons arrested under s 41 Terrorism Act 2000 may present special risks, not only to custody staff but to any individual who comes into contact with the detainee. Code H 3.6 imposes a duty on the custody officer to obtain information from the investigation team in order to be able properly to assess and minimize any such risk.

Where it appears to the officer that the person may:

- be mentally disordered or otherwise mentally vulnerable;
- be under the age of 17; or

- have difficulty hearing, speaking, or understanding English,

then that person will fall within a special group of detained persons for whom there are additional provisions that must be complied with whilst they are in police detention. These are considered as a separate topic in Chapter 7.

4.3.6 **Charging**

As soon as practicable after an arrested person arrives at the police station, or, in the case of a person arrested at the police station, as soon as practicable after his arrest, the custody officer must determine whether he has before him sufficient evidence to charge that person with the offence for which he was arrested, and may detain him at the police station for such period as is necessary to enable him to do so (s 37(1), (10)). In making that determination the custody officer will invariably rely on the information given to him by the arresting officer; he is entitled to do so, and to assume that the arrest was a lawful one.

Where the custody officer considers that there is insufficient evidence to charge, the detained person must be released (either with or without bail) unless the custody officer has reasonable grounds for believing that detention without charge is necessary in order to 'secure or preserve evidence relating to an offence for which he is under arrest or to obtain such evidence by questioning him' (s 37(2), (3)). This may include an interview, search, or identification procedure.

Where authorization to detain is given, the custody officer must, as soon as practicable, make a written record of the grounds for the detention (s 37(4)). Unless the person to be detained is incapable of understanding what is being said to him, asleep, violent or likely to become violent, or is in urgent need of medical help or attention, then the record of the grounds for his detention must be made in his presence and he must be informed by the custody officer of those grounds (s 37(5), (6), Code C 3.23).

Where the custody officer determines that he does have sufficient evidence to charge the person arrested with the offence for which he was arrested, then s 37(7) provides the custody officer with five options. They are that the person arrested shall be:

- released without charge and on bail for the purpose of enabling the Director of Public Prosecutions (DPP) to make a decision under s 37B;
- kept in police detention for the purpose of enabling the DPP to make a decision under s 37B;
- released without charge and on bail but not for s 37B purposes;
- released without charge and without bail; or
- charged.

Although s 37(7A) states that the decision as to which of the above routes to follow is that of the custody officer, in making that decision custody officers must comply with guidance issued by the DPP (s 37A(3); Code C 16.1A). The fifth version of the Director's Guidance on Charging was issued on 6 May 2013; the introduction states that '[p]olice officers and prosecutors must comply with this Guidance to ensure that charging and other prosecution decisions are fair and consistent and fully comply with PACE, the PACE Codes of Practice and the Code for Crown Prosecutors'.

What amounts to 'sufficient evidence'?

Paragraph 8 of the Director's Guidance on Charging states that cases should not be charged by the police or referred to prosecutors unless the Full Code Test is met. There are two elements to the test; the evidential test—that there is sufficient evidence to provide a realistic prospect of conviction (the tribunal of fact, properly directed, would be more likely than not to convict the defendant of the charge alleged); and the public interest test. In certain circumstances where there is insufficient evidence available to meet the evidential element of the Full Code Test, the lower Threshold Test may be applied. This test is met if:

- there is at least a reasonable suspicion that the person to be charged has committed the offence; and
- there are reasonable grounds for believing that further evidence (sufficient to meet the Full Code Test) will become available within a reasonable period; and
- a charge is in the public interest.

This lower Threshold Test can be applied where the seriousness or the circumstances of the case justifies the making of an immediate charging decision; there are continuing substantial grounds to object to bail in accordance with the Bail Act 1976; and in all the circumstances of the case it is proper to do so.

If there is sufficient evidence to charge, what must the custody officer do then?

If the custody officer determines that there is sufficient evidence to charge, the next step depends upon whether the offence is one for which the police have responsibility to charge in accordance with the Guidance, or whether it is an offence which must be referred to the CPS for a charging decision to be made.

If responsibility for charging lies with the police, then provided the Full Code Test is met, including a determination that a charge is in the public interest, then the suspect should be charged. It will then be for the custody officer to determine whether the suspect should be released (with or without bail) or should be kept in police detention in accordance with s 38.

The use of the Threshold Test will rarely be appropriate in cases for which the police have the responsibility for charging and will never be appropriate in those cases that are not punishable with imprisonment (Guidance para 14).

Where the charging decision is one that rests with the Crown Prosecution Service (CPS), if the custody officer considers that there is sufficient evidence to charge, a referral will be made to the Crown Prosecutors setting out the reasons why it is considered that there is sufficient evidence to charge and why a prosecution would be in the public interest (Guidance para 5).

Clearly it can take time to report to, consult with, and obtain a decision from the CPS. Under s 37(7)(a)(ii), an arrested person may be kept in detention whilst this takes place. This provision cannot, however, be used to extend the period of time in which a person can be kept in police detention, should be relied upon only where a quick decision on charge can be expected, and only where the release of the person on bail pending a decision has been considered to be inappropriate.

If it proves impossible to obtain a prosecutor's authority to charge before the expiry of any relevant time limits, and if the continued detention of the suspect is justifiable, a Police Inspector may authorize the charging of an offence that would otherwise fall to be determined by a prosecutor and apply the Threshold Test to do so. Where this happens, the case must be referred to a prosecutor as soon as possible following charge for review (Guidance para 20).

Where the person is suitable for bail, the custody officer may release the detained person on pre-charge bail, with or without conditions in accordance with s 37(7)(a)(i) pending the DPP's decision. In these circumstances, the suspect should be informed that they are being released on bail in order to enable the DPP to make a decision under s 37B; Code C 16.1B. Thereafter the custody officer must act in accordance with the decision made by the DPP.

If the prosecutor is not satisfied that the evidential test is met, it will then be for the custody officer to determine whether the suspect may continue to be detained (if time limits permit) or be released on bail, or released without charge and the case concluded (Guidance para 12).

There may be circumstances where, although the custody officer feels that there is sufficient evidence to charge, nevertheless it is not thought appropriate to do so at that stage—where there are outstanding enquiries or investigations to be conducted, for example. In those circumstances, the custody officer may release the detained person under s 37(7)(b). Following the implementation of the Police and Justice Act 2006, conditions may be attached to bail.

If there is insufficient evidence to charge, what must the custody officer do then?

As previously stated, the Full Code Test must be applied to all cases. If the Full Code Test cannot be met, the officer or prosecutor will have to consider whether or not it is appropriate to apply the lower Threshold Test. This is likely to depend upon the nature and complexity of the investigation and the bail risk presented by the suspect. If no further evidence can be or will be obtained, then the suspect should be released without charge. If the further evidence necessary to meet the Full Code Test is obtainable and can be gathered before the time limits on detention expire, or, if not, if the suspect can properly be released with or without bail pending charge, then the Threshold Test is unlikely to be appropriate. This is likely to be the position in the vast majority of cases in which the police make the charging decision and it would therefore rarely be the case that it would be necessary for the police to apply any lower test than the Full Code Test. In those circumstances the suspect should be released with or without bail pending receipt of the further evidence required to charge.

The Threshold Test will more often be deployed by prosecutors where the case is a serious or complex one and where it would not be appropriate to release the defendant pending receipt of all the evidence.

In what cases can the police make the charging decisions?

Under the Guidance, the police may charge:

- any summary only offence (including criminal damage where the value of the loss or damage is less than £5,000) irrespective of plea;
- any offence of retail theft (shoplifting) or attempted retail theft, irrespective of plea, provided it is suitable for sentence in the Magistrates' Court;
- any either way offence anticipated as a guilty plea and suitable for sentence in a Magistrates' Court, provided it is not:
  - a case requiring the DPP's consent to prosecute;
  - a case involving a death;
  - connected with terrorist activity or official secrets;
  - classified as a Hate Crime or Domestic Violence under CPS policies;
  - an offence of Violent Disorder or Affray;
  - causing Grievous Bodily Harm or Wounding, or Actual Bodily Harm;
  - a Sexual Offences Act offence committed by or upon a person under 18;
  - an offence under the Licensing Act 2003.

In all other cases then, under the Guidance, the charging decision is the responsibility of Crown Prosecutors (Guidance para 15).

4.3.7 Bail

Section 38(1) requires that where a person arrested for an offence, otherwise than under a warrant endorsed for bail, is charged with an offence, the custody officer shall order his release from police detention with or without bail.

There are a number of exceptions to this requirement. They are:

(i) Flow diagram on charging decisions

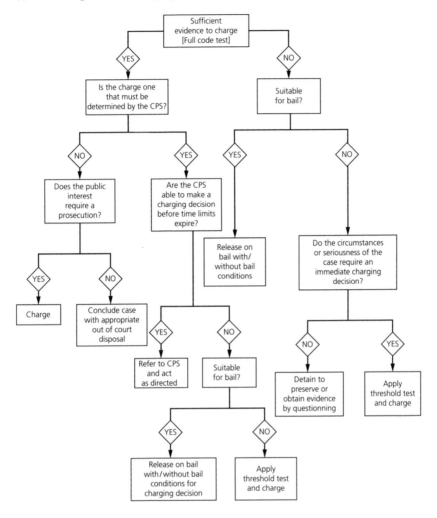

- where there is doubt about the arrested person's real name or address;
- where the custody officer has reasonable grounds for believing that the person arrested will fail to answer bail;
- where, in the case of a person arrested for an imprisonable offence, the custody officer has reasonable grounds for believing that detention is necessary to prevent the commission of further offences;
- where detention is necessary to enable a sample to be taken from the arrested person under s 63B (testing for the presence of Class A drugs)—but only for a period of up to six hours after charge;
- where, in the case of a person arrested for an offence which is not an imprisonable offence, the custody officer has reasonable grounds for believing that detention is necessary to prevent physical injury to another person or to prevent loss of or damage to property;
- where the custody officer has reasonable grounds for believing that detention is necessary to prevent the person arrested from interfering with the administration of justice or with the investigation of an offence;
- where the custody officer has reasonable grounds for believing that the detention of the person arrested is necessary for his own protection;
- the offence with which the person is charged where the charge is murder.

An arrested juvenile may additionally be refused bail if the custody officer has reasonable grounds for believing that he ought to be detained in his own interests (s 38(1)(b)(ii)).

In determining whether or not there exist reasonable grounds to believe that the person arrested will fail to answer bail, commit further offences, injure another person, or cause loss or damage to property, or interfere with the administration of justice, the custody officer must have regard to:

- the nature and seriousness of the offence;
- the character, antecedents, associations, and community ties of the arrested person;
- the arrested person's previous bail record;
- the strength of the evidence together with any other relevant consideration (s 38(2A)).

Where a custody officer authorizes the continued detention of a person who has been charged, he shall as soon as practicable make a written record of the grounds for his detention in the presence of the person charged and shall at the same time inform him of those grounds (s 38(3), (4)).

The requirement to inform the person charged of the reasons for his detention and to make a written record of the grounds in his presence does not apply where the person charged is:

- incapable of understanding what is said to him;
- violent or likely to become violent;
- in urgent need of medical attention.

Release on bail from detention may be with, or without conditions which must be both relevant and necessary (see further para 4.8). Where the release on bail is pre-charge, the police have no power subsequently to vary those conditions. Where, therefore, a person breaches the conditions imposed pre-charge and is again released on bail, any conditions attached must be the same as they were previously.

4.3.8 **Treatment**

It is the duty of the custody officer to ensure that all persons in police detention at the police station are treated in accordance with the Act and the Codes, and that all matters which are required by the Act and Codes to be recorded are recorded in the custody records (s 39(1)), save that where the custody of a detained person has been transferred by the custody officer to an investigating officer or to an officer who has charge of that detained person outside the police station, then that other officer will bear the responsibility of ensuring that he is treated in accordance with the provisions of the Act and the Codes, and on returning the detained person to the custody of the custody officer, must confirm that the Act and Codes have been so complied with (s 39(2), (3)).

That the responsibility for the care and treatment of a detained person falls squarely on the custody officer's shoulders is made clear by s 39(6). Where an officer of a higher rank than the custody officer gives directions relating to a person in police detention which are at variance with any decision made or action taken, or which would have been made or taken by the custody officer in the performance of a duty imposed upon him by the Act, then the custody officer must at once refer the matter to an officer of at least the rank of superintendent or above.

The provisions relating to the care and treatment of detained persons are to be found in Codes C 8 and 9 and are dealt with further in Chapter 5.

4.4 **Reviews**

Periodic reviews of the detention of each person held in police detention in connection with the investigation of an offence must be carried out by a 'review officer' throughout the period in which a person is detained, both before and after charge. In basic terms, the review officer must ask himself is the person's continued detention really necessary? When the review takes place before charge there are essentially two questions: is there sufficient evidence to charge, and if not, is the person's continued detention necessary in order to secure or preserve evidence relating to an offence or to obtain such evidence through questioning?

The identity of the review officer depends upon when the review is carried out, whether pre- or post-charge. Where the detained person has been arrested but not yet charged, an officer of at least the rank of inspector who has not been directly involved in the investigation will carry out the reviews. After charge, the review officer will be the custody officer (s 40(1)).

The importance of the role of the review officer is underlined in s 40(11); if an officer of a higher rank than the custody officer gives directions relating to a person in police detention and those directions are at variance with any decision or action made or which would have been made by the review officer in the performance of his duties, then the review officer must immediately refer the matter to an officer of at least the rank of superintendent.

A separate regime applies to those persons arrested under the Terrorism Act 2000 s 41 or detained under Sch 7 of that Act. Details of the procedures to be followed can be found in Code H, section 14.

4.4.1 **How often must a person's detention be reviewed?**

The timetable for reviews of detention is set out at s 40(3):

- the first review shall be no later than six hours after detention was first authorized;
- the second review shall be no later than nine hours after the first;
- subsequent reviews shall take place at intervals of not more than nine hours apart.

A review may be postponed if, in all the circumstances at the time, it is not practicable to carry out the review at the specified time. Section 40(4)(b) provides two examples of when it might not be practicable to carry out a review. The first is where at the time of the review the detained person is being questioned by the police and the review officer considers that to interrupt the questioning for the purposes of a review would prejudice the investigation in connection with which he is being questioned; the second is that there is no review officer readily available at the specified time.

Where any review has been postponed (whether for one of the reasons described in s 40(4)(b), or for any other reason), the reasons for that postponement must be recorded by the review officer on the custody record (s 40(7)), and the postponed review must take place as soon as practicable thereafter (s 40(5)).

It is important to note, however, that the postponement of a review does not affect the timetable laid down in s 40(3); a subsequent review must take place within the time limit measured from the time when the postponed review should have taken place, not from when it actually did take place.

4.4.2 **What tests are applied in a review of detention?**

Where the detention of a person who has not been charged is under review, the review officer applies the same tests as the custody officer under s 37(1)–(6) when first considering the necessity for detention following arrest; that is, whether there is sufficient evidence to charge, and if not, whether his detention without being charged is necessary to secure or preserve evidence relating to an offence for which he is under arrest or to obtain such evidence by questioning him. Where continued detention is authorized, the person whose detention is authorized must be informed of the grounds for that decision and a written record must be made of them in his presence, unless he is incapable of understanding what is being said to him, asleep, violent or likely to become so, or is in urgent need of medical attention (s 40(8)).

Where a person is in police detention under s 37(9) or s 37D(5), that is, where he is unfit, the purpose of the review is to establish whether he is yet in a fit state (s 40(9)).

Where the person whose detention is under review has been charged (s 38(1)–(6B)) 'Duties of custody officer after charge' apply (s 40(10)). As the review officer will at this stage be the custody officer, the only effect of s 40(10) is to provide a timetable for the custody officer acting as a review officer to review his original decision under s 38 (whether or not to allow the person charged to be released on bail).

In all cases, the review officer must, before determining whether or not to authorize a person's continued detention, remind the detainee (unless asleep) of his right to free legal advice (Code C 15.4) and give the detained person (unless asleep) or any solicitor available at the time of the review the opportunity to make representations about that continued detention, either orally or in writing (s 40(12), (13)). Where it appears likely that a detainee will be asleep at the latest time a review or authorization to extend detention may take place, the officer should (subject to legal obligations and time constraints) bring forward the procedure to allow the detainee to make representations (Note 15C). Reasonable efforts should be made to give the solicitor or appropriate adult sufficient notice of the time the decision is expected to be made so that they can make themselves available to make representations whether in person at the station or by telephone 'or other electronic means' (Note 15CA).

The review officer may refuse to hear oral representations from the detained person under review if it appears from his behaviour or because of his condition that he is unfit to make such representations (s 40(14)).

4.4.3 **How may reviews be carried out?**

Reviews may be carried out in person, or by telephone, or, where facilities exist and the conditions set out in s 45A are satisfied, by use of video-conferencing.

Under s 45A an officer who is not present in the police station but who has access to the use of video-conferencing facilities enabling him to communicate with persons in that station may use those facilities to carry out:

- the functions of a custody officer under ss 37, 38, or 40 where the arrested person is at a police station that is not a designated police station, provided that the officer is a custody officer at a designated police station; and

- a review under s 40(1)(b)—review of a person arrested but not charged by an officer of at least the rank of inspector.

Where video-conferencing facilities are used for the purpose of carrying out a s 40 review, the detained person or his solicitor must still be given the opportunity to make representations either through the video-conferencing facilities or in writing by fax or e-mail. A record of the review must be made in the custody record, but the obligation for making that record may be delegated to another officer.

Where video-conferencing facilities do not exist or it is not practicable to use them, a review may be carried out by telephone (s 40A). Again, the obligations relating to the making of records are retained but transferred to another officer, and an opportunity for representations to be made must again be provided, either orally over the telephone to the review officer, or in writing where facilities exist for the immediate transmission of those written representations (fax or e-mail).

A record must be made in the custody record of the fact that the detainee was reminded of his right to free legal advice, the grounds for and extent of any delay in a review, the reasons for and details surrounding a telephone review, and the outcome of any review, extension, or application to extend (Code C 15.12–15.16).

4.5 Limits on Detention (Section 41)

The basic rule set out in s 41 is that no person shall be kept in police detention for longer than 24 hours after the time (referred to as 'the relevant time') at which he arrived at the relevant police station, or the time of arrest, whichever is the earlier. To this basic rule there are a number of variations:

- where a person is arrested outside England and Wales, the 24 hours runs from the time at which he arrives at a police station in England or Wales in the police area in which the offence is being investigated, or 24 hours after his entry into England or Wales, whichever is the earlier (s 41(2)(a));
- where a person attends at a police station either voluntarily or in the company of a constable without having been arrested, and is arrested at the police station, the 24 hours runs from the time of his arrest (s 41(c));
- where a person attends a police station to answer bail under s 30A, the 24 hours runs from the time he arrives at the police station (s 41(ca));
- where a person's arrest is sought in area A but he is arrested in area B although not questioned there, the 24 hours runs from the time at which he arrives in the first police station in area A or from the time 24 hours after the time of his arrest whichever is the earlier (s 41(3));
- where a person is in police detention in area A but his arrest is sought in area B and he is taken to area B for the purposes of investigation without having previously been questioned, the 24 hours runs from the time 24 hours after he

leaves the place at which he was detained in area A or the time at which he arrives at the first police station in area B, whichever is the earlier (s 41(5));

- where a person in police detention is removed to hospital for treatment, any time during which he was questioned shall count towards the 24 hours but any other time (whether whilst in hospital or on journeys to and from it) shall not form part of the calculation (s 41(6));
- where a person already under arrest is arrested for a further offence under s 31, any calculations taken from the time of arrest are taken from the time of the original not subsequent arrest (s 41(4)).

On the expiry of the 24-hour limit, a person who is in police detention but who has not been charged must be released, with or without bail, unless an extension of the 24-hour period has been authorized under ss 42 or 43 (s 41(7), (8)).

Where an extension period has been authorized, and a detained person has been released, the time limits cannot be circumvented by re-arresting without a warrant for the original offence unless there is new evidence justifying such a re-arrest or that re-arrest comes as a result of a failure to answer to police bail under s 46A (s 41(9)).

4.6 Extensions of Detention (Sections 42–44)

The 24-hour period may be extended after the second review to up to 36 hours where an officer of the rank of at least superintendent who is responsible for the police station at which the person is being detained has reasonable grounds for believing that:

- the detention of the person without charge is necessary to secure or preserve evidence relating to an offence for which he is under arrest or to obtain such evidence by questioning him;
- an offence for which he is under arrest is an indictable offence; and
- the investigation is being conducted diligently and expeditiously (s 42(1)).

Where the extension period authorized expires less than 36 hours after the relevant time, a further extension period up to that time limit may be authorized if the authorizing officer is satisfied that the conditions set out above still apply (s 42(2)).

The extension period cannot be authorized retrospectively, neither can it be given in early anticipation that an extended period of time might be needed. Section 42(4) states that no authorization to extend up to 36 hours shall be given more than 24 hours after the relevant time, or before the second review of detention under s 40 has been carried out.

Again, the detained person must be told of his right to free legal advice and he (if fit to do so) or his solicitor (if available) must be given the opportunity to make representations either orally or in writing before the decision to authorize continued detention is made.

A detainee cannot be held incommunicado for longer than 36 hours. Where, therefore, continued detention is authorized, and where the detained person has not previously exercised his right under s 56 to have someone informed of his arrest, or under s 58 to consult with a solicitor, the authorizing officer must:

- inform him of that right;
- decide whether he should be permitted to exercise it;
- record the decision in the custody record; and
- if the authorizing officer has refused to permit the detained person to exercise those rights, record the grounds for that decision in the custody record.

After the expiration of the 36-hour period, if the detained person has not yet been charged he must be released from custody, with or without bail, unless a warrant of further detention has been obtained in accordance with s 43.

If he is released, he cannot be re-arrested without warrant for the same offence unless new evidence justifying such a course of action has come to light, or unless the arrest is carried out under s 46A, failure to answer to or comply with conditions of police bail.

4.6.1 Warrants of further detention

If further time is required to hold a person in detention in order to secure, pre-serve, or obtain evidence through questioning for an indictable offence, an application can be made on oath by a constable to a magistrates' court for a warrant of further detention authorizing the keeping of that person in police detention for a further period of up to 36 hours.

The application can only be heard where it is supported by an information, where a copy of that information has been given to the detained person, and where the detained person has been brought before the court for the hearing (s 43(2)).

The information must state:

- the nature of the offence;
- the general nature of the evidence;
- what inquiries have already been carried out and what further inquiries are proposed;
- the reasons for believing that the continued detention of the person is neces-sary for the purposes of such further inquiries (s 43(14)).

The detained person is entitled to be legally represented at the hearing, although may be kept in police detention during any adjournment of the case necessary in order to obtain that legal representation (s 43(3)).

The application may be made at any time before the expiry of the 36 hours after the relevant time. There is a degree of leeway permitted to cover the situ-ation in which it is not practicable for the court to sit at the time when ordinarily the application would be made; in these circumstances s 43(5)(b) allows a further six hours after the expiry of the 36-hour limit within which the application must be made. The person may be kept in police detention during this extra period but a note must be made in the custody record of that fact and the reasons for it (s 43(6)).

Police must be careful not to regard the extra six hours grace as forming part of the ordinary time limits; if an application is made after the expiry of the 36-hour period and it appears to the magistrates that it would have been reasonable to have made the application prior to the expiry of that period, 'the court shall dismiss the application' (s 43(7)). Regard should be had to Note 15D which states that an application to a magistrates' court for a warrant of further detention or extension under ss 43 or 44 should be made between 10am and 9pm, and if possible during normal court hours.

The task of the magistrates' court is to consider whether they are satisfied that there are reasonable grounds for believing that a person's further detention is justified. To conclude that it is and that a warrant should be issued, they must be satisfied of three things:

- that the detention is necessary to secure or preserve evidence relating to an offence for which he is under arrest or to obtain such evidence by questioning him;
- that the offence is an indictable offence; and
- that the investigation is being conducted diligently and expeditiously (s 43(5)).

Where the magistrates' court is not so satisfied at the time of the application they may adjourn the hearing (although the period of that adjournment must not exceed the expiry of the original 36-hour period) or refuse the application (s 43(8)).

If the application is refused, the person concerned must either be charged or released with or without bail within 24 hours from the relevant time or before the expiry of such longer period of time as has been authorized under s 42 (s 43(15), (16)).

No further application may be made unless supported by new evidence (s 43(17)).

Where the application is granted a warrant of further detention will be issued authorizing the person to be kept in police detention for the period stated in it which shall be for the period that the magistrates' court deems appropriate having regard to the evidence before it, but which shall not exceed 36 hours (s 43(10)–(12)).

Prior to the expiry of the warrant, the person to whom it relates must be charged or released either with or without bail unless the warrant is extended.

4.6.2 Extension of warrants

Where, having heard an application on oath supported by an information, a magistrates' court is satisfied that there are reasonable grounds for believing that the further detention of a person to whom the application relates is justified, the court may further extend the application of the warrant for such period as it thinks fit, but which shall not be longer than 36 hours or end later than 96 hours after the relevant time.

If a warrant is extended for a period that brings the total period of detention to less than 96 hours, the court may further extend the warrant until that maximum period is reached (s 44(1)–(4)).

4.7 Detention after Charge (Section 46)

Section 46 sets out the procedure and timetable for bringing a person who has been kept in police detention following charge, or who is detained by a local authority under s 38(6), before a magistrates' court.

The primary aim is that such a person should be brought before the magistrates' court in the same local justice area as the police station at which he was charged as soon as practicable, and in any event no later than the first court sitting after he is charged with the offence.

Where, however, the court is not due to be sitting that day or the following day, or where the person is taken to a magistrates' court in an area other than that in which the police station at which he was charged is situated, then s 46 provides for the 'designated officer' for the relevant local justice area to make arrangements for a magistrates' court to sit.

4.8 Bail and Arrest (Sections 46A and 47)

Where a person has been released on bail with a duty to re-attend at the police station but fails to do so at the appointed time, that person may be arrested without warrant (s 46A(1)).

Where a person has been released on bail under s 37, s 37C(2)(b), or s 37CA(2)(b), he may be arrested without warrant if a constable has reasonable grounds for suspecting that he has breached his bail conditions.

Conditions may be attached to a grant of bail where a person is released either before charge under s 37—release on bail for a charging decision to be made, or for any other reason, or after charge under s 38(1). Any conditions attached must be relevant and proportionate, and limited to those necessary to secure the person's surrender to custody, prevent reoffending whilst on bail, and to ensure that the person does not interfere with witnesses or otherwise obstruct justice. Where the person is under 17, conditions may also be imposed for that person's welfare or in their own interests. A condition may not be imposed of residence in a bail hostel, neither can any surety, security or recognizance be taken (Explanatory notes to Police and Justice Act 2006). Any conditions that are imposed may, on application, be varied by a magistrates' court (s 47(1E)).

Where bail is granted, that bail may be either to appear before a magistrates' court on a date not later than the first court sitting after he has been charged (unless the case cannot be accommodated until a later date), or to re-attend at the police station, whether for a live link preliminary hearing under s 57C of the Crime and Disorder Act 1998, or for any other reason, unless written notice is given that he need not attend at that time (s 46(3)–(4)).

Practical Guidance

4.9 Case Study

Jones, a 19-year-old youth, is arrested for burglary by DC Potts and taken to the police station where detention is authorized at 11am by the custody officer, Sergeant Brown.

It is now 4pm and Jones has been in custody for five hours. What are Sergeant Brown's responsibilities in respect of reviewing Jones's detention?

As Jones has not at this stage been charged Sergeant Brown should ensure that before the expiry of six hours from when detention was authorized an officer of not less rank than inspector is notified of the need to review Jones's detention.

Sergeant Brown discovers the duty inspector is engaged at a serious incident and will not be available for some hours. The chief inspector volunteers to carry out the review but must do so immediately as he has to leave the station. How should Sergeant Brown deal with this situation?

It is not necessary to wait for the expiry of six hours before the first review and Sergeant Brown should use the chief inspector to carry out the initial review of detention. It should be noted that the nine-hour period in respect of the next review commences at the time of the first review and not after six hours. Therefore if Jones's detention is reviewed at 4pm the next review should take place not later than 1am the next day. As Jones is likely to be asleep at this time, consideration should be given to bringing forward the review to allow him to make representations.

Having completed all his enquiries DC Potts asks Sergeant Brown to charge Jones with burglary. How should Sergeant Brown deal with this request?

Sergeant Brown must comply with the Director's Guidance on Charging. He should first of all decide whether the 'Full Code Test' is met; that is, whether there is sufficient evidence to provide a realistic prospect of conviction, and that it is in the public interest to proceed. Assuming that the test is met, then as the offence of burglary is an 'either way' offence, in accordance with the current

Guidance the police could only charge if (a) a guilty plea is anticipated and (b) the offence is suitable for sentence in the Magistrates' Court. If Jones is of previous good character and if the burglary was a low value burglary of a non-dwelling then this might be the case, but if the burglary is of a dwelling and/or if Jones had previous convictions for other offences of dishonesty then the case would almost certainly be committed for sentence to the Crown Court. In these circumstances the charging decision rests with the Crown Prosecution Service, and Sergeant Brown must refer the case to them.

Jones is charged with burglary and DC Potts suggests that bail would not be appropriate as Jones is unlikely to attend court. How should Sergeant Brown deal with the question of bail?

Sergeant Brown is obliged by s 38 of PACE to release Jones either with or without bail unless one or more of the conditions in s 38(i)–(vi) is satisfied. Sergeant Jones should ascertain from DC Potts on what basis he considers Jones will fail to appear at court and decide whether this and any other relevant information provide him with reasonable grounds to conclude that Jones will indeed fail to appear at court. If so satisfied, then Sergeant Jones may refuse to bail Jones and keep him in custody pending a court appearance.

If Sergeant Brown decides to bail Jones but is then ordered by the detective chief inspector to keep Jones in custody, how should he deal with this situation?

This would be a difficult situation for any custody officer to deal with but Sergeant Brown's duties are clear. As the detective chief inspector's order is at variance with a decision made in the performance of Sergeant Brown's duty under the detention provisions of the Act, then he should respectfully refuse to carry out the order. Sergeant Brown should then refer the matter to an officer of at least the rank of superintendent responsible for that station (s 39(6)). The superintendent or above will then be responsible for deciding whether Jones is given bail. Sergeant Brown should comply with the superintendent's decision and ensure a full entry is created in the custody record.

How should Sergeant Brown respond if the detective inspector at the station offered to carry out the review?

Sergeant Brown should ascertain if the detective inspector has had any direct involvement in the case. If not, then there is no reason why a detective officer of the appropriate rank should not carry out the review. If the detective inspector has had direct involvement then he or she cannot act as a reviewing officer for that particular case.

Treatment: Part V

Law and Commentary

5.1 Introduction

Sections 53 to 65 form Part V of the Act which is entitled 'Questioning and Treatment of Persons by the Police'. Part V encompasses disparate but important provisions relating to the rights and treatment of detainees, interviews, and identification.

Sections 53 to 55 provide for the detainee to be searched, both to ascertain what items the person searched is in possession of, but also to assist in identifying the detained person. At the end of Part V ss 61 to 64 provide the police with the power to take fingerprints, impressions of footwear, intimate and other samples, photographs, and to test the detainee for the presence of Class A drugs.

In between these two 'bookends' are provisions giving rights to the detainee; notably the right to have someone informed of their arrest and the right to legal advice. The sections of the Act are expanded upon substantially in Code C of the Codes of Practice which also sets out minimum standards for the conditions in which a person is held in police detention. In addition, it is in Code C (rather than in the substantive sections of the Act) that there can be found the extremely important provisions relating to police interviews.

Juveniles and other vulnerable detainees, referred to in the Code as 'special groups' have additional rights and safeguards applicable to their detention.

For ease of reference and convenience the provisions relating to interviews, identification, and vulnerable witnesses are dealt with in separate chapters. This chapter is concerned with the rights and treatment of detainees.

5.2 Rights of Detainees

As was seen in Chapter 4, all detainees, whether brought to the police station under arrest or arrested at the police station having gone there voluntarily, have the same three basic rights under Code C which can be exercised at any time. They are:

- the right to have someone informed of their arrest;
- the right to consult privately with a solicitor and the provision of free legal advice;
- the right to consult the Codes of Practice (Code C 3.1).

The detainee must be told about these rights in clear terms at the outset of their detention, and must also be served with a written notice which sets out:

- those rights;
- the arrangements for obtaining legal advice;

- the right to a copy of the custody record after leaving police detention; and,
- the caution (Code C 3.2).

Each detainee should also be given a 'notice of entitlements' which lists their entitlements whilst in custody to, for example:

- reasonable standards of physical comfort;
- adequate food and drink;
- access to toilets and washing facilities, clothing, medical attention, and exercise where practicable (Code C 3.2; Note 3A).

Foreign nationals or citizens of independent Commonwealth countries must be told that they have the right, on request, to communicate at any time with their High Commission, Embassy, or Consulate, and the right to have their High Commission, Embassy, or Consulate informed of their whereabouts and the grounds for their detention (Code C 3.3; Code C 7).

Juveniles, the mentally disordered or otherwise mentally vulnerable, and those who have difficulty communicating (whether because of disability or for any other reason) have a substantial number of additional rights and safeguards. These are covered in detail in Chapter 8.

Although the rights set out in the Act and Codes relate to detainees, Code C 1A makes it clear that those who are not in detention but who are voluntarily present at the police station in order to assist in an investigation 'should be treated with no less consideration'. In particular they should be offered refreshments and have 'an absolute right' to obtain legal advice or to communicate at will with anyone outside the police station. In addition, if they are not arrested but cautioned in accordance with Code C 10, they must be told that they are not under arrest and are not obliged to remain at the police station, and informed that if they do remain, then they are entitled to free and independent legal advice (Code C 3.21).

Code C 8 sets out the standards to be applied for accommodation: cells must be adequately cleaned, heated, and ventilated; clean bedding, toilet and washing facilities, and meals must be provided; where practicable outdoor exercise should be offered; and additional restraints kept to a minimum.

Code C 9 provides for the care and treatment of detainees. All detainees should be visited every hour (more frequently if any risks were identified on risk assessment); clinical attention should be obtained as soon as practicable where requested by the detainee or where it appears to the custody officer that the person appears to be suffering from a physical illness or mental disorder, is injured, or for any other reason appears to need clinical attention; arrangements must be made to provide medication or other treatment as directed; and any complaints made by the detainee must be reported as soon as possible to a senior officer (inspector or above) not connected with the investigation.

Code C does not apply to those detained under the Terrorism Act 2000 (C 1.11). Code H applies to such detainees who, it is recognized, may be held in detention for long periods of time and may have special needs. The provisions emphasize the need to offer appropriate exercise, food, clothing and reading materials as well as the need to provide the detainee with the opportunity to carry out religious observance.

5.2.1 Right to have someone informed when arrested

Section 56 provides a detainee with the right, if he so requests, to have one friend, relative, or other person 'known to him or who is likely to take an interest in his welfare' told of his arrest and detention.

The right is exercisable by the detainee, not only when first arrested and held in police custody, but if he is transferred from one place to another (eg between different police stations), on each transfer (s 56(8)).

Although the right is only exercisable on request, the detainee must be informed by the custody officer of the existence of the right and asked if he wants to exercise it (Code C 3.5).

If the detainee does choose to exercise his right to have someone informed, his request must be carried out as soon as practicable (s 56(1)).

Code H provides additional entitlements for a person detained following arrest under s 41 of the Terrorism Act 2000. Such persons may be detained for lengthy periods and where possible should be allowed visits from family and friends as well as from 'official visitors' (Code H 5.4, Note 5B, 5C).

What if the named person cannot be contacted?

If the person nominated by the detainee cannot be contacted, then he may name up to two alternative persons. If neither of those are contactable further attempts can be made at the discretion of the custody officer or investigating officer (Code C 5.1).

If the detainee is unable to nominate someone who is readily contactable, Note 5C urges the police to themselves consider who may be able to offer advice or support.

Are there any circumstances in which the exercise of the right can be delayed?

An officer of the rank of at least inspector can authorize a delay for up to 36 hours from the relevant time (as defined in s 41(2)) where the person is in police detention for an indictable offence, and he has reasonable grounds for believing that informing the named person of the arrest will:

- lead to interference with or harm to evidence connected with an indictable offence; or
- lead to interference with or physical injury to other persons; or

- lead to the alerting of other persons suspected of having committed an indictable offence but not yet arrested for it; or
- hinder the recovery of any property obtained as a result of such an offence; or
- hinder the recovery of the value of the property constituting the benefit to a detainee of his criminal conduct (as defined in Part 2 of PACE) (s 56(5), (5A); Annex B 1, 2).

Where a delay for any of these reasons is authorized, that authorization must be confirmed in writing and the detainee informed of the reasons as soon as practicable. The decision and the reasons for it must also be noted in the detainee's custody record. As soon as the grounds for authorizing delay cease to exist, the detainee must be asked whether he wants to exercise this right and have his custody record noted accordingly (Annex B 6).

Additional entitlements to contact

In addition to the right conferred by s 56, the detainee is also entitled to himself telephone one person 'for a reasonable time' and must be provided with writing materials if he wishes to write a letter (Code C 5.6).

If necessary, an interpreter should be provided to assist with the translation, either of the phone call or letter (Note 5A).

There is no obligation on the custody officer to inform the detainee directly of these entitlements, however they must be set out in the notice of entitlements which must be given to the detainee under Code C 3.2

As well as contact made by the detainee with someone outside, it may be that a friend, relative, or any other person interested in his welfare may themselves seek information about the detainee's whereabouts. Unless reasons for withholding this information apply (as listed previously), then the information shall be given if the detainee agrees (Code C 5.5). Moreover, at the custody officer's discretion and subject to practicalities, the detainee may receive visits (Code C 5.4; Note 5B).

Can these entitlements be delayed?

The entitlements conferred by Code C 5.6 may not only be delayed but may be refused if the person is detained for any arrestable or indictable offence, and an officer of the rank of inspector or above considers that communication by letter or telephone may result in one of the consequences as set out in s 56(5) and (5A) and repeated in Annex B (hindrance of the investigation of the offence or recovery of the value of the benefit to the detainee of his criminal conduct).

They may also be delayed or refused if the person is detained under the Terrorism Act 2000 and Annex B of Code H applies.

A record must be kept of any communications made or refused (Code C 5.8).

5.2.2 **Right to legal advice (Section 58)**

Section 58(1) provides every person arrested and held in custody with the right, if he so requests, to consult with a solicitor at any time. The consultation may be in person, by telephone, or in writing, depending on the circumstances of the arrest, but however the consultation is conducted, it is a fundamental right that the detainee should be allowed to have that communication in private (Code C 6.1; Note 6J).

A qualification to this right comes in Code H 6.5 where in certain circumstances an officer of the rank of Commander or Assistant Chief Constable may give a direction that a detainee arrested under s 41 of the Terrorism Act 2000 may only consult with a solicitor within the sight and hearing of a 'qualified officer'. Even for such detainees it is recognized that the right to consult privately with a solicitor is fundamental and would only exceptionally be interfered with (Code H, Note 6I).

The right to legal advice is of fundamental importance. The custody officer must not only inform the detainee of the right at an early stage, but must provide him with written details of the arrangements for obtaining such advice (Code A 3.2) and ask him whether or not he wishes to exercise that right (Code C 3.5).

Moreover, posters in English, Welsh, and the main minority ethnic or European languages advertising the right to legal advice should be displayed in a prominent position not only in the charging area of each police station as required by Code C 6.3, but wherever such an advertisement is likely to be helpful and it is practicable to do so (Code C, Note 6H).

It is important that nothing is said to a detainee to influence his choice of solicitor or to dissuade him from seeking legal advice (Code C 6.4).

Where an arrested person does seek legal advice and requests a private consultation with a solicitor, the fact of the request and the time at which it was made must be noted in the custody record and the request complied with as soon as practicable (s 58(2), (4)).

The procedure for arranging for the provision of legal advice is set out in Note 6B: where a detainee asks for free legal advice, the Defence Solicitor Call Centre (DSCC) must be informed; they will determine whether the advice should be limited to telephone advice provided by CDS Direct, or whether to make arrangements for advice to be given in person by a solicitor at the police station. Alternatively, where advice is not limited to telephone advice, or where the detainee is willing to pay for legal advice himself, he can ask for advice from a named solicitor. If that named solicitor cannot be contacted, the detainee may choose up to two alternatives. If neither alternative can be contacted then further attempts may be made at the custody officer's discretion, or the DSCC may be contacted to arrange for advice.

If the detainee decides that he does not wish to exercise his right to consult with a solicitor he should be reminded that he can speak to a solicitor on the telephone. If he continues to decline legal advice he should be asked why and any reasons given noted on the custody record (Code C 6.5).

He is not, however, obliged to give any reasons and should not be pressed to do so (Code C, Note 6K).

Even if a detainee declines legal advice on being initially offered it, the right continues throughout his time in police detention and can be exercised at any time. He must in addition be reminded of his entitlement at specified points throughout his detention, in particular before interview, and on detention reviews.

If a solicitor attends the police station to see a particular detainee, that person must be advised of that fact and asked if they would like to see the solicitor, even if he has previously waived his right to legal advice (Code C 6.15).

Can access to legal advice be delayed?

Compliance with the request may be delayed for the same reasons as set out in s 56 and Code C, Annex B above in relation to the right not to be held incommunicado but only where the officer who authorizes that delay has reasonable grounds for believing that the solicitor will do something (whether inadvertently or otherwise) which will result in one of those consequences, in which case, the detainee must be allowed to choose another solicitor.

The fact that an authorization to delay notification of arrest under s 56 has been given does not necessarily mean that a delay in access to legal advice will also be authorized.

Code C, Note B3 notes that a decision to delay access to a nominated solicitor will be rarely made, and only where it can be shown that the detainee is capable of misleading the solicitor, and that 'there is a more than substantial risk' that the detainee will be able to pass information that will lead to one of the specified consequences.

Delay in providing access to legal advice can only be authorized by an officer of the rank of superintendent or above (s 58(6), (8)).

Where authorization for a delay is given, it must be confirmed in writing and the detainee must be informed of the reasons for the decision which must be noted in his custody record.

The detainee must be informed that he may exercise his right to consult privately with a solicitor as soon as the reason for authorizing the delay has ceased to exist, and in any event within 36 hours of the relevant time as defined in s 41(2) (s 58(11), (5); Code C, Annex B 6).

5.3 Searches (Section 54)

5.3.1 Searches of detained persons

Section 54(1), supplemented by Code C 4.1, provides that the custody officer 'shall ascertain everything that a person has with him' when in police detention.

This does not, however, mean that the detainee must be searched; s 54(6) makes it clear that a search need only be carried out where the custody officer considers it necessary to do so in order to fulfil his duty under subsection (1). Similarly, the extent of the search should be limited to that which the custody officer considers necessary for the purposes of subsection (1) and may not in any event involve the removal of more than the outer clothing.

Where a search is carried out, it should be conducted by a constable of the same sex as the person to be searched (s 54(8), (9)). A new Annex L to Code C deals with establishing the gender of persons for the purpose of searching with particular reference to transgender and transvestite persons.

What can be seized?

Anything found on a search can be seized and retained (s 54(3)). However, clothing and 'personal effects' (defined in Code C 4.3 as 'items a detainee may lawfully need, use or refer to while in detention' but not including cash or valuables) may only be seized where the custody officer believes that the detainee may use them:

- to cause physical injury to himself or another person;
- to damage property;
- to interfere with evidence; or
- to assist him to escape (s 54(4)(a)).

A search for any items that may be used for such purposes may be conducted at any time during which a person is in police detention, whether at a police station or elsewhere (s 54(6A)).

Clothes and personal effects may also be seized where the custody officer has reasonable grounds to believe that they may be evidence relating to an offence (s 54(4)(b)).

In the event that anything is seized, the person searched must be told the reasons for the seizure unless that is impracticable either because the detainee is violent or at risk of becoming violent, or is incapable of understanding what is said (s 54(5)).

If any item of clothing or personal effects is seized, the reason for that seizure must be recorded (Code C 4.5).

There is no mandatory requirement to keep records of any other items seized; however, in practice a record is made, both of property noted to be in possession of the detainee and of the items seized which is usually attached to or forms part of the custody record. Where any record is made, the detainee should be invited to check and sign it (Code C 4.4).

In the event that clothing is seized, whether under this section or for any other reason (eg hygiene), adequate replacement clothing must be provided (Code C 8.5).

Section 43(2) of the Terrorism Act 2000 additionally allows a constable to search a detainee arrested under s 41 of the same Act, for anything that may constitute evidence that he is a terrorist (Code H, Note 4D).

Where the person has attended the police station in answer to live link bail, a constable may 'at any time' search that person or any article in that person's possession. No authority appears to be necessary for such a search to take place, neither is there any requirement to record that a search has taken place or that items have been seized as a result, although a record 'may' be made. Where items are found which may:

- jeopardize the maintenance of order in the police station;
- put the safety of any person in the police station at risk;
- be evidence of, or in relation to, an offence,

such items may be seized and retained where necessary

- for use as evidence at trial;
- for forensic examination or for investigation in connection with an offence;
- to establish its lawful owner where there are reasonable grounds for believing that it has been obtained in consequence of the commission of an offence (s 54B).

5.3.2 Intimate searches

An intimate search is defined in Annex A of Code C of the Codes of Practice as 'the physical examination of a person's body orifices other than the mouth'.

As it is recognized that such searches carry with them inherent risks, Note for Guidance A1 advises that every reasonable effort should be made to persuade the detainee to hand the item over voluntarily and without the need for a search. In such circumstances a registered medical practitioner or nurse should be available to provide assistance to the detainee.

An intimate search can only be carried out where an officer of at least the rank of inspector has reasonable grounds for believing that the detainee has concealed upon him either:

- something which he could use to cause physical injury to himself or others whilst in police detention or the custody of a court; or
- a Class A drug which he intended either to supply to another or to export,

and the officer has reasonable grounds for believing that such an item or drug cannot be found without an intimate search (s 55(1), (2)).

Note for Guidance A2 makes it clear that authorization for an intimate search should only be given where there are real grounds for believing that a relevant item has been concealed and where there is no other alternative to such a search taking place.

If the object of the search is to recover a Class A drug, the detainee must first give his consent in writing. He must be warned that a refusal without good cause may harm his case if it comes to trial (Code A, Annex A, 2(b); 2B).

Where can an intimate search be carried out?

An intimate search can only be carried out at:

- a police station (but not where it is a drug search);
- a hospital;
- a registered medical practitioner's surgery; or
- some other place used for medical purposes (s 55(8)).

Who may carry out the search?

An intimate search should be carried out by either a registered medical practitioner or a registered nurse unless an officer of at least the rank of inspector considers that this is not practicable, in which case the search can be carried out by a constable of the same sex as the person to be searched (s 55(5)–(7)).

At least two people in addition to the detainee should be present during the search; subject to that, the number of people present should be kept to the minimum necessary and (unless a medical practitioner or nurse) should be of the same sex as the person searched (Annex A6).

Although the Act provides for a constable to carry out a search if it is 'not practicable' for the search to be carried out by a registered medical practitioner or nurse, Note for Guidance A4 states that this should only happen as a matter of last resort and in circumstances where the authorizing officer is satisfied that the detainee might use the article for causing a 'sufficiently severe' injury to himself or another.

Where the intimate search is a search for a Class A drug intended by the suspected person for supply or export, then the search may only be carried out by a registered medical practitioner or nurse at a hospital, surgery, or other medical premises.

Anything found in the course of the search which the custody officer believes may be used by the detainee:

- to cause physical injury to himself or another person;
- to damage property;
- to interfere with evidence; or
- to assist him to escape,

may be seized and retained (s 55(12)(a)).

A custody officer may also cause to be seized anything found which he has reasonable grounds for believing may be evidence relating to an offence (s 55(12)(b)).

The detainee must be told the reason for the seizure unless he is violent, at risk of becoming violent, or is incapable of understanding what is said to him (s 55(13)).

Records

Authorization for an intimate search must be given or confirmed in writing (s 55(3)).

Section 55(10) states that a record must be made in the custody record of the parts of the body that have been searched and the reason for that search.

Annex A7 expands the requirement for documentation to include details of who carried out the search, who was present, why it was thought that the article could only be removed through an intimate search, and the result.

If the intimate search was carried out by a police officer instead of a registered medical practitioner or nurse, the reasons must be recorded (Code C, Annex A8).

5.3.3 X-rays and ultrasound scans

Where an officer of the rank of inspector or above has reasonable grounds for believing that a suspect who has been arrested and is in police detention may have swallowed a Class A drug that he was, prior to his arrest, intending either to supply to another or to export, then that officer may authorize either an X-ray and/or an ultrasound scan to be carried out on the suspect (s 55A(1)).

An X-ray or scan authorized under this section must be carried out by a 'suitably qualified person'—that is, a registered nurse or registered medical practitioner, and only at a hospital, surgery or other medical premises.

An X-ray or ultrasound can only be carried out if the suspect gives his consent in writing. However, if he fails to give his consent without good cause, then that refusal can be taken into account by a judge in deciding whether there is a case to answer or to grant an application for dismissal, and a court or jury can draw adverse inferences from the refusal.

The suspect must be warned of these consequences by a police officer or member of police staff; the appropriate words of the warning can be found at Note K2 of Annex K of Code C.

A refusal may be taken into account against the suspect only where that refusal was without good cause. Understandably, perhaps, a suspect may have some concerns about the effects of undergoing an X-ray or ultrasound scan. Note for Guidance K1 therefore suggests that the medical practitioner or nurse should explain the procedure to the suspect to allay any concerns. As well as being good medical practice, following such a course of action may have the added benefit of removing any argument of 'good cause' for refusing to undergo the procedure.

A record must be made in the custody record of the authorization, the grounds upon which it was given, the warning, written consent (or refusal), and details of where the procedure took place, who carried it out, who else was present, and the result.

5.3.4 Strip searches

There are no substantive provisions in the Act governing the conduct of strip searches which are instead dealt with only in the Codes of Practice at Code C, Annex A.

A strip search is defined at Annex A9 as 'a search involving the removal of more than outer clothing [which] includes shoes and socks'. The purpose of a strip search is to remove an article which the detainee would not be allowed to keep. A strip search should not be carried out as a matter of routine, but only where it is reasonably considered that such an article might have been concealed and where a strip search is considered necessary to remove that article.

The Code is silent on the question of authorization although, as with other searches, the authority of the custody officer should be obtained. However, as a strip search may well result in the establishment of reasonable grounds to carry out an intimate search, the safer course may well be to obtain the authority of an inspector. As with the conduct of an intimate search, a strip search should be carried out quickly and with sensitivity. Annex A11(d) states that 'every effort shall be made to secure the detainee's co-operation and minimise embarrassment'. Accordingly, the detainee should not have to remove all his clothes at once and should be allowed to re-dress as soon as the procedure is complete, the search must be carried out by an officer of the same sex as the detainee, and the search should take place in a private area.

Ordinarily, if the strip search will expose intimate body parts, two people other than the detainee should be present (Annex A11(c)).

Body orifices may be visually inspected but may not be touched. To do so would constitute an intimate search. If, therefore, it appears likely on visual inspection that an article is within a body orifice, then the detainee should be asked to hand the item over (Annex A11(f)). If he refuses to do so, then an intimate search will need to be authorized and conducted in accordance with s 55 and Part A of Annex A.

A record must be made on the custody record detailing the reason for the strip search, the identities of those present, and the result (Annex A12).

5.3.5 Searches to establish identity

A detainee may also be searched or examined in order to ascertain whether he has any identifying mark or otherwise to help facilitate identification. The provisions relating to these searches (found at s 54 and in Code D) are dealt with in Chapter 6.

5.4 Fingerprints

The provisions relating to the taking of fingerprints and impressions of footwear are dealt with in Chapter 6.

5.5 Samples (Section 63)

There are a number of provisions dealing with the taking of both intimate and non-intimate samples. As these are primarily taken for the purpose of confirming or eliminating the identification of a suspect as the offender they are more conveniently dealt with in Chapter 6. The exception is where a sample is taken for the purpose of ascertaining whether a detainee has taken Class A drugs; these provisions are dealt with here.

5.5.1 **Drug testing**

In certain circumstances, a non-intimate sample, including a sample of urine may be taken from a person in police detention in order to ascertain whether he has a specified Class A drug in his body (s 63B(1)).

Where by notification by the Secretary of State the relevant arrangements are in place (whether at a specified police station or for a police area as a whole), samples may be requested for these purposes from detainees over the age of 14. Where notification has not been given, they apply to detainees who have reached the age of 18.

The circumstances in which such a sample can be requested are where either:

- the detainee has been charged with a 'trigger offence'; or
- the detainee has been charged with an offence and an officer of at least the rank of inspector has reasonable grounds for suspecting that the misuse of a specified Class A drug caused or contributed to the offence.

'Trigger offences' are defined in Sch 6 of the Criminal Justice and Court Services Act 2000 as:

- theft, robbery, burglary, obtaining property by deception, handling stolen goods, and attempts to commit any of those offences;
- aggravated burglary, taking a motor vehicle or other conveyance without authority, aggravated vehicle taking, going equipped for burglary, theft, or cheat;
- offences under ss 4, 5(2) and 5(3) of the Misuse of Drugs Act 1971—that is, production, supply, possession and possession with intent to supply where the drug in question is a Class A drug;
- begging, persistent begging.

'Specified Class A drugs' are defined in the Criminal Justice (Specified Class A Drugs) Order 2001 Art 2 as:

- cocaine, its salts and any preparation or other product containing cocaine or its salts; and
- diamorphine, its salts and any preparation or other product containing diamorphine or its salts.

As a non-intimate sample cannot be taken without consent, the police can only request a detainee to give such a sample. However, failure without good cause to give a sample when requested under s 63B is a summary offence punishable with up to three months' imprisonment (s 63B(8); s 63C(1)).

The detainee must be warned of the possible consequences if he fails to give consent before the sample is formally requested (s 63B(5)).

Where a sample has been taken, the information derived from it may be disclosed for the purposes of informing decisions taken about bail, supervision, and sentencing, and to ensure that the person is given appropriate advice and treatment. A non-intimate sample taken for the purposes of drug-testing cannot be used for any other purpose (eg identification).

A record must be made, in the detainee's custody record where applicable, of any authorization given under s 63B(2)(b) and the grounds for suspicion that led to that authorization.

Practical Guidance

5.6 Case Study (Detainee's Rights)

Jones, a 19-year-old youth, is arrested for burglary and taken to the police station where detention is authorized at 11am. DC Potts takes charge of the case and reasonably suspects that some of the property stolen during the burglary may be at Jones' house. Fearing that if allowed to make a phone call Jones will alert others to dispose of the property DC Potts asks the custody officer, Sergeant Brown, not to allow Jones to make a phone call or contact a solicitor until a search of his house has been carried out. Jones requests a solicitor, asks that his brother is informed of his arrest, and that he be allowed to make a phone call.

Can Sergeant Brown prevent Jones from making a phone call and contacting a solicitor?

As Jones' brother is a person likely to take an interest in his welfare then Jones is entitled to have notification of his arrest sent to him. He is also entitled to speak on the telephone for a reasonable period and to consult and communicate privately with a solicitor at any time (s 56/58 of PACE). Sergeant Brown has a duty to facilitate these rights unless delay is authorized by the Act—s 56(2)–(5A). Sergeant Brown cannot authorize delay himself but should ensure the necessary conditions are fully met before seeking authority from an officer of appropriate rank. The offence for which Jones is under arrest is an indictable offence so the first condition is met. Sergeant Brown should ensure that there are reasonable grounds to believe that informing Jones' brother of Jones' whereabouts, allowing Jones to make a phone call, and contacting a solicitor will hinder the recovery of any property obtained as a result of having committed burglary. In the case of preventing Jones from making a phone call and informing his brother, on the facts it is reasonable to delay communication until steps have been taken to search his premises. However, in respect of refusing access to a solicitor this is much harder to justify. There must be reasonable grounds to believe the solicitor Jones wants to contact will inadvertently or otherwise pass on a message or act in some other way that will hinder the recovery of stolen property (Code of Practice C, Annex B3). This is a difficult condition to satisfy. Only on rare occasions will a delay in access to a solicitor be justified. The Code of Practice makes clear that the fact that the grounds for delaying notification of arrest may be satisfied does not automatically mean the grounds for delaying access to legal advice will also be satisfied (Code of Practice C, Annex B5).

Only an officer of at least the rank of inspector may authorize delay in having someone informed of Jones' whereabouts and speaking to someone on the phone. In the case of delay in contacting a solicitor the authority of an officer of at least superintendent rank is required. Sergeant Brown should make a record in the custody record of the request for notification, and request to see a solicitor, and the action taken. If delay is authorized then as soon as practicable a further record should be made in the custody record of the grounds, and Jones informed of them (Code of Practice Code C, Annex B13).

Assuming the request to delay legal advice is turned down, how should Sergeant Brown deal with a request from Jones to have legal advice from a friend who is a first year student studying law at university?

Jones has a right to consult and communicate privately with a solicitor. The Code of Practice states that 'solicitor' means, a person holding a current practicing certificate or an accredited or probationary representative. Sergeant Brown should therefore explain this to Jones and refuse the request. He should make an entry in the custody record and remind Jones that free independent legal advice is available from the duty solicitor.

When informed that notification to his brother is being delayed, Jones states that he is a citizen of the Irish Republic and asks that the embassy be informed of his arrest. How should Sergeant Brown deal with this request?

Nationals of foreign countries including the Republic of Ireland may communicate at any time with the appropriate High Commission, Embassy, or Consulate. This right may not be interfered with and therefore Sergeant Brown should ensure the appropriate Embassy is informed of Jones' whereabouts and make an entry.

6

Identification: Part V, Code D

Law and Commentary

6.1 Introduction

Part V of the Act contains a number of important sections dealing with procedures that can take place in order to help facilitate identification, both to establish the identity of the suspect but also to identify the suspect as the offender. The methods by which a suspect may be identified are varied; a suspect may be searched or examined for any identifying features, fingerprints and footwear impressions may be taken for comparison with those found at a scene, and physical samples (both intimate and non-intimate) can be taken from the suspect's person to obtain a DNA profile. Amendments to the Act provided for by the Crime and Security Act 2010 give the police additional powers to take fingerprints and DNA samples from people arrested, charged or convicted of a recordable offence, or who have been convicted overseas of a serious sexual or violent offence.

Further proposed amendments to s 64 of PACE contained in s 14 of the Crime and Security Act 2010 were designed to meet the ruling of the European Court of Human Rights in *S and Marper v United Kingdom* [2008] ECHR 1581 that the existing provisions in PACE permitting the indiscriminate retention of DNA from unconvicted individuals violated Art 8 of the European Convention. These proposed amendments were never brought into force and are repealed by Sch 9 of the Protection of Freedoms Act 2012. When Chapter 1 of Part 1 of that Act is brought into force (expected to be October 2013), it will insert new sections 63D to 63U into PACE providing a new framework for the destruction, retention, and use of fingerprints and DNA profiles derived from samples.

The comprehensive provisions concerning the identification of a suspect by witnesses are to be found, not in the Act, but in Code D which 'concerns the principal methods used by police to identify people in connection with the investigation of offences and the keeping of accurate and reliable criminal records' (Code D 1.1). In the latest version of Code D, which applies to any identification procedure carried out after midnight on 6 March 2011, the procedure to be followed depends upon whether the identification is of a suspect by an eye-witness (Code D.3(A)), or is evidence of recognition from a film, photograph, or other image.

6.2 Searches to Ascertain Identity (Section 54A)

Under s 54A, a detainee (other than one detained at a police station to be searched under a stop and search power) may be searched and/or examined by a constable of the same sex as the person to be searched:

- in order to ascertain whether he has any mark that would tend to identify him as a person involved in the commission of an offence; or

- to facilitate the ascertainment of his identity.

Authority for such a search or examination can only be given by an officer of at least the rank of inspector (s 54(1)). If given orally, the authorization must be confirmed in writing as soon as practicable (s 54(4)).

6.2.1 When can authorization be given?

If the purpose of the examination or search is to find an identifying mark, then authorization can only be given if:

- the detainee has refused to consent to such a search or examination; or
- it is not practicable to obtain such consent, for example, where the detainee is unfit to give consent (s 54(2); Code D, Note 5D).

If the purpose of the examination or search is to facilitate identification, then authorization can only be given where:

- the detainee has refused to identify himself; or
- the officer has reasonable grounds for suspecting that the detainee is not who he claims to be (s 54(3)).

A 'mark' includes features and injuries. An 'identifying mark' is a mark which either facilitates the ascertainment of the detainee's identity or his identification as a person involved in the commission of an offence (s 54A(12)). Where an identifying mark (as defined) is found, it may be photographed by a constable of the same sex as the person searched, either with or without the consent of the detainee (s 54A(5)–(7)).

The use to which such a photograph (which is defined to include any visual image however produced) can be put is wide. Section 54A(9) and (10) provide that a photograph of the identifying mark can be used by or disclosed to any person for any purpose related to the prevention or detection of crime, the investigation of an offence or the conduct of a prosecution whether in the United Kingdom or abroad. Examples of how a photograph might be used for such purposes are listed in Code D, Note 5B.

A photograph taken of an identifying mark under this section may be retained but may only be used for the purposes set out above (Code D 5.6). If a person refuses to cooperate with a search, examination, or photograph, a constable may use reasonable force to search, examine, or photograph the person without his consent (Code D 5.9).

Any search or examination under s 54A should be kept to the minimum necessary to achieve the desired purpose. If it is necessary to remove more than a person's outer clothing to properly search or examine him, then the search must be carried out in accordance with the provisions of Code C, Annex A, 11 (ie strip searches) (Code D 5.10).

6.3 **Fingerprints (Sections 61, 63A, and 64)**

A person may give consent in writing at a police station for his fingerprints to be taken. There are however numerous situations in which a constable can take fingerprints from a person without consent; where necessary, the constable may use reasonable force to do so (s 117).

Fingerprints may be taken from a person without consent in the following situations in which either:

- fingerprints have not previously been taken in the course of an investigation, or
- fingerprints have been taken, but they either did not constitute a complete set, or were not of sufficient quality to allow satisfactory analysis.

Those situations are where the person has been:

- detained at a police station as a consequence of arrest for a recordable offence—s 61(3);
- detained at a police station and charged with or informed that he will be reported for a recordable offence—s 61(4);
- arrested for a recordable offence and released—s 61(5A);
- not detained, but charged with or informed that he will be reported for a recordable offence—s 61(5B).

Fingerprints may also be taken without consent under s 61(6)—where the person has been convicted, cautioned, or has been warned or reprimanded for a recordable offence and has not had his fingerprints taken since he was convicted, cautioned, warned, or reprimanded; and under s 61(6D)—where the person has been convicted of an offence overseas which would have constituted a qualifying offence if done in England or Wales, and he has not had his fingerprints taken on a previous occasion under this subsection. Fingerprints can only be taken without consent under these subsections where authorized by an officer of at least the rank of inspector who is satisfied that the taking of fingerprints is necessary to assist in the prevention or detection of crime.

In two situations, fingerprints can be taken without consent in order to establish identity. These are under s 61(4A)—where a person has answered to bail at a court or police station, and the court or an officer of at least the rank of inspector authorizes fingerprints to be taken in order to ascertain identity for the reasons set out in s 61(4B); and s 61(6A)—by virtue of which a constable may take the fingerprints of a person who he reasonably suspects is committing or attempting to commit an offence or who has committed or has attempted to commit an offence and either the name of the person cannot be readily ascertained by the constable, or the constable has reasonable grounds for doubting whether the name given by the person is correct. Note that fingerprints taken under s 61(6A) do not count as fingerprints taken in the course of an investigation (s 61(6C)), and must be destroyed as soon as they have fulfilled the purpose for which they were taken (s 64(1BA)).

In all cases where fingerprints are taken without consent, the person shall first be informed of:

- the reason for taking the fingerprints,
- the power by virtue of which the fingerprints are taken, and
- (where authorization was required) the fact that authorization was given.

A record must be made of these matters which shall be on the custody record if the person is detained at a police station—s 61(7).

Whether the fingerprints are taken with or without consent, the person shall also be told before they are taken that they may be the subject of a speculative search, and a record made of the fact that he has been so informed—s 61(7A).

Where a speculative search takes place, fingerprints or information derived from them may be checked against other fingerprints or information contained in records to which the person carrying out the check has access held by other law-enforcement agencies as listed in s 63A.

Schedule 2A to the Act, added by the Crime and Security Act 2010, sets out powers to require attendance at a police station for fingerprints and/or other samples to be taken and the time limits within which such powers must be exercised.

6.4 **Impressions of Footwear (Sections 61A and 63A)**

Section 61A allows impressions of a person's footwear to be taken. The provisions mirror subsections (1), (2), (3), (3A), (7A), and (7) of s 61 which deals with fingerprints.

Section 61A(2) states that an impression of a person's footwear may be taken with consent, which must be given in writing if he is at the police station. An impression of footwear can only be taken without consent by a constable and where:

- the person is detained at a police station and has either been
- detained in consequence of his arrest for a recordable offence, or has been charged with or informed that he will be reported for a recordable offence, and either,
- he has not had an impression of his footwear taken previously in the course of the investigation of the offence or if it has, that impression was incomplete or of insufficient quality for comparison or analysis (s 61A(3), (4)).

As with fingerprints, whether the impression is taken with or without consent, the person from whom it is taken must be told in advance that it may be subject to a speculative search as described above and set out at s 63A and a record must be made in his custody record that he has been informed of this possibility (s 61A(5)).

Where the impression is taken without consent, the person must be told the reason why and the reason recorded in his custody record (s 61A(6)).

6.5 **Samples (Sections 62, 63, 63A, and 65)**

6.5.1 **Intimate samples**

An intimate sample is defined in section 65 of the Act as:

- a sample of blood, semen or any other tissue fluid, urine, or pubic hair;
- a dental impression;
- a swab taken from any part of a person's genitals (including pubic hair) or from a person's body orifice other than the mouth.

An intimate sample can only be taken from a person in police detention where the detainee has given written consent, and where the taking of the sample has been authorized by an officer of at least the rank of inspector (s 62(1)).

An intimate sample may also be taken from a person who is not in police detention where he has already in the course of the investigation provided two non-intimate samples for the same means of analysis as it is intended to subject the intimate sample (eg DNA testing), but where those two non-intimate samples have proved to be insufficient.

The person from whom the intimate sample was taken would still need to give written consent and the taking of the sample must be authorized by an officer of at least the rank of inspector (s 62(1A)).

In either case, authorization can only be given where the authorizing officer has reasonable grounds for believing that the person from whom it is to be taken has been involved in a recordable offence and that the sample will tend to prove or disprove his involvement (s 62(2)).

Section 62(2A) provides one further situation in which an intimate sample may be taken with consent and where authorization has been given by an officer of at least the rank of inspector; namely, where two or more intimate samples have been taken from a person convicted of an offence outside England and Wales, but which have proved insufficient for analysis. Before authorization can be given, the officer must be satisfied that taking the sample is necessary to assist in the prevention of crime.

In each case before an intimate sample is taken from a person he must be informed of the reason for taking the sample, the fact that authorization has been given, and the provision under which it has been given, and, where the sample has been taken at a police station, the fact that the sample may be the subject of a speculative search as set out at s 63A.

Details of the authorization, grounds, notification of the possibility of a speculative search, and consent must all be recorded in the person's custody record as
soon as practicable after the sample has been taken (s 62(7), (8)).

A constable may require a person to attend a police station for the purpose of
taking an intimate sample from him under s 62(1A) or (2A) if two or more intimate samples suitable for the same means of analysis have been taken but have
proved insufficient (Schedule 2 Part 2).

By whom may the sample be taken?

If the sample to be taken is a dental impression, then it must be taken by a
registered dentist. In all other cases (save a sample of urine) the sample may
only be taken by a registered medical practitioner or other healthcare professional (s 62(9A)).

What if consent is withheld?

If consent is refused without good cause, then in any subsequent proceedings
adverse inferences may be drawn by a court, judge, or jury (s 62(10)).

The suspect must be made aware of the possible consequences and be reminded of his entitlement to free legal advice (Code D 6.3(b)).

Note that none of the above provisions apply to the taking of a specimen for
the purposes of ss 4–11 of the Road Traffic Act 1988.

6.5.2 Non-intimate samples

Section 63 deals with the taking of non-intimate samples.

A non-intimate sample is:

- a sample of hair (other than pubic hair). Hair may be cut or plucked, but if the
  latter, a sample no bigger than is reasonably necessary. The suspect should be
  allowed a reasonable choice as to what part of the body the hair is taken
  from;
- a sample from or under a nail;
- a swab taken from the mouth or any other non-intimate part of the body;
- saliva;
- a skin impression (Code D6).

Unlike intimate samples which can only be taken if they have been authorized
and if the appropriate written consent has been given, a non-intimate sample
can be taken without consent in a number of situations, using reasonable force
if necessary (s 117). The provisions governing many of these situations mirror
the corresponding provisions in s 61 for the taking of fingerprints without
consent.

A non-intimate sample may be taken from a person without consent in the following situations:

1. Where a person has been detained at a police station as a consequence of arrest for a recordable offence, and:
   - has not had a sample of the same type from the same part of the body taken in course of the investigation, or
   - has had such a sample but it was insufficient—s 63(2B).
2. Where a person is held in custody by the police on the authority of the court, and:
   - the taking of the sample is authorized by an officer of at least the rank of inspector who has reasonable grounds for suspecting the involvement of the person in a recordable offence and for believing that the sample will tend to confirm or disprove his involvement (note that the sample shall not be a skin impression if one has already been taken from the same part of the body and has not proved insufficient)— s 63(3), (4), (5A).
3. Where a person has been arrested for a recordable offence and released, and:
   - is on bail, but has not had a non-intimate sample of the same type from the same part of the body taken in the course of the investigation, or
   - has had a non-intimate sample taken but it was not suitable for the same means of analysis or was insufficient—s 63(3ZA).
4. Where a person has been charged with or informed that he will be reported for a recordable offence, and:
   - has not had a non-intimate sample taken in the course of the investigation, or
   - has had a non-intimate sample taken but it was not suitable for the same means of analysis or was insufficient, or
   - has had a non-intimate sample taken but the sample has been destroyed pursuant to s 63R or any other enactment, and
   - it is disputed whether a DNA profile relevant to the proceedings is derived from the sample—s 63(3A).
5. Where a person has been convicted, cautioned, warned, or reprimanded for a recordable offence and:
   - has not had a non-intimate sample taken since convicted, cautioned, warned, or reprimanded, or
   - such a sample has been taken but it was not suitable for the same means of analysis, or it proved insufficient, and
   - authority has been given by an officer of at least the rank of inspector who is satisfied that it is necessary to take the sample to assist in the prevention or detection of crime—s 63(3B).

6. Where a person has been convicted of an offence overseas which would have constituted a qualifying offence if done in England or Wales, and:
   - has not had a non-intimate sample taken on a previous occasion under this subsection, or
   - such a sample has been taken but it was not suitable for the same means of analysis, or it proved insufficient, and
   - authority has been given by an officer of at least the rank of inspector who is satisfied that it is necessary to take the sample to assist in the prevention or detection of crime—s 63(3E).

7. A non-intimate sample may also be taken from a person without consent if he is a person to whom s 2 of the Criminal Evidence (Amendment) Act 1997 applies (persons detained following acquittal on grounds of insanity or finding of unfitness to plead)—s 63(3C).

In all cases where under a power conferred by this section a non-intimate sample is taken without consent, before the sample is taken an officer shall inform the person of:

- the reason for taking the sample
- the power by virtue of which it is taken
- where authorization is required, the fact that authorization has been given.

These matters must be recorded as soon as practicable after the sample is taken; on the custody record if the person is detained at a police station.

If a sample is taken at a police station (whether with or without consent), the person must be informed before the sample is taken that it may be the subject of a speculative search.

Part 3 of Sch 2 sets out the powers to require a person to attend a police station for the purpose of taking a non-intimate sample from him, and provides time limits for the exercise of those powers.

6.6 Retention and Destruction of Fingerprints, Footwear Impressions, and Samples (Section 64)

Following the decision in *S and Marper v UK* [2008] ECHR 1581, the Government brought forward provisions in ss 14 to 23 of the Crime and Security Act 2010 which contained provisions to be found in 14 new subsections of s 64 of PACE. These provisions were never brought into force and are now repealed by Sch 9 of the Protection of Freedoms Act 2012 which received Royal Assent on 1 May 2012. Chapter 1 of the 2012 Act replaces the existing framework contained in Part 5 of PACE whereby fingerprints and DNA profiles taken from a person arrested for, charged with, or convicted of a recordable offence could be retained indefinitely, with a new framework, set out in 17 new lengthy subsections to an amended s 63.

6.6.1 **The Basic Rule—s 63D**

The basic rule, set out in a new s 63D, provides that fingerprints and DNA profiles derived from samples taken from a person under any power conferred by Part 5 of PACE or which were taken by the police with the consent of the person from whom they were taken in connection with the investigation of an offence by the police ('s 63D material') must be destroyed if:

- it appears to the responsible chief officer of police that either the taking of the fingerprint or sample from which the DNA profile was derived was unlawful, or,
- the fingerprint or sample was taken from a person in connection with that person's arrest, and the arrest was unlawful or based on mistaken identity.

In any other case, s 63 material must be destroyed unless it is retained under any power conferred by sections 63E to 63O, or (if it ceases to be retained under any of those powers) under any other such power which applies to it—see the exceptions and exclusions listed in s 63U.

The provisions contained within s 63 are complex. The maximum period for which a fingerprint or DNA profile can be retained is dependent on numerous factors; most important of which are the age of the person from whom the fingerprint or DNA profile has been obtained, and whether he has been arrested, charged, or convicted of a 'recordable offence' (see s 118), a 'qualifying offence' (serious violent, sexual, and terrorist offences as set out in s 65A(2)), or an 'excluded offence' (a recordable offence which is not a qualifying offence committed when the person was under 18—see s 63F(11)). But it is not just the age of the offender or seriousness of the offence which determines the retention period; other factors may include: whether the offender is arrested, charged, or convicted; his antecedent history; the type and length of sentence imposed; the circumstances of the alleged victim of the offence.

In certain cases the consent of the 'Commissioner for the Retention and Use of Biometric Material' is required for material to be retained. Dependent on the section, application can be made to a District Judge for an order to extend the retention period, or to a Crown Court on appeal against such an extension.

There is no substitute for studying the relevant subsections themselves, but in outline, the relevant retention periods are as set out in Table 6.1. In all cases where the person has previously been convicted of a recordable offence which is not an excluded offence, the retention period is indefinite. A conviction includes a caution, warning, reprimand, finding of not guilty by reason of insanity, or a finding that a person under a disability has done the act charged—s 65B.

In all cases, s 63D(5) permits a person's s 63D material to be retained for a reasonable period to enable a speculative search to be carried out if the responsible chief officer of police considers such a search to be desirable.

139

Table 6.1

Subsection	Offender/Offence	Retention Period	Authorization/Extension
s 63I	Adult Conviction All crimes	Indefinite	

s 63F(4)	Adult
	Charged but not
	   convicted
	Qualifying offence
		3 years	Extendable by a court on
			   application for up to 2
			   years

s 63F(5)	Adult
	Arrested but not
	   charged or convicted
	Qualifying offence
		3 years	Authorization required
			   by the Commissioner
			   (s 63G)
			Extendable by a court on
			   application for up to 2
			   years

s 63H	Adult Arrested or charged but not convicted Recordable offence	None	
s 63I, K	Under 18 Convicted Qualifying offence	Indefinite	

s 63K	Under 18
	Convicted
	Recordable offence
		1st conviction—5 years +
		   length of any custodial
		   sentence (where custodial
		   term less than 5 years—
		   otherwise, indefinite)
		2nd conviction—indefinite	

s 63F(4)	Under 18
	Charged but not
	   convicted
	Qualifying offence
		3 years	Extendable by a court on
			   application for up to 2
			   years

s 63F(5)	Under 18
	Arrested but not
	   charged or convicted
	Qualifying offence
		3 years	Authorization required
			   by the Commissioner
			   (s 63G)
			Extendable by a court on
			   application for up to 2
			   years

s 63H	Under 18 Arrested or charged but not convicted Recordable offence	None	

s 63J	Persons convicted overseas	Indefinite	
s 63L	Persons given a penalty notice s 2 CJPA 2001	2 years	
s 63M	National security	2 years	Renewable. Subject to review by the Commissioner
s 63N	63D material given voluntarily	Until it has fulfilled the purpose for which it was taken.	
s 63R	Biological DNA samples	Until a DNA profile has been obtained, or 6 months (whichever is sooner)	Application may be made to a court for an order to retain if sample likely to be needed in proceedings

Impressions of footwear may be retained for as long as is necessary for purposes related to the prevention or detection of crime, the investigation of an offence, or the conduct of a prosecution—s 63S.

Section 63T sets out the restrictions on the use to which material to which ss 63D, 63R and 63S applies can be put. It is important to note that once the time period for the retention of such material has expired, such material 'must not' be used in evidence against the person to whom the material relates or be used for the purposes of the investigation of any offence.

Section 64 sets out further provisions relating to the use and destruction of fingerprints, footwear impressions, and samples taken in connection with the investigation of an offence. Section 64(1A) provides that unless they are required to be destroyed in accordance with s 64(3), they may be retained after they have fulfilled the purposes for which they were taken, but shall not be used by any person except for purposes related to the prevention or detection of crime, the investigation of an offence, the conduct of a prosecution, or the identification of a deceased person.

Where the fingerprint, footwear impression, or sample was taken from a person in connection with the investigation of an offence, but that person is not suspected of having committed the offence, the fingerprint, impression, or sample must be destroyed as soon as it has fulfilled the purpose for which it was taken, unless either:

- it was taken for the purposes of the investigation of an offence of which a person has been convicted; and a sample, fingerprint, or impression of footwear was

also taken from the convicted person for the purpose of that investigation—
s 64(3AA); or
- the person gives written consent for the fingerprint, sample, or impression of
footwear to be retained—s 64(3AC).

6.7 **Photographs (Section 64A)**

Section 64A, as amended by the Serious Organised Crime and Police Act,
provides the police with wide powers to photograph suspects.

A person may be photographed, with or without their consent, if they
have been:

- detained at a police station;
- arrested by a constable for an offence;
- taken into custody by a constable after being arrested for an offence by
a person other than a constable;
- made subject to a requirement to wait with a community support officer
under para 2(3) or (3A) of Sch 4 to the Police Reform Act 2002;
- required to leave a locality under s 27 of the Violent Crime Reduction
Act 2007;
- given certain fixed penalty notices as set out at s 64A(1B)(d)–(g).

The person taking the photograph may require the removal (or may, using reasonable force, remove himself) any item or substance worn on or over the whole
or any part of the head or face of the person to be photographed (s 64A(2)).

Consent is not required before taking the photograph and if necessary a
photograph may be taken covertly or by the use of reasonable force (Code D
5.14).

Any photograph taken may be retained and disclosed for purposes related to
the prevention or detection of (any) crime, or the investigation of (any) offence
or conduct of a prosecution (s 64A(4)).

The person photographed must be informed of the purpose of the photograph, the grounds on which authority has been obtained for the photograph
if applicable, and the purposes for which the photograph may be used, disclosed, or retained, either before the photograph is taken, or afterwards if it is
taken covertly (Code D 5.15).

A record must be made detailing the identity of the officer who took the
photograph, the purpose of the photograph, whether the photograph was taken
with or without consent, details of any authority given, and details of the
circumstances and identities of those present where any force was used.

A person who is suspected on reasonable grounds of involvement in a criminal offence but who is at a police station voluntarily and is therefore not in
police detention may also be photographed, but may not be subjected to any
force in order to do so (Code D 5.21).

Photographs or other images of a person not detained must be destroyed unless the person is either charged, prosecuted, or informed that they may be prosecuted for a recordable offence; is cautioned, given a warning or a reprimand for a recordable offence (see para 3.3.1); or gives 'informed consent' in writing for the photograph to be retained. 'Informed consent' means that they must be fully appraised of the purposes to which that photograph could in future be put (Code D 5.22).

A photograph includes any visual image however recorded, including a video or other film (s 64A(6)).

A photograph may only be taken by a constable (s 64A(3)).

6.8 **Identification by Witnesses (Code D)**

The important provisions concerning the practice and procedure of the identification of a suspect by witnesses are contained entirely within Code D. The procedures are intended to test the witness's ability to identify a person they saw on a previous occasion (for example, committing an offence or at the scene of a crime), to obtain evidence of recognition and to test a person's claim that they recognize someone shown in an image as a person known to them, and to provide safeguards against the dangers of a mistaken identification.

6.8.1 **Part A—Identification of a suspect by an eye-witness**

Part A 'applies when an eye-witness has seen the offender committing the crime, or in any other circumstances which tend to prove or disprove the involvement of the person they saw in the crime, for example, close to the scene of the crime immediately before or immediately after it was committed'.

The identification procedure to be adopted depends in the first instance on whether or not the identity of the suspect is known to the police. The identity of the suspect will be 'known' when there is sufficient information known to the police to justify the arrest of a person for suspected involvement in an offence (Code D 3.4).

6.8.2 **Identification where the suspect's identity is not known**

Such cases are covered in Code D 3.2 and 3.3 and allow for a witness to be taken to a particular place to see whether they can identify the relevant person, or for the witness to be shown photographs or other images from which an identification might be made.

The first of these situations most commonly occurs where an offence takes place in a particular locality to which the police are called and arrive within a short period of time. The witness may then be driven around that area or any other relevant place in the hope that the offender might be spotted by the witness and an identification made. Whilst Code D 3.2 allows for the fact that the circumstances in which such an identification might be made cannot be controlled in the same way as formal identification procedures, nevertheless, insofar as possible, measures should be adopted to ensure that the witness's identification is independent and to safeguard against the possibility of a mistaken identification.

Where practicable therefore:

- an accurate and legible record should be made of the first description of a suspect given by a witness before the witness is asked to make any identification;
- the witness's attention should not be directed towards any particular person save where it appears that a witness may be in danger of overlooking a possible suspect because they are, for example, only looking in one direction;
- where there is more than one witness, they should be kept separate so that independent identifications can be made;
- a detailed record should be kept by the officer or other member of police staff accompanying the witness of all the circumstances surrounding the identification.

Photographs

In accordance with Code D 3.3 and Annex E, a witness may be shown up to 12 photographs (including drawings or computerized images) at a time and told that a photograph of the person that they saw may or may not be amongst them. They should further be told that if they cannot make a positive identification they should say so, but that they should not make a decision until they have viewed all 12 photographs.

Where a positive identification is made from photographs then no other witnesses should be asked to view the photographs but instead, as the identity of the suspect is now 'known', formal identification procedures should be held. The suspect and his legal representative must be told before any formal identification procedures that the witness has previously been shown photographs or other similar images.

Again, as with a 'street identification', measures should be put in place to ensure that any identification is made independently. So, prior to being shown any photographs at all, the supervising officer (sergeant or above) must confirm that the first description of the suspect given by the witness has been recorded; the photographs shown should, so far as possible, be of the same type; only one witness at a time should be shown the photographs; witnesses must not be allowed to communicate with each other; the witness must not be prompted or guided in their selection.

All photographs shown must be retained, whether or not a positive identification was made, and a record, signed by the supervising officer, must be kept of all the circumstances surrounding the showing of the photographs and any identification subsequently made.

After any identification procedure has been carried out the eye-witness must be asked if they have seen any film, photograph, or image relating to the offence or any description of the suspect which has been broadcast in the media or on any social networking site, and a record must be made of the details of the circumstances in which such an image was seen—Code D 3.29.

6.8.3 Identification procedures where the identity of the suspect is known

A formal identification procedure in accordance with Code D must be held where:

- the identity of the suspect is known to the police (that is, where there is sufficient information to justify the arrest of an individual on suspicion of involvement in an offence); and
- the suspect is available (that is, available and willing to take part in an identification procedure that it is practicable to arrange within a reasonable period of time); and
- the suspect disputes being the person the witness claims to have seen; and either
- the witness has purported to identify the suspect prior to formal procedures (eg in a street identification or from photographs); or,
- there is a witness available who has not previously been given the opportunity to identify the suspect who may be able to make an identification (Code D 3.12).

An identification procedure may additionally be held where the officer in charge of the investigation considers that it would be useful (Code D 3.13). An example might be where, although not positively raised as an issue by the suspect at the time of the investigation, the circumstances are such that it is clear to the police that identification will be in issue.

Where the witness has only been able to give evidence of a very general nature, whether of appearance or of clothing, but has not been able to describe any facial features, identification procedures need not be held as there would be no reasonable possibility that he would be able to make an identification (*R v Gayle* [1999] EWCA Crim 450).

Code D 3.12 provides further examples of situations in which an identification procedure would serve no useful purpose: where the suspect admits being at the scene and gives an account that is not contradicted by the eyewitness; or where the identifying witness recognizes the offender, and it is not disputed that the suspect and the witness are known to each other. Some caution is needed, however, in ascertaining whether or not the purported recognition is accepted. If the suspect disputes the recognition, identification procedures must still be held (*R v Harris* (2003) 147 SJ 237, CA; [2003] EWCA Crim 174).

Where there is more than one witness who claims that they would be able to recognize the offender, each should attend the identification procedure. If it were otherwise, the police could, where they had one positive identification, avoid the risk of another witness failing to make an identification and thus diluting their case (*R v Gojra and Dhir* [2011] Crim LR 311 CA).

What form can the identification procedure take?

There are three primary forms of identification procedure which in order of preference are:

- video identification;
- identification parade;
- group identification.

Whichever procedure is adopted, the suspect must be informed orally and in writing of:

- the purposes of the procedure;
- their entitlement to free legal advice;
- the conduct of the procedure, including their right to be represented;
- the first description given by any witness who is to attend the procedure;
- whether the witness has previously been shown any photographs or other images by the police.

They must also be warned that:

- they do not need to consent to or cooperate with any procedure but that if they do not their refusal may be given in evidence at court and the police may proceed to make other arrangements to test a witness's ability to identify them which could include an identification from images taken covertly;
- if they significantly alter their appearance prior to the procedure taking place, then evidence of that change may be given in court and other forms of identification considered;
- a moving image or photograph may be taken of them when they attend for the procedure.

A copy of the written notice setting out the above should be signed after reading by the suspect and retained by the officer supervising the identification (the identification officer).

Who decides which procedure should be used?

The identification officer and the officer in charge of the investigation should consult to determine which form of identification procedure should be offered. Almost invariably, the suspect should be offered a video identification unless it is not practicable in which case the suspect should be offered an identification parade (Code D 3.14). Before any option is offered, the suspect must be reminded of his entitlement to free legal advice.

The suspect and his solicitor may make representations why another form of procedure from that offered should take place, and if appropriate the identification officer should make arrangements for another form of procedure to take place if suitable and practicable (Code D 3.15).

Any representations made and the reasons for any resultant decisions must be recorded (Code D 3.16).

Who is the identification officer?

The identification officer will be an officer of at least the rank of inspector who will be responsible for the arrangements for and conduct of the identification procedure. The identification officer may delegate some or all of the tasks connected with arrangements and procedures to another officer or police staff; however, he will retain supervisory control and must be able to intervene or to be contacted as necessary.

No officer involved in the investigation of the offence should act as the identification officer or otherwise take part in the procedures except as specifically provided for in the Code (Code D 3.11).

6.8.4 **Video identification**

A video identification will comprise a set of images including the suspect and at least eight other people who resemble the suspect in age, height and general appearance. As far as possible the images will show the suspect and all other people in the same positions or carrying out the same sequence of movements under identical conditions. If the suspect has any distinctive feature— eg a scar—the feature may be concealed or replicated (electronically or otherwise) by the identification officer. Although the choice is for the identification officer, Annex A, 2A states that where a witness makes reference to a particular feature the feature should, if practicable, be replicated; if the suspect has a feature that the witness has not referred to, however, it should be concealed. If this is not done, there is a risk that the witness will pick out the suspect only because he is the only person on the parade with that feature; the value of any identification in those circumstances may be substantially diminished—*R v Pecco (unreported)* 22 April 2010—CLW/10/27/2. The images shown must be moving images, unless the suspect does not consent, or is unavailable, or has a physical feature that can neither be concealed nor replicated. In those circumstances, any suitable still or moving images may be used. In practice the head and shoulders of each individual is shown against a plain background, face on and then, by turning to each side, in profile.

The set of images must be shown to the suspect and his representative prior to being shown to a witness and any objections to the images noted and resolved where practicable.

Conduct of the video identification

A video identification must be carried out in accordance with the provisions in Annex A of Code D.

The suspect and his solicitor must be given reasonable notification of the time and place of the video identification and the solicitor given the opportunity to be present. If no representative is able to be present, the procedure must itself be recorded on video.

If the suspect refuses to cooperate with identification procedures or is otherwise 'unavailable', a video-identification may still be held using any suitable still or moving images, obtained covertly if necessary.

Only one witness at a time may be shown the images and steps must be taken to ensure that there is no contact or communication between a witness who has seen the images and one who has not that might compromise the independence of any identification made.

The witness must be told before viewing the images that the person they saw on a specified earlier occasion may or may not appear in the images and that if they cannot make a positive identification they should say so.

If the witness is or appears to be mentally disordered or vulnerable or a juvenile, then a 'pre-trial support person', who should not themselves be or be likely to be a witness, should be present unless the witness states that they do not want a support person to be present (Code D 2.15A; Code D, Note 2AB).

Care must be taken not to prompt an identification whether by directing the witness's attention to a particular image, reminding him of his earlier description, or in any other way. A witness may, however, view all or some of the images as many times as they like and may ask to have a particular image frozen for them to study.

All relevant material used in the course of a video identification must be retained and kept securely.

A record must be kept on forms provided for the purpose of the conduct of the video identification procedure and of any identification made.

6.8.5 Identification parades

Code D 3.7 defines an identification parade as one where 'the witness sees the suspect in a line of others who resemble the suspect'. Identification procedures must be conducted in accordance with Annex B of Code D.

Before the identification parade begins, the suspect must be given a reasonable opportunity to have a solicitor or friend present, must be reminded of the procedures for the conduct of the identification parade, and must be cautioned.

The parade must be conducted in the presence and hearing of the suspect and his solicitor or friend unless the parade is being conducted in a room with a screen separating the participants in the parade from the identifying witness, in which case everything said to or by any witness at the parade must be said in the solicitor's or friend's presence unless the parade is itself recorded on video.

The parade must consist of at least eight other people in addition to the suspect who shall as closely as possible resemble him in age, height, and general appearance; any identifying features (such as a scar or tattoo) should, with the agreement of the suspect and his solicitor, be concealed (however, this can be removed at the request of the viewing witness).

Separate parades should be held for each suspect save that where there are two suspects of a similar appearance they may stand on the same parade with at least 12 other participants.

If there are any objections from the suspect or his solicitor about the arrangements for or composition of the parade, steps should be taken to resolve those objections where practicable; any objections should be formally recorded.

The suspect may choose where in the line to stand and may if he wishes alter his position after each witness has viewed the parade.

Conduct of the parade

As with any other form of identification procedure, care must be taken to ensure that any identification made is independent. Arrangements must therefore be made to ensure that witnesses do not communicate with each other, see any member of the parade including the suspect, or see or be reminded of any picture or description given of the suspect.

The witness must be told that the person that they saw on a specified earlier occasion may or may not be present, and if they cannot make a positive identification they should say so. They should be asked to look at each person on the parade at least twice before making any identification.

If a witness viewing the parade wishes to hear a participant speak, or see them move, or adopt a particular posture, they must be asked whether they can make an identification on the basis of physical appearance alone. They should also be reminded if they ask to hear a particular person speak that participants have been chosen on the basis only of physical appearance. The person may then, however, be asked to speak, move, or adopt the position requested by the witness. They may also be asked to remove anything used to conceal an identifying mark at the request of the witness.

If the witness is mentally disordered, vulnerable, or a juvenile, a pre-trial support person should be present but must take care not to prompt an identification by the witness.

It not infrequently occurs that a witness purports to make an identification after the parade has ended. Where this occurs, the suspect and his solicitor should be informed, and consideration given to allowing the witness a further opportunity to identify the suspect.

A video recording of the conduct of the parade should normally be made and must be made where the parade takes place behind a screen separating the parade from the viewing witness and where no representative of the suspect is present.

A formal record must be made of the details of the conduct of the parade and any comments made by either the witness or the suspect about the parade or identifications.

6.8.6 Group identification

A group identification is when the witness sees the suspect in an informal group of people, and may take place either with the suspect's cooperation and consent, or covertly.

Group identifications will usually be carried out in a public place; they should only be conducted in a police station or prison if the group identification involves a prison inmate, or for other reasons of safety, security, or practicability.

A group identification will by its very nature be harder to control than a video identification or identification parade; nevertheless the same principles of fairness and independence apply to group identifications as much as to the more formal procedures. The measures to be adopted to ensure so far as possible that these can be achieved are set out in Annex C to Code D.

Location

The location chosen for the group identification to take place should be one in which there are likely to be groups of people (whether stationary or moving) that the suspect can join, and where the numbers and types of people that are likely to be present might be reasonably expected to include those of a broadly similar appearance to the defendant. Annex C4 gives as examples of locations that might fit these requirements a shopping centre or a bus or railway station.

Where the identification is to take place covertly, then the choice of location will of necessity be restricted to those public places known to be frequented by the suspect.

Conduct

The suspect should, unless the procedure is to be conducted covertly, be given a reasonable opportunity to have a solicitor or friend present who will remain with the witness and those conducting the procedure. The witness and others observing the procedure (including a pre-trial support person if applicable) may be concealed from the group they are observing if it assists with the conduct of the identification, or the witness may be asked to himself move among the group and to take a closer look where practicable to confirm any identification made.

The suspect will be told to join a group of people, whether moving or stationary, and may choose and/or change his position within that group.

The person conducting the parade shall remind the witness that the person they saw on a previous specified occasion may or may not be in the group and tell them that if they cannot make a positive identification they should say so. The witness's attention should then be directed towards the group and the witness asked to point out any person they think they saw on the previous occasion.

A witness should be allowed as long as is reasonably necessary to observe and compare members of the group before attempting to make an identification.

If the suspect unreasonably delays joining the group, or deliberately conceals himself from the witness's sight, then his conduct may be treated as a refusal to cooperate.

Only one witness at a time should view a group identification, and arrangements must be made to ensure that there is no contamination between witnesses, or that they are reminded of any picture or description of the suspect.

A video or colour photograph should be taken of the location used for the group identification either during or immediately after the procedure, or at a later date if not practicable to do it at the time.

A formal record must be made of all the details surrounding the group identification.

6.8.7 **Confrontations**

Where the identity of a suspect is known but the suspect is unavailable, for example because he has refused to cooperate, the identification officer may arrange for the suspect to be directly confronted by the witness (Code D 3.23).

A confrontation must be carried out in accordance with Annex D.

The confrontation should normally take place in a police station, and must be in the presence of the suspect's solicitor or friend unless this would cause unreasonable delay. If no representative is present, the confrontation should be recorded on video.

Prior to the confrontation taking place, the witness must be warned that the person he is about to see may or may not be the person that he saw on a previous specified occasion. The witness should then be shown the suspect and asked, 'Is this the person?'

Although the suspect's consent is not required for a confrontation to take place, no force can be used to make the suspect's face visible to the witness.

6.8.8 **Part B—Evidence of recognition**

For the first time, in the most recent version of Code D, guidance is given on the procedure to be followed and records kept where any person—including a police officer—views an image of a person (in whatever format) and is asked whether they recognize that individual as someone known to them.

This guidance is both welcome and timely given the plethora of cases now heard in court in which a witness has carried out their own researches on Facebook or other internet sites to find a photo of the suspect, or someone who they think (or who they have been told) resembles the suspect. In *R v Alexander and McGill* (1 November 2012) 177 JP 73 (CA) the court commented that if identifications occur through Facebook, it is incumbent on the police and the prosecutor to take steps to obtain, in as much detail as possible, evidence relating to the initial identification, including the images that were looked at, and a statement in relation to what happened. The details to be included in any statement or record where a witness has purported to recognize a suspect in an image (whether still or otherwise) are set out at Code D 3.36.

Code D 3.35 specifies that the images should be shown 'on an individual basis to avoid the possibility of collusion and...mistaken recognition'. This of course presupposes that the police are in control of the procedure (rather than the uncontrolled but common situation where a witness himself finds a picture of the suspect) but it recognizes the inherent dangers in this sort of identification by recognition and the efforts that should be made to minimize them. To this end, it is important to ensure that nothing is said or shown to the witness which provides them with information that may compromise the independence and thus the admissibility and value of the evidence of recognition—Note 3G.

A record of the circumstances and conditions under which the person was provided with the opportunity to make a recognition is set out at Code D 3.36; the record should include the information that the witness had about the identity of the suspect, the circumstances in which the image was viewed, how the viewing was controlled, and by whom, the reason why the witness claims to recognize the person in the image, and any doubt expressed by the witness. The record may be made by the officer or member of police staff who shows the images, or by the person who views the images and makes the recognition himself. What may at first sight seem a rather odd provision (permitting the person who views the image to himself record matters that may, for example, cast doubt upon the reliability and accuracy of his own purported recognition), was presumably a pragmatic addition given the increase in CCTV evidence and the use of police officers to identify known offenders from such images.

Practical Guidance

6.9 Case Study 1 (fingerprints, searches, and examinations)

PC Smith is on mobile patrol and sees White driving a car along the High Street. PC Smith was present in court three months before when White, a youth well known to local police, was disqualified for a drink-drive offence. PC Smith stops the vehicle and questions White who refuses to answer questions but states that he is not disqualified and his name is Clark.

Can PC Smith arrest White for driving whilst disqualified?

See para 3.10 Case Study. White's arrest in order to take fingerprints to ascertain his correct name (s 24(5)(a) and for the prompt and effective investigation of the offence (s 24(5)(e)) would provide a reason to arrest.

Once at the station White's fingerprints could be taken without his consent under the provisions of s 61(3)(a) and (b) of PACE and checked against the fingerprints taken when he was arrested in respect of the original offence that led to his disqualification (s 63A(1)(b)).

Once at the station PC Smith recalls that White, who is still denying his identity, has a distinctive tattoo on his back. When requested by the custody officer to show his back, White refuses. How should this situation be dealt with?

Section 54A(1) allows a detainee to be examined to establish whether he has any mark or feature that would tend to identify him and to photograph any identifying marks. An examination to establish a suspect's identity may be carried out without the detainee's consent only where authorized by an officer of at least the rank of inspector. As an examination of White's back may facilitate the ascertainment of his identity, and as White has withheld consent then authority from an appropriate officer should be sought to carry out such an examination and photograph the tattoo. The examination and taking of the photograph may only be carried out by a police officer of the same sex using reasonable force (ss 54A and 117 PACE, Code D 5.9). As the examination will require the removal of more than outer clothing then the Code of Practice requires the examination be conducted in a place where White cannot be seen by anyone who does not need to be present or any member of the opposite sex (Code of Practice D 5.10 and C. Annex A11(a)–(g)).

6.10 Case Study 2 (footwear impressions)

Jones, a 19-year-old youth, has been arrested for burglary and has been taken to the police station.

DC Potts has discovered a footprint left at the scene of the burglary and requests permission to take an impression of Jones's footwear. When asked to cooperate Jones refuses. How should Sergeant Brown deal with this situation?

Sergeant Brown should inform Jones of the reason why an impression is needed and that the impression may be retained and may be the subject of a speculative search. In addition Jones should be informed that if he is subsequently acquitted of the burglary offence the impression will be destroyed and he may witness the destruction (Code of Practice D 4.19(a)–(c)). If Jones refuses to cooperate then as he is in custody for a recordable offence and has not previously had an impression taken of his footwear, a police officer may use reasonable force to take the impression without Jones's consent.

6.11 Case Study 3 (non-intimate samples)

Jan is in custody for grievous bodily harm and gives written authority for a sample of head hair to be taken from her. DC Harley, the officer in the case, takes possession of the sample intending to take it by hand for DNA analysis. The officer misplaces the sample and requests that a further sample be obtained from the prisoner. However, Jan now refuses to give written authority and DC Harley asks Inspector Lister to authorize the use of force to take another sample. How should Inspector Lister deal with this request?

A sample of hair is a non-intimate sample and can be taken without the appropriate consent and by use of reasonable force if necessary. However, in this case a sample of hair has already been taken and the only occasion a second sample can be taken of the same type and from the same part of the body is where the first proved insufficient. Inspector Lister should advise DC Harley that as the sample of hair was lost then without Jan's written consent, no more hair may be taken from her head. He could advise that if another type of non-intimate sample, such as a nail clipping, could be used for the purposes of DNA analysis and this would tend to prove or disprove Jan's involvement in a recordable offence, then the sample can be taken with Jan's consent. If Jan should refuse to give consent Inspector Lister can authorize the taking of the sample using reasonable force (s 63 PACE; Code of Practice D paras 6.5–6.6).

6.12 Case Study 4 (fingerprints, use of force)

Curtis has been charged with theft and refuses to allow his fingerprints to be taken. He has an arm injury and suffers from high blood pressure. He is aggressive and indicates he will do all he can to prevent anyone taking his fingerprints. The Forensic Medical Examiner (FME) has previously certified that Curtis is fit to be detained. PS Simpson, the custody officer, is unsure about how to deal with Curtis and seeks advice from Inspector North. What advice should Inspector North give to PS Simpson?

Inspector North should advise PS Simpson that as Curtis is in custody and has been charged with a recordable offence then s 61 of PACE provides the power to take his fingerprints without consent. In addition, reasonable force may be used if necessary. Whilst the power is clear the actual taking of the fingerprints by force can provide real difficulties. The first priority should be to use all reasonable persuasion to encourage Curtis to give his authority and allow officers to take his fingerprints. The Codes of Practice require that certain information is given to Curtis before the fingerprints are taken and if video/audio recording facilities are available in the custody area it is sensible to ensure the giving of this information is recorded on tape. If Curtis still refuses to give his consent then in view of his condition it is good practice to call the FME to carry out an examination before any force is used. The FME should also be asked to remain whilst the fingerprints are taken. The taking of the fingerprints by force from a person who is resisting is extremely difficult and great care needs to be taken to avoid causing injury. A record must be made of the circumstances in which force was used to take fingerprints (Code D 4.8). In those circumstances, it would be sensible to record the taking of the prints on video if at all possible.

6.13 **Case Study 5 (identification procedures)**

Whilst walking home from work late at night, Lyndsey is struck from behind by a man who then steals her handbag from her and runs away across a common towards a residential area. When she has managed to recover from the shock, Lyndsey is able to make her way to a nearby pub from where the landlord calls the police on her behalf.

The police arrive within a matter of minutes and PC Swift asks Lyndsey if she can describe the person who attacked her. She states that he was in his late teens or early 20s, over 6ft, well built and was wearing dark clothing and a green 'beanie' cap; she is unable to describe any facial features. At this stage, there appear to be no other witnesses.

What should PC Swift do?

At this stage, the identity of the attacker is not known; however Lyndsey has been able to provide a general description of the man together with a description of his clothing. The area towards which he was running is known and thanks to the prompt arrival of the police a very short time has elapsed since the commission of the offence. PC Swift should note the description given by Lyndsey and then take her on a 'drive round' the area towards which the offender made off to see whether she can identify the person who attacked her.

PC Swift puts out details of the attack and the description of the offender over his radio and begins to drive towards the residential area towards which the attacker ran. During the drive, PC Swift receives information from PC Price that a member of the public, Adam King, has observed a man discarding a handbag in Kingston Avenue, which he has handed to the police; the handbag appears to belong to Lyndsey and the detailed description given by Adam matches that given by Lyndsey.

What should PC Swift do now?

Code D 3.2 permits the police to drive a witness to a particular locality to see if they can identify the person they saw on a previous occasion; PC Swift can therefore drive Lyndsey to Kingston Avenue and the surrounding streets in which it would appear that the offender may still be present. However, Code D 3.2(b) states that care must be taken not to direct the witness's attention to any individual unless, taking account of all the circumstances this cannot be avoided. Such an 'unavoidable' situation might exist where a suspect has already been stopped by the police and is standing with them when the witness arrives on the scene.

In a street adjacent to Kingston Avenue, Lyndsey points out a man wearing a green 'beanie' hat and dark clothing as the person who attacked her, telling PC Swift that she recognizes him because of his hat. PC Price arrives at the location moments later and arrests the man, Cyrus on suspicion of robbery.

What duties does PC Swift have now in respect of the identification?

PC Swift should ensure that, in accordance with Code D 3.2(e), a detailed record is made of the time, place and circumstances of the identification made, together with details of the weather, lighting conditions, whether the witness's attention was drawn to the suspect for any reason, and what comments if any were made by either the witness or the suspect.

Cyrus is searched but no stolen property is found on him. He is interviewed by DC Booth and makes no comment; however, he does submit a short pre-prepared statement in which he says that he was simply walking home from a night out with friends, he never attacked anyone and is not guilty of any offence.

What should DC Booth do?

Although he has not said so directly, it is clear from the terms of Cyrus's pre-prepared statement that he disputes that he was correctly identified by Lyndsey. Under Code D 3.12, wherever a witness has purported to identify a suspect, or there is a witness who may reasonably be able to identify a suspect, and where the suspect disputes the correctness of the identification, then an identification procedure 'shall be held'. DC Booth should therefore ask Cyrus whether he is willing to take part in an identification procedure, which should be a video identification unless such a procedure is not practicable.

Cyrus agrees to a video identification, but his solicitor, Mr Atkins, expresses concern that such a procedure may be unfair because Cyrus has a very noticeable scar running across his right cheek.

What, if anything, should DC Booth do to take account of the solicitor's objection?

All the images shown on the identification video should be of people who are as like to the suspect in terms of their facial and general physical appearance as possible, and this extends to distinctive physical features. DC Booth should arrange for the images to be modified so that either all the people shown have the same scar replicated on their image, or the scar should be concealed on the image of the defendant. The choice is for DC Booth to make, however Annex A, 2A states that where a feature is referred to by a witness it should be replicated and, where it is not, should be concealed.

Which witnesses should attend the identification procedure?

There are two potential witnesses; Lyndsey and Adam. Adam gave the police a detailed description of the man he saw discarding Lyndsey's handbag, including facial features such as a scar to his cheek. There is therefore a reasonable chance that Adam will be able to make a positive identification and he should be asked to attend the procedure. As he did make a reference to the scar, DC Booth should, as stated above, arrange for all the images shown to be electronically manipulated to replicate the same scar on each person's face. Lyndsey made a street identification of Cyrus before the identification procedure; on an initial reading of Code D 3.12 therefore, she should attend the procedure. However, the same paragraph of the Code states that no identification procedure need be held if it would serve no useful purpose. Although Lyndsey gave a general description to the police and made a street identification, her identification was based upon recognition of clothing, not facial features, which she was unable to describe. Although DC Booth may feel that it is worth a chance asking Lyndsey to attend the identification procedure, there is no requirement under the Act or Code for her to do so as it is highly unlikely that she would be able to make a positive identification and thus 'no useful purpose' would be achieved by requiring her to attend.

6.14 **Case Study 6 (identification procedures)**

In October, Stuart, Robert, and Richard, attend the opening night of a new club, Chill. On leaving the club at the end of the evening, they are accosted by a group of men – none of whom they know – one of whom produces a knife with which he stabs Richard before running away. In due course, police take statements from each of the three men: Stuart describes the man with the knife as 6', slim build, ginger hair, wearing a blue jacket; Robert is unable to provide a description; Richard describes the man as 5'9", light brown greasy hair, wearing a grey or light blue top.

Two months later, Stuart and Robert find a Facebook page for Chill on which are posted approximately 200 photos of the opening night. They agree together that a ginger-haired man wearing a grey t-shirt shown in two of the pictures is the man with the knife. They print the pictures off and take them to show Richard, who also agrees. They then inform the investigating officer— DC Moore. What should DC Moore do?

'Identification by Facebook' is becoming prevalent but is fraught with problems, particularly where there have been discussions between the witnesses which may compromise their independence. DC Moore should make every effort to ensure that as much information is collated about the circumstances in which the Facebook pictures were found and viewed. Part B of Code D 3 applies. Statements from each of the three men should be taken covering the matters set out in Code D 3.36. DC Moore should also ensure that he retains not just copies of the photos that the witnesses believe show the suspect, but all the other photos that were posted on the Facebook site of the opening night.

PC Alcock, an officer with good local knowledge, is asked to view the photos in accordance with Code C 3.36. He recognizes the man shown as Pond. Pond is arrested. In interview, Pond agrees that he was at Chill's opening night, and accepts that he is the man shown in the photos, but he denies any knowledge of or involvement in the stabbing. What should DC Moore do?

Identity is clearly in issue. As the suspect's identity is 'known' one of the identification procedures as set out in Code D Part A 3.5–3.10 must be used in accordance with Code D 3.12. Stuart, Robert, and Richard should all attend such a procedure and it should be made clear to both Pond and the officer in charge of the identification procedure that all three men have previously seen and identified Pond from a photograph.

Interviews: Part V, Codes C, E, and F

Law and Commentary

7.1 Introduction

Perhaps surprisingly, there are no substantive provisions within the Act itself dealing with this important topic. Instead, s 60 imposes a duty on the Secretary of State to make an order requiring that interviews with suspects are tape recorded and to issue a code of practice in connection with such interviews; s 60A provides the Secretary of State with the power (as opposed to a duty) to make a similar order and to issue a code of practice for the visual recording of interviews.

The Code of Practice that applies is Code E although there are also important relevant provisions in Code C, especially Code C 10–14. Code F applies to the audio-visual recording of interviews. Both Codes E and F were updated with effect from 1 May 2010 with amendments in keeping with the advance of technology covering the use of digital recordings.

Officers who conduct interviews should also have regard to Home Office Circular 26/1995 (1995) 159 JPN 303 which provides national guidelines on the preparation of records of interviews in accordance with Code E Note 5A.

7.2 What is an Interview?

An interview is defined in Code C 11.1A as 'the questioning of a person regarding their involvement or suspected involvement in a criminal offence or offences' which must be carried out under caution.

The basic rules are that:

- if the suspect is under arrest, the interview should take place at a police station or other authorized place of detention;
- the suspect is entitled to free legal advice before and during his interview;
- the interview must be carried out under caution;
- the interview must be recorded.

It is important to recognize that *any* questioning regarding a person's involvement or suspected involvement in an offence can constitute an interview, however short that questioning may be and wherever it takes place. Accordingly an exchange between a police officer and a suspect at the scene of an offence or during a search may be held to amount to an interview if the questioning is about the suspect's involvement in an offence; the relevant provisions of Code C will therefore apply, breaches of which—in particular the requirement to caution the suspect and to record the contents of the interview—may lead to the exclusion of the interview. Note, however, that the trigger for the application of Code C 11.1 is that the person is a 'suspect'. As was stated in

Hughes v DPP [2010] EWHC 515, applying *R (Ridehalgh) v DPP* [2005] EWHC 1100 (Admin):

> Where police officers question people, in any circumstances in the course of possible investigations relating to the commission of a criminal offence, there inevitably comes a time when it begins to occur to them that an offence might have been committed. They need to make further enquiries to establish whether there are grounds for suspecting the particular person, the potential defendant, of committing the offence. If the stage comes when there are such grounds, then the duty to caution arises.

7.3 Voluntary Interviews

A distinction can be drawn between a 'voluntary interview', where the suspect has not been arrested (see Code G Note 2F), and an interview that takes place after arrest.

A voluntary interview may take place at the police station or any other location, including premises for which the interviewer requires the interviewee's consent to remain—for example, the person's home. A proposed amendment to Code E (new 1.12) specifies that where an interview takes place of a suspect who has not been arrested at a location other than a police station, the 'interview room' should be regarded as including 'any place or location which the interviewer is satisfied will enable the interview to be conducted and recorded in accordance with [the] Code and where the suspect is present voluntarily'. Where there is any doubt as to the suitability of a location for an interview to take place then a proposed new Note 1A states that an officer of the rank of sergeant or above should be consulted.

Code C 3.21 makes it clear that wherever a voluntary interview is held, the interviewee may leave at will unless they are arrested (see Code G), and they must be informed when cautioned that they are not under arrest, are not obliged to remain but that if they do so, they are entitled to free and independent legal advice. Where the interview takes place in a location for which the interviewer requires the interviewee's consent to remain, the right to leave allows the person to withdraw their consent and to require the interviewer to leave.

Codes E and F (audio and visual recording of interviews) apply and should be followed 'insofar as they can be applied to suspects who are not under arrest'—Code C 3.21. In practice, many voluntary interviews not carried out at a police station will not be recorded on tape but in writing.

7.4 Interviews at the Police Station

If a suspect has been arrested, they must only be interviewed about an offence in a police station 'or other authorised place of detention' unless that would cause a delay which would be likely to:

- lead to interference with, or harm to, evidence connected with an offence;
- lead to interference with, or physical harm to, other people; or
- serious loss of or damage to property; or
- alert other people suspected of committing an offence but not yet arrested for it; or
- hinder the recovery of property obtained in consequence of the commission of an offence (Code C 11.1).

Once the risk which has necessitated an urgent interview has passed, the questioning must stop.

Where the interview does take place at a police station, then insofar as it is practicable, the interview must take place in a room which is adequately heated, lit, and ventilated (Code C 12.4).

However if a suspect who has been detained before charge in order to obtain evidence by questioning refuses to cooperate by either refusing to leave their cell, or by trying to leave the interview room, the interview can if necessary be conducted in their cell (Code C 12.5).

If an interview room is not used, a record must be made of the reasons why and any consequent actions taken (Code C 12.11).

7.4.1 The role of the custody officer

If an officer wishes to interview a suspect held in police detention, then he will require the consent of the custody officer who will be responsible for deciding whether or not to transfer custody of the detainee to the interviewing officer. Where custody is transferred to an investigating officer, so too is the responsibility for the detainee's care and safe custody in accordance with the provisions of the Code (Code C 12.1). If during the course of the interview a complaint is made by or on behalf of the interview concerning the provisions of Codes, or if it appears to the interviewer that the interviewee may have been treated improperly, the interviewer is required to record such matters in the custody record and bring the matter to the attention of the custody officer (Code C 12.9).

Before making the decision to transfer, the custody officer will need to assess whether or not the detainee is fit enough to be interviewed. This will require an assessment of the detainee's mental and physical state carried out if necessary in consultation with the interviewing officer and an appropriate health professional. The custody officer should also, as part of this assessment, consider what safeguards might be appropriate if the interview was permitted to proceed. Annex G provides helpful guidance on the factors to be taken into account when assessing a detainee's fitness to be interviewed.

If, following an assessment, the custody officer considers that an interview would cause significant harm to the detainee's physical or mental state, then he must not permit the interview to proceed.

A vulnerable suspect should always be considered to be at risk. (For consideration of the appropriate provisions relating to such suspects, see Chapter 8.)

A record must be made of the time and reason why the detainee is no longer in the custody of the custody officer and the reason for any refusal to deliver him out of that custody (Code C 12.10).

The custody officer must in addition have in mind Code C 12.2 in deciding when a detainee should be interviewed. Code C 12.2 provides that in every 24-hour period a detainee must be allowed a continuous period of at least eight hours rest free from questioning, travel, or any interruption in connection with the investigation concerned. The rest period may, however, be interrupted or delayed if there are reasonable grounds for believing that not interrupting or delaying the period would:

- involve a risk of harm to people or serious loss of, or damage to, property; or
- delay unnecessarily the person's release from custody; or
- otherwise prejudice the outcome of the investigation.

If the rest period is interrupted or delayed for any of the above reasons, then a new period must be allowed.

The rest period may also be interrupted or delayed:

- at the request of the detainee, his legal representative or appropriate adult; or
- in order to comply with legal obligations or duties under Code C 15 (reviews and extensions of detention); or
- in order to take action required under Code C 9 (provisions relating to the care and treatment of detained persons) or in accordance with medical advice.

As well as determining whether and when an interview can start, as will be seen, the custody officer also has an important role in determining when questioning should be brought to an end.

Once the interviewing process has commenced, care should be taken to ensure that there are adequate breaks to allow for the provision of meals or other refreshments. Breaks of at least 45 minutes should be taken at mealtimes and short (15-minute) refreshment breaks should be provided at approximately two-hour intervals, subject to the interviewing officer's discretion to delay breaks if there are reasonable grounds to believe that it would:

- involve a risk of harm to people or serious loss of, or damage to property;
- unnecessarily delay the detainee's release;
- otherwise prejudice the outcome of the investigation (Code C 12.8).

Any decision to delay a break in the interview must be recorded together with the reasons (Code C 12.12).

7.5 **The Conduct of Interviews (Code C and Annex B and C)**

7.5.1 **Legal advice**

At the outset of an interview the interviewer must remind the detainee that he has the right to free legal advice and that the interview can be delayed in order to obtain such advice (Code C 11.2). The detainee must not, however, be told (except in answer to a direct question) that the period for which they are liable to be detained or the time taken to complete the interview might be reduced if they do not require legal advice or a solicitor present (Code C Note 6ZA).

The arrangements which enable detainees to obtain legal advice are set out in Code C Note 6B).

Can an interview take place in the absence of a solicitor if the detainee has requested legal advice?

If a detainee does want legal advice then the basic rule is that he must not be interviewed until he has received it. Or, if in the course of an interview the detainee indicates that he wishes to take legal advice then the interview must stop until such advice has been received.

Despite the apparently absolute terms of this provision, there are nevertheless a number of situations in which the police may proceed with an interview in the absence of a solicitor, notwithstanding that the detainee has requested legal advice. They are where:

- an officer of the rank of superintendent or above has reasonable grounds for believing that access to a solicitor will result in one of the consequences set out at Annex B1 or 2; or
- an officer of superintendent rank or above has reasonable grounds to believe that the delay occasioned in waiting for a solicitor to arrive might lead to one of the consequences set out in Annex B1; or
- a solicitor has been contacted and agreed to attend but where an officer of the rank of superintendent or above has reasonable grounds to believe that the delay caused in awaiting his arrival would cause unreasonable delay to the process of investigation; or
- the detainee's nominated solicitor cannot be contacted, has indicated that he does not wish to be contacted, or having been contacted declines to attend, and the detainee has refused the duty solicitor, and an officer of inspector rank or above has agreed to the interview proceeding; or
- the detainee has changed his mind about wanting legal advice and states that they no longer wish to speak to a solicitor. In these circumstances:
  - an officer of the rank of inspector or above must speak to the detainee to ask why he has changed his mind;

- reasonable efforts must be made to ascertain the solicitor's expected time of arrival and notify him of the suspect's change of mind and any reason given for it;
- a record must be made in the custody record of the suspect's change of mind, reason, and outcome of enquiries with the solicitor;
- the detainee must be informed of the outcome of the enquiries and must confirm in writing by signing the custody record that he wants the interview to proceed without speaking to a solicitor or a solicitor being present;
- an officer of the rank of inspector or above must be satisfied that it is proper for the interview to proceed in these circumstances and give written authority to that effect;
- at the outset of the interview, the interviewer must remind the suspect of his right to legal advice and ensure that there is recorded on the interview record confirmation that: the detainee has changed his mind about legal advice; that authority to proceed has been given; that if the solicitor arrives before the interview is completed the detainee will be informed without delay and allowed to speak to the solicitor if required; and that the detainee may ask for legal advice at any time during the interview (Code C 6.6).

The consequences set out in Annex B that would permit the appropriate officer to authorize an interview notwithstanding the fact that the suspect has not been permitted to exercise his right to legal advice are when the officer has reasonable grounds to believe that exercising that right would lead to:

- interference with, or harm to, evidence connected with an indictable offence; or
- interference with or physical harm to, other people; or
- alerting other suspects who have yet to be arrested; or
- hindering the recovery of property obtained as a result of the offence;

or where:

- the person detained for an indictable offence has benefited from their criminal conduct; and
- the recovery of the value of the property constituting the benefit will be hindered by the exercise of the right.

In considering whether it would be appropriate to continue or start an interview in the absence of a solicitor where it has been established that a solicitor is willing to attend, the police should obtain from the solicitor an estimate of how long it will take for him to arrive and if it appears that the delay might lead to one of the consequences in Annex B1, or to an unreasonable delay to the investigation, should if necessary give the detainee the opportunity to obtain legal advice from an alternative source (Code C Note 6A).

Are the police obliged to give pre-interview disclosure?

Code C 10.3 states that a person who is arrested must be informed as soon as practicable after their arrest of the fact of their arrest and the grounds for it. Note for Guidance 10B clarifies that this means that the suspect must be informed of the nature of the suspected offence, when and where it was committed and the reasons why arrest is considered necessary. Although there is no requirement to give any additional information prior to interview, in practice some pre-interview disclosure is almost invariably given, although the quality and quantity of that disclosure will depend on the case. The interviewing officer will need to bear in mind that if no or no adequate disclosure is given, the defence could argue that the legal representative was unable to give proper legal advice to the suspect; in those circumstances there is a risk that not only would the suspect be advised to exercise his right to silence in interview, but that no adverse inferences would be drawn from that silence (see *Ward v Police Service of Northern Ireland* [2007] UKHL 50).

Can the police refuse to allow a solicitor to attend an interview?

A detainee is entitled to have the benefit of the presence of a solicitor throughout their interview unless one of the exceptions outlined above applies (Code C 6.8).

In exceptional circumstances, a solicitor can be required to leave an interview if their conduct is such that the interview cannot be conducted properly.

Where this occurs, the interview should be stopped and the interviewer should consult a senior officer, ideally an officer of the rank of superintendent or above, but if such an officer is not available, then an inspector, not concerned in the investigation, who will subsequently have to report the matter to a superintendent.

As in any of the other possible situations in which an interview could proceed without legal advice being available to a detainee who has requested it, the removal of a solicitor should be a matter of last resort. It should be remembered that the role of a solicitor at the police station, and in interview, is to protect the legal rights of their client. This may involve advice not to answer some or all questions; it may involve intervention to prevent what a solicitor regards as improper questions being put or seeking to stop the interview in order to give his client further advice. None of these would be grounds for seeking the removal of the solicitor, however frustrating his actions may be to the officers conducting the interview. Note 6D states that it is only when the solicitor's conduct 'prevents or unreasonably obstructs proper questions being put to the suspect or the suspect's response being recorded' that consideration should be given to removing the solicitor. Some indication of how serious the conduct would have to be is given in Code C 6.11; that consideration should be given to reporting the solicitor to the Solicitors Regulation Authority and (if the solicitor is a duty solicitor) the Legal Services Commission. Even then, the authorizing officer should first speak to the solicitor in question about his conduct and if a decision is made to remove him should give the suspect the opportunity to consult with and have present in interview an alternative solicitor (Code C 6.10).

Where a solicitor is excluded, Note for Guidance 6E points out that the authorizing officer will need to be able to satisfy a court that his decision was appropriate. To do so, he may have himself needed to witness the conduct that led to his decision to exclude.

7.5.2 **Cautions**

Before any questions (or further questions) are put to a suspect about his involvement in an offence, he must be cautioned (Code C 10.1).

The words of the caution are:

> You do not have to say anything. But it may harm your defence if you do not mention when questioned something that you later rely on in court. Anything that you do say may be given in evidence. (Code C 10.5)

It is important that the person cautioned understands what this means and the possible implications of it. If necessary, therefore, the meaning of the caution should be explained by the officer who gives it. Moreover, the person being questioned must, under Code C 11.1A, be informed of the true nature of the offence about which he is being questioned so that he can make an informed choice whether or not to answer questions.

Note that the caution is required before there is any questioning about a suspect's involvement in a criminal offence—the same definition as that for an interview. A person need not be cautioned if the questions are 'for other necessary purposes' such as seeking to ascertain someone's identity, or for the proper and effective conduct of a search where those questions fall short of an 'interview' (Code C 10.1); so, for example, in *R v Senior* [2004] 2 Cr App R 12, CA, a case involving customs officers (bound by the Codes), no caution was required prior to questioning two suspects in a drug-smuggling operation about the ownership of a suitcase where the identity of the owner was unclear, but was something that it was necessary to ascertain before any other questions were put.

Moreover, a caution is only required where the person being questioned is suspected—there must therefore be reasonable grounds to suspect a person of involvement in an offence before a caution is required when questioning. Where, objectively, grounds for suspicion are present, a caution should be administered (*R v Hunt* [1992] Crim LR 582, CA; *R v Nelson and Rose* [1998] 2 Cr App R 399, CA).

As the caution must be given before any questions 'or further questions' are put, if there is a break in the course of an interview, the police should on resumption ensure that the suspect understands that he is still under caution; the safest course may well be to give the caution in full again (Code C 10.8).

A failure to give the caution where required is likely to be regarded by the courts as a significant and substantial breach of the Code and may render the evidence inadmissible. The courts will in this regard assess the 'fairness' of the conduct. Although the Code extends beyond those in police custody, the courts have tended to differentiate between a failure to give a caution when a suspect was in the custody of or otherwise vulnerable to pressure from the police, and the situation in which incriminating comments have been given by a suspect to, for example, an undercover police officer, but in circumstances where those comments have been made voluntarily—albeit in ignorance of the person to whom they have been talking (*R v Christou and Wright* [1992] 95 Cr App R 264, CA).

The police cannot, however, take advantage by such a method in order to circumvent the Code—if that was the effect of any action by the police, then irrespective of their intention the courts would be likely to regard it as unfair and to exclude the evidence obtained. See *R (CC) v Commr of Police of the Metropolis* [2012] 1 WLR 1913, QBD.

Code C does not apply to terrorism suspects to whom Code H applies, or who are detained for examination under Sch 7 of the Terrorism Act 2000. Paragraph 2 of Sch 7 permits an examining officer to question a person at a port or border area for reasons connected with travel into, out of or (if by air) within the country, for the purpose of determining whether he is concerned with acts of terrorism. This power of questioning cannot however be used if the predominant purpose was something other than to establish whether a person was a terrorist within the meaning of s 40(1)(b) of TACT. If therefore a person suspected of immigration offences was questioned under Sch 7 TACT in order to secure evidence or admissions relating to such offences, such an interview would be unlawful and any admissions secured within such an interview or any subsequent interview carried out under PACE may be ruled inadmissible.

What are the consequences if a suspect interviewed under caution refuses to answer some or all of the questions put to him?

If a suspect who is being interviewed in accordance with the Act and Codes fails, having been cautioned, to mention a fact that he later relies on in his defence, that being a fact that he could reasonably have been expected to mention when questioned, a court or jury may draw 'such inferences from the failure as appear proper' (s 34 Criminal Justice and Public Order Act 1994).

This only applies, however, where the person questioned has been given the opportunity to have legal advice (whether from a nominated solicitor or the duty solicitor). Where access to legal advice has been denied under Annex B, or an interview has commenced in circumstances where the detainee has asked for legal advice but before he has had the opportunity to speak to his solicitor, then no adverse inference can be drawn and a shorter caution should be applied which is:

> You do not have to say anything, but anything you do say may be given in evidence. (Code C, Annex C 1–2)

If the position changes then the person interviewed must be re-cautioned appropriately. So, for example, if a suspect wished to have the benefit of legal advice, but Annex B applied and authority was given to withhold access to legal advice, no adverse inference could be drawn from any failure in the course of that interview to mention facts later relied on in evidence and the shorter caution should be given. If Annex B subsequently ceases to apply and the suspect is permitted then to consult with a solicitor, on resuming the interview the suspect must be re-cautioned in the terms set out in Code 10.5. Annex C Note C2 sets out some suggested wording to be used when re-cautioning either because the restriction on adverse inferences begins or ceases to apply.

7.5.3 Special warnings

If a detainee on being interviewed fails or refuses to answer questions satisfactorily or at all, when asked to account for objects, marks, or substances or marks on objects found:

- on his person; or
- in or on his clothing or footwear; or
- otherwise in his possession; or
- in any place in which he is at the time of his arrest;

or he fails or refuses to answer questions satisfactorily or at all, when asked to account for his presence at a place at or about the time the offence for which he has been arrested is alleged to have been committed and it is reasonably believed that his presence at that time and place may be attributable to his participation in the commission of the offence, then under ss 36 and 37 of the Criminal Justice and Public Order Act 1994, an adverse inference may be drawn, but only where:

- the restriction in Annex C on drawing adverse inferences from silence does not apply (see previously);
- the person being questioned is under arrest; and
- the person being questioned has been given a special warning (Code 10.10; Note 10F).

In giving the warning, the suspect being interviewed must be told in ordinary language:

- what offence is being investigated;
- what fact they are being asked to account for;

169

- that this fact may be due to them taking part in the commission of the offence;
- that a court may draw a proper inference if they fail or refuse to account for this fact;
- that a record is being made of the interview and it may be given in evidence if they are brought to trial (Code C 10.11).

If the suspect is a juvenile or mentally vulnerable, this information must only be given in the presence of the appropriate adult (Code C 10.11A).

7.5.4 Content of interviews

When questioning, Code C Note 11B advises the interviewing officer to have in mind para 3.5 of the Criminal Procedure and Investigations Act 1996 Code of Practice which states that the investigator must pursue all reasonable lines of enquiry whether they point towards or away from the suspect. The interviewer must, however, be careful not to do or say anything which might be considered to be an inducement or amount to oppression or anything else that might subsequently render the contents of the interview unsafe and inadmissible. Accordingly, Code C 11.5 states that 'no interviewer may try to obtain answers or elicit a statement by the use of oppression'. Neither, save when explaining the terms of the caution or special warning or otherwise explaining to the suspect the legal consequences of refusing to cooperate or answer questions, should the police indicate what action they will take as a result of anything that the suspect says or does except in answer to a direct question, and only then when the action is itself proper and warranted (Code C 11.5).

So, for example, an interviewer should not indicate to a person being questioned that he will get bail if he cooperates—that could be regarded as an inducement that might result in a finding that any answers given in response were unreliable and therefore inadmissible in evidence. Neither should the interviewer give such an indication in response to a direct question, the question of bail being a matter for the custody officer. The interviewer should bear in mind that he may also have to satisfy a court that nothing was said or done to influence the suspect in any breaks within or between interviews. Accordingly, Code C Note 10E suggests that at the beginning of any new or resumed interview, the interviewing officer should summarize the reason for the break and confirm this with the suspect. He would also be well advised following any break to ask the suspect to confirm that no questions or other discussions relating to the offence have taken place in the course of the break.

Before the interview begins the interviewer must identify to the suspect all those present in the interview, and as already stated, remind him of his right to free legal advice (if applicable) and caution or re-caution the suspect.

Following these preliminaries, at the outset of the interview the interviewing officer must put to the suspect any 'significant statement' or silence and ask the suspect whether he confirms or denies that statement or silence and whether he wishes to add anything to it (Code C 11.4).

Any record that has been made of a significant statement or silence should be shown to the suspect in interview and he should be asked to sign it to confirm its accuracy if he has not already done so. Any refusal to sign or disagreement with the contents of any such record should be recorded (Code C Note 11E).

A significant statement is defined in Code C 11.4A as 'one which appears capable of being used in evidence against the suspect, in particular a direct admission of guilt'. A significant silence is defined in the same section as 'a failure or refusal to answer a question or answer satisfactorily when under caution' in circumstances which might give rise to an adverse inference under the Criminal Justice and Public Order Act 1994. Comments made outside the context of an interview which do not amount in themselves to a significant statement but which nevertheless might be relevant to an offence should if possible also be recorded and put to a suspect for him to read, sign, and indicate whether and to what extent he agrees or disagrees with its contents (Code C 11.13).

7.5.5 Ending the interview

Section 37 of the Act provides that where there is insufficient evidence to charge a suspect, the custody officer may authorize his detention for such period as is necessary (subject to review) to obtain such evidence—*inter alia*, by questioning. When the custody officer has sufficient evidence to charge the person with the offence for which he was arrested that person must either be charged or released with or without bail.

If, in the course of the interview, sufficient evidence has been gained to charge, must the interview immediately be brought to an end? Code C 11.6 states that the interview of a person about an offence with which that person has not been charged must cease when:

- the investigating officer is satisfied that all the questions considered relevant to obtaining accurate and reliable information about the offence have been put to the suspect, including allowing the suspect an opportunity to give an innocent explanation and asking questions to test if the explanation is accurate and reliable;
- the investigating officer has taken account of any other available evidence; and
- the investigating officer or, in the case of a detained suspect, the custody officer, reasonably believes that there is sufficient evidence to provide a realistic prospect of conviction if the person was prosecuted.

Accordingly, once the interviewing officer concludes that he has sufficient evidence for a prosecution to succeed, he should ask the person being interviewed if he has anything further to say, and once he has said all he wishes, the interview should be terminated and the person brought before the custody officer to be charged or otherwise dealt with.

7.5.6 Post-charge interviews

Notwithstanding the mandatory terms of Code 11.6, exceptionally, a further interview of the detainee may be necessary after charge to:

- prevent or minimize harm or loss to some other person, or the public;
- to clear up an ambiguity in a previous answer or statement;
- in the interests of justice for the detainee to have put to them, and to have the opportunity to comment on, information concerning the offence which has come to light since they were charged or informed that they might be prosecuted—Code C 16.5.

Prior to any further interview the suspect must be reminded of their right to legal advice and cautioned in the following terms: 'You do not have to say anything, but anything you do say may be given in evidence'. It follows from the terms of the caution that no adverse inference could be drawn from a failure to mention facts or answer questions in a post-charge interview.

Where an interview after charge has taken place a full and proper record must be made of all questions put and answers given. This may be done by audio or visual recording of the interview, or by way of a written record which must be signed by the detainee, interviewer, and any other persons present—Code C 16.9. Proposed amendments to Code E will specify that where there is a post-charge interview in respect of an indictable offence, or where an interviewer wants to tell a person post-charge about the contents of a written statement or interview conducted with another person, unless the person has been arrested and the interview or information is given at a location other than at a police station, that interview, or information should be audio-recorded.

7.6 Interview Records (Codes C and E)

An accurate record must be made of every interview, whether it is conducted at a police station or elsewhere (Code C 11.7).

Where the interview takes place at a police station, audio-recording must be used unless the custody officer gives authorization not to audio-record the interview in circumstances where it is not reasonably practicable to do so due to the unavailability of equipment, whether due to equipment failure, or because the person to be interviewed refuses to go into or remain in a suitable interview room and no portable recording equipment is available. In those circumstances the interview must be recorded in writing.

Interviews may be audio-recorded using removable media (audio or audio/visual taping) to which Code E 2 to 6 apply, or via a secure digital network, to which Code E 7 applies. See also Code F in this regard.

7.6.1 **Tape-recording**

Section 60 of the Act imposes on the Secretary of State a duty to issue a code of practice for the tape-recording of interviews with suspects at police stations and to make an order requiring that some or all such interviews as specified are tape-recorded.

The applicable code of practice in this regard is Code E which provides detailed guidance on the audio-recording of interviews from the type of tapes and tape-machines to use, or what to do if a tape breaks, to sections dealing with the maintenance of tape security following an interview. There is substantial overlap with, and indeed repetition of some of the provisions of Code C, and the two codes must accordingly be read together.

The primary provision in Code E is E 3.1(a) which states that the interviews of all persons who are interviewed about an indictable offence at a police station, under caution and in accordance with the provisions of Code C must be audio-recorded.

An interview must also be audio-recorded where an officer asks further questions after the suspect has been charged or told that he may be prosecuted for an offence, or where an officer wants to tell such a person about any written statement or interview with another person.

The only exceptions to the above are where either it is not practicable to use audio-recording because the recording equipment or the facilities to use it are not available and the custody officer has reasonable grounds to consider that the interview should not be delayed; or where it is clear from the outset that no prosecution will follow (Code E 3.3). A further possible but highly unusual scenario would be where a suspect will not cooperate with the interview procedure and the custody officer gives authority for the interview to be conducted in the suspect's cell and no portable equipment is available (Code E 3.4).

If the interview is not tape-recorded for one of these reasons, it must nevertheless be recorded in writing, as must the reason for departing from the normal procedure which the authorizing officer may well need to justify in court.

Where an interview is tape-recorded, the recording should be done openly. Two tapes should be used simultaneously, one of which will become the master copy and the other the working copy. The tapes should be clean and unused and should be unwrapped or opened in the presence of the suspect (Code E 4.3).

At the outset the interviewer should ask all persons present, including the suspect, to speak to identify themselves—this will in due course have the very practical effect of aiding voice recognition.

As well as identifying the persons present, reminding the suspect of his entitlement to free legal advice, and cautioning the suspect, the interviewer should in addition at the commencement of a tape-recorded interview state that the interview is being tape-recorded, state the time, date, and place of interview, and tell the suspect that he will be given a notice about what will happen to the tapes (Code E 4.4).

If the suspect objects to the interview being tape-recorded, the interviewer should ask for the suspect to state his objections on tape. When he has done so (or if he refuses to do so) the interviewer has a discretion whether to continue to record the interview or to turn the tape off and record any further questions and answers in writing (Code E 4.8). It might reasonably be supposed, however, that such a course of action would be a risky one to take.

If the reason for wanting the tape turned off is that the suspect wants to tell the interviewer about other matters not directly connected with the offence and that it is these matters that they are unwilling to speak about on tape, then an opportunity should be provided at the conclusion of the interview for this to be done (Code E 4.10).

Where any complaints are made by the suspect in the course of the interview the custody officer must be informed (Code C 12.9). Ideally, the tape should be allowed to run whilst the custody officer speaks to the suspect and deals with the matter of complaint (Code E Note 4E). However, if the complaint is about a matter unconnected with the interview then the interviewer may at his discretion continue the interview and bring the matter to the attention of the custody officer as soon as practicable after the interview has concluded (Code E Note 4F).

If an interview is suspended for a break to be taken, that fact and the time of the break should be recorded on tape. If the break is a short one and all parties remain in the interview room the tape-recorder can simply be turned off; when the interview recommences it should be recorded on the same tapes. If, however, the suspect leaves the room in the course of a break, then the tapes should be removed and dealt with in the same way as if the interview had concluded (Code E 4.12, 4.13).

At the conclusion of the interview the suspect must be asked whether there is anything he would like to clarify or add, following which the time should be recorded and the tape switched off. The master tape must then be sealed, the suspect and his legal representative or appropriate adult if any asked to sign the seal, and the tape then treated as an exhibit (Code E 4.18).

Once sealed the seal of a master tape required in criminal proceedings may not be broken by a police officer save in the presence of a representative of the Crown Prosecution Service and on notice to the defendant or his legal representative who is entitled to be present (Code E 6.2).

If a suspect is charged or informed that he will be prosecuted, he is entitled to a copy of the tape, and at the conclusion of the interview must be given a notice detailing his entitlement to the tape, the arrangements for access to the tape, and how it is to be used (Code E 4.19).

Whether or not a suspect is ultimately prosecuted, all master tapes of interviews must be kept in secure conditions and treated in the same way as an exhibit (Code E 6.1).

7.6.2 **Video recording**

The Secretary of State has a 'duty' under s 60 of the Act to issue a code of practice and to make an order requiring the tape-recording of interviews. Under s 61 he has a 'power' to issue a code of practice in connection with and to make an order requiring the visual recording of interviews. The applicable Code of Practice is Code F, which broadly mirrors the provisions applicable to tape-recorded interviews in Code E. The provisions in Code C relating to interviews and the drawing of adverse inferences apply equally here as to interviews recorded either on audio tape or in writing.

At the outset, Code F makes clear that there is no statutory requirement to visually record interviews. Nevertheless, although there is no requirement at the present time that interviews should be visually recorded, there are obvious benefits in doing so. In particular, Code F 3.1(d) and (e) draw attention to the fact that it could be considered appropriate to visually record an interview that takes place with or in the presence of a deaf or deaf/blind or speech impaired person who uses sign language to communicate, or where the interview has taken place with or in the presence of anyone who requires an appropriate adult.

7.6.3 **Secure digital network**

The requirements for recording using a secure digital network (which does not involve the use of removable media) are set out at Code E 7 and closely follow the requirements for interviews conducted using other formats.

In the event of an equipment failure that cannot be quickly rectified, the interview should continue using removable media (audio or audio-visual taping) unless such equipment is unavailable, in which case authority should be sought from the custody officer in accordance with Code E 3.3 to complete the interview record in writing.

Code E 7.16, 7.17 contain requirements to ensure the security and integrity of secure digital network interview records, and emphasize the need to strictly control and monitor necessary access to those records.

7.6.4 **Writing**

Where an interview is recorded in writing, that record must be made on forms provided for that purpose or in the interviewer's pocket book (Code C 11.7(c)).

The record must be made contemporaneously with the interview unless this would not be practicable or would interfere with the conduct of the interview. If the record is not made in the course of the interview then it must be made as soon as practicable thereafter and must include within it the reason why it could not be made during the interview (Code C 11.8, 11.10).

Where possible the suspect, his legal representative, or appropriate adult if present during the interview should be given the opportunity to read the record of interview and sign it as correct. If the suspect cannot read, then the record should be read over to him (Code C 11.11, 11.12).

The written record should so far as possible be a verbatim transcript of the questions and answers or an adequate and accurate summary.

7.7 Written Statements under Caution (Code C, Annex D)

Annex D1 of Code C states that 'a person shall always be invited to write down what they want to say'. Despite the seemingly mandatory requirement of the provision, in reality it will be little used, as Code C Note 12A makes it clear that there would normally be no necessity for a written statement where the interview was recorded or taped contemporaneously or where a written record of interview has been signed by the interviewee. A suspect may, however, be asked if he wants to make a statement or he may himself ask to do so. Any statement then made must include at the outset a declaration that the writer makes the statement of his own free will and understands that it is under caution, the words of which will follow. The exact wording to be included is set out in full at Annex D2.

If a detainee asks to make a written statement under caution either on or after being charged or informed that they may be prosecuted for an offence then they may do so. Again the appropriate version of the caution must be included at the outset.

If the detainee wishes, they may ask a police officer to write the statement for them. In these circumstances the officer writing the statement must use the exact words spoken by the person making the statement. If any clarification is required the questions and answers concerning the clarification must be included. At the conclusion of the statement taking the person who made the statement must be given the opportunity to read the statement himself, to make any corrections, alterations, and additions, to confirm that it is correct, and to sign a declaration to that effect. If the person cannot or will not read the statement it should be read to him.

Practical Guidance

7.8 Case Study 1

Green is in custody having been arrested for theft. DC Potts wishes to interview him, but Green requests legal advice from his regular solicitor. Having followed the procedure set out in Code C Note 6B, Green's solicitor is contacted and agrees to attend. An hour later, Green's solicitor has still not arrived and Green informs DC Potts that he wishes to go ahead with the interview without legal representation.

What, if anything should DC Potts do?

Although a detainee has the right to legal advice, he is under no obligation to have it. He can therefore decline legal representation. Where a detainee originally requested a solicitor but then changes his mind the interviewing officer will need to follow Code C 6.6(d). An officer of inspector rank or above should be informed. That officer must speak to Green and ask him why he has changed his mind, should make reasonable efforts to ascertain the time of the solicitor's expected arrival, and notify the detainee of the outcome of those enquiries. If the detainee then confirms in writing that he wishes the interview to proceed in the absence of his solicitor, and if the inspector is satisfied that it is proper for the interview to proceed, he may give authority to that effect.

The inspector is unable to contact Green's solicitor, Green maintains his position that the interview should go ahead, and having considered the position the inspector gives authority for the interview to proceed. The interview commences; it is audio-recorded in accordance with Code E.

After about ten minutes Green asks DC Potts not to record the interview on tape. How should DC Potts deal with this request?

DC Potts should explain to Smith that the Codes of Practice require him to record his objections to the audio recording on tape and ascertain what they are. Once Smith has stated on tape what his objections are or refused to do so, DC Potts should consider whether to continue the recording (Code E 4.8). If he chooses not to do so, he should then turn the recorder off. DC Potts should then commence the interview again and make a contemporaneous written record of the questions and answers. He should caution Smith again, repeat any special warnings, and remind him of his right to free legal advice. If possible, DC Potts should also obtain the assistance of a colleague to record the interview and to act as a witness in case Smith should subsequently dispute the accuracy of the written record. Once the interview has been completed DC Potts should ensure Smith is given the opportunity to read the written account and sign it as correct. It is good practice to go through the record of each question and answer and, if the interviewee agrees with the accuracy, ask him to initial each answer as well as signing the foot of each page (Codes of Practice C, paras 11.7–11.11, E 4.8).

Whilst the interview is in progress, Green's solicitor arrives at the police station. What action should be taken?

Green must be informed without delay that his solicitor has arrived and, if he wishes, the interview must be suspended in order for him to speak to his solicitor.

In due course Green is charged with theft although the investigation continues. As a consequence, DC Potts receives further evidence which casts doubt on some of the answers that Green gave in interview. DC Potts wants to ask him about these further matters. Can he re-interview Green?

Code C 11.6 states that an interview must cease when the custody officer reasonably believes that there is sufficient evidence to provide a realistic prospect of conviction. A detainee may not be interviewed about an offence after charge save in specific circumstances as set out in Code C 16.5. One of those circumstances is that further information has come to light since charge and that it is in the interests of justice that the detainee should have the opportunity to comment on it. DC Potts can therefore re-interview Green.

At the outset of the re-interview, Green states that he does not wish to answer questions but wants to provide a statement.

At the outset of the interview, DC Potts must caution Green in the following terms: 'You do not have to say anything, but anything you do say may be given in evidence.' Green therefore has the right not to say anything, and no adverse inference can be drawn from his refusal to answer questions (Code C—Annex C 1(b)). He does however have the right to make a statement, which should, in accordance with Code C—Annex D 4, commence with this statement which Green should sign: 'I make this statement of my own free will. *I understand that I do not have to say anything. This statement may be given in evidence.*'

7.9 **Case Study 2**

PC Smith is called to an address where a burglar alarm has been activated. She sees Dean, a known criminal loitering in the vicinity. PC Smith approaches Dean, who appears to be the worse for wear for drink. She notices that he is carrying a CD player and asks him where he got it from. Dean states that he is keeping it for a friend who he refuses to name. PC Smith then receives further information via her personal radio confirming that a house nearby has been broken into and a CD player stolen. PC Smith then arrests Dean on suspicion of burglary and cautions him. Dean is placed in the rear of PC Smith's police car to await a van to transport him to the police station. While they are waiting, PC Smith again asks Dean where he got the CD player from and Dean admits that he stole it in the course of the burglary. PC Smith, realizing the significance of what has been said, hurriedly makes a note in her notebook and asks Dean to sign it, which he does without reading it.

After being booked into custody, Dean is examined by the forensic medical examiner and is deemed unfit for interview due to alcohol consumption.

After a night's rest, Dean is interviewed by PC Smith. On the advice of his solicitor Dean gives a pre-prepared statement in which he denies any wrongdoing. After the interview, Dean's solicitor makes an official complaint against PC Smith for abusing her authority by interviewing his client away from the police station and whilst he was drunk.

Did PC Smith's initial questions amount to an interview?

There can be a fine line between questions asked to establish if reasonable grounds to arrest exist and conducting an interview. Any questioning of a *suspect* regarding their involvement in a criminal offence is classified as an interview; but police officers may regularly regard a person as 'suspicious' without having sufficient grounds to regard them as a suspect for an offence and, moreover, are entitled to ask questions of those who are not 'suspects' in the course of their investigations without such questioning amounting to an interview. Here, it is at least arguable that at the time of the initial questioning Dean was not a suspect for an offence and that therefore the questions did not amount to an interview.

At what point does Dean become a suspect?

When it is confirmed to PC Smith that a burglary has occurred and that a CD player was stolen, those facts together with Dean's known background, his proximity to the scene of the crime, and his possession of an item that may have been stolen in the course of that burglary, clearly provide reasonable grounds to suspect him of involvement in the offence. At this point, PC Smith quite properly arrested and cautioned him.

Were PC Smith's subsequent questions an interview?

As Dean has been arrested as a suspect, no further questioning should take place; any such questioning would be classed as an interview which should take place at the police station and in accordance with the Codes of Practice. PC Smith's actions would probably be viewed as an attempt to circumvent the Codes and any questions and answers would almost certainly be excluded under s 78(1).

What if Dean had volunteered the information given in the car?

The position would be different if Dean's 'confession' was made spontaneously rather than as a result of questioning. Had that been the situation, PC Smith's actions of recording the comments made and asking Dean to sign them would be entirely appropriate. PC Smith should then draw those comments to the attention of the custody officer on arrival at the station and they should be raised at the outset of the recorded interview. It may well be that an application would be made to exclude those comments as unreliable due to Dean's inebriated state, but PC Smith's actions could not be criticized.

8

The Detention and Treatment of Vulnerable Suspects

Law and Commentary

8.1 Introduction

The law recognizes that there are particular classes of detainee who may have difficulty in understanding the significance of procedures, questioning, and the implication of any replies they make to such questioning. Such detainees, described in Code C 3(b) as 'special groups' are deemed in need of special protection. Code C provides a number of safeguards covering the detention, treatment, and questioning of the members of such groups.

As it is recognized that those who may have limited understanding or be otherwise vulnerable may be liable to give misleading, unreliable, or self-incriminating evidence, consequently it must be recognized that any breach of the safeguards designed to protect their interests may well give rise to a subsequent successful application to exclude any evidence thereafter obtained.

8.2 The Special Groups

8.2.1 Which detainees form the 'special groups'?

Those for whom special safeguards exist are:

- juveniles;
- the mentally disordered or otherwise mentally vulnerable;
- those who appear to be deaf, or about whom there is doubt about their hearing or speaking ability or ability to understand English;
- those who are blind, seriously visually impaired, or unable to read.

8.2.2 Who is a juvenile?

In the current version of Code C, a juvenile is a person under the age of 17. This will change following the decision in *R (HC (a child, by his litigation friend CC)) v Secretary of State for the Home Department*—25 April 2013 which held that to give a 17-year-old no additional rights and protections than those given to an adult was to act incompatibly with Art 8 read with the United Nations Convention on the Rights of the Child, which requires a 17-year-old detainee to be treated according to the principle that his best interests are a primary consideration. The Court of Appeal accordingly determined that by failing to amend Code C so as to distinguish between those aged 17 and those aged 18 or over, the Secretary of State was in breach of her obligations under the Human Rights Act 1998. Code C will inevitably be amended in the light of this ruling, and the same rights and protections should be afforded to those aged under 18, as are currently only available to those under 17.

When determining the age of the detainee, proof of age is not required, and the law errs on the side of caution; accordingly it is sufficient that someone appears to be under 17 (18). If they do, then in the absence of clear evidence to the contrary they must be treated as a juvenile (Code C 1.5).

8.2.3 What is meant by 'mentally vulnerable or otherwise mentally disordered'?

Again, where there is any uncertainty or room for doubt about the mental state of a detainee then the detainee must be regarded as vulnerable. Therefore, if an officer has any suspicion, or is told in good faith that a person of any age may be mentally disordered or otherwise mentally vulnerable, or is mentally incapable of understanding the significance of questions or their replies, then that person is to be treated as mentally vulnerable in the absence of clear evidence to dispel that suspicion (Code C 1.4; Annex E 1).

A detainee is 'mentally vulnerable' if, because of their mental state or capacity, they may not understand the significance of what is said, of questions, or their replies.

'Mental disorder' is defined in the Mental Health Act 1983 as 'any disorder or disability of mind' (Code C, Note 1G).

8.3 Initial Steps

8.3.1 What initial steps must be taken when a juvenile is detained?

Where a juvenile is detained, the custody officer must as soon as practicable inform the appropriate adult of the grounds of the juvenile's detention and whereabouts, and ask them to come to the station to see the detainee (Code C 3.15).

All detainees are entitled under s 56 of PACE to have a friend, relative, or some other person likely to take an interest in his welfare informed of his arrest. Where the person detained is a juvenile, s 57 places the police under an additional duty to take such steps as are practicable to identify the person responsible for the juvenile's welfare (who may or may not be the person acting as the appropriate adult) and inform them of the facts of his arrest.

Section 57 must be read together with Code C 3.13. That provides that where it appears to the custody officer that the detainee is under 17 (18), he must as soon as practicable ascertain the identity of a person responsible for their welfare and inform that person:

- that the juvenile has been arrested;
- why they have been arrested; and
- where they are detained.

The relevant person may be:

- a parent or guardian;
- (if the juvenile is in local authority care, or is being otherwise looked after under the Children Act 1989), a person appointed by that organization to have responsibility for the juvenile's welfare;
- any other person who has for the time being assumed responsibility for the juvenile's welfare.

If the juvenile is under a court order, the 'responsible officer' who supervises or otherwise monitors the juvenile should also be informed; for example a member of the Youth Offending Team or the contractor providing electronic monitoring (Code C 3.14). Consideration should also be given to contacting the juvenile's parents, even where there is no legal obligation to inform them (eg because the juvenile is in local authority care), or where the juvenile is not living with them (Code C, Note 3C).

A juvenile therefore has the right, in common with all detainees, to have someone informed of the circumstances of his detention under s 56, and the police have a duty to inform the person responsible for the juvenile's welfare under s 57 and Code 3.13, and to inform and secure the attendance at the police station of an appropriate adult (who may or may not be the person responsible for the juvenile's welfare). Additionally, they should consider informing the juvenile's parents if not already informed under one of the categories listed. In practice, however, it is usually a parent who is informed both as the person responsible for the juvenile's welfare and as the appropriate adult.

Note that a juvenile cannot be held incommunicado. Even where Annex B of Code C applies (delay in notifying arrest or allowing access to legal advice in certain specified situations), the appropriate adult and the person responsible for the juvenile detainee's welfare must be contacted, informed of the circumstances of arrest, and asked to attend the police station to see the detainee (Note B1).

8.3.2 What initial steps must be taken when a suspect who may have a mental or physical disorder is detained?

The custody officer must determine whether the detainee might be in need of medical treatment or attention—whether due to a physical illness or injury, or because of a mental disorder or for any other reason (eg the effects of drink or drugs). Wherever there is any doubt the custody officer must err on the side of caution and take steps to ensure that the detainee receives appropriate clinical attention as soon as reasonably practicable (Code C 9.5).

This applies irrespective of whether or not the detainee has asked for medical assistance and irrespective of whether he has received clinical attention elsewhere (Code C 9.5A).

Note 9C warns that when assessing whether or not a detainee requires clinical attention and if so what, it is important to bear in mind that there may be hidden and serious causes for a detainee's apparent condition. A detainee who appears to be drunk may in fact have sustained an injury, particularly a head injury that might not be immediately obvious; a detainee who is behaving abnormally may have a physical or mental illness; a detainee who is dependent on drink or drugs may experience harmful effects within a short time of being deprived of their supply. Wherever there is any doubt, or where the need is urgent, the police must act immediately to call a health care professional or an ambulance.

A mentally disordered or otherwise mentally vulnerable person who has been detained under s 136 of the Mental Health Act 1983 must be assessed as soon as possible and should whenever practicable be taken to hospital for that purpose (Code 9D—see further, Chapter 10 of the Mental Health Act 1983 Code of Practice). Where the assessment takes place at the police station, an approved mental health professional and a registered medical practitioner (but not the appropriate adult) must be called to the police station as soon as possible to carry that assessment out. Once the detainee has been assessed and suitable arrangements have been made for their treatment and care they can no longer be detained under s 136. Neither can their detention continue under s 136 if, having examined them, a registered medical practitioner concludes that they are not mentally disordered within the meaning of the Act (Code C 3.16).

Where the detainee is mentally disordered or otherwise mentally vulnerable, an appropriate adult must be notified, apprised of the circumstances of the person's detention and whereabouts, and asked to come to the station to see the detainee (Code C 3.15). It should be noted however that under Code C 3.16, the presence of the appropriate adult is not required where an assessment is carried out in accordance with the requirements in Code C 3.16; an appropriate adult has no role in any assessment process.

As with juveniles, the right to have an appropriate adult informed under Code C 3.15 applies even where the police could in the case of a non-vulnerable detainee have delayed notification of arrest or access to legal advice in accordance with Annex B.

8.3.3 What initial steps should be taken if the detainee has difficulty communicating?

It is a pre-requisite that a detainee should be able to understand what is taking place and to be able to communicate effectively. Many of the safeguards provided by PACE and Code C are directed to ensure this. The custody officer must therefore check to determine whether a detainee requires help to check documentation or an interpreter in order to facilitate communication (Code C 3.5(c)(ii)).

If the detainee appears to be deaf, or if there is doubt about his hearing or speaking ability, or ability to understand English, and effective communication cannot be established, the custody officer must as soon as practicable call an interpreter for assistance (Code C 3.12).

If the detainee is blind, seriously visually impaired, or unable to read, a person not involved in the investigation (eg a solicitor, relative, or—in the case of a juvenile or mentally vulnerable detainee—an appropriate adult) must be made available to help them check any documentation (Code 3.20).

8.4 **Who can Act as an Appropriate Adult?**

The categories of people who can act as an appropriate adult differ according to whether the detainee is a juvenile or is mentally disordered or otherwise mentally vulnerable.

Where the detainee is a juvenile, the appropriate adult can be:

- the parent, guardian, or, if in the care of a local authority or voluntary organization, a person representing that authority or organization;
- a social worker of a local authority social services department;
- failing these, some other responsible adult aged 18 or over who is not a police officer or employed by the police (Code C 1.7(a)).

A person, including a parent or guardian, should not act as an appropriate adult if he or she:

- is suspected of involvement in the offence;
- is the victim;
- is a witness;
- is involved in the investigation;
- has received admissions prior to attending to act as the appropriate adult;
- is a parent or guardian estranged from the juvenile and the juvenile expressly and specifically objects to their presence;
- is a social worker or member of a Youth Offending Team in whose presence the juvenile has admitted the offence at a time other than when (s)he is acting as the appropriate adult;
- is a solicitor or independent custody visitor present at the police station in that capacity (Code C, Note 1B, C, F);
- (in the case of a detainee arrested under s 41 the Terrorism Act 2000) is suspected of involvement in the commission, preparation or instigation of acts of terrorism (Code H, Note 1B).

Where the detainee is mentally disordered or otherwise mentally vulnerable, the appropriate adult can be:

185

- a relative, guardian, or other person responsible for their care or custody;
- someone experienced in dealing with mentally disordered or mentally vulnerable people but who is not a police officer or employed by the police;
- failing these, some other responsible adult aged 18 or over who is not a police officer or employed by the police (Code C 1.7(b)).

Note 1D advises that it may be more satisfactory if the appropriate adult for a mentally disordered or otherwise mentally vulnerable person is someone experienced or trained in their care, rather than a relative lacking such qualifications. Notwithstanding the guidance, if the detainee prefers a relative to a better qualified stranger or objects to a particular person, then their wishes should, if practicable, be respected.

As for juveniles, a solicitor or independent custody visitor who is present at the police station in that capacity cannot also act as the appropriate adult (Note 1F).

8.4.1 What is the role of the appropriate adult?

It is the appropriate adult's role to ensure that a vulnerable detainee understands the procedures and their rights and is able to exercise those rights effectively. Code C identifies various procedures that must be carried out or repeated in the presence of the appropriate adult, gives the appropriate adult certain rights to oversee procedures, and details specific responsibilities that the appropriate adult will have. In particular, the appropriate adult has a responsibility to give the detainee advice and assistance, and this must be made known to the detainee who must in addition be told that they can consult privately with the appropriate adult at any time (Code C 3.18).

8.4.2 What are the rights and responsibilities of the appropriate adult?

As it is essential that the detainee should understand his rights, those rights (as enshrined in Code C 3.1–3.5) must be given in the presence of the appropriate adult. If those rights were given prior to the appropriate adult's attendance at the police station, they must be given again and in his presence once he has arrived (Code C 3.17).

It is equally important that the vulnerable detainee should understand the implication of matters put to him and his replies (or lack of them). A vulnerable detainee cannot therefore be given a special warning under ss 36 and 37 of the Criminal Justice and Public Order Act 1994 (adverse inferences which may be drawn where a suspect fails or refuses to account for any objects, marks, or substances found) unless the appropriate adult is present. Similarly, whenever a caution is given, it must be given, or repeated, in the presence of the appropriate adult (Code C 10.12).

The appropriate adult must be permitted to inspect a detainee's custody record as soon as practicable after their arrival at the police station, at any other time whilst the person is detained, and (on giving reasonable notice) after the detainee has left police detention (Code C 2.4; 2.5).

Moreover, the detainee, appropriate adult, or legal representative is entitled to be given a copy of the custody record on request within 12 months of the time when the detainee leaves police detention or is brought before a court (Code C 2.4A).

8.5 **When is an Interpreter Required?**

An interpreter may be required either for reasons of disability (a speech or hearing impediment) or language. The underlying intention is to ensure that the detainee understands the procedure, what is put to him, and the significance of his replies.

The custody officer should establish at an early stage whether or not a detainee may require an interpreter. Where effective communication cannot be established with a detainee who is or appears to be deaf, or where there are doubts about their ability to hear, speak, or understand English, then a suitably qualified interpreter should be made available at public expense. The interpreter will need to explain the offence to the detainee and any information given by the custody officer.

8.5.1 **Who can act as an interpreter?**

Whenever possible, Note 13A advises that interpreters should be provided in accordance with the national arrangements approved or prescribed by the Secretary of State. A police officer or member of the police staff may, in certain circumstances, interpret, but only if the detainee (and where applicable the appropriate adult) give their consent in writing, or if in the interview is either audio or visually recorded in accordance with Codes E or F.

As the interpreter must be impartial, a police officer or member of the police staff cannot interpret where that interpretation is required for the purpose of obtaining legal advice (Code C 13.9). The requirement of impartiality extends beyond the use of police staff as interpreters. In *R v West London Youth Court, ex p J* [2001] 1 WLR 2368, it was held that it was wrong for a male relative acting as the appropriate adult for an 11-year-old girl to additionally take on the role of an interpreter. The interpreter had to be wholly impartial and an appropriate adult was not impartial as his function was to assist the person being questioned.

8.6 **Legal Advice**

Advising a vulnerable detainee of the right to free and independent legal advice is one of the main roles of the appropriate adult. Where the detainee is a juvenile, is mentally disordered, or is otherwise mentally vulnerable, the appropriate adult should always consider whether legal advice from a solicitor is required and has the right to ask for a solicitor to attend if this would be in the best interests of the detainee, even where the detainee has indicated that he does not want legal advice. The decision whether to receive legal advice is, however, ultimately that of the detainee. Accordingly he cannot be forced to see a solicitor if he does not wish to do so (Code C 6.5A).

Where the detainee does agree to see a solicitor he has the right to consult with that solicitor in private which includes, if he wishes, the absence of the appropriate adult (Code C, Note 1E).

As already referred to, where the detainee cannot communicate with the solicitor because of language, hearing, or speech difficulties an interpreter must be called. In this situation the interpreter may not be a police officer or civilian support staff.

8.7 **Interviews**

A juvenile or person who is mentally disordered or otherwise mentally vulnerable must not be interviewed regarding their (suspected) involvement in a criminal offence, or be asked to provide or sign a written statement under caution or record of interview in the absence of an appropriate adult (Code C 11.15).

The only exception to this is where an officer of at least the rank of superintendent considers that delaying the interview will:

- lead to interference with, or harm to, evidence connected with an offence;
- lead to interference with or physical harm to other people;
- lead to serious loss of, or damage to property;
- alert other suspects yet to be arrested;
- hinder the recovery of property obtained as a result of the commission of an offence (Code C 11.1).

Where any of these risks exists, an urgent interview may be authorized where the authorizing officer is satisfied that carrying out the interview in such circumstances would not significantly harm the detainee's physical or mental state (Code C 11.18). Once sufficient information has been obtained to avert the risks set out above, then the interview must cease (Code C 11.19).

Similarly, any detainee who:

- appears unable to appreciate the significance of questions and their answers;
- appears unable to understand what is happening because of the effects of drink, drugs, or any illness, ailment, or condition;
- has difficulty understanding English or has a hearing disability and who does not have an interpreter present,

may not be interviewed unless the interview is an urgent one and the authorizing officer is satisfied that no significant harm to the detainee will result.

Guidance to assist in the assessment of how a detainee's physical or mental state might be affected in interview is set out at Annex G to Code C.

The reason why there is such a need for caution in interviewing a vulnerable detainee is made clear in Note for Guidance 11C; that whilst a juvenile or mentally vulnerable detainee may well be capable of providing reliable evidence there is an acknowledged risk that the evidence given may instead be unreliable, misleading, or self-incriminating. Special care should therefore be taken. As well as ensuring that an appropriate adult is involved whenever there is any doubt about the detainee's age or mental state or capacity, corroboration of any facts admitted in interview should be obtained whenever possible.

Where the appropriate adult is present in an interview their role is an active one. The appropriate adult shall be informed that they are not expected to act simply as an observer, but are there to:

- advise the person being interviewed;
- observe whether the interview is being conducted properly and fairly; and
- facilitate communication with the person being interviewed (Code C 11.17).

An appropriate adult present at an interview should be given an opportunity to read and sign the interview record or any written statement taken down during interview (Code 11.12).

A 'person capable of interpreting' must be present during interview if:

- the interviewee has difficulty understanding English;
- the interviewer cannot speak the person's own language;
- the interviewee wants an interpreter to be present.

The only exception is where an urgent interview is authorized (Code C 13.2).

Where an interpreter is present, the interviewer must ensure that the interpreter makes a note of the interview at the time, in the person's language, for use in the event of the interpreter being called to give evidence, and certifies its accuracy. Accordingly, the interview should proceed at such a pace as allows sufficient time for the interpreter to note each question and answer after it is put, given, and interpreted. At the conclusion of the interview, the interviewee should be allowed to read the record or have it read to them and should sign it as correct or indicate the respects in which they consider it inaccurate (Code C 13.3).

If the detainee wishes to give a statement to the police (eg a pre-prepared statement instead of answering questions in interview), and that statement is given in a foreign language, the interpreter must record the statement in the language in which it is made, and the detainee be invited to sign it. The statement will at a later date need to be translated into English (Code C 13.4).

If a person appears to be deaf, or there is doubt about their hearing or speaking ability, they can be interviewed in the absence of an interpreter, but only where they agree in writing to such a course, or an urgent interview is authorized (Code 13.5).

189

As with an interview in a foreign language, the interpreter must be given the opportunity to read the interview record and certify its accuracy in the event of the interpreter being called to give evidence (Code 13.7).

An interpreter should also be called if a juvenile is to be interviewed and the appropriate adult appears to be deaf or there is doubt about their hearing or speaking ability, unless they agree in writing to proceeding without one or it is an urgent interview (Code C 13.6). Note that this only applies where the appropriate adult is also the parent or guardian of the juvenile.

Action taken to call an interpreter and any agreement to be interviewed in the absence of an interpreter must be recorded (Code C 13.11).

Code 11.1 states that an interview must be carried out at a police station 'or other authorised place of detention' unless the interview is an urgent one as defined above. Juveniles may be interviewed at their place of education, but only in exceptional circumstances and only when the principal or their nominee agrees. Where this happens, every effort should be made to notify the parent(s) or some other person responsible for the juvenile's welfare, and the appropriate adult (if this is a different person) that the police want to interview the juvenile, and reasonable time should be allowed to enable the appropriate adult to be present at the interview. If awaiting the arrival of the appropriate adult would cause unreasonable delay then the principal or their nominee can act as the appropriate adult for the purposes of the interview unless the offence of which the juvenile is suspected is an offence against the educational establishment (Code C 11.16).

Wards of court

Where a juvenile is a ward of court and the police wish to interview him, they must act in accordance with the Practice Direction (Criminal Proceedings: Consolidation), para 5 [2002] 1 WLR 2870. Other than in exceptional cases where immediate action is necessary, the police must apply to the wardship court for leave. Paragraph 5.3 of the Practice Direction acknowledges that it would be an exceptional case justifying immediate action where the police wish to interview a ward who is suspected by the police of having committed a criminal act. The police must act in accordance with the relevant provisions of Code C and notify the parent or other appropriate adult and the reporting officer (if applicable) and supply the reporting officer with a copy of any interview or statement made by the ward.

8.8 Detention

The necessity for continued detention of any detainee must be reviewed periodically throughout the detention period. A review of detention may take place in person or by telephone, or, where facilities exist, by video-conferencing.

In determining how the review should take place, the review officer must take full account of the needs of the person in custody. Where the detainee is:

- a juvenile; or
- mentally vulnerable; or
- in need of medical attention (other than for routine minor ailments)

then ordinarily the review should be conducted in person (C 15.3C).

Without a warrant of further detention, under s 42(1) the maximum period for which the police can authorize detention for an indictable offence is 36 hours. However, whether authorization is in fact given for an extension of detention of a juvenile or mentally vulnerable person beyond 24 hours will depend upon the circumstances of the case, and in particular:

- the detainee's special vulnerability;
- the legal obligation to provide an opportunity for representations to be made prior to a decision about extending detention;
- the need to consult and consider the views of any appropriate adult; and
- any alternatives to police custody (Code C 15.2A).

Before authorizing the continued detention of a juvenile or mentally vulnerable person, the authorizing officer, who must be of the rank of superintendent or above, must give the detainee, his solicitor if available, the appropriate adult if available, and (at his discretion) any other people having an interest in the detainee's welfare, the opportunity to make representations (Code C 15.3).

'Available' includes being contactable in time to enable the relevant person to make representations, whether by telephone or in person. Note 15CA states that 'reasonable efforts' should be made to notify the solicitor or appropriate adult of the time that a decision is expected to be made so that they can make themselves 'available'.

8.8.1 What are the standards of treatment for a vulnerable detainee?

Sections 8 and 9 of Code C set out provisions for the conditions of detention and the care and treatment of detained persons. Together with the Guidance on the Safer Detention and Handling of Persons in Police Custody (2012) they cover the provision of accommodation, toilet and washing facilities, clothing, food, and access to healthcare. It is clear from Code C 1.12 that these are to be considered the minimum standards of treatment. Certain of the provisions relate specifically to the treatment of juveniles and other vulnerable detainees.

Accommodation in cells

A juvenile must not be placed in a police cell unless there is no other secure accommodation available and the custody officer considers either that it is necessary to place them in a cell for the purposes of practical supervision, or that a cell provides more comfortable accommodation than other secure accommodation available (Code C 8.8). If a juvenile is placed in a cell the reason must be recorded (Code C 8.10).

In no circumstances may a juvenile be placed in a cell with a detained adult (Code C 8.8).

Use of restraints

Restraints may only be used in a locked cell where absolutely necessary. The restraint equipment must be approved for use, reasonable and necessary in the circumstances, and used to ensure the safety of the detainee and others. Particular care must be taken in deciding to use any form of restraint where the detainee is deaf, mentally disordered, or otherwise mentally vulnerable (Code C 8.2).

If any restraint is used, it must be recorded (Code C 8.11).

Checks

Detainees should normally be visited every hour. Juveniles and mentally vulnerable detainees should, however, be visited more frequently wherever possible (Code 9.3; Note 9B).

Unless otherwise directed by a health professional, those detainees suspected of being under the influence of drink or drugs, or of having swallowed drugs, or whose level of consciousness raises concern should be visited and roused at least every half hour and their condition assessed (Code C 9.3).

Where there is any doubt about the condition of a detainee, an appropriate healthcare professional should be called.

Medical treatment

Where a detainee requests a clinical examination, an appropriate health care professional must be called as soon as practicable to assess the detainee's clinical needs (Code C 9.8).

If a health care professional is called to examine or treat a detainee, the custody officer shall ask for their opinion about any risks or problems which the police need to take into account when making decisions about the detainee's continued detention; when to carry out an interview; and the need for safeguards (Code C 9.13).

It is important that the custody officer ensures that he fully understands any directions given by the healthcare professional, particularly in relation to the frequency of visits or need for observation (Code C 9.14; Note 9F).

A record must be made in the custody record of:

- arrangements made for an examination by a health care professional due to an allegation of assault or the use of unreasonable force by the police on the detainee;

- any arrangements made to secure clinical attention where the detainee appeared to be suffering from physical illness, mental disorder, was injured, or appeared to need clinical attention;
- any request by the detainee for clinical attention and arrangements made in response;
- the injury, ailment, condition, or other reason which made it necessary to arrange clinical attention;
- any clinical directions and advice given to the police by the health care professional concerning the care and treatment of the detainee;
- the responses received when attempting to rouse a detainee in accordance with the procedures in Annex H (a series of criteria used to measure the detainee's level of rousability) in order to chart any change in the detainee's consciousness level and arrange clinical treatment if appropriate (Code C 9.15).

8.9 **Intimate Searches**

8.9.1 **What is an 'intimate search'?**

An intimate search is defined in Annex A of Code C as 'the physical examination of a person's body orifices other than the mouth'. Attention is drawn to the risks associated with intrusive searches.

Intimate searches may only take place where authorized by an officer of the rank of inspector or above who has reasonable grounds for believing that the person may have concealed on themselves anything which they could and might use to cause injury to themselves or another, or a Class A drug which they intended to supply or export to another, and where an intimate search is the only way to recover such items (Annex A2).

Ordinarily, the search must be carried out by a registered medical practitioner or registered nurse and may only take place at a hospital, surgery, or other medical premises, or at the police station (Annex A3, 4).

Where the search is for an object that might be used to cause injury and where it is not practicable for a medical practitioner or nurse to carry out the search, then an officer of at least the rank of inspector may authorize a police officer of the same sex as the detainee to carry out the search; but only following a risk assessment and as a matter of last resort (Annex A3, 3A, 6).

Where the person to be searched is a juvenile, or is mentally vulnerable, an appropriate adult of the same sex must be present during the search unless the detainee specifically requests a particular adult of the opposite sex who is readily available. An intimate search of a juvenile may only take place in the absence of the appropriate adult where the juvenile signifies in the presence of the appropriate adult that he does not want the appropriate adult to be present during the search, and the appropriate adult agrees. Where that happens, a record must be made of the juvenile's decision which the appropriate adult must sign (Annex A5).

If the intimate search is a drug search in accordance with Annex A2(b), a detainee must give consent in writing. Where the detainee is a juvenile or is mentally vulnerable or disordered, the seeking and giving of consent must take place in the presence of the appropriate adult. Where a juvenile is under 14, the juvenile's parent or guardian must give consent (Annex A 2B).

Any intimate search must be carried out with proper regard to the sensitivity and vulnerability of the detainee (Annex A6).

A record must be made of the details of the search (Annex A7).

8.10 Strip Searches

8.10.1 What is a strip search?

A strip search is defined in Code C, Annex A9 as 'a search involving the removal of more than outer clothing'. Strip searches are not to be carried out routinely, but may only be carried out where the authorizing officer reasonably believes that a detainee may have concealed an article which the detainee would not be allowed to keep (Code C, Annex B10).

The officer carrying out the strip search must be of the same sex as the detainee; no-one of the opposite sex to the detainee may be present save for an appropriate adult who has been specifically requested by the detainee (Annex B11(b)).

Except in cases of urgency where there is a risk of serious harm to the detainee or others, whenever a strip search involves exposure of intimate body parts, there must be at least two people present other than the detainee, one of whom must be the appropriate adult where the search is of a juvenile or mentally vulnerable person unless either the search is urgent, or the juvenile signifies in the presence of the appropriate adult that he does not want the adult to be present during the search and the adult agrees. In such circumstances, a record must be made of the juvenile's decision and signed by the appropriate adult (Annex B11(c)).

As with intimate searches, the guidance makes it clear that proper regard must be had to the sensitivity and vulnerability of the detainee (Annex B11(d)).

8.11 Drug Testing

In some (but not all) police areas or stations within police areas, provisions are in force under s 63B and Code C 17 providing police with the powers to take a sample of urine or a non-intimate sample from a detained person in order to test whether he has Class A drugs in his body. The power is not a blanket one; the detainee must either have been arrested for or been charged with a 'trigger offence' (see Code C Note 17E) or an officer of at least the rank of inspector has reasonable grounds for suspecting that the misuse by that person of any specified Class A drug caused or contributed either to the trigger offence where the detainee has been arrested but not charged with that offence, or to any offence with which the detainee has been charged (whether a trigger offence or not).

The detainee can only be requested to provide the sample; it cannot be taken by force. However, he must be warned before the request is made that if he fails to provide a sample without good cause then he may be liable to prosecution (s 63B(4)(5)).

A detainee who is under the age of 18 can only be requested to provide a sample if he has been charged with an offence as set out in s 63B(2), (s 63B(3)). A sample cannot be requested of a juvenile under the age of 14.

Where the detainee is under 17 (18), the request for the sample, the warning of the consequences of refusal and (where applicable) the grounds for authorization, and the taking of the sample may not take place other than in the presence of an appropriate adult (s 63B(5A)).

An appropriate adult for the purposes of this section means:

- the person's parent or guardian or, if he is in the care of a local authority or voluntary organization, a person representing that authority or organization; or
- a social worker of a local authority; or
- if none of the above is available, any responsible person aged 18 or over who is not a police officer or a person employed by the police.

8.12 **Charging**

When the officer in charge of the investigation reasonably believes that there is sufficient evidence to provide a realistic prospect of conviction, he must immediately inform the custody officer who is responsible for considering whether the detainee should be charged.

Where the detainee is a juvenile or mentally disordered or mentally vulnerable, any resulting action shall be taken in the presence of the appropriate adult if they are present at the time, and if they are not, then the provisions must be complied with again in their presence when they arrive unless the detainee has previously been released (Code C 16.6). However, there is no power to detain a person and delay action under the charging procedures solely to await the presence of an appropriate adult. Neither can bail be refused or delayed simply because an appropriate adult is not available. Rather, 'reasonable efforts' should be made to give sufficient notice to the appropriate adult to enable that person to be present. If the appropriate adult is not or cannot be present, then the detainee should be released on bail to return at such a time when the appropriate adult is present unless bail is deemed unsuitable in the appropriate adult's absence (Note 16C).

When a juvenile or mentally disordered or mentally vulnerable detainee is charged, a written notice showing particulars of the offence, the precise offence in law with which he has been charged, the officer's name, and the case reference number should be given to the appropriate adult (Code C 16.3).

If, after the detainee has been charged with or informed that they may be prosecuted for an offence, an officer wants to tell them about any written statement or interview with another person relating to such an offence, the detainee shall either be handed a copy of the written statement or the content of the interview record brought to their attention. Where the detainee cannot read, the document shall be read to them. Where the detainee is a juvenile, mentally disordered, or otherwise mentally vulnerable, the appropriate adult shall also be given a copy, or the interview record brought to their attention (Code 16.4, 16.4A).

8.13 **Bail**

Following charge, a person must be released from police detention either with or without bail. Continued detention can only be authorized if one of the situations set out in s 38(1)(a) applies. For a juvenile detainee there are two further situations in which bail can be refused, and those are where the custody officer has reasonable grounds for believing that the juvenile ought to be detained in his own interests (s 38(1)(b)(ii)), or where the offence with which the person is charged is murder (s 38(1)(c)).

Where detention is authorized under this section that detention must be secured in local authority accommodation, not at the police station, unless one of the exceptions set out in s 38(6) applies. They are that:

- it is impracticable (for reasons that the custody officer must certify), or
- the juvenile is over 12 years old, no secure accommodation is available, and keeping him in other local authority accommodation would not be adequate to protect the public from serious harm.

What is meant by 'serious harm'?

'Serious harm' is not defined in the act, save in relation to a charge for a violent or sexual offence where it is construed as 'death or serious personal injury, whether physical or psychological, occasioned by further such offences committed by him' (s 38(6A)).

What is meant by 'impracticable'?

Note for Guidance 16D provides some assistance on the meaning of 'impractical' in s 38(6)(a). Neither a juvenile's behaviour, nor the nature of the offence, nor the unavailability of secure local authority accommodation would make a transfer to local authority accommodation 'impracticable'; impracticability relates to transport and travel arrangements. The lack of available secure accommodation may, however, be a relevant factor under s 38(6)(b) where the juvenile is over 12 years of age and where other local authority accommodation would not be adequate to protect the public from serious harm.

Where bail is granted, the release on bail cannot be delayed pending the arrival of an appropriate adult unless the absence of the appropriate adult gives rise to one of the grounds for continued detention after charge in accordance with s 38.

Practical Guidance

8.14 **Case Study 1**

PC Harvey arrests a 14-year-old juvenile for handling stolen goods and takes him before PS Morris, the custody officer. The juvenile refuses to provide any details in respect of his identity but states he is 18 years old. PS Morris considers he looks much younger. How should PS Morris deal with the prisoner?

As the prisoner appears to be under 17 (18) years then in the absence of clear evidence to the contrary and despite the stated age, PS Morris should treat him as a juvenile for the purpose of the Codes of Practice (Codes of Practice C 1.5).

PC Harvey wishes to interview the prisoner who still refuses to provide any personal details. The Social Services have indicated there will be a two-hour delay before a social worker can attend to act as an appropriate adult. John, a civilian employee at the station, has experience of working with underprivileged youths and runs a local youth centre. He offers to sit in at the interview as an appropriate adult. How should PS Morris respond to John's offer?

As John is employed by the police he is specifically excluded from acting in the role of appropriate adult. PS Morris should therefore decline the offer and delay the interview until a social worker can attend the station (Code C 1.7).

PC Harvey establishes the juvenile's name and his address; he also receives reliable information that other stolen goods can be found at the address. The officer obtains written authority from an inspector to search the premises. The juvenile now gives his personal details and requests that his parents are informed of his whereabouts. PC Harvey requests that notification be delayed pending the search of the premises. How should PC Harvey's request be dealt with?

The Codes of Practice requires the custody officer to inform the parents of a detained juvenile of the arrest, where the person is detained, and why the person was arrested. This right is in addition to the right not to be held incommunicado and cannot be interfered with. The custody officer should therefore make arrangements for the parents to be informed as soon as practicable. If the address were nearby, an option would be for officers to attend and inform the parents personally. The premises could then be searched under the authority of s 18 of PACE and little opportunity would have been provided for the occupants to dispose of any stolen goods.

8.15 Case Study 2

Police are called to a disturbance at a public house. On arrival they find that one of the pub windows has been smashed, as have several chairs, and a victim is on the ground being treated for obvious injuries by paramedics. Members of the public point out Nicolas Grabarczyk, a Romanian man who is stumbling around nearby muttering to himself. The police attempt to arrest him, but he puts up violent resistance. Eventually police manage to take him to the ground where he is restrained with force. He is handcuffed, placed in a van, and conveyed to the police station where he continues to act aggressively. The custody sergeant decides that he is a danger to himself and others; what should he do?

The custody sergeant should have in mind Code C, Note 9C. There could be a number of reasons for Grabarczyk's behaviour. His behaviour could be consistent with the effects of drink or drugs, he could have a mental disorder, or he could have sustained a head injury in the course either of the arrest or during the incident that preceded it. The custody sergeant should urgently seek medical assistance, whether by calling an ambulance or by seeking the advice of an appropriate healthcare professional. As there are concerns about the risk that Grabarczyk may present, the healthcare professional should be asked for advice about a safe and appropriate care plan, any risks or problems that the police should be aware of, and the need for safeguards—Code C 9.13. Such advice will be essential when carrying out a risk assessment in accordance with Code 3.6–3.10 and if contemplating—eg—the use of additional restraints in the cell under Code 8.2. Assuming that Grabarczyk is suffering from the effects of alcohol or drugs rather than a mental or physical condition that requires his removal to hospital, he should be checked every half-hour in accordance with Code C9.3 and Annex H.

A medical professional attends the station but is unable to communicate with Grabarczyk who is unable to speak or understand English. A Romanian-speaking police officer offers to assist; is he able to do so?

The custody officer should make arrangements for an interpreter to attend as soon as possible in accordance with Code C3.12. It may take some time however for the interpreter to arrive, and in the circumstances, provided that Grabarczyk agrees, a police officer may act as an interpreter.

The medical professional determines that Grabarczyk is suffering from nothing more than excess alcohol; he is fit to detain and will be fit to interview after a specified period. The interpreter has still not arrived, but the Romanian-speaking officer has been invaluable in explaining his rights to Grabarczyk including the right to free legal advice which Grabarczyk wishes to have. A solicitor attends. The interpreter does not. Grabarczyk has by now built up a good rapport with the Romanian-speaking officer and wants him to provide all further interpretation. Can he?

No. Code C 13.9 is clear; even though the suspect wishes the officer to continue to provide assistance, and even though a police officer or other member of police staff may provide interpretation, that assistance cannot be given where it is required for the purpose of obtaining legal advice. The custody officer will need to explain this to Grabarczyk and continue with efforts to secure an independent interpreter in accordance with national arrangements (Code C, Note 13A).

9

Evidence: Part VIII

Law and Commentary

9.1 Introduction

In early versions of the Act, important provisions relating to evidence in criminal proceedings could be found in both Part VII (Documentary Evidence in Criminal Proceedings) and Part VIII (Evidence in Criminal Proceedings—General). Now, however, Part VII is all but obsolete; s 69, which dealt with evidence derived from computer records, has been repealed, and s 68, which concerned the admissibility of documentary evidence, was replaced by ss 23 to 28 of the Criminal Justice Act 1998, which in turn has been replaced by corresponding provisions in the Criminal Justice Act 2003. The only remaining section in Part VII relates to proving the contents of a document by the production of a microfilm copy of it.

Part VIII by contrast retains enormous importance. Arguably, some of the sections contained within it, in particular ss 76 (confessions) and 78 (exclusion of unfair evidence) are among the most significant of the entire Act. Other sections deal with proof of previous convictions and acquittals where that evidence is admissible in evidence (ss 73–75), confessions, by the accused (s 76), a co-accused (s 76A), and special provisions dealing with confessions by the 'mentally handicapped' (s 77), as well as miscellaneous provisions that provide the courts with the power to exclude evidence (s 78), deal with the competence and compellability of the accused's spouse (ss 80–80A), and the necessity to give advance notice of expert evidence.

9.2 Convictions and Acquittals (Sections 73 to 75)

Section 73 provides one way of proving, where it is necessary to do so, that a person has been convicted or acquitted of an offence in the United Kingdom or a member state (other than the United Kingdom). The extension to convictions and acquittals in member states was made by amendments in the Coroners and Justice Act 2009. A 'member state' is not defined in PACE. It denotes a state that is party to treaties of the European Union: European Communities Act 1972, s 1(2) and Sch 1, Pt II.

Section 73 is not the only way by which such matters can be proved; s 73(4) makes it clear that:

> [t]he method of proving a conviction or acquittal authorised by this section shall be in addition to and not to the exclusion of any other authorised manner of proving a conviction or acquittal.

9.2.1 Whose convictions and acquittals can be proved?

The provisions apply both to the accused and to persons other than the accused. Further, where there is a joint trial of defendants for a joint offence, it has been held that analogous principles apply which permit a court to take account of its own finding that one accused is guilty (even if founded on a confession which would not ordinarily be admissible against a co-accused) and use that finding as evidence against the accused: *R v Hayter* [2005] UKHL 6; *Persad v Trinidad and Tobago* [2007] UKPC 51.

9.2.2 **How are convictions and acquittals proved?**

All that s 73 requires in relation to convictions or acquittals in the United Kingdom is the production of a signed certificate or memorandum of conviction or acquittal, together with proof that the person named in the certificate is the person whose conviction or acquittal is to be proved. In the case of convictions or acquittals in a member state, proof consists of a certificate, signed by the proper officer of the court (a person who would be the proper officer of the EU Court if that court were in the United Kingdom) where the conviction or acquittal took place, giving details of the offence, of the conviction or acquittal, and of any sentence.

9.2.3 **What does proof of a conviction or acquittal establish?**

Section 73 is silent as to what a conviction or acquittal may go to prove, or when such evidence may be admissible.

The Act provides no assistance in relation to either the effect of, or the admissibility of, an acquittal. Nor does the Act provide any help on when proof of a conviction may be admissible.

The Act does, however, deal with the *effect* of the admissibility of evidence of a conviction in s 74. By virtue of that section, where it is admissible to prove the conviction of a person, whether the accused or a person other than the accused, evidence of his conviction by or before a court in the United Kingdom or any other member state or a Service court (court-martial or Standing Civilian Court) outside the United Kingdom is admissible as proof that he did commit the offence for which he was convicted unless the contrary is proved.

Furthermore, not only can the fact of conviction be proved as set out in s 73, but (where admissible) the facts upon which the conviction was based can be adduced in evidence through either

(a) the contents of any document which is admissible as evidence of the conviction, and

(b) the contents of the information, complaint, indictment or charge-sheet on which the person in question was convicted or, in the case of a conviction of an offence by a court in a member state (other than the United Kingdom), any document produced in relation to the proceedings for that offence which fulfils a purpose similar to any such document or documents (s 75(1)).

It follows that s 74 is designed to be used where it is relevant and admissible to show that a person *committed* the offence in question, and not simply the fact that he was convicted of it (*R v Smith* [2007] EWCA Crim 2105). Proving the conviction is merely the means by which it may be proved that the person committed the offence.

9.2.4 **When will a conviction or acquittal be admissible?**

The admissibility of a conviction or acquittal is governed by the common law and by the bad character provisions of Part 11, Chapter 1 of The Criminal Justice Act 2003.

The circumstances in which evidence of an acquittal is admissible are likely to be rare. Where an earlier acquittal is arguably attributable to some aspect of the evidence which is common to both trials and/or otherwise relevant to an issue in the second, evidence of the acquittal may be admissible in the later trial. However, the acquittal is not conclusive proof of innocence and it does not mean that all relevant issues that arose in the previous matter for which the person was acquitted were resolved in his favour: *R v Terry* [2005] 2 Cr App R 7 (CA).

Where a conviction is directly relevant to proceedings as constituting a necessary ingredient or direct evidence of the offence alleged, it will be *prima facie* admissible. Otherwise, its admissibility will be governed by the bad character provisions of the Criminal Justice Act 2003. Where it is *prima facie* admissible, there remains a discretion in the judge to exclude it under s 78 (and account needs to be taken of the discretionary exclusionary provisions in the 2003 Act). The guiding principle in the exercise of that discretion was described at para 16 of *R v Derk Nathan Smith* [2007] EWCA Crim 2105, in which the court referred to case law summarized in *R v Kempster* [1989] 1 WLR 1125 (CA) and then went on to say:

> ...That line of cases indicates that section 74 should be sparingly applied. The reason is because the evidence that a now absent co-accused has pleaded guilty may carry in the minds of the jury enormous weight, but it is nevertheless evidence which cannot properly be tested in the trial of the remaining defendant. That is particularly so where the issue is such that the absent co-defendant who has pleaded guilty could not, or scarcely could, be guilty of the offence unless the present defendant were also. In both those situations the court needs to consider with considerable care whether the evidence of the conviction would have a disproportionate and unfair effect upon the trial. With those cases can be contrasted the kind of case in which there is little or no issue that the offence was committed, and the real live issue is whether the present defendant was party to it or not. In those circumstances, commonly, the pleas of guilty of other co-defendants can properly be admitted to reinforce the evidence that the offence did occur, leaving the jury independently to consider whether the guilt of the present defendant is additionally proved.

9.3 **Confessions (Sections 76, 76A, and 77)**

Section 76 deals with the important topic of the admissibility of confessions made by an accused person and their exclusion where the prosecution fail to prove that the confession was, or may have been obtained as a result of oppression, or anything else said or done which was likely to render that confession unreliable.

Although the best known, s 76 is not the only provision in the Act that is concerned with confession evidence. Section 76A, inserted by the Criminal Justice Act 2003, sets out parallel grounds for the admission or exclusion of confessions made by an accused person where their admission is sought by a co-accused rather than the prosecution. In practice, often submissions to exclude confessions are made, additionally or alternatively, under s 78.

Section 77 imposes a duty on the courts to direct themselves or a jury to treat a case that depends wholly or substantially upon the confession of a mentally handicapped person with caution.

9.3.1 **Section 76: confessions which the prosecution seek to adduce**

The wording of s 76 (1)–(3), taken together, define the scope of the section. It applies to 'where the prosecution proposes to give in evidence a confession made by an accused person'. It is prospective in its effect in that once the evidence is in, s 76 (and s 78) can have no application (although there may be other remedies such as appropriate directions by the judge or by exclusion under s 82(3)): *R v Sat-Bhambra* (1989) 88 Cr App R 55 (CA).

Insofar as it is relevant to a matter in issue in proceedings, the prosecution may adduce in evidence a confession made by an accused person. In order to be admissible, however, two further tests must be met, namely that the confession was not obtained either:

(a) by oppression of the person who made it; or
(b) in consequence of anything said or done which was likely, in the circumstances existing at the time, to render unreliable any confession which might be made in consequence thereof (s 76(2)).

Where there is an issue as to how the confession was obtained, whether that issue is raised by a party to the proceedings or by the court of its own motion, the prosecution are required to prove beyond reasonable doubt that the confession was not obtained in either of the ways set out in s 76(2).

What is perhaps surprising given that s 76(2)(b) is concerned with the reliability or otherwise of the confession, is that the *truth* of the confession is irrelevant to any determination. It may be thought that if a confession is true, then it must also be reliable. The Act is quite specific, however, that if the prosecution are unable to prove to the required standard that the confession has not been obtained through oppression or in consequence of anything said or done likely to render it unreliable then the court 'shall not' allow it to be admitted in evidence 'notwithstanding that it may be true'.

What is a confession?

A confession is defined in s 82(1) as including 'any statement wholly or partly adverse to the person who made it, whether made to a person in authority or not and whether made in words or otherwise'.

It can be seen from the above definition that a confession for the purposes of ss 76 to 77 does not necessarily mean 'I did it'; rather, any statement, whether made orally or in writing, in which a person amongst other things admits relevant matters that are adverse to him is a confession. However, the question is to be judged at the time that the statement was made and s 76 does not apply to a statement intended by the maker to be exculpatory or neutral and which appears to be so on its face, but which becomes damaging to him at the trial because, for example, its contents can then be shown to be evasive or false or inconsistent with the maker's evidence on oath: *R v Hasan (Aytach)* [2005] UKHL 22.

What is meant by oppression?

Section 76(8) states that oppression 'includes torture, inhuman or degrading treatment, and the use or threat of violence (whether or not amounting to torture)', but conduct need not be so extreme to be oppressive; for example, in *R v Paris, Abdullai and Miller* (1993) 97 Cr App R 99, prolonged questioning of the defendant in which accusations were made in a hostile and intimidating way, where the strength of the prosecution evidence was exaggerated to the suspect and where the police made it clear that they would continue to question him until he agreed with their version of events, was found by the Court of Appeal to have amounted to oppression; and in *R v Mushtaq* [2005] 1 WLR 1513, HL, the House of Lords approved the definition of oppression used in *R v Prager* [1972] 1 WLR 260, CA as:

> ...questioning which by its nature, duration or other circumstances (including the fact of custody) excites hopes (such as the hope of release) or fears, or so affects the mind of the subject that his will crumbles and he speaks when otherwise he would have stayed silent.

What is meant by 'in consequence of anything said or done'?

Two obvious points arise when considering whether a confession should be excluded under s 76(2)(b). First, the confession must have been obtained 'in consequence' of something said or done by another. In other words, there must be a link between the making of the confession and the thing said or done. Secondly, whatever the thing said or done, it must have been something which was likely 'in the circumstances existing at the time' to render the subsequent confession unreliable.

This second factor means, of course, that the particular characteristics of the defendant have to be taken into account as well as, for example, the type of offence about which he is being questioned. So, for example, a court may conclude that to tell a suspect that he will have to remain in police custody until a matter is resolved is unlikely to render unreliable a confession subsequently made by a man of reasonable firmness and intelligence who is being questioned about a serious offence, but a different conclusion may be reached where the 'threat' is made to a vulnerable person who is being questioned about something comparatively minor.

It should also be noted that the 'circumstances existing at the time' could include omitting to do something. In particular, a failure to comply with the Codes of Practice may result in the exclusion of evidence; so where an interview takes place ('something said or done') where there had been a failure to caution the defendant or to make him aware of his right to legal advice ('the circumstances existing at the time'), that omission may well be judged likely to render unreliable any confession which is made as a result.

What is meant by 'likely ... to render unreliable'?

The Act means what it says. The court is only required to look at whether the oppression or the thing said or done was *likely* to make the subsequent confession unreliable. Unreliability is both fact and, indeed, defendant specific. It does not have to be shown that the confession was in fact unreliable, or that it was untrue. The truth or otherwise of the confession made is irrelevant to the test that has to be adopted.

General propositions

The following observations about s 76 can be made;

- the definition of oppression in s 76(8) is not exhaustive; a wider test as set out in *R v Mushtaq* has been approved (see para 9.3.1);
- there must be a link under s 76(2)(b) between the thing said and done and the confession subsequently made;
- the 'circumstances existing at the time' can include the physical and mental characteristics of the defendant—whether or not known to the police at the time—and can include omitting to do something that should have been done under the Act or Codes as well as doing something that the police are prohibited from doing;
- not every breach of the Act or Codes will render a subsequent confession unreliable—all the circumstances existing at the time will be considered;
- the courts are only concerned with whether the conduct is likely to render a confession made as a result unreliable. It is not necessary to show that it did render the confession unreliable; nor is it relevant to consider whether or not the confession is or might be true.

Note, however, that a confession may be excluded under s 78 as well as under s 76.

9.3.2 **Section 76A**

This new section, inserted by s 128(1) of the Criminal Justice Act 2003, sets out identical tests governing the admissibility of a confession made by one defendant which a co-defendant wishes to adduce in his own case. The only difference is that whereas under s 76(2) the prosecution must satisfy the tests beyond reasonable doubt, a co-defendant need only do so on the balance of probabilities. In the same case, therefore, a confession may be ruled inadmissible for use by the prosecution, but admissible for a co-defendant. The remedy in such a situation is likely to be either an application by the defendant whose confession it is for a ruling excluding the admission of that evidence under s 78, or an application for separate trials. Note that a co-defendant's confession is not admissible under s 76A where the co-defendant has pleaded guilty and therefore is not party to the trial, although it may be admitted under the hearsay provisions of the Criminal Justice Act 2003 (*R v Finch* [2007] EWCA Crim 36).

9.3.3 **What are the consequences when a confession is ruled inadmissible?**

Where a confession has been ruled inadmissible, no further reference to it can be made in the course of the trial unless made by the person whose confession it is. Subsection 4(a) of both s 76 and s 76A does, however, permit evidence to be given of any facts discovered as a result of the confession. So, for example, if a suspect being questioned about a burglary admits that he committed the offence and tells the police where he has hidden the stolen property, and where that confession is excluded under s 76, evidence may be given that the police went to a particular location and recovered the stolen items, but no evidence can be given to explain how it was that they came to discover that that was the place at which the items would be found, as to do so would be to admit evidence of the confession which has been excluded, and this is inadmissible unless adduced by the defendant himself (s 76(5)).

Subsection 4(b) also allows evidence of an excluded confession to be given where it is relevant to show that the defendant 'speaks, writes or expresses himself in a particular way'. This will, however, be limited to only so much as is strictly necessary. So, for example, it might be relevant and necessary to demonstrate that the defendant speaks with a particular accent; sufficient of a tape-recorded interview which has otherwise been excluded might be played for this purpose, but the early uncontentious introductory comments may be sufficient.

9.3.4 **Confessions by mentally handicapped persons**

Where a case depends 'wholly or substantially' upon a confession made by a mentally handicapped person, and where that confession was not made in the presence of an 'independent person', the judge must warn the jury that there is a special need for caution before convicting the accused in reliance on the confession, and explain why (s 77(1)).

Where there is no jury (eg in summary proceedings before the magistrates or where a judge is sitting without a jury), the court must treat the case as one in which there is a special need for caution before convicting the accused on his confession (s 77(2), (2A)).

What is meant by 'mentally handicapped'

Mentally handicapped is defined in s 77(3) as '...a state of arrested or incomplete development of mind which includes significant impairment of intelligence and social functioning'. It is not clear why the term 'mentally handicapped' was used rather than 'mentally vulnerable' or 'mentally disordered' as in Code C; however, it is likely that someone who met the test of mentally vulnerable or mentally disordered as set out in Code C, Note 1G, would equally meet the definition of mentally handicapped in s 77(3).

What does 'wholly or substantially' mean?

The test to be applied has been held to be whether the prosecution case is substantially less strong without the confession than it is with it (*R v Campbell* [1995] 1 Cr App R 522 (CA)).

Who is 'an independent person'?

The 'independent person' must, for the purposes of the Act, be someone other than the person to whom the confession was made. Where, therefore, a confession was made to a friend, that person cannot be an independent person (*R v Bailey* [1995] 2 Cr App R 262, (CA)); neither can a police officer or person 'employed for or engaged on, police purposes', who are specifically excluded from the definition by s 77(3). An independent person is most likely to be the appropriate adult. A solicitor can also be an independent person for these purposes when attending the police station in a professional capacity.

9.4 Exclusion of Unfair Evidence (Sections 78 and 82(3))

Tucked towards the back of the Act under the heading 'Miscellaneous' is perhaps the best known of all the provisions in the entire Act; and arguably the one with the most far-reaching effects. Section 78(1) states that:

> [I]n any proceedings the court may refuse to allow evidence on which the prosecution proposes to rely to be given if it appears to the court that, having regard to all the circumstances, including the circumstances in which the evidence was obtained, the admission of the evidence would have such an adverse effect on the fairness of the proceedings that the court ought not to admit it.

9.4.1 **When will Section 78 apply?**

No hard and fast rules can be applied to the application of this section; nor are there any uniform guidelines. The power to exclude evidence under this section of the Act is entirely a matter for the discretion of the judge in the particular circumstances of the case before him. In each case, the test that the judge has to apply is whether or not the admission of the evidence would have such an adverse effect on the fairness of the case that he ought not to admit the challenged evidence. Unfortunately for the defendant, this produces uncertain results; what is considered unfair by one judge may be considered fair by another. The Court of Appeal will not interfere with the exercise of a judge's discretion under s 78 save where it can be shown that he has failed to exercise his discretion or has otherwise come to a conclusion that no reasonable judge could have reached. Moreover, although there is voluminous case law on s 78, as each case turns on its own facts caution must be applied in seeking to gain any general guidance as to what may or may not be excluded under this section; the same conduct or misconduct may result in different conclusions depending on all the other circumstances in the case. Some general points can, however, be made:

- Like s 76, s 78 is prospective in its effect because it allows the court to 'refuse to allow evidence on which the prosecution proposes to rely to be given'. It therefore has no application once the evidence is in.
- Section 78 can be invoked in respect of any evidence irrespective of any other powers that the court has to exclude evidence. So, for example, a court may refuse to exclude the evidence of a confession under s 76 but nevertheless exclude it under s 78.
- Evidence is frequently sought to be excluded where it has been obtained in breach of the Act or Codes. Not every breach will, however, result in exclusion; normally the breach must have been significant and substantial. However, it is the effect of the breach that is important rather than the nature of it. So, a failure to caution prior to interviewing a vulnerable person in police detention for the first time may lead to the exclusion of that interview, whereas a court would be less likely to hold that the failure to caution had such an adverse effect on the fairness of proceedings that evidence was required to be excluded where the person interviewed was a career criminal with substantial experience of police interviews.
- Although not designed to penalize officers who fail to act appropriately, s 78 specifically permits a court to look at how evidence was obtained. Evidence may therefore be excluded where it was obtained improperly or through unlawful means. However there is no obligation to exclude such evidence, merely a discretion to do so.
- Although evidence will often be excluded where a police officer has acted in bad faith, there is no requirement for bad faith to be shown although it will undoubtedly form part of the 'circumstances of the case'. The circumstances

of the particular case may call for the exclusion of evidence even where the officer has acted entirely properly. So, for example, where a mentally disordered person was interviewed in the absence of an appropriate adult, the evidence obtained therein might be excluded even though the officer had no reason to suspect that the person was mentally disordered.

• The judge must consider fairness to both sides.

• Although no reference is made to the burden or standard of proof, and although the court may raise s 78 of its own motion, almost invariably the issue is raised by the defence. The practical effect is that the burden of persuading the judge first that there is an issue to be decided and then that the issue should be resolved by the exclusion of the evidence rests on the defence.

9.4.2 Section 82(3)

The power to exclude evidence at common law is unaffected by Part VIII PACE. Section 82(3) states:

> Nothing in this Part of this Act shall prejudice any power of a court to exclude evidence (whether by preventing questions from being put or otherwise) at its discretion.

In practice, given the wide scope of s 76 and s 78 to deal with most challenges to the fairness of evidence, the applicability of s 82(3) is limited. However, it remains of importance where evidence can no longer be challenged through s 76 and s 78 because it is already in: see *R v Sat-Bhambra* (referred to at para 9.3.1). This may arise where, after the evidence has been admitted, new grounds emerge for challenging it. The discretion is wide enough to capture any ground of challenge that might have been made under s 76 and s 78. In *Scott v R* [1989] AC 1242 (PC), the Privy Council held that the 'discretion of a judge to ensure a fair trial includes a power to exclude the admission of a deposition' but that the discretion should only be exercised where 'directions cannot ensure a fair trial'. The discretion is often described as permitting the exclusion of evidence that is more prejudicial than probative (which, though an old formulation, suggests the modern concept of proportionality): see eg *Neilly v R* [2012] UKPC 12 at para 10.

9.5 Time for Taking an Accused's Evidence (Section 79)

Section 79 provides that where the defendant is to give evidence and will also be calling one or more further witnesses of fact, then the defendant should give his evidence first 'unless the court in its discretion otherwise directs'.

9.6 **Evidence from an Accused's Spouse or Civil Partner (Section 80)**

Under s 80(2), the husband, wife, or civil partner of a defendant is compellable to give evidence on behalf of his or her spouse or civil partner unless either:

(a) he or she is also charged in any proceedings, or
(b) the offence with which his or her spouse or civil partner is charged is a 'specified offence' that is one which:
  • involves an assault on, or injury or threat of injury to the wife, husband, or civil partner, or to a person who was under 16 at the material time;
  • is a sexual offence alleged to have been committed against a person who was at the material time under 16;
  • consists of attempting or conspiring to commit, or of aiding, abetting, counselling, or procuring or inciting the commission of any such offence as set out above.

Where the offence is a 'specified offence' then a spouse or civil partner *is* compellable to give evidence on behalf of any other person charged in the proceedings (that is, not his or her spouse or civil partner), or on behalf of the prosecution.

What is meant by 'charged in any proceedings'?

This means charged *and* liable to be convicted. So it does not apply where, for example, the person has already pleaded guilty, or where a charge has been subsequently withdrawn (s 80(4A)). Note that the term used in s 80(4) is 'any proceedings', not 'the same proceedings'. So, for example, if for whatever reason separate trials had been ordered of a husband and wife who were each charged with an offence or offences arising out of the same facts, then one spouse could not be compelled to give evidence for or against the other.

The proceedings must be criminal proceedings including those taking place before a court-martial whether in the United Kingdom or elsewhere.

What is 'the material time'?

The material time is the date upon which the specified offence was alleged to have been committed.

What is meant by 'a sexual offence'?

Section 80(7) defines a sexual offence as an offence under the Protection of Children Act 1978, or Part I of the Sexual Offences Act 2003.

Is a spouse compellable if divorced?

Section 80(5) provides that once divorced, a person is treated as if they had never been married and is therefore compellable to give evidence for or against their former spouse. It makes no difference whether the offence about which they are giving evidence occurred before, during or after the end of the marriage. Section 80(5A) sets out an identical rule for civil partners.

Section 80 has no applicability at all to common-law partners or to second or subsequent wives in a polygamous marriage.

Under s 80A, the prosecution are prohibited from making any comment about the failure of a compellable witness to give evidence on behalf of their spouse or civil partner.

9.7 Expert Evidence (Section 81)

Section 81 provides for the making of rules requiring a party to criminal proceedings to make advance disclosure to the other side of any expert evidence proposed to be adduced, and prohibiting such evidence from being adduced where advance disclosure has not been made as required except with the leave of the court.

The current rules made under this section are to be found in Part 33 of the Criminal Procedure Rules 2010.

Practical Guidance

9.8 Case Study 1 (confessions; section 76)

DC Potts is investigating a recent theft in which a large amount of cash has been stolen. The owner of the property from where the cash was taken informs DC Potts that he suspects that his 18-year-old son, James, may have been responsible. DC Potts establishes that James has a drug addiction and has stolen from his father in the past, but that the police were not informed on those occasions. James does not live at his father's address but does have keys and visits frequently. DC Potts asks the victim to notify him should he become aware of James' whereabouts.

The next day, the victim attends the police station with James and informs DC Potts that James was indeed responsible for the theft and produces a handwritten note of confession, made by the father but signed by James. DC Potts takes a statement from the victim who explains how he informed James that unless he told the truth he would no longer provide him with financial support, following which James 'broke down' and admitted stealing the money to spend on drugs. DC Potts arrests James, but at a subsequent interview and following advice from his solicitor, James remains silent.

Is the evidence so far obtained sufficient to found a conviction?

An admission does not have to be made to a police officer to come within the ambit of s 82(1); the signed note was adverse to James and, therefore, would amount to a confession within the meaning of the Act. However, whilst admissible evidence under s 76(1), the confession would be vulnerable to an application under s 76(2)(b); in this particular case, James' admission appears to have been made under threat of losing the allowance provided by his father; it could be argued that this was the only reason why he made the confession he did and that for this reason it is unreliable and should be excluded. DC Potts would accordingly be well advised to undertake further enquiries to obtain additional evidence—for example a s 18(1) search of James' address.

9.9 Case Study 2 (interviews; breach of Code E; section 78)

PC Smith has arrested Vazon, a seasoned criminal with many convictions, for burglary and interviews him on tape. PC Smith properly cautions Vazon at the start of the interview, which is conducted in accordance with the Codes of Practice. Vazon gives 'no comment' answers to all questions asked. After 30 minutes, Vazon asks for a break. On resuming the interview PC Smith introduces all those present, but forgets to remind Vazon that he is still under caution. In this second part of the interview, Vazon has a change of heart and unexpectedly admits the offence. Later, when transcribing the tape, PC Smith realizes his mistake.

Has there been a breach of the Codes?

Code E 4.14 states that after any break in an interview the suspect should be reminded that he is under caution, and if there is any doubt the caution must be given in full again. PC Smith's failure to remind Vazon of the caution is a breach of the Code.

Would the interview be excluded?

Any breach of the Codes may give rise to an application for the exclusion of evidence thereafter obtained under either s 76 (confessions) or s 78 (fairness); however it is not every breach that would result in such a determination. Determinations in reported cases in which s 76 or s 78 arguments have arisen are very fact specific. Much depends on the nature of the breach, the reason for it, the motivation of the officer and facts known about the offender. Here, Vazon is an experienced criminal who has been interviewed many times before and who could therefore be expected to be well aware of his rights. There is no suggestion that his admissions in this case were made other than voluntarily and fully in the knowledge that they could be used against him. It is unlikely therefore that any application to exclude would succeed. The outcome may well be different if the person interviewed is an inexperienced or vulnerable suspect, particularly if they do not have the benefit of legal advice.

As well as reminding the suspect of the caution, it is also good practice for the interviewing officer to demonstrate that nothing untoward has occurred during a break that might encourage a suspect to make admissions, by summarizing on tape the reasons for the break and asking the suspect whether he agrees with the accuracy of the summary given (Code E Note 4G).

9.10 Case Study 3 (interviews; sections 76 and 78)

PC Jones, a relatively inexperienced officer is dealing with Brown who is in custody for burglary. Brown has a large number of convictions and is a prolific offender. PC Jones had reasonable grounds to arrest Brown, but with nothing else the evidence is weak and unlikely to lead to a conviction. PC Jones carries out an interview during which Brown, who is not represented, says nothing. Feeling somewhat frustrated, PC Jones calls a break and decides to apply some pressure. During the break, when the recording equipment is turned off, PC Jones informs Brown that the results of a forensic examination have just been received and that Brown's fingerprints have been identified inside the premises where the burglary occurred. In fact, no forensic evidence to connect Brown to the offence has been obtained. Brown, who did in fact commit the offence, believes that the game is up and makes a full admission during the second part of the interview and identifies where the proceeds of the burglary are hidden; these are subsequently recovered.

Was PC Jones' tactic justified?

Whilst there is no obligation to disclose any information pre-interview, it is important that neither the suspect nor his legal representative (if any) are misled. In this case, PC Jones has told a blatant lie. Brown has made a full admission, but only as a consequence of the deceit practised upon him by PC Jones.

Would the admissions subsequently made be excluded?

Brown's admissions are adverse to him and accordingly amount to a confession within the meaning of s 82(1). Challenging the improper conduct by way of s 76 is not altogether straightforward. It could be argued that PC Jones' actions in deceiving Brown would be likely to render the resulting confession unreliable. The fact that the proceeds of the burglary were subsequently found at the location stated by Brown would not retrospectively legitimize PC Jones' actions or provide any real grounds to rebut such an application. Conversely, it might be argued that only a person who had actually committed the offence would fall for the trick; so Brown's confession is not unreliable although it was obtained in an underhand and improper manner. Nor does the trick fall squarely within what is usually meant by oppression. However, s 78 looks like a better fit.

It allows the court to exclude evidence 'having regard to all the circumstances, including the circumstances in which the evidence was obtained' where 'the admission of the evidence would have such an adverse effect on the fairness of the proceedings that the court ought not to admit it'. The fact that the evidence was obtained in an improper fashion does not mean that the court is bound to exclude the evidence. However, the courts take a dim view of such behaviour by the police. In this case, where PC Jones has been shown to have told a deliberate lie, there would undoubtedly be adverse criticism by the court of his actions. (Such comments may well be disclosable in other cases in which PC Jones gives evidence. Disciplinary proceedings may well follow.) Further, the evidence may well be excluded by the judge.

If the admissions are excluded, would the evidence found as a result of those admissions also be excluded?

The fact that the admissions are excluded does not automatically render the evidence of the finding of the proceeds of the crime as a result of those admissions inadmissible (s 76(4)(a)); however, no mention could be made of how the police came by the items, and, in the absence of any forensic link to Brown, such evidence would not strengthen the prosecution's case against him.

Contents of Appendices

Appendix 4

Appendix 5

Appendix 9

Appendix 1

Police and Criminal Evidence Act 1984

1984 Chapter 60

Supplementary

PART III
ARREST

PART IV
DETENTION

Detention—conditions and duration

Act

Detention—miscellaneous

PART V
QUESTIONING AND TREATMENT OF PERSONS BY POLICE

Part VI
Codes of Practice—General

Act

Part VII
Documentary Evidence in Criminal Proceedings

Part VIII
Evidence in Criminal Proceedings—General

Convictions and acquittals

Confessions

Miscellaneous

Part VIII
Supplementary

Part IX
Police Complaints and Discipline

The Police Complaints Authority

Handling of complaints etc.

Amendments of Discipline Provisions

PART X
POLICE—GENERAL

PART XI
MISCELLANEOUS AND SUPPLEMENTARY

SCHEDULES

Act

Police and Criminal Evidence Act 1984

1984 Chapter 60

An Act to make further provision in relation to the powers and duties of the police, persons in police detention, criminal evidence, police discipline and complaints against the police; to provide for arrangements for obtaining the views of the community on policing and for a rank of deputy chief constable; to amend the law relating to the Police Federations and Police Forces and Police Cadets in Scotland; and for connected purposes.

[31st October 1984]

BE IT ENACTED by the Queen's most Excellent Majesty, by and with the advice and consent of the Lords Spiritual and Temporal, and Commons, in this present Parliament assembled, and by the authority of the same, as follows:—

PART I

POWERS TO STOP AND SEARCH

1 Power of constable to stop and search persons, vehicles etc

(1) A constable may exercise any power conferred by this section—

    (a) in any place to which at the time when he proposes to exercise the power the public or any section of the public has access, on payment or otherwise, as of right or by virtue of express or implied permission; or

    (b) in any other place to which people have ready access at the time when he proposes to exercise the power but which is not a dwelling.

(2) Subject to subsection (3) to (5) below, a constable—

    (a) may search—

        (i) any person or vehicle;

        (ii) anything which is in or on a vehicle,

        for stolen or prohibited articles[, any article to which subsection (8A) below applies or any firework to which subsection (8B) below applies][1]; and

    (b) may detain a person or vehicle for the purpose of such a search.

(3) This section does not give a constable power to search a person or vehicle or anything in or on a vehicle unless he has reasonable grounds for suspecting that he will find stolen or prohibited articles [or [, any article to which subsection (8A) below applies or any firework to which subsection (8B) below applies][2][3].

(4) If a person is in a garden or yard occupied with and used for the purposes of a dwelling or on other land so occupied and used, a constable may not search him in the exercise of the power conferred by this section unless the constable has reasonable grounds for believing—

    (a) that he does not reside in the dwelling; and

---

[1] Amended by SOCAPA 2005, s 115(1), (2).

[2] Amended by SOCAPA 2005, s 115(1), (3).

[3] Amended by Criminal Justice Act 1988, s 140(1)(a)(ii).

Act

(b) that he is not in the place in question with the express or implied permission of a person who resides in the dwelling.

(5) If a vehicle is in a garden or yard occupied with and used for the purposes of a dwelling or on other land so occupied and used, a constable may not search the vehicle or anything in or on it in the exercise of the power conferred by this section unless he has reasonable grounds for believing—

(a) that the person in charge of the vehicle does not reside in the dwelling; and

(b) that the vehicle is not in the place in question with the express or implied permission of a person who resides in the dwelling.

(6) If in the course of such a search a constable discovers an article which he has reasonable grounds for suspecting to be a stolen or prohibited article[, an article to which subsection (8A) below applies or a firework to which subsection (8B) below applies]⁴, he may seize it.

(7) An article is prohibited for the purposes of this Part of this Act if it is—

(a) an offensive weapon; or

(b) an article—

   (i) made or adapted for use in the course of or in connection with an offence to which this sub-paragraph applies; or

   (ii) intended by the person having it with him for such use by him or by some other person.

(8) The offences to which subsection (7)(b)(i) above applies are—

(a) burglary;

(b) theft;

(c) offences under section 12 of the Theft Act 1968 (taking motor vehicle or other conveyance without authority); [...]⁵

[(d) fraud (contrary to section 1 of the Fraud Act 2006)];⁶ and

(e) offences under section 1 of the Criminal Damage Act 1971 (destroying or damaging property)]⁷.

[(8A) This subsection applies to any article in relation to which a person has committed, or is committing or is going to commit an offence under section 139 of the Criminal Justice Act 1988]⁸.]⁹

[(8B) This subsection applies to any firework which a person possesses in contravention of a prohibition imposed by fireworks regulations.

(8C) In this section—

(a) 'firework' shall be construed in accordance with the definition of 'fireworks' in section 1(1) of the Fireworks Act 2003; and

(b) 'fireworks regulations' has the same meaning as in that Act.]¹⁰

(9) In this Part of this Act 'offensive weapon' means any article—

(a) made or adapted for use for causing injury to persons; or

(b) intended by the person having it with him for such use by him or by some other person.

---

⁴ Amended by SOCAPA 2005, s 115(1), (4).
⁵ Repealed by the Criminal Justice Act 2003, s 332, Sch 37, Pt 1.
⁶ Substituted by Fraud Act 2006, Sch 1, para 21.
⁷ Amended by the Criminal Justice Act 2003, s 1(2).
⁸ Amended by LASPOA 2012, Sch 26, para 3.
⁹ Amended by the Criminal Justice Act 1988, s 140(1)(c).
¹⁰ Amended by SOCAPA 2005, s 115(1), (5).

2 Provisions relating to search under section 1 and other powers

(1) A constable who detains a person or vehicle in the exercise—
    (a) of the power conferred by section 1 above; or
    (b) of any other power—
        (i) to search a person without first arresting him; or
        (ii) to search a vehicle without making an arrest,
    need not conduct a search if it appears to him subsequently—
        (i) that no search is required; or
        (ii) that a search is impracticable.

(2) If a constable contemplates a search, other than a search of an unattended vehicle, in the exercise—
    (a) of the power conferred by section 1 above; or
    (b) of any other power, except the power conferred by section 6 below and the power conferred by section 27(2) of the Aviation Security Act 1982—
        (i) to search a person without first arresting him; or
        (ii) to search a vehicle without making an arrest,
    it shall be his duty, subject to subsection (4) below, to take reasonable steps before he commences the search to bring to the attention of the appropriate person—
        (i) if the constable is not in uniform, documentary evidence that he is a constable; and
        (ii) whether he is in uniform or not, the matters specified in subsection (3) below;
    and the constable shall not commence the search until he has performed that duty.

(3) The matters referred to in subsection (2)(ii) above are—
    (a) the constable's name and the name of the police station to which he is attached;
    (b) the object of the proposed search;
    (c) the constable's grounds for proposing to make it; and
    (d) the effect of section 3(7) or (8) below, as may be appropriate.

(4) A constable need not bring the effect of section 3(7) or (8) below to the attention of the appropriate person if it appears to the constable that it will not be practicable to make the record in section 3(1) below.

(5) In this section 'the appropriate person' means—
    (a) if the constable proposes to search a person, that person; and
    (b) if he proposes to search a vehicle, or anything in or on a vehicle, the person in charge of the vehicle.

(6) On completing a search of an unattended vehicle or anything in or on such a vehicle in the exercise of any such power as is mentioned in subsection (2) above a constable shall leave a notice—
    (a) stating that he has searched it;
    (b) giving the name of the police station to which he is attached;
    (c) stating that an application for compensation for any damage caused by the search may be made to that police station; and
    (d) stating the effect of section 3(8) below.

(7) The constable shall leave the notice inside the vehicle unless it is not reason-
     ably practicable to do so without damaging the vehicle.

(8) The time for which a person or vehicle may be detained for the purposes of such
     a search is such time as is reasonably required to permit a search to be carried out
     either at the place where the person or vehicle was first detained or nearby.

(9) Neither the power conferred by section 1 above nor any other power to detain
     and search a person without first arresting him or to detain and search a vehi-
     cle without making an arrest is to be construed—
     (a) as authorising a constable to require a person to remove any of his cloth-
          ing in public other than an outer coat, jacket or gloves; or
     (b) as authorising a constable not in uniform to stop a vehicle.

(10) This section and section 1 above apply to vessels, aircraft and hovercraft as
     they apply to vehicles.

3 Duty to make records concerning searches

(1) Where a constable has carried out a search in the exercise of any such power as
     is mentioned in section 2(1) above, other than a search—
     (a) under section 6 below; or
     (b) under section 27(2) of the Aviation Security Act 1982,
     [a record shall be made][11] in writing unless it is not practicable to do so.

[(2) If a record of a search is required to be made by subsection (1) above—
     (a) in a case where the search results in a person being arrested and taken to a
          police station, the constable shall secure that the record is made as part of
          the person's custody record;
     (b) in any other case, the constable shall make the record on the spot, or, if that is
          not practicable, as soon as practicable after the completion of the search.][12]

(3)–(5) [...][13]

(6) The record of a search of a person or a vehicle—
     (a) shall state—
          (i)   the object of the search;
          (ii) the grounds for making it;
          (iii) the date and time when it was made;
          (iv) the place where it was made;
          [(v) except in the case of a search of an unattended vehicle, the ethnic
                origins of the person searched or the person in charge of the vehicle
                searched (as the case may be); and][14]
     (b) shall identify the constable [who carried out the search][15].

[(6A) The requirement in subsection (6)(a)(v) above for a record to state a person's
     ethnic origins is a requirement to state—
     (a) the ethnic origins of the person described by the person, and
     (b) if different, the ethnic origins of the person as perceived by the constable.][16]

---

[11] Amended by the Crime and Security Act 2010, s1(2).
[12] Amended by the Crime and Security Act 2010, s 1(2).
[13] Repealed by the Crime and Security Act 2010, s 1(4).
[14] s 3(6)(a)(v) substituted for s 3(6)(a)(v) and (vi) by the Crime and Security Act 2010, s 1(5)(a).
[15] Amended by the Crime and Security Act 2010, s 1(5)(b).
[16] Amended by the Crime and Security Act 2010, s 1(6).

(7) [If a record of a search of a person has been made under this section,][17] the
     person who was searched shall be entitled to a copy of the record if he asks for
     one before the end of the period specified in subsection (9) below.

(8) If—

     (a) the owner of a vehicle which has been searched or the person who was in charge
          of the vehicle at the time when it was searched asks for a copy of the record of
          the search before the end of the period specified in subsection (9) below; and

     [(b) a record of the search of the vehicle has been made under this section,][18]

     the person who made the request shall be entitled to a copy.

(9) The period mentioned in subsections (7) and (8) above is the period of [3
     months][19] beginning with the date on which the search was made.

(10) The requirements imposed by this section with regard to records of searches of
     vehicles shall apply also to records of searches of vessels, aircraft and hovercraft.

4 Road checks

(1) This section shall have effect in relation to the conduct of road checks by police
     officers for the purpose of ascertaining whether a vehicle is carrying—

     (a) a person who has committed an offence other than a road traffic offence or
          a [vehicle][20] excise offence;

     (b) a person who is a witness to such an offence;

     (c) a person intending to commit such an offence; or

     (d) a person who is unlawfully at large.

(2) For the purposes of this section a road check consists of the exercise in a locality
     of the power conferred by [section 163 of the Road Traffic Act 1988][21] in such a
     way as to stop during the period for which its exercise in that way in that local-
     ity continues all vehicles or vehicles selected by any criterion.

(3) Subject to subsection (5) below, there may only be such a road check if a police
     officer of the rank of superintendent or above authorises it in writing.

(4) An officer may only authorise a road check under subsection (3) above—

     (a) for the purpose specified in subsection (1)(a) above, if he has reasonable
          grounds—

          (i)   for believing that the offence is [an indictable offence][22]; and

          (ii) for suspecting that the person is, or is about to be, in the locality in
                which vehicles would be stopped if the road check were authorised;

     (b) for the purpose specified in subsection (1)(b) above, if he has reasonable
          grounds for believing that the offence is [an indictable offence][23];

     (c) for the purpose specified in subsection (1)(c) above, if he has reasonable
          grounds—

          (i)   for believing that the offence would be [an indictable offence][24]; and

          (ii) for suspecting that the person is, or is about to be, in the locality in
                which vehicles would be stopped if the road check were authorised;

---

[17] Amended by the Crime and Security Act 2010, s 1(7).
[18] Amended by the Crime and Security Act 2010, s 1(8).
[19] Amended by the Crime and Security Act 2010, s 1(9).
[20] Amended by the Vehicle Excise and Registration Act 1994, s 63, Sch 3, para 19.
[21] Amended by the Road Traffic (Consequential Provisions) Act 1988, s 4, Sch 3, para 27.
[22] Amended by SOCAPA 2005, s 111, Sch 7, Pt 3, para 43(1), (2)(a).
[23] ibid.
[24] ibid.

(d) for the purpose specified in subsection (1)(d) above, if he has reasonable grounds for suspecting that the person is, or is about to be, in that locality.

Act

(5) An officer below the rank of superintendent may authorise such a road check if it appears to him that it is required as a matter of urgency for one of the purposes specified in subsection (1) above.

(6) If an authorisation is given under subsection (5) above, it shall be the duty of the officer who gives it—

(a) to make a written record of the time at which he gives it; and

(b) to cause an officer of the rank of superintendent or above to be informed that it has been given.

(7) The duties imposed by subsection (6) above shall be performed as soon as it is practicable to do so.

(8) An officer to whom a report is made under subsection (6) above may, in writing, authorise the road check to continue.

(9) If such an officer considers that the road check should not continue, he shall record in writing—

(a) the fact that it took place; and

(b) the purpose for which it took place.

(10) An officer giving an authorisation under this section shall specify the locality in which vehicles are to be stopped.

(11) An officer giving an authorisation under this section, other than an authorisation under subsection (5) above—

(a) shall specify a period, not exceeding seven days, during which the road check may continue; and

(b) may direct that the road check—

(i) shall be continuous; or

(ii) shall be conducted at specified times,

during that period.

(12) If it appears to an officer of the rank of superintendent or above that a road check ought to continue beyond the period for which it has been authorised he may, from time to time, in writing specify a further period, not exceeding seven days, during which it may continue.

(13) Every written authorisation shall specify—

(a) the name of the officer giving it;

(b) the purpose of the road check; and

(c) the locality in which vehicles are to be stopped.

(14) The duties to specify the purposes of a road check imposed by subsections (9) and (13) above include duties to specify any relevant [indictable offence][25].

(15) Where a vehicle is stopped in a road check, the person in charge of the vehicle at the time when it is stopped shall be entitled to obtain a written statement of the purpose of the road check if he applies for such a statement not later than the end of the period of twelve months from the day on which the vehicle was stopped.

(16) Nothing in this section affects the exercise by police officers of any power to stop vehicles for purposes other than those specified in subsection (1) above.

---

[25] Amended by SOCAPA 2005, s 111, Sch 7, Pt 3, para 43(1), (2)(b).

5 Reports of recorded searches and of road checks

(1)   Every annual report—

[(a) under section 22 of the Police Act 1996; or][26]

(b) made by the Commissioner of Police of the Metropolis,

shall contain information—

    (i) about searches recorded under section 3 above which have been carried out in the area to which the report relates during the period to which it relates; and

    (ii) about road checks authorised in that area during that period under section 4 above.

(1A) [...][27]

(2)   The information about searches shall not include information about specific searches but shall include—

(a) the total numbers of searches in each month during the period to which the report relates—

    (i) for stolen articles;

    (ii) for offensive weapons [or articles to which section 1(8A) above applies][28]; and

    (iii) for other prohibited articles;

(b) the total number of persons arrested in each such month in consequence of searches of each of the descriptions specified in paragraph (a)(i) to (iii) above.

(3)   The information about road checks shall include information—

(a) about the reason for authorising each road check; and

(b) about the result of each of them.

6 Statutory undertakers etc

(1)   A constable employed by statutory undertakers may stop, detain and search any vehicle before it leaves a goods area included in the premises of the statutory undertakers.

[(1A) Without prejudice to any powers under subsection (1) above, a constable employed [by the [British Transport Police Authority][29]][30] may stop, detain and search any vehicle before it leaves a goods area which is included in the premises of any successor of the British Railways Board and is used wholly or mainly for the purposes of a relevant undertaking.][31]

(2)   In this section 'goods area' means any area used wholly or mainly for the storage or handling of goods[, and 'successor of the British Railways Board' and 'relevant undertaking' have the same meaning as in the Railways Act 1993 (Consequential Modifications) Order 1999][32].

(3)–(4) [...][33]

---

[26] Amended by the Police Act 1996, s 103, Sch 7, para 34.

[27] Repealed by SOCAPA 2005, ss 59, 174(2), Sch 4, paras 43, 44, Sch 17, Pt 2.

[28] Amended by the Criminal Justice Act 1988, s 140(2).

[29] Amended by SI 2004/1573, art 12(1)(e).

[30] Amended by the Transport Act 2000, s 217, Sch 18, Pt 1, para 5.

[31] Amended by SI 1999/1998, art 5(1).

[32] Amended by SI 1999/1998, art 5(2).

[33] Repealed by the Energy Act 2004, s 197(9), Sch 23, Pt 1.

7 Part I—supplementary

(1)   The following enactments shall cease to have effect—

(a) section 8 of the Vagrancy Act 1824;

(b) section 66 of the Metropolitan Police Act 1839;

(c) section 11 of the Canals (Offences) Act 1840;

(d) section 19 of the Pedlars Act 1871;

(e) section 33 of the County of Merseyside Act 1980; and

(f) section 42 of the West Midlands County Council Act 1980.

(2)   There shall also cease to have effect—

(a) so much of any enactment contained in an Act passed before 1974, other than—

(i) an enactment contained in a public general Act; or

(ii) an enactment relating to statutory undertakers,

as confers power on a constable to search for stolen or unlawfully obtained goods; and

(b) so much of any enactment relating to statutory undertakers as provides that such a power shall not be exercisable after the end of a specified period.

(3)   In this Part of this Act 'statutory undertakers' means persons authorised by any enactment to carry on any railway, light railway, road transport, water transport, canal, inland navigation, dock or harbour undertaking.

PART II

POWERS OF ENTRY, SEARCH AND SEIZURE

Search warrants

8 Power of justice of the peace to authorise entry and search of premises

(1)   If on an application made by a constable a justice of the peace is satisfied that there are reasonable grounds for believing—

(a) that [an indictable offence][34] has been committed; and

(b) that there is material on premises [mentioned in subsection (1A) below][35] which is likely to be of substantial value (whether by itself or together with other material) to the investigation of the offence; and

(c) that the material is likely to be relevant evidence; and

(d) that it does not consist of or include items subject to legal privilege, excluded material or special procedure material; and

(e) that any of the conditions specified in subsection (3) below applies [in relation to each set of premises specified in the application][36],

he may issue a warrant authorising a constable to enter and search the premises.

[(1A) The premises referred to in subsection (1)(b) above are—

(a) one or more sets of premises specified in the application (in which case the application is for a 'specific premises warrant'); or

---

[34] Amended by SOCAPA 2005, s 111, Sch 7, Pt 3, para 43(1), (3).

[35] Amended by SOCAPA 2005, s 113(1), (2), (3)(a).

[36] Amended by SOCAPA 2005, s 113(1), (2), (3)(b).

(b) any premises occupied or controlled by a person specified in the application, including such sets of premises as are so specified (in which case the application is for an 'all premises warrant').

(1B) If the application is for an all premises warrant, the justice of the peace must also be satisfied—

(a) that because of the particulars of the offence referred to in paragraph (a) of subsection (1) above, there are reasonable grounds for believing that it is necessary to search premises occupied or controlled by the person in question which are not specified in the application in order to find the material referred to in paragraph (b) of that subsection; and

(b) that it is not reasonably practicable to specify in the application all the premises which he occupies or controls and which might need to be searched.][37]

[(1C) The warrant may authorise entry to and search of premises on more than one occasion if, on the application, the justice of the peace is satisfied that it is necessary to authorise multiple entries in order to achieve the purpose for which he issues the warrant.

(1D) If it authorises multiple entries, the number of entries authorised may be unlimited, or limited to a maximum.][38]

(2) A constable may seize and retain anything for which a search has been authorised under subsection (1) above.

(3) The conditions mentioned in subsection (1)(e) above are—

(a) that it is not practicable to communicate with any person entitled to grant entry to the premises;

(b) that it is practicable to communicate with a person entitled to grant entry to the premises but it is not practicable to communicate with any person entitled to grant access to the evidence;

(c) that entry to the premises will not be granted unless a warrant is produced;

(d) that the purpose of a search may be frustrated or seriously prejudiced unless a constable arriving at the premises can secure immediate entry to them.

(4) In this Act 'relevant evidence', in relation to an offence, means anything that would be admissible in evidence at a trial for the offence.

(5) The power to issue a warrant conferred by this section is in addition to any such power otherwise conferred.

[(6) This section applies in relation to a relevant offence (as defined in section 28D(4) of the Immigration Act 1971) as it applies in relation to [an indictable offence][39]][40].

[(7) Section 4 of the Summary Jurisdiction (Process) Act 1881 (execution of process of English courts in Scotland) shall apply to a warrant issued on the application of an officer of Revenue and Customs under this section by virtue of section 114 below.][41]

---

[37] Amended by SOCAPA 2005, s 113(1), (2), (4).
[38] Amended by SOCAPA 2005, s 114(1), (2).
[39] Amended by SOCAPA 2005, s 111, Sch 7, Pt 3, para 43(1), (3).
[40] Amended by the Immigration and Asylum Act 1999, s 169(1), Sch 14, para 80(1), (2).
[41] Added by Finance Act 2007, s 86.

Act

9 Special provisions as to access

(1)   A constable may obtain access to excluded material or special procedure material for the purposes of a criminal investigation by making an application under Schedule 1 below and in accordance with that Schedule.

(2)   Any Act (including a local Act) passed before this Act under which a search of premises for the purposes of a criminal investigation could be authorised by the issue of a warrant to a constable shall cease to have effect so far as it relates to the authorisation of searches—
   (a) for items subject to legal privilege; or
   (b) for excluded material; or
   (c) for special procedure material consisting of documents or records other than documents.

[(2A) Section 4 of the Summary Jurisdiction (Process) Act 1881 (c 24) (which includes provision for the execution of process of English courts in Scotland) and section 29 of the Petty Sessions (Ireland) Act 1851 (c 93) (which makes equivalent provision for execution in Northern Ireland) shall each apply to any process issued by a circuit judge[42] under Schedule 1 to this Act as it applies to process issued by a magistrates' court under the Magistrates' Courts Act 1980 (c 43).][43]

10 Meaning of 'items subject to legal privilege'

(1)   Subject to subsection (2) below, in this Act 'items subject to legal privilege' means—
   (a) communications between a professional legal adviser and his client or any person representing his client made in connection with the giving of legal advice to the client;
   (b) communications between a professional legal adviser and his client or any person representing his client or between such an adviser or his client or any such representative and any other person made in connection with or in contemplation of legal proceedings and for the purposes of such proceedings; and
   (c) items enclosed with or referred to in such communications and made—
      (i)   in connection with the giving of legal advice; or
      (ii) in connection with or in contemplation of legal proceedings and for the purposes of such proceedings,
      when they are in the possession of a person who is entitled to possession of them.

(2)   Items held with the intention of furthering a criminal purpose are not items subject to legal privilege.

11 Meaning of 'excluded material'

(1)   Subject to the following provisions of this section, in this Act 'excluded material' means—
   (a) personal records which a person has acquired or created in the course of any trade, business, profession or other occupation or for the purposes of any paid or unpaid office and which he holds in confidence;

---

[42] Prospectively amended by the Courts Act 2003, s 65, Sch 4, para 5.
[43] Amended by the Criminal Justice and Police Act 2001, s 86(1).

    (b) human tissue or tissue fluid which has been taken for the purposes of diagnosis or medical treatment and which a person holds in confidence;

    (c) journalistic material which a person holds in confidence and which consists—
      (i) of documents; or
      (ii) of records other than documents.

(2) A person holds material other than journalistic material in confidence for the purposes of this section if he holds it subject—

    (a) to an express or implied undertaking to hold it in confidence; or

    (b) to a restriction on disclosure or an obligation of secrecy contained in any enactment, including an enactment contained in an Act passed after this Act.

(3) A person holds journalistic material in confidence for the purposes of this section if—

    (a) he holds it subject to such an undertaking, restriction or obligation; and

    (b) it has been continuously held (by one or more persons) subject to such an undertaking, restriction or obligation since it was first acquired or created for the purposes of journalism.

12 Meaning of 'personal records'

(1) In this Part of this Act 'personal records' means documentary and other records concerning an individual (whether living or dead) who can be identified from them and relating—

    (a) to his physical or mental health;

    (b) to spiritual counselling or assistance given or to be given to him; or

    (c) to counselling or assistance given or to be given to him, for the purposes of his personal welfare, by any voluntary organisation or by any individual who—

      (i) by reason of his office or occupation has responsibilities for his personal welfare; or

      (ii) by reason of an order of a court has responsibilities for his supervision.

13 Meaning of 'journalistic material'

(1) Subject to subsection (2) below, in this Act 'journalistic material' means material acquired or created for the purposes of journalism.

(2) Material is only journalistic material for the purposes of this Act if it is in the possession of a person who acquired or created it for the purposes of journalism.

(3) A person who receives material from someone who intends that the recipient shall use it for the purposes of journalism is to be taken to have acquired it for those purposes.

14 Meaning of 'special procedure material'

(1) In this Act 'special procedure material' means—

    (a) material to which subsection (2) below applies; and

    (b) journalistic material, other than excluded material.

(2) Subject to the following provisions of this section, this subsection applies to material, other than items subject to legal privilege and excluded material, in the possession of a person who—

    (a) acquired or created it in the course of any trade, business, profession or other occupation or for the purpose of any paid or unpaid office; and

      (b) holds it subject—

          (i)   to an express or implied undertaking to hold it in confidence; or

          (ii) to a restriction or obligation such as is mentioned in section 11(2)(b) above.

(3)   Where material is acquired—

      (a) by an employee from his employer and in the course of his employment; or

      (b) by a company from an associated company,

    it is only special procedure material if it was special procedure material immediately before the acquisition.

(4)   Where material is created by an employee in the course of his employment, it is only special procedure material if it would have been special procedure material had his employer created it.

(5)   Where material is created by a company on behalf of an associated company, it is only special procedure material if it would have been special procedure material had the associated company created it.

(6)   A company is to be treated as another's associated company for the purposes of this section if it would be so treated under [section 449 of the Corporation Tax Act 2010].[44]

15 Search warrants—safeguards

(1)   This section and section 16 below have effect in relation to the issue to constables under any enactment, including an enactment contained in an Act passed after this Act, of warrants to enter and search premises; and an entry on or search of premises under a warrant is unlawful unless it complies with this section and section 16 below.

(2)   Where a constable applies for any such warrant, it shall be his duty—

      (a) to state—

          (i)   the ground on which he makes the application; [...][45]

          (ii)   the enactment under which the warrant would be issued; [and][46]

          [(iii) if the application is for a warrant authorising entry and search on more than one occasion, the ground on which he applies for such a warrant, and whether he seeks a warrant authorising an unlimited number of entries, or (if not) the maximum number of entries desired;][47]

      [(b) to specify the matters set out in subsection (2A)below; and][48]

      (c) to identify, so far as is practicable, the articles or persons to be sought.

[(2A) The matters which must be specified pursuant to subsection (2)(b) above are—

      [(a) if the application relates to one or more sets of premises specified in the application, each set of premises which it is desired to enter and search;][49]

---

[44] Words substituted by Corporation Tax Act 2010, Sch 1, para 193 (1 April 2010, and has effect for corporation tax purposes for accounting periods ending on or after that day, and for income tax and capital gains tax purposes, for the tax year 2010–11 and subsequent tax years, subject to transitional provisions and savings specified in 2010: Sch 2).

[45] Repealed by SOCAPA 2005, ss 114(1), (3), (4)(a), 174(2), Sch 17, Pt 2.

[46] Amended by SOCAPA 2005, s 114(1), (3), (4)(b).

[47] Amended by SOCAPA 2005, s 114(1), (3), (4)(c).

[48] Amended by SOCAPA 2005, s 113(1), (5), (6).

[49] Amended by SI 2005/3496, art 7(1), (2)(a).

(b) [if the application relates to any premises occupied or controlled by a person specified in the application—][50]

    (i)   as many sets of premises which it is desired to enter and search as it is reasonably practicable to specify;

    (ii) the person who is in occupation or control of those premises and any others which it is desired to enter and search;

    (iii) why it is necessary to search more premises than those specified under sub-paragraph (i); and

    (iv) why it is not reasonably practicable to specify all the premises which it is desired to enter and search.][51]

(3)   An application for such a warrant shall be made ex parte and supported by an information in writing.

(4)   The constable shall answer on oath any question that the justice of the peace or judge hearing the application asks him.

(5)   A warrant shall authorise an entry on one occasion only [unless it specifies that it authorises multiple entries][52].

[(5A) If it specifies that it authorises multiple entries, it must also specify whether the number of entries authorised is unlimited, or limited to a specified maximum.][53]

(6)   A warrant—

    (a) shall specify—

       (i)   the name of the person who applies for it;

       (ii) the date on which it is issued;

       (iii) the enactment under which it is issued; and

      [(iv) each set of premises to be searched, or (in the case of an all premises warrant) the person who is in occupation or control of premises to be searched, together with any premises under his occupation or control which can be specified and which are to be searched; and][54]

    (b) shall identify, so far as is practicable, the articles or persons to be sought.

[(7)   Two copies shall be made of a [warrant][55] (see section 8(1A)(a) above) which specifies only one set of premises and does not authorise multiple entries; and as many copies as are reasonably required may be made of any other kind of warrant.][56]

(8)   The copies shall be clearly certified as copies.

16 Execution of warrants

(1)   A warrant to enter and search premises may be executed by any constable.

(2)   Such a warrant may authorise persons to accompany any constable who is executing it.

---

[50] Amended by SI 2005/3496, art 7(1), (2)(b).

[51] Amended by SOCAPA 2005, s 113(1), (5), (7).

[52] Amended by SOCAPA 2005, s 114(1), (3), (5).

[53] Amended by SOCAPA 2005, s 114(1), (3), (6).

[54] Amended by SOCAPA 2005, s 113(1), (5), (8).

[55] Amended by SI 2005/3496, art 7(1), (3).

[56] Amended by SOCAPA 2005, s 114(1), (3), (7).

[(2A) A person so authorised has the same powers as the constable whom he accompanies in respect of—

(a) the execution of the warrant, and

(b) the seizure of anything to which the warrant relates.

(2B) But he may exercise those powers only in the company, and under the supervision, of a constable.][57]

(3) Entry and search under a warrant must be within [three months][58] from the date of its issue.

[(3A) If the warrant is an all premises warrant, no premises which are not specified in it may be entered or searched unless a police officer of at least the rank of inspector has in writing authorised them to be entered.][59]

[(3B) No premises may be entered or searched for the second or any subsequent time under a warrant which authorises multiple entries unless a police officer of at least the rank of inspector has in writing authorised that entry to those premises.][60]

(4) Entry and search under a warrant must be at a reasonable hour unless it appears to the constable executing it that the purpose of a search may be frustrated on an entry at a reasonable hour.

(5) Where the occupier of premises which are to be entered and searched is present at the time when a constable seeks to execute a warrant to enter and search them, the constable—

(a) shall identify himself to the occupier and, if not in uniform, shall produce to him documentary evidence that he is a constable;

(b) shall produce the warrant to him; and

(c) shall supply him with a copy of it.

(6) Where—

(a) the occupier of such premises is not present at the time when a constable seeks to execute such a warrant; but

(b) some other person who appears to the constable to be in charge of the premises is present,

subsection (5) above shall have effect as if any reference to the occupier were a reference to that other person.

(7) If there is no person present who appears to the constable to be in charge of the premises, he shall leave a copy of the warrant in a prominent place on the premises.

(8) A search under a warrant may only be a search to the extent required for the purpose for which the warrant was issued.

(9) A constable executing a warrant shall make an endorsement on it stating—

(a) whether the articles or persons sought were found; and

(b) whether any articles were seized, other than articles which were sought[,][61] [and, unless the warrant is a [...][62] warrant specifying one set of premises

---

[57] Amended by the Criminal Justice Act 2003, s 2.

[58] Amended by SOCAPA 2005, s 114(1), (8)(a).

[59] Amended by SOCAPA 2005, s 113(1), (9)(a).

[60] Amended by SOCAPA 2005, s 114(1), (8)(b).

[61] Amended by SOCAPA 2005, s 113(1), (9)(b).

[62] Repealed by SI 2005/3496, art 8.

only, he shall do so separately in respect of each set of premises entered and searched, which he shall in each case state in the endorsement][63].

[(10) A warrant shall be returned to the appropriate person mentioned in subsection (10A) below—

    (a) when it has been executed; or

    (b) in the case of a specific premises warrant which has not been executed, or an all premises warrant, or any warrant authorising multiple entries, upon the expiry of the period of three months referred to in subsection (3) above or sooner.

(10A) The appropriate person is—

    (a) if the warrant was issued by a justice of the peace, the designated officer for the local justice area in which the justice was acting when he issued the warrant;

    (b) if it was issued by a judge, the appropriate officer of the court from which he issued it.][64]

(11) A warrant which is returned under subsection (10) above shall be retained for 12 months from its return—

    (a) by the [designated officer for the local justice area][65], if it was returned under paragraph (i) of that subsection; and

    (b) by the appropriate officer, if it was returned under paragraph (ii).

(12) If during the period for which a warrant is to be retained the occupier of [premises][66] to which it relates asks to inspect it, he shall be allowed to do so.

Entry and search without search warrant

17 Entry for purpose of arrest etc

(1) Subject to the following provisions of this section, and without prejudice to any other enactment, a constable may enter and search any premises for the purpose—

    (a) of executing—

        (i) a warrant of arrest issued in connection with or arising out of criminal proceedings; or

        (ii) a warrant of commitment issued under section 76 of the Magistrates' Courts Act 1980;

    (b) of arresting a person for an [indictable][67] offence;

    (c) of arresting a person for an offence under—

        (i) section 1 (prohibition of uniforms in connection with political objects) [...][68] of the Public Order Act 1936;

        (ii) any enactment contained in sections 6 to 8 or 10 of the Criminal Law Act 1977 (offences relating to entering and remaining on property);

      [(iii) section 4 of the Public Order Act 1986 (fear or provocation of violence);][69]

---

[63] Amended by SOCAPA 2005, s 113(1), (9)(b).

[64] s 16(1)–(10A) substituted for s 16(10) by SOCAPA 2005, s 114(1), (8)(c).

[65] Amended by the Courts Act 2003, s 109(1), Sch 8, para 281(1), (3).

[66] Amended by SOCAPA 2005, s 113(1), (9)(c).

[67] Amended by SOCAPA 2005, s 111, Sch 7, Pt 3, para 43(1), (4).

[68] Repealed by the Public Order Act 1986, s 40(3), Sch 3.

[69] Amended by the Public Order Act 1986, s 40(2), Sch 2, para 7.

Act

[(iiia) section 4 (driving etc when under influence of drink or drugs) or 163 (failure to stop when required to do so by constable in uniform) of the Road Traffic Act 1988;

(iiib) section 27 of the Transport and Works Act 1992 (which relates to offences involving drink or drugs);][70]

[(iv) section 76 of the Criminal Justice and Public Order Act 1994 (failure to comply with interim possession order);][71]

[(v) any of sections 4, 5, 6(1) and (2), 7 and 8(1) and (2) of the Animal Welfare Act 2006 (offences relating to the prevention of harm to animals);][72]

[(vi)] section 144 of the Legal Aid, Sentencing and Punishment of Offenders Act 2012 (squatting in a residential building).][73]

[(ca) of arresting, in pursuance of section 32(1A) of the Children and Young Persons Act 1969, any child or young person who has been remanded [to local authority accommodation or youth detention accommodation under section 91 of the Legal Aid, Sentencing and Punishment of Offenders Act 2012][74];

[(caa) of arresting a person for an offence to which section 61 of the Animal Health Act 1981 applies;][75]

(cb) of recapturing any person who is, or is deemed for any purpose to be, unlawfully at large while liable to be detained—

   (i) in a prison, remand centre, young offender institution or secure training centre, or

   (ii) in pursuance of [section 92 of the Powers of Criminal Courts (Sentencing) Act 2000][76] (dealing with children and young persons guilty of grave crimes), in any other place;][77]

(d) of recapturing [any person whatever][78] who is unlawfully at large and whom he is pursuing; or

(e) of saving life or limb or preventing serious damage to property.

(2) Except for the purpose specified in paragraph (e) of subsection (1) above, the powers of entry and search conferred by this section—

(a) are only exercisable if the constable has reasonable grounds for believing that the person whom he is seeking is on the premises; and

(b) are limited, in relation to premises consisting of two or more separate dwellings, to powers to enter and search—

   (i) any parts of the premises which the occupiers of any dwelling comprised in the premises use in common with the occupiers of any other such dwelling; and

---

[70] Amended by SOCAPA 2005, s 111, Sch 7, Pt 4, para 58(a).

[71] Amended by the Criminal Justice and Public Order Act 1994, s 168(2), Sch 10, para 53(a).

[72] Added by Animal Welfare Act 2006, s 24 (6 April 2007; SI 2007/499).

[73] Amended by LASPOA 2012, s 144(8)(a).

[74] Amended by LASPOA 2012, Sch 12, para 21 (3 December 2012 subject to savings as specified in SI 2012/2906 art 7(2)).

[75] Amended by SOCAPA 2005, s 111, Sch 7, Pt 4, para 58(b).

[76] Amended by the Powers of Criminal Courts (Sentencing) Act 2000, s 165(1), Sch 9, para 95.

[77] Amended by the Prisoners (Return to Custody) Act 1995, s 2(1).

[78] ibid.

(ii) any such dwelling in which the constable has reasonable grounds for believing that the person whom he is seeking may be.

(3) The powers of entry and search conferred by this section are only exercisable for the purposes specified in subsection (1)(c)(ii) [, (iv) or (vi)]⁷⁹ above by a constable in uniform.

(4) The power of search conferred by this section is only a power to search to the extent that is reasonably required for the purpose for which the power of entry is exercised.

(5) Subject to subsection (6) below, all the rules of common law under which a constable has power to enter premises without a warrant are hereby abolished.

(6) Nothing in subsection (5) above affects any power of entry to deal with or prevent a breach of the peace.

18 Entry and search after arrest

(1) Subject to the following provisions of this section, a constable may enter and search any premises occupied or controlled by a person who is under arrest for an [indictable]⁸⁰ offence, if he has reasonable grounds for suspecting that there is on the premises evidence, other than items subject to legal privilege, that relates—
  (a) to that offence; or
  (b) to some other [indictable]⁸¹ offence which is connected with or similar to that offence.

(2) A constable may seize and retain anything for which he may search under subsection (1) above.

(3) The power to search conferred by subsection (1) above is only a power to search to the extent that is reasonably required for the purpose of discovering such evidence.

(4) Subject to subsection (5) below, the powers conferred by this section may not be exercised unless an officer of the rank of inspector or above has authorised them in writing.

[(5) A constable may conduct a search under subsection (1)—
  (a) before the person is taken to a police station or released on bail under section 30A, and
  (b) without obtaining an authorisation under subsection (4),
  if the condition in subsection (5A) is satisfied.

(5A) The condition is that the presence of the person at a place (other than a police station) is necessary for the effective investigation of the offence.]⁸²

(6) If a constable conducts a search by virtue of subsection (5) above, he shall inform an officer of the rank of inspector or above that he has made the search as soon as practicable after he has made it.

(7) An officer who—
  (a) authorises a search; or
  (b) is informed of a search under subsection (6) above, shall make a record in writing—

---

⁷⁹ Amended by LASPOA 2012, s 144(8)(b).
⁸⁰ Amended by SOCAPA 2005, s 111, Sch 7, Pt 3, para 43(1), (5).
⁸¹ ibid.
⁸² Amended by the Criminal Justice Act 2003, s 12, Sch 1, paras 1, 2.

Act

     (i) of the grounds for the search; and

    (ii) of the nature of the evidence that was sought.

(8) If the person who was in occupation or control of the premises at the time of the search is in police detention at the time the record is to be made, the officer shall make the record as part of his custody record.

Seizure etc

19 General power of seizure etc

(1) The powers conferred by subsections (2), (3) and (4) below are exercisable by a constable who is lawfully on any premises.

(2) The constable may seize anything which is on the premises if he has reasonable grounds for believing—

    (a) that it has been obtained in consequence of the commission of an offence; and

    (b) that it is necessary to seize it in order to prevent it being concealed, lost, damaged, altered or destroyed.

(3) The constable may seize anything which is on the premises if he has reasonable grounds for believing—

    (a) that it is evidence in relation to an offence which he is investigating or any other offence; and

    (b) that it is necessary to seize it in order to prevent the evidence being concealed, lost, altered or destroyed.

(4) The constable may require any information which is [stored in any electronic form][83] and is accessible from the premises to be produced in a form in which it can be taken away and in which it is visible and legible [or from which it can readily be produced in a visible and legible form][84] if he has reasonable grounds for believing—

    (a) that—

       (i) it is evidence in relation to an offence which he is investigating or any other offence; or

      (ii) it has been obtained in consequence of the commission of an offence; and

    (b) that it is necessary to do so in order to prevent it being concealed, lost, tampered with or destroyed.

(5) The powers conferred by this section are in addition to any power otherwise conferred.

(6) No power of seizure conferred on a constable under any enactment (including an enactment contained in an Act passed after this Act) is to be taken to authorise the seizure of an item which the constable exercising the power has reasonable grounds for believing to be subject to legal privilege.

20 Extension of powers of seizure to computerised information

(1) Every power of seizure which is conferred by an enactment to which this section applies on a constable who has entered premises in the exercise of a power conferred by an enactment shall be construed as including a power to require any

---

[83] Amended by the Criminal Justice and Police Act 2001, s 70, Sch 2, Pt 2, para 13(1)(a), (2)(a).
[84] Amended by the Criminal Justice and Police Act 2001, s 70, Sch 2, Pt 2, para 13(1)(b), (2)(a).

information [stored in any electronic form][85] and accessible from the premises to be produced in a form in which it can be taken away and in which it is visible and legible [or from which it can readily be produced in a visible and legible form][86].

(2) This section applies—

    (a) to any enactment contained in an Act passed before this Act;

    (b) to sections 8 and 18 above;

    (c) to paragraph 13 of Schedule 1 to this Act; and

    (d) to any enactment contained in an Act passed after this Act.

21 Access and copying

(1) A constable who seizes anything in the exercise of a power conferred by any enactment, including an enactment contained in an Act passed after this Act, shall, if so requested by a person showing himself—

    (a) to be the occupier of premises on which it was seized; or

    (b) to have had custody or control of it immediately before the seizure,

    provide that person with a record of what he seized.

(2) The officer shall provide the record within a reasonable time from the making of the request for it.

(3) Subject to subsection (8) below, if a request for permission to be granted access to anything which—

    (a) has been seized by a constable; and

    (b) is retained by the police for the purpose of investigating an offence,

    is made to the officer in charge of the investigation by a person who had custody or control of the thing immediately before it was so seized or by someone acting on behalf of such a person, the officer shall allow the person who made the request access to it under the supervision of a constable.

(4) Subject to subsection (8) below, if a request for a photograph or copy of any such thing is made to the officer in charge of the investigation by a person who had custody or control of the thing immediately before it was so seized, or by someone acting on behalf of such a person, the officer shall—

    (a) allow the person who made the request access to it under the supervision of a constable for the purpose of photographing or copying it; or

    (b) photograph or copy it, or cause it to be photographed or copied.

(5) A constable may also photograph or copy, or have photographed or copied, anything which he has power to seize, without a request being made under subsection (4) above.

(6) Where anything is photographed or copied under subsection (4)(b) above, the photograph or copy shall be supplied to the person who made the request.

(7) The photograph or copy shall be so supplied within a reasonable time from the making of the request.

(8) There is no duty under this section to grant access to, or to supply a photograph or copy of, anything if the officer in charge of the investigation for the purposes of which it was seized has reasonable grounds for believing that to do so would prejudice—

    (a) that investigation;

---

[85] Amended by the Criminal Justice and Police Act 2001, s 70, Sch 2, Pt 2, para 13(1)(a), (2)(a).

[86] Amended by the Criminal Justice and Police Act 2001, s 70, Sch 2, Pt 2, para 13(1)(b), (2)(a).

Act

(b) the investigation of an offence other than the offence for the purposes of investigating which the thing was seized; or

(c) any criminal proceedings which may be brought as a result of—

    (i) the investigation of which he is in charge; or

    (ii) any such investigation as is mentioned in paragraph (b) above.

[(9) The references to a constable in subsections (1), (2), (3)(a) and (5) include a person authorised under section 16(2) to accompany a constable executing a warrant.][87]

22 Retention

(1) Subject to subsection (4) below, anything which has been seized by a constable or taken away by a constable following a requirement made by virtue of section 19 or 20 above may be retained so long as is necessary in all the circumstances.

(2) Without prejudice to the generality of subsection (1) above—

    (a) anything seized for the purposes of a criminal investigation may be retained, except as provided by subsection (4) below—

        (i) for use as evidence at a trial for an offence; or

        (ii) for forensic examination or for investigation in connection with an offence; and

    (b) anything may be retained in order to establish its lawful owner, where there are reasonable grounds for believing that it has been obtained in consequence of the commission of an offence.

(3) Nothing seized on the ground that it may be used—

    (a) to cause physical injury to any person;

    (b) to damage property;

    (c) to interfere with evidence; or

    (d) to assist in escape from police detention or lawful custody,

may be retained when the person from whom it was seized is no longer in police detention or the custody of a court or is in the custody of a court but has been released on bail.

(4) Nothing may be retained for either of the purposes mentioned in subsection (2)(a) above if a photograph or copy would be sufficient for that purpose.

(5) Nothing in this section affects any power of a court to make an order under section 1 of the Police (Property) Act 1897.

[(6) This section also applies to anything retained by the police under section 28H(5) of the Immigration Act 1971.][88]

[(7) The reference in subsection (1) to anything seized by a constable includes anything seized by a person authorised under section 16(2) to accompany a constable executing a warrant.][89]

Supplementary

23 Meaning of 'premises' etc

In this Act—

'premises' includes any place and, in particular, includes—

---

[87] Amended by the Criminal Justice Act 2003, s 12, Sch 1, paras 1, 3.

[88] Amended by the Immigration and Asylum Act 1999, s 169(1), Sch 14, para 80(1), (3).

[89] Amended by the Criminal Justice Act 2003, s 12, Sch 1, paras 1, 4.

(a)   any vehicle, vessel, aircraft or hovercraft;

(b)   any offshore installation; [...][90]

[(ba)   any renewable energy installation;][91]

(c)   any tent or movable structure; [...][92]

'offshore installation' has the meaning given to it by section 1 of the Mineral
Workings (Offshore Installations) Act 1971;

['renewable energy installation' has the same meaning as in Chapter 2 of Part 2
of the Energy Act 2004][93].

PART III
ARREST

[24 Arrest without warrant: constables

(1) A constable may arrest without a warrant—

    (a) anyone who is about to commit an offence;

    (b) anyone who is in the act of committing an offence;

    (c) anyone whom he has reasonable grounds for suspecting to be about to
commit an offence;

    (d) anyone whom he has reasonable grounds for suspecting to be committing
an offence.

(2) If a constable has reasonable grounds for suspecting that an offence has been
committed, he may arrest without a warrant anyone whom he has reasonable
grounds to suspect of being guilty of it.

(3) If an offence has been committed, a constable may arrest without a warrant—

    (a) anyone who is guilty of the offence;

    (b) anyone whom he has reasonable grounds for suspecting to be guilty of it.

(4) But the power of summary arrest conferred by subsection (1), (2) or (3) is exercisable only if the constable has reasonable grounds for believing that for any of
the reasons mentioned in subsection (5) it is necessary to arrest the person in
question.

(5) The reasons are—

    (a) to enable the name of the person in question to be ascertained (in the case
where the constable does not know, and cannot readily ascertain, the person's name, or has reasonable grounds for doubting whether a name given
by the person as his name is his real name);

    (b) correspondingly as regards the person's address;

    (c) to prevent the person in question—

       (i)   causing physical injury to himself or any other person;

       (ii)   suffering physical injury;

       (iii) causing loss of or damage to property;

       (iv) committing an offence against public decency (subject to subsection
(6)); or

       (v)   causing an unlawful obstruction of the highway;

---

[90] Amended by the Energy Act 2004, s 103(2)(a).

[91] Amended by the Energy Act 2004, s 103(2)(a).

[92] Repealed by the Energy Act 2004, s 197(9), Sch 23, Pt 1.

[93] Amended by the Energy Act 2004, s 103(2)(b).

(d) to protect a child or other vulnerable person from the person in question;

(e) to allow the prompt and effective investigation of the offence or of the conduct of the person in question;

(f) to prevent any prosecution for the offence from being hindered by the disappearance of the person in question.

(6) Subsection (5)(c)(iv) applies only where members of the public going about their normal business cannot reasonably be expected to avoid the person in question.][94]

[24A Arrest without warrant: other persons

(1) A person other than a constable may arrest without a warrant—

(a) anyone who is in the act of committing an indictable offence;

(b) anyone whom he has reasonable grounds for suspecting to be committing an indictable offence.

(2) Where an indictable offence has been committed, a person other than a constable may arrest without a warrant—

(a) anyone who is guilty of the offence;

(b) anyone whom he has reasonable grounds for suspecting to be guilty of it.

(3) But the power of summary arrest conferred by subsection (1) or (2) is exercisable only if—

(a) the person making the arrest has reasonable grounds for believing that for any of the reasons mentioned in subsection (4) it is necessary to arrest the person in question; and

(b) it appears to the person making the arrest that it is not reasonably practicable for a constable to make it instead.

(4) The reasons are to prevent the person in question—

(a) causing physical injury to himself or any other person;

(b) suffering physical injury;

(c) causing loss of or damage to property; or

(d) making off before a constable can assume responsibility for him.

[(5) This section does not apply in relation to an offence under Part 3 or 3A of the Public Order Act 1986.[95]][96]

25 General arrest conditions

[...][97]

26 Repeal of statutory powers of arrest without warrant or order

(1) Subject to subsection (2) below, so much of any Act (including a local Act) passed before this Act as enables a constable—

(a) to arrest a person for an offence without a warrant; or

(b) to arrest a person otherwise than for an offence without a warrant or an order of a court,

shall cease to have effect.

---

[94] ss 24–24A substituted for s 24 by SOCAPA 2005, s 110(1).

[95] New subsection (5) prospectively inserted by the Racial and Religious Hatred Act 2006, s 2 (1 October 2007).

[96] Inserted by SOCAPA 2005, s 110(1).

[97] Repealed by SOCAPA 2005, ss 110(2), 174(2), Sch 17, Pt 2, para 1.

(2)   Nothing in subsection (1) above affects the enactments specified in Schedule 2 to this Act.

27 Fingerprinting of certain offenders

[...][98]

(4)   The Secretary of State may by regulations make provision for recording in national police records convictions for such offences as are specified in the regulations.

[...][99]

[(4A) In subsection (4) 'conviction' includes—

       (a)   a caution within the meaning of Part 5 of the Police Act 1997; and

       (b)   a reprimand or warning given under section 65 of the Crime and Disorder Act 1998.][100]

(5)   Regulations under this section shall be made by statutory instrument and shall be subject to annulment in pursuance of a resolution of either House of Parliament.

28 Information to be given on arrest

(1)   Subject to subsection (5) below, where a person is arrested, otherwise than by being informed that he is under arrest, the arrest is not lawful unless the person arrested is informed that he is under arrest as soon as is practicable after his arrest.

(2)   Where a person is arrested by a constable, subsection (1) above applies regardless of whether the fact of the arrest is obvious.

(3)   Subject to subsection (5) below, no arrest is lawful unless the person arrested is informed of the ground for the arrest at the time of, or as soon as is practicable after, the arrest.

(4)   Where a person is arrested by a constable, subsection (3) above applies regardless of whether the ground for the arrest is obvious.

(5)   Nothing in this section is to be taken to require a person to be informed—

       (a)   that he is under arrest; or

       (b)   of the ground for the arrest,

if it was not reasonably practicable for him to be so informed by reason of his having escaped from arrest before the information could be given.

29 Voluntary attendance at police station etc

Where for the purpose of assisting with an investigation a person attends voluntarily at a police station or at any other place where a constable is present or accompanies a constable to a police station or any such other place without having been arrested—

       (a)   he shall be entitled to leave at will unless he is placed under arrest;

       (b)   he shall be informed at once that he is under arrest if a decision is taken by a constable to prevent him from leaving at will.

---

[98] s 27(1)–(3) repealed by the Crime and Security Act 2010, s 6(3).
[99] Repealed by the Criminal Justice and Police Act 2001, Sch 7(2)(1), para 1.
[100] Amended by the Protection of Freedoms Act 2012, s 85.

Act

30 Arrest elsewhere than at police station

[(1) Subsection (1A) applies where a person is, at any place other than a police station—

    (a) arrested by a constable for an offence, or

    (b) taken into custody by a constable after being arrested for an offence by a person other than a constable.

(1A) The person must be taken by a constable to a police station as soon as practicable after the arrest.

(1B) Subsection (1A) has effect subject to section 30A (release on bail) and subsection (7) (release without bail).][101]

(2) Subject to subsections (3) and (5) below, the police station to which an arrested person is taken under [subsection (1A)][102] above shall be a designated police station.

(3) A constable to whom this subsection applies may take an arrested person to any police station unless it appears to the constable that it may be necessary to keep the arrested person in police detention for more than six hours.

(4) Subsection (3) above applies—

    (a) to a constable who is working in a locality covered by a police station which is not a designated police station; and

    (b) to a constable belonging to a body of constables maintained by an authority other than a [local policing body][103].

(5) Any constable may take an arrested person to any police station if—

    (a) either of the following conditions is satisfied—

        (i) the constable has arrested him without the assistance of any other constable and no other constable is available to assist him;

        (ii) the constable has taken him into custody from a person other than a constable without the assistance of any other constable and no other constable is available to assist him; and

    (b) it appears to the constable that he will be unable to take the arrested person to a designated police station without the arrested person injuring himself, the constable or some other person.

(6) If the first police station to which an arrested person is taken after his arrest is not a designated police station, he shall be taken to a designated police station not more than six hours after his arrival at the first police station unless he is released previously.

[(7) A person arrested by a constable at any place other than a police station must be released without bail if the condition in subsection (7A) is satisfied.

(7A) The condition is that, at any time before the person arrested reaches a police station, a constable is satisfied that there are no grounds for keeping him under arrest or releasing him on bail under section 30A.][104]

(8) A constable who releases a person under subsection (7) above shall record the fact that he has done so.

---

[101] Amended by the Criminal Justice Act 2003, s 4(1), (2).
[102] Amended by the Criminal Justice Act 2003, s 4(1), (3).
[103] Amended by the Police Reform and Social Responsibility Act 2011, Sch 16(3), para 161.
[104] Amended by the Criminal Justice Act 2003, s 4(1), (4).

(9)   The constable shall make the record as soon as is practicable after the release.

[(10)   Nothing in subsection (1A) or in section 30A prevents a constable delaying taking a person to a police station or releasing him on bail if the condition in subsection (10A) is satisfied.

(10A)   The condition is that the presence of the person at a place (other than a police station) is necessary in order to carry out such investigations as it is reasonable to carry out immediately.

(11)   Where there is any such delay the reasons for the delay must be recorded when the person first arrives at the police station or (as the case may be) is released on bail.][105]

(12)   Nothing in [subsection (1A) or section 30A][106] above shall be taken to affect—
        (a) paragraphs 16(3) or 18(1) of Schedule 2 to the Immigration Act 1971;
        (b) section 34(1) of the Criminal Justice Act 1972; or
        [(c) any provision of the Terrorism Act 2000.][107]

(13)   Nothing in subsection (10) above shall be taken to affect paragraph 18(3) of Schedule 2 to the Immigration Act 1971.

[30A Bail elsewhere than at police station

(1)   A constable may release on bail a person who is arrested or taken into custody in the circumstances mentioned in section 30(1).

(2)   A person may be released on bail under subsection (1) at any time before he arrives at a police station.

(3)   A person released on bail under subsection (1) must be required to attend a police station.

[(3A)   Where a constable releases a person on bail under subsection (1)—
        (a) no recognizance for the person's surrender to custody shall be taken from the person,
        (b) no security for the person's surrender to custody shall be taken from the person or from anyone else on the person's behalf,
        (c) the person shall not be required to provide a surety or sureties for his surrender to custody, and
        (d) no requirement to reside in a bail hostel may be imposed as a condition of bail.

(3B)   Subject to subsection (3A), where a constable releases a person on bail under subsection (1) the constable may impose, as conditions of the bail, such requirements as appear to the constable to be necessary—
        (a) to secure that the person surrenders to custody,
        (b) to secure that the person does not commit an offence while on bail,
        (c) to secure that the person does not interfere with witnesses or otherwise obstruct the course of justice, whether in relation to himself or any other person, or

---

[105] Amended by the Criminal Justice Act 2003, s 4(1), (5).

[106] Amended by the Criminal Justice Act 2003, s 4(1), (6).

[107] Amended by the Terrorism Act 2000, ss 125(1), Sch 15, para 5(1), (2); for savings see the Terrorism Act 2000, s 129(1)(b) and SI 2001/421, art 2.

(d) for the person's own protection or, if the person is under the age of 17, for the person's own welfare or in the person's own interests.

(4) Where a person is released on bail under subsection (1), a requirement may be imposed on the person as a condition of bail only under the preceding provisions of this section.][108]

(5) The police station which the person is required to attend may be any police station.][109]

[30B Bail under section 30A: notices

(1) Where a constable grants bail to a person under section 30A, he must give that person a notice in writing before he is released.

(2) The notice must state—
(a) the offence for which he was arrested, and
(b) the ground on which he was arrested.

(3) The notice must inform him that he is required to attend a police station.

(4) It may also specify the police station which he is required to attend and the time when he is required to attend.

[(4A) If the person is granted bail subject to conditions under section 30A(3B), the notice also–
(a) must specify the requirements imposed by those conditions,
(b) must explain the opportunities under sections 30CA(1) and 30CB(1) for variation of those conditions, and
(c) if it does not specify the police station at which the person is required to attend, must specify a police station at which the person may make a request under section 30CA(1)(b).][110]

(5) If the notice does not include the information mentioned in subsection (4), the person must subsequently be given a further notice in writing which contains that information.

(6) The person may be required to attend a different police station from that specified in the notice under subsection (1) or (5) or to attend at a different time.

(7) He must be given notice in writing of any such change as is mentioned in subsection (6) but more than one such notice may be given to him.][111]

[30C Bail under section 30A: supplemental

(1) A person who has been required to attend a police station is not required to do so if he is given notice in writing that his attendance is no longer required.

(2) If a person is required to attend a police station which is not a designated police station he must be—
(a) released, or
(b) taken to a designated police station,
not more than six hours after his arrival.

(3) Nothing in the Bail Act 1976 applies in relation to bail under section 30A.

---

[108] Section 30A(3A)–(4) substituted for s 30A(4) by Police and Justice Act 2006, Sch 6, para 2.
[109] Inserted by the Criminal Justice Act 2003, s 4(1), (7).
[110] Added by Police and Justice Act 2006, Sch 6, para 3.
[111] Inserted by the Criminal Justice Act 2003, s 4(1), (7).

(4) Nothing in section 30A or 30B or in this section prevents the re-arrest without a warrant of a person released on bail under section 30A if new evidence justifying a further arrest has come to light since his release.][112]

[30CA Bail under section 30A: variation of conditions by police

(1) Where a person released on bail under section 30A(1) is on bail subject to conditions—
   (a) a relevant officer at the police station at which the person is required to attend, or
   (b) where no notice under section 30B specifying that police station has been given to the person, a relevant officer at the police station specified under section 30B(4A)(c), may, at the request of the person but subject to subsection (2), vary the conditions.

(2) On any subsequent request made in respect of the same grant of bail, subsection (1) confers power to vary the conditions of the bail only if the request is based on information that, in the case of the previous request or each previous request, was not available to the relevant officer considering that previous request when he was considering it.

(3) Where conditions of bail granted to a person under section 30A(1) are varied under subsection (1)—
   (a) paragraphs (a) to (d) of section 30A(3A) apply,
   (b) requirements imposed by the conditions as so varied must be requirements that appear to the relevant officer varying the conditions to be necessary for any of the purposes mentioned in paragraphs (a) to (d) of section 30A(3B), and
   (c) the relevant officer who varies the conditions must give the person notice in writing of the variation.

(4) Power under subsection (1) to vary conditions is, subject to subsection (3)(a) and (b), power—
   (a) to vary or rescind any of the conditions, and
   (b) to impose further conditions.

(5) In this section 'relevant officer', in relation to a designated police station, means a custody officer but, in relation to any other police station—
   (a) means a constable [...][113] who is not involved in the investigation of the offence for which the person making the request under subsection (1) was under arrest when granted bail under section 30A(1), if such a constable [...][114] is readily available, and
   (b) if no such constable [...][115] is readily available—
      (i) means a constable other than the one who granted bail to the person, if such a constable is readily available, and
      (ii) if no such constable is readily available, means the constable who granted bail.][116]

---

[112] ibid.
[113] Words repealed by Policing and Crime Act 2009, Sch 8(13), para 1.
[114] Ibid.
[115] Ibid.
[116] Added by Police and Justice Act 2006, Sch 6, para 14.

Act

[30CB Bail under section 30A: variation of conditions by court

(1) Where a person released on bail under section 30A(1) is on bail subject to conditions, a magistrates' court may, on an application by or on behalf of the person, vary the conditions if—

    (a) the conditions have been varied under section 30CA(1) since being imposed under section 30A(3B),

    (b) a request for variation under section 30CA(1) of the conditions has been made and refused, or

    (c) a request for variation under section 30CA(1) of the conditions has been made and the period of 48 hours beginning with the day when the request was made has expired without the request having been withdrawn or the conditions having been varied in response to the request.

(2) In proceedings on an application for a variation under subsection (1), a ground may not be relied upon unless—

    (a) in a case falling within subsection (1)(a), the ground was relied upon in the request in response to which the conditions were varied under section 30CA(1), or

    (b) in a case falling within paragraph (b) or (c) of subsection (1), the ground was relied upon in the request mentioned in that paragraph, but this does not prevent the court, when deciding the application, from considering different grounds arising out of a change in circumstances that has occurred since the making of the application.

(3) Where conditions of bail granted to a person under section 30A(1) are varied under subsection (1)—

    (a) paragraphs (a) to (d) of section 30A(3A) apply,

    (b) requirements imposed by the conditions as so varied must be requirements that appear to the court varying the conditions to be necessary for any of the purposes mentioned in paragraphs (a) to (d) of section 30A(3B), and

    (c) that bail shall not lapse but shall continue subject to the conditions as so varied.

(4) Power under subsection (1) to vary conditions is, subject to subsection (3)(a) and (b), power—

    (a) to vary or rescind any of the conditions, and

    (b) to impose further conditions.][117]

[30D Failure to answer to bail under section 30A

(1) A constable may arrest without a warrant a person who—

    (a) has been released on bail under section 30A subject to a requirement to attend a specified police station, but

    (b) fails to attend the police station at the specified time.

(2) A person arrested under subsection (1) must be taken to a police station (which may be the specified police station or any other police station) as soon as practicable after the arrest.

---

[117] Added by Police and Justice Act 2006, Sch 6(2), para 4.

[(2A) A person who has been released on bail under section 30A may be arrested without a warrant by a constable if the constable has reasonable grounds for suspecting that the person has broken any of the conditions of bail.

(2B) A person arrested under subsection (2A) must be taken to a police station (which may be the specified police station mentioned in subsection (1) or any other police station) as soon as practicable after the arrest.][118]

(3) In subsection (1), 'specified' means specified in a notice under subsection (1) or (5) of section 30B or, if notice of change has been given under subsection (7) of that section, in that notice.

(4) For the purposes of—

(a) section 30 (subject to the obligation in subsection (2) [and (2B)][119], and

(b) section 31,

an arrest under this section is to be treated as an arrest for an offence.][120]

31 Arrest for further offence

(1) Where—

(a) a person—

(i) has been arrested for an offence; and

(ii) is at a police station in consequence of that arrest; and

(b) it appears to a constable that, if he were released from that arrest, he would be liable to arrest for some other offence,

he shall be arrested for that other offence.

32 Search upon arrest

(1) A constable may search an arrested person, in any case where the person to be searched has been arrested at a place other than a police station, if the constable has reasonable grounds for believing that the arrested person may present a danger to himself or others.

(2) Subject to subsections (3) to (5) below, a constable shall also have power in any such case—

(a) to search the arrested person for anything—

(i) which he might use to assist him to escape from lawful custody; or

(ii) which might be evidence relating to an offence; and

[(b) if the offence for which he has been arrested is an indictable offence, to enter and search any premises in which he was when arrested or immediately before he was arrested for evidence relating to the offence][121].

(3) The power to search conferred by subsection (2) above is only a power to search to the extent that is reasonably required for the purpose of discovering any such thing or any such evidence.

(4) The powers conferred by this section to search a person are not to be construed as authorising a constable to require a person to remove any of his clothing in public other than an outer coat, jacket or gloves [but they do authorise a search of a person's mouth][122].

---

[118] Added by Police and Justice Act 2006, Sch 6, para 5(2).
[119] Words substituted by Police and Justice Act 2006, Sch 6(2), para 5(3).
[120] Added by Criminal Justice Act 2003, s 4(7).
[121] Amended by SOCAPA 2005, s 111, Sch 7(3), para 43(1), (6).
[122] Amended by the Criminal Justice and Public Order Act 1994, s 59(2).

Act

(5) A constable may not search a person in the exercise of the power conferred by subsection (2)(a) above unless he has reasonable grounds for believing that the person to be searched may have concealed on him anything for which a search is permitted under that paragraph.

(6) A constable may not search premises in the exercise of the power conferred by subsection (2)(b) above unless he has reasonable grounds for believing that there is evidence for which a search is permitted under that paragraph on the premises.

(7) In so far as the power of search conferred by subsection (2)(b) above relates to premises consisting of two or more separate dwellings, it is limited to a power to search—

(a) any dwelling in which the arrest took place or in which the person arrested was immediately before his arrest; and

(b) any parts of the premises which the occupier of any such dwelling uses in common with the occupiers of any other dwellings comprised in the premises.

(8) A constable searching a person in the exercise of the power conferred by subsection (1) above may seize and retain anything he finds, if he has reasonable grounds for believing that the person searched might use it to cause physical injury to himself or to any other person.

(9) A constable searching a person in the exercise of the power conferred by subsection (2)(a) above may seize and retain anything he finds, other than an item subject to legal privilege, if he has reasonable grounds for believing—

(a) that he might use it to assist him to escape from lawful custody; or

(b) that it is evidence of an offence or has been obtained in consequence of the commission of an offence.

(10) Nothing in this section shall be taken to affect the power conferred by [section 43 of the Terrorism Act 2000][123].

33 Execution of warrant not in possession of constable

[...][124]

PART IV
DETENTION

Detention—conditions and duration

34 Limitations on police detention

(1) A person arrested for an offence shall not be kept in police detention except in accordance with the provisions of this Part of this Act.

(2) Subject to subsection (3) below, if at any time a custody officer—

(a) becomes aware, in relation to any person in police detention, that the grounds for the detention of that person have ceased to apply; and

(b) is not aware of any other grounds on which the continued detention of that person could be justified under the provisions of this Part of this Act,

---

[123] Amended by the Terrorism Act 2000, s 125(1), Sch 15, para 5(1), (3).
[124] Repealed by the Access to Justice Act 1999, s 106, Sch 15(V)(8) para 1; for transitional provisions see SI 2001/168, arts 2(b), 3.

it shall be the duty of the custody officer, subject to subsection (4) below, to order his immediate release from custody.

(3) No person in police detention shall be released except on the authority of a custody officer at the police station where his detention was authorised or, if it was authorised at more than one station, a custody officer at the station where it was last authorised.

(4) A person who appears to the custody officer to have been unlawfully at large when he was arrested is not to be released under subsection (2) above.

(5) A person whose release is ordered under subsection (2) above shall be released without bail unless it appears to the custody officer—

(a) that there is need for further investigation of any matter in connection with which he was detained at any time during the period of his detention; or

[(b) that, in respect of any such matter, proceedings may be taken against him or he may be reprimanded or warned under section 65 of the Crime and Disorder Act 1998,][125]

and, if it so appears, he shall be released on bail.

(6) For the purposes of this Part of this Act a person arrested under [section 6D of the Road Traffic Act 1988][126] [or section 30(2) of the Transport and Works Act 1992 (c 42)][127] is arrested for an offence.

[(7) [For the purposes of this Part a person who—

(a) attends a police station to answer to bail granted under section 30A,

(b) returns to a police station to answer to bail granted under this Part, or

(c) is arrested under section 30D or 46A,

is to be treated as arrested for an offence and that offence is the offence in connection with which he was granted bail.][128]

[But this subsection is subject to section 47(6) (which provides for the calculation of certain periods, where a person has been granted bail under this Part, by reference to time when the person is in police detention only.)][129]][130]

[(8) Subsection (7) does not apply in relation to a person who is granted bail subject to the duty mentioned in section 47(3)(b) and who either—

(a) attends a police station to answer to such bail, or

(b) is arrested under section 46A for failing to do so, (provision as to the treatment of such persons for the purposes of this Part being made by section 46ZA).][131]

35 Designated police stations

(1) The chief officer of police for each police area shall designate the police stations in his area which, subject to [sections 30(3) and (5), 30A(5) and 30D(2)][132],

---

[125] Amended by the Criminal Justice and Court Services Act 2000, s 56(2).

[126] Amended by the Railways and Transport Safety Act 2003, s 107, Sch 7, para 12.

[127] Amended by the Police Reform Act 2002, s 53(1).

[128] Amended by the Criminal Justice Act 2003, s 12, Sch 1, paras 1, 5.

[129] Amended by the Police (Detention and Bail) Act, s 1(2) (deemed always to have had effect since insertion of 1984, s 34(7) on 10 April 1995).

[130] Amended by the Criminal Justice and Public Order Act 1994, s 29(3).

[131] Added by Police and Justice Act 2006, s 46(2) (1 April 2007 for purposes specified in SI 2007/709, art 3(n); 14 November 2008 for purposes specified in SI 2008/2785, art 2 and not yet in force otherwise).

[132] Amended by the Criminal Justice Act 2003, s 12, Sch 1, paras 1, 6.

Act

are to be the stations in that area to be used for the purpose of detaining arrested persons.

(2)   A chief officer's duty under subsection (1) above is to designate police stations appearing to him to provide enough accommodation for that purpose.

[(2A) The Chief Constable of the British Transport Police Force may designate police stations which (in addition to those designated under subsection (1) above) may be used for the purpose of detaining arrested persons.][133]

(3)   Without prejudice to section 12 of the Interpretation Act 1978 (continuity of duties) a chief officer—

(a) may designate a station which was not previously designated; and

(b) may direct that a designation of a station previously made shall cease to operate.

(4)   In this Act 'designated police station' means a police station designated under this section.

36 Custody officers at police stations

(1)   One or more custody officers shall be appointed for each designated police station.

(2)   A custody officer for [a police station designated under section 35(1) above][134] shall be appointed—

(a) by the chief officer of police for the area in which the designated police station is situated; or

(b) by such other police officer as the chief officer of police for that area may direct.

[(2A) A custody officer for a police station designated under section 35(2A) above shall be appointed—

(a) by the Chief Constable of the British Transport Police Force; or

(b) by such other member of that Force as that Chief Constable may direct.][135]

[(3)   No officer may be appointed a custody officer unless he is of at least the rank of sergeant.][136]

(4)   An officer of any rank may perform the functions of a custody officer at a designated police station if a custody officer is not readily available to perform them.

(5)   Subject to the following provisions of this section and to section 39(2) below, none of the functions of a custody officer in relation to a person shall be performed by an officer who at the time when the function falls to be performed is involved in the investigation of an offence for which that person is in police detention at that time.

(6)   Nothing in subsection (5) above is to be taken to prevent a custody officer—

(a) performing any function assigned to custody officers—

(i) by this Act; or

(ii) by a code of practice issued under this Act;

---

[133] Amended by the Anti-terrorism, Crime and Security Act 2001, s 101, Sch 7, paras 11, 12.
[134] Amended by the Anti-terrorism, Crime and Security Act 2001, s 101, Sch 7, paras 11, 13(1).
[135] Amended by the Anti-terrorism, Crime and Security Act 2001, s 101, Sch 7, paras 11, 13(1), (3).
[136] Substituted by Policing and Crime Act 2009, Sch 7, para.123(3)(a) (12 January 2010).

(b) carrying out the duty imposed on custody officers by section 39 below;

(c) doing anything in connection with the identification of a suspect; or

(d) doing anything under [sections 7 and 8 of the Road Traffic Act 1988][137].

(7) Where an arrested person is taken to a police station which is not a designated police station, the functions in relation to him which at a designated police station would be the functions of a custody officer shall be performed—

(a) by an officer who is not involved in the investigation of an offence for which he is in police detention, if such an officer is readily available; and

(b) if no such officer is readily available, by the officer who took him to the station or any other officer.

[(7A) Subject to subsection (7B), subsection (7) applies where a person attends a police station which is not a designated station to answer to bail granted under section 30A as it applies where a person is taken to such a station.

(7B) Where subsection (7) applies because of subsection (7A), the reference in subsection (7)(b) to the officer who took him to the station is to be read as a reference to the officer who granted him bail.][138]

(8) References to a custody officer in the following provisions of this Act include references to an officer other than a custody officer who is performing the functions of a custody officer by virtue of subsection (4) or (7) above.

(9) Where by virtue of subsection (7) above an officer of a force maintained by a police authority who took an arrested person to a police station is to perform the functions of a custody officer in relation to him, the officer shall inform an officer who—

(a) is attached to a designated police station; and

(b) is of at least the rank of inspector,

that he is to do so.

(10) The duty imposed by subsection (9) above shall be performed as soon as it is practicable to perform it.

37 Duties of custody officer before charge

(1) Where—

(a) a person is arrested for an offence—

(i) without a warrant; or

(ii) under a warrant not endorsed for bail, [...][139]

(b) [...][140]

the custody officer at each police station where he is detained after his arrest shall determine whether he has before him sufficient evidence to charge that person with the offence for which he was arrested and may detain him at the police station for such period as is necessary to enable him to do so.

(2) If the custody officer determines that he does not have such evidence before him, the person arrested shall be released either on bail or without bail, unless the custody officer has reasonable grounds for believing that his detention without being charged is necessary to secure or preserve evidence relating to

---

[137] Amended by the Road Traffic (Consequential Provisions) Act 1988, s 4, Sch 3, para 27(3).

[138] Amended by the Criminal Justice Act 2003, s 12, Sch 1, paras 1, 7.

[139] Repealed by the Criminal Justice and Public Order Act 1994, ss 29(4)(a), 168(3), Sch 11.

[140] ibid.

Act

an offence for which he is under arrest or to obtain such evidence by questioning him.

(3)   If the custody officer has reasonable grounds for so believing, he may authorise the person arrested to be kept in police detention.

(4)   Where a custody officer authorises a person who has not been charged to be kept in police detention, he shall, as soon as is practicable, make a written record of the grounds for the detention.

(5)   Subject to subsection (6) below, the written record shall be made in the presence of the person arrested who shall at that time be informed by the custody officer of the grounds for his detention.

(6)   Subsection (5) above shall not apply where the person arrested is, at the time when the written record is made—

(a) incapable of understanding what is said to him;

(b) violent or likely to become violent; or

(c) in urgent need of medical attention.

(7)   Subject to section 41(7) below, if the custody officer determines that he has before him sufficient evidence to charge the person arrested with the offence for which he was arrested, the person arrested—

[(a) [shall be—

(i)   released without charge and on bail, or

(ii) kept in police detention, for the purpose of enabling the Director of Public Prosecutions to make a decision under section 37B below][141]

(b) shall be released without charge and on bail but not for that purpose,

(c) shall be released without charge and without bail, or

(d) shall be charged].[142]

[(7A) The decision as to how a person is to be dealt with under subsection (7) above shall be that of the custody officer.

(7B) Where a person is [dealt with under subsection (7)(a)][143] above, it shall be the duty of the custody officer to inform him that he is being released[, or (as the case may be) detained,][144] to enable the Director of Public Prosecutions to make a decision under section 37B below.][145]

(8)   Where—

(a) a person is released under subsection (7)(b) [or (c)][146] above; and

(b) at the time of his release a decision whether he should be prosecuted for the offence for which he was arrested has not been taken,

it shall be the duty of the custody officer so to inform him.

[(8A) Subsection (8B) applies if the offence for which the person is arrested is one in relation to which a sample could be taken under section 63B below and the custody officer—

(a) is required in pursuance of subsection (2) above to release the person arrested and decides to release him on bail, or

---

[141] Section 37(7)(a)(i) and (ii) and words substituted for words by Police and Justice Act 2006, s 11.

[142] Amended by the Criminal Justice Act 2003, s 28, Sch 2, para 2(2).

[143] Words substituted by Police and Justice Act 2006, Sch 14, para 9(a).

[144] Words inserted by Police and Justice Act 2006, Sch 14, para 9(b).

[145] Amended by the Criminal Justice Act 2003, s 28, Sch 2, para 2(3).

[146] Amended by the Criminal Justice Act 2003, s 28, Sch 2, paras 1, 2(1), (4).

(b) decides in pursuance of subsection (7)(a) or (b) above to release the person without charge and on bail.

(8B) The detention of the person may be continued to enable a sample to be taken under section 63B, but this subsection does not permit a person to be detained for a period of more than 24 hours after the relevant time.][147]

(9) If the person arrested is not in a fit state to be dealt with under subsection (7) above, he may be kept in police detention until he is.

(10) The duty imposed on the custody officer under subsection (1) above shall be carried out by him as soon as practicable after the person arrested arrives at the police station or, in the case of a person arrested at the police station, as soon as practicable after the arrest.

(11)–(14) [...][148]

(15) In this Part of this Act—

'arrested juvenile' means a person arrested with or without a warrant who appears to be under the age of 17 [...][149];

'endorsed for bail' means endorsed with a direction for bail in accordance with section 117(2) of the Magistrates' Courts Act 1980.

[**37A Guidance**

(1) The Director of Public Prosecutions may issue guidance—

(a) for the purpose of enabling custody officers to decide how persons should be dealt with under section [37(7) above or 37C(2) or 37CA(2)][150] below, and

(b) as to the information to be sent to the Director of Public Prosecutions under section 37B(1) below.

(2) The Director of Public Prosecutions may from time to time revise guidance issued under this section.

(3) Custody officers are to have regard to guidance under this section in deciding how persons should be dealt with under section 37(7) above or 37C(2) [or 37CA(2)][151] below.

(4) A report under section 9 of the Prosecution of Offences Act 1985 (report by DPP to Attorney General) must set out the provisions of any guidance issued, and any revisions to guidance made, in the year to which the report relates.

(5) The Director of Public Prosecutions must publish in such manner as he thinks fit—

(a) any guidance issued under this section, and

(b) any revisions made to such guidance.

(6) Guidance under this section may make different provision for different cases, circumstances or areas.][152]

---

[147] Amended by the Drugs Act 2005, s 23(1), Sch 1, paras 1, 2.
[148] Repealed by the Criminal Justice Act 1991, ss 72, 101(2), Sch 13.
[149] Repealed by the Children Act 1989, s 108(7), Sch 15.
[150] Amended by the Police and Justice Act 2006, Sch 6(3), para 8(2).
[151] Words inserted by Police and Justice Act 2006, Sch 6(3), para 8(2) (1 April 2007).
[152] Inserted by the Criminal Justice Act 2003, s 28, Sch 2, paras 1, 3.

[37B Consultation with the Director of Public Prosecutions

(1) Where a person is [dealt with under section 37(7)(a)][153] above, an officer involved in the investigation of the offence shall, as soon as is practicable, send to the Director of Public Prosecutions such information as may be specified in guidance under section 37A above.

(2) The Director of Public Prosecutions shall decide whether there is sufficient evidence to charge the person with an offence.

(3) If he decides that there is sufficient evidence to charge the person with an offence, he shall decide—

(a) whether or not the person should be charged and, if so, the offence with which he should be charged, and

(b) whether or not the person should be given a caution and, if so, the offence in respect of which he should be given a caution.

(4) The Director of Public Prosecutions [shall give notice][154] of his decision to an officer involved in the investigation of the offence.

[(4A) Notice under subsection (4) above shall be in writing, but in the case of a person kept in police detention under section 37(7)(a) above it may be given orally in the first instance and confirmed in writing subsequently.][155]

(5) If his decision is—

(a) that there is not sufficient evidence to charge the person with an offence, or

(b) that there is sufficient evidence to charge the person with an offence but that the person should not be charged with an offence or given a caution in respect of an offence,

a custody officer shall give the person notice in writing that he is not to be prosecuted.

(6) If the decision of the Director of Public Prosecutions is that the person should be charged with an offence, or given a caution in respect of an offence, the person shall be charged or cautioned accordingly.

(7) But if his decision is that the person should be given a caution in respect of the offence and it proves not to be possible to give the person such a caution, he shall instead be charged with the offence.[156]

[(8) For the purposes of this section, a person is to be charged with an offence either—

[(a) when he is in police detention after returning to a police station to answer bail or is otherwise in police detention at a police station, or][157]

(b) in accordance with section 29 of the Criminal Justice Act 2003.][158]

(9) In this section 'caution' includes—

[(a) a conditional caution within the meaning of Part 3 of the Criminal Justice Act 2003 [...][159]][160]

---

[153] Words substituted by Police and Justice Act 2006, Sch 14, para 10(2) (15 January 2007).

[154] Words substituted by Police and Justice Act 2006, Sch 14, para 10(3).

[155] Added by Police and Justice Act 2006, Sch 14, para 10(4).

[156] New subsection (8) prospectively inserted by the Criminal Justice Act 2003, s 28, Sch 2, paras 1, 3: see below.

[157] Amended by the Police and Justice Act 2006, Sch 14, para 10(5).

[158] Subsection 8 inserted by the Criminal Justice Act 2003, s 28, Sch 2, paras 1, 3 (1 October 2007; SI 2007/2874).

[159] Added by Criminal Justice and Immigration Act 2008, Sch 26(2), para 20(1)(a) (16 November in relation to the areas specified in SI 2009/2780, art 2(2); not yet in force otherwise).

[160] Added by Criminal Justice Act 2003, Sch 2, para 3 (3 July; SI 2004/1629).

Act

[(aa) a youth conditional caution within the meaning of Chapter 1 of Part 4 of the Crime and Disorder Act 1998, and][161]

(b) a warning or reprimand under section 65 of that Act].[162]

[37C Breach of bail following release under section 37(7)(a)

(1) This section applies where—
  (a) a person released on bail under section 37(7)(a) above or subsection (2)(b) below is arrested under section 46A below in respect of that bail, and
  (b) at the time of his detention following that arrest at the police station mentioned in section 46A(2) below, notice under section 37B(4) above has not been given.
(2) The person arrested—
  (a) shall be charged, or
  (b) shall be released without charge, either on bail or without bail.
(3) The decision as to how a person is to be dealt with under subsection (2) above shall be that of a custody officer.
(4) A person released on bail under subsection (2)(b) above shall be released on bail subject to the same conditions (if any) which applied immediately before his arrest.][163]

[37CA Breach of bail following release under section 37(7)(b)

(1) This section applies where a person released on bail under section 37(7)(b) above or subsection (2)(b) below—
  (a) is arrested under section 46A below in respect of that bail, and
  (b) is being detained following that arrest at the police station mentioned in section 46A(2) below.
(2) The person arrested—
  (a) shall be charged, or
  (b) shall be released without charge, either on bail or without bail.
(3) The decision as to how a person is to be dealt with under subsection (2) above shall be that of a custody officer.
(4) A person released on bail under subsection (2)(b) above shall be released on bail subject to the same conditions (if any) which applied immediately before his arrest.][164]

[37D Release [on bail under section 37][165]: further provision

(1) Where a person is released on bail under section [37, 37C(2)(b) or 37CA(2)(b)][166] above, a custody officer may subsequently appoint a different time, or an additional time, at which the person is to attend at the police station to answer bail.
(2) The custody officer shall give the person notice in writing of the exercise of the power under subsection (1).

---

[161] Added by Criminal Justice and Immigration Act 2008, Sch 26(2), para 20(1)(a) (16 November 2009 in relation to the areas specified in SI 2009/2780, art 2(2); not yet in force otherwise).
[162] Words substituted by Criminal Justice and Immigration Act 2008, Sch 26(2), para 20(1)(b) (16 November 2009 in relation to the areas specified in SI 2009/2780, art 2(2); not yet in force otherwise).
[163] Added by Criminal Justice Act 2003, Sch 2, para 3 (29 January 2004; SI 2004/81).
[164] Added by Police and Justice Act 2006, Sch 6, para 8(1) (1 April 2007).
[165] Words substituted by Police and Justice Act 2006, Sch 6(3), para 9(2) (1 April 2007).
[166] Words substituted by Police and Justice Act 2006, Sch 6(3), para 9(1).

Act

(3)   The exercise of the power under subsection (1) shall not affect the conditions (if any) to which bail is subject.

(4)   Where a person released on bail under section 37(7)(a) or 37C(2)(b) above returns to a police station to answer bail or is otherwise in police detention at a police station, he may be kept in police detention to enable him to be dealt with in accordance with section 37B or 37C above or to enable the power under subsection (1) above to be exercised.

[(4A) Where a person released on bail under section 37(7)(b) or 37CA(2)(b) above returns to a police station to answer bail or is otherwise in police detention at a police station, he may be kept in police detention to enable him to be dealt with in accordance with section 37CA above or to enable the power under subsection (1) above to be exercised.

(5)   If the person mentioned in subsection (4) or (4A) above is not in a fit state to enable him to be dealt with as mentioned in that subsection or to enable the power under subsection (1) above to be exercised, he may be kept in police detention until he is.][167]

(6)   Where a person is kept in police detention by virtue of subsection (4)[, (4a)][168] or (5) above, section 37(1) to (3) and (7) above (and section 40(8) below so far as it relates to section 37(1) to (3)) shall not apply to the offence in connection with which he was released on bail under section [37(7), 37C(2)(b) or 37CA(2)(b)][169] above.][170]

38 Duties of custody officer after charge

(1)   Where a person arrested for an offence otherwise than under a warrant endorsed for bail is charged with an offence, the custody officer shall[, subject to section 25 of the Criminal Justice and Public Order Act 1994,][171] order his release from police detention, either on bail or without bail, unless—

(a) if the person arrested is not an arrested juvenile—

    (i)   his name or address cannot be ascertained or the custody officer has reasonable grounds for doubting whether a name or address furnished by him as his name or address is his real name or address;

    [(ii)   the custody officer has reasonable grounds for believing that the person arrested will fail to appear in court to answer to bail;

    (iii)   in the case of a person arrested for an imprisonable offence, the custody officer has reasonable grounds for believing that the detention of the person arrested is necessary to prevent him from committing an offence;

    [(iiia) in a case where a sample may be taken from the person under section 63B below, the custody officer has reasonable grounds for believing that the detention of the person is necessary to enable the sample to be taken from him;][172]

[167] Section 37D(4A) and (5) substituted for s 37D(5) by Police and Justice Act 2006, Sch 6, para 10(2).
[168] Words inserted by Police and Justice Act 2006, Sch 6, para 10(3)(a).
[169] Words substituted by Police and Justice Act 2006, Sch 6, para 10(3)(b).
[170] Added by Criminal Justice Act 2003, Sch 2, para 3 (29 January 2004; SI 2004/81).
[171] Amended by the Criminal Justice and Public Order Act 1994, s 168(2), Sch 10, para 54.
[172] Amended by the Drugs Act 2005, s 23(1), Sch 1, paras 1, 3(a).

(iv) in the case of a person arrested for an offence which is not an imprisonable offence, the custody officer has reasonable grounds for believing that the detention of the person arrested is necessary to prevent him from causing physical injury to any other person or from causing loss of or damage to property;

(v) the custody officer has reasonable grounds for believing that the detention of the person arrested is necessary to prevent him from interfering with the administration of justice or with the investigation of offences or of a particular offence; or

(vi) the custody officer has reasonable grounds for believing that the detention of the person arrested is necessary for his own protection;][173]

(b) if he is an arrested juvenile—

(i) any of the requirements of paragraph (a) above is satisfied [(but, in the case of paragraph (a)(iiia) above, only if the arrested juvenile has attained the minimum age)][174]; or

(ii) the custody officer has reasonable grounds for believing that he ought to be detained in his own interests[;][175]

[(c) the offence with which the person is charged is murder.][176]

(2)   If the release of a person arrested is not required by subsection (1) above, the custody officer may authorise him to be kept in police detention [but may not authorise a person to be kept in police detention by virtue of subsection (1)(a)(iiia) after the end of the period of six hours beginning when he was charged with the offence][177].

[(2A) The custody officer, in taking the decisions required by subsection (1)(a) and (b) above (except (a)(i) and (vi) and (b)(ii)), shall have regard to the same considerations as those which a court is required to have regard to in taking the corresponding decisions under paragraph [2(1) of Part I of Schedule 1 to the Bail Act 1976][178] [(disregarding [paragraphs 1(A) and 2(2)][179] of that Part)[180].][181]

(3)   Where a custody officer authorises a person who has been charged to be kept in police detention, he shall, as soon as practicable, make a written record of the grounds for the detention.

(4)   Subject to subsection (5) below, the written record shall be made in the presence of the person charged who shall at that time be informed by the custody officer of the grounds for his detention.

(5)   Subsection (4) above shall not apply where the person charged is, at the time when the written record is made—

---

[173] Amended by the Criminal Justice and Public Order Act 1994, s 28(2).
[174] Amended by the Criminal Justice Act 2003, s 5(1), (2)(a)(ii).
[175] Added by Coroners and Justice Act 2009, Sch 21, para 77.
[176] Added by Coroners and Justice Act 2009, Sch 21, para 77.
[177] Amended by the Criminal Justice and Court Services Act 2000, s 57(1), (3)(b).
[178] Amended by the Criminal Justice Act 2003, s 331, Sch 36, Pt 1, para 5(a).
[179] Amended by the Legal Aid, Sentencing and Punishment of Offenders Act 2012, Sch 11, para 34.
[180] Amended by the Criminal Justice Act 2003, s 331, Sch 36, Pt 1, para 5(b).
[181] Amended by the Criminal Justice and Public Order Act 1994, s 28(3), (4).

Act

      (a) incapable of understanding what is said to him;

      (b) violent or likely to become violent; or

      (c) in urgent need of medical attention.

[(6)   Where a custody officer authorises an arrested juvenile to be kept in police detention under subsection (1) above, the custody officer shall, unless he certifies—

      (a) that, by reason of such circumstances as are specified in the certificate, it is
impracticable for him to do so; or

      (b) in the case of an arrested juvenile who has attained the [age of 12 years][182],
that no secure accommodation is available and that keeping him in other
local authority accommodation would not be adequate to protect the
public from serious harm from him,

    secure that the arrested juvenile is moved to local authority accommodation.

(6A)   In this section—

    'local authority accommodation' means accommodation provided by or on
behalf of a local authority (within the meaning of the Children Act 1989);

    ['minimum age' means the age specified in [section 63B(3)(b) below][183];][184]

    'secure accommodation' means accommodation provided for the purpose of
restricting liberty;

    ['sexual offence' means an offence specified in Part 2 of Schedule 15 to the
Criminal Justice Act 2003;

    'violent offence' means murder or an offence specified in Part 1 of that
Schedule;][185]

    and any reference, in relation to an arrested juvenile charged with a violent or
sexual offence, to protecting the public from serious harm from him shall be
construed as a reference to protecting members of the public from death or
serious personal injury, whether physical or psychological, occasioned by further such offences committed by him.][186]

[(6B) Where an arrested juvenile is moved to local authority accommodation under
subsection (6) above, it shall be lawful for any person acting on behalf of the
authority to detain him.][187]

(7)   A certificate made under subsection (6) above in respect of an arrested juvenile
shall be produced to the court before which he is first brought thereafter.

[(7A) In this section 'imprisonable offence' has the same meaning as in Schedule 1
to the Bail Act 1976.][188]

(8)   In this Part of this Act 'local authority' has the same meaning as in the
[Children Act 1989][189].

39 Responsibilities in relation to persons detained

(1)   Subject to subsections (2) and (4) below, it shall be the duty of the custody
officer at a police station to ensure—

---

[182] Amended by the Criminal Justice and Public Order Act 1994, s 24.

[183] Amended by the Drugs Act 2005, s 23(1), Sch 1, paras 1, 3(b).

[184] Amended by the Criminal Justice Act 2003, s 5(1), (2)(b).

[185] Amended by the Criminal Justice Act 2003, s 304, Sch 32, Pt 1, para 44.

[186] Amended by the Criminal Justice Act 1991, s 59.

[187] Amended by the Children Act 1989, s 108(5), Sch 13, para 53(2).

[188] Amended by the Criminal Justice and Public Order Act 1994, s 28(3), (4).

[189] Amended by the Children Act 1989, s 108(5), Sch 13, para 53(3).

(a) that all persons in police detention at that station are treated in accordance with this Act and any code of practice issued under it and relating to the treatment of persons in police detention; and

(b) that all matters relating to such persons which are required by this Act or by such codes of practice to be recorded are recorded in the custody records relating to such persons.

(2) If the custody officer, in accordance with any code of practice issued under this Act, transfers or permits the transfer of a person in police detention—

(a) to the custody of a police officer investigating an offence for which that person is in police detention; or

(b) to the custody of an officer who has charge of that person outside the police station,

the custody officer shall cease in relation to that person to be subject to the duty imposed on him by subsection (1)(a) above; and it shall be the duty of the officer to whom the transfer is made to ensure that he is treated in accordance with the provisions of this Act and of any such codes of practice as are mentioned in subsection (1) above.

(3) If the person detained is subsequently returned to the custody of the custody officer, it shall be the duty of the officer investigating the offence to report to the custody officer as to the manner in which this section and the codes of practice have been complied with while that person was in his custody.

(4) If an arrested juvenile is [moved to local authority accommodation][190] under section 38(6) above, the custody officer shall cease in relation to that person to be subject to the duty imposed on him by subsection (1) above.

[...][191]

(6) Where—

(a) an officer of higher rank than the custody officer gives directions relating to a person in police detention; and

(b) the directions are at variance—

(i) with any decision made or action taken by the custody officer in the performance of a duty imposed on him under this Part of this Act; or

(ii) with any decision or action which would but for the directions have been made or taken by him in the performance of such a duty,

the custody officer shall refer the matter at once to an officer of the rank of superintendent or above who is responsible for the police station for which the custody officer is acting as custody officer.

40 Review of police detention

(1) Reviews of the detention of each person in police detention in connection with the investigation of an offence shall be carried out periodically in accordance with the following provisions of this section—

(a) in the case of a person who has been arrested and charged, by the custody officer; and

---

[190] Amended by the Children Act 1989, s 108(5), Sch 13, para 54.
[191] Repealed by the Children Act 1989, s 108(7), Sch 15 para 1.

Act

(b) in the case of a person who has been arrested but not charged, by an officer of at least the rank of inspector who has not been directly involved in the investigation.

(2) The officer to whom it falls to carry out a review is referred to in this section as a 'review officer'.

(3) Subject to subsection (4) below—

(a) the first review shall be not later than six hours after the detention was first authorised;

(b) the second review shall be not later than nine hours after the first;

(c) subsequent reviews shall be at intervals of not more than nine hours.

(4) A review may be postponed—

(a) if, having regard to all the circumstances prevailing at the latest time for it specified in subsection (3) above, it is not practicable to carry out the review at that time;

(b) without prejudice to the generality of paragraph (a) above—

(i) if at that time the person in detention is being questioned by a police officer and the review officer is satisfied that an interruption of the questioning for the purpose of carrying out the review would prejudice the investigation in connection with which he is being questioned; or

(ii) if at that time no review officer is readily available.

(5) If a review is postponed under subsection (4) above it shall be carried out as soon as practicable after the latest time specified for it in subsection (3) above.

(6) If a review is carried out after postponement under subsection (4) above, the fact that it was so carried out shall not affect any requirement of this section as to the time at which any subsequent review is to be carried out.

(7) The review officer shall record the reasons for any postponement of a review in the custody record.

(8) Subject to subsection (9) below, where the person whose detention is under review has not been charged before the time of the review, section 37(1) to (6) above shall have effect in relation to him, but with [the modifications specified in subsection (8A).][192]

[(8A) The modifications are—

(a) the substitution of references to the person whose detention is under review for references to the person arrested;

(b) the substitution of references to the review officer for references to the custody officer; and

(c) in subsection (6), the insertion of the following paragraph after paragraph (a)—

'(aa) asleep;'.][193]

(9) Where a person has been kept in police detention by virtue of [section 37(9) or 37D(5)][194] above, section 37(1) to (6) shall not have effect in relation to him but it shall be the duty of the review officer to determine whether he is yet in a fit state.

---

[192] Amended by the Police Reform Act 2002, s 52(1).
[193] Amended by the Police Reform Act 2002, s 52(2).
[194] Amended by the Criminal Justice Act 2003, s 28, Sch 2, paras 1, 4.

(10)   Where the person whose detention is under review has been charged before
        the time of the review, [section 38(1) to (6B)][195] above shall have effect in
        relation to him, with [the modifications specified in subsection (10A)][196].

[(10A) The modifications are—
        (a) the substitution of a reference to the person whose detention is under review
            for any reference to the person arrested or to the person charged; and
        (b) in subsection (5), the insertion of the following paragraph after para-
            graph (a)—
            '(aa) asleep;'.][197]

(11)   Where—
        (a) an officer of higher rank than the review officer gives directions relating
            to a person in police detention; and
        (b) the directions are at variance—
            (i) with any decision made or action taken by the review officer in the
                 performance of a duty imposed on him under this Part of this Act; or
            (ii) with any decision or action which would but for the directions have
                 been made or taken by him in the performance of such a duty,
        the review officer shall refer the matter at once to an officer of the rank of
        superintendent or above who is responsible for the police station for which the
        review officer is acting as review officer in connection with the detention.

(12)   Before determining whether to authorise a person's continued detention the
        review officer shall give—
        (a) that person (unless he is asleep); or
        (b) any solicitor representing him who is available at the time of the review,
        an opportunity to make representations to him about the detention.

(13)   Subject to subsection (14) below, the person whose detention is under review
        or his solicitor may make representations under subsection (12) above either
        orally or in writing.

(14)   The review officer may refuse to hear oral representations from the person
        whose detention is under review if he considers that he is unfit to make such
        representations by reason of his condition or behaviour.

[40A Use of telephone for review under s 40

[(1)   A review under section 40(1)(b) may be carried out by means of a discussion,
        conducted by telephone, with one or more persons at the police station
        where the arrested person is held.

(2)   But subsection (1) does not apply if—
        (a) the review is of a kind authorised by regulations under section 45A to be
            carried out using video-conferencing facilities; and
        (b) it is reasonably practicable to carry it out in accordance with those
            regulations.][198]

(3)   Where any review is carried out under this section by an officer who is not
        present at the station where the arrested person is held—

---

[195] Amended by the Police Reform Act 2002, s 52(3)(a).
[196] ibid.
[197] Amended by the Police Reform Act 2002, s 52(4).
[198] Amended by the Criminal Justice Act 2003, s 6.

Act

(a) any obligation of that officer to make a record in connection with the carrying out of the review shall have effect as an obligation to cause another officer to make the record;

(b) any requirement for the record to be made in the presence of the arrested person shall apply to the making of that record by that other officer; and

(c) the requirements under section 40(12) and (13) above for—

    (i) the arrested person, or

    (ii) a solicitor representing him,

to be given any opportunity to make representations (whether in writing or orally) to that officer shall have effect as a requirement for that person, or such a solicitor, to be given an opportunity to make representations in a manner authorised by subsection (4) below.

(4) Representations are made in a manner authorised by this subsection—

(a) in a case where facilities exist for the immediate transmission of written representations to the officer carrying out the review, if they are made either—

    (i) orally by telephone to that officer; or

    (ii) in writing to that officer by means of those facilities;

    and

(b) in any other case, if they are made orally by telephone to that officer.

(5) In this section 'video-conferencing facilities' has the same meaning as in section 45A below.][199]

41 Limits on period of detention without charge

(1) Subject to the following provisions of this section and to sections 42 and 43 below, a person shall not be kept in police detention for more than 24 hours without being charged.

(2) The time from which the period of detention of a person is to be calculated (in this Act referred to as 'the relevant time')—

(a) in the case of a person to whom this paragraph applies, shall be—

    (i) the time at which that person arrives at the relevant police station; or

    (ii) the time 24 hours after the time of that person's arrest,

whichever is the earlier;

(b) in the case of a person arrested outside England and Wales, shall be—

    (i) the time at which that person arrives at the first police station to which he is taken in the police area in England or Wales in which the offence for which he was arrested is being investigated; or

    (ii) the time 24 hours after the time of that person's entry into England and Wales,

whichever is the earlier;

(c) in the case of a person who—

    (i) attends voluntarily at a police station; or

    (ii) accompanies a constable to a police station without having been arrested,

and is arrested at the police station, the time of his arrest;

---

[199] Inserted by the Criminal Justice and Police Act 2001, s 73(1), (2).

[(ca) in the case of a person who attends a police station to answer to bail granted under section 30A, the time when he arrives at the police station;][200]

(d) in any other case, except where subsection (5) below applies, shall be the time at which the person arrested arrives at the first police station to which he is taken after his arrest.

(3) Subsection (2)(a) above applies to a person if—

(a) his arrest is sought in one police area in England and Wales;

(b) he is arrested in another police area; and

(c) he is not questioned in the area in which he is arrested in order to obtain evidence in relation to an offence for which he is arrested;

and in sub-paragraph (i) of that paragraph 'the relevant police station' means the first police station to which he is taken in the police area in which his arrest was sought.

(4) Subsection (2) above shall have effect in relation to a person arrested under section 31 above as if every reference in it to his arrest or his being arrested were a reference to his arrest or his being arrested for the offence for which he was originally arrested.

(5) If—

(a) a person is in police detention in a police area in England and Wales ('the first area'); and

(b) his arrest for an offence is sought in some other police area in England and Wales ('the second area'); and

(c) he is taken to the second area for the purposes of investigating that offence, without being questioned in the first area in order to obtain evidence in relation to it,

the relevant time shall be—

(i) the time 24 hours after he leaves the place where he is detained in the first area; or

(ii) the time at which he arrives at the first police station to which he is taken in the second area,

whichever is the earlier.

(6) When a person who is in police detention is removed to hospital because he is in need of medical treatment, any time during which he is being questioned in hospital or on the way there or back by a police officer for the purpose of obtaining evidence relating to an offence shall be included in any period which falls to be calculated for the purposes of this Part of this Act, but any other time while he is in hospital or on his way there or back shall not be so included.

(7) Subject to subsection (8) below, a person who at the expiry of 24 hours after the relevant time is in police detention and has not been charged shall be released at that time either on bail or without bail.

(8) Subsection (7) above does not apply to a person whose detention for more than 24 hours after the relevant time has been authorised or is otherwise permitted in accordance with section 42 or 43 below.

(9) A person released under subsection (7) above shall not be re-arrested without a warrant for the offence for which he was previously arrested unless new evi-

---

[200] Amended by the Criminal Justice Act 2003, s 12, Sch 1, paras 1, 8.

Act

dence justifying a further arrest has come to light since his release[; but this subsection does not prevent an arrest under section 46A below][201].

42 Authorisation of continued detention

(1) Where a police officer of the rank of superintendent or above who is responsible for the police station at which a person is detained has reasonable grounds for believing that—
  (a) the detention of that person without charge is necessary to secure or preserve evidence relating to an offence for which he is under arrest or to obtain such evidence by questioning him;
  [(b) an offence for which he is under arrest is an [indictable][202] offence; and][203]
  (c) the investigation is being conducted diligently and expeditiously,
  he may authorise the keeping of that person in police detention for a period expiring at or before 36 hours after the relevant time.
(2) Where an officer such as is mentioned in subsection (1) above has authorised the keeping of a person in police detention for a period expiring less than 36 hours after the relevant time, such an officer may authorise the keeping of that person in police detention for a further period expiring not more than 36 hours after that time if the conditions specified in subsection (1) above are still satisfied when he gives the authorisation.
(3) If it is proposed to transfer a person in police detention to another police area, the officer determining whether or not to authorise keeping him in detention under subsection (1) above shall have regard to the distance and the time the journey would take.
(4) No authorisation under subsection (1) above shall be given in respect of any person—
  (a) more than 24 hours after the relevant time; or
  (b) before the second review of his detention under section 40 above has been carried out.
(5) Where an officer authorises the keeping of a person in police detention under subsection (1) above, it shall be his duty—
  (a) to inform that person of the grounds for his continued detention; and
  (b) to record the grounds in that person's custody record.
(6) Before determining whether to authorise the keeping of a person in detention under subsection (1) or (2) above, an officer shall give—
  (a) that person; or
  (b) any solicitor representing him who is available at the time when it falls to the officer to determine whether to give the authorisation,
  an opportunity to make representations to him about the detention.
(7) Subject to subsection (8) below, the person in detention or his solicitor may make representations under subsection (6) above either orally or in writing.
(8) The officer to whom it falls to determine whether to give the authorisation may refuse to hear oral representations from the person in detention if he considers that he is unfit to make such representations by reason of his condition or behaviour.

---

[201] Amended by the Criminal Justice and Public Order Act 1994, s 29(4)(b).
[202] Amended by SOCAPA 2005, s 111, Sch 7, Pt 3, para 43(1), (7).
[203] Amended by the Criminal Justice Act 2003, s 7.

(9) Where—
- (a) an officer authorises the keeping of a person in detention under subsection (1) above; and
- (b) at the time of the authorisation he has not yet exercised a right conferred on him by section 56 or 58 below,

the officer—
- (i) shall inform him of that right;
- (ii) shall decide whether he should be permitted to exercise it;
- (iii) shall record the decision in his custody record; and
- (iv) if the decision is to refuse to permit the exercise of the right, shall also record the grounds for the decision in that record.

(10) Where an officer has authorised the keeping of a person who has not been charged in detention under subsection (1) or (2) above, he shall be released from detention, either on bail or without bail, not later than 36 hours after the relevant time, unless—
- (a) he has been charged with an offence; or
- (b) his continued detention is authorised or otherwise permitted in accordance with section 43 below.

(11) A person released under subsection (10) above shall not be re-arrested without a warrant for the offence for which he was previously arrested unless new evidence justifying a further arrest has come to light since his release[; but this subsection does not prevent an arrest under section 46A below][204].

43 Warrants of further detention

(1) Where, on an application on oath made by a constable and supported by an information, a magistrates' court is satisfied that there are reasonable grounds for believing that the further detention of the person to whom the application relates is justified, it may issue a warrant of further detention authorising the keeping of that person in police detention.

(2) A court may not hear an application for a warrant of further detention unless the person to whom the application relates—
- (a) has been furnished with a copy of the information; and
- (b) has been brought before the court for the hearing.

(3) The person to whom the application relates shall be entitled to be legally represented at the hearing and, if he is not so represented but wishes to be so represented—
- (a) the court shall adjourn the hearing to enable him to obtain representation; and
- (b) he may be kept in police detention during the adjournment.

(4) A person's further detention is only justified for the purposes of this section or section 44 below if—
- (a) his detention without charge is necessary to secure or preserve evidence relating to an offence for which he is under arrest or to obtain such evidence by questioning him;
- (b) an offence for which he is under arrest is [an indictable offence][205]; and

---

[204] Amended by the Criminal Justice and Public Order Act 1994, s 29(4)(b).
[205] Amended by SOCAPA 2005, s 111, Sch 7, Pt 3, para 43(1), (8).

(c) the investigation is being conducted diligently and expeditiously.

(5) Subject to subsection (7) below, an application for a warrant of further detention may be made—

    (a) at any time before the expiry of 36 hours after the relevant time; or

    (b) in a case where—

        (i) it is not practicable for the magistrates' court to which the application will be made to sit at the expiry of 36 hours after the relevant time; but

        (ii) the court will sit during the 6 hours following the end of that period, at any time before the expiry of the said 6 hours.

(6) In a case to which subsection (5)(b) above applies—

    (a) the person to whom the application relates may be kept in police detention until the application is heard; and

    (b) the custody officer shall make a note in that person's custody record—

        (i) of the fact that he was kept in police detention for more than 36 hours after the relevant time; and

        (ii) of the reason why he was so kept.

(7) If—

    (a) an application for a warrant of further detention is made after the expiry of 36 hours after the relevant time; and

    (b) it appears to the magistrates' court that it would have been reasonable for the police to make it before the expiry of that period,

the court shall dismiss the application.

(8) Where on an application such as is mentioned in subsection (1) above a magistrates' court is not satisfied that there are reasonable grounds for believing that the further detention of the person to whom the application relates is justified, it shall be its duty—

    (a) to refuse the application; or

    (b) to adjourn the hearing of it until a time not later than 36 hours after the relevant time.

(9) The person to whom the application relates may be kept in police detention during the adjournment.

(10) A warrant of further detention shall—

    (a) state the time at which it is issued;

    (b) authorise the keeping in police detention of the person to whom it relates for the period stated in it.

(11) Subject to subsection (12) below, the period stated in a warrant of further detention shall be such period as the magistrates' court thinks fit, having regard to the evidence before it.

(12) The period shall not be longer than 36 hours.

(13) If it is proposed to transfer a person in police detention to a police area other than that in which he is detained when the application for a warrant of further detention is made, the court hearing the application shall have regard to the distance and the time the journey would take.

(14) Any information submitted in support of an application under this section shall state—

    (a) the nature of the offence for which the person to whom the application relates has been arrested;

    (b) the general nature of the evidence on which that person was arrested;

    (c) what inquiries relating to the offence have been made by the police and what further inquiries are proposed by them;

    (d) the reasons for believing the continued detention of that person to be necessary for the purposes of such further inquiries.

(15) Where an application under this section is refused, the person to whom the application relates shall forthwith be charged or, subject to subsection (16) below, released, either on bail or without bail.

(16) A person need not be released under subsection (15) above—

    (a) before the expiry of 24 hours after the relevant time; or

    (b) before the expiry of any longer period for which his continued detention is or has been authorised under section 42 above.

(17) Where an application under this section is refused, no further application shall be made under this section in respect of the person to whom the refusal relates, unless supported by evidence which has come to light since the refusal.

(18) Where a warrant of further detention is issued, the person to whom it relates shall be released from police detention, either on bail or without bail, upon or before the expiry of the warrant unless he is charged.

(19) A person released under subsection (18) above shall not be re-arrested without a warrant for the offence for which he was previously arrested unless new evidence justifying a further arrest has come to light since his release[; but this subsection does not prevent an arrest under section 46A below.][206]

44 Extension of warrants of further detention

(1) On an application on oath made by a constable and supported by an information a magistrates' court may extend a warrant of further detention issued under section 43 above if it is satisfied that there are reasonable grounds for believing that the further detention of the person to whom the application relates is justified.

(2) Subject to subsection (3) below, the period for which a warrant of further detention may be extended shall be such period as the court thinks fit, having regard to the evidence before it.

(3) The period shall not—

    (a) be longer than 36 hours; or

    (b) end later than 96 hours after the relevant time.

(4) Where a warrant of further detention has been extended under subsection (1) above, or further extended under this subsection, for a period ending before 96 hours after the relevant time, on an application such as is mentioned in that subsection a magistrates' court may further extend the warrant if it is satisfied as there mentioned; and subsections (2) and (3) above apply to such further extensions as they apply to extensions under subsection (1) above.

(5) A warrant of further detention shall, if extended or further extended under this section, be endorsed with a note of the period of the extension.

(6) Subsections (2), (3), and (14) of section 43 above shall apply to an application made under this section as they apply to an application made under that section.

---

[206] Amended by the Criminal Justice and Public Order Act 1994, s 29(4)(b).

(7) Where an application under this section is refused, the person to whom the application relates shall forthwith be charged or, subject to subsection (8) below, released, either on bail or without bail.

(8) A person need not be released under subsection (7) above before the expiry of any period for which a warrant of further detention issued in relation to him has been extended or further extended on an earlier application made under this section.

45 Detention before charge—supplementary

(1) In sections 43 and 44 of this Act 'magistrates' court' means a court consisting of two or more justices of the peace sitting otherwise than in open court.

(2) Any reference in this Part of this Act to a period of time or a time of day is to be treated as approximate only.

[45A Use of video-conferencing facilities for decisions about detention

(1) Subject to the following provisions of this section, the Secretary of State may by regulations provide that, in the case of an arrested person who is held in a police station, some or all of the functions mentioned in subsection (2) may be performed (notwithstanding anything in the preceding provisions of this Part) by an officer who—

    (a) is not present in that police station; but
    (b) has access to the use of video-conferencing facilities that enable him to communicate with persons in that station.

(2) Those functions are—

    (a) the functions in relation to an arrested person taken to[, or answering to bail at,][207] a police station that is not a designated police station which, in the case of an arrested person taken to a station that is a designated police station, are functions of a custody officer under section 37, 38 or 40 above; and
    (b) the function of carrying out a review under section 40(1)(b) above (review, by an officer of at least the rank of inspector, of the detention of person arrested but not charged).

(3) Regulations under this section shall specify the use to be made in the performance of the functions mentioned in subsection (2) above of the facilities mentioned in subsection (1) above.

(4) Regulations under this section shall not authorise the performance of any of the functions mentioned in subsection (2)(a) above by such an officer as is mentioned in subsection (1) above unless he is a custody officer for a designated police station.

(5) Where any functions mentioned in subsection (2) above are performed in a manner authorised by regulations under this section—

    (a) any obligation of the officer performing those functions to make a record in connection with the performance of those functions shall have effect as an obligation to cause another officer to make the record; and

---

[207] Amended by the Criminal Justice Act 2003, s 12, Sch 1, paras 1, 9.

      (b) any requirement for the record to be made in the presence of the arrested person shall apply to the making of that record by that other officer.

(6) Where the functions mentioned in subsection (2)(b) are performed in a manner authorised by regulations under this section, the requirements under section 40(12) and (13) above for—

      (a) the arrested person, or

      (b) a solicitor representing him,

to be given any opportunity to make representations (whether in writing or orally) to the person performing those functions shall have effect as a requirement for that person, or such a solicitor, to be given an opportunity to make representations in a manner authorised by subsection (7) below.

(7) Representations are made in a manner authorised by this subsection—

      (a) in a case where facilities exist for the immediate transmission of written representations to the officer performing the functions, if they are made either—

            (i) orally to that officer by means of the video-conferencing facilities used by him for performing those functions; or

            (ii) in writing to that officer by means of the facilities available for the immediate transmission of the representations;

      and

      (b) in any other case if they are made orally to that officer by means of the video-conferencing facilities used by him for performing the functions.

(8) Regulations under this section may make different provision for different cases and may be made so as to have effect in relation only to the police stations specified or described in the regulations.

(9) Regulations under this section shall be made by statutory instrument and shall be subject to annulment in pursuance of a resolution of either House of Parliament.

(10) Any reference in this section to video-conferencing facilities, in relation to any functions, is a reference to any facilities (whether a live television link or other facilities) by means of which the functions may be performed with the officer performing them, the person in relation to whom they are performed and any legal representative of that person all able to both see and to hear each other.][208]

Detention—miscellaneous

46 Detention after charge

(1) Where a person—

      (a) is charged with an offence; and

      (b) after being charged—

            (i) is kept in police detention; or

            (ii) is detained by a local authority in pursuance of arrangements made under section 38(6) above,

he shall be brought before a magistrates' court in accordance with the provisions of this section.

---

[208] Inserted by the Criminal Justice and Police Act 2001, s 73(1), (3).

Act

(2) If he is to be brought before a magistrates' court [in the local justice][209] area in which the police station at which he was charged is situated, he shall be brought before such a court as soon as is practicable and in any event not later than the first sitting after he is charged with the offence.

(3) If no magistrates' court [in that area][210] is due to sit either on the day on which he is charged or on the next day, the custody officer for the police station at which he was charged shall inform the [designated officer][211] for the area that there is a person in the area to whom subsection (2) above applies.

(4) If the person charged is to be brought before a magistrates' court [in a local justice][212] area other than that in which the police station at which he was charged is situated, he shall be removed to that area as soon as is practicable and brought before such a court as soon as is practicable after his arrival in the area and in any event not later than the first sitting of a magistrates' court [in that area][213] after his arrival in the area.

(5) If no magistrates' court [in that area][214] is due to sit either on the day on which he arrives in the area or on the next day—
   (a) he shall be taken to a police station in the area; and
   (b) the custody officer at that station shall inform the [designated officer][215] for the area that there is a person in the area to whom subsection (4) applies.

(6) Subject to subsection (8) below, where [the designated officer for a local justice][216] area has been informed—
   (a) under subsection (3) above that there is a person in the area to whom subsection (2) above applies; or
   (b) under subsection (5) above that there is a person in the area to whom subsection (4) above applies, [the designated officer][217] shall arrange for a magistrates' court to sit not later than the day next following the relevant day.

(7) In this section 'the relevant day'—
   (a) in relation to a person who is to be brought before a magistrates' court [in the local justice][218] area in which the police station at which he was charged is situated, means the day on which he was charged; and
   (b) in relation to a person who is to be brought before a magistrates' court [in any other local justice][219] area, means the day on which he arrives in the area.

(8) Where the day next following the relevant day is Christmas Day, Good Friday or a Sunday, the duty of the [designated officer][220] under subsection (6) above is a duty to arrange for a magistrates' court to sit not later than the first day after the relevant day which is not one of those days.

---

[209] Amended by the Courts Act 2003, s 109(1), Sch 8, para 282(1), (2).
[210] Amended by the Courts Act 2003, s 109(1), Sch 8, para 282(1), (3)(a).
[211] Amended by the Courts Act 2003, s 109(1), Sch 8, para 282(1), (3)(b).
[212] Amended by the Courts Act 2003, s 109(1), Sch 8, para 282(1), (4)(a).
[213] Amended by the Courts Act 2003, s 109(1), Sch 8, para 282(1), (4)(b).
[214] Amended by the Courts Act 2003, s 109(1), Sch 8, para 282(1), (5)(a).
[215] Amended by the Courts Act 2003, s 109(1), Sch 8, para 282(1), (5)(b)
[216] Amended by the Courts Act 2003, s 109(1), Sch 8, para 282(1), (6)(a).
[217] Amended by the Courts Act 2003, s 109(1), Sch 8, para 282(1), (6)(b).
[218] Amended by the Courts Act 2003, s 109(1), Sch 8, para 282(1), (7)(a).
[219] Amended by the Courts Act 2003, s 109(1), Sch 8, para 282(1), (7)(b).
[220] Amended by the Courts Act 2003, s 109(1), Sch 8, para 282(1), (8).

(9)   Nothing in this section requires a person who is in hospital to be brought before a court if he is not well enough.

[46ZA Persons granted live link bail

(1)   This section applies in relation to bail granted under this Part subject to the duty mentioned in section 47(3)(b) ('live link bail').

(2)   An accused person who attends a police station to answer to live link bail is not to be treated as in police detention for the purposes of this Act.

(3)   Subsection (2) does not apply in relation to an accused person if—

      [...][221]

    (b) [at any time before the beginning of proceedings in relation to a live link direction under section 57C of the Crime and Disorder Act 1998 in relation to the accused person,][222] a constable informs him that a live link will not be available for his use for the purposes of that section; [or]

      [...][223]

    (d) the court determines for [any reason][224] not to give such a direction.

(4)   If [paragraph (b) or (d) of subsection (3) applies][225] in relation to a person, he is to be treated for the purposes of this Part—

    (a) as if he had been arrested for and charged with the offence in connection with which he was granted bail, and

    (b) as if he had been so charged at the time when that paragraph first applied in relation to him.

(5)   An accused person who is arrested under section 46A for failing to attend at a police station to answer to live link bail, and who is brought to a police station in accordance with that section, is to be treated for the purposes of this Part—

    (a) as if he had been arrested for and charged with the offence in connection with which he was granted bail, and

    (b) as if he had been so charged at the time when he is brought to the station.

(6)   Nothing in subsection (4) or (5) affects the operation of section 47(6).][226]

[46A Power of arrest for failure to answer to police bail

(1)   A constable may arrest without a warrant any person who, having been released on bail under this Part of this Act subject to a duty to attend at a police station, fails to attend at that police station at the time appointed for him to do so.

[(1ZA) The reference in subsection (1) to a person who fails to attend at a police station at the time appointed for him to do so includes a reference to a person who—

    (a) attends at a police station to answer to bail granted subject to the duty mentioned in section 47(3)(b), but

---

[221] Repealed by Coroners and Justice Act 2009, s 107(2)(a)(i).

[222] Words substituted by Coroners and Justice Act 2009, s 107(2)(a)(ii).

[223] Repealed by Coroners and Justice Act 2009, Pt 3 c.4 s 107(2)(a)(iii).

[224] Words substituted by Coroners and Justice Act 2009, s 107(2)(a)(iv).

[225] Words substituted by Coroners and Justice Act 2009, s 107(2)(b).

[226] Added by Police and Justice Act 2006, s 46(3) (1 April 2007 for purposes specified in SI 2007/709 art 3(n); 14 November 2008 for purposes specified in SI 2008/2785, art 2; 3 October 2011 for purposes specified in SI 2011/2144 art 2, and not yet in force otherwise).

Act

(b) leaves the police station at any time before the beginning of proceedings in relation to a live link direction under section 57C of the Crime and Disorder Act 1998 in relation to him [...][227].][228]

[(1ZB) The reference in subsection (1) to a person who fails to attend a police station at the time appointed for the person to do so includes a reference to a person who—

(a) attends at a police station to answer to bail granted subject to the duty mentioned in section 47(3)(b), but

(b) refuses to be searched under section 54B.][229]

[(1A) A person who has been released on bail under [section 37, 37C(2)(b) or 37CA(2)(b)][230] above may be arrested without warrant by a constable if the constable has reasonable grounds for suspecting that the person has broken any of the conditions of bail.][231]

(2) A person who is arrested under this section shall be taken to the police station appointed as the place at which he is to surrender to custody as soon as practicable after the arrest.

(3) For the purposes of—

(a) section 30 above (subject to the obligation in subsection (2) above), and

(b) section 31 above,

an arrest under this section shall be treated as an arrest for an offence.][232]

47 Bail after arrest

(1) [Subject to the following provisions of this section][233], a release on bail of a person under this Part of this Act shall be a release on bail granted in accordance with [sections 3, 3A, 5 and 5A of the Bail Act 1976 as they apply to bail granted by a constable][234].

[(1A) The normal powers to impose conditions of bail shall be available to him where a custody officer releases a person on bail under [section 37 above or section 38(1)][235] (including that subsection as applied by section 40(10) above) but not in any other cases.

In this subsection, 'the normal powers to impose conditions of bail' has the meaning given in section 3(6) of the Bail Act 1976.][236]

[(1B) No application may be made under section 5B of the Bail Act 1976 if a person is released on bail under section [37, 37C(2)(b) or 37CA(2)(b)][237] above.

---

[227] Words repealed by Coroners and Justice Act 2009, s 107(3).

[228] Added by Police and Justice Act 2006, s 46(4) (1 April 2007 for purposes specified in SI 2007/709, art 3(n); 14 November 2008 for purposes specified in SI 2008/2785, art 2; 3 October 2011 for purposes specified in SI 2011/2144 art 2, and not yet in force otherwise).

[229] Added by Coroners and Justice Act 2009, s 108(2).

[230] Words substituted by Police and Justice Act 2006, Sch 6(3), para 7.

[231] Amended by the Criminal Justice Act 2003, s 28, Sch 2, paras 1, 5.

[232] Inserted by the Criminal Justice and Public Order Act 1994, s 29(2).

[233] Amended by the Criminal Justice Act 2003, s 28, Sch 2, paras 1, 6(1), (2).

[234] Amended by the Criminal Justice and Public Order Act 1994, s 27(1)(a).

[235] Word substituted by Police and Justice Act 2006, Sch 6(3), para 6.

[236] Amended by the Criminal Justice and Public Order Act 1994, s 27(1)(b).

[237] Words substituted by Police and Justice Act 2006, Sch 6(3), para 11.

(1C) Subsections (1D) to (1F) below apply where a person released on bail under section [37, 37C(2)(b) or 37CA(2)(b)][238] above is on bail subject to conditions.

(1D) The person shall not be entitled to make an application under section 43B of the Magistrates' Courts Act 1980.

(1E) A magistrates' court may, on an application by or on behalf of the person, vary the conditions of bail; and in this subsection 'vary' has the same meaning as in the Bail Act 1976.

(1F) Where a magistrates' court varies the conditions of bail under subsection (1E) above, that bail shall not lapse but shall continue subject to the conditions as so varied.][239]

(2) Nothing in the Bail Act 1976 shall prevent the re-arrest without warrant of a person released on bail subject to a duty to attend at a police station if new evidence justifying a further arrest has come to light since his release.

(3) Subject to [subsections (3A) and (4)][240] below, in this Part of this Act references to 'bail' are references to bail subject to a duty—

    [(a) to appear before a magistrates' court at such time and such place as the custody officer may appoint;

    (b) to attend at such police station as the custody officer may appoint at such time as he may appoint for the purposes of—

       (i) proceedings in relation to a live link direction under section 57C of the Crime and Disorder Act 1998 (use of live link direction at preliminary hearings where accused is at police station); and

       (ii) any preliminary hearing in relation to which such a direction is given; or

    (c) to attend at such police station as the custody officer may appoint at such time as he may appoint for purposes other than those mentioned in paragraph (b).][241]

[(3A) Where a custody officer grants bail to a person subject to a duty to appear before a magistrates' court, he shall appoint for the appearance—

    (a) a date which is not later than the first sitting of the court after the person is charged with the offence; or

    (b) where he is informed by the [designated officer for the relevant local justice][242] area that the appearance cannot be accommodated until a later date, that later date.][243]

(4) Where a custody officer has granted bail to a person subject to a duty to appear at a police station, the custody officer may give notice in writing to that person that his attendance at the police station is not required.

    [...][244]

---

[238] Words substituted by Police and Justice Act 2006, Sch 6(3), para 11.

[239] Amended by the Criminal Justice Act 2003, s 28, Sch 2, paras 1, 6(1), (4).

[240] Amended by the Crime and Disorder Act 1998, s 46(1).

[241] Section 47(3)(a)–(c) substituted for s 47(3)(a) and (b) and words by Police and Justice Act 2006, s 46(5)(a) (1 April 2007 for purposes specified in SI 2007/709, art 3(n); 14 November 2008 for purposes specified in SI 2008/2785, art 2, 3 October 2011 for purposes specified in SQ 2011/2144, art 2, and not yet in force otherwise).

[242] Amended by the Courts Act 2003, s 109(1), Sch 8, para 283.

[243] Amended by the Crime and Disorder Act 1998, s 46(2).

[244] Repealed by the Criminal Justice and Public Order Act 1994, ss 29(4)(c), 168(3), Sch 11.

Act

(6) Where a person [who has been granted bail [under this Part]²⁴⁵ and either has attended at the police station in accordance with the grant of bail or has been arrested under section 46A above is detained at a police station]²⁴⁶, any time during which he was in police detention prior to being granted bail shall be included as part of any period which falls to be calculated under this Part of this Act [and any time during which he was on bail shall not be so included]²⁴⁷.

(7) Where a person who was released on bail [under this Part]²⁴⁸ subject to a duty to attend at a police station is re-arrested, the provisions of this Part of this Act shall apply to him as they apply to a person arrested for the first time[; but this subsection does not apply to a person who is arrested under section 46A above or has attended a police station in accordance with the grant of bail (and who accordingly is deemed by section 34(7) above to have been arrested for an offence)]²⁴⁹ [or to a person to whom section 46ZA(4) or (5) applies]²⁵⁰

(8) In the Magistrates' Courts Act 1980—

(a) the following section shall be substituted for section 43—

43 'Bail on arrest

(1) Where a person has been granted bail under the Police and Criminal Evidence Act 1984 subject to a duty to appear before a magistrates' court, the court before which he is to appear may appoint a later time as the time at which he is to appear and may enlarge the recognizances of any sureties for him at that time.

(2) The recognizance of any surety for any person granted bail subject to a duty to attend at a police station may be enforced as if it were conditioned for his appearance before a magistrates' court for the petty sessions area in which the police station named in the recognizance is situated.'; and

(b) the following subsection shall be substituted for section 117(3)—

'(3) Where a warrant has been endorsed for bail under subsection (1) above—

(a) where the person arrested is to be released on bail on his entering into a recognizance without sureties, it shall not be necessary to take him to a police station, but if he is so taken, he shall be released from custody on his entering into the recognizance; and

(b) where he is to be released on his entering into a recognizance with sureties, he shall be taken to a police station on his arrest, and the custody officer there shall (subject to his approving any surety tendered in compliance with the endorsement) release him from custody as directed in the endorsement.'.

[47A Early administrative hearings conducted by justices' clerks

Where a person has been charged with an offence at a police station, any requirement imposed under this Part for the person to appear or be brought before a

²⁴⁵ Amended by the Criminal Justice Act 2003, s 12, Sch 1, paras 1, 10(a).
²⁴⁶ Amended by the Criminal Justice and Public Order Act 1994, s 29(4)(d).
²⁴⁷ Amended by the Police (Detention and Bail) Act 2011, s 1(1) (1 June 1991: insertion deemed always to have had effect; that is from the original commencement of 1984 s 47 on 1 January 1986).
²⁴⁸ Amended by the Criminal Justice Act 2003, s 12, Sch 1, paras 1, 10(b).
²⁴⁹ Amended by the Criminal Justice and Public Order Act 1994, s 29(4)(e).
²⁵⁰ Words inserted by Police and Justice Act 2006, s 46(5)(b) (1 April 2007 for purposes specified in SI 2007/709, art 3(n); 14 November 2008 for purposes specified in SI 2008/2785, art 2; 3 October 2011 for purposes specified in SI 2011/2144 art 2, and not yet in force otherwise).

magistrates' court shall be taken to be satisfied if the person appears or is brought before [a justices' clerk]²⁵¹ in order for the clerk to conduct a hearing under section 50 of the Crime and Disorder Act 1998 (early administrative hearings).]²⁵²

48 Remands to police detention

In section 128 of the Magistrates' Courts Act 1980—

(a) in subsection (7) for the words 'the custody of a constable' there shall be substituted the words 'detention at a police station';

(b) after subsection (7) there shall be inserted the following subsection—

'(8) Where a person is committed to detention at a police station under subsection (7) above—

(a) he shall not be kept in such detention unless there is a need for him to be so detained for the purposes of inquiries into other offences;

(b) if kept in such detention, he shall be brought back before the magistrates' court which committed him as soon as that need ceases;

(c) he shall be treated as a person in police detention to whom the duties under section 39 of the Police and Criminal Evidence Act 1984 (responsibilities in relation to persons detained) relate;

(d) his detention shall be subject to periodic review at the times set out in section 40 of that Act (review of police detention).'.

49 Police detention to count towards custodial sentence

(1) In subsection (1) of section 67 of the Criminal Justice Act 1967 (computation of custodial sentences) for the words from 'period', in the first place where it occurs, to 'the offender' there shall be substituted the words 'relevant period, but where he'.

(2) The following subsection shall be inserted after that subsection—

'(1A) In subsection (1) above 'relevant period' means—

(a) any period during which the offender was in police detention in connection with the offence for which the sentence was passed; or

(b) any period during which he was in custody—

(i) by reason only of having been committed to custody by an order of a court made in connection with any proceedings relating to that sentence or the offence for which it was passed or any proceedings from which those proceedings arose; or

(ii) by reason of his having been so committed and having been concurrently detained otherwise than by order of a court.'.

(3) The following subsections shall be added after subsection (6) of that section—

'(7) A person is in police detention for the purposes of this section—

(a) at any time when he is in police detention for the purposes of the Police and Criminal Evidence Act 1984; and

(b) at any time when he is detained under section 12 of the Prevention of Terrorism (Temporary Provisions) Act 1984.

---

²⁵¹ Amended by the Courts Act 2003, s 109(1), Sch 8, para 284; for transitional provisions see SI 2005/911, arts 2–5.

²⁵² Inserted by the Crime and Disorder Act 1998, s 119, Sch 8, para 62.

Act

(8) No period of police detention shall be taken into account under this section unless it falls after the coming into force of section 49 of the Police and Criminal Evidence Act 1984.'.

50 Records of detention

(1) Each police force shall keep written records showing on an annual basis—
   (a) the number of persons kept in police detention for more than 24 hours and subsequently released without charge;
   (b) the number of applications for warrants of further detention and the results of the applications; and
   (c) in relation to each warrant of further detention—
      (i) the period of further detention authorised by it;
      (ii) the period which the person named in it spent in police detention on its authority; and
      (iii) whether he was charged or released without charge.

(2) Every annual report—
   [(a) under section 22 of the Police Act 1996; or][253]
   (b) made by the Commissioner of Police of the Metropolis,
   shall contain information about the matters mentioned in subsection (1) above in respect of the period to which the report relates.

51 Savings

Nothing in this Part of this Act shall affect—
   (a) the powers conferred on immigration officers by section 4 of and Schedule 2 to the Immigration Act 1971 (administrative provisions as to control on entry etc);
   [(b) the powers conferred by virtue of section 41 of, or Schedule 7 to, the Terrorism Act 2000 (powers of arrest and detention);][254]
   [...][255]
   (d) any right of a person in police detention to apply for a writ of habeas corpus or other prerogative remedy.

52 Children

   [...][256]

PART V
QUESTIONING AND TREATMENT OF PERSONS BY POLICE

53 Abolition of certain powers of constables to search persons

(1) Subject to subsection (2) below, there shall cease to have effect any Act (including a local Act) passed before this Act in so far as it authorises—
   (a) any search by a constable of a person in police detention at a police station; or

---

[253] Amended by the Police Act 1996, s 103, Sch 7, para 35.
[254] Amended by the Terrorism Act 2000, s 125(1), Sch 15, para 5(1), (4); for savings see the Terrorism Act 2000, s 129(1)(b) and SI 2001/421, art 2.
[255] Repealed by Armed Forces Act 2006, Sch 17, para 1.
[256] Repealed by the Children Act 1989, s 108(7), Sch 15.

(b) an intimate search of a person by a constable;
and any rule of common law which authorises a search such as is mentioned in paragraph (a) or (b) above is abolished.

(2)   [...][257]

54 Searches of detained persons

(1)   The custody officer at a police station shall ascertain [...][258] everything which a person has with him when he is—

(a) brought to the station after being arrested elsewhere or after being committed to custody by an order or sentence of a court; or

[(b) arrested at the station or detained there [, as a person falling within section 34(7), under section 37 above][259] [or as a person to whom section 46ZA(4) or (5) applies].[260]][261]

[(2) The custody officer may record or cause to be recorded all or any of the things which he ascertains under subsection (1).

(2A) In the case of an arrested person, any such record may be made as part of his custody record.][262]

(3)   Subject to subsection (4) below, a custody officer may seize and retain any such thing or cause any such thing to be seized and retained.

(4)   Clothes and personal effects may only be seized if the custody officer—

(a) believes that the person from whom they are seized may use them—

(i)   to cause physical injury to himself or any other person;

(ii) to damage property;

(iii) to interfere with evidence; or

(iv) to assist him to escape; or

(b) has reasonable grounds for believing that they may be evidence relating to an offence.

(5)   Where anything is seized, the person from whom it is seized shall be told the reason for the seizure unless he is—

(a) violent or likely to become violent; or

(b) incapable of understanding what is said to him.

(6)   Subject to subsection (7) below, a person may be searched if the custody officer considers it necessary to enable him to carry out his duty under subsection (1) above and to the extent that the custody officer considers necessary for that purpose.

[(6A) A person who is in custody at a police station or is in police detention otherwise than at a police station may at any time be searched in order to ascertain whether he has with him anything which he could use for any of the purposes specified in subsection (4)(a) above.

---

[257] Repealed by the Prevention of Terrorism (Temporary Provisions) Act 1989, s 25(2), Sch 9, Pt 1.

[258] Repealed by the Criminal Justice Act 2003, ss 8(1), 332, Sch 37(1), para 1.

[259] Amended by the Criminal Justice and Public Order Act 1994, s 168(2), Sch 10, para 55.

[260] Words inserted by Police and Justice Act 2006, s 46(6) (1 April 2007 for purposes specified in SI 2007/709, art 3(n); 14 November 2008 for purposes specified in SI 2008/2785, art 2; 3 October 2011 for purposes specified in SI 2011/2144, art 2, and not yet in force otherwise).

[261] Section 54(1)(b) substituted by the Criminal Justice Act 1988, s 147(a).

[262] Amended by the Criminal Justice Act 2003, s 8(2).

(6B) Subject to subsection (6C) below, a constable may seize and retain, or cause to be seized and retained, anything found on such a search.

(6C) A constable may only seize clothes and personal effects in the circumstances specified in subsection (4) above.][263]

(7) An intimate search may not be conducted under this section.

(8) A search under this section shall be carried out by a constable.

(9) The constable carrying out a search shall be of the same sex as the person searched.

[54A Searches and examination to ascertain identity

(1) If an officer of at least the rank of inspector authorises it, a person who is detained in a police station may be searched or examined, or both—

(a) for the purpose of ascertaining whether he has any mark that would tend to identify him as a person involved in the commission of an offence; or

(b) for the purpose of facilitating the ascertainment of his identity.

(2) An officer may only give an authorisation under subsection (1) for the purpose mentioned in paragraph (a) of that subsection if—

(a) the appropriate consent to a search or examination that would reveal whether the mark in question exists has been withheld; or

(b) it is not practicable to obtain such consent.

(3) An officer may only give an authorisation under subsection (1) in a case in which subsection (2) does not apply if—

(a) the person in question has refused to identify himself; or

(b) the officer has reasonable grounds for suspecting that that person is not who he claims to be.

(4) An officer may give an authorisation under subsection (1) orally or in writing but, if he gives it orally, he shall confirm it in writing as soon as is practicable.

(5) Any identifying mark found on a search or examination under this section may be photographed—

(a) with the appropriate consent; or

(b) if the appropriate consent is withheld or it is not practicable to obtain it, without it.

(6) Where a search or examination may be carried out under this section, or a photograph may be taken under this section, the only persons entitled to carry out the search or examination, or to take the photograph, are [constables][264].

(7) A person may not under this section carry out a search or examination of a person of the opposite sex or take a photograph of any part of the body of a person of the opposite sex.

(8) An intimate search may not be carried out under this section.

(9) A photograph taken under this section—

(a) may be used by, or disclosed to, any person for any purpose related to the prevention or detection of crime, the investigation of an offence or the conduct of a prosecution; and

(b) after being so used or disclosed, may be retained but may not be used or disclosed except for a purpose so related.

---

[263] Amended by the Criminal Justice Act 1988, s 147(b).
[264] Amended by the Police Reform Act 2002, s 107(1), Sch 7, para 9(2).

(10) In subsection—
    (a) the reference to crime includes a reference to any conduct which—
        (i) constitutes one or more criminal offences (whether under the law of a part of the United Kingdom or of a country or territory outside the United Kingdom); or
        (ii) is, or corresponds to, any conduct which, if it all took place in any one part of the United Kingdom, would constitute one or more criminal offences;
    and
    (b) the references to an investigation and to a prosecution include references, respectively, to any investigation outside the United Kingdom of any crime or suspected crime and to a prosecution brought in respect of any crime in a country or territory outside the United Kingdom.

(11) In this section—
    (a) references to ascertaining a person's identity include references to showing that he is not a particular person; and
    (b) references to taking a photograph include references to using any process by means of which a visual image may be produced, and references to photographing a person shall be construed accordingly.

(12) In this section 'mark' includes features and injuries; and a mark is an identifying mark for the purposes of this section if its existence in any person's case facilitates the ascertainment of his identity or his identification as a person involved in the commission of an offence.

[(13) Nothing in this section applies to a person arrested under an extradition arrest power.][265][266]

[54B Searches of persons answering to live link bail

(1) A constable may search at any time—
    (a) any person who is at a police station to answer to live link bail; and
    (b) any article in the possession of such a person.

(2) If the constable reasonably believes a thing in the possession of the person ought to be seized on any of the grounds mentioned in subsection (3), the constable may seize and retain it or cause it to be seized and retained.

(3) The grounds are that the thing—
    (a) may jeopardise the maintenance of order in the police station;
    (b) may put the safety of any person in the police station at risk; or
    (c) may be evidence of, or in relation to, an offence.

(4) The constable may record or cause to be recorded all or any of the things seized and retained pursuant to subsection (2).

(5) An intimate search may not be carried out under this section.

(6) The constable carrying out a search under subsection (1) must be of the same sex as the person being searched.

(7) In this section 'live link bail' means bail granted under Part 4 of this Act subject to the duty mentioned in section 47(3)(b).][267]

---

[265] Amended by the Extradition Act 2003, s 169(1), (2); for savings see SI 2003/3103, arts 3–4.
[266] Inserted by the Anti-terrorism, Crime and Security Act 2001, s 90(1).
[267] Added by Coroners and Justice Act 2009, s 108(1).

[54C Power to retain articles seized

(1) Except as provided by subsections (2) and (3), a constable may retain a thing seized under section 54B until the time when the person from whom it was seized leaves the police station.

(2) A constable may retain a thing seized under section 54B in order to establish its lawful owner, where there are reasonable grounds for believing that it has been obtained in consequence of the commission of an offence.

(3) If a thing seized under section 54B may be evidence of, or in relation to, an offence, a constable may retain it—

(a) for use as evidence at a trial for an offence; or

(b) for forensic examination or for investigation in connection with an offence.

(4) Nothing may be retained for either of the purposes mentioned in subsection (3) if a photograph or copy would be sufficient for that purpose.

(5) Nothing in this section affects any power of a court to make an order under section 1 of the Police (Property) Act 1897.

(6) The references in this section to anything seized under section 54B include anything seized by a person to whom paragraph 27A of Schedule 4 to the Police Reform Act 2002 applies.][268]

55 Intimate searches

(1) Subject to the following provisions of this section, if an officer of at least the rank of [inspector][269] has reasonable grounds for believing—

(a) that a person who has been arrested and is in police detention may have concealed on him anything which—

(i) he could use to cause physical injury to himself or others; and

(ii) he might so use while he is in police detention or in the custody of a court; or

(b) that such a person—

(i) may have a Class A drug concealed on him; and

(ii) was in possession of it with the appropriate criminal intent before his arrest,

he may authorise [an intimate search][270] of that person.

(2) An officer may not authorise an intimate search of a person for anything unless he has reasonable grounds for believing that it cannot be found without his being intimately searched.

(3) An officer may give an authorisation under subsection (1) above orally or in writing but, if he gives it orally, he shall confirm it in writing as soon as is practicable.

[(3A) A drug offence search shall not be carried out unless the appropriate consent has been given in writing.

(3B) Where it is proposed that a drug offence search be carried out, an appropriate officer shall inform the person who is to be subject to it—

(a) of the giving of the authorisation for it; and

(b) of the grounds for giving the authorisation.][271]

---

[268] Added by Coroners and Justice Act 2009, s 108(1).
[269] Amended by the Criminal Justice and Police Act 2001, s 79.
[270] Amended by the Criminal Justice Act 1988, s 170(1), Sch 15, paras 97, 99.
[271] Amended by the Drugs Act 2005, s 3(1), (2).

(4)   An intimate search which is only a drug offence search shall be by way of examination by a suitably qualified person.

(5)   Except as provided by subsection (4) above, an intimate search shall be by way of examination by a suitably qualified person unless an officer of at least the rank of [inspector][272] considers that this is not practicable.

(6)   An intimate search which is not carried out as mentioned in subsection (5) above shall be carried out by a constable.

(7)   A constable may not carry out an intimate search of a person of the opposite sex.

(8)   No intimate search may be carried out except—

(a) at a police station;

(b) at a hospital;

(c) at a registered medical practitioner's surgery; or

(d) at some other place used for medical purposes.

(9)   An intimate search which is only a drug offence search may not be carried out at a police station.

(10)   If an intimate search of a person is carried out, the custody record relating to him shall state—

(a) which parts of his body were searched; and

(b) why they were searched.

[(10A) If the intimate search is a drug offence search, the custody record relating to that person shall also state—

(a) the authorisation by virtue of which the search was carried out;

(b) the grounds for giving the authorisation; and

(c) the fact that the appropriate consent was given.][273]

(11)   The information required to be recorded by [subsections (10) and (10A)][274] above shall be recorded as soon as practicable after the completion of the search.

(12)   The custody officer at a police station may seize and retain anything which is found on an intimate search of a person, or cause any such thing to be seized and retained—

(a) if he believes that the person from whom it is seized may use it—

(i)   to cause physical injury to himself or any other person;

(ii) to damage property;

(iii) to interfere with evidence; or

(iv) to assist him to escape; or

(b) if he has reasonable grounds for believing that it may be evidence relating to an offence.

(13)   Where anything is seized under this section, the person from whom it is seized shall be told the reason for the seizure unless he is—

(a) violent or likely to become violent; or

(b) incapable of understanding what is said to him.

[(13A) Where the appropriate consent to a drug offence search of any person was refused without good cause, in any proceedings against that person for an offence—

---

[272] Amended by the Criminal Justice and Police Act 2001, s 79.
[273] Amended by the Drugs Act 2005, s 3(1), (3).
[274] Amended by the Drugs Act 2005, s 3(1), (4).

(a) the court, in determining whether there is a case to answer;

(b) a judge, in deciding whether to grant an application made by the accused under paragraph 2 of Schedule 3 to the Crime and Disorder Act 1998 (applications for dismissal); and

(c) the court or jury, in determining whether that person is guilty of the offence charged,

may draw such inferences from the refusal as appear proper.][275]

(14) Every annual report—

[(a) under section 22 of the Police Act 1996; or][276]

(b) made by the Commissioner of Police of the Metropolis,

shall contain information about searches under this section which have been carried out in the area to which the report relates during the period to which it relates.

[...][277]

(15) The information about such searches shall include—

(a) the total number of searches;

(b) the number of searches conducted by way of examination by a suitably qualified person;

(c) the number of searches not so conducted but conducted in the presence of such a person; and

(d) the result of the searches carried out.

(16) The information shall also include, as separate items—

(a) the total number of drug offence searches; and

(b) the result of those searches.

(17) In this section—

'the appropriate criminal intent' means an intent to commit an offence under—

(a) section 5(3) of the Misuse of Drugs Act 1971 (possession of controlled drug with intent to supply to another); or

(b) section 68(2) of the Customs and Excise Management Act 1979 (exportation etc with intent to evade a prohibition or restriction);

['appropriate officer' means—

(a) a constable,

(b) a person who is designated as a detention officer in pursuance of section 38 of the Police Reform Act 2002 if his designation applies paragraph 33D of Schedule 4 to that Act[;]

[...][278]][279]

'Class A drug' has the meaning assigned to it by section 2(1)(b) of the Misuse of Drugs Act 1971;

'drug offence search' means an intimate search for a Class A drug which an officer has authorised by virtue of subsection (1)(b) above; and

'suitably qualified person' means—

[275] Amended by the Drugs Act 2005, s 3(1), (5).
[276] Amended by the Police Act 1996, s 103, Sch 7(II), para 36.
[277] Repealed by SOCAPA 2005, ss 59, 174(2), Sch 4, paras 43, 45, Sch 17, Pt 2.
[278] Repealed by Policing and Crime Act 2009, Sch 8, para 1.
[279] Definition inserted by the Drugs Act 2005, s 3(6).

297

(a)　a registered medical practitioner; or

(b)　a registered nurse.

[55A　**X-rays and ultrasound scans**

(1) If an officer of at least the rank of inspector has reasonable grounds for believing that a person who has been arrested for an offence and is in police detention—

(a)　may have swallowed a Class A drug, and

(b)　was in possession of it with the appropriate criminal intent before his arrest,

the officer may authorise that an x-ray is taken of the person or an ultrasound scan is carried out on the person (or both).

(2) An x-ray must not be taken of a person and an ultrasound scan must not be carried out on him unless the appropriate consent has been given in writing.

(3) If it is proposed that an x-ray is taken or an ultrasound scan is carried out, an appropriate officer must inform the person who is to be subject to it—

(a)　of the giving of the authorisation for it, and

(b)　of the grounds for giving the authorisation.

(4) An x-ray may be taken or an ultrasound scan carried out only by a suitably qualified person and only at—

(a)　a hospital,

(b)　a registered medical practitioner's surgery, or

(c)　some other place used for medical purposes.

(5) The custody record of the person must also state—

(a)　the authorisation by virtue of which the x-ray was taken or the ultrasound scan was carried out,

(b)　the grounds for giving the authorisation, and

(c)　the fact that the appropriate consent was given.

(6) The information required to be recorded by subsection (5) must be recorded as soon as practicable after the x-ray has been taken or ultrasound scan carried out (as the case may be).

(7) Every annual report—

(a)　under section 22 of the Police Act 1996, or

(b)　made by the Commissioner of Police of the Metropolis,

must contain information about x-rays which have been taken and ultrasound scans which have been carried out under this section in the area to which the report relates during the period to which it relates.

(8) The information about such x-rays and ultrasound scans must be presented separately and must include—

(a)　the total number of x-rays;

(b)　the total number of ultrasound scans;

(c)　the results of the x-rays;

(d)　the results of the ultrasound scans.

(9) If the appropriate consent to an x-ray or ultrasound scan of any person is refused without good cause, in any proceedings against that person for an offence—

(a)　the court, in determining whether there is a case to answer,

(b)　a judge, in deciding whether to grant an application made by the accused under paragraph 2 of Schedule 3 to the Crime and Disorder Act 1998 (applications for dismissal), and

(c) the court or jury, in determining whether that person is guilty of the offence charged,

may draw such inferences from the refusal as appear proper.

Act

(10) In this section 'the appropriate criminal intent', 'appropriate officer', 'Class A drug' and 'suitably qualified person' have the same meanings as in section 55 above.][280]

56 Right to have someone informed when arrested

(1) Where a person has been arrested and is being held in custody in a police station or other premises, he shall be entitled, if he so requests, to have one friend or relative or other person who is known to him or who is likely to take an interest in his welfare told, as soon as is practicable except to the extent that delay is permitted by this section, that he has been arrested and is being detained there.

(2) Delay is only permitted—
   (a) in the case of a person who is in police detention for [an indictable offence][281]; and
   (b) if an officer of at least the rank of [inspector][282] authorises it.

(3) In any case the person in custody must be permitted to exercise the right conferred by subsection (1) above within 36 hours from the relevant time, as defined in section 41(2) above.

(4) An officer may give an authorisation under subsection (2) above orally or in writing but, if he gives it orally, he shall confirm it in writing as soon as is practicable.

(5) [Subject to subsection (5A) below][283] an officer may only authorise delay where he has reasonable grounds for believing that telling the named person of the arrest—
   (a) will lead to interference with or harm to evidence connected with [an indictable offence][284] or interference with or physical injury to other persons; or
   (b) will lead to the alerting of other persons suspected of having committed such an offence but not yet arrested for it; or
   (c) will hinder the recovery of any property obtained as a result of such an offence.

[(5A) An officer may also authorise delay where he has reasonable grounds for believing that—
   (a) the person detained for [the indictable offence][285] has benefited from his criminal conduct, and
   (b) the recovery of the value of the property constituting the benefit will be hindered by telling the named person of the arrest.

(5B) For the purposes of subsection (5A) above the question whether a person has benefited from his criminal conduct is to be decided in accordance with Part 2 of the Proceeds of Crime Act 2002.][286]

---

[280] Inserted by the Drugs Act 2005, s 5(1).
[281] Amended by SOCAPA 2005, s 111, Sch 7, Pt 3, para 43(1), (9)(a).
[282] Amended by the Criminal Justice and Police Act 2001, s 74.
[283] Amended by the Drug Trafficking Offences Act 1986, s 32(1).
[284] Amended by SOCAPA 2005, s 111, Sch 7, Pt 3, para 43(1), (9)(a).
[285] Amended by SOCAPA 2005, s 111, Sch 7, Pt 3, para 43(1), (9)(b).
[286] Amended by the Proceeds of Crime Act 2002, s 456, Sch 11, paras 1, 14(1), (2).

(6)   If a delay is authorised—
      (a) the detained person shall be told the reason for it; and
      (b) the reason shall be noted on his custody record.
(7)   The duties imposed by subsection (6) above shall be performed as soon as is
      practicable.
(8)   The rights conferred by this section on a person detained at a police station or
      other premises are exercisable whenever he is transferred from one place to
      another; and this section applies to each subsequent occasion on which they
      are exercisable as it applies to the first such occasion.
(9)   There may be no further delay in permitting the exercise of the right conferred
      by subsection (1) above once the reason for authorising delay ceases to
      subsist.
[(10) Nothing in this section applies to a person arrested or detained under the ter-
      rorism provisions.][287]

57 Additional rights of children and young persons

The following subsections shall be substituted for section 34(2) of the Children and
Young Persons Act 1933—

'(2) Where a child or young person is in police detention, such steps as are practi-
      cable shall be taken to ascertain the identity of a person responsible for his
      welfare.
(3)   If it is practicable to ascertain the identity of a person responsible for the wel-
      fare of the child or young person, that person shall be informed, unless it is not
      practicable to do so—
      (a) that the child or young person has been arrested;
      (b) why he has been arrested; and
      (c) where he is being detained.
(4)   Where information falls to be given under subsection (3) above, it shall be
      given as soon as it is practicable to do so.
(5)   For the purposes of this section the persons who may be responsible for the
      welfare of a child or young person are—
      (a) his parent or guardian; or
      (b) any other person who has for the time being assumed responsibility for his
           welfare.
(6)   If it is practicable to give a person responsible for the welfare of the child or
      young person the information required by subsection (3) above, that person
      shall be given it as soon as it is practicable to do so.
(7)   If it appears that at the time of his arrest a supervision order, as defined in sec-
      tion 11 of the Children and Young Persons Act 1969, is in force in respect of
      him, the person responsible for his supervision shall also be informed as
      described in subsection (3) above as soon as it is reasonably practicable to
      do so.
(8)   The reference to a parent or guardian in subsection (5) above is—
      (a) in the case of a child or young person in the care of a local authority, a
           reference to that authority; and

---

[287] Amended by the Terrorism Act 2000, s 125(1), Sch 15, para 5(1), (5).

Act

(b) in the case of a child or young person in the care of a voluntary organisation in which parental rights and duties with respect to him are vested by
virtue of a resolution under section 64(1) of the Child Care Act 1980, a
reference to that organisation.

(9) The rights conferred on a child or young person by subsections (2) to (8) above
are in addition to his rights under section 56 of the Police and Criminal
Evidence Act 1984.

(10) The reference in subsection (2) above to a child or young person who is in
police detention includes a reference to a child or young person who has been
detained under the terrorism provisions; and in subsection (3) above 'arrest'
includes such detention.

(11) In subsection (10) above 'the terrorism provisions' has the meaning assigned to
it by section 65 of the Police and Criminal Evidence Act 1984'.

58 Access to legal advice

(1) A person arrested and held in custody in a police station or other premises shall
be entitled, if he so requests, to consult a solicitor privately at any time.

(2) Subject to subsection (3) below, a request under subsection (1) above and the
time at which it was made shall be recorded in the custody record.

(3) Such a request need not be recorded in the custody record of a person who
makes it at a time while he is at a court after being charged with an offence.

(4) If a person makes such a request, he must be permitted to consult a solicitor as
soon as is practicable except to the extent that delay is permitted by this section.

(5) In any case he must be permitted to consult a solicitor within 36 hours from
the relevant time, as defined in section 41(2) above.

(6) Delay in compliance with a request is only permitted—
(a) in the case of a person who is in police detention for [an indictable
offence][288]; and
(b) if an officer of at least the rank of superintendent authorises it.

(7) An officer may give an authorisation under subsection (6) above orally or in
writing but, if he gives it orally, he shall confirm it in writing as soon as is
practicable.

(8) [Subject to subsection (8A) below][289] an officer may only authorise delay where
he has reasonable grounds for believing that the exercise of the right conferred
by subsection (1) above at the time when the person detained desires to exercise it—
(a) will lead to interference with or harm to evidence connected with [an
indictable offence][290] or interference with or physical injury to other persons; or
(b) will lead to the alerting of other persons suspected of having committed
such an offence but not yet arrested for it; or
(c) will hinder the recovery of any property obtained as a result of such an
offence.

[288] Amended by SOCAPA 2005, s 111, Sch 7, Pt 3, para 43(1), (10)(a).
[289] Amended by the Drug Trafficking Offences Act 1986, s 32(2).
[290] Amended by SOCAPA 2005, s 111, Sch 7, Pt 3, para 43(1), (10)(a).

[(8A) An officer may also authorise delay where he has reasonable grounds for believing that—

(a) the person detained for [the indictable offence][291] has benefited from his criminal conduct, and

(b) the recovery of the value of the property constituting the benefit will be hindered by the exercise of the right conferred by subsection (1) above.

(8B) For the purposes of subsection (8A) above the question whether a person has benefited from his criminal conduct is to be decided in accordance with Part 2 of the Proceeds of Crime Act 2002.][292]

(9) If delay is authorised—

(a) the detained person shall be told the reason for it; and

(b) the reason shall be noted on his custody record.

(10) The duties imposed by subsection (9) above shall be performed as soon as is practicable.

(11) There may be no further delay in permitting the exercise of the right conferred by subsection (1) above once the reason for authorising delay ceases to subsist.

[(12) Nothing in this section applies to a person arrested or detained under the terrorism provisions.][293]

59 Legal aid for persons at police stations

[…][294]

60 Tape-recording of interviews

(1) It shall be the duty of the Secretary of State—

(a) to issue a code of practice in connection with the tape-recording of interviews of persons suspected of the commission of criminal offences which are held by police officers at police stations; and

(b) to make an order requiring the tape-recording of interviews of persons suspected of the commission of criminal offences, or of such descriptions of criminal offences as may be specified in the order, which are so held, in accordance with the code as it has effect for the time being.

(2) An order under subsection (1) above shall be made by statutory instrument and shall be subject to annulment in pursuance of a resolution of either House of Parliament.

[60A Visual recording of interviews

(1) The Secretary of State shall have power—

(a) to issue a code of practice for the visual recording of interviews held by police officers at police stations; and

(b) to make an order requiring the visual recording of interviews so held, and requiring the visual recording to be in accordance with the code for the time being in force under this section.

[291] Amended by SOCAPA 2005, s 111, Sch 7, Pt 3, para 43(1), (10)(b).
[292] Amended by the Proceeds of Crime Act 2002, s 456, Sch 11, paras 1, 14(1), (3).
[293] Amended by the Terrorism Act 2000, s 125(1), Sch 15, para 5(1), (6).
[294] Repealed by the Legal Aid Act 1988, s 45(2), (3), Sch 6.

Act

(2)   A requirement imposed by an order under this section may be imposed in rela-
      tion to such cases or police stations in such areas, or both, as may be specified
      or described in the order.
(3)   An order under subsection (1) above shall be made by statutory instrument
      and shall be subject to annulment in pursuance of a resolution of either House
      of Parliament.
(4)   In this section—
      (a) references to any interview are references to an interview of a person sus-
          pected of a criminal offence; and
      (b) references to a visual recording include references to a visual recording in
          which an audio recording is comprised.][295]

61 Fingerprinting

(1)   Except as provided by this section no person's fingerprints may be taken with-
      out the appropriate consent.
(2)   Consent to the taking of a person's fingerprints must be in writing if it is given
      at a time when he is at a police station.
[(3) The fingerprints of a person detained at a police station may be taken without
      the appropriate consent if—
      (a) he is detained in consequence of his arrest for a recordable offence; and
      (b) he has not had his fingerprints taken in the course of the investigation of
          the offence by the police.][296]
[(3A) [Where a person mentioned in paragraph (a) of subsection (3) or (4) has
      already had his fingerprints taken in the course of the investigation of the
      offence by the police][297], that fact shall be disregarded for the purposes of that
      subsection if—
      (a) the fingerprints taken on the previous occasion do not constitute a com-
          plete set of his fingerprints; or
      (b) some or all of the fingerprints taken on the previous occasion are not of
          sufficient quality to allow satisfactory analysis, comparison or matching
          (whether in the case in question or generally).][298]
[(4) The fingerprints of a person detained at a police station may be taken without
      the appropriate consent if—
      (a) he has been charged with a recordable offence or informed that he will be
          reported for such an offence; and
      (b) he has not had his fingerprints taken in the course of the investigation of
          the offence by the police.][299]
[(4A) The fingerprints of a person who has answered to bail at a court or police sta-
      tion may be taken without the appropriate consent at the court or station if—
      (a) the court, or
      (b) an officer of at least the rank of inspector,
      authorises them to be taken.

---

[295] Inserted by the Criminal Justice and Police Act 2001, s 76(1).
[296] Amended by the Criminal Justice Act 2003, s 9(1), (2).
[297] Amended by the Criminal Justice Act 2003, s 9(1), (3).
[298] Amended by the Criminal Justice and Police Act 2001, s 78(3).
[299] Amended by the Criminal Justice Act 2003, s 9(1), (2).

(4B) A court or officer may only give an authorisation under subsection (4A) if—
  (a) the person who has answered to bail has answered to it for a person whose fingerprints were taken on a previous occasion and there are reasonable grounds for believing that he is not the same person; or
  (b) the person who has answered to bail claims to be a different person from a person whose fingerprints were taken on a previous occasion.][300]
(5) An officer may give an authorisation under [subsection (4A)][301] above orally or in writing but, if he gives it orally, he shall confirm it in writing as soon as is practicable.
[(5A) The fingerprints of a person may be taken without the appropriate consent if (before or after the coming into force of this subsection) he has been arrested for a recordable offence and released and—
  (a) in the case of a person who is on bail, he has not had his fingerprints taken in the course of the investigation of the offence by the police; or
  (b) in any case, he has had his fingerprints taken in the course of that investigation but subsection (3A)(a) or (b) above applies.][302]
(5B) The fingerprints of a person not detained at a police station may be taken without the appropriate consent if (before or after the coming into force of this subsection) he has been charged with a recordable offence or informed that he will be reported for such an offence and—
  (a) he has not had his fingerprints taken in the course of the investigation of the offence by the police; or
  (b) he has had his fingerprints taken in the course of that investigation but subsection (3A)(a) or (b) above applies.][303]
(6) Subject to this section, the fingerprints of a person may be taken without the appropriate consent if (before or after the coming into force of this subsection)—
  (a) he has been convicted of a recordable offence,
  (b) he has been given a caution in respect of a recordable offence which, at the time of the caution, he has admitted, or
  (c) he has been warned or reprimanded under section 65 of the Crime and Disorder Act 1998 for a recordable offence, and
  either of the conditions mentioned in subsection (6ZA) below is met.
(6ZA) The conditions referred to in subsection (6) above are—
  (a) the person has not had his fingerprints taken since he was convicted, cautioned or warned or reprimanded;
  (b) he has had his fingerprints taken since then but subsection (3A)(a) or (b) above applies.
(6ZB) Fingerprints may only be taken as specified in subsection (6) above with the authorisation of an officer of at least the rank of inspector.
(6ZC) An officer may only give authorisation under subsection (6ZB) above if the officer is satisfied that taking the fingerprints is necessary to assist in the prevention or detection of crime.][304]

[300] Amended by the Criminal Justice and Police Act 2001, s 78(4).
[301] Amended by the Criminal Justice Act 2003, s 9(1), (4).
[302] Amended by the Crime and Security Act 2010, s 2(1).
[303] Amended by the Crime and Security Act 2010, s 2(2).
[304] Sections 61(6)–(6ZC) substituted for s 61(6) by the Crime and Security Act 2010, s 2(3).

Act

[(6A) A constable may take a person's fingerprints without the appropriate consent if—
    (a) the constable reasonably suspects that the person is committing or attempting to commit an offence, or has committed or attempted to commit an offence; and
    (b) either of the two conditions mentioned in subsection (6B) is met.

(6B) The conditions are that—
    (a) the name of the person is unknown to, and cannot be readily ascertained by, the constable;
    (b) the constable has reasonable grounds for doubting whether a name furnished by the person as his name is his real name.

(6C) The taking of fingerprints by virtue of subsection (6A) does not count for any of the purposes of this Act as taking them in the course of the investigation of an offence by the police.][305]

[(6D) Subject to this section, the fingerprints of a person may be taken without the appropriate consent if—
    (a) under the law in force in a country or territory outside England and Wales the person has been convicted of an offence under that law (whether before or after the coming into force of this subsection and whether or not he has been punished for it);
    (b) the act constituting the offence would constitute a qualifying offence if done in England and Wales (whether or not it constituted such an offence when the person was convicted); and
    (c) either of the conditions mentioned in subsection (6E) below is met.

(6E) The conditions referred to in subsection (6D)(c) above are—
    (a) the person has not had his fingerprints take on a previous occasion under subsection (6D) above;
    (b) he has had his fingerprints taken on a previous occasion under that section but subsection (3A)(a) or (b) above applies.

(6F) Fingerprints may only be taken as specified in subsection (6D) above with the authorisation of an officer of at least the rank of inspector.

(6G) An officer may only give an authorisation under subsection (6F) above if the officer is satisfied that taking the fingerprints is necessary to assist in the prevention or detection of crime.][306]

[(7) Where a person's fingerprints are taken without the appropriate consent by virtue of any power conferred by this section—
    (a) before the fingerprints are taken, the person shall be informed of—
        (i) the reason for taking the fingerprints;
        (ii) the power by virtue of which they are taken; and
        (iii) in a case where the authorisation of the court or an officer is required for the exercise of the power, the fact that the authorisation has been given; and
    (b) those matters shall be recorded as soon as practicable after the fingerprints are taken.][307]

---

[305] Subsections (6A)–(6C) inserted by the SOCAPA 2005, s 117(1), (2).
[306] Amended by the Crime and Security Act 2010, s 3(1).
[307] Amended by the Crime and Security Act 2010, s 4(1).

[(7A) If a person's fingerprints are taken at a police station, [or by virtue of [subsection (4A), (6A)][308] at a place other than a police station,][309] whether with or without the appropriate consent—

    (a) before the fingerprints are taken, an officer shall inform him that they may be the subject of a speculative search; and

    (b) the fact that the person has been informed of this possibility shall be recorded as soon as is practicable after the fingerprints have been taken.][310]

(8) If he is detained at a police station when the fingerprints are taken, [the matters referred to in subsection (7)(a)(i) to (iii) above][311] [and, in the case falling within subsection (7A) above, the fact referred to in paragraph (b) of that subsection][312] shall be recorded on his custody record.

[(8B) Any power under this section to take the fingerprints of a person without the appropriate consent, if not otherwise specified to be exercisable by a constable, shall be exercisable by a constable.][313]

(9) Nothing in this section—

    (a) affects any power conferred by paragraph 18(2) of Schedule 2 to the Immigration Act 1971; or

    [(b) applies to a person arrested or detained under the terrorism provisions][314].

[(10) Nothing in this section applies to a person arrested under an extradition arrest power.][315]

[61A Impressions of footwear

(1) Except as provided by this section, no impression of a person's footwear may be taken without the appropriate consent.

(2) Consent to the taking of an impression of a person's footwear must be in writing if it is given at a time when he is at a police station.

(3) Where a person is detained at a police station, an impression of his footwear may be taken without the appropriate consent if—

    (a) he is detained in consequence of his arrest for a recordable offence, or has been charged with a recordable offence, or informed that he will be reported for a recordable offence; and

    (b) he has not had an impression taken of his footwear in the course of the investigation of the offence by the police.

(4) Where a person mentioned in paragraph (a) of subsection (3) above has already had an impression taken of his footwear in the course of the investigation of the offence by the police, that fact shall be disregarded for the purposes of that subsection if the impression of his footwear taken previously is—

    (a) incomplete; or

    (b) is not of sufficient quality to allow satisfactory analysis, comparison or matching (whether in the case in question or generally).

---

[308] Amended by the Crime and Security Act 2010, s 4(2)(a).

[309] Words inserted by SOCAPA 2005, s 117(4)(a).

[310] Amended by the Criminal Justice and Public Order Act 1994, s 168(2), Sch 10, para 56(a).

[311] Amended by the Crime and Security Act 2010, s 4(3).

[312] Amended by the Criminal Justice and Public Order Act 1994, s 168(2), Sch 10, para 56(b).

[313] Amended by the Crime and Security Act 2010, s 2(4).

[314] Amended by the Terrorism Act 2000, s 125(1), Sch 15, para 5(1), (7); for savings see the Terrorism Act 2000, s 129(1)(b) and SI 2001/421, art 2.

[315] Amended by the Extradition Act 2003, s 169(1), (3); for savings see SI 2003/3103, arts 2–4.

(5)　If an impression of a person's footwear is taken at a police station, whether with or without the appropriate consent—

(a)　before it is taken, an officer shall inform him that it may be the subject of a speculative search; and

(b)　the fact that the person has been informed of this possibility shall be recorded as soon as is practicable after the impression has been taken, and if he is detained at a police station, the record shall be made on his custody record.

(6)　In a case where, by virtue of subsection (3) above, an impression of a person's footwear is taken without the appropriate consent—

(a)　he shall be told the reason before it is taken; and

(b)　the reason shall be recorded on his custody record as soon as is practicable after the impression is taken.

(7)　The power to take an impression of the footwear of a person detained at a police station without the appropriate consent shall be exercisable by any constable.

(8)　Nothing in this section applies to any person—

(a)　arrested or detained under the terrorism provisions;

(b)　arrested under an extradition arrest power.][316]

62 Intimate samples

(1)　[Subject to section 63B below,][317] an intimate sample may be taken from a person in police detention only—

(a)　if a police officer of at least the rank of [inspector][318] authorises it to be taken; and

(b)　if the appropriate consent is given.

[(1A)　An intimate sample may be taken from a person who is not in police detention but from whom, in the course of the investigation of an offence, two or more non-intimate samples suitable for the same means of analysis have been taken which have proved insufficient—

(a)　if a police officer of at least the rank of [inspector][319] authorises it to be taken; and

(b)　if the appropriate consent is given.][320]

(2)　An officer may only give an authorisation [under subsection (1) or (1A) above][321] if he has reasonable grounds—

(a)　for suspecting the involvement of the person from whom the sample is to be taken in a [recordable offence][322]; and

(b)　for believing that the sample will tend to confirm or disprove his involvement.

---

[316] Inserted by SOCAPA 2005, s 118(1), (2).

[317] Amended by the Criminal Justice and Court Services Act 2000, s 74, Sch 7, Pt II, paras 76, 78.

[318] Amended by the Criminal Justice and Police Act 2001, s 80(1).

[319] Amended by the Criminal Justice and Police Act 2001, s 80(1).

[320] Amended by the Criminal Justice and Public Order Act 1994, ss 54(2), 168(2), Sch 10, paras 57(a), 62(4)(a).

[321] Amended by the Criminal Justice and Public Order Act 1994, s 54(3).

[322] ibid.

(3) An officer may give an authorisation under subsection (1) [or (1A)][323] [or (2A)][324] above orally or in writing but, if he gives it orally, he shall confirm it in writing as soon as is practicable.

(4) The appropriate consent must be given in writing.

[(5) Before an intimate sample is taken from a person, an officer shall inform him of the following—

(a) the reason for taking the sample;

(b) the fact that authorisation has been given and the provision of this section under which it has been given; and

(c) if the sample was taken at a police station, the fact that the sample may be the subject of a speculative search.

(6) The reason referred to in subsection (5)(a) above must include, except in a case where the sample is taken under subsection (2A) above, a statement of the nature of the offence in which it is suspected that the person has been involved.

(7) After an intimate sample has been taken from a person, the following shall be recorded as soon as practicable—

(a) the matters referred to in subsection (5)(a) and (b) above;

(b) if the sample was taken at a police station, the fact that the person has been informed as specified in subsection (5)(c) above; and

(c) the fact that the appropriate consent was given.][325]

(8) If an intimate sample is taken from a person detained at a police station, the matters required to be recorded by subsection (7) [...][326] above shall be recorded in his custody record.

[(9) In the case of an intimate sample which is a dental impression, the sample may be taken from a person only by a registered dentist.

(9A) In the case of any other form of intimate sample, except in the case of a sample of urine, the sample may be taken from a person only by—

(a) a registered medical practitioner; or

(b) a registered health care professional.][327]

(10) Where the appropriate consent to the taking of an intimate sample from a person was refused without good cause, in any proceedings against that person for an offence—

(a) the court, in determining—

[...][328]

(ii) whether there is a case to answer; and

---

[323] Amended by the Criminal Justice and Public Order Act 1994, s 54(4).

[324] Amended by the Crime and Security Act 2010, s 3(3).

[325] s 65(5)–(7) substituted for s 65(5)–(7A) by the Crime and Security Act 2010, s 4(4).

[326] Repealed by the Crime and Security Act 2010, s 4(5).

[327] Amended by the Police Reform Act 2002, s 54(1).

[328] Repealed by the Criminal Justice Act 2003, Sch 37(4) para 1 (18 June 2012: repeal has effect on 18 June 2012 in relation to the relevant local justice areas specified in SI 2012/1320 art 4(1)(d) and purposes specified in SI 2012/1320 art 4(3) subject to savings specified in SI 2012/1320 art 5; 5 November 2012 in relation to local justice areas specified in SI 2012/2574 art 2(1)(d) and purposes specified in SI 2012/2574 art 2(3) subject to saving provisions specified in SI 2012/2574 arts 3 and 4; not yet in force otherwise).

Act

[(aa) a judge, in deciding whether to grant an application made by the accused under [paragraph 2 of Schedule 3 to the Crime and Disorder Act 1998 (applications for dismissal); and][329]
[...][330][331]

(b) the court or jury, in determining whether that person is guilty of the offence charged,

may draw such inferences from the refusal as appear proper [...][332]

(11) Nothing in this section [applies to the taking of a specimen for the purposes of any of the provisions of][333] [sections 4 to 11 of the Road Traffic Act 1988][334] [or of sections 26 to 38 of the Transport and Works Act 1992][335].

[(12) Nothing in this section applies to a person arrested or detained under the terrorism provisions; and subsection (1A) shall not apply where the non-intimate samples mentioned in that subsection were taken under paragraph 10 of Schedule 8 to the Terrorism Act 2000.][336]

63 Other samples

(1) Except as provided by this section, a non-intimate sample may not be taken from a person without the appropriate consent.

(2) Consent to the taking of a non-intimate sample must be given in writing.

[(2A) A non-intimate sample may be taken from a person without the appropriate consent if two conditions are satisfied.

(2B) The first is that the person is in police detention in consequence of his arrest for a recordable offence.

(2C) The second is that—

(a) he has not had a non-intimate sample of the same type and from the same part of the body taken in the course of the investigation of the offence by the police, or

(b) he has had such a sample taken but it proved insufficient.][337]

(3) A non-intimate sample may be taken from a person without the appropriate consent if—

(a) he [...][338] is being held in custody by the police on the authority of a court; and

---

[329] Amended by the Criminal Justice Act 2003, Sch 3(2), para 56(2)(b) (9 May 2005 in relation to cases sent for trial under 1998 s 51 or s 51A(3)(d); 18 June 2012 in relation to the relevant local justice areas subject to savings as specified in SI 2012/1320 art 5; 18 June 2012 for purposes specified in SI 2012/1230 art 4(3) subject to savings as specified in SI 2012/1320 art 5; 5 November 2012 in relation to the relevant local justice areas and purposes specified in SI 2012/2574 art 2(3) subject to saving provisions specified in SI 2012/2574 arts 3 and 4; not yet in force otherwise).

[330] Ibid.

[331] Amended by the Criminal Justice and Public Order Act 1994, Sch 9, para 24.

[332] Repealed by the Criminal Justice and Public Order Act 1994, s 168(3), Sch 11.

[333] Amended by the Police Reform Act 2002, s 53(2)(a).

[334] Amended by the Road Traffic (Consequential Provisions) Act 1988, s 4, Sch 3, para 27.

[335] Amended by the Police Reform Act 2002, s 53(2)(b).

[336] Amended by the Terrorism Act 2000, s 125(1), Sch 15, para 5(1), (8); for savings see the Terrorism Act 2000, s 129(1)(b) and SI 2001/421, art 2.

[337] Amended by the Criminal Justice Act 2003, s 10(1), (2).

[338] Repealed by the Criminal Justice Act 2003, ss 10(1), (3), 332, Sch 37, Pt 1.

(b) an officer of at least the rank of [inspector][339] authorises it to be taken without the appropriate consent.

[(3ZA) A non-intimate sample may be taken from a person without the appropriate consent if (before or after the coming into force of this subsection) he has been arrested for a recordable offence and released and—

    (a) in the case of a person who is on bail, he has not had a non-intimate sample of the same type and from the same part of the body taken from him in the course of the investigation of the offence by the police; or

    (b) in any case, he has had a non-intimate sample taken from him in the course of that investigation but—

       (i) it was not suitable for the same means of analysis, or

       (ii) it proved insufficient.][340]

[(3A) A non-intimate sample may be taken from a person (whether or not he is in police detention or held in custody by the police on the authority of a court) without the appropriate consent if he has been charged with a recordable offence or informed that he will be reported for such an offence and—

    (a) he has not had a non-intimate sample taken from him in the course of the investigation of the offence by the police; or

    (b) he has had a non-intimate sample taken from him in the course of the investigation but—

       (i) it was not suitable for the same means of analysis, or

       (ii) it proved insufficient; or

    (c) he has had non-intimate sample taken from him in the course of that investigation and—

       (i) the sample has been destroyed pursuant to section 64ZA below or any other enactment, and

       (ii) it is disputed, in relation to any proceedings relating to the offence, whether a DNA profile relevant to the proceedings is derived from the sample.][341]

[(3B) Subject to this section, a non-intimate sample may be taken from a person without the appropriate consent if (before or after the coming into force of this subsection) —

    (a) he has been convicted of a recordable offence,

    (b) he has been given a caution in respect of a recordable offence which, at the time of the caution, he has admitted, or

    (c) he has been warned or reprimanded under section 65 of the Crime and Disorder Act 1998 for a recordable offence, and

either of the conditions mentioned in subsection (3BA) below is met.

(3BA) The conditions referred to in subsection (3B) above are—

    (a) a non-intimate sample has not been taken from the person since he was convicted, cautioned or warned or reprimanded;

    (b) such a sample has been taken from him since then but—

       (i) it was not suitable for the same means of analysis, or

       (ii) it proved insufficient.

---

[339] Amended by the Criminal Justice and Police Act 2001, s 80(1).
[340] Amended by the Crime and Security Act 2010, s 2(5).
[341] Amended by the Crime and Security Act 2010, s 2(6).

(3BB)   A non-intimate sample may only be taken as specified in subsection (3B) above with the authorisation of an officer of at least the rank of inspector.

(3BC)   An officer may only give an authorisation under subsection (3BB) above if the officer is satisfied that taking the sample is necessary to assist in the prevention or detection of crime.][342]

[(3C)   A non-intimate sample may also be taken from a person without the appropriate consent if he is a person to whom section 2 of the Criminal Evidence (Amendment) Act 1997 applies (persons detained following acquittal on grounds of insanity or finding of unfitness to plead).][343]

[(3E)   Subject to this section, a non-intimate sample may be taken without the appropriate consent from a person if—

(a)   under the law in force in a country or territory outside England and Wales the person has been convicted of an offence under that law (whether before or after the coming into force of this subsection and whether or not he has been punished for it);

(b)   the act constituting the offence would constitute a qualifying offence if done in England and Wales (whether or not it constituted such an offence when the person was convicted); and

(c)   either of the conditions mentioned in subsection (3F) below is met.

(3F)   The conditions referred to in subsection (3E)(c) above are—

(a)   the person has not had a non-intimate sample taken from him on a previous occasion under subsection (3E) above;

(b)   he has had such sample taken from him on a previous occasion under that subsection but—

(i)   the sample was not suitable for the same means of analysis, or

(ii)   it proved insufficient.

(3G)   A non-intimate sample may only be taken as specified in subsection (3E) above with the authorisation of an officer of at least the rank of inspector.

(3H)   An officer may only give an authorisation under subsection (3G) above if the officer is satisfied that taking the sample is necessary to assist in the prevention or detection of crime.][344]

(4)   An officer may only give an authorisation under subsection (3) above if he has reasonable grounds—

(a)   for suspecting the involvement of the person from whom the sample is to be taken in a [recordable offence][345]; and

(b)   for believing that the sample will tend to confirm or disprove his involvement.

(5)   An officer may give an authorisation under subsection (3) above orally or in writing but, if he gives it orally, he shall confirm it in writing as soon as is practicable.

[(5A)   An officer shall not give an authorisation under subsection (3) above for the taking from any person of a non-intimate sample consisting of a skin impression if—

---

[342] Amended by the Crime and Security Act 2010, s 2(7).

[343] Amended by the Criminal Evidence (Amendment) Act 1997, s 2(2).

[344] Amended by the Crime and Security Act 2010, s 3(4).

[345] Amended by the Criminal Justice and Public Order Act 1994, s 55(3).

      (a) a skin impression of the same part of the body has already been taken from that person in the course of the investigation of the offence; and

      (b) the impression previously taken is not one that has proved insufficient.][346]

[(6)   Where a non-intimate sample is taken from a person without the appropriate consent by virtue of any power conferred by this section—

      (a) before the sample is taken, an officer shall inform him of—

          (i)   the reason for taking the sample;

          (ii) the power by virtue of which it is taken; and

          (iii) in a case where the authorisation of an officer is required for the exercise of the power, the fact that the authorisation has been given; and

      (b) those matters shall be recorded as soon as practicable after the sample is taken.

(7)   The reason referred to in subsection (6)(a)(i) above must include, except in a case where the non-intimate sample is taken under subsection (3B) or (3E) above, a statement of the nature of the offence in which it is suspected that the person has been involved.][347]

[(8B) If a non-intimate sample is taken from a person at a police station, whether with or without the appropriate consent—

      (a) before the sample is taken, an officer shall inform him that it may be the subject of a speculative search; and

      (b) the fact that the person has been informed of this possibility shall be recorded as soon as practicable after the sample has been taken.][348]

(9)   If a non-intimate sample is taken from a person detained at a police station, the matters required to be recorded by [subsection (6) or (8B)][349] above shall be recorded in his custody record.

[(9ZA) The power to take a non-intimate sample from a person without the appropriate consent shall be exercisable by any constable.][350]

[(9A) Subsection (3B) above shall not apply to [—][351]

      [(a) any person convicted before 10th April 1995 unless he is a person to whom section 1 of the Criminal Evidence (Amendment) Act 1997 applies (persons imprisoned or detained by virtue of pre-existing conviction for sexual offence etc.); or

      (b) a person given a caution before 10th April 1995.][352]][353]

[(10) Nothing in this section applies to a person arrested or detained under the terrorism provisions.][354]

[(11) Nothing in this section applies to a person arrested under an extradition arrest power.][355]

---

[346] Amended by the Criminal Justice and Police Act 2001, s 80(3).

[347] Amended by the Crime and Security Act, s 4(7).

[348] Amended by the Criminal Justice and Public Order Act 1994, ss 55(2), 168(2), Sch 10, para 58(a).

[349] Amended by the Crime and Security Act 2010, s 4(8).

[350] Amended by the Police Reform Act 2002, s 107(1), Sch 7, para 9(4).

[351] Amended by the Crime and Security Act 2010, s 2(8).

[352] Ibid.

[353] Amended by the Criminal Evidence (Amendment) Act 1997, s 1(2).

[354] Amended by the Terrorism Act 2000, s 125(1), Sch 15, para 5(1), (9).

[355] Amended by the Extradition Act 2003, s 169(1), (4); (1 January 2004 subject to savings specified in SI 2003/3103 arts 3–4).

[63A Fingerprints and samples: supplementary provisions

[(1)   Where a person has been arrested on suspicion of being involved in a recordable
offence or has been charged with such an offence or has been informed that he
will be reported for such an offence, fingerprints[, impressions of footwear][356] or
samples or the information derived from samples taken under any power conferred by this Part of this Act from the person may be checked against—

    (a) other fingerprints[, impressions of footwear][357] or samples to which the
person seeking to check has access and which are held by or on behalf of
[any one or more relevant law-enforcement authorities or which][358] are
held in connection with or as a result of an investigation of an offence;

    (b) information derived from other samples if the information is contained
in records to which the person seeking to check has access and which are
held as mentioned in paragraph (a) above.

[(1ZA) Fingerprints taken by virtue of section 61(6A) above may be checked against
other fingerprints to which the person seeking to check has access and which
are held by or on behalf of any one or more relevant law-enforcement authorities or which are held in connection with or as a result of an investigation of
an offence.][359]

[(1A)   In subsection (1) [and (1ZA)][360] above 'relevant law-enforcement authority'
means—

    (a) a police force;

    [(b) the Serious Organised Crime Agency;][361]

    (d) a public authority (not falling within paragraphs (a) to (c)) with func-
tions in any part of the British Islands which consist of or include the
investigation of crimes or the charging of offenders;

    (e) any person with functions in any country or territory outside the United
Kingdom which—

      (i) correspond to those of a police force; or

      (ii) otherwise consist of or include the investigation of conduct contrary
to the law of that country or territory, or the apprehension of persons
guilty of such conduct;

    (f) any person with functions under any international agreement which
consist of or include the investigation of conduct which is—

      (i) unlawful under the law of one or more places,

      (ii) prohibited by such an agreement, or

      (iii) contrary to international law,

    or the apprehension of persons guilty of such conduct.

(1B)   The reference in subsection (1A) above to a police force is a reference to any
of the following—

    (a) any police force maintained under section 2 of the Police Act 1996 (c 16)
(police forces in England and Wales outside London);

---

[356] Amended by SOCAPA 2005, s 118(1), (3)(a).
[357] ibid.
[358] Amended by the Criminal Justice and Police Act 2001, s 81(1).
[359] Amended by the SOCAPA 2005, s 117(5)(a).
[360] Words inserted by SOCAPA 2005, s 117(5)(b).
[361] Amended by SOCAPA 2005, s 59, Sch 4, paras 43, 46.

(b) the metropolitan police force;

(c) the City of London police force;

(d) any police force maintained under or by virtue of section 1 of the Police (Scotland) Act 1967 (c 77);

(e) the Police Service of Northern Ireland;

(f) the Police Service of Northern Ireland Reserve;

(g) the Ministry of Defence Police;

(h) the [Royal Navy Police][362];

(i) the Royal Military Police;

(j) the Royal Air Force Police;

[...][363]

(l) the British Transport Police;

(m) the States of Jersey Police Force;

(n) the salaried police force of the Island of Guernsey;

(o) the Isle of Man Constabulary.

(1C) Where—

(a) fingerprints[, impressions of footwear][364] or samples have been taken from any person in connection with the investigation of an offence but otherwise than in circumstances to which subsection (1) above applies, and

(b) that person has given his consent in writing to the use in a speculative search of the fingerprints[, of the impressions of footwear][365] or of the samples and of information derived from them,

the fingerprints [or impressions of footwear][366] or, as the case may be, those samples and that information may be checked against any of the fingerprints[, impressions of footwear][367], samples or information mentioned in paragraph (a) or (b) of that subsection.

(1D) A consent given for the purposes of subsection (1C) above shall not be capable of being withdrawn.][368]][369]

[(1E) Where fingerprints or samples have been taken from any persons under section 61(6) or 63(3B) above (persons convicted etc), the fingerprints or samples, or information derived from the samples, may be checked against any of the fingerprints, samples or information mentioned in subsection (1)(a) or (b) above.

(1F) Where fingerprints or samples have been taken from any person under section 61(6D), 62(2A) or 63(3E) above (offences outside England and Wales etc), the fingerprints or samples, or information derived from the samples, may be checked against any of the fingerprints, samples or information mentioned in subsection (1)(a) or (b) above.][370]

---

[362] Amended by the Armed Forces Act 2006, Sch 17, para 1 (31 October 2009; SI 2009/1167).

[363] Repealed by the Armed Forces Act 2006, Sch 17, para 1 (31 October 2009; SI 2009/1167).

[364] Amended by SOCAPA 2005, s 118(1), (3)(b)(i).

[365] Amended by SOCAPA 2005, s 118(1), (3)(b)(ii).

[366] Amended by SOCAPA 2005, s 118(1), (3)(b)(iii).

[367] Amended by SOCAPA 2005, s 118(1), (3)(b)(iv).

[368] Amended by the Criminal Justice and Police Act 2001, s 81(2).

[369] Amended by the Criminal Procedure and Investigations Act 1996, s 64(1).

[370] Amended by the Crime and Security Act 2010, s 5(1).

(2)   Where a sample of hair other than pubic hair is to be taken the sample may be
       taken either by cutting hairs or by plucking hairs with their roots so long as no
       more are plucked than the person taking the sample reasonably considers to
       be necessary for a sufficient sample.

(3)   Where any power to take a sample is exercisable in relation to a person the
       sample may be taken in a prison or other institution to which the Prison Act
       1952 applies.

[(3A) Where—

       (a) the power to take a non-intimate sample under section 63(3B) above is
            exercisable in relation to any person who is detained under Part III of the
            Mental Health Act 1983 in pursuance of—
            (i)   a hospital order or interim hospital order made following his convic-
                  tion for the recordable offence in question, or
            (ii) a transfer direction given at a time when he was detained in pursuance
                  of any sentence or order imposed following that conviction, or
       (b) the power to take a non-intimate sample under section 63(3C) above is
            exercisable in relation to any person,
       the sample may be taken in the hospital in which he is detained under that
       Part of that Act.
       Expressions used in this subsection and in the Mental Health Act 1983 have
       the same meaning as in that Act.

(3B)   Where the power to take a non-intimate sample under section 63(3B) above
       is exercisable in relation to a person detained in pursuance of directions of the
       Secretary of State under [section 92 of the Powers of Criminal Courts
       (Sentencing) Act 2000][371] the sample may be taken at the place where he is so
       detained.][372]

[(4)   Schedule 2A (fingerprinting and samples: power to require attendance at police
       station) shall have effect.][373][374]

[63AA Inclusion of DNA profiles on National DNA Database

(1)   This section applies to a DNA profile which is derived from a DNA sample and which
       is retained under any power conferred by any of sections 63E to 63L (including those
       sections as applied by section 63P).

(2)   A DNA profile to which this section applies must be recorded on the National DNA
       Database.][375]

[63AB National DNA Database Strategy Board

(1)   The Secretary of State must make arrangements for a National DNA Database
       Strategy Board to oversee the operation of the National DNA Database.

(2)   The National DNA Database Strategy Board must issue guidance about the
       destruction of DNA profiles which are, or may be, retained under this Part of this
       Act.

---

[371] Amended by the Powers of Criminal Courts (Sentencing) Act 2000, s 165(1), Sch 9, para 97.
[372] Amended by the Criminal Evidence (Amendment) Act 1997, s 3.
[373] Amended by the Crime and Security Act 2010, s 6(1).
[374] Amended by the Criminal Justice and Public Order Act 1994, s 56.
[375] Added by the Protection of Freedoms Act 2012, s 23 (date to be appointed).

(3) A chief officer of a police force in England and Wales must act in accordance with guidance issued under subsection (2).

(4) The National DNA Database Strategy Board may issue guidance about the circumstances in which applications may be made to the Commissioner for the Retention and Use of Biometric Material under section 63G.

(5) Before issuing any such guidance, the National DNA Database Strategy Board must consult the Commissioner for the Retention and Use of Biometric Material.

(6) The Secretary of State must publish the governance rules of the National DNA Database Strategy Board and lay a copy of the rules before Parliament.

(7) The National DNA Database Strategy Board must make an annual report to the Secretary of State about the exercise of its functions.

(8) The Secretary of State must publish the report and lay a copy of the published report before Parliament.

(9) The Secretary of State may exclude from publication any part of the report if, in the opinion of the Secretary of State, the publication of that part would be contrary to the public interest or prejudicial to national security.][376]

[63B Testing for presence of Class A drugs

(1) A sample of urine or a non-intimate sample may be taken from a person in police detention for the purpose of ascertaining whether he has any specified Class A drug in his body if [—

    (a) either the arrest condition or the charge condition is met;

    (b) both the age condition and the request condition are met; and

    (c) the notification condition is met in relation to the arrest condition, the charge condition or the age condition (as the case may be).][377]

[(1A) The arrest condition is that the person concerned has been arrested for an offence but has not been charged with that offence and either—

    (a) the offence is a trigger offence; or

    (b) a police officer of at least the rank of inspector has reasonable grounds for suspecting that the misuse by that person of a specified Class A drug caused or contributed to the offence and has authorised the sample to be taken.][378]

(2) [The charge condition is either][379]—

    (a) that the person concerned has been charged with a trigger offence; or

    (b) that the person concerned has been charged with an offence and a police officer of at least the rank of inspector, who has reasonable grounds for suspecting that the misuse by that person of any specified Class A drug caused or contributed to the offence, has authorised the sample to be taken.

[(3) The age condition is—

    (a) if the arrest condition is met, that the person concerned has attained the age of 18;

    (b) if the charge condition is met, that he has attained the age of 14.][380]

---

[376] Added by the Protection of Freedoms Act 2012, s 24 (date to be appointed).
[377] Amended by the Drugs Act 2005, s 7(1), (2), (13), (14).
[378] Amended by the Drugs Act 2005, s 7(1), (3), (13), (14).
[379] Amended by the Drugs Act 2005, s 7(1), (4), (13), (14).
[380] Amended by the Drugs Act 2005, s 7(1), (5), (13), (14).

Act

(4)   The [request][381] condition is that a police officer has requested the person concerned to give the sample.

[(4A) The notification condition is that—

    (a) the relevant chief officer has been notified by the Secretary of State that appropriate arrangements have been made for the police area as a whole, or for the particular police station, in which the person is in police detention, and

    (b) the notice has not been withdrawn.

(4B)   For the purposes of subsection (4A) above, appropriate arrangements are arrangements for the taking of samples under this section from whichever of the following is specified in the notification—

    (a) persons in respect of whom the arrest condition is met;

    (b) persons in respect of whom the charge condition is met;

    (c) persons who have not attained the age of 18.][382]

(5)   Before requesting the person concerned to give a sample, an officer must—

    (a) warn him that if, when so requested, he fails without good cause to do so he may be liable to prosecution, and

    (b) in a case within subsection [(1A)(b) or][383] (2)(b) above, inform him of the giving of the authorisation and of the grounds in question.

[(5A) In the case of a person who has not attained the age of 17—

    (a) the making of the request under subsection (4) above;

    (b) the giving of the warning and (where applicable) the information under subsection (5) above; and

    (c) the taking of the sample,

may not take place except in the presence of an appropriate adult.][384]

[(5B) If a sample is taken under this section from a person in respect of whom the arrest condition is met no other sample may be taken from him under this section during the same continuous period of detention but—

    (a) if the charge condition is also met in respect of him at any time during that period, the sample must be treated as a sample taken by virtue of the fact that the charge condition is met;

    (b) the fact that the sample is to be so treated must be recorded in the person's custody record.

(5C)   Despite subsection (1)(a) above, a sample may be taken from a person under this section if—

    (a) he was arrested for an offence (the first offence),

    (b) the arrest condition is met but the charge condition is not met,

    (c) before a sample is taken by virtue of subsection (1) above he would (but for his arrest as mentioned in paragraph (d) below) be required to be released from police detention,

    (d) he continues to be in police detention by virtue of his having been arrested for an offence not falling within subsection (1A) above, and

---

[381] Amended by the Drugs Act 2005, s 7(1), (6), (13), (14).
[382] Amended by the Drugs Act 2005, s 7(1), (7), (13), (14).
[383] Amended by the Drugs Act 2005, s 7(1), (8), (13), (14).
[384] Amended by the Criminal Justice Act 2003, s 5(1), (3)(b).

    (e) the sample is taken before the end of the period of 24 hours starting with the time when his detention by virtue of his arrest for the first offence began.

(5D) A sample must not be taken from a person under this section if he is detained in a police station unless he has been brought before the custody officer.][385]

(6) A sample may be taken under this section only by a person prescribed by regulations made by the Secretary of State by statutory instrument.

No regulations shall be made under this subsection unless a draft has been laid before, and approved by resolution of, each House of Parliament.

[[(6A) The Secretary of State may by order made by statutory instrument amend—

    (a) paragraph (a) of subsection (3) above, by substituting for the age for the time being specified a different age specified in the order, or different ages so specified for different police areas so specified;

    (b) paragraph (b) of that subsection, by substituting for the age for the time being specified a different age specified in the order.][386]

(6B) A statutory instrument containing an order under subsection (6A) above shall not be made unless a draft of the instrument has been laid before, and approved by a resolution of, each House of Parliament.][387]

(7) Information obtained from a sample taken under this section may be disclosed—

    (a) for the purpose of informing any decision about granting bail in criminal proceedings (within the meaning of the Bail Act 1976) to the person concerned;

    [(aa) for the purpose of informing any decision about the giving of a conditional caution under Part 3 of the Criminal Justice Act 2003 [or a youth conditional caution under Chapter 1 of Part 4 of the Crime and Disorder Act 1998][388] to the person concerned;][389]

    (b) where the person concerned is in police detention or is remanded in or committed to custody by an order of a court or has been granted such bail, for the purpose of informing any decision about his supervision;

    (c) where the person concerned is convicted of an offence, for the purpose of informing any decision about the appropriate sentence to be passed by a court and any decision about his supervision or release;

    [(ca) for the purpose of an assessment which the person concerned is required to attend by virtue of section 9(2) or 10(2) of the Drugs Act 2005;

    (cb) for the purpose of proceedings against the person concerned for an offence under section 12(3) or 14(3) of that Act;][390]

    (d) for the purpose of ensuring that appropriate advice and treatment is made available to the person concerned.

(8) A person who fails without good cause to give any sample which may be taken from him under this section shall be guilty of an offence.

[[...][391]

---

[385] Amended by the Drugs Act 2005, s 7(1), (9), (13), (14).

[386] Amended by the Drugs Act 2005, s 7(1), (10), (13), (14).

[387] Amended by the Criminal Justice Act 2003, s 5(1), (3)(c).

[388] Words inserted by Criminal Justice and Immigration Act 2008, Sch 26(2), para 20(2) (16 November 2009 in relation to the areas specified in SI 2009/2780, art 2(2); not yet in force otherwise).

[389] Amended by the Drugs Act 2005, s 7(1), (11), (13), (14).

[390] Amended by the Drugs Act 2005, s 23(1), Sch 1, paras 1, 4.

[391] Repealed by the Drugs Act 2005, ss 7(1), (12)–(14), 23(2), Sch 2.

Act

(10) In this section—

'appropriate adult', in relation to a person who has not attained the age of 17, means—

(a) his parent or guardian or, if he is in the care of a local authority or voluntary organisation, a person representing that authority or organisation; or

(b) a social worker of a local authority [...][392]; or

(c) if no person falling within paragraph (a) or (b) is available, any responsible person aged 18 or over who is not a police officer or a person employed by the police;

'relevant chief officer' means—

(a) in relation to a police area, the chief officer of police of the police force for that police area; or

(b) in relation to a police station, the chief officer of police of the police force for the police area in which the police station is situated.][393]][394]

[63C Testing for presence of Class A drugs: supplementary

(1) A person guilty of an offence under section 63B above shall be liable on summary conviction to imprisonment for a term not exceeding three months, or to a fine not exceeding level 4 on the standard scale, or to both.

(2) A police officer may give an authorisation under section 63B above orally or in writing but, if he gives it orally, he shall confirm it in writing as soon as is practicable.

(3) If a sample is taken under section 63B above by virtue of an authorisation, the authorisation and the grounds for the suspicion shall be recorded as soon as is practicable after the sample is taken.

(4) If the sample is taken from a person detained at a police station, the matters required to be recorded by subsection (3) above shall be recorded in his custody record.

(5) Subsections (11) and (12) of section 62 above apply for the purposes of section 63B above as they do for the purposes of that section; and section 63B above does not prejudice the generality of sections 62 and 63 above.

(6) In section 63B above—

'Class A drug' and 'misuse' have the same meanings as in the Misuse of Drugs Act 1971;

'specified' (in relation to a Class A drug) and 'trigger offence' have the same meanings as in Part III of the Criminal Justice and Court Services Act 2000.][395]

[63D Destruction of fingerprints and DNA profiles

(1) This section applies to—

(a) fingerprints—

(i) taken from a person under any power conferred by this Part of this Act, or

(ii) taken by the police, with the consent of the person from whom they were taken, in connection with the investigation of an offence by the police, and

---

[392] Repealed by the Children Act 2004, s 64, Sch 5, Pt 4.
[393] Amended by the Criminal Justice Act 2003, s 5(1), (3)(d).
[394] Inserted by the Criminal Justice and Courts Services Act 2000, s 57(1), (2).
[395] Inserted by the Criminal Justice and Courts Services Act 2000, s 57(1), (2).

   (b) *a DNA profile derived from a DNA sample taken as mentioned in paragraph (a)(i) or (ii).*

(2) *Fingerprints and DNA profiles to which this section applies ('section 63D material') must be destroyed if it appears to the responsible chief officer of police that—*

   (a) *the taking of the fingerprint or, in the case of a DNA profile, the taking of the sample from which the DNA profile was derived, was unlawful, or*

   (b) *the fingerprint was taken, or, in the case of a DNA profile, was derived from a sample taken, from a person in connection with that person's arrest and the arrest was unlawful or based on mistaken identity.*

(3) *In any other case, section 63D material must be destroyed unless it is retained under any power conferred by sections 63E to 63O (including those sections as applied by section 63P).*

(4) *Section 63D material which ceases to be retained under a power mentioned in subsection (3) may continue to be retained under any other such power which applies to it.*

(5) *Nothing in this section prevents a speculative search, in relation to section 63D material, from being carried out within such time as may reasonably be required for the search if the responsible chief officer of police considers the search to be desirable.*][396]

[63E Retention of section 63D material pending investigation or proceedings

(1) *This section applies to section 63D material taken (or, in the case of a DNA profile, derived from a sample taken) in connection with the investigation of an offence in which it is suspected that the person to whom the material related has been involved.*

(2) *The material may be retained until the conclusion of the investigation of the offence or, where the investigation gives rise to proceedings against the person for the offence, until the conclusion of those proceedings.*][397]

[63F Retention of section 63D material: persons arrested for or charged with a qualifying offence

(1) *This section applies to section 63D material which—*

   (a) *relates to a person who is arrested for, or charged with, a qualifying offence but is not convicted of that offence, and*

   (b) *was taken (or, in the case of a DNA profile, derived from a sample taken) in connection with the investigation of the offence.*

(2) *If the person has previously been convicted of a recordable offence which is not an excluded offence, or is so convicted before the material is required to be destroyed by virtue of this section, the material may be retained indefinitely.*

(3) *Otherwise, material falling within subsection (4) or (5) may be retained until the end of the retention period specified in subsection (6).*

(4) *Material falls within this subsection if it—*

   (a) *relates to a person who is charged with a qualifying offence but is not convicted of that offence, and*

   (b) *was taken (or, in the case of a DNA profile, derived from a sample taken) in connection with the investigation of that offence.*

(5) *Material falls within this subsection if—*

---

[396] Added by the Protection of Freedoms Act 2012, s 1 (date to be appointed).
[397] Added by the Protection of Freedoms Act 2012, s 2 (date to be appointed).

(a) it relates to a person who is arrested for a qualifying offence but is not charged with that offence,

(b) it was taken (or, in the case of a DNA profile, derived from a sample taken) in connection with the investigation of the offence, and

(c) the Commissioner for the Retention and Use of Biometric Material has consented under section 63G to the retention of the material.

(6)   The retention period is—

(a) in the case of fingerprints, the period of 3 years beginning with the date on which the fingerprints were taken, and

(b) in the case of a DNA profile, the period of 3 years beginning with the date on which the DNA sample from which the profile was derived was taken (or, if the profile was derived from more than one DNA sample, the date on which the first of those samples was taken).

(7)   The responsible chief officer of police or a specified chief officer of police may apply to a District Judge (Magistrates' Courts) for an order extending the retention period.

(8)   An application for an order under subsection (7) must be made within the period of 3 months ending on the last day of the retention period.

(9)   An order under subsection (7) may extend the retention period by a period which—

(a) begins with the end of the retention period, and

(b) ends with the end of the period of 2 years beginning with the end of the retention period.

(10) The following persons may appeal to the Crown Court against an order under subsection (7), or a refusal to make such an order—

(a) the responsible chief officer of police;

(b) a specified chief officer of police;

(c) the person from whom the material was taken.

(11) In this section—

'excluded offence', in relation to a person, means a recordable offence—

(a) which—

(i)   is not a qualifying offence,

(ii) is the only recordable offence of which the person has been convicted, and

(iii) was committed when the person was aged under 18, and

(b) for which the person was not given a relevant custodial sentence of 5 years or more,

'relevant custodial sentence' has the meaning given by section 63K(6),

'a specified chief officer of police' means—

(a) the chief officer of the police force of the area in which the person from whom the material was taken resides, or

(b) a chief officer of police who believes that the person is in, or is intending to come to, the chief officer's area.][398]

[63G Retention of section 63D material by virtue of section 63F(5): consent of Commissioner

(1)   The responsible chief officer of police may apply under subsection (2) or (3) to the Commissioner for the retention and Use of Biometric Material for consent to the retention of section 63D material which falls within section 63F(5)(a) and (b).

---

[398] Added by the Protection of Freedoms Act 2012, s 3 (date to be appointed).

(2)   The responsible chief officer of police may make an application under this subsection if the responsible chief officer of police considers that the material was taken (or, in the case of a DNA profile, derived from a sample take) in connection with the investigation of an offence where any alleged victim of the offence was, at the time of the offence—
  (a) under the age of 18,
  (b) a vulnerable adult, or
  (c) associated with the person to whom the material relates.

(3)   The responsible chief officer of police may make an application under this subsection if the responsible chief officer of police considers that—
  (a) the material is not material to which subsection (2) relates, but
  (b) the retention of the material is necessary to assist in the prevention or detection of crime.

(4)   The Commissioner may, on an application under this section, consent to the retention of material to which the application relates if the Commissioner considers that it is appropriate to retain the material.

(5)   But where notice is given under subsection (6) in relation to the application, the Commissioner must, before deciding whether or not to give consent, consider any representations by the person to whom the material relates which are made within the period of 28 days beginning with the day on which the notice is given.

(6)   The responsible chief officer of police must give to the person to whom the material relates notice of—
  (a) an application under this section, and
  (b) the right to make representations.

(7)   A notice under subsection (6) may, in particular, be given to a person by—
  (a) leaving it at the person's usual or last known address (whether residential or otherwise),
  (b) sending it to the person by post at that address, or
  (c) sending it to the person by email or other electronic means.

(8)   The requirement in subsection (6) does not apply if the whereabouts of the person to whom the material relates is not known and cannot, after reasonable inquiry, be ascertained by the responsible chief officer of police.

(9)   An application or notice under this section must be in writing.

(10) In this section—
  'victim' includes intended victim,
  'vulnerable adult' means a person aged 18 or over whose ability to protect himself or herself from violence, abuse or neglect is significantly impaired through physical or mental disability or illness, through old age or otherwise,
  and the reference in subsection (2)(c) to a person being associated with another person is to be read in accordance with section 62(3) to (7) of the Family Law Act 1996.][399]

[63H Retention of section 63D material: persons arrested for or charged with a minor offence

(1)   This section applies to section 63D material which—
  (a) relates to a person who—
     (i) is arrested for or charged with a recordable offence other than a qualifying offence,

---

[399] Added by the Protection of Freedoms Act 2012, s 3 (date to be appointed).

(ii) *if arrested for or charged with more than one offence arising out of a single course of action, is not also arrested for or charged with a qualifying offence, and*

(iii) *is not convicted of the offence or offences in respect of which the person is arrested or charged, and*

(b) *was taken (or, in the case of a DNA profile, derived from a sample taken) in connection with the investigation of the offence or offences in respect of which the person is arrested or charged.*

(2) *If the person has previously been convicted of a recordable offence which is not an excluded offence, the material may be retained indefinitely.*

(3) *In this section 'excluded offence' has the meaning given by section 63F(11).]*[400]

[63I Retention of material: persons convicted of a recordable offence

(1) *This section applies, subject to subsection (3), to—*

(a) *section 63D material which—*

(i) *relates to a person who is convicted of a recordable offence, and*

(ii) *was taken (or, in the case of a DNA profile, derived from a sample taken) in connection with the investigation of the offence, or*

(b) *material taken under section 61(6) or 63(3B) which relates to a person who is convicted of a recordable offence.*

(2) *The material may be retained indefinitely.*

(3) *This section does not apply to section 63D material to which section 63K applies.]*[401]

[63J Retention of material: persons convicted of an offence outside England and Wales

(1) *This section applies to material falling within subsection (2) relating to a person who is convicted of an offence under the law of any country or territory outside England and Wales.*

(2) *Material falls within this subsection if it is—*

(a) *fingerprints taken from the person under section 61(6D) (power to take fingerprints without consent in relation to offences outside of England and Wales), or*

(b) *a DNA profile derived from a DNA sample taken from the person under section 62(2A) or 63(3E) (powers to take intimate and non-intimate samples in relation to offences outside England and Wales).*

(3) *The material may be retained indefinitely.]*[402]

[63K Retention of section 63D material: exception for persons under 18 convicted of first minor offence

(1) *This section applies to section 63D material which—*

(a) *relates to a person who—*

(i) *is convicted of a recordable offence other than a qualifying offence,*

(ii) *has not previously been convicted of a recordable offence, and*

(iii) *is aged under 18 at the time of the offence, and*

(b) *was taken (or, in the case of a DNA profile, derived from a sample taken) in connection with the investigation of the offence.*

---

[400] Added by the Protection of Freedoms Act 2012, s 4 (date to be appointed).
[401] Added by the Protection of Freedoms Act 2012, s 5 (date to be appointed).
[402] Added by the Protection of Freedoms Act 2012, s 6 (date to be appointed).

(2) Where the person is given a relevant custodial sentence of less than 5 years in respect of the offence, the material may be retained until the end of the period consisting of the term of the sentence plus 5 years.

(3) Where the person is given a relevant custodial sentence of 5 years or more in respect of the offence, the material may be retained indefinitely.

(4) Where the person is given a sentence other than a relevant custodial sentence in respect of the offence, the material may be retained until—

    (a) in the case of fingerprints, the end of the period of 5 years beginning with the date on which the fingerprints were taken, and

    (b) in the case of a DNA profile, the end of the period of 5 years beginning with—

        (i) the date on which the DNA sample from which the profile was derived was taken, or

        (ii) if the profile was derived from more than one DNA sample, the date on which the first of those samples was taken.

(5) But if, before the end of the period within which material may be retained by virtue of this section, the person is again convicted of a recordable offence, the material may be retained indefinitely.

(6) In this section, 'relevant custodial sentence' means any of the following—

    (a) a custodial sentence within the meaning of section 76 of the Powers of Criminal Courts (Sentencing) Act 2000;

    (b) a sentence of a period of detention and training (excluding any period of supervision) which a person is liable to serve under an order under section 211 of the Armed Forces Act 2006 or a secure training order.][403]

[63L Retention of section 63D material: persons given a penalty notice

(1) This section applies to section 63D material which—

    (a) relates to a person who is given a penalty notice under section 2 of the Criminal Justice and Police Act 2001 and in respect of whom no proceedings are brought for the offence to which the notice relates, and

    (b) was taken (or, in the case of a DNA profile, derived from a sample taken) from the person in connection with the investigation of the offence to which the notice relates.

(2) The material may be retained—

    (a) in the case of fingerprints, for a period of 2 years beginning with the date on which the fingerprints were taken,

    (b) in the case of a DNA profile, for a period of 2 years beginning with—

        (i) the date on which the DNA sample from which the profile was derived was taken, or

        (ii) if the profile was derived from more than one DNA sample, the date on which the first of those samples was taken.][404]

[63M Retention of section 63D material for purposes of national security

(1) Section 63D material may be retained for as long as a national security determination made by the responsible chief officer of police has effect in relation to it.

---

[403] Added by the Protection of Freedoms Act 2012, s 7 (date to be appointed).
[404] Added by the Protection of Freedoms Act 2012, s 8 (date to be appointed).

Act

(2) A national security determination is made if the responsible chief officer of police determines that it is necessary for any section 63D material to be retained for the purposes of national security.

(3) A national security determination—

    (a) must be made in writing,

    (b) has effect for a maximum of 2 years beginning with the date on which it is made, and

    (c) may be renewed.][405]

[63N Retention of section 63D material given voluntarily

(1) This section applies to the following section 63D material—

    (a) fingerprints taken with the consent of the person from whom they were taken, and

    (b) a DNA profile derived from a DNA sample taken with the consent of the person from whom the sample was taken.

(2) Material to which this section applies may be retained until it has fulfilled the purpose for which it was taken or derived.

(3) Material to which this section applies which relates to—

    (a) a person who is convicted of a recordable offence, or

    (b) a person who has previously been convicted of a recordable offence (other than a person who has only one exempt conviction),

    may be retained indefinitely.

(4) For the purposes of subsection (3)(b), a conviction is exempt if it is in respect of a recordable offence, other than a qualifying offence, committed when the person is aged under 18.][406]

[63O Retention of section 63D material with consent

(1) This section applies to the following material—

    (a) fingerprints (other than fingerprints taken under section 61(6A) to which section 63D applies), and

    (b) a DNA profile to which section 63D applies.

(2) If the person to whom the material relates consents to material to which this section applies being retained, the material may be retained for as long as that person consents to it being retained.

(3) Consent given under this section—

    (a) must be in writing, and

    (b) can be withdrawn at any time.][407]

[63P Section 63D material obtained for one purpose and used for another

(1) Subsection (2) applies if section 63D material which is taken (or, in the case of a DNA profile, derived from sample taken) from a person in connection with the investigation of an offence leads to the person to whom the material relates being arrested for or charged with, or convicted of, an offence other than the offence under investigation.

(2) Sections 63E to 63O and sections 63Q and 63T have effect in relation to the material as if the material was taken (or, in the case of a DNA profile, derived from a sample

---

[405] Added by the Protection of Freedoms Act 2012, s 9 (date to be appointed).

[406] Added by the Protection of Freedoms Act 2012, s 10 (date to be appointed).

[407] Added by the Protection of Freedoms Act 2012, s 11 (date to be appointed).

taken) in connection with the investigation of the offence in respect of which the person is arrested or charged.][408]

[63Q   Destruction of copies of section 63D material

(1) If fingerprints are required by section 63D to be destroyed, any copies of the fingerprints held by the police must also be destroyed.

(2) If a DNA profile is required by that section to be destroyed, no copy may be retained by the police expert in a form which does not include information which identifies the person to whom the DNA profile relates.][409]

[63R   Destruction of samples

(1) This section applies to samples—

    (a) taken from a person under any power conferred by this Part of this Act, or

    (b) taken by the police, with the consent of the person from whom they were taken, in connection with the investigation of an offence by the police.

(2) Samples to which this section applies must be destroyed if it appears to the responsible chief officer of police that—

    (a) the taking of the samples was unlawful, or

    (b) the samples were taken from a person in connection with that person's arrest and the arrest was unlawful or based on mistaken identity.

(3) Subject to this, the rule in subsection (4) or (as the case may be) (5) applies.

(4) A DNA sample to which this section applies must be destroyed—

    (a) as soon as a DNA profile has been derived from the sample, or

    (b) if sooner, before the end of the period of 6 months beginning with the date on which the sample was taken.

(5) Any other sample to which this section applies must be destroyed before the end of the period of 6 months beginning with the date on which it was taken.

(6) The responsible chief officer of police may apply to a District Judge (Magistrates' Courts) for an order to retain a sample to which this section applies beyond the date on which the sample would otherwise be required to be destroyed by virtue of subsection (4) or (5) if—

    (a) the sample was taken from a person in connection with the investigation of a qualifying offence, and

    (b) the responsible chief officer of police considers that the condition in subsection (7) is met.

(7) The condition is that, having regard to the nature and complexity of other material that is evidence in relation to the offence, the sample is likely to be needed in any proceedings for the offence for the purposes of—

    (a) disclosure to, or use by, a defendant, or

    (b) responding to any challenge by a defendant in respect of the admissibility of material that is evidence on which the prosecution proposes to rely.

(8) An application under subsection (6) must be made before the date on which the sample would otherwise be required to be destroyed by virtue of subsection (4) or (5).

(9) If, on an application made by the responsible chief officer of police under subsection (6), the District Judge (Magistrates' Courts) is satisfied that the condition in subsection (7) is met, the District judge may make an order under this subsection which—

---

[408] Added by the Protection of Freedoms Act 2012, s 12 (date to be appointed).
[409] Added by the Protection of Freedoms Act 2012, s 13 (date to be appointed).

(a) allows the sample to be retained for a period of 12 months beginning with the date on which the sample would otherwise be required to be destroyed by virtue of subsection (4) or (5), and

(b) may be renewed (on one or more occasions) for a further period of not more than 12 months from the end of the period when the order would otherwise cease to have effect.

(10) An application for an order under subsection (9) (other than an application for renewal)—

(a) may be made without notice of the application having been given to the person from whom the sample was taken, and

(b) may be heard and determined in private in the absence of that person.

(11) A sample retained by virtue of an order under subsection (9) must not be used other than for the purposes of any proceedings for the offence in connection with which the sample was taken.

(12) A sample that ceases to be retained by virtue of an order under subsection (9) must be destroyed.

(13) Nothing in this section prevents a speculative search, in relation to samples to which this section applies, from being carried out within such time as may reasonably be required for the search if the responsible chief officer of police considers the search to be desirable.][410]

[63S Destruction of impressions of footwear

(1) This section applies to impressions of footwear—

(a) taken from a person under any power conferred by this Part of this Act, or

(b) taken by the police, with the consent of the person from whom they were taken, in connection with the investigation of an offence by the police.

(2) Impressions of footwear to which this section applies must be destroyed unless they are retained under subsection (3).

(3) Impressions of footwear may be retained for as long as is necessary for purposes related to the prevention or detection of crime, the investigation of an offence or the conduct of a prosecution.][411]

[63T Use of retained material

(1) Any material to which section 63D, 63R or 63S applies must not be used other than—

(a) in the interests of national security,

(b) for the purposes of a terrorist investigation,

(c) for purposes related to the prevention or detection of crime, the investigation of an offence or the conduct of a prosecution, or

(d) for the purposes related to the identification of a deceased person or of the person to whom the material relates.

(2) Material which is required by section 63D, 63R or 63R to be destroyed must not at any time after it is required to be destroyed be used—

(a) in evidence against the person to whom the material relates, or

(b) for the purposes of the investigation of any offence.

(3) In this section—

(a) the reference to using material includes a reference to allowing any check to be made against it and to disclosing it to any person,

(b) the reference to crime includes a reference to any conduct which—

---

[410] Added by the Protection of Freedoms Act 2012, s 14 (date to be appointed).
[411] Added by the Protection of Freedoms Act 2012, s 15 (date to be appointed).

> (i) constitutes one or more criminal offences (whether under the law of England and Wales or of any country or territory outside England and Wales), or
>
> (ii) is, or corresponds to, any conduct which, if it all took place in England and Wales, would constitute one or more criminal offences, and
>
> (c) the references to an investigation and to a prosecution include references, respectively, to any investigation outside England and Wales of any crime or suspected crime and to a prosecution brought in respect of any crime in a country or territory outside of England and Wales.][412]

[63U Exclusions for certain regimes

(1)   Sections 63D to 63T do not apply to material to which paragraphs 20A to 20J of Schedule 8 to the Terrorism Act 2000 (destruction, retention and use of material taken from terrorist suspects) apply.

(2)   Any reference in those sections to a person being arrested for, or charged with, an offence does not include a reference to a person—

   (a) being arrested under section 41 of the Terrorism Act 2000, or

   (b) being charged with an offence following arrest under that section.

(3)   Sections 63D to 63T do not apply to material which paragraph 8 of Schedule 4 to the International Criminal Court Act 2001 (requirement to destroy material) applies.

(4)   Sections 63D to 63T do not apply to material to which paragraph 6 of Schedule 6 to the Terrorism Prevention and Investigation Measures Act 2011 (requirement to destroy material) applies.

(5)   Sections 63D to 63Q, 63S and 63T do not apply to material which is, or may become, disclosable under—

   (a) the Criminal Procedure and Investigations Act 1996, or

   (b) a code of practice prepared under section 23 of that Act and in operation by virtue of an order under section 25 of that Act.

(6)   Sections 63D to 63T do not apply to material which—

   (a) is taken from a person, but

   (b) relates to another person.

(7)   Nothing in sections 63D to 63T affects any power conferred by—

   (a) paragraph 18(2) of Schedule 2 to the Immigration Act 1971 (power to take reasonable steps to identify a person detained), or

   (b) section 20 of the Immigration and Asylum Act 1999 (disclosure of police information to the Secretary of State for use for immigration purposes).][413]

64 Destruction of fingerprints and samples

[(1A) Where—

   (a) fingerprints[, impressions of footwear][414] or samples are taken from a person in connection with the investigation of an offence, and

   (b) subsection (3) below does not require them to be destroyed,

   the fingerprints[, impressions of footwear][415] or samples may be retained after they have fulfilled the purposes for which they were taken but shall not be used

---

[412] Added by the Protection of Freedoms Act 2012, s 16 (date to be appointed).
[413] Added by the Protection of Freedoms Act 2012, s 17 (date to be appointed).
[414] Amended by SOCAPA 2005, s 118(1), (4)(a).
[415] ibid.

by any person except for purposes related to the prevention or detection of crime, the investigation of an offence[, the conduct of a prosecution or the identification of a deceased person or of the person from whom a body part came][416].

(1B)   In subsection (1A) above—

(a) the reference to using a fingerprint [or an impression of footwear][417] includes a reference to allowing any check to be made against it under section 63A(1) or (1C) above and to disclosing it to any person;

(b) the reference to using a sample includes a reference to allowing any check to be made under section 63A(1) or (1C) above against it or against information derived from it and to disclosing it or any such information to any person;

(c) the reference to crime includes a reference to any conduct which—

(i) constitutes one or more criminal offences (whether under the law of a part of the United Kingdom or of a country or territory outside the United Kingdom); or

(ii) is, or corresponds to, any conduct which, if it all took place in any one part of the United Kingdom, would constitute one or more criminal offences;

and

(d) the references to an investigation and to a prosecution include references, respectively, to any investigation outside the United Kingdom of any crime or suspected crime and to a prosecution brought in respect of any crime in a country or territory outside the United Kingdom.][418]

[(1BA) Fingerprints taken from a person by virtue of section 61(6A) above must be destroyed as soon as they have fulfilled the purpose for which they were taken.][419]

(3) If—

(a) fingerprints[, impressions of footwear][420] or samples are taken from a person in connection with the investigation of an offence; and

(b) that person is not suspected of having committed the offence,

they must[, except as provided in [the following provisions of this section][421],][422] be destroyed as soon as they have fulfilled the purpose for which they were taken.

[(3AA) Samples[, fingerprints and impressions of footwear][423] are not required to be destroyed under subsection (3) above if—

(a) they were taken for the purposes of the investigation of an offence of which a person has been convicted; and

(b) a sample[, fingerprint, (or as the case may be) an impression of footwear][424] was also taken from the convicted person for the purposes of that investigation.

---

[416] Amended by SOCAPA 2005, s 117(6), (7).

[417] Amended by SOCAPA 2005, s 118(1), (4)(b).

[418] Amended by the Criminal Justice and Police Act 2001, s 82(1), (2), (6).

[419] Amended by SOCAPA 2005, s 117(6), (8).

[420] Amended by SOCAPA 2005, s 118(1), (4)(c).

[421] Amended by the Criminal Justice and Police Act 2001, s 82(1), (3).

[422] Amended by the Criminal Justice and Public Order Act 1994, s 57(2).

[423] Amended by SOCAPA 2005, s 118(1), (4)(d)(i).

[424] Amended by SOCAPA 2005, s 118(1), (4)(d)(ii).

(3AB) Subject to subsection (3AC) below, where a person is entitled under [subsection (1BA) or (3)][425] above to the destruction of any fingerprint[, impression of footwear][426] or sample taken from him (or would be but for subsection (3AA) above), neither the fingerprint[, nor the impression of footwear,][427] nor the sample, nor any information derived from the sample, shall be used—

(a) in evidence against the person who is or would be entitled to the destruction of that fingerprint[, impression of footwear][428] or sample; or

(b) for the purposes of the investigation of any offence;

and subsection (1B) above applies for the purposes of this subsection as it applies for the purposes of subsection (1A) above.

(3AC) Where a person from whom a fingerprint[, impression of footwear][429] or sample has been taken consents in writing to its retention—

(a) that [fingerprint [, impression of footwear][430] or][431] sample need not be destroyed under subsection (3) above;

(b) subsection (3AB) above shall not restrict the use that may be made of the fingerprint[, impression of footwear][432] or sample or, in the case of a sample, of any information derived from it; and

(c) that consent shall be treated as comprising a consent for the purposes of section 63A(1C) above[.

This subsection does not apply to fingerprints taken from a person by virtue of section 61(6A) above.].[433]

and a consent given for the purpose of this subsection shall not be capable of being withdrawn.

(3AD) For the purposes of subsection (3AC) above it shall be immaterial whether the consent is given at, before or after the time when the entitlement to the destruction of the fingerprint[, impression of footwear][434] or sample arises.][435]

(4) [...][436]

[(5) If fingerprints [or impressions of footwear][437] are destroyed—

(a) any copies of the fingerprints [or impressions of footwear][438] shall also be destroyed; and

(b) any chief officer of police controlling access to computer data relating to the fingerprints [or impressions of footwear][439] shall make access to the data impossible, as soon as it is practicable to do so.][440]

---

[425] Amended by SOCAPA 2005, s 117(1), (9).
[426] Amended by SOCAPA 2005, s 118(1), (4)(e)(i).
[427] Amended by SOCAPA 2005, s 118(1), (4)(e)(ii).
[428] Amended by SOCAPA 2005, s 118(1), (4)(e)(i).
[429] Amended by SOCAPA 2005, s 118(1), (4)(f).
[430] Amended by SOCAPA 2005, s 118(1), (4)(f).
[431] Amended by SOCAPA 2005, s 117(6), (10)(a).
[432] ibid.
[433] Prospectively amended by SOCAPA 2005, s 117(1), (10)(b).
[434] Amended by SOCAPA 2005, s 118(1), (4)(g).
[435] Amended by the Criminal Justice and Police Act 2001, s 82(1), (4), (6).
[436] Repealed by the Criminal Justice and Police Act 2001, s 137, Sch 7, Pt 2(1).
[437] Amended by SOCAPA 2005, s 118(1), (4)(h).
[438] ibid.
[439] ibid.
[440] Amended by the Criminal Justice Act 1988, s 148.

Act

(6)   A person who asks to be allowed to witness the destruction of his finger-prints [or impressions of footwear]⁴⁴¹ or copies of them shall have a right to witness it.

[(6A)   If—

(a)   subsection (5)(b) above falls to be complied with; and

(b)   the person to whose fingerprints [or impressions of footwear]⁴⁴² the data relate asks for a certificate that it has been complied with,

such a certificate shall be issued to him, not later than the end of the period of three months beginning with the day on which he asks for it, by the responsible chief officer of police or a person authorised by him or on his behalf for the purposes of this section.

(6B)   In this section—

[...]⁴⁴³

'the responsible chief officer of police' means the chief officer of police in whose [police]⁴⁴⁴ area the computer data were put on to the computer.]⁴⁴⁵

(7)   Nothing in this section—

(a)   affects any power conferred by paragraph 18(2) of Schedule 2 to the Immigration Act 1971 [or section 20 of the Immigration and Asylum Act 1999 (c 33) (disclosure of police information to the Secretary of State for use for immigration purposes)]⁴⁴⁶; or

(b)   applies to a person arrested or detained under the terrorism provisions.

[64ZA   Destruction of samples]

(1)   A DNA sample to which section 64 applies must be destroyed—

(a)   as soon as a DNA profile has been derived from the sample, or

(b)   if sooner, before the end of the period of 6 months beginning with the date on which the sample was taken.

(2)   Any other sample to which section 64 applies must be destroyed before the end of the period of 6 months beginning with the date on which it was taken.]⁴⁴⁷

[64ZB   Destruction of data given voluntarily

(1)   This section applied to—

(a)   fingerprints or impressions of footwear taken in connection with the investigation of an offence with the consent of the person from whom they were taken, and

(b)   a DNA profile derived from a DNA sample taken in connection with the investigation of an offence with the consent of the person from whom the sample was taken.

(2)   Material to which this section applies must be destroyed as soon as it has fulfilled the purpose for which it was taken or derived, unless it is—

(a)   material relating to a person who is convicted of the offence,

---

⁴⁴¹ Amended by SOCAPA 2005, s 118(1), (4)(i).

⁴⁴² Amended by SOCAPA 2005, s 118(1), (4)(j).

⁴⁴³ Repealed by the Police Act 1996, s 103, Sch 7, Pt II, para 37, Sch 9, Pt I.

⁴⁴⁴ Amended by the Police Act 1996, s 103, Sch 7, Pt II, para 37.

⁴⁴⁵ Amended by the Criminal Justice Act 1988, s 148.

⁴⁴⁶ Amended by the Criminal Justice and Police Act 2001, s 82(1), (5).

⁴⁴⁷ Added by the Crime and Security Act 2010, s 14(2) (date to be appointed).

(b) *material relating to a person who has previously been convicted of a recordable offence other than a person who has only one exempt conviction,*

(c) *material in relation to which any of sections 64ZC to 64ZH applies, or*

(d) *material which is not required to be destroyed by virtue of consent given under section 64ZL.*

(3) *If material to which this section applies leads to the person to whom the material relates being arrested or charged with an offence other than the offence under investigation—*

  (a) *the material is not required to be destroyed by virtue of this section, and*

  (b) *sections 64ZD to 64ZH have effect in relation to the material as if the material was taken (or, in the case of a DNA profile, was derived from material taken) in connection with the investigation of the offence in respect of which the person is arrested or charged.*][448]

[64ZC Destruction of data relating to a person subject to a control order

(1) *This section applies to material falling within subsection (2) relating to a person who—*

  (a) *has no previous convictions or only one exempt conviction, and*

  (b) *is subject to a control order.*

(2) *Material falls within this subsection if it is—*

  (a) *fingerprints taken from the person, or*

  (b) *a DNA profile derived from a DNA sample taken from a person.*

(3) *The material must be destroyed before the end of the period of 2 years beginning with the date on which the person ceases to be subject to a control order.*

(4) *This section ceases to have effect in relation to the material if the person is convicted—*

  (a) *in England and Wales or Northern Ireland of a recordable offence, or*

  (b) *in Scotland of an offence which is punishable by imprisonment,*

before the material is required to be destroyed by virtue of this section.

(5) *For the purposes of subsection (1)—*

  (a) *a person has no previous convictions if the person has not previously been convicted—*

    (i) *in England and Wales or Northern Ireland of a recordable offence, or*

    (ii) *in Scotland of an offence which is punishable by imprisonment, and*

  (b) *if the person has been previously convicted of a recordable offence in England and Wales or Northern Ireland, the conviction is exempt if it is in respect of a recordable offence other than a qualifying offence, committed when the person is aged under 18.*

(6) *For the purposes of that subsection—*

  (a) *a person is to be treated as having been convicted of an offence if—*

    (i) *he has been given a caution in England and Wales or Northern Ireland in respect of the offence which, at the time of the caution, he has admitted, or*

    (ii) *he has been warned or reprimanded under section 65 of the Crime and Disorder Act 1998 for the offence, and*

  (b) *if a person is convicted of more than one offence arising out of a single course of action,*

those convictions are to be treated as a single conviction.

(7) *In this section—*

  (a) *'recordable offence' has, in relation to a conviction in Northern Ireland, the meaning given by Article 2(2) of the Police and Criminal Evidence (Northern Ireland) Order 1989, and*

---

[448] Added by the Crime and Security Act 2010, s 14(2) (date to be appointed).

Act

(b) 'qualifying offence' has, in relation to a conviction in respect of a recordable offence committed in northern Ireland, the meaning given by Article 53A of that Order.][449]

[64ZD Destruction of data relating to persons not convicted

(1) This section applies to material falling within subsection (2) relating to a person who—
    (a) has no previous convictions or only one exempt conviction,
    (b) is arrested for or charged with a recordable offence, and
    (c) is aged 18 or over at the time of the alleged offence.
(2) Material falls within this subsection if it is—
    (a) fingerprints or impressions of footwear taken from the person in connection with the investigation of the offence, or
    (b) a DNA profile derived from a DNA sample so taken.
(3) The material must be destroyed—
    (a) in the case of fingerprints or impressions of footwear, before the end of the period of 6 years beginning with the date on which the fingerprints or impressions were taken,
    (b) in the case of a DNA profile, before the end of the period of 6 years beginning with the date on which the DNA sample from which the profile was derived was taken (or, if the profile was derived from more than one DNA sample, the date on which the first of those samples was taken).
(4) But if, before the material is required to be destroyed by virtue of this section, the person is arrested for or charged with a recordable offence the material may be further retained until the end of the period of 6 years beginning with the date of the arrest or charge.
(5) This section ceases to have effect in relation to the material if the person is convicted of a recordable offence before the material is required to be destroyed by virtue of this section.][450]

[64ZE Destruction of data relating to persons under 18 not convicted: recordable offences other than qualifying offences

(1) This section applies to material falling within subsection (2) relating to a person who—
    (a) has no previous convictions or only one exempt conviction,
    (b) is arrested for or charged with a recordable offence other than a qualifying offence, and
    (c) is aged under 18 at the time of the alleged offence.
(2) Material falls within this subsection if it is—
    (a) fingerprints or impressions of footwear taken from the person in connection with the investigation of the offence, or
    (b) a DNA profile derived from a DNA sample so taken.
(3) The material must be destroyed—
    (a) in the case of fingerprints or impressions of footwear, before the end of the period of 3 years beginning with the date on which the fingerprints or impressions were taken,
    (b) in the case of a DNA profile, before the end of the period of 3 years beginning with the date on which the DNA sample from which the profile was derived was taken

---

[449] Added by the Crime and Security Act 2012, s 14(2) (date to be appointed).
[450] Added by the Crime and Security Act 2012, s 14(2) (date to be appointed).

(or, if the profile was derived from more than one DNA sample, the date on which the first of those samples was taken).

(4) But if, before the material is required to be destroyed by virtue of this section, the person is arrested for or charged with a recordable offence—

  (a) where the person is aged 18 or over at the time of the alleged offence, the material may be further retained until the end of the period of 6 years beginning with the date of the arrest or charge,

  (b) where—
    (i) the alleged offence is not a qualifying offence, and
    (ii) the person is aged under 18 at the time of the alleged offence,
    the material may be further retained until the end of the period of three years beginning with the date of the arrest or charge,

  (c) where—
    (i) the alleged offence is a qualifying offence, and
    (ii) the person is aged under 16 at the time of the alleged offence,
    the material may be further retained until the end of the period of 3 years beginning with the date of the arrest or charge,

  (d) where—
    (i) the alleged offence is a qualifying offence, and
    (ii) the person is aged 16 or 17 at the time of the alleged offence,
    the material may be further retained until the end of the period of 6 years beginning with the date of the arrest or charge,

  (e) where—
    (i) the person is convicted of the offence,
    (ii) the offence is not a qualifying offence,
    (iii) the person is aged under 18 at the time of the offence, and
    (iv) the person has no previous convictions,
    the material may be further retained until the end of the period of 5 years beginning with the date of the arrest or charge.

(5) This section ceases to have effect in relation to the material if, before the material is required to be destroyed by virtue of this section, the person—

  (a) is convicted of a recordable offence and is aged 18 or over at the time of the offence,
  (b) is convicted of a qualifying offence, or
  (c) having a previous exempt conviction of a recordable offence.][451]

[64ZF **Destruction of data relating to persons under 16 not convicted: qualifying offences**

(1) This section applies to material falling within subsection (2) relating to a person who—

  (a) has no previous convictions or only one exempt conviction,
  (b) is arrested for or charged with a qualifying offence, and
  (c) is aged under 16 at the time of the alleged offence.

(2) Material falls within this subsection if it is—

  (a) fingerprints or impressions of footwear taken from the person in connection with the investigation of the offence, or
  (b) a DNA profile derived from a DNA sample so taken.

---

[451] Added by the Crime and Security Act 2010, s 14(2) (date to be appointed).

Act

(3) The material must be destroyed—

    (a) in the case of fingerprints or impressions of footwear, before the end of the period of 3 years beginning with the date on which the fingerprints or impressions were taken,

    (b) in the case of a DNA profile, before the end of the period of 3 years beginning with the date on which the DNA sample from which the profile was derived was taken (or, if the profile was derived from more than one DNA sample, the date on which the first of those samples was taken).

(4) But if, before the material is required to be destroyed by virtue of this section, the person is arrested for or charged with a recordable offence—

    (a) where the person is aged 18 or over at the time of the alleged offence, the material may be further retained until the end of the period of 6 years beginning with the date of the arrest or charge,

    (b) where—

        (i) the alleged offence is not a qualifying offence, and

        (ii) the person is aged under 18 at the time of the alleged offence,

    the material may be further retained until the end of the period of 3 years beginning with the date of the arrest or charge,

    (c) where—

        (i) the alleged offence is a qualifying offence, and

        (ii) the person is aged under 16 at the time of the alleged offence,

    the material may be further retained until the end of the period of 3 years beginning with the date of the arrest or charge,

    (d) where—

        (i) the alleged offence is a qualifying offence, and

        (ii) the person is aged 16 or 17 at the time of the alleged offence,

    the material may be further retained until the end of the period of 6 years beginning with the date of the arrest or charge,

    (e) where—

        (i) the person is convicted of the offence,

        (ii) the offence is not a qualifying offence,

        (iii) the person is aged under 18 at the time of the offence, and

        (iv) the person has no previous convictions,

    the material may be further retained until the end of the period of 5 years beginning with the date of the arrest or charge.

(5) This section ceases to have effect in relation to the material if, before the material is required to be destroyed by virtue of this section, the person—

    (a) is convicted of a recordable offence and is aged 18 or over at the time of the offence,

    (b) is convicted of a qualifying offence, or

    (c) having a previous exempt conviction, is convicted of a recordable offence.][452]

[64ZG Destruction of data relating to persons aged 16 or 17 not convicted: qualifying offences

(1) This section applies to material falling within subsection (2) relating to a person who—

    (a) has no previous convictions or only one exempt conviction,

---

[452] Added by the Crime and Security Act 2012, s 14(2) (date to be appointed).

      (b) *is arrested for or charged with a qualifying offence, and*

      (c) *is aged 16 or 17 at the time of the alleged offence.*

  (2) *Material falls within this subsection if it is—*

      (a) *fingerprints or impressions of footwear taken from the person in connection with the investigation of the offence, or*

      (b) *a DNA profile derived from a DNA sample so taken.*

  (3) *The material must be destroyed—*

      (a) *in the case of fingerprints or impressions of footwear, before the end of the period of 6 years beginning with the date on which the fingerprints or impressions were taken,*

      (b) *in the case of a DNA profile, before the end of the period of 6 years beginning with the date on which the DNA sample from which the profile was derived was taken (or, if the profile was derived from more than one DNA sample, the date on which the first of those samples was taken).*

  (4) *But if, before the material is required to be destroyed by virtue of this section, the person is arrested for or charged with a recordable offence—*

      (a) *where the person is aged 18 or over at the time of the alleged offence, the material may be further retained until the end of the period of 6 years beginning with the date of the arrest or charge,*

      (b) *where—*

         (i) *the alleged offence is not a qualifying offence, and*

         (ii) *the person is aged under 18 at the time of the alleged offence,*

      the material may be further retained until the end of the date of the arrest or charge,

      (c) *where—*

         (i) *the alleged offence is a qualifying offence, and*

         (ii) *the person is aged 16 or 17 at the time of the alleged offence,*

      the material may be further retained until the end of the period of 6 years beginning with the date of the arrest or charge,

      (d) *where—*

         (i) *the person is convicted of the offence,*

         (ii) *the offence is not a qualifying offence,*

         (iii) *the person is aged under 18 at the time of the offence, and*

         (iv) *the person has no previous convictions,*

      the material may be further retained until the end of the period of 5 years beginning with the date of the arrest or charge.

  (5) *This section ceases to have effect in relation to the material if, before the material is required to be destroyed by virtue of this section, the person—*

      (a) *is convicted of a recordable offence, and is aged 18 or over at the time of the offence,*

      (b) *is convicted of a qualifying offence, or*

      (c) *having a previous exempt conviction, is convicted of a recordable offence.*][453]

[64ZH Destruction of data relating to persons under 18 convicted of a recordable offence other than a qualifying offence

  (1) *This section applies to material falling within subsection (2) relating to a person who—*

      (a) *has no previous convictions,*

---

[453] Added by the Crime and Security Act 2010, s 14(2) (date to be appointed).

Act

    (b) is convicted of a recordable offence other than a qualifying offence, and

    (c) is aged under 18 at the time of the offence.

(2) Material falls within this subsection if it is—

    (a) fingerprints or impressions of footwear taken from the person in connection with the investigation of the offence, or

    (b) a DNA profile derived from a DNA sample so taken.

(3) The material must be destroyed—

    (a) in the case of fingerprints or impressions of footwear, before the end of the period of 5 years beginning with the date on which the fingerprints or impressions were taken,

    (b) in the case of a DNA profile, before the end of the period of 5 years beginning with the date on which the DNA sample from which the profile was derived was taken (or, if the profile was derive from more than one DNA sample, the date on which the first of those samples was taken).

(4) But if, before the material is required to be destroyed by virtue of this section, the person is arrested for or charged with a recordable offence—

    (a) where the person is aged 18 or over at the time of the alleged offence, the material may be further retained until the end of the period of 6 years beginning with the date of the arrest of charge,

    (b) where—

        (i) the alleged offence is not a qualifying offence, and

        (ii) the person is aged under 18 at the time of the alleged offence,

    the material may be further retained until the end of the period of 3 years beginning with the date of the arrest or charge,

    (c) where—

        (i) the alleged offence is a qualifying offence, and

        (ii) the person is aged under 16 at the time of the alleged offence,

    the material may be further retained until the end of the period of 3 years beginning with the date of the arrest or charge,

    (d) where—

        (i) the alleged offence is a qualifying offence, and

        (ii) the person is aged 16 or 17 at the time of the alleged offence,

    the material may be further retained until the end of the period of 6 years beginning with the date of the arrest or charge.

(5) This section ceases to have effect in relation to the material if the person is convicted of a further recordable offence before the material is required to be destroyed by virtue of this section.][454]

[64ZI Sections 64ZB to 64ZH: supplementary provision

(1) Any reference in section 64ZB or sections 64ZD to 64ZH to a person being charged with an offence includes a reference to a person being informed that he will be reported for an offence.

(2) For the purposes of those sections—

    (a) a person has no previous convictions if the person has not previously been convicted of a recordable offence, and

    (b) if the person has been previously convicted of a recordable offence, the conviction is exempt if it is in respect of a recordable offence other than a qualifying offence, committed when the person is aged under 18.

---

[454] Added by the Crime and Security Act 2010, s 14(2) (date to be appointed).

(3) For the purposes of those sections, a person is to be treated as having been convicted of an offence if—

    (a) he has been given a caution in respect of the offence which, at the time of the caution, he has admitted, or

    (b) he has been warned or reprimanded under section 65 of the Crime and Disorder Act 1998 for the offence.

(4) If a person is convicted of more than one offence arising out of a single course of action, those convictions are to be treated as a single conviction for the purpose of any provision of those sections relating to an exempt, first or subsequent conviction.

(5) Subject to the completion of any speculative search that the responsible chief officer of police considers necessary or desirable, material falling within any of sections 64ZD to 64ZH must be destroyed immediately if it appears to the chief police officer that—

    (a) the arrest was unlawful,

    (b) the taking of the fingerprints, impressions of footwear or DNA sample concerned was unlawful,

    (c) the arrest was based on mistaken identity, or

    (d) other circumstances relating to the arrest or the alleged offence mean that is is appropriate to destroy the material.

(6) 'Responsible chief officer of police' means the chief officer of police for the police area—

    (a) in which the samples, fingerprints or impressions of footwear were taken, or

    (b) in the case of a DNA profile, in which the sample from which the DNA profile was derived was taken.][455]

[64ZJ Destruction of fingerprints taken under section 61(6A)

Fingerprints taken from a person by virtue of section 61(6A) (taking fingerprints for the purposes of identification) must be destroyed as soon as they have fulfilled the purpose for which they were taken.][456]

[64ZK Retention for purposes of national security

(1) Subsection (2) applies if the responsible chief officer of police determines that it is necessary for—

    (a) a DNA profile to which section 64 applies, or

    (b) fingerprints to which section 64 applies, other than fingerprints taken under section 61(6A),

    to be retained for the purposes of national security.

(2) Where this subsection applies—

    (a) the material is not required to be destroyed in accordance with sections 64ZB to 64ZH, and

    (b) section 64ZN(2) does not apply to the material,

    for as long as the determination has effect.

(3) A determination under subsection (1) has effect for a maximum of 2 years beginning with the date on which the material would otherwise be required to be destroyed, but a determination may be renewed.

(4) 'Responsible chief officer of police' means the chief officer of police for the police area—

    (a) in which the fingerprints were taken, or

---

[455] Added by the Crime and Security Act 2010, s 14(2) (date to be appointed).

[456] Added by the Crime and Security Act 2010, s 14(2) (date to be appointed).

(b) in the case of a DNA profile, in which the sample from which the DNA profile was derived was taken.][457]

Act

[64ZL Retention with consent

(1) If a person consents in writing to the retention of fingerprints, impressions of footwear or a DNA profile to which section 64 applies, other than fingerprints taken under section 61(6A)—

(a) the material is not required to be destroyed in accordance with sections 64ZB to 64ZH, and

(b) section 64ZN(2) does not apply to the material.

(2) It is immaterial for the purposes of subsection (1) whether the consent is given at, before or after the time when the entitlement to the destruction of the material arises.

(3) Consent given under this section can be withdrawn at any time.][458]

[64ZM Destruction of copies, and notification of destruction

(1) If fingerprints or impressions of footwear are required to be destroyed by virtue of any of sections 64ZB to 64ZJ, any copies of the fingerprints or impressions of footwear must also be destroyed.

(2) If a DNA profile is required to be destroyed by virtue of any of those sections, no copy may be kept except in a form which does not include information which identifies the person to whom the DNA profile relates.

(3) If a person makes a request to the responsible chief officer of police to be notified when anything relating to the person is destroyed under any of sections 64ZA to 64ZJ, the responsible chief officer of police or a person authorised by the chief officer or on the chief officer's behalf must within three months of the request issue the person with a certificate recording the destruction.

(4) 'Responsible chief officer of police' means the chief officer of police for the police area—

(a) in which the samples, fingerprints or impressions of footwear have been destroyed were taken, or

(b) in the case of a DNA profile which has been destroyed, in which the samples from which the DNA profile was derived were taken.][459]

[64ZN Use of retained material

(1) Any material to which section 64 applies which is retained after it has fulfilled the purpose for which it was taken or derived must not be used other than—

(a) in the interests of national security,

(b) for the purposes of a terrorist investigation,

(c) for purposes related to the prevention or detection of crime, the investigation of an offence or the conduct of a prosecution, or

(d) for purposes related to the identification of a deceased person or of the person to whom the material relates.

(2) Material which is required to be destroyed by virtue of any of sections 64ZA to 64ZJ, or of section 64ZM, must not at any time after it is required to be destroyed be used—

(a) in evidence against the person to whom the material relates, or

(b) for the purposes of the investigation of any offence.

---

[457] Added by the Crime and Security Act 2010, s 14(2) (date to be appointed).
[458] Added by the Crime and Security Act 2010, s 14(2) (date to be appointed).
[459] Added by the Crime and Security Act 2010, s 14(2) (date to be appointed).

(3)   *In this section—*
  (a)   *the reference to using material includes a reference to allowing any check to be made against it and to disclosing it to any person,*
  (b)   *the reference to crime includes a reference to any conduct which—*
    (i)   *constitutes one or more criminal offences (whether under the law of a part of the United Kingdom or of a country or territory outside the United Kingdom), or*
    (ii)   *is, or corresponds to, any conduct which, if it all took place in any one part of the united Kingdom, would constitute one or more criminal offences, and*
  (c)   *the references to an investigation and to a prosecution include references, respectively, to any investigation outside the United Kingdom of any crime or suspected crime and to a prosecution brought in respect of any crime in a country or territory outside the United Kingdom.]*[460]

[64A Photographing of suspects etc

(1)   A person who is detained at a police station may be photographed—
  (a)   with the appropriate consent; or
  (b)   if the appropriate consent is withheld or it is not practicable to obtain it, without it.

[(1A) A person falling within subsection (1B) below may, on the occasion of the relevant event referred to in subsection (1B), be photographed elsewhere than at a police station—
  (a)   with the appropriate consent; or
  (b)   if the appropriate consent is withheld or it is not practicable to obtain it, without it.

(1B)   A person falls within this subsection if he has been—
  (a)   arrested by a constable for an offence;
  (b)   taken into custody by a constable after being arrested for an offence by a person other than a constable;
  (c)   made subject to a requirement to wait with a community support officer under paragraph 2(3) or (3B) of Schedule 4 to the Police Reform Act 2002 ('the 2002 Act');
  [(ca) given a direction by a constable under section 27 of the Violent Crime Reduction Act 2006;][461]
  (d)   given a penalty notice by a constable in uniform under Chapter 1 of Part 1 of the Criminal Justice and Police Act 2001, a penalty notice by a constable under section 444A of the Education Act 1996, or a fixed penalty notice by a constable in uniform under section 54 of the Road Traffic Offenders Act 1988;
  (e)   given a notice in relation to a relevant fixed penalty offence (within the meaning of paragraph 1 of Schedule 4 to the 2002 Act) by a community support officer by virtue of a designation applying that paragraph to him; […][462]

---

[460] Added by the Crime and Security Act 2010, s 14(2) (date to be appointed).
[461] Added by Violent Crime Reduction Act 2006, s 27(7).
[462] Word repealed by Police and Justice Act 2006, Sch 15(2), para 1 (1 April 2007; SI 2007/709).

(f)   given a notice in relation to a relevant fixed penalty offence (within the meaning of paragraph 1 of Schedule 5 to the 2002 Act) by an accredited person by virtue of accreditation specifying that that paragraph applies to him[; or][463]

[(g)   given a notice in relation to a relevant fixed penalty offence (within the meaning of Schedule 5A to the 2002 Act) by an accredited inspector by virtue of accreditation specifying that paragraph 1 of Schedule 5A to the 2002 Act applies to him.][464]][465]

(2) A person proposing to take a photograph of any person under this section—

(a)   may, for the purpose of doing so, require the removal of any item or substance worn on or over the whole or any part of the head or face of the person to be photographed; and

(b)   if the requirement is not complied with, may remove the item or substance himself.

(3) Where a photograph may be taken under this section, the only persons entitled to take the photograph are [constables.][466]

[...][467]

(4) A photograph taken under this section—

(a)   may be used by, or disclosed to, any person for any purpose related to the prevention or detection of crime, the investigation of an offence or the conduct of a prosecution [or to the enforcement of a sentence][468]; and

(b)   after being so used or disclosed, may be retained but may not be used or disclosed except for a purpose so related.

(5) In subsection (4)—

(a)   the reference to crime includes a reference to any conduct which—

(i)   constitutes one or more criminal offences (whether under the law of a part of the United Kingdom or of a country or territory outside the United Kingdom); or

(ii)   is, or corresponds to, any conduct which, if it all took place in any one part of the United Kingdom, would constitute one or more criminal offences;

and

(b)   the references to an investigation and to a prosecution include references, respectively, to any investigation outside the United Kingdom of any crime or suspected crime and to a prosecution brought in respect of any crime in a country or territory outside the United Kingdom[; and][469]

[(c)   'sentence' includes any order made by a court in England and Wales when dealing with an offender in respect of his offence][470].

---

[463] Amended by the Police and Justice Act 2006, Sch 14, para 11.

[464] Added by the Police and Justice Act 2006, Sch 14, para 11.

[465] Amended by SOCAPA 2005, s 116(1), (2).

[466] Amended by the Police Reform Act 2002, s 107(1), Sch 7, para 9(5).

[467] Amended by the Police Reform Act 2002, s 107(1), Sch 7, para 9(5).

[468] Amended by SOCAPA 2005, s 116(1), (3).

[469] Amended by SOCAPA 2005, s 116(1), (4).

[470] Amended by SOCAPA 2005, s 116(1), (4).

(6)   References in this section to taking a photograph include references to using any process by means of which a visual image may be produced; and references to photographing a person shall be construed accordingly.

[(6A) In this section, a 'photograph' includes a moving image, and corresponding expressions shall be construed accordingly.][471]

[(7)   Nothing in this section applies to a person arrested under an extradition arrest power.][472][473]

65 Part V—supplementary

[(1)   In this Part of this Act—

'analysis', in relation to a skin impression, includes comparison and matching;

'appropriate consent' means—

(a)   in relation to a person who has attained the age of 17 years, the consent of that person;

(b)   in relation to a person who has not attained that age but has attained the age of 14 years, the consent of that person and his parent or guardian; and

(c)   in relation to a person who has not attained the age of 14 years, the consent of his parent or guardian;

[...][474]

['extradition arrest power' means any of the following—

(a)   a Part 1 warrant (within the meaning given by the Extradition Act 2003) in respect of which a certificate under section 2 of that Act has been issued;

(b)   section 5 of that Act;

(c)   a warrant issued under section 71 of that Act;

(d)   a provisional warrant (within the meaning given by that Act);][475]

['fingerprints', in relation to any person, means a record (in any form and produced by any method) of the skin pattern and other physical characteristics or features of—

(a)   any of that person's fingers; or

(b)   either of his palms;][476]

'intimate sample' means—

(a)   a sample of blood, semen or any other tissue fluid, urine or pubic hair;

(b)   a dental impression;

[(c)   a swab taken from any part of a person's genitals (including pubic hair) or from a person's body orifice other than the mouth;][477]

'intimate search' means a search which consists of the physical examination of a person's body orifices other than the mouth;

---

[471] Amended by SOCAPA 2005, s 116(1), (5).

[472] Amended by the Extradition Act 2003, s 169(1), (5); for savings see SI 2003/3103, arts 3–4.

[473] Added by the Anti-terrorism, Crime and Security Act 2001, s 92.

[474] Repealed by the Proceeds of Crime Act 2002, s 457, Sch 12, para 1 (24 March 2003 as SI 2003/333).

[475] Amended by the Extradition Act 2003, s 169(1), (6); for savings see SI 2003/3103, arts 3–4.

[476] Amended by the Criminal Justice and Police Act 2001, s 78(8).

[477] Amended by SOCAPA 2005, s 119(1), (2).

Act

'non-intimate sample' means—
(a) a sample of hair other than pubic hair;
(b) a sample taken from a nail or from under a nail;
[(c) a swab taken from any part of a person's body other than a part from which a swab taken would be an intimate sample;][478]
(d) saliva;
(e) a skin impression;
['offence' in relation to any country or territory outside England and Wales, includes an act punishable under the law of that country or territory, however it is described;][479]
'registered dentist' has the same meaning as in the Dentists Act 1984;
'skin impression' in relation to any person, means any record (other than a fingerprint) which is a record (in any form and produced by any method) of the skin pattern and other physical characteristics of features of the whole or any part of his foot or of any other part of his body;
'registered health care professional' means a person (other than a medical practitioner) who is—
(a) a registered nurse; or
(b) a registered member of a health care profession which is designated for the purposes of this paragraph by an order made by the Secretary of State;
'speculative search' in relation to a person's fingerprints or samples, means such a check against other fingerprints or samples or against information derived from other samples as is referred to in section 63A(1) above;
'sufficient' and 'insufficient', in relation to a sample, means (subject to subsection (2) below) sufficient or insufficient (in point of quantity or quality) for the purpose of enabling information to be produced by the means of analysis used or to be used in relation to the sample.
'the terrorism provisions' means section 41 of the Terrorism Act 2000, and any provision of Schedule 7 to that Act conferring a power of detention; and
'terrorism' has the meaning given in section 1 of that Act.
[...][480][481]
[(1A) A health care profession is any profession mentioned in section 60(2) of the Health Act 1999 (c 8) other than the profession of practising medicine and the profession of nursing.
(1B) An order under subsection (1) shall be made by statutory instrument and shall be subject to annulment in pursuance of a resolution of either House of Parliament.][482]
[(2) References in this Part of this Act to a sample's proving insufficient include references to where, as a consequence of—
(a) the loss, destruction or contamination of the whole or any part of the sample,
(b) any damage to the whole or a part of the sample, or

---

[478] Amended by SOCAPA 2005, s 119(1), (3).
[479] Added by the Crime and Security Act 2010, s 3(5).
[480] Repealed by the Proceeds of Crime Act 2002, Sch 12, para 1 (24 March 2003 as SI 2003/333).
[481] Existing text renumbered as s 65(1), definitions amended and s 65(2) inserted by the Criminal Justice and Police Act 2001, part 3, s 80.
[482] Amended by the Police Reform Act 2002, s 54(3).

    (c) the use of the whole or a part of the sample for an analysis which produced no results or which produced results some or all of which must be regarded, in the circumstances, as unreliable,

the sample has become unavailable or insufficient for the purpose of enabling information, or information of a particular description, to be obtained by means of analysis of the sample.][483]

(3) For the purposes of this Part, a person has in particular been convicted of an offence under the law of a country or territory outside England and Wales if—

    (a) a court exercising jurisdiction under the law of that country or territory has made in respect of such an offence a finding equivalent to a finding that the person is not guilty by reason of insanity; or

    (b) such a court has made in respect of such an offence a finding equivalent to a finding that the person is under a disability and did the act charged against him in respect of the offence.][484]

[65A 'Qualifying offence'

(1) In this Part, 'qualifying offence' means—

    (a) an offence specified in subsection (2) below, or

    (b) an ancillary offence relating to such an offence.

(2) The offences referred to in subsection (1)(a) above are—

    (a) murder;

    (b) manslaughter;

    (c) false imprisonment;

    (d) kidnapping;

    (e) an offence under section 4, 16, 18, 20 to 24 or 47 of the Offences Against the Person Act 1861;

    (f) an offence under section 2 or 3 of the Explosive Substances Act 1883;

    (g) an offence under section 1 of the Children and Young Persons Act 1933;

    (h) an offence under section 4(1) of the Criminal Law Act 1967 committed in relation to murder;

    (i) an offence under sections 16 to 18 of the Firearms Act 1968;

    (j) an offence under section 9 or 10 of the Theft Act 1968 or an offence under section 12A of that Act involving an accident which caused a person's death;

    (k) an offence under section 1 of the Criminal Damage Act 1971 required to be charged as arson;

    (l) an offence under section 1 of the Protection of Children Act 1978;

    (m) an offence under section 1 of the Aviation Security Act 1982;

    (n) an offence under section 2 of the Child Abduction Act 1984;

    (o) an offence under section 9 of the Aviation and Maritime Security Act 1990;

    (p) an offence under any of sections 1 to 19, 25, 26, 30 to 41, 47 to 50, 52, 53, 57 to 59, 61 to 67, 69 and 70 of the Sexual Offences Act 2003;

    (q) an offence under section 5 of the Domestic Violence, Crime and Victims Act 2004;

---

[483] Existing text renumbered as s 65(1), definitions amended and s 65(2) inserted by the Criminal Justice and Police Act 2001, s 80.

[484] Added by the Crime and Security Act 2010, s 3(6).

Act

     (r) an offence for the time being listed in section 41(1) of the Counter-Terorism Act 2008.

(3) The Secretary of State may by order made by statutory instrument amend sub-section (2) above.

(4) A statutory instrument containing an order under subsection (3) above shall not be made unless a draft of the instrument has been laid befor, and approved by resolution of, each House of Parliament.

(5) In subsection (1)(b) above, 'ancillary offence', in relation to an offence, means—

     (a) aiding, abetting, counselling or procuring the commission of the offence;

     (b) an offence under Part 2 of the Serious Crime Act 2007 (encouraging or assisting crime) in relation to the offence (including, in relation to times before the commencement of that Part, an offence of incitement);

     (c) attempting or conspiring to commit the offence.][485]

[65B Persons convicted of an offence

(1) For the purposes of this Part, any reference to a person who is convicted of an offence includes a reference to—

     (a) a person who has been given a caution in respect of the offence which, at the time of the caution, the person has admitted,

     (b) a person who has been warned or reprimanded under section 65 of the Crime and Disorder Act 1998 for the offence,

     (c) a person who has been found not guilty of the offence by reason of insanity, or

     (d) a person who has been found to be under a disability and to have done the act charged in respect of the offence.

(2) This Part, so far as it relates to persons convicted of an offence, has effect despite any-thing in the Rehabilitation of Offenders Act 1974.

(3) But a person is not to be treated as having been convicted of an offence if that convic-tion is a disregarded conviction of caution by virtue of section 92 of the Protection of Freedoms Act 2012.

(4) If a person is convicted of more than one offence arising out of a single course of action, those convictions are to be treated as a single conviction for the purposes of calculating under sections 63F, 63H and 63N whether the person has been convicted of only one offence.

(5) See also section 65(3) (which deals with findings equivalent to those mentioned in subsection (1)(c) or (d) by courts which exercise jurisdiction under the laws of countries or territories outside England and Wales).][486]

PART VI
CODES OF PRACTICE—GENERAL

66 Codes of practice

[(1) The Secretary of State shall issue codes of practice in connection with—

     (a) the exercise by police officers of statutory powers—

          (i) to search a person without first arresting him;

          [...][487]

---

[485] Added by the Crime and Security Act 2010, s 7.
[486] Added by the Protection of Freedoms Act 2012, s 18(5) (date to be appointed).
[487] Repealed by SOCAPA 2005, ss 110(3)(a), 174(2), Sch 17, Pt 2, para 1.

            (ii) to search a vehicle without making an arrest; [or

            (iii) to arrest a person;][488]

      (b) the detention, treatment, questioning and identification of persons by police officers;

      (c) searches of premises by police officers; and

      (d) the seizure of property found by police officers on persons or premises.

(2) Codes shall (in particular) include provision in connection with the exercise by police officers of powers under section 63B above.][489]

[(3) Nothing in this section requires the Secretary of State to issue a code of practice in relation to any matter falling within the code of practice issued under section 47AB(2) of the Terrorism Act 2000 (as that code is altered or replaced from time to time) (code of practice in relation to terrorism powers to search persons and vehicles and to stop and search in specified locations).][490]

67 Codes of practice—supplementary

[(1) In this section, 'code' means a code of practice under section 60, 60A or 66.

(2) The Secretary of State may at any time revise the whole or any part of a code.

(3) A code may be made, or revised, so as to—

      (a) apply only in relation to one or more specified areas,

      (b) have effect only for a specified period,

      (c) apply only in relation to specified offences or descriptions of offender.

(4) Before issuing a code, or any revision of a code, the Secretary of State must consult—

      [[(a) such persons as appear to the Secretary of State to represent the views of police and crime commissioners,][491]

      [(aa) the Mayor's Office for Policing and Crime,][492]

      [(ab) the Common Council of the City of London,][493]

      (b) the Association of Chief Police Officers of England, Wales and Northern Ireland,][494]

      (c) the General Council of the Bar,

      (d) the Law Society of England and Wales,

      (e) the Institute of Legal Executives, and

      (f) such other persons as he thinks fit.

(5) A code, or a revision of a code, does not come into operation until the Secretary of State by order so provides.

(6) The power conferred by subsection (5) is exercisable by statutory instrument.

(7) An order bringing a code into operation may not be made unless a draft of the order has been laid before Parliament and approved by a resolution of each House.

(7A) An order bringing a revision of a code into operation must be laid before Parliament if the order has been made without a draft having been so laid and approved by a resolution of each House.

---

[488] Amended by SOCAPA 2005, s 110(3)(b).

[489] Amended by the Criminal Justice and Court Services Act 2000, s 57(1), (4).

[490] Added by the Protection of Freedoms Act 2012, Sch 9(5), para 21.

[491] Amended by the Police Reform and Social Responsibility Act 2011, Sch 16(3), para 163(2).

[492] Added by the Police Reform and Social Responsibility Act 2011, Sch 16(3), para 163(2).

[493] Added by the Police Reform and Social Responsibility Act 2011, Sch 16(3), para 163(2).

[494] Substituted by Police and Justice Act 2006, Sch 4, para 1.

(7B) When an order or draft of an order is laid, the code or revision of a code to which it relates must also be laid.

(7C) No order or draft of an order may be laid until the consultation required by subsection (4) has taken place.

(7D) An order bringing a code, or a revision of a code, into operation may include transitional or saving provisions.][495]

(8) [...][496]

(9) Persons other than police officers who are charged with the duty of investigating offences or charging offenders shall in the discharge of that duty have regard to any relevant provision of [...][497] a code.

[(9A) Persons on whom powers are conferred by—

(a) any designation under section 38 or 39 of the Police Reform Act 2002 (c 30) (police powers for [civilian staff][498]), or

(b) any accreditation under section 41 of that Act (accreditation under community safety accreditation schemes),

shall have regard to any relevant provision of a code [...][499] in the exercise or performance of the powers and duties conferred or imposed on them by that designation or accreditation.][500]

(10) A failure on the part—

(a) of a police office to comply with any provision of [...][501] a code; [...][502]

(b) of any person other than a police officer who is charged with the duty of investigating offences or charging offenders to have regard to any relevant provision of [...][503] a code in the discharge of that duty, [or

(c) of a person designated under section 38 or 39 or accredited under section 41 of the Police Reform Act 2002 (c 30) to have regard to any relevant provision of [...][504] a code in the exercise or performance of the powers and duties conferred or imposed on him by that designation or accreditation,][505]

shall not of itself render him liable to any criminal or civil proceedings.

(11) In all criminal and civil proceedings any [...][506] code shall be admissible in evidence; and if any provision of [...][507] a code appears to the court or tribunal conducting the proceedings to be relevant to any question arising in the proceedings it shall be taken into account in determining that question.

[(12) In subsection (11) 'criminal proceedings' includes service proceedings.

(13) In this section 'service proceedings' means proceedings before a court (other than a civilian court) in respect of a service offence; and 'service offence' and

[495] Amended by the Criminal Justice Act 2003, s 11(1).
[496] Repealed by the Police Act 1996, s 103, Sch 9, Pt II.
[497] Repealed by the Criminal Justice Act 2003, s 332, Sch 37, Pt 1.
[498] Amended by the Police Reform and Social Responsibility Act 2011, Sch 16(3), para 163(3).
[499] Repealed by the Criminal Justice Act 2003, s 332, Sch 37, Pt 1.
[500] Amended by the Police Reform Act 2002, s 107(1), Sch 7, para 9(7).
[501] Repealed by the Criminal Justice Act 2003, s 332, Sch 37, Pt 1.
[502] Repealed by the Police Reform Act 2002, s 107(2), Sch 8.
[503] Repealed by the Criminal Justice Act 2003, s 332, Sch 37, Pt 1.
[504] ibid.
[505] Amended by the Police Reform Act 2002, s 107(1), Sch 7, para 9(8).
[506] Repealed by the Criminal Justice Act 2003, s 332, Sch 37, Pt 1.
[507] ibid.

'civilian court' here have the same meanings as in the Armed Forces Act 2006.][508]

PART VII
DOCUMENTARY EVIDENCE IN CRIMINAL PROCEEDINGS

68 Evidence from documentary records

[...][509]

69 Evidence from computer records

[...][510]

70 Provisions supplementary to sections 68 and 69

[...][511]

71 Microfilm copies

In any proceedings the contents of a document may (whether or not the document is still in existence) be proved by the production of an enlargement of a microfilm copy of that document or of the material part of it, authenticated in such manner as the court may approve.
[...][512]

72 Part VII—supplementary

(1)   In this Part of this Act—
['copy', in relation to a document, means anything onto which information recorded in the document has been copied, by whatever means and whether directly or indirectly, and 'statement' means any representation of fact, however made; and][513]
'proceedings' means criminal proceedings, including [service proceedings].[514]

[(1A) In subsection (1) 'service proceedings' means proceedings before a court (other than a civilian court) in respect of a service offence; and 'service offence' and 'civilian court' here have the same meanings as in the Armed Forces Act 2006.][515]

(2)   Nothing in this Part of this Act shall prejudice any power of a court to exclude evidence (whether by preventing questions from being put or otherwise) at its discretion.

---

[508] Section 67(12)–(13) substituted for s 67(12) by Armed Forces Act 2006, Sch 16, para 101.

[509] Repealed by the Criminal Justice Act 1988, s 170(2), Sch 16.

[510] Repealed by the Youth Justice and Criminal Evidence Act 1999, ss 60, 67(3), Sch 6.

[511] Repealed by the Youth Justice and Criminal Evidence Act 1999, s 67(3), Sch 6.

[512] Words repealed by the Criminal Justice Act 2003, Sch 37(4), para 1 (18 June 2012: repeal has effect on 18 June 2012 in relation to the relevant local justice areas specified in SI 2012/1320 art 4(1)(d) and purposes specified in SI 2012/1320 art 4(3) subject to savings specified in SI 2012/1320 art 5; 5 November 2012 in relation to local justice areas specified in SI 2012/2574 art 2(1)(d) and purposes specified in SI 2012/2574 art 2(3) subject to saving provisions specified in SI 2012/2574 arts 3 and 4; not yet in force otherwise).

[513] Amended by the Civil Evidence Act 1995, s 15(1), Sch 1, para 9(2).

[514] Words substituted for paras (a)–(c) in the definition of proceedings by Armed Forces Act 2006, Sch 16, para 102(2).

[515] Added by Armed Forces Act 2006, Sch 16, para 102(3).

PART VIII
EVIDENCE IN CRIMINAL PROCEEDINGS—GENERAL

Convictions and acquittals

Act

73 Proof of convictions and acquittals

(1) Where in any proceedings the fact that a person has in the United Kingdom [or any other member State][516] been convicted or acquitted of an offence otherwise than by a Service court is admissible in evidence, it may be proved by producing a certificate of conviction or, as the case may be, of acquittal relating to that offence, and proving that the person named in the certificate as having been convicted or acquitted of the offence is the person whose conviction or acquittal of the offence is to be proved.

(2) For the purposes of this section a certificate of conviction or of acquittal—

    (a) shall, as regards a conviction or acquittal on indictment, consist of a certificate, signed by the [proper officer][517] of the court where the conviction or acquittal took place, giving the substance and effect (omitting the formal parts) of the indictment and of the conviction or acquittal; and

    (b) shall, as regards a conviction or acquittal on a summary trial, consist of a copy of the conviction or of the dismissal of the information, signed by the [proper officer][518] of the court where the conviction or acquittal took place or by the [proper officer][519] of the court, if any, to which a memorandum of the conviction or acquittal was sent; [and

    (c) shall, as regards a conviction or acquittal by a court in a member State (other than the United Kingdom), consist of a certificate, signed by the proper officer of the court where the conviction or acquittal took place, giving details of the offence, of the conviction or acquittal, and of any sentence;][520]

and a document purporting to be a duly signed certificate of conviction or acquittal under this section shall be taken to be such a certificate unless the contrary is proved.

[(3) In subsection (2) above 'proper officer' means—

    (a) in relation to a magistrates' court in England and Wales, the [designated officer][521] for the court; and

    (b) in relation to any other court [in the United Kingdom][522], the clerk of the court, his deputy or any other person having custody of the court record[, and

    (c) in relation to any court in another member State ('the EU court'), a person who would be the proper officer of the EU court if that court were in the United Kingdom.][523][524]

---

[516] Amended by the Coroners and Justice Act 2009, Sch 17, para 13(2).

[517] Amended by the Access to Justice Act 1999, s 90(1), Sch 13, paras 125, 128(1), (2).

[518] ibid.

[519] ibid.

[520] Amended by the Coroners and Justice Act 2009, Sch 17, para 13(3).

[521] Amended by the Courts Act 2003, s 109(1), Sch 8, para 285; for transitional provisions see SI 2005/911, arts 2–5.

[522] Amended by the Coroners and Justice Act 2009, Sch 17, para 13(4)(a).

[523] Amended by the Coroners and Justice Act 2009, Sch 17, para 13(4)(b).

[524] Amended by the Access to Justice Act 1999, s 90(1), Sch 13, paras 125, 128(1), (3).

(4) The method of proving a conviction or acquittal authorised by this section shall be in addition to and not to the exclusion of any other authorised manner of proving a conviction or acquittal.

74 Conviction as evidence of commission of offence

(1) In any proceedings the fact that a person other than the accused has been convicted of an offence by or before any court in the United Kingdom [or any other member State][525] or by a Service court outside the United Kingdom shall be admissible in evidence for the purpose of proving [that that person committed that offence, where evidence of his having done so is admissible][526] is given.

(2) In any proceedings in which by virtue of this section a person other than the accused is proved to have been convicted of an offence by or before any court in the United Kingdom [or any other member State][527] or by a Service court outside the United Kingdom, he shall be taken to have committed that offence unless the contrary is proved.

(3) In any proceedings where evidence is admissible of the fact that the accused has committed an offence, [...][528] if the accused is proved to have been convicted of the offence—

   (a) by or before any court in the United Kingdom [or any other member State][529]; or

   (b) by a Service court outside the United Kingdom,

   he shall be taken to have committed that offence unless the contrary is proved.

(4) Nothing in this section shall prejudice—

   (a) the admissibility in evidence of any conviction which would be admissible apart from this section; or

   (b) the operation of any enactment whereby a conviction or a finding of fact in any proceedings is for the purposes of any other proceedings made conclusive evidence of any fact.

75 Provisions supplementary to section 74

(1) Where evidence that a person has been convicted of an offence is admissible by virtue of section 74 above, then without prejudice to the reception of any other admissible evidence for the purpose of identifying the facts on which the conviction was based—

   (a) the contents of any document which is admissible as evidence of the conviction; and

   [(b) the contents of—

      (i) the information, complaint, indictment or charge-sheet on which the person in question was convicted, or

      (ii) in the case of a conviction of an offence by a court in a member State (other than the United Kingdom), any document produced in relation

---

[525] Amended by the Coroners and Justice Act 2009, Sch 17, para 14(2).
[526] Amended by the Criminal Justice Act 2003, s 331, Sch 36, Pt 5, para 85(1), (2).
[527] Amended by the Coroners and Justice Act 2009, Sch 17, para 14(3).
[528] Repealed by the Criminal Justice Act 2003, ss 331, 332, Sch 36, Pt 5, para 85(1), (3), Sch 37, Pt 5.
[529] Amended by the Coroners and Justice Act 2009, Sch 17, para 14(4).

Act

to the proceedings for that offence which fulfils a purpose similar to any document or documents specified in sub-paragraph (1),][530]

shall be admissible in evidence for that purpose.

(2) Where in any proceedings the contents of any document are admissible in evidence by virtue of subsection (1) above, a copy of that document, or of the material part of it, purporting to be certified or otherwise authenticated by or on behalf of the court or authority having custody of that document shall be admissible in evidence and shall be taken to be a true copy of that document or part unless the contrary is shown.

(3) Nothing in any of the following—

  (a) [section 14 of the Powers of Criminal Courts (Sentencing) Act 2000][531] (under which a conviction leading to probation or discharge is to be disregarded except as mentioned in that section);

  [(aa) section 187 of the Armed Forces Act 2006 (which makes similar provision in respect of service convictions);][532]

  (b) [section 247 of the Criminal Procedure (Scotland) Act 1995][533] (which makes similar provision in respect of convictions on indictment in Scotland); and

  (c) section 8 of the Probation Act (Northern Ireland) 1950 (which corresponds to section 13 of the Powers of Criminal Courts Act 1973) or any legislation which is in force in Northern Ireland for the time being and corresponds to that section,

shall affect the operation of section 74 above; and for the purposes of that section any order made by a court of summary jurisdiction in Scotland under [section 228 or section 246(3) of the said Act of 1995][534] shall be treated as a conviction.

(4) Nothing in section 74 above shall be construed as rendering admissible in any proceedings evidence of any conviction other than a subsisting one.

Confessions

76 Confessions

(1) In any proceedings a confession made by an accused person may be given in evidence against him in so far as it is relevant to any matter in issue in the proceedings and is not excluded by the court in pursuance of this section.

(2) If, in any proceedings where the prosecution proposes to give in evidence a confession made by an accused person, it is represented to the court that the confession was or may have been obtained—

  (a) by oppression of the person who made it; or

  (b) in consequence of anything said or done which was likely, in the circumstances existing at the time, to render unreliable any confession which might be made by him in consequence thereof,

---

[530] Amended by the Coroners and Justice Act 2009, Sch 17, para 15.

[531] Amended by the Powers of Criminal Courts (Sentencing) Act 2000, s 165(1), Sch 9, para 98.

[532] Added by Armed Forces Act 2006, Sch 16, para 103 (31 October 2009).

[533] Amended by the Criminal Procedure (Consequential Provisions) (Scotland) Act 1995, s 5, Sch 4, para 55(a).

[534] Amended by the Criminal Procedure (Consequential Provisions) (Scotland) Act 1995, s 5, Sch 4, para 55(b).

the court shall not allow the confession to be given in evidence against him except in so far as the prosecution proves to the court beyond reasonable doubt that the confession (notwithstanding that it may be true) was not obtained as aforesaid.

(3) In any proceedings where the prosecution proposes to give in evidence a confession made by an accused person, the court may of its own motion require the prosecution, as a condition of allowing it to do so, to prove that the confession was not obtained as mentioned in subsection (2) above.

(4) The fact that a confession is wholly or partly excluded in pursuance of this section shall not affect the admissibility in evidence—
  (a) of any facts discovered as a result of the confession; or
  (b) where the confession is relevant as showing that the accused speaks, writes or expresses himself in a particular way, of so much of the confession as is necessary to show that he does so.

(5) Evidence that a fact to which this subsection applies was discovered as a result of a statement made by an accused person shall not be admissible unless evidence of how it was discovered is given by him or on his behalf.

(6) Subsection (5) above applies—
  (a) to any fact discovered as a result of a confession which is wholly excluded in pursuance of this section; and
  (b) to any fact discovered as a result of a confession which is partly so excluded, if the fact is discovered as a result of the excluded part of the confession.

(7) Nothing in Part VII of this Act shall prejudice the admissibility of a confession made by an accused person.

(8) In this section 'oppression' includes torture, inhuman or degrading treatment, and the use or threat of violence (whether or not amounting to torture).
[....] [535]

[76A Confessions may be given in evidence for co-accused

(1) In any proceedings a confession made by an accused person may be given in evidence for another person charged in the same proceedings (a co-accused) in so far as it is relevant to any matter in issue in the proceedings and is not excluded by the court in pursuance of this section.

(2) If, in any proceedings where a co-accused proposes to give in evidence a confession made by an accused person, it is represented to the court that the confession was or may have been obtained—
  (a) by oppression of the person who made it; or
  (b) in consequence of anything said or done which was likely, in the circumstances existing at the time, to render unreliable any confession which might be made by him in consequence thereof,
the court shall not allow the confession to be given in evidence for the co-accused except in so far as it is proved to the court on the balance of probabilities that the confession (notwithstanding that it may be true) was not so obtained.

---

[535] Repealed by the Criminal Justice Act 2003, Sch 37(4), para 1 (18 June 2012: repeal has effect on 18 June 2012 in relation to the relevant local justice areas specified in SI 2012/1320 art 4(1)(d) and purposes specified in SI 2012/1320 art 4(3) subject to savings specified in SI 2012/1320 art 5; 5 November 2012 in relation to local justice areas specified in SI 2012/2574 art 2(1)(d) and purposes specified in SI 2012/2574 art 2(3) subject to saving provisions specified in SI 2012/2574 arts 3 and 4; not yet in force otherwise).

Act

(3) Before allowing a confession made by an accused person to be given in evidence for a co-accused in any proceedings, the court may of its own motion require the fact that the confession was not obtained as mentioned in subsection (2) above to be proved in the proceedings on the balance of probabilities.

(4) The fact that a confession is wholly or partly excluded in pursuance of this section shall not affect the admissibility in evidence—

(a) of any facts discovered as a result of the confession; or

(b) where the confession is relevant as showing that the accused speaks, writes or expresses himself in a particular way, of so much of the confession as is necessary to show that he does so.

(5) Evidence that a fact to which this subsection applies was discovered as a result of a statement made by an accused person shall not be admissible unless evidence of how it was discovered is given by him or on his behalf.

(6) Subsection (5) above applies—

(a) to any fact discovered as a result of a confession which is wholly excluded in pursuance of this section; and

(b) to any fact discovered as a result of a confession which is partly so excluded, if the fact is discovered as a result of the excluded part of the confession.

(7) In this section 'oppression' includes torture, inhuman or degrading treatment, and the use or threat of violence (whether or not amounting to torture).][536]

77 Confessions by mentally handicapped persons

(1) Without prejudice to the general duty of the court at a trial on indictment [with a jury][537] to direct the jury on any matter on which it appears to the court appropriate to do so, where at such a trial—

(a) the case against the accused depends wholly or substantially on a confession by him; and

(b) the court is satisfied—

(i) that he is mentally handicapped; and

(ii) that the confession was not made in the presence of an independent person,

the court shall warn the jury that there is special need for caution before convicting the accused in reliance on the confession, and shall explain that the need arises because of the circumstances mentioned in paragraphs (a) and (b) above.

(2) In any case where at the summary trial of a person for an offence it appears to the court that a warning under subsection (1) above would be required if the trial were on indictment [with a jury][538], the court shall treat the case as one in which there is a special need for caution before convicting the accused on his confession.

---

[536] Inserted by the Criminal Justice Act 2003, s 128; for savings see the Criminal Justice Act 2004, s 141 and SI 2005/950, art 2(1), Sch 1, para 6.

[537] The words 'with a jury' in square brackets inserted by the Criminal Justice Act 2003, s 331, Sch 36, Pt 4, para 48(1), (2) (24 July 2006 in relation to England and Wales; 8 January 2007 otherwise).

[538] The words 'with a jury' in square brackets inserted by the Criminal Justice Act 2003, s 331, Sch 36, Pt 4, para 48(1), (3) (24 July 2006 in relation to England and Wales; 8 January 2007 otherwise).

[(2A) In any case where at the trial on indictment without a jury of a person for an offence it appears to the court that a warning under subsection (1) above would be required if the trial were with a jury, the court shall treat the case as one in which there is a special need for caution before convicting the accused on his confession.]⁵³⁹

(3)   In this section—

'independent person' does not include a police officer or a person employed for, or engaged on, police purposes;

'mentally handicapped', in relation to a person, means that he is in a state of arrested or incomplete development of mind which includes significant impairment of intelligence and social functioning; and

'police purposes' has the meaning assigned to it by [section 101(2) of the Police Act 1996]⁵⁴⁰.

Miscellaneous

78 Exclusion of unfair evidence

(1)   In any proceedings the court may refuse to allow evidence on which the prosecution proposes to rely to be given if it appears to the court that, having regard to all the circumstances, including the circumstances in which the evidence was obtained, the admission of the evidence would have such an adverse effect on the fairness of the proceedings that the court ought not to admit it.

(2)   Nothing in this section shall prejudice any rule of law requiring a court to exclude evidence.

[...]⁵⁴¹

79 Time for taking accused's evidence

If at the trial of any person for an offence—

(a) the defence intends to call two or more witnesses to the facts of the case; and

(b) those witnesses include the accused,

the accused shall be called before the other witness or witnesses unless the court in its discretion otherwise directs.

80   [...]⁵⁴² Compellability of accused's spouse [or civil partner]⁵⁴³

(1)   [...]⁵⁴⁴

---

⁵³⁹ New subsection (2A) prospectively inserted by the Criminal Justice Act 2003, s 331, Sch 36, Pt 4, para 48(1), (4) (24 July 2006 in relation to England and Wales; 8 January 2007 otherwise).

⁵⁴⁰ Amended by the Police Act 1996, s 103, Sch 7, para 38.

⁵⁴¹ Repealed by the Criminal Justice Act 2003, Sch 37(4), para 1 (18 June 2012: repeal has effect on 18 June 2012 in relation to the relevant local justice areas specified in SI 2012/1320 art 4(1)(d) and purposes specified in SI 2012/1320 art 4(3) subject to savings specified in SI 2012/1320 art 5; 5 November 2012 in relation to local justice areas specified in SI 2012/2574 art 2(1)(d) and purposes specified in SI 2012/2574 art 2(3) subject to saving provisions specified in SI 2012/2574 arts 3 and 4; not yet in force otherwise).

⁵⁴² Repealed by the Youth Justice and Criminal Evidence Act 1999, s 67(1), Sch 4, paras 12, 13(1), (4).

⁵⁴³ Amended by the Civil Partnership Act 2004, s 261(1), Sch 27, para 97(1), (4).

⁵⁴⁴ Repealed by the Youth Justice and Criminal Evidence Act 1999, s 67(1), (3), Sch 4, paras 12, 13(1), (2), Sch 6.

[(2) In any proceedings the [spouse or civil partner]^{545} of a person charged in the proceedings shall, subject to subsection (4) below, be compellable to give evidence on behalf of that person.

(2A) In any proceedings the [spouse or civil partner]^{546} of a person charged in the proceedings shall, subject to subsection (4) below, be compellable—

    (a) to give evidence on behalf of any other person charged in the proceedings but only in respect of any specified offence with which that other person is charged; or

    (b) to give evidence for the prosecution but only in respect of any specified offence with which any person is charged in the proceedings.

(3) In relation to the [spouse or civil partner]^{547} of a person charged in any proceedings, an offence is a specified offence for the purposes of subsection (2A) above if—

    (a) it involves an assault on, or injury or a threat of injury to, the [spouse or civil partner]^{548} or a person who was at the material time under the age of 16;

    (b) it is a sexual offence alleged to have been committed in respect of a person who was at the material time under that age; or

    (c) it consists of attempting or conspiring to commit, or of aiding, abetting, counselling, procuring or inciting the commission of, an offence falling within paragraph (a) or (b) above.

(4) No person who is charged in any proceedings shall be compellable by virtue of subsection (2) or (2A) above to give evidence in the proceedings.

(4A) References in this section to a person charged in any proceedings do not include a person who is not, or is no longer, liable to be convicted of any offence in the proceedings (whether as a result of pleading guilty or for any other reason).]^{549}

(5) In any proceedings a person who has been but is no longer married to the accused shall be [...]^{550} compellable to give evidence as if that person and the accused had never been married.

[(5A) In any proceedings a person who has been but is no longer the civil partner of the accused shall be compellable to give evidence as if that person and the accused had never been civil partners.]^{551}

(6) Where in any proceedings the age of any person at any time is material for the purposes of subsection (3) above, his age at the material time shall for the purposes of that provision be deemed to be or to have been that which appears to the court to be or to have been his age at that time.

(7) In subsection (3)(b) above 'sexual offence' means an offence under [...]^{552} the Protection of Children Act 1978 [or Part 1 of the Sexual Offences Act 2003]^{553}.

---

^{545} Amended by the Civil Partnership Act 2004, s 261(1), Sch 27, para 97(1), (2).
^{546} ibid.
^{547} ibid.
^{548} ibid.
^{549} Amended by the Youth Justice and Criminal Evidence Act 1999, s 67(1), Sch 4, paras 12, 13(1), (3).
^{550} Repealed by the Youth Justice and Criminal Evidence Act 1999, s 67(1), (3), Sch 4, paras 12, 13(1), (4), Sch 6.
^{551} Amended by the Civil Partnership Act 2004, s 261(1), Sch 27, para 97(1), (3).
^{552} Repealed by the Sexual Offences Act 2003, s 140, Sch 7.
^{553} Amended by the Sexual Offences Act 2003, s 139, Sch 6, para 28(1), (2).

Act

(8)   [...]⁵⁵⁴

(9)   Section 1(d) of the Criminal Evidence Act 1898 (communications between
husband and wife) and section 43(1) of the Matrimonial Causes Act 1965 (evidence as to marital intercourse) shall cease to have effect.

80A [Rule where accused's spouse [or civil partner]⁵⁵⁵ not compellable

The failure of the [spouse or civil partner]⁵⁵⁶ of a person charged in any proceedings to give evidence in the proceedings shall not be made the subject of
any comment by the prosecution.]⁵⁵⁷

81 Advance notice of expert evidence in crown court

(1)   [Criminal Procedure Rules]⁵⁵⁸ may make provision for—
      (a) requiring any party to proceedings before the court to disclose to the other
           party or parties any expert evidence which he proposes to adduce in the
           proceedings; and
      (b) prohibiting a party who fails to comply in respect of any evidence with
           any requirement imposed by virtue of paragraph (a) above from adducing
           that evidence without the leave of the court.

(2)   [Criminal Procedure Rules]⁵⁵⁹ made by virtue of this section may specify the
kinds of expert evidence to which they apply and may exempt facts or matters
of any description specified in the rules.

PART VIII—SUPPLEMENTARY

82 Part VIII—Interpretation

(1)   In this Part of this Act—
      'confession' includes any statement wholly or partly adverse to the person
      who made it, whether made to a person in authority or not and whether made
      in words or otherwise;
      [...]⁵⁶⁰;
      'proceedings' means criminal proceedings, including [service proceedings;]⁵⁶¹
      'Service court' means a court-martial or [the Court Martial or the Service
      Civilian Court].⁵⁶²

[(1A) In subsection (1) 'service proceedings' means proceedings before a court (other
than a civilian court) in respect of a service offence; and 'service offence' and 'civilian court' here have the same meanings as in the Armed Forces Act 2006.]⁵⁶³

(2)   [...]⁵⁶⁴

---

⁵⁵⁴ Repealed by the Youth Justice and Criminal Evidence Act 1999, s 67(1), (3), Sch 4, paras 12, 13(1), (2), Sch 6.
⁵⁵⁵ Amended by the Civil Partnership Act 2004, s 261(1), Sch 27, para 98(b).
⁵⁵⁶ Amended by the Civil Partnership Act 2004, s 261(1), Sch 27, para 98(a).
⁵⁵⁷ Inserted by the Youth Justice and Criminal Evidence Act 1999, s 67(1), Sch 4, paras 12, 14.
⁵⁵⁸ Amended by the Courts Act 2003, s 109(1), Sch 8, para 286; for savings see SI 2004/2066, art 3.
⁵⁵⁹ ibid.
⁵⁶⁰ Definition repealed by Armed Forces Act 2006, Sch 17, para 1 (31 October 2009; SI 2009/1167).
⁵⁶¹ Words substituted for paras (a)–(c) in the definition of proceedings by Armed Forces Act 2006, Sch 16, para 104(2)(b).
⁵⁶² Words substituted by Armed Forces Act 2006, Sch 16, para 104(2)(c).
⁵⁶³ Added by Armed Forces Act 2006, Sch 16, para 104(3).
⁵⁶⁴ Repealed by Armed Forces Act 2006, Sch 17, para 1 (31 October 2009; SI 2009/1167).

(3) Nothing in this Part of this Act shall prejudice any power of a court to exclude evidence (whether by preventing questions from being put or otherwise) at its discretion.

Act

PART IX
POLICE COMPLAINTS AND DISCIPLINE

The Police Complaints Authority

83 Establishment of the police complaints authority

[...]⁵⁶⁵

Handling of complaints etc.

84 Preliminary

[...]⁵⁶⁶

85 Investigation of complaints: standard procedure

[...]⁵⁶⁷

86 Investigation of complaints against senior officers

[...]⁵⁶⁸

87 References of complaints to authority

[...]⁵⁶⁹

88 References of other matters to authority

[...]⁵⁷⁰

89 Supervision of investigations by authority

[...]⁵⁷¹

90 Steps to be taken after investigation—general

[...]⁵⁷²

91 Steps to be taken where accused has admitted charges

[...]⁵⁷³

92 Powers of Authority to direct reference of reports etc. to Director of Public Prosecutions

[...]⁵⁷⁴

---

⁵⁶⁵ Repealed by the Police Act 1996, s 103, Sch 9, Pt II.
⁵⁶⁶ ibid.
⁵⁶⁷ ibid.
⁵⁶⁸ ibid.
⁵⁶⁹ ibid.
⁵⁷⁰ ibid.
⁵⁷¹ ibid.
⁵⁷² ibid.
⁵⁷³ ibid.
⁵⁷⁴ ibid.

93 Powers of Authority as to disciplinary charges

[...]575

94 Disciplinary tribunals

[...]576

95 Information as to the manner of dealing with complaints etc.

[...]577

96 Constabularies maintained by authorities other than police authorities

[...]578

97 Reports

[...]579

98 Restriction on disclosure of information

[...]580

99 Regulations

[...]581

100 Regulations—supplementary

[...]582

101 Discipline regulations

[...]583

102 Representation at disciplinary proceedings

[...]584

103 Disciplinary appeals

[...]585

104 Restrictions on subsequent proceedings

[...]586

105 Guidelines concerning discipline, complaints etc.

[...]587

---

575 ibid.
576 ibid.
577 ibid.
578 ibid.
579 ibid.
580 ibid.
581 ibid.
582 ibid.
583 ibid.
584 ibid.
585 ibid.
586 ibid.
587 ibid.

PART X
POLICE—GENERAL

Act

106 Arrangements for obtaining the views of the community on policing

[...]⁵⁸⁸

107 Police officers performing duties of higher rank

[(1) For the purpose of any provision of this Act or any other Act under which a power in respect of the investigation of offences or the treatment of persons in police custody is exercisable only by or with the authority of a police officer of at least the rank of superintendent, an officer of the rank of chief inspector shall be treated as holding the rank of superintendent if

(a) he has been authorised by an officer holding a rank above the rank of superintendent to exercise the power or, as the case may be, to give his authority for its exercise, or

(b) he is acting during the absence of an officer holding the rank of superintendent who has authorised him, for the duration of that absence, to exercise the power or, as the case may be, to give his authority for its exercise.]⁵⁸⁹

(2) For the purpose of any provision of this Act or any other Act under which such a power is exercisable only by or with the authority of an officer of at least the rank of inspector, an officer of the rank of sergeant shall be treated as holding the rank of inspector if he has been authorised by an officer of at least the rank of [superintendent]⁵⁹⁰ to exercise the power or, as the case may be, to give his authority for its exercise.

108 [...]⁵⁹¹

109 Amendments relating to police federations

[...]⁵⁹²

110 [...]⁵⁹³

111 Regulations for Police Forces and Police Cadets—Scotland

(1) In section 26 to the Police (Scotland) Act 1967 (regulations as to government and administration of police forces)—

(a) after subsection (1) there shall be inserted the following subsection—

'(1A) Regulations under this section may authorise the Secretary of State, the police authority or the chief constable to make provision for any purpose specified in the regulations.'; and

---

⁵⁸⁸ Repealed by the Police Act 1996, s 103(3), Sch 9, Pt I.
⁵⁸⁹ Amended by the Police and Magistrates' Courts Act 1994, s 44, Sch 5, Pt II, para 35.
⁵⁹⁰ ibid.
⁵⁹¹ Repealed by Statute Law (Repeals) Act 2008, Sch 1, para 1.
⁵⁹² Repealed by the Police Act 1996, s 103(3), Sch 9, Pt I.
⁵⁹³ Repealed by Statute Law (Repeals) Act 2008, Sch 1, para 1.

(b) at the end there shall be inserted the following subsection—
    '(10) Any statutory instrument made under this section shall be subject to annulment in pursuance of a resolution of either House of Parliament.'.

(2) In section 27 of the said Act of 1967 (regulations for police cadets) in subsection (3) for the word '(9)' there shall be substituted the words '(1A), (9) and (10)'.

112 Metropolitan police officers

[...]⁵⁹⁴

113 Application of Act to Armed Forces

[(1) The Secretary of State may by order make provision in relation to—
    (a) investigations of service offences,
    (b) persons arrested under a power conferred by or under the Armed Forces Act 2006,
    (c) persons charged under that Act with service offences,
    (d) persons in service custody, or
    (e) persons convicted of service offences, which is equivalent to that made by any provision of Part 5 of this Act (or this Part of this Act so far as relating to that Part), subject to such modifications as the Secretary of State considers appropriate.]⁵⁹⁵

(2) Section 67(9) above shall not have effect in relation to investigations of [service offences]⁵⁹⁶.

(3) The Secretary of State shall issue a code of practice, or a number of such codes, for persons other than police officers who are [concerned with–]⁵⁹⁷
    [(a) the exercise of powers conferred by or under Part 3 of the Armed Forces Act 2006; or
    (b) investigations of service offences.]⁵⁹⁸

[(3A) In subsections (4) to (10), 'code' means a code of practice under subsection (3).]⁵⁹⁹

(4) Without prejudice to the generality of subsection (3) above, a code [...]⁶⁰⁰ may contain provisions, in connection with [the powers mentioned in subsection (3)(a) above or the [investigations]⁶⁰¹ mentioned in subsection (3)(b) above]⁶⁰², as to the following matters—
    (a) the tape-recording of interviews;
    (b) searches of persons and premises; and
    (c) the seizure of things found on searches.

---

⁵⁹⁴ Repealed by Police Act 1996 c 16 Sch 9(I) para 1.
⁵⁹⁵ Substituted by Armed Forces Act 2006, Sch 16, para 105(2).
⁵⁹⁶ Words substituted by Armed Forces Act 2006, Sch 16, para 105(3).
⁵⁹⁷ Words substituted by Armed Forces Act 2006, Sch 16, para 105(4).
⁵⁹⁸ Words substituted by Armed Forces Act 2006, Sch 16, para 105(4).
⁵⁹⁹ Amended by the Criminal Justice Act 2003, s 11(2), (3).
⁶⁰⁰ Repealed by the Criminal Justice Act 2003, s 332, Sch 37, Pt 1.
⁶⁰¹ Word substituted by Armed Forces Act 2006, Sch 16, para 105(5).
⁶⁰² Amended by the Armed Forces Act 2001, s 13(1), (4); for transitional provisions see SI 2003/2268, arts 3, 4.

Act

[(5)   The Secretary of State may at any time revise the whole or any part of a code.

(6)   A code may be made, or revised, so as to—

(a) apply only in relation to one or more specified areas,

(b) have effect only for a specified period,

(c) apply only in relation to specified offences or descriptions of offender.

(7)   The Secretary of State must lay a code, or any revision of a code, before Parliament.]603

(8)   A failure on the part of any person to comply with any provision of a code [...]604 shall not of itself render him liable to any criminal or civil proceedings except those to which this subsection applies.

[(9)   Subsection (8) above applies to proceedings in respect of an offence under a provision of Part 1 of the Armed Forces Act 2006 other than section 42 (criminal conduct).]605

(10)   In all criminal and civil proceedings any [...]606 code shall be admissible in evidence and if any provision of [...]607 a code appears to the court or tribunal conducting the proceedings to be relevant to any question arising in the proceedings it shall be taken into account in determining that question.

(11)   [...]608

(12)   Parts VII and VIII of this Act have effect for the purposes of [service proceedings (a)–(c)]609—

subject to any modifications which the Secretary of State may by order specify.

[(12A) In this section–

'service offence' has the meaning given by section 50 of the Armed Forces Act 2006;

'criminal proceedings' includes service proceedings;

'service proceedings' means proceedings before a court (other than a civilian court) in respect of a service offence; and

'civilian court' has the meaning given by section 374 of the Armed Forces Act 2006;

and section 376(1) and (2) of that Act (meaning of 'convicted' in relation to summary hearings and the SAC) apply for the purposes of subsection (1)(e) above as they apply for the purposes of that Act.]610

(13)   An order under this section shall be made by statutory instrument and shall be subject to annulment in pursuance of a resolution of either House of Parliament.

[(14) Section 373(5) and (6) of the Armed Forces Act 2006 (supplementary provisions) apply in relation to an order under this section as they apply in relation to an order under that Act.]611

---

603 Amended by the Criminal Justice Act 2003, s 11(2), (4).

604 Repealed by the Criminal Justice Act 2003, s 332, Sch 37, Pt 1.

605 Substituted by Armed Forces Act 2006, Sch 16, para 105(6).

606 Words repealed by Criminal Justice Act 2003 c. 44 Sch 37(1) para 1 (January 20, 2004; SI 2004/81).

607 ibid.

608 Repealed by Armed Forces Act 2006, Sch 17, para 1 (31 October 2009; SI 2009/1167).

609 Words substituted for s 113(12)(a)–(c) by Armed Forces Act 2006, Sch 16, para 105(8).

610 Added by Armed Forces Act 2006, Sch 16, para 105(9).

611 Added by Armed Forces Act 2006, Sch 16, para 105(10).

114 [Application of Act to Revenue and Customs][612]

(1)   'Arrested', 'arresting', 'arrest' and 'to arrest' shall respectively be substituted for 'detained', 'detaining', 'detention' and 'to detain' wherever in the customs and excise Acts, as defined in section 1(1) of the Customs and Excise Management Act 1979, those words are used in relation to persons.

(2)   The Treasury may by order direct—

(a) that any provision of this Act which relates to investigations of offences conducted by police officers or to persons detained by the police shall apply, subject to such modifications as the order may specify, to [investigations conducted by officers of Revenue and Customs][613] or to [persons detained by officers of Revenue and Customs;][614] and

(b) that, in relation to [investigations of offences conducted by officers of Revenue and Customs][615]

(i) this Act shall have effect as if the following sections[616] were inserted after section 14—

'14A Exception for [Revenue and Customs][617]

Material in the possession of a person who acquired or created it in the course of any trade, business, profession or other occupation or for the purpose of any paid or unpaid office [and which relates to a matter in relation to which Her Majesty's Revenue and Customs have functions,][618] is neither excluded material nor special procedure material for the purposes of any enactment such as is mentioned in section 9(2) above.'

[14B Revenue and Customs: restriction on other powers to apply for production of documents

(1) An officer of Revenue and Customs may make an application for the delivery of, or access to, documents under a provision specified in subsection (3) only if the condition in subsection (2) is satisfied.

(2) The condition is that the officer thinks that an application under Schedule 1 would not succeed because the material required does not consist of or include special procedure material.

(3) The provisions are—

(a) section 20BA of, and Schedule 1AA to, the Taxes Management Act 1970 (serious tax fraud);

(b) paragraph 11 of Schedule 11 to the Value Added Tax Act 1994 (VAT);

(c) paragraph 4A of Schedule 7 to the Finance Act 1994 (insurance premium tax);

---

[612] Words substituted by Finance Act 2007, s 82(11).
[613] Words substituted by Finance Act 2007, s 82(2)(a).
[614] Words substituted by Finance Act 2007, s 82(2)(b).
[615] Words substituted by Finance Act 2007, s 82(3).
[616] Word substituted by Finance Act 2007, s 82(4).
[617] Modified by Finance Act 2007, s 82.
[618] Modified by Finance Act 2007, s 82.

Act

(d) paragraph 7 of Schedule 5 to the Finance Act 1996 (landfill tax);
(e) paragraph 131 of Schedule 6 to the Finance Act 2000 (climate change levy);
(f) paragraph 8 of Schedule 7 to the Finance Act 2001 (aggregates levy);
(g) Part 6 of Schedule 13 to the Finance Act 2003 (stamp duty land tax)[619]; and
(ii) section 55 above shall have effect as if it related only to things such as are mentioned in subsection (1)(a) of that section.

[(d) that where an officer of Revenue and Customs searches premises in reliance on a warrant under section 8 of, or paragraph 12 of Schedule 1 to, this Act (as applied by an order under this subsection) the officer shall have the power to search persons found on the premises—
(i) in such cases and circumstances as are specified in the order, and
(ii) subject to any conditions specified in the order; and
(e) that powers and functions conferred by a provision of this Act (as applied by an order under this subsection) may be exercised only by officers of Revenue and Customs acting with the authority (which may be general or specific) of the Commissioners for Her Majesty's Revenue and Customs.][620]

[(2A) A certificate of the Commissioners that an officer of Revenue and Customs had authority under subsection (2)(e) to exercise a power or function conferred by a provision of this Act shall be conclusive evidence of that fact.][621]

(3) [An order under subsection (2)—
(a) may make provision that applies generally or only in specified cases or circumstances,
(b) may make different provision for different cases or circumstances,
(c) may, in modifying a provision, in particular impose conditions on the exercise of a function, and
(d) shall not be taken to limit a power under section 164 of the Customs and Excise Management Act 1979.][622]

(4) [...][623]

(5) An order under this section shall be made by statutory instrument and shall be subject to annulment in pursuance of a resolution of either House of Parliament.

[114A Power to apply Act to officers of the Secretary of State etc

(1) The Secretary of State may by order direct that—
(a) the provisions of Schedule 1 to this Act so far as they relate to special procedure material, and
(b) the other provisions of this Act so far as they relate to the provisions falling within paragraph (a) above,

---

[619] Modified by Finance Act 2007, s 82.
[620] Added by Finance Act 2007, s 82(8).
[621] Added by Finance Act 2007, s 82(9).
[622] Substituted by Finance Act 2007, s 82(10).
[623] Repealed by the Commissioners for Revenue and Customs Act 2005, ss 50(6), 52(2), Sch 4, para 31, Sch 5.

shall apply, with such modifications as may be specified in the order, for the purposes of investigations falling within subsection (2) as they apply for the purposes of investigations of offences conducted by police officers.

(2) An investigation falls within this subsection if—

    (a) it is conducted by an officer of the department of [the Secretary of State for Business, Innovation and Skills][624] or by another person acting on that Secretary of State's behalf;

    (b) it is conducted by that officer or other person in the discharge of a duty to investigate offences; and

    (c) the investigation relates to [an indictable offence][625] or to anything which there are reasonable grounds for suspecting has involved the commission of [an indictable offence][626].

(3) The investigations for the purposes of which provisions of this Act may be applied with modifications by an order under this section include investigations of offences committed, or suspected of having been committed, before the coming into force of the order or of this section.

(4) An order under this section shall be made by statutory instrument and shall be subject to annulment in pursuance of a resolution of either House of Parliament.][627]

115 Expenses

Any expenses of a Minister of the Crown incurred in consequence of the provisions of this Act, including any increase attributable to those provisions in sums payable under any other Act, shall be defrayed out of money provided by Parliament.

116 Meaning of 'serious arrestable offence'

[...][628]

117 Power of constable to use reasonable force

Where any provision of this Act—

    (a) confers a power on a constable; and

    (b) does not provide that the power may only be exercised with the consent of some person, other than a police officer,

the officer may use reasonable force, if necessary, in the exercise of the power.

118 General interpretation

(1) In this Act—

    [...][629]

    [...][630]

    'designated police station' has the meaning assigned to it by section 35 above;

    'document' [means anything in which information of any description is recorded.][631];

---

[624] Words substituted by Secretary of State for Business, Innovation and Skills Order 2009, SI 2009/2748, Sch 1, para 3.

[625] Amended by SOCAPA 2005, s 111, Sch 7, Pt 3, para 43(1), (11).

[626] ibid.

[627] Inserted by the Criminal Justice and Police Act 2001, s 85.

[628] Repealed by SOCAPA 2005, ss 111, 174(2), Sch 7, Pt 3, para 43(1), (12), Sch 17, Pt 2.

[629] Repealed by SOCAPA 2005, ss 111, 174(2), Sch 7, Pt 1, para 24(1), (2), Sch 17, Pt 2.

[630] Repealed by the Railways and Transport Safety Act 2003, Sch 5, para 4(2)(c).

[631] Amended by the Civil Evidence Act 1995, s 15(1), Sch 1, para 9(3).

Act

[...]632

'item subject to legal privilege' has the meaning assigned to it by section 10 above;

'parent or guardian' means—

(a) in the case of a child or young person in the care of a local authority, that authority;[...]633

(b) [...]634;

'premises' has the meaning assigned to it by section 23 above;

'recordable offence' means any offence to which regulations under section 27 above apply;

'vessel' includes any ship, boat, raft or other apparatus constructed or adapted for floating on water.

(2) [Subject to subsection (2A)]635 a person is in police detention for the purposes of this Act if—

[(a) he has been taken to a police station after being arrested for an offence or after being arrested under section 41 of the Terrorism Act 2000, or]636

(b) he is arrested at a police station after attending voluntarily at the station or accompanying a constable to it,

and is detained there or is detained elsewhere in the charge of a constable, except that a person who is at a court after being charged is not in police detention for those purposes.

[(2A) Where a person is in another's lawful custody by virtue of paragraph 22, 34(1) or 35(3) of Schedule 4 to the Police Reform Act 2002, he shall be treated as in police detention.]637

119 Amendments and repeals

(1) The enactments mentioned in Schedule 6 to this Act shall have effect with the amendments there specified.

(2) The enactments mentioned in Schedule 7 to this Act (which include enactments already obsolete or unnecessary) are repealed to the extent specified in the third column of that Schedule.

(3) The repeals in Parts II and IV of Schedule 7 to this Act have effect only in relation to criminal proceedings.

120 Extent

(1) Subject to the following provisions of this section, this Act extends to England and Wales only.

(2) The following extend to Scotland only—

[...]638

section 111;

section 112(1); and

---

632 Repealed by the Criminal Justice and Public Order Act 1994, s 168(3), Sch 11.

633 Repealed by the Children Act 1989, s 108(7), Sch 15.

634 ibid.

635 Amended by the Police Reform Act 2002, s 107(1), Sch 7, para 9(9).

636 Amended by the Terrorism Act 2000, s 125(1), Sch 15, para 5(1), (12); for savings see the Terrorism Act 2000, s 129(1)(b) and SI 2001/421, art 2.

637 Amended by the Police Reform Act 2002, s 107(9), Sch 7, para 9(9).

638 Entries repealed by Statute Law (Repeals) Act 2008, Sch 1(6), para 1.

section 119(2), so far as it relates to the provisions of the Pedlars Act 1871 repealed by Part VI of Schedule 7.

(3)   The following extend to Northern Ireland only—
      section 6(4), and
      section 112(2).

(4)   The following extend to England and Wales and Scotland—
      section 6(1) and (2);
      section 7;
      [...] and[639]
      section 119(2), so far as it relates to section 19 of the Pedlars Act 1871.

(5)   The following extend to England and Wales, Scotland and Northern Ireland—
      section 6(3);
      [section 9(2A);] and [640]
      section 114(1).

[(6) Nothing in subsection (1) affects–
      (a) the extent of section 113(1) to (7) and (12) to (14);
      (b) the extent of the relevant provisions so far as they relate to service proceedings.][641]

(8)   In this section 'the relevant provisions' means—
      [(a) section 67(11) to (13);][642]
      (c) Parts VII and VIII of this Act, except paragraph 10 of Schedule 3;
      [(d) section 113(8) to (10).][643]

[(8A) In this section 'service proceedings' means proceedings before a court (other than a civilian court) in respect of a service offence; and 'service offence' and 'civilian court' here have the same meanings as in the Armed Forces Act 2006.

(8B) Section 384 of the Armed Forces Act 2006 (Channel Islands, Isle of Man and British overseas territories) applies in relation to the provisions mentioned in subsection (6)(a) and (b) above as it applies in relation to that Act.][644]
      Section 119(1), so far as it relates to any provision amended by Part II of Schedule 6, extends to any place to which that provision extends.

(10) Section 119(2), so far as it relates—
      (a) to any provision contained in—
           the Army Act 1955;
           the Air Force Act 1955;
           the Armed Forces Act 1981; or
           the Value Added Tax Act 1983;
      (b) to any provision mentioned in Part VI of Schedule 7, other than section 18 of the Pedlars Act 1871,
      extends to any place to which that provision extends.

---

[639] Entries repealed by Statute Law (Repeals) Act 2008, Sch 1(6), para 1.

[640] Entry repealed by Statute Law (Repeals) Act 2008, Sch 1, para 1 (21 July 2008) and entry inserted by Criminal Justice and Police Act 2001, s 86(2).

[641] Section 120(6) substituted for s 120(6) and (7) by Armed Forces Act 2006, Sch 16, para 106(2).

[642] Section 120(8)(a) substituted for s 120(8)(a) and (b) by Armed Forces Act 2006, Sch 16, para 106(3)(a).

[643] Section 120(8)(d) substituted for s 120(8)(d)–(e) by Armed Forces Act 2006, Sch 16, para 106(3)(b).

[644] Section 120(8A)–(8B) substituted for s 120(9) by Armed Forces Act 2006, Sch 16, para 106(4).

(11) So far as any of the following—
section 115;
in section 118, the definition of 'document';
this section;
section 121; and
section 122,
has effect in relation to any other provision of this Act, it extends to any place
to which that provision extends.

121 Commencement

(1) This Act, except section 120 above, this section and section 122 below, shall
come into operation on such day as the Secretary of State may by order made
by statutory instrument appoint, and different days may be so appointed for
different provisions and for different purposes.
(2) Different days may be appointed under this section for the coming into force of
section 60 above in different areas.
(3) When an order under this section provides by virtue of subsection (2) above
that section 60 above shall come into force in an area specified in the order, the
duty imposed on the Secretary of State by that section shall be construed as a
duty to make an order under it in relation to interviews in that area.
(4) An order under this section may make such transitional provision as appears to
the Secretary of State to be necessary or expedient in connection with the provisions thereby brought into operation.

122 Short title

This Act may be cited as the Police and Criminal Evidence Act 1984.

SCHEDULES
SCHEDULE 1
SPECIAL PROCEDURE

Section 9

Making of orders by circuit judge

1 If on an application made by a constable a circuit judge is satisfied that one or
other of the sets of access conditions is fulfilled, he may make an order under
paragraph 4 below.
2 The first set of access conditions is fulfilled if—
(a) there are reasonable grounds for believing—
(i) that [an indictable offence][645] has been committed;
(ii) that there is material which consists of special procedure material or also
includes special procedure material and does not also include excluded
material on premises specified in the application[, or on premises occupied or controlled by a person specified in the application (including all
such premises on which there are reasonable grounds for believing that
there is such material as it is reasonably practicable so to specify)][646];

---

[645] Amended by SOCAPA 2005, s 111, Sch 7, Pt 3, para 43(1), (13).
[646] Amended by SOCAPA 2005, s 113(1), (10), (11).

(iii) that the material is likely to be of substantial value (whether by itself or together with other material) to the investigation in connection with which the application is made; and

(iv) that the material is likely to be relevant evidence;

(b) other methods of obtaining the material—

(i) have been tried without success; or

(ii) have not been tried because it appeared that they were bound to fail; and

(c) it is in the public interest, having regard—

(i) to the benefit likely to accrue to the investigation if the material is obtained; and

(ii) to the circumstances under which the person in possession of the material holds it,

that the material should be produced or that access to it should be given.

3 The second set of access conditions is fulfilled if—

(a) there are reasonable grounds for believing that there is material which consists of or includes excluded material or special procedure material on premises specified in the application[, or on premises occupied or controlled by a person specified in the application (including all such premises on which there are reasonable grounds for believing that there is such material as it is reasonably practicable so to specify)][647];

(b) but for section 9(2) above a search of [such premises][648] for that material could have been authorised by the issue of a warrant to a constable under an enactment other than this Schedule; and

(c) the issue of such a warrant would have been appropriate.

4 An order under this paragraph is an order that the person who appears to the circuit judge to be in possession of the material to which the application relates shall—

(a) produce it to a constable for him to take away; or

(b) give a constable access to it,

not later than the end of the period of seven days from the date of the order or the end of such longer period as the order may specify.

5 Where the material consists of information [stored in any electronic form][649]—

(a) an order under paragraph 4(a) above shall have effect as an order to produce the material in a form in which it can be taken away and in which it is visible and legible [or from which it can readily be produced in a visible and legible form][650]; and

(b) an order under paragraph 4(b) above shall have effect as an order to give a constable access to the material in a form in which it is visible and legible.

6 For the purposes of sections 21 and 22 above material produced in pursuance of an order under paragraph 4(a) above shall be treated as if it were material seized by a constable.

---

[647] ibid.

[648] Amended by SOCAPA 2005, s 113(1), (10), (12).

[649] Amended by the Criminal Justice and Police Act 2001, s 70, Sch 2, Pt 2, para 14(a).

[650] Amended by the Criminal Justice and Police Act 2001, s 70, Sch 2, Pt 2, para 14(b).

Notices of applications for orders

7   An application for an order under paragraph 4 above shall be made inter partes.
8   Notice of an application for such an order may be served on a person either by delivering it to him or by leaving it at his proper address or by sending it by post to him in a registered letter or by the recorded delivery service.
9   Such a notice may be served—
     (a) on a body corporate, by serving it on the body's secretary or clerk or other similar officer; and
     (b) on a partnership, by serving it on one of the partners.
10   For the purposes of this Schedule, and of section 7 of the Interpretation Act 1978 in its application to this Schedule, the proper address of a person, in the case of secretary or clerk or other similar officer of a body corporate, shall be that of the registered or principal office of that body, in the case of a partner of a firm shall be that of the principal office of the firm, and in any other case shall be the last known address of the person to be served.
11   Where notice of an application for an order under paragraph 4 above has been served on a person, he shall not conceal, destroy, alter or dispose of the material to which the application relates except—
     (a) with the leave of a judge; or
     (b) with the written permission of a constable,
     until—
     (i) the application is dismissed or abandoned; or
     (ii) he has complied with an order under paragraph 4 above made on the application.

Issue of warrants by circuit judge

12   If on an application made by a constable a circuit judge—
     (a) is satisfied—
         (i) that either set of access conditions is fulfilled; and
         (ii) that any of the further conditions set out in paragraph 14 below is also fulfilled [in relation to each set of premises specified in the application][651] [or (as the case may be) all premises occupied or controlled by the person referred to in paragraph 2(a)(ii) or 3(a), including such sets of premises as are specified in the application (an 'all premises warrant')][652]; or
     (b) is satisfied—
         (i) that the second set of access conditions is fulfilled; and
         (ii) that an order under paragraph 4 above relating to the material has not been complied with,
     he may issue a warrant authorising a constable to enter and search the premises.
[12A The judge may not issue an all premises warrant unless he is satisfied—
     (a) that there are reasonable grounds for believing that it is necessary to search premises occupied or controlled by the person in question which are not specified in the application, as well as those which are, in order to find the material in question; and

---

[651] Amended by SOCAPA 2005, s 113(1), (10), (13)(a).
[652] Amended by SOCAPA 2005, s 113(1), (10), (13)(b).

(b) that it is not reasonably practicable to specify all the premises which he occupies or controls which might need to be searched.][653]

13 A constable may seize and retain anything for which a search has been authorised under paragraph 12 above.

14 The further conditions mentioned in paragraph 12(a)(ii) above are—

(a) that it is not practicable to communicate with any person entitled to grant entry to the premises [...][654];

(b) that it is practicable to communicate with a person entitled to grant entry to the premises but it is not practicable to communicate with any person entitled to grant access to the material;

(c) that the material contains information which—

(i) is subject to a restriction or obligation such as is mentioned in section 11(2)(b) above; and

(ii) is likely to be disclosed in breach of it if a warrant is not issued;

(d) that service of notice of an application for an order under paragraph 4 above may seriously prejudice the investigation.

15 (1) If a person fails to comply with an order under paragraph 4 above, a circuit judge may deal with him as if he had committed a contempt of the Crown Court.

(2) Any enactment relating to contempt of the Crown Court shall have effect in relation to such a failure as if it were such a contempt.

Costs

16 The costs of any application under this Schedule and of anything done or to be done in pursuance of an order made under it shall be in the discretion of the judge.

Interpretation[655]

[17 In this Schedule "judge" means [a judge of the High Court, a Circuit judge, a Recorder][656] [, a qualifying judge advocate (within the meaning of the Senior Courts Act 1981)][657] or a District Judge (Magistrates' Courts).]

[SCHEDULE 1A

SPECIFIC OFFENCES WHICH ARE ARRESTABLE OFFENCES][658

[...][659]

[27B An offence under section 21(1), 27(1) or 31(1) of the London Olympic Games and Paralympics Games Act 2006 (unauthorised advertising, trading and ticket-sales).][660]

---

[653] Amended by SOCAPA 2005, s 113(1), (10), (14).

[654] Repealed by SOCAPA 2005, ss 113(1), (10), (15), 174(2), Sch 17, Pt 2.

[655] New para 17 added by Courts Act 2003, Sch 4, para 6(2) (date to be appointed).

[656] Substituted by SOCAPA 2005, s 114(9) (date to be appointed).

[657] Inserted by Armed Forces Act 2011 c 18 Sch 2(2) para 11(2) (date to be appointed). (The insertion came into force on 2 April 2012 but cannot take effect until the insertion of Sch 1 para 17.)

[658] Inserted by the Police Reform Act 2002, s 48(1), (5), Sch 6.

[659] Repealed by SOCAPA 2005, ss 111, 174(2), Sch 7, Pt 1, para 24(1), (3), Sch 17, Pt 2.

[660] Added by the London Olympic Games and Paralympic Games Act 2006, s 39(1) (date to be appointed).

SCHEDULE 2
PRESERVED POWERS OF ARREST

Section 26

Act

[...]661	[...]662
[...]663	[...]664
[...]665	[...]666
[...]667	[...]668
1952 c 52	Section 49 of the Prison Act 1952.
1952 c 67	Section 13 of the Visiting Forces Act 1952.
[...]669	[...]670
1969 c 54	[Section 32 of the Children and Young Persons Act 1969.]671
1971 c 77	Section 24(2) of the Immigration Act 1971 and paragraphs 17, 24 and 33 of Schedule 2 and paragraph 7 of Schedule 3 to that Act.
[...]672	
1976 c 63	Section 7 of the Bail Act 1976.
[...]673 1983 c 20	[...]674 Sections 18, 35(10), 36(8), 38(7), 136(1) and 138 of the Mental Health Act 1983.
[...]675 1984 c 47	Section 5(5) of the Repatriation of Prisoners Act 1984.

SCHEDULE 2A
FINGERPRINTING AND SAMPLES: POWER TO REQUIRE
ATTENDANCE AT POLICE STATION

PART I
FINGERPRINTING

[1 Persons arrested and released

(1) A constable may require a person to attend a police station for the purpose of taking his fingerprints under section 61(5A).

---

661 Repealed by SOCAPA 2005, ss 111, 174(2), Sch 7, Pt 1, para 24(1), (4), Sch 17, Pt 2.

662 ibid.

663 ibid.

664 ibid.

665 Repealed by the Civil Contingencies Act 2004, s 32(2), Sch 3.

666 ibid.

667 Repealed by SOCAPA 2005, ss 111, 174(2), Sch 7, Pt 1, para 24(1), (4), Sch 17, Pt 2.

668 ibid.

669 Entries repealed by Armed Forces Act 2006, Sch 17, para 1 (31 October 2009; SI 2009/1167).

670 Entries repealed subject to transitory provisions specified in SI 2005/3495 art 2(2) by Serious Organised Crime and Police Act 2005 c. 15 Sch 17(2) para 1 (1 January 2006: repeal has effect subject to transitory provisions specified in SI 2005/3495 art 2(2)).

671 Amended by the Children Act 1989, s 108(5), (6), Sch 13, para 55.

672 Repealed by the Road Traffic (Consequential Provisions) Act 1988, s 3(1), Sch 1, Pt 1.

673 Repealed by SOCAPA 2005, ss 111, 174(2), Sch 7, Pt 1, para 24(1), (4), Sch 17, Pt 2.

674 Entry repealed by Electoral Administration Act 2006, Sch 2, para 1 (1 January 2007; SI 2006/3412).

675 Entry relating to the Prevention of Terrorism (Temporary Provisions) Act 1984 repealed by Prevention of Terrorism (Temporary Provisions) Act 1989, s 25(2), Sch 9, Pt I.

(2) The power under sub-paragraph (1) above may not be exercised in a case falling within section 61(5A)(b) (fingerprints taken on previous occasion insufficient etc.) after the end of the period of six months beginning with the day on which the appropriate officer was informed that section 61(3A)(a) or (b) applied.

(3) In sub-paragraph (2) above 'appropriate officer' means the officer investigating the offence for which the person was arrested.][676]

[2 Persons charged etc

(1) A constable may require a person to attend a police station for the purpose of taking his fingerprints under section 61(5B).

(2) The power under sub-paragraph (1) above may not be exercised after the end of the period of six months beginning with—

(a) in a case falling within section 61(5B)(a) (fingerprints not taken previously), the day on which the person was charged or informed that he would be reported, or

(b) in a case falling within section 61(5B)(b) (fingerprints taken on previous occasions insufficient etc.), the day on which the appropriate officer was informed that section 61(3A)(a) or (b) applied.

(3) In sub-paragraph (2)(b) above 'appropriate officer' means the officer investigating the offence for which the person was charged or informed that he would be reported.][677]

[3 Persons convicted etc of an offence in England and Wales

(1) A constable may require a person to attend a police station for the purpose of taking his fingerprints under section 61(6).

(2) Where the condition in section 61(6ZA)(a) is satisfied (fingerprints not taken previously), the power under sub-paragraph (1) above may not be exercised after the end of the period of two years beginning with—

(a) the day on which the person was convicted, cautioned or warned or reprimanded, or

(b) if later, the day on which this Schedule comes into force.

(3) Where the condition in section 61(6ZA)(b) is satisfied (fingerprints taken on a previous occasion insufficient etc.), the power under sub-paragraph (1) above may not be exercised after the end of the period of two years beginning with—

(a) the day on which the appropriate officer was informed that section 61(3A) (a) or (b) applied, or

(b) if later, the day on which this Schedule comes into force.

(4) In sub-paragraph (3)(a) above, 'appropriate officer' means an officer of the police force which investigated the offence in question.

(5) Sub-paragraphs (2) and (3) above do not apply where the offence is a qualifying offence (whether or not it was such an offence at the time of the conviction, caution or warning or reprimand).][678]

---

[676] Added by the Crime and Security Act 2010, s 6(2) (7 March 2011 as SI 2011/414).
[677] Added by the Crime and Security Act 2010, s 6(2) (7 March 2011 as SI 2011/414).
[678] Added by the Crime and Security Act 2010, s 6(2) (7 March 2011 as SI 2011/414).

4 Persons subject to a control order

[...][679]

[5 Persons convicted etc of an offence outside England and Wales

A constable may require a person to attend a police station for the purpose of taking his fingerprints under section 61(6D).][680]

[6 Multiple attendance

(1) Where a person's fingerprints have been taken under section 61 on two occasions in relation to any offence, he may not under this Schedule be required to attend a police station to have his fingerprints taken under that section in relation to that offence on a subsequent occasion without the authorisation of an officer of at least the rank of inspector.

(2) Where an authorisation is given under sub-paragraph (1) above—

    (a) the fact of the authorisation, and

    (b) the reasons for giving it,

shall be recorded as soon as practicable after it has been given.][681]

PART II

INTIMATE SAMPLES

[7 Persons suspected to be involved in an offence

A constable may require a person to attend a police station for the purpose of taking an intimate sample from him under section 62(1A) if, in the course of the investigation of an offence, two or more non-intimate samples suitable for the same means of analysis have been taken from him but have proved insufficient.][682]

[8 Persons convicted etc of an offence outside England and Wales

A constable may require a person to attend a police station for the purpose of taking a sample from him under section 62(2A) if two or more non-intimate samples suitable for the same means of analysis have been taken from him under section 63(3E) but have proved insufficient.][683]

PART III

NON-INTIMATE SAMPLES

[9 Persons arrested and released

(1) A constable may require a person to attend a police station for the purpose of taking a non-intimate sample from him under section 63(3ZA).

(2) The power under sub-paragraph (1) above may not be exercised in a case falling within section 63(3ZA)(b) (sample taken on a previous occasion not suitable etc.)

---

[679] Repealed, never in force, by the Terrorism Prevention and Investigation Measures Act 2011, Sch 7(1), para 2 (15 December 2011: repeal has effect subject to transnational and saving provision specified in 2011 c 23 Sch 8).

[680] Added by the Crime and Security Act 2010, s 6(2) (7 March 2011 as SI 2011/414).

[681] Added by the Crime and Security Act 2010, s 6(2) (7 March 2011 as SI 2011/414).

[682] Added by the Crime and Security Act 2010, s 6(2) (7 March 2011 as SI 2011/414).

[683] Added by the Crime and Security Act 2010, s 6(2) (7 March 2011 as SI 2011/414).

after the end of the period of six months beginning with the day on which the appropriate officer as informed of the matters specified in section 63(3ZA)(b)(i) or (ii).

(3) In sub-paragraph (2) above, 'appropriate officer' means the officer investigating the offence for which the person was arrested.][684]

[10 Persons charged etc

(1) A constable may require a person to attend a police station for the purpose of taking a non-intimate sample from him under section 63(3A).

(2) The power under sub-paragraph (1) above may not be exercised in a case falling within section 63(3A)(a) (sample not taken previously) after the end of the period of six months beginning with the day on which he was charged or informed that he would be reported.

(3) The power under sub-paragraph (1) above may not be exercised in a case falling within section 63(3A)(b) (sample taken on a previous occasion not suitable etc.) after the end of the period of six months beginning with the day on which the appropriate officer was informed of the matters specified in section 63(3A)(b)(i) or (ii).

(4) In sub-paragraph (3) above 'appropriate officer' means the officer investigating the offence for which the person was charged or informed that he would be reported.][685]

[11 Persons convicted etc of an offence in England and Wales

(1) A constable may require a person to attend a police station for the purpose of taking a non-intimate sample from him under section 63(3B).

(2) Where the condition in section 63(3BA)(a) is satisfied (sample not taken previously), the power under sub-paragraph (1) above may not be exercised after the end of the period of two years beginning with—
(a) the day on which the person was convicted, cautioned or warned or reprimanded, or
(b) if later, the day on which this Schedule comes into force.

(3) Where the condition in section 63(3BA)(b) is satisfied (sample taken on a previous occasion not suitable etc.), the power under sub-paragraph (1) above may not be exercised after the end of the period of two years beginning with—
(a) the day on which an appropriate officer was informed of the matters specified in section 63(3BA)(b)(i) or (ii), or
(b) if later, the day on which this Schedule comes into force.

(4) In sub-paragraph (3)(a) above 'appropriate officer' means an officer of the police force which investigated the offence in question.

(5) Sub-paragraphs (2) and (3) above do not apply where—
(a) the offence is a qualifying offence (whether or not it was such an offence at the time of the conviction, caution or warning or reprimand), or
(b) he was convicted before 10th April 1995 and is a person to whom section 1 of the Criminal Evidence (Amendment) Act 1997 applies.][686]

---

[684] Added by the Crime and Security Act 2010, s 6(2) (7 March 2011 as SI 2011/414).
[685] Added by the Crime and Security Act 2010, s 6(2) (March 7 2011 as SI 2011/414).
[686] Added by the Crime and Security Act 2010, s 6(2) (7 March 2011 as SI 2011/414).

Act

12 Persons subject to a control order

[...][687]

[13 Persons convicted etc of an offence outside England and Wales

A constable may require a person to attend a police station for the purpose of taking a non-intimate sample from him section 63(3E).][688]

[14 Multiple exercise of power

(1) Where a non-intimate sample has been taken from a person under section 63 on two occasions in relation to any offence, he may not under this Schedule be required to attend a police station to have another such sample taken from him under that section in relation to that offence on a subsequent occasion without the authorisation of an officer of at least the rank of inspector.

(2) Where an authorisation is given under sub-paragraph (1) above—
    (a) the fact of the authorisation, and
    (b) the reasons for giving it,
shall be recorded as soon as practicable after it has been given.][689]

Part IV
General and Supplementary

[15 Requirement to have power to take fingerprints or sample

(1) A power conferred by this Schedule to require a person to attend a police station for the purposes of taking fingerprints or a sample under any provision of this Act may be exercised only in a case where the fingerprints or sample may be taken from the person under that provision (and, in particular, if any necessary authorisation for taking the fingerprints or sample under that provision has been obtained).][690]

[16 Date and time of attendance

(1) A requirement under this Schedule—
    (a) shall give the person a period of at least seven days within which he must attend the police station; and
    (b) may direct him so to attend at a specified time of day or between specified times of day.

(2) In specifying a period of time or times of day for the purposes of sub-paragraph (1) above, the constable shall consider whether the fingerprints or sample could reasonably be taken at a time when the person is for any other reason required to attend the police station.

(3) A requirement under this Schedule may specify a period shorter than seven days if—

---

[687] Repealed, never in force, by the Terrorism Prevention and Investigation Measures Act 2011, Sch 7(1), para 2 (15 December 2011: repeal has effect subject to transitional and saving provision specified in 2011 c 23 Sch 8).

[688] Added by the Crime and Security Act 2010, s 6(2) (7 March 2011 as SI 2011/414).

[689] Added by the Crime and Security Act 2010, s 6(2) (7 March 2011 as SI 2011/414).

[690] Added by the Crime and Security Act 2010, s 6(2) (7 March 2011 as SI 2011/414).

(a) there is an urgent need for the fingerprints or sample for the purposes of the investigation of an offence; and

(b) the shorter period is authorised by an officer of at least the rank of inspector.

(4) Where an authorisation is given under sub-paragraph (3)(b) above—

(a) the fact of the authorisation, and

(b) the reasons or giving it,

shall be recorded as soon as practicable after it has been given.

(5) If the constable giving a requirement under this Schedule and the person to whom it is given so agree, it may be varied so as to specify any period within which, or date or time at which, the person must attend; but a variation shall not have effect unless confirmed by the constable in writing.][691]

[17 Enforcement

A constable may arrest without warrant a person who has failed to comply with a requirement under this Schedule.][692]

SCHEDULE 3

PROVISIONS SUPPLEMENTARY TO SECTIONS 68 AND 69

Section 70

PART I

PROVISIONS SUPPLEMENTARY TO SECTION 68

[...][693]

PART II

PROVISIONS SUPPLEMENTARY TO SECTION 69

[...][694]

PART III

PROVISIONS SUPPLEMENTARY TO SECTIONS 68 AND 69

13— [...][695]
14— [...][696]
15— [...][697]

SCHEDULE 4

THE POLICE COMPLAINTS AUTHORITY

Section 83

---

[691] Added by the Crime and Security Act 2010, s 6(2) (7 March 2011 as SI 2011/414).
[692] Added by the Crime and Security Act 2010, s 6(2) (7 March 2011 as SI 2011/414).
[693] Repealed by the Criminal Justice Act 1988, s 170(2), Sch 16.
[694] Repealed by the Youth Justice and Criminal Evidence Act 1999, s 67(3), Sch 6.
[695] Repealed by the Criminal Justice Act 1988, s 170(2), Sch 16.
[696] Repealed by the Youth Justice and Criminal Evidence Act 1999, s 67(3), Sch 6.
[697] ibid.

Act

PART I
GENERAL

[...]⁶⁹⁸

PART II
TRANSITIONAL

[...]⁶⁹⁹

SCHEDULE 5
SERIOUS ARRESTABLE OFFENCES

Section 116

PART I
OFFENCES MENTIONED IN SECTION 116(2)(A)

[...]⁷⁰⁰

PART II
OFFENCES MENTIONED IN SECTION 116(2)(B)

[...]⁷⁰¹

SCHEDULE 6
MINOR AND CONSEQUENTIAL AMENDMENTS

Section 119

PART I
ENGLAND AND WALES

Game Act 1831 (c. 32)

1. The following section shall be inserted after section 31 of the Game Act 1831—
    'Powers of constables in relation to trespassers
    31A. The powers conferred by section 31 above to require a person found on
    land as mentioned in that section to quit the land and to tell his christian
    name, surname, and place of abode shall also be exercisable by a police
    constable.'.

Metropolitan Police Act 1839 (c. 47)

2. In section 39 of the Metropolitan Police Act 1839 (fairs within the metropolitan
    police district) after the word 'amusement' there shall be inserted the words
    'shall be guilty of an offence'.

Railway Regulation Act 1840 (c. 97)

3. In section 16 of the Railway Regulation Act 1840 (persons obstructing officers of
    railway company or trespassing upon railway) for the words from 'and' in the
    third place where it occurs to 'justice,' in the third place where it occurs there

---

⁶⁹⁸ Repealed by the Police Act 1996, s 103, Sch 9, Pt II.
⁶⁹⁹ ibid.
⁷⁰⁰ Repealed by SOCAPA 2005, ss 111, 174(2), Sch 7, Pt 3, para 43(1), (14), Sch 17, Pt 2.
⁷⁰¹ ibid.

shall be substituted the words ', upon conviction by a magistrates' court, at the discretion of the court,'.

London Hackney Carriages Act 1843 (c. 86)

4. In section 27 of the London Hackney Carriages Act 1843 (no person to act as driver of carriage without consent of proprietor) for the words after 'constable' there shall be substituted the words 'if necessary, to take charge of the carriage and every horse in charge of any person unlawfully acting as a driver and to deposit the same in some place of safe custody until the same can be applied for by the proprietor.'.

Town Gardens Protection Act 1863 (c. 13)

5. In section 5 of the Town Gardens Protection Act 1863 (penalty for injuring garden) for the words from the beginning to 'district' there shall be substituted the words 'Any person who throws any rubbish into any such garden, or trespasses therein, or gets over the railings or fence, or steals or damages the flowers or plants, or commits any nuisance therein, shall be guilty of an offence and'.

Parks Regulation Act 1872 (c. 15)

6. The following section shall be substituted for section 5 of the Parks Regulation Act 1872 (apprehension of offender whose name or residence is not known)—
    '5. Any person who—
    (a) within the view of a park constable acts in contravention of any of the said regulations in the park where the park constable has jurisdiction; and
    (b) when required by any park constable or by any police constable to give his name and address gives a false name or false address,
    shall be liable on summary conviction to a penalty of an amount not exceeding level 1 on the standard scale, as defined in section 75 of the Criminal Justice Act 1982.'

Dogs (Protection of Livestock) Act 1953 (c. 28)

7. In the Dogs (Protection of Livestock) Act 1953 the following section shall be inserted after section 2—
    'Power of justice of the peace to authorise entry and search
    2A. If on an application made by a constable a justice of the peace is satisfied that there are reasonable grounds for believing—
    (a) that an offence under this Act has been committed; and
    (b) that the dog in respect of which the offence has been committed is on premises specified in the application,
    he may issue a warrant authorising a constable to enter and search the premises in order to identify the dog.'.

Army Act 1955 (c. 18)

Air Force Act 1955 (c. 19)

8. [...][702]

---

[702] Repealed by Armed Forces Act 2006, Sch 17, para 1 (31 October 2009; SI 2009/1167).

Act

Sexual Offences Act 1956 (c. 69)

9. [...][703]

Game Laws (Amendment) Act 1960 (c. 36)

10. In subsection (1) of section 2 of the Game Laws (Amendment) Act 1960 (power of police to enter on land) for the words 'purpose of exercising any power conferred on him by the foregoing section' there shall be substituted the words 'purpose—
    (a) of exercising in relation to him the powers under section 31 of the Game Act 1831 which section 31A of that Act confers on police constables; or
    (b) of arresting him in accordance with section 25 of the Police and Criminal Evidence Act 1984.'.

11. In subsection (1) of section 4 of that Act (enforcement powers) for the words from 'under', in the first place where it occurs, to 'thirty-one' there shall be substituted the words ', in accordance with section 25 of the Police and Criminal Evidence Act 1984, for an offence under section one or section nine of the Night Poaching Act 1828, or under section thirty'.

Betting, Gaming and Lotteries Act 1963 (c. 2)

12. [...][704]

Deer Act 1963 (c. 36)

13. [...][705]

Police Act 1964 (c. 48)

14. [...][706]
15. [...][707]
16. [...][708]

Criminal Law Act 1967 (c. 58)

17. [...][709]

Theatres Act 1968 (c. 54)

18. In section 15(1) of the Theatres Act 1968 (powers of entry and inspection) for the words 'fourteen days' there shall be substituted the words 'one month'.

Children and Young Persons Act 1969 (c. 54)

19. In the Children and Young Persons Act 1969—
    (a) [...][710]
    (b) the following section shall be substituted for section 29—
    29. 'Recognisance on release of arrested child or young person

---

[703] Repealed by the Sexual Offences Act 2003, Sch 7, para 1.

[704] Repealed by Gambling Act 2005, Sch 17, para 1 (1 September 2007; SI 2006/3272).

[705] Repealed by the Deer Act 1991, Sch 4, para 1.

[706] Repealed by the Police and Magistrates' Courts Act 1994, Sch 9, Pt I, para 1.

[707] ibid.

[708] Repealed by the Police Officers (Central Service) Act 1989, s 3, Schedule.

[709] Repealed by SOCAPA 2005, s 174(2), Sch 17, Pt 2, para 1; for transitional provisions see SI 2005/3495, art 2(2).

[710] Repealed by the Children Act 1989, s 108, Sch 15, para 1.

A child or young person arrested in pursuance of a warrant shall not be released unless he or his parent or guardian (with or without sureties) enters into a recognisance for such amount as the custody officer at the police station where he is detained considers will secure his attendance at the hearing of the charge; and the recognisance entered into in pursuance of this section may, if the custody officer thinks fit, be conditioned for the attendance of the parent or guardian at the hearing in addition to the child or young person.'.

Immigration Act 1971 (c. 77)

20. In section 25(3) of the Immigration Act 1971 for the words 'A constable or' there shall be substituted the word 'An'.

Criminal Justice Act 1972 (c. 71)

21. In subsection (1) of section 34 of the Criminal Justice Act 1972 (powers of constable to take drunken offender to treatment centre) for the words from the beginning to 'section the' there shall be substituted the words 'On arresting an offender for an offence under—
    (a) section 12 of the Licensing Act 1872; or
    (b) section 91(1) of the Criminal Justice Act 1967,
    a'.

Child Care Act 1980 (c. 5)

22. [...][711]

Deer Act 1980 (c. 49)

23. [...][712]

Animal Health Act 1981 (c. 22)

24. In subsection (5) of section 60 of the Animal Health Act 1981 (enforcement powers) for the words 'a constable or other officer' there shall be substituted the words 'an officer other than a constable'.

Wildlife and Countryside Act 1981 (c. 69)

25. In subsection (2) of section 19 of the Wildlife and Countryside Act 1981 (enforcement powers) after the words 'subsection (1)' there shall be inserted the words 'or arresting a person, in accordance with section 25 of the Police and Criminal Evidence Act 1984, for such an offence'.

Mental Health Act 1983 (c. 20)

26. In section 135(4) of the Mental Health Act 1983 for the words 'the constable to whom it is addressed', in both places where they occur, there shall be substituted the words 'a constable'.

Prevention of Terrorism (Temporary Provisions) Act 1984 (c. 8)

27. [...][713]

---

[711] ibid.
[712] Repealed by the Deer Act 1991, Sch 4, para 1.
[713] Repealed by the Prevention of Terrorism (Temporary Provisions) Act 1989, s 25(2), Sch 9, Pt I.

Act

PART II
OTHER AMENDMENTS

Army Act 1955 (c. 18)

28. [...]⁷¹⁴

Air Force Act 1955 (c. 19)

29. [...]⁷¹⁵

Police (Scotland) Act 1967 (c. 77)

30. In section 6(2) of the Police (Scotland) Act 1967 (constables below rank of assistant chief constable) for the words 'an assistant chief constable or a constable holding the office of deputy chief constable' there shall be substituted the words 'a deputy chief constable or an assistant chief constable'.
31. In section 7(1) of that Act (ranks) after the words 'chief constable,' there shall be inserted the words 'deputy chief constable,'.
32. In section 26(7) of that Act (disciplinary authority) immediately before the words 'deputy chief constable' there shall be inserted the word 'any'.
33. In section 31(2) of that Act (compulsory retirement of chief constable etc.) for the words 'the deputy or an assistant chief constable' there shall be substituted the words 'a deputy or assistant chief constable'.

Courts-Martial (Appeals) Act 1968 (c. 20)

34. [...]⁷¹⁶

House of Commons Disqualification Act 1975 (c. 24)

Northern Ireland Assembly Disqualification Act 1975 (c. 25)

35. In Part II of Schedule 1 to the House of Commons Disqualification Act 1975 and Part II of Schedule 1 to the Northern Ireland Assembly Disqualification Act 1975 (bodies of which all members are disqualified under those Acts) there shall be inserted at the appropriate place in alphabetical order—
'The Police Complaints Authority'.

Armed Forces Act 1976 (c. 52)

36. [...]⁷¹⁷

Customs and Excise Management Act 1979 (c. 2)

37. The following subsection shall be substituted for section 138(4) of the Customs and Excise Management Act 1979—
'(4) Where any person has been arrested by a person who is not an officer—
(a) by virtue of this section; or
(b) by virtue of section 24 of the Police and Criminal Evidence Act 1984 in its application to offences under the customs and excise Acts,

---

⁷¹⁴ Repealed by Armed Forces Act 2006, Sch 17, para 1 (31 October 2009; SI 2009/1167).
⁷¹⁵ Repealed by Armed Forces Act 2006, Sch 17, para 1 (31 October 2009; SI 2009/1167).
⁷¹⁶ Repealed by Armed Forces Act 2001 c 19 Sch 7(5) para 1 (11 May 2001).
⁷¹⁷ ibid.

the person arresting him shall give notice of the arrest to an officer at the nearest convenient office of customs and excise.'.

38. In section 161 of that Act—
   (a) in subsection (3), for the words from 'that officer' to the end of the subsection there shall be substituted the words 'any officer and any person accompanying an officer to enter and search the building or place named in the warrant within one month from that day'; and
   (b) in subsection (4), for the words 'person named in a warrant under subsection (3) above' there shall be substituted the words 'other person so authorised'.

Betting and Gaming Duties Act 1981 (c. 63)

39. [...][718]

Car Tax Act 1983 (c. 53)

40. [...][719]

Value Added Tax Act 1983 (c. 55)

41. [...][720]

SCHEDULE 7
REPEALS

Section 119

PART I

ENACTMENTS REPEALED IN CONSEQUENCE OF PARTS I TO V

Chapter	Short Title	Extent of Repeal
5 Geo 4 c 83	Vagrancy Act 1824	Section 8.
		Section 13.
1 & 2 Will 4 c 32	Game Act 1831	In section 31, the words 'or for any police constable'.
2 & 3 Vict c 47	Metropolitan Police Act 1839	Section 34.
		In section 38, the words from 'it' to 'and' in the sixth place where it occurs.
		In section 39, the words 'to take into custody'.
		In section 47, the words 'take into custody' and the words ', and every person so found'.
		In section 54, the words from 'And' to the end of the section.
		In section 62, the words from 'may' in the first place where it occurs to 'and' in the second place where it occurs.

---

[718] Repealed by Finance Act 2007, Sch 27(5)(1), para 1 (8 November 2007: commencement order SI).
[719] Repealed by the Statute Law (Repeals) Act 2004, Sch 1, Pt 9.
[720] Repealed by the Value Added Tax Act 1994, Sch 15, para 1.

		Sections 63 to 67.
3 & 4 Vict c 50	Canals (Offences) Act 1840	The whole Act.
5 & 6 Vict c 55	Railway Regulation Act 1842	In section 17, the words 'or for any special constable duly appointed,'.
8 & 9 Vict c 20	Railways Clauses Consolidation Act 1845	In section 104, the words 'and all constables, gaolers, and police officers,'.
10 & 11 Vict c 89	Town Police Clauses Act 1847	In section 15, the words 'may be taken into custody, without a warrant, by any constable, or' and the words from 'Provided' to the end of the section.
		In section 28, the words from 'and' in the first place where it occurs to 'offence' in the second place where it occurs.
14 & 15 Vict c 19	Prevention of Offences Act 1851	Section 11.
23 & 24 Vict c 32	Ecclesiastical Courts Jurisdiction Act 1860	In section 3, the words 'constable or'.
24 & 25 Vict c 100	Offences against the Person Act 1861	In section 65, the words 'in the daytime'.
34 & 35 Vict c 96	Pedlars Act 1871	Sections 18 and 19.
35 & 36 Vict c 93	Pawnbrokers Act 1872	In section 36, the words, 'within the hours of business,'.
38 & 39 Vict c 17	Explosives Act 1875	In section 78, the words 'a constable, or'.
52 & 53 Vict c 18	Indecent Advertisements Act 1889	Section 6.
52 & 53 Vict c 57	Regulation of Railways Act 1889	In section 5(2), the words 'or any constable'.
8 Edw 7 c 66	Public Meeting Act 1908	In section 1, in subsection (3) the words from 'and' in the sixth place where it occurs to the end of the subsection.
1 & 2 Geo 5 c 28	Official Secrets Act 1911	In section 9(1) the words 'named therein'.
15 & 16 Geo 5 c 71	Public Health Act 1925	Section 74(2) and (3).
23 & 24 Geo 5 c 12	Children and Young Persons Act 1933	Section 10(2).
		Section 13(1) and (2).
		In section 40, in subsection (1) the words 'named therein' and in subsection (4) the words 'addressed to and'.
11 & 12 Geo 6 c 58	Criminal Justice Act 1948	Section 68.
1 & 2 Eliz 2 c 14	Prevention of Crime Act 1953	Section 1(3).
3 & 4 Eliz 2 c 28	Children and Young Persons (Harmful Publications) Act 1955	In section 3(1), the words 'named therein'.

Act

4 & 5 Eliz 2 c 69	Sexual Offences Act 1956	Section 40.
		In section 43(1), the word 'named'.
5 & 6 Eliz 2 c 53	Naval Discipline Act 1957	In section 106(1), the words from 'may' in the first place where it occurs to 'and'.
7 & 8 Eliz 2 c 66	Obscene Publications Act 1959	In section 3(1), the words, 'within fourteen days from the date of the warrant,'.
8 & 9 Eliz 2 c 36	Game Laws (Amendment) Act 1960	
1963 c 2	Betting, Gaming and Lotteries Act 1963	In section 51(1), the words 'at any time within fourteen days from the time of the issue of the warrant' and the words 'arrest and'.
1963 c 36	Deer Act 1963	Section 5(1)(c).
1964 c 26	Licensing Act 1964	Section 187(5).
1967 c 58	Criminal Law Act 1967	Section 2.
1968 c 27	Firearms Act 1968	In section 46(1), the words 'named therein'.
		Section 50.
1968 c 52	Caravan Sites Act 1968	Section 11(5).
1968 c 60	Theft Act 1968	Section 12(3).
		Section 26(2).
1968 c 65	Gaming Act 1968	Section 5(2).
		In section 43, in subsection (4), the words 'at any time within fourteen days from the time of the issue of the warrant', and in subsection (5)(b), the words 'arrest and'.
1970 c 30	Conservation of Seals Act 1970	Section 4(1)(a).
1971 c 38	Misuse of Drugs Act 1971	Section 24.
1971 c 77	Immigration Act 1971	In Schedule 2, in paragraph 17(2), the words 'acting for the police area in which the premises are situated,' and the words 'at any time or times within one month from the date of the warrant'.
1972 c 20	Road Traffic Act 1972	Section 19(3).
		Section 164(2).
1972 c 27	Road Traffic (Foreign Vehicles) Act 1972	Section 3(2).
1972 c 71	Criminal Justice Act 1972	Section 34(3).
1973 c 57	Badgers Act 1973	Section 10(1)(b).
1974 c 6	Biological Weapons Act 1974	In section 4(1), the words 'named therein'.
1976 c 32	Lotteries and Amusements Act 1976	In section 19, the words 'at any time within 14 days from the time of the issue of the warrant'.
1976 c 58	International Carriage of Perishable Foodstuffs Act 1976	Section 11(6).

Act

1977 c 45	Criminal Law Act 1977	Section 11.
		Section 62.
1979 c 2	Customs and Excise Management Act 1979	In section 138, in subsections (1) and (2), the words 'or constable'.
1980 c 43	Magistrates' Courts Act 1980.	Section 49.
1980 c 49	Deer Act 1980	Section 4(1)(c).
1980 c 66	Highways Act 1980	Section 137(2).
1980 c x	County of Merseyside Act 1980	Section 33.
1980 c xi	West Midlands County Council Act 1980	Section 42.
1981 c 14	Public Passenger Vehicles Act 1981	Section 25(2).
1981 c 22	Animal Health Act 1981	In section 60, subsection (3), in subsection (4) the words 'or apprehending', and in subsection (5) the words 'constable or', in the second place where they occur.
1981 c 42	Indecent Displays (Control) Act 1981	Section 2(1).
		In section 2(3), the words 'within fourteen days from the date of issue of the warrant'.
1981 c 47	Criminal Attempts Act 1981	Section 9(4).
1981 c 69	Wildlife and Countryside Act 1981	Section 19(1)(c).
1982 c 48	Criminal Justice Act 1982	Section 34.
1983 c 2	Representation of the People Act 1983	In section 97(3), the words from 'and' in the fifth place where it occurs to 'him' in the third place where it occurs.
		[...][721]
1983 c 20	Mental Health Act 1983	In section 135, in subsections (1) and (2), the words 'named in the warrant'.

PART II
ENACTMENTS REPEALED IN RELATION TO CRIMINAL
PROCEEDINGS IN CONSEQUENCE OF PART VII

Chapter	Short Title	Extent of Repeal
1971 c liv	Cornwall County Council Act 1971	Section 98(4).
1971 c xlvii	Hampshire County Council Act 1972	Section 86(2).

[721] Repealed by the Representation of the People Act 1985, s 28, Sch 5.

PART III

ENACTMENTS REPEALED GENERALLY IN
CONSEQUENCE OF PART VII

Chapter	Short Title	Extent of Repeal
3 & 4 Eliz 2 c 18	Army Act 1955	In section 198(1), the words 'of this section and of sections 198A and 198B of this Act'.
		Sections 198A and 198B.
3 & 4 Eliz 2 c 19	Air Force Act 1955	In section 198(1), the words 'of this section and of sections 198A and 198B of this Act'.
		Sections 198A and 198B.
1965 c 20	Criminal Evidence Act 1965	The whole Act.
1969 c 48	Post Office Act 1969	In section 93(4), the words 'the Criminal Evidence Act 1965 and'.
		In Schedule 4, paragraph 77.
1981 c 55	Armed Forces Act 1981	Section 9.
1981 c xviii	County of Kent Act 1981	Section 82.
1983 c 55	Value Added Tax Act 1983	In Schedule 7, paragraph 7(7) and (8).

PART IV

ENACTMENTS REPEALED IN RELATION TO
CRIMINAL PROCEEDINGS IN CONSEQUENCE OF PART VIII

Chapter	Short Title	Extent of Repeal
14 & 15 Vict c 99	Evidence Act 1851	Section 13.
28 & 29 Vict c 18	Criminal Procedure Act 1865	In section 6, the words from 'and a certificate' onwards.
34 & 35 Vict c 112	Prevention of Crimes Act 1871	Section 18 except the words 'A previous conviction in any one part of the United Kingdom may be proved against a prisoner in any other part of the United Kingdom'.

PART V

ENACTMENTS REPEALED GENERALLY IN
CONSEQUENCE OF PART VIII

Chapter	Short Title	Extent of Repeal
16 & 17 Vict c 83	Evidence (Amendment) Act 1853	Section 3.
46 & 47 Vict c 3	Explosive Substances Act 1883	Section 4(2).

Act

58 & 59 Vict c 24	Law of Distress Amendment Act 1895	Section 5.
61 & 62 Vict c 36	Criminal Evidence Act 1898	In section 1, the words 'and the wife or husband, as the case may be, of the person so charged', the words (in paragraph (b)) 'or of the wife or husband, as the case may be, of the person so charged' and paragraphs (c) and (d).
		Section 4.
		In section 6(1), the words from 'notwithstanding' to the end.
		The Schedule.
4 & 5 Geo 5 c 58	Criminal Justice Administration Act 1914	Section 28(3).
19 & 20 Geo 5 c 34	Infant Life (Preservation) Act 1929	Section 2(5).
23 & 24 Geo 5 c 12	Children and Young Persons Act 1933	Section 15.
		Section 26(5).
4 & 5 Eliz 2 c 69	Sexual Offences Act 1956	Section 12(2) and (3).
		Section 15(4) and (5).
		Section 16(2) and (3).
		Section 39.
		In Schedule 3, the entry relating to section 15 of the Children and Young Persons Act 1933.
8 & 9 Eliz 2 c 33	Indecency with Children Act 1960	In section 1, subsection (2) and in subsection (3) the words 'except in section 15 (which relates to the competence as a witness of the wife or husband of the accused)'.
1965 c 72	Matrimonial Causes Act 1965	Section 43(1).
1968 c 60	Theft Act 1968	Section 30(3).
1970 c 55	Family Income Supplements Act 1970	Section 12(5).
1973 c 38	Social Security Act 1973	In Schedule 23, paragraph 4.
1975 c 14	Social Security Act 1975	Section 147(6).
1975 c 16	Industrial Injuries and Diseases (Old Cases) Act 1975	Section 10(4).
1975 c 61	Child Benefit Act 1975	Section 11(8).
1976 c 71	Supplementary Benefits Act 1976	Section 26(5).

1977 c 45	Criminal Law Act 1977	In section 54(3), the words 'subsection (2) (competence of spouse of accused to give evidence)'.
1978 c 37	Protection of Children Act 1978	Section 2(1).
1979 c 18	Social Security Act 1979	Section 16.
1980 c 43	Magistrates' Courts Act 1980	In Schedule 7, paragraph 4.
1982 c 24	Social Security and Housing Benefits Act 1982	Section 21(6).

PART VI

MISCELLANEOUS REPEALS

Chapter	Short Title	Extent of Repeal
2 & 3 Vict c 47	Metropolitan Police Act 1839	Section 7.
34 & 35 Vict c 96	Pedlars Act 1871	In section 18, the words from 'or' where secondly occurring to 'Act,' and the words from 'and forthwith' to the end of the section.
1964 c 48	Police Act 1964	Section 49.
		Section 50.
1967 c 77	Police (Scotland) Act 1967	Section 5(3) and section 17(6).
1972 c 11	Superannuation Act 1972	In Schedule 1, the reference to the Police Complaints Board.
1975 c 24	House of Commons Disqualification Act 1975	In Part II of Schedule 1, the entry relating to the Police Complaints Board.
1975 c 25	Northern Ireland Assembly Disqualification Act 1975	In Part II of Schedule 1, the entry relating to the Police Complaints Board.
1976 c 46	Police Act 1976	Section 1(1) to (4).
		Sections 2 to 13.
		Section 14(2).
		In the Schedule, paragraphs 1 to 3, in paragraph 4, the words 'remuneration' and 'allowances' and paragraphs 5 to 13.

Appendix 2

Code A: PACE Code of Practice for the Exercise by Police Officers of Statutory Powers of Stop and Search; Police Officers and Police Staff of Requirements to Record Public Encounters

This code applies to any search by a police officer and the recording of public encounters taking place after midnight on 06 March 2011.

GENERAL

This code of practice must be readily available at all police stations for consultation by police officers, police staff, detained persons and members of the public.

The notes for guidance included are not provisions of this code, but are guidance to police officers and others about its application and interpretation. Provisions in the annexes to the code are provisions of this code.

This code governs the exercise by police officers of statutory powers to search a person or a vehicle without first making an arrest. The main stop and search powers to which this code applies are set out in Annex A, but that list should not be regarded as definitive. [See *Note 1*]

In addition, it covers requirements on police officers and police staff to record encounters not governed by statutory powers. This code does not apply to:

(a) the powers of stop and search under;
   (i) Aviation Security Act 1982, section 27(2);
   (ii) Police and Criminal Evidence Act 1984, section 6(1) (which relates specifically to powers of constables employed by statutory undertakers on the premises of the statutory undertakers).
(b) searches carried out for the purposes of examination under Schedule 7 to the Terrorism Act 2000 and to which the Code of Practice issued under paragraph 6 of Schedule 14 to the Terrorism Act 2000 applies.

1 PRINCIPLES GOVERNING STOP AND SEARCH

1.1 Powers to stop and search must be used fairly, responsibly, with respect for people being searched and without unlawful discrimination. The Equality Act 2010 makes it unlawful for police officers to discriminate against, harass or victimise any person on the grounds of the 'protected characteristics' of age, disability, gender reassignment, race, religion or belief, sex and sexual orientation, marriage and civil partnership, pregnancy and maternity when using their powers. When police forces are carrying out their functions they also have a duty to have regard to the need to eliminate unlawful discrimination, harassment and victimisation and to take steps to foster good relations.

1.2 The intrusion on the liberty of the person stopped or searched must be brief and detention for the purposes of a search must take place at or near the location of the stop.

1.3 If these fundamental principles are not observed the use of powers to stop and search may be drawn into question. Failure to use the powers in the proper manner reduces their effectiveness. Stop and search can play an important role in the detection and prevention of crime, and using the powers fairly makes them more effective.

1.4 The primary purpose of stop and search powers is to enable officers to allay or confirm suspicions about individuals without exercising their power of arrest. Officers may be required to justify the use or authorisation of such powers, in relation both to individual searches and the overall pattern of their activity in this regard, to their supervisory officers or in court. Any misuse of the powers is likely to be harmful to policing and lead to mistrust of the police. Officers must also be able to explain their actions to the member of the public searched. The misuse of these powers can lead to disciplinary action.

1.5 An officer must not search a person, even with his or her consent, where no power to search is applicable. Even where a person is prepared to submit to a search voluntarily, the person must not be searched unless the necessary legal power exists, and the search must be in accordance with the relevant power and the provisions of this Code. The only exception, where an officer does not require a specific power, applies to searches of persons entering sports grounds or other premises carried out with their consent given as a condition of entry.

2 EXPLANATION OF POWERS TO STOP AND SEARCH

2.1 This code applies to powers of stop and search as follows:
  (a) powers which require reasonable grounds for suspicion, before they may be exercised; that articles unlawfully obtained or possessed are being carried, or under Section 43 of the Terrorism Act 2000 that a person is a terrorist;
  (b) authorised under section 60 of the Criminal Justice and Public Order Act 1994, based upon a reasonable belief that incidents involving serious violence may take place or that people are carrying dangerous instruments or offensive weapons within any locality in the police area or that it is expedient to use the powers to find such instruments or weapons that have been used in incidents of serious violence;
  (c) authorised under section 44(1) of the Terrorism Act 2000 based upon a consideration that the exercise of the power is necessary for the prevention of acts of terrorism (see *paragraph 2.18A*), and
  (d) powers to search a person who has not been arrested in the exercise of a power to search premises (see Code B paragraph 2.4).

Searches requiring reasonable grounds for suspicion

2.2 Reasonable grounds for suspicion depend on the circumstances in each case. There must be an objective basis for that suspicion based on facts, information, and/or intelligence which are relevant to the likelihood of finding an article of a certain kind or, in the case of searches under section 43 of the Terrorism Act 2000, to the likelihood that the person is a terrorist. Reasonable suspicion can never be supported on the basis of personal factors. It must rely on intelligence or information about, or some specific behaviour by, the person concerned. For example, unless the police have a description of a suspect, a person's physical appearance (including any of the 'protected characteristics' set out in the Equality Act 2010 (see *paragraph 1.1*), or the fact that the person is known to have a previous conviction, cannot be used alone or in combination with each other, or in combination with any other factor, as the reason for searching that person. Reasonable suspicion cannot be based on generalisations or stereotypical images of certain groups or categories of people as more likely to be involved in criminal activity.

2.3 Reasonable suspicion may also exist without specific information or intelligence and on the basis of the behaviour of a person. For example, if an officer encounters someone on the street at night who is obviously trying to hide something, the officer may (depending on the other surrounding circumstances) base such suspicion on the fact that this kind of behaviour is often linked to stolen or prohibited articles being carried. Similarly, for the purposes of section 43 of the Terrorism Act 2000, suspicion that a person is a terrorist may arise from the person's behaviour at or near a location which has been identified as a potential target for terrorists.

2.4 However, reasonable suspicion should normally be linked to accurate and current intelligence or information, such as information describing an article being carried, a suspected offender, or a person who has been seen carrying a type of article known to have been stolen recently from premises in the area. Searches based on accurate and current intelligence or information are more likely to be effective. Targeting searches in a particular area at specified crime problems increases their effectiveness and minimises inconvenience to law-abiding members of the public. It also helps in justifying the use of searches both to those who are searched and to the public. This does not however prevent stop and search powers being exercised in other locations where such powers may be exercised and reasonable suspicion exists.

2.5 Searches are more likely to be effective, legitimate, and secure public confidence when reasonable suspicion is based on a range of factors. The overall use of these powers is more likely to be effective when up to date and accurate intelligence or information is communicated to officers and they are well-informed about local crime patterns.

2.6 Where there is reliable information or intelligence that members of a group or gang habitually carry knives unlawfully or weapons or controlled drugs, and wear a distinctive item of clothing or other means of identification to indicate their membership of the group or gang, that distinctive item of clothing or other means of identification may provide reasonable grounds to stop and search a person. [See *Note 9*]

2.7   A police officer may have reasonable grounds to suspect that a person is in innocent possession of a stolen or prohibited article or other item for which he or she is empowered to search. In that case the officer may stop and search the person even though there would be no power of arrest.

2.8   Under section 43(1) of the Terrorism Act 2000 a constable may stop and search a person whom the officer reasonably suspects to be a terrorist to discover whether the person is in possession of anything which may constitute evidence that the person is a terrorist. These searches may only be carried out by an officer of the same sex as the person searched (see Annex F). An authorisation under section 44(1) of the Terrorism Act 2000 allows vehicles to be stopped and searched by a constable in uniform who reasonably suspects that articles which could be used in connection with terrorism will be found in the vehicle or in anything in or on that vehicle. See paragraph 2.18A below.

2.9   An officer who has reasonable grounds for suspicion may detain the person concerned in order to carry out a search. Before carrying out a search the officer may ask questions about the person's behaviour or presence in circumstances which gave rise to the suspicion. As a result of questioning the detained person, the reasonable grounds for suspicion necessary to detain that person may be confirmed or, because of a satisfactory explanation, be eliminated. [See Notes 2 and 3] Questioning may also reveal reasonable grounds to suspect the possession of a different kind of unlawful article from that originally suspected. Reasonable grounds for suspicion however cannot be provided retrospectively by such questioning during a person's detention or by refusal to answer any questions put.

2.10 If, as a result of questioning before a search, or other circumstances which come to the attention of the officer, there cease to be reasonable grounds for suspecting that an article is being carried of a kind for which there is a power to stop and search, no search may take place. [See Note 3] In the absence of any other lawful power to detain, the person is free to leave at will and must be so informed.

2.11 There is no power to stop or detain a person in order to find grounds for a search. Police officers have many encounters with members of the public which do not involve detaining people against their will. If reasonable grounds for suspicion emerge during such an encounter, the officer may search the person, even though no grounds existed when the encounter began. If an officer is detaining someone for the purpose of a search, he or she should inform the person as soon as detention begins.

Searches authorised under section 60 of the Criminal Justice and Public Order Act 1994

2.12 Authority for a constable in uniform to stop and search under section 60 of the Criminal Justice and Public Order Act 1994 may be given if the authorising officer reasonably believes:

(a) that incidents involving serious violence may take place in any locality in the officer's police area, and it is expedient to use these powers to prevent their occurrence;

(b) that persons are carrying dangerous instruments or offensive weapons without good reason in any locality in the officer's police area or

(c) that an incident involving serious violence has taken place in the officer's police area, a dangerous instrument or offensive weapon used in the incident is being carried by a person in any locality in that police area, and it is expedient to use these powers to find that instrument or weapon.

2.13   An authorisation under section 60 may only be given by an officer of the rank of inspector or above and in writing, or orally if paragraph 2.12(c) applies and it is not practicable to give the authorisation in writing. The authorisation (whether written or oral) must specify the grounds on which it was given, the locality in which the powers may be exercised and the period of time for which they are in force. The period authorised shall be no longer than appears reasonably necessary to prevent, or seek to prevent incidents of serious violence, or to deal with the problem of carrying dangerous instruments or offensive weapons or to find a dangerous instrument or offensive weapon that has been used. It may not exceed 24 hours. An oral authorisation given where paragraph 2.12(c) applies must be recorded in writing as soon as practicable. [See Notes 10–13]

Code A

2.14   An inspector who gives an authorisation must, as soon as practicable, inform an officer of or above the rank of superintendent. This officer may direct that the authorisation shall be extended for a further 24 hours, if violence or the carrying of dangerous instruments or offensive weapons has occurred, or is suspected to have occurred, and the continued use of the powers is considered necessary to prevent or deal with further such activity or to find a dangerous instrument or offensive weapon that has been used. That direction must be given in writing unless it is not practicable to do so, in which case it must be recorded in writing as soon as practicable afterwards. [See Note 12]

2.14A The selection of persons and vehicles under section 60 to be stopped and, if appropriate, searched should reflect an objective assessment of the nature of the incident or weapon in question and the individuals and vehicles thought likely to be associated with that incident or those weapons (see Notes 10 and 11). The powers must not be used to stop and search persons and vehicles for reasons unconnected with the purpose of the authorisation. When selecting persons and vehicles to be stopped in response to a specific threat or incident, officers must take care not to discriminate unlawfully against anyone on the grounds of any of the protected characteristics set out in the Equality Act 2010 (see paragraph 1.1).

2.14B The driver of a vehicle which is stopped under section 60 and any person who is searched under section 60 are entitled to a written statement to that effect if they apply within twelve months from the day the vehicle was stopped or the person was searched. This statement is a record which states that the vehicle was stopped or (as the case may be) that the person was searched under section 60 and it may form part of the search record or be supplied as a separate record.

Powers to require removal of face coverings

2.15   Section 60AA of the Criminal Justice and Public Order Act 1994 also provides a power to demand the removal of disguises. The officer exercising the power must reasonably believe that someone is wearing an item wholly or mainly for the purpose of concealing identity. There is also a power to seize such items where the officer believes that a person intends to wear them for this purpose. There is no power to stop and search for disguises. An officer may seize any such item which is discovered when exercising a power of search for something else, or which is being carried, and which the officer reasonably believes is intended to be used for concealing anyone's identity. This power can only be used if an authorisation given under section 60 or under section 60AA is in force. [See Note 4]

2.16   Authority under section 60AA for a constable in uniform to require the removal of disguises and to seize them may be given if the authorising officer reasonably believes that activities may take place in any locality in the officer's police area that are likely to involve the commission of offences and it is expedient to use these powers to prevent or control these activities.

2.17   An authorisation under section 60AA may only be given by an officer of the rank of inspector or above, in writing, specifying the grounds on which it was given, the locality in which the powers may be exercised and the period of time for which they are in force. The period authorised shall be no longer than appears reasonably necessary to prevent, or seek to prevent the commission of offences. It may not exceed 24 hours. [See Notes 10–13]

2.18   An inspector who gives an authorisation, must, as soon as practicable, inform an officer of or above the rank of superintendent. This officer may direct that the authorisation shall be extended for a further 24 hours, if crimes have been committed, or are suspected to have been committed, and the continued use of the powers is considered necessary to prevent or deal with further such activity. This direction must also be given in writing at the time or as soon as practicable afterwards. [See *Note 12*]

Searches authorised under section 44 of the Terrorism Act 2000

2.18A The European Court of Human Rights has ruled that the stop and search powers under sections 44 to 47 of the Terrorism Act 2000 are not compatible with the right to a private life under Article 8 of the European Convention on Human Rights. Neither the European Court ruling nor the provisions of this Code can amend these statutory provisions. However, in an oral statement made by the Home Secretary in the House of Commons on 8 July 2010, interim guidelines were announced pending a review (with a view to legislative amendment) of these provisions to ensure that police do not exercise any powers under section 44 in a way which would be incompatible with Convention rights. Under these guidelines:

(i)   Authorisations under section 44(1) should be given, and may be confirmed by the Secretary of State, only:
- in relation to searches of vehicles and anything in or on vehicles, but not searches of drivers or passengers or anything being carried by a driver or passenger; and
- if such searches are considered necessary for the prevention of acts of terrorism.

Note: Section 44(3) provides that an authorising officer may give an authorisation when they consider it is 'expedient' for the prevention of acts of terrorism, but the test now to be applied is that of necessity—taking account of all of the circumstances.

(ii)   A search of a vehicle or of anything in or on a vehicle under section 44(1) should only be carried out if it is reasonably suspected that articles which could be used in connection with terrorism will be found in the vehicle or in anything in or on that vehicle.

Note: This now applies despite the provision in section 45(1)(b) which allows the power to be exercised whether or not the constable has grounds for suspecting the presence of such articles.

(iii) Authorisations to search pedestrians, drivers of vehicles and passengers in vehicles and anything carried by a driver or passenger, are not to be given under section 44(1) or (2) and if given, will not be confirmed. For these searches police must rely on the power under section 43 which requires the person who may be searched to be reasonably suspected of being a terrorist, but does not authorise the removal of headgear or footwear in public.

Code **A**

The provisions of paragraphs 2.1, 2.8, 2.19 to 2.26, 3.5, Annex A paragraphs 15 and 16 and Annex C paragraph 1 are amended by this Code to reflect these guidelines.

2.19   An officer of the rank of assistant chief constable (or equivalent) or above, may give authority under section 44(1) of the Terrorism Act 2000 for a constable in uniform to exercise the power to stop and search any vehicle and anything in or on any vehicle, in the whole or any part or parts of the authorising officer's police area. An authorisation may only be given if the officer considers it is necessary for the prevention of acts of terrorism.

2.20   If an authorisation is given orally at first, it must be confirmed in writing by the officer who gave it as soon as reasonably practicable.

2.21   When giving an authorisation, the officer must specify the geographical area in which the power may be used, and the time and date that the authorisation ends (up to a maximum of 28 days from the time the authorisation was given). [See Notes 12 and 13]

2.22   The officer giving an authorisation under section 44(1) must cause the Secretary of State to be informed, as soon as reasonably practicable, that such an authorisation has been given. An authorisation which is not confirmed by the Secretary of State within 48 hours of its having been given, shall have effect up until the end of that 48 hour period or the end of the period specified in the authorisation (whichever is the earlier). [See Note 14]

2.23   Following notification of the authorisation, the Secretary of State may:
(i)   cancel the authorisation with immediate effect or with effect from such other time as he or she may direct;
(ii)   confirm it but for a shorter period than that specified in the authorisation; or
(iii) confirm the authorisation as given.

2.24   When an authorisation under section 44(1) is given, a constable in uniform may exercise the power:
(a)   only for the purpose of stopping and searching a vehicle and anything in or on a vehicle for articles of a kind which could be used in connection with terrorism (see paragraph 2.25); and

(b) only if there are reasonable grounds for suspecting the presence of such articles. See paragraphs 2.2 to 2.11, "Searches requiring reasonable grounds for suspicion".

2.24A When a Community Support Officer on duty and in uniform has been conferred powers under Section 44(1) of the Terrorism Act 2000 by a Chief Officer of their force, the exercise of this power must comply with the requirements of this Code of Practice, including the recording requirements.

2.25 Paragraphs 2.2 to 2.11 above ("Searches requiring reasonable grounds for suspicion") are to be applied to the stopping and searching of vehicles when an authorisation under section 44(1) is given.

2.26 The powers under sections 43 and 44(1) of the Terrorism Act 2000 allow a constable to search only for articles which could be used for terrorist purposes. However, this would not prevent a search being carried out under other powers if, in the course of exercising these powers, the officer formed reasonable grounds for suspicion.

Powers to search in the exercise of a power to search premises

2.27 The following powers to search premises also authorise the search of a person, not under arrest, who is found on the premises during the course of the search:
(a) section 139B of the Criminal Justice Act 1988 under which a constable may enter school premises and search the premises and any person on those premises for any bladed or pointed article or offensive weapon;
(b) under a warrant issued under section 23(3) of the Misuse of Drugs Act 1971 to search premises for drugs or documents but only if the warrant specifically authorises the search of persons found on the premises; and
(c) under a search warrant or order issued under paragraph 1, 3 or 11 of Schedule 5 to the Terrorism Act 2000 to search premises and any person found there for material likely to be of substantial value to a terrorist investigation.

2.28 Before the power under section 139B of the Criminal Justice Act 1988 may be exercised, the constable must have reasonable grounds to believe that an offence under section 139A of the Criminal Justice Act 1988 (having a bladed or pointed article or offensive weapon on school premises) has been or is being committed. A warrant to search premises and persons found therein may be issued under section 23(3) of the Misuse of Drugs Act 1971 if there are reasonable grounds to suspect that controlled drugs or certain documents are in the possession of a person on the premises.

2.29 The powers in paragraph 2.27 do not require prior specific grounds to suspect that the person to be searched is in possession of an item for which there is an existing power to search. However, it is still necessary to ensure that the selection and treatment of those searched under these powers is based upon objective factors connected with the search of the premises, and not upon personal prejudice.

3 CONDUCT OF SEARCHES

3.1 All stops and searches must be carried out with courtesy, consideration and respect for the person concerned. This has a significant impact on public confidence in the police. Every reasonable effort must be made to minimise the embarrassment that a person being searched may experience. [See Note 4]

3.2 The co-operation of the person to be searched must be sought in every case, even if the person initially objects to the search. A forcible search may be made only if it has been established that the person is unwilling to co-operate or resists. Reasonable force may be used as a last resort if necessary to conduct a search or to detain a person or vehicle for the purposes of a search.

3.3 The length of time for which a person or vehicle may be detained must be reasonable and kept to a minimum. Where the exercise of the power requires reasonable suspicion, the thoroughness and extent of a search must depend on what is suspected of being carried, and by whom. If the suspicion relates to a particular article which is seen to be slipped into a person's pocket, then, in the absence of other grounds for suspicion or an opportunity for the article to be moved elsewhere, the search must be confined to that pocket. In the case of a small article which can readily be concealed, such as a drug, and which might be concealed anywhere on the person, a more extensive search may be necessary. In the case of searches mentioned in paragraph 2.1(b), (c), and (d), which do not require reasonable grounds for suspicion, officers may make any reasonable search to look for items for which they are empowered to search. [See Note 5]

Code **A**

3.4 The search must be carried out at or near the place where the person or vehicle was first detained. [See Note 6]

3.5 There is no power to require a person to remove any clothing in public other than an outer coat, jacket or gloves except under section 60AA of the Criminal Justice and Public Order Act 1994 (which empowers a constable to require a person to remove any item worn to conceal identity). [See Notes 4 and 6] A search in public of a person's clothing which has not been removed must be restricted to superficial examination of outer garments. This does not, however, prevent an officer from placing his or her hand inside the pockets of the outer clothing, or feeling round the inside of collars, socks and shoes if this is reasonably necessary in the circumstances to look for the object of the search or to remove and examine any item reasonably suspected to be the object of the search. For the same reasons, subject to the restrictions on the removal of headgear, a person's hair may also be searched in public (see paragraphs 3.1 and 3.3).

3.6 Where on reasonable grounds it is considered necessary to conduct a more thorough search (e.g. by requiring a person to take off a T-shirt), this must be done out of public view, for example, in a police van unless paragraph 3.7 applies, or police station if there is one nearby. [See Note 6] Any search involving the removal of more than an outer coat, jacket, gloves, headgear or footwear, or any other item concealing identity, may only be made by an officer of the same sex as the person searched and may not be made in the presence of anyone of the opposite sex unless the person being searched specifically requests it. [See Annex F and Notes 4, 7 and 8]

3.7 Searches involving exposure of intimate parts of the body must not be conducted as a routine extension of a less thorough search, simply because nothing is found in the course of the initial search. Searches involving exposure of intimate parts of the body may be carried out only at a nearby police station or other nearby location which is out of public view (but not a police vehicle). These searches must be conducted in accordance with paragraph 11 of Annex A to Code C except that an intimate search mentioned in paragraph 11(f) of Annex A to Code C may not be authorised or carried out under any stop and search powers. The other provisions of Code C do not apply to the conduct and recording of searches of persons detained at police stations in the exercise of stop and search powers. [See *Note 7*]

Steps to be taken prior to a search

3.8 Before any search of a detained person or attended vehicle takes place the officer must take reasonable steps, if not in uniform (see *paragraph 3.9*), to show their warrant card to the person to be searched or in charge of the vehicle to be searched and whether or not in uniform, to give that person the following information:

(a) that they are being detained for the purposes of a search;

(b) the officer's name (except in the case of enquiries linked to the investigation of terrorism, or otherwise where the officer reasonably believes that giving his or her name might put him or her in danger, in which case a warrant or other identification number shall be given) and the name of the police station to which the officer is attached;

(c) the legal search power which is being exercised; and

(d) a clear explanation of:

  (i)   the object of the search in terms of the article or articles for which there is a power to search; and

  (ii) in the case of:
  - the power under section 60 of the Criminal Justice and Public Order Act 1994 (see *paragraph 2.1(b)*), the nature of the power, the authorisation and the fact that it has been given;
  - the power under section 44 of the Terrorism Act 2000, the nature of the power, the authorisation and the fact that it has been given and the grounds for suspicion; (see *paragraph 2.1(c)* and *2.18A*)
  - all other powers requiring reasonable suspicion (see *paragraph 2.1(a)*), the grounds for that suspicion.

(e) that they are entitled to a copy of the record of the search if one is made (see section 4 below) if they ask within 3 months from the date of the search and:

  (i)   if they are not arrested and taken to a police station as a result of the search and it is practicable to make the record on the spot, that immediately after the search is completed they will be given, if they request, either:
  - a copy of the record, or
  - a receipt which explains how they can obtain a copy of the full record or access to an electronic copy of the record, or

  (ii) if they are arrested and taken to a police station as a result of the search, that the record will be made at the station as part of their custody record and they will be given, if they request, a copy of their custody record which includes a record of the search as soon as practicable whilst they are at the station. [See *Note 16*]

3.9 Stops and searches under the powers mentioned in paragraphs 2.1(b), and (c) may be undertaken only by a constable in uniform.

3.10 The person should also be given information about police powers to stop and search and the individual's rights in these circumstances.

3.11 If the person to be searched, or in charge of a vehicle to be searched, does not appear to understand what is being said, or there is any doubt about the person's ability to understand English, the officer must take reasonable steps to bring information regarding the person's rights and any relevant provisions of this Code to his or her attention. If the person is deaf or cannot understand English and is accompanied by someone, then the officer must try to establish whether that person can interpret or otherwise help the officer to give the required information.

Code **A**

4 RECORDING REQUIREMENTS

(a) Searches which do not result in an arrest

4.1 When an officer carries out a search in the exercise of any power to which this Code applies and the search does not result in the person searched or person in charge of the vehicle searched being arrested and taken to a police station, a record must be made of it, electronically or on paper, unless there are exceptional circumstances which make this wholly impracticable (e.g. in situations involving public disorder or when the recording officer's presence is urgently required elsewhere). If a record is to be made, the officer carrying out the search must make the record on the spot unless this is not practicable, in which case, the officer must make the record as soon as practicable after the search is completed. [See *Note 16.*]

4.2 If the record is made at the time, the person who has been searched or who is in charge of the vehicle that has been searched must be asked if they want a copy and if they do, they must be given immediately, either:
- a copy of the record, or
- a receipt which explains how they can obtain a copy of the full record or access to an electronic copy of the record

4.2A An officer is not required to provide a copy of the full record or a receipt at the time if they are called to an incident of higher priority. [See *Note 21*]

(b) Searches which result in an arrest

4.2B If a search in the exercise of any power to which this Code applies results in a person being arrested and taken to a police station, the officer carrying out the search is responsible for ensuring that a record of the search is made as part of their custody record. The custody officer must then ensure that the person is asked if they want a copy of the record and if they do, that they are given a copy as soon as practicable. [See *Note 16*].

(c) Record of search

4.3 The record of a search must always include the following information:
(a) A note of the self-defined ethnicity, and if different, the ethnicity as perceived by the officer making the search, of the person searched or of the person in charge of the vehicle searched (as the case may be); [See *Note 18*]
(b) The date, time and place the person or vehicle was searched [See *Note 6*];
(c) The object of the search in terms of the article or articles for which there is a power to search;

(d) In the case of:
   - the power under section 60 of the Criminal Justice and Public Order Act 1994 (see *paragraph 2.1(b)*), the nature of the power, the authorisation and the fact that it has been given; [See *Note 17*]
   - the power under section 44 of the Terrorism Act 2000, the nature of the power, the authorisation and the fact that it has been given and the grounds for suspicion; [see *paragraphs 2.1(c) and 2.18A and Note 17*]
   - all other powers requiring reasonable suspicion (see *paragraph 2.1(a)*), the grounds for that suspicion.

(e) subject to paragraph 3.8(b), the identity of the officer carrying out the search. [See *Note 15*]

4.3A For the purposes of completing the search record, there is no requirement to record the name, address and date of birth of the person searched or the person in charge of a vehicle which is searched and the person is under no obligation to provide this information.

4.4   Nothing in paragraph 4.3 requires the names of police officers to be shown on the search record or any other record required to be made under this code in the case of enquiries linked to the investigation of terrorism or otherwise where an officer reasonably believes that recording names might endanger the officers. In such cases the record must show the officers' warrant or other identification number and duty station.

4.5   A record is required for each person and each vehicle searched. However, if a person is in a vehicle and both are searched, and the object and grounds of the search are the same, only one record need be completed. If more than one person in a vehicle is searched, separate records for each search of a person must be made. If only a vehicle is searched, the self-defined ethnic background of the person in charge of the vehicle must be recorded, unless the vehicle is unattended.

4.6   The record of the grounds for making a search must, briefly but informatively, explain the reason for suspecting the person concerned, by reference to the person's behaviour and/or other circumstances.

4.7   Where officers detain an individual with a view to performing a search, but the need to search is eliminated as a result of questioning the person detained, a search should not be carried out and a record is not required. [See *paragraph 2.10, Notes 3* and *22A*]

4.8   After searching an unattended vehicle, or anything in or on it, an officer must leave a notice in it (or on it, if things on it have been searched without opening it) recording the fact that it has been searched.

4.9   The notice must include the name of the police station to which the officer concerned is attached and state where a copy of the record of the search may be obtained and how (if applicable) an electronic copy may be accessed and where any application for compensation should be directed.

4.10 The vehicle must if practicable be left secure.

4.10A *Not used*

4.10B *Not used*

Recording of encounters not governed by statutory powers

4.11 *Not used*

4.12   There is no national requirement for an officer who requests a person in a public place to account for themselves, i.e. their actions, behaviour, presence in an area or possession of anything, to make any record of the encounter or to give the person a receipt. [See *Notes 22A* and *22B*]

4.12A *Not used*

4.13   *Not used*

4.14   *Not used*

4.15   *Not used*

4.16   *Not used*

4.17   *Not used*

4.18   *Not used*

4.19   *Not used*

4.20   *Not used*

Code **A**

5 MONITORING AND SUPERVISING THE USE OF STOP AND SEARCH POWERS

5.1 Supervising officers must monitor the use of stop and search powers and should consider in particular whether there is any evidence that they are being exercised on the basis of stereotyped images or inappropriate generalisations. Supervising officers should satisfy themselves that the practice of officers under their supervision in stopping, searching and recording is fully in accordance with this Code. Supervisors must also examine whether the records reveal any trends or patterns which give cause for concern, and if so take appropriate action to address this.

5.2 Senior officers with area or force-wide responsibilities must also monitor the broader use of stop and search powers and, where necessary, take action at the relevant level.

5.3 Supervision and monitoring must be supported by the compilation of comprehensive statistical records of stops and searches at force, area and local level. Any apparently disproportionate use of the powers by particular officers or groups of officers or in relation to specific sections of the community should be identified and investigated.

5.4 In order to promote public confidence in the use of the powers, forces in consultation with police authorities must make arrangements for the records to be scrutinised by representatives of the community, and to explain the use of the powers at a local level. [See *Note 19*].

Notes for guidance

Officers exercising stop and search powers

1   *This code does not affect the ability of an officer to speak to or question a person in the ordinary course of the officer's duties without detaining the person or exercising any element of compulsion. It is not the purpose of the code to prohibit such encounters between the police and the community with the co-operation of the person concerned and neither does it affect the principle that all citizens have a duty to help police officers to prevent crime and discover offenders. This is a civic rather than a legal duty; but when a police officer is trying to discover whether, or by whom, an offence has been committed he or she may question any person from whom useful information might be*

obtained, subject to the restrictions imposed by Code C. A person's unwillingness to reply does not alter this entitlement, but in the absence of a power to arrest, or to detain in order to search, the person is free to leave at will and cannot be compelled to remain with the officer.

2   *In some circumstances preparatory questioning may be unnecessary, but in general a brief conversation or exchange will be desirable not only as a means of avoiding unsuccessful searches, but to explain the grounds for the stop/search, to gain co- operation and reduce any tension there might be surrounding the stop/search.*

3   *Where a person is lawfully detained for the purpose of a search, but no search in the event takes place, the detention will not thereby have been rendered unlawful.*

4   *Many people customarily cover their heads or faces for religious reasons for example, Muslim women, Sikh men, Sikh or Hindu women, or Rastafarian men or women. A police officer cannot order the removal of a head or face covering except where there is reason to believe that the item is being worn by the individual wholly or mainly for the purpose of disguising identity, not simply because it disguises identity. Where there may be religious sensitivities about ordering the removal of such an item, the officer should permit the item to be removed out of public view. Where practicable, the item should be removed in the presence of an officer of the same sex as the person and out of sight of anyone of the opposite sex [see Annex F].*

5   *A search of a person in public should be completed as soon as possible.*

6   *A person may be detained under a stop and search power at a place other than where the person was first detained, only if that place, be it a police station or elsewhere, is nearby. Such a place should be located within a reasonable travelling distance using whatever mode of travel (on foot or by car) is appropriate. This applies to all searches under stop and search powers, whether or not they involve the removal of clothing or exposure of intimate parts of the body (see paragraphs 3.6 and 3.7) or take place in or out of public view. It means, for example, that a search under the stop and search power in section 23 of the Misuse of Drugs Act 1971 which involves the compulsory removal of more than a person's outer coat, jacket or gloves cannot be carried out unless a place which is both nearby the place they were first detained and out of public view, is available. If a search involves exposure of intimate parts of the body and a police station is not nearby, particular care must be taken to ensure that the location is suitable in that it enables the search to be conducted in accordance with the requirements of paragraph 11 of Annex A to Code C.*

7   *A search in the street itself should be regarded as being in public for the purposes of paragraphs 3.6 and 3.7 above, even though it may be empty at the time a search begins. Although there is no power to require a person to do so, there is nothing to prevent an officer from asking a person voluntarily to remove more than an outer coat, jacket or gloves in public.*

8   *Not used*

9   *Other means of identification might include jewellery, insignias, tattoos or other features which are known to identify members of the particular gang or group.*

Authorising officers

10   *The powers under section 60 are separate from and additional to the normal stop and search powers which require reasonable grounds to suspect an individual of carrying an offensive weapon (or other article). Their overall purpose is to prevent serious violence and the widespread carrying of weapons which might lead to persons being seriously*

injured by disarming potential offenders or finding weapons that have been used in circumstances where other powers would not be sufficient. They should not therefore be used to replace or circumvent the normal powers for dealing with routine crime problems. A particular example might be an authorisation to prevent serious violence or the carrying of offensive weapons at a sports event by rival team supporters when the expected general appearance and age range of those likely to be responsible, alone, would not be sufficiently distinctive to support reasonable suspicion (see paragraph 2.6). The purpose of the powers under section 60AA is to prevent those involved in intimidatory or violent protests using face coverings to disguise identity.

Code **A**

11 Authorisations under section 60 require a reasonable belief on the part of the authorising officer. This must have an objective basis, for example: intelligence or relevant information such as a history of antagonism and violence between particular groups; previous incidents of violence at, or connected with, particular events or locations; a significant increase in knife-point robberies in a limited area; reports that individuals are regularly carrying weapons in a particular locality; information following an incident in which weapons were used about where the weapons might be found or in the case of section 60AA previous incidents of crimes being committed while wearing face coverings to conceal identity.

12 It is for the authorising officer to determine the period of time during which the powers mentioned in paragraph 2.1 (b) and (c) may be exercised. The officer should set the mini-mum period he or she considers necessary to deal with the risk of violence, the carrying of knives or offensive weapons, or terrorism or to find dangerous instruments or weapons that have been used. A direction to extend the period authorised under the powers mentioned in paragraph 2.1(b) may be given only once. Thereafter further use of the powers requires a new authorisation. There is no provision to extend an authorisation of the powers mentioned in paragraph 2.1(c); further use of the powers requires a new authorisation.

13 It is for the authorising officer to determine the geographical area in which the use of the powers is to be authorised. In doing so the officer may wish to take into account factors such as the nature and venue of the anticipated incident or the incident which has taken place, the number of people who may be in the immediate area of that incident, their access to surrounding areas and the anticipated or actual level of violence. The officer should not set a geographical area which is wider than that he or she believes necessary for the purpose of preventing anticipated violence, the carrying of knives or offensive weapons, acts of terrorism, finding a dangerous instrument or weapon that has been used or, in the case of section 60AA, the prevention of commission of offences. It is particularly important to ensure that constables exercising such powers are fully aware of where they may be used. If the area specified is smaller than the whole force area, the officer giving the authorisation should specify either the streets which form the boundary of the area or a divisional boundary within the force area. If the power is to be used in response to a threat or incident that straddles police force areas, an officer from each of the forces concerned will need to give an authorisation.

14 An officer who has authorised the use of powers under section 44(1) of the Terrorism Act 2000 must take immediate steps to send a copy of the authorisation to the National Joint Unit, Metropolitan Police Special Branch, who will forward it to the Secretary of State. The Secretary of State should be informed of the reasons for the authorisation. The National Joint Unit will inform the force concerned, within 48 hours of the autho-

risation being made, whether the Secretary of State has confirmed or cancelled or altered the authorisation. See paragraph 2.18A.

Recording

15 *Where a stop and search is conducted by more than one officer the identity of all the officers engaged in the search must be recorded on the record. Nothing prevents an officer who is present but not directly involved in searching from completing the record during the course of the encounter.*

16 *When the search results in the person searched or in charge of a vehicle which is searched being arrested, the requirement to make the record of the search as part of the person's custody record does not apply if the person is granted "street bail" after arrest (see section 30A of PACE) to attend a police station and is not taken in custody to the police station. An arrested person's entitlement to a copy of the search record which is made as part of their custody record does not affect their entitlement to a copy of their custody record or any other provisions of PACE Code C section 2 (Custody records).*

17 *It is important for monitoring purposes to specify whether the authority for exercising a stop and search power was given under section 60 of the Criminal Justice and Public Order Act 1994, or under section 44(1) of the Terrorism Act 2000.*

18 *Officers should record the self-defined ethnicity of every person stopped according to the categories used in the 2001 census question listed in Annex B. The person should be asked to select one of the five main categories representing broad ethnic groups and then a more specific cultural background from within this group. The ethnic classification should be coded for recording purposes using the coding system in Annex B. An additional "Not stated" box is available but should not be offered to respondents explicitly. Officers should be aware and explain to members of the public, especially where concerns are raised, that this information is required to obtain a true picture of stop and search activity and to help improve ethnic monitoring, tackle discriminatory practice, and promote effective use of the powers. If the person gives what appears to the officer to be an "incorrect" answer (e.g. a person who appears to be white states that they are black), the officer should record the response that has been given and then record their own perception of the person's ethnic background by using the PNC classification system. If the "Not stated" category is used the reason for this must be recorded on the form.*

19 *Arrangements for public scrutiny of records should take account of the right to confidentiality of those stopped and searched. Anonymised forms and/or statistics generated from records should be the focus of the examinations by members of the public.*

20 *Not used*

21 *In situations where it is not practicable to provide a written copy of the record or immediate access to an electronic copy of the record or a receipt of the search at the time (see paragraph 4.2A above), the officer should consider giving the person details of the station which they may attend for a copy of the record. A receipt may take the form of a simple business card which includes sufficient information to locate the record should the person ask for copy, for example, the date and place of the search, a reference number or the name of the officer who carried out the search (unless paragraph 4.4 applies).*

22 *Not used*

22A *Where there are concerns which make it necessary to monitor any local dispropor-*
tionality, forces have discretion to direct officers to record the self-defined ethnicity of
persons they request to account for themselves in a public place or who they detain
with a view to searching but do not search. Guidance should be provided locally and
efforts made to minimise the bureaucracy involved. Records should be closely moni-
tored and supervised in line with paragraphs 5.1 to 5.4 and forces can suspend or re-
instate recording of these encounters as appropriate.

22B *A person who is asked to account for themselves should, if they request, be given infor-*
mation about how they can report their dissatisfaction about how they have been
treated.

Code **A**

Definition of Offensive Weapon

23 *'Offensive weapon' is defined as any article made or adapted for use for causing injury*
to the person, or intended by the person having it with him for such use or by someone
else. There are three categories of offensive weapons: those made for causing injury to
the person; those adapted for such a purpose; and those not so made or adapted, but
carried with the intention of causing injury to the person. A firearm, as defined by sec-
tion 57 of the Firearms Act 1968, would fall within the definition of offensive weapon
if any of the criteria above apply.

24 *Not used*

25 *Not used*

Annex A—Summary of Main Stop and Search Powers

This table relates to stop and search powers only. Individual statutes below may contain other police powers of entry, search and seizure

Power	Object of search	Extent of search	Where exercisable
Unlawful articles general			
1. Public Stores Act 1875, s6	HM Stores stolen or unlawfully obtained	Persons, vehicles and vessels	Anywhere where the constabulary powers are exercisable
2. Firearms Act 1968, s47	Firearms	Persons and vehicles	A public place, or anywhere in the case of reasonable suspicion of offences of carrying firearms with criminal intent or trespassing with firearms
3. Misuse of Drugs Act 1971, s23	Controlled drugs	Persons and vehicles	Anywhere
4. Customs and Excise Management Act 1979, s163	Goods: (a) on which duty has not been paid; (b) being unlawfully removed, imported or exported; (c) otherwise liable to forfeiture to HM Customs and Excise	Vehicles and vessels only	Anywhere

Power	Object of search	Extent of search	Where exercisable
5. Aviation Security Act 1982, s27(1)	Stolen or unlawfully obtained goods	Airport employees and vehicles carrying airport employees or aircraft or any vehicle in a cargo area whether or not carrying an employee	Any designated airport
6. Police and Criminal Evidence Act 1984, s1	Stolen goods; articles for use in certain Theft Act offences; offensive weapons, including bladed or sharply-pointed articles (except folding pocket knives with a bladed cutting edge not exceeding 3 inches); prohibited possession of a category 4 (display grade) firework, any person under 18 in possession of an adult firework in a public place.	Persons and vehicles	Where there is public access
	Criminal Damage: Articles made, adapted or intended for use in destroying or damaging property	Persons and vehicles	Where there is public access
7. Sporting events (Control of Alcohol etc.) Act 1985, s7	Intoxicating liquor	Persons, coaches and trains	Designated sports grounds or coaches and trains travelling to or from a designated sporting event
8. Crossbows Act 1987, s4	Crossbows or parts of crossbows (except crossbows with a draw weight of less than 1.4 kilograms)	Persons and vehicles	Anywhere except dwellings
9. Criminal Justice Act 1988 s139B	Offensive weapons, bladed or sharply pointed article	Persons	School premises
Evidence of game and wildlife offences			
10. Poaching Prevention Act 1862, s2	Game or poaching equipment	Persons and vehicles	A public place
11. Deer Act 1991, s12	Evidence of offences under the Act	Persons and vehicles	Anywhere except dwellings
12. Conservation of Seals Act 1970, s4	Seals or hunting equipment	Vehicles only	Anywhere

Power	Object of search	Extent of search	Where exercisable
13. Badgers Act 1992, s11	Evidence of offences under the Act	Persons and vehicles	Anywhere
14. Wildlife and Countryside Act 1981, s19	Evidence of wildlife offences	Persons and vehicles	Anywhere except dwellings
Other			
15. Terrorism Act 2000, s43(1)	Anything which may constitute evidence that the person is a terrorist	Persons	Anywhere
16. Terrorism Act 2000, s44(1)	Articles of a kind which could be used in connection with terrorism	Vehicles, and anything in or on vehicles (See paragraph 2.18A)	Anywhere within the area or locality authorised under subsection (1)
17. Not used			
18. Paragraphs 7 and 8 of Schedule 7 to the Terrorism Act 2000	Anything relevant to determining if a person being examined falls within section 40(1)(b)	Persons, vehicles, vessels etc. (Note: These searches are subject to the Code of Practice issued under paragraph 6 of Schedule 14 to the Terrorism Act 2000)	*Ports and airports*
19. Section 60 Criminal Justice and Public Order Act 1994	Offensive weapons or dangerous instruments to prevent incidents of serious violence *or to deal with the carrying of such items or find such items which have been used in incidents of serious violence*	Persons and vehicles	Anywhere within a locality authorised under subsection (1)

Code **A**

Annex B—Self-Defined Ethnic Classification Categories

White	*W*
A. White—British	W1
B. White—Irish	W2
C. Any other White background	W9
Mixed	**M**
D. White and Black Caribbean	M1
E. White and Black African	M2
F. White and Asian	M3
G. Any other Mixed Background	M9
Asian/Asian—British	***A***
H. Asian—Indian	A1
I. Asian—Pakistani	A2
J. Asian—Bangladeshi	A3
K. Any other Asian background	A9
Black/Black—British	***B***

L. Black—Caribbean	B1
M. Black African	B2
N. Any other Black background	B9
Other	**O**
O. Chinese	O1
P. Any other	O9
Not Stated	**NS**

Annex C—Summary of Powers of Community Support Officers to Search and Seize

The following is a summary of the search and seizure powers that may be exercised by a community support officer (CSO) who has been designated with the relevant powers in accordance with Part 4 of the Police Reform Act 2002.

When exercising any of these powers, a CSO must have regard to any relevant provisions of this Code, including section 3 governing the conduct of searches and the steps to be taken prior to a search.

1. Powers to stop and search not requiring consent

Designation	Power conferred	Object of Search	Extent of Search	Where Exercisable
Police Reform Act 2002, Schedule 4, paragraph 15	Terrorism Act 2000, s.44(1)(a) and (d) and 45(2) *(See paragraph 2.18A)*	Items intended to be used in connection with terrorism.	(a) Vehicles or anything carried in or on the vehicle	Anywhere within area of locality authorised and in the company and under the supervision of a constable.

2. Powers to search requiring the consent of the person and seizure

A CSO may detain a person using reasonable force where necessary as set out in Part 1 of Schedule 4 to the Police Reform Act 2002. If the person has been lawfully detained, the CSO may search the person provided that person gives consent to such a search in relation to the following:

Designation	Powers conferred	Object of Search	Extent of Search	Where Exercisable
Police Reform Act 2002, Schedule 4, paragraph 7A	(a) Criminal Justice and Police Act 2001, s12(2)	(a) Alcohol or a container for alcohol	(a) Persons	(a) Designated public place
	(b) Confiscation of Alcohol (Young Persons) Act 1997, s1	(b) Alcohol	(b) Persons under 18 years old	(b) Public place
	(c) Children and Young Persons Act 1933, section 7(3)	(c) Tobacco or cigarette papers	(c) Persons under 16 years old found smoking	(c) Public place

3 Powers to search not requiring the consent of the person and seizure

A CSO may detain a person using reasonable force where necessary as set out in Part 1 of Schedule 4 to the Police Reform Act 2002. If the person has been lawfully detained, the CSO may search the person without the need for that person's consent in relation to the following:

Designation	Power conferred	Object of Search	Extent of Search	Where Exercisable
Police Reform Act 2002, Schedule 4, paragraph 2A	Police and Criminal Evidence Act 1984, s.32	(a) Objects that might be used to cause physical injury to the person or the CSO.	Persons made subject to a requirement to wait.	Any place where the requirement to wait has been made.
		(b) Items that might be used to assist escape.		

Code A

4 Powers to seize without consent

This power applies when drugs are found in the course of any search mentioned above.

Designation	Power conferred	Object of Seizure	Where Exercisable
Police Reform Act 2002, Schedule 4, paragraph 7B	*Police Reform Act 2002, Schedule 4, paragraph 7B*	Controlled drugs in a person's possession.	Any place where the person is in possession of the drug.

ANNEX D—DELETED

ANNEX E—DELETED

ANNEX F—ESTABLISHING GENDER OF PERSONS FOR
THE PURPOSE OF SEARCHING

1. Certain provisions of this and other Codes explicitly state that searches and other procedures may only be carried out by, or in the presence of, persons of the same sex as the person subject to the search or other procedure. (See *paragraphs 2.8 and 3.6 and Note 4 of this Code, Code C paragraph 4.1 and Annex A paragraphs 5, 6, 11 and 12 (searches, strip and intimate searches of detainees under sections 54 and 55 of PACE), Code D paragraph 5.5 and Note 5F (searches, examinations and photographing of detainees under section 54A of PACE) and 6.9 (taking samples) and Code H paragraph 4.1 and Annex A paragraphs 6, 7 and 12 (searches, strip and intimate searches under sections 54 and 55 of PACE and 43(2) of the Terrorism Act of persons arrested under section 41 of the Terrorism Act 2000)*.

2. All searches should be carried out with courtesy, consideration and respect for the person concerned. Police officers should show particular sensitivity when dealing with transsexual or transvestite persons (see *Notes F1* and *F2*). The following approach is designed to minimise embarrassment and secure the co-operation of the person subject to the search.

409

(a) Consideration

3. At law, the gender of an individual is their gender as registered at birth unless they possess a gender recognition certificate as issued under section 9 of the Gender Recognition Act 2004, in which case the person's gender is the acquired gender.

    (a) If there is no doubt as to the sex of a person, or there is no reason to suspect that the person is not the sex that they appear to be, they should be dealt with as that sex.

    (b) A person who possesses a gender recognition certificate must be treated as their acquired gender.

    (c) If the police are not satisfied that the person possesses a gender recognition certificate and there is doubt as to a person's gender, the person should be asked what gender they consider themselves to be. If the person expresses a preference to be dealt with as a particular gender, they should be asked to sign the search record, the officer's notebook or, if applicable, their custody record, to indicate and confirm their preference. If appropriate, the person should be treated as being that gender.

    (d) If a person is unwilling to make such an election, efforts should be made to determine the predominant lifestyle of the person. For example, if they appear to live predominantly as a woman, they should be treated as such.

    (e) If there is still doubt, the person should be dealt with according to the sex that they were born.

5. Once a decision has been made about which gender an individual is to be treated as, where possible before an officer searches that person, the officer should be advised of the doubt as to the person's gender. This is important so as to maintain the dignity of the officer(s) concerned.

(b) Documentation

6. Where the gender of the detainee is established under *paragraphs 2(b)* to *(e)* above the decision should be recorded either on the search record, in the officer's notebook or, if applicable, in the person's custody record.

7. Where the person elects which gender they consider themselves to be under *paragraph 2(c)* but is not treated as their elected gender, the reason must be recorded in the search record, in the officer's notebook or, if applicable, in the person's custody record.

Note for Guidance

F1   Transsexual means a person who is proposing to undergo, is undergoing or has undergone a process (or part of a process) for the purpose of gender reassignment which is a protected characteristic under the Equality Act 2010 (see paragraph 1.1) by changing physiological or other attributes of their sex. It would apply to a woman making the transition to being a man and a man making the transition to being a woman as well as to a person who has only just started out on the process of gender reassignment and to a person who has completed the process. Both would share the characteristic of gender reassignment with each having the characteristics of one sex, but with certain characteristics of the other sex.

F2   Transvestite means a person of one gender who dresses in the clothes of a person of the opposite gender.

F3   Similar principles will apply to police officers and police staff whose duties involve carrying out, or being present at, any of the searches and other procedures mentioned in paragraph 1. Chief officers are responsible for providing corresponding operational guidance and instructions for the deployment of any transsexual officers and staff under their direction and control.

Code **A**

Appendix 3
Code B: PACE Code of Practice for Searches of Premises by Police Officers and the Seizure of Property Found by Police Officers on Persons or Premises

This code applies to applications for warrants made after midnight on 06 March 2011 and to searches and seizures taking place after midnight on 06 March 2011.

1 INTRODUCTION

1.1   This Code of Practice deals with police powers to:
- search premises
- seize and retain property found on premises and persons

1.1A These powers may be used to find:
- property and material relating to a crime
- wanted persons
- children who abscond from local authority accommodation where they have been remanded or committed by a court

1.2   A justice of the peace may issue a search warrant granting powers of entry, search and seizure, e.g. warrants to search for stolen property, drugs, firearms and evidence of serious offences. Police also have powers without a search warrant. The main ones provided by the Police and Criminal Evidence Act 1984 (PACE) include powers to search premises:
- to make an arrest
- after an arrest

1.3   The right to privacy and respect for personal property are key principles of the Human Rights Act 1998. Powers of entry, search and seizure should be fully and clearly justified before use because they may significantly interfere with the occupier's privacy. Officers should consider if the necessary objectives can be met by less intrusive means.

1.3A Powers to search and seize must be used fairly, responsibly, with respect for people who occupy premises being searched or are in charge of property being seized and without unlawful discrimination. The Equality Act 2010 makes it unlawful for police officers to discriminate against, harass or victimise any person on the grounds of the 'protected characteristics' of age, disability, gender reassignment, race, religion or belief, sex and sexual orientation, marriage and civil partnership, pregnancy and maternity when using their powers. When police forces are carrying out their functions they also have a duty to have regard to the need to eliminate unlawful discrimination, harassment and victimisation and to take steps to foster good relations.

1.4   In all cases, police should therefore:
  - exercise their powers courteously and with respect for persons and property
  - only use reasonable force when this is considered necessary and proportionate to the circumstances

1.5   If the provisions of PACE and this Code are not observed, evidence obtained from a search may be open to question.

2 GENERAL

2.1 This Code must be readily available at all police stations for consultation by:
  - police officers
  - police staff
  - detained persons
  - members of the public

2.2 The *Notes for Guidance* included are not provisions of this Code.

2.3 This Code applies to searches of premises:
  (a) by police for the purposes of an investigation into an alleged offence, with the occupier's consent, other than:
    - routine scene of crime searches;
    - calls to a fire or burglary made by or on behalf of an occupier or searches following the activation of fire or burglar alarms or discovery of insecure premises;
    - searches when *paragraph 5.4* applies;
    - bomb threat calls;
  (b) under powers conferred on police officers by PACE, sections 17, 18 and 32;
  (c) undertaken in pursuance of search warrants issued to and executed by constables in accordance with PACE, sections 15 and 16. See *Note 2A*;
  (d) subject to *paragraph 2.6*, under any other power given to police to enter premises with or without a search warrant for any purpose connected with the investigation into an alleged or suspected offence. See *Note 2B*.

For the purposes of this Code, 'premises' as defined in PACE, section 23, includes any place, vehicle, vessel, aircraft, hovercraft, tent or movable structure and any offshore installation as defined in the Mineral Workings (Offshore Installations) Act 1971, section 1. See *Note 2D*

2.4 A person who has not been arrested but is searched during a search of premises should be searched in accordance with Code A. See *Note 2C*

2.5 This Code does not apply to the exercise of a statutory power to enter premises or to inspect goods, equipment or procedures if the exercise of that power is not dependent on the existence of grounds for suspecting that an offence may have been committed and the person exercising the power has no reasonable grounds for such suspicion.

2.6 This Code does not affect any directions or requirements of a search warrant, order or other power to search and seize lawfully exercised in England or Wales that any item or evidence seized under that warrant, order or power be handed over to a police force, court, tribunal, or other authority outside England or Wales. For example, warrants and orders issued in Scotland or Northern Ireland, see *Note 2B(f)* and search warrants and powers provided for in sections 14 to 17 of the Crime (International Co-operation) Act 2003.

Code **B**

2.7   When this Code requires the prior authority or agreement of an officer of at
      least inspector or superintendent rank, that authority may be given by a ser-
      geant or chief inspector authorised to perform the functions of the higher rank
      under PACE, section 107.
2.8   Written records required under this Code not made in the search record shall,
      unless otherwise specified, be made:
      • in the recording officer's pocket book ('pocket book' includes any official
        report book issued to police officers) or
      • on forms provided for the purpose
2.9   Nothing in this Code requires the identity of officers, or anyone accompanying
      them during a search of premises, to be recorded or disclosed:
      (a) in the case of enquiries linked to the investigation of terrorism; or
      (b) if officers reasonably believe recording or disclosing their names might put
          them in danger.
      In these cases officers should use warrant or other identification numbers and
      the name of their police station. Police staff should use any identification
      number provided to them by the police force. See *Note 2E*
2.10 The 'officer in charge of the search' means the officer assigned specific duties
      and responsibilities under this Code. Whenever there is a search of premises to
      which this Code applies one officer must act as the officer in charge of the
      search. See *Note 2F*
2.11 In this Code:
      (a) 'designated person' means a person other than a police officer, designated
          under the Police Reform Act 2002, Part 4 who has specified powers and
          duties of police officers conferred or imposed on them. See *Note 2G*
      (b) any reference to a police officer includes a designated person acting in the
          exercise or performance of the powers and duties conferred or imposed on
          them by their designation.
      (c) a person authorised to accompany police officers or designated persons in
          the execution of a warrant has the same powers as a constable in the execu-
          tion of the warrant and the search and seizure of anything related to the
          warrant. These powers must be exercised in the company and under the
          supervision of a police officer. See *Note 3C*.
2.12 If a power conferred on a designated person:
      (a) allows reasonable force to be used when exercised by a police officer, a des-
          ignated person exercising that power has the same entitlement to use force;
      (b) includes power to use force to enter any premises, that power is not exercis-
          able by that designated person except:
          (i) in the company and under the supervision of a police officer; or
          (ii) for the purpose of:
              • saving life or limb; or
              • preventing serious damage to property.
2.13 Designated persons must have regard to any relevant provisions of the Codes of
      Practice.

Notes for guidance

*2A   PACE sections 15 and 16 apply to all search warrants issued to and executed by con-
      stables under any enactment, e.g. search warrants issued by a:*

    (a) *justice of the peace under the:*
- *Theft Act 1968, section 26—stolen property;*
- *Misuse of Drugs Act 1971, section 23—controlled drugs;*
- *PACE, section 8—evidence of an indictable offence;*
- *Terrorism Act 2000, Schedule 5, paragraph 1;*
- *Prevention of Terrorism Act 2005, section 7C – monitoring compliance with control order (see paragraph 10.1).*

    (b) *Circuit judge under:*
- *PACE, Schedule 1;*
- *Terrorism Act 2000, Schedule 5, paragraph 11.*

2B *Examples of the other powers in paragraph 2.3(d) include:*

    (a) *Road Traffic Act 1988, section 6E(1) giving police power to enter premises under section 6E(1) to:*
- *require a person to provide a specimen of breath; or*
- *arrest a person following*
  - *— a positive breath test;*
  - *— failure to provide a specimen of breath;*

    (b) *Transport and Works Act 1992, section 30(4) giving police powers to enter premises mirroring the powers in (a) in relation to specified persons working on transport systems to which the Act applies;*

    (c) *Criminal Justice Act 1988, section 139B giving police power to enter and search school premises for offensive weapons, bladed or pointed articles;*

    (d) *Terrorism Act 2000, Schedule 5, paragraphs 3 and 15 empowering a superintendent in urgent cases to give written authority for police to enter and search premises for the purposes of a terrorist investigation;*

    (e) *Explosives Act 1875, section 73(b) empowering a superintendent to give written authority for police to enter premises, examine and search them for explosives;*

    (f) *search warrants and production orders or the equivalent issued in Scotland or Northern Ireland endorsed under the Summary Jurisdiction (Process) Act 1881 or the Petty Sessions (Ireland) Act 1851 respectively for execution in England and Wales.*

    (g) *Sections 7A and 7B of the Prevention of Terrorism Act 2005, searches connected with the enforcement of control orders (see paragraph 10.1).*

2C *The Criminal Justice Act 1988, section 139B provides that a constable who has reasonable grounds to believe an offence under the Criminal Justice Act 1988, section 139A has or is being committed may enter school premises and search the premises and any persons on the premises for any bladed or pointed article or offensive weapon. Persons may be searched under a warrant issued under the Misuse of Drugs Act 1971, section 23(3) to search premises for drugs or documents only if the warrant specifically authorises the search of persons on the premises. Powers to search premises under certain terrorism provisions also authorise the search of persons on the premises, for example, under paragraphs 1, 2, 11 and 15 of Schedule 5 to the Terrorism Act 2000 and section 52 of the Anti-terrorism, Crime and Security Act 2001.*

2D *The Immigration Act 1971, Part III and Schedule 2 gives immigration officers powers to enter and search premises, seize and retain property, with and without a search warrant. These are similar to the powers available to police under search warrants issued by a justice of the peace and without a warrant under PACE, sections 17, 18, 19 and*

Code B

32 except they only apply to specified offences under the Immigration Act 1971 and immigration control powers. For certain types of investigations and enquiries these powers avoid the need for the Immigration Service to rely on police officers becoming directly involved. When exercising these powers, immigration officers are required by the Immigration and Asylum Act 1999, section 145 to have regard to this Code's corresponding provisions. When immigration officers are dealing with persons or property at police stations, police officers should give appropriate assistance to help them discharge their specific duties and responsibilities.

2E   *The purpose of paragraph 2.9(b) is to protect those involved in serious organised crime investigations or arrests of particularly violent suspects when there is reliable information that those arrested or their associates may threaten or cause harm to the officers or anyone accompanying them during a search of premises. In cases of doubt, an officer of inspector rank or above should be consulted.*

2F   *For the purposes of paragraph 2.10, the officer in charge of the search should normally be the most senior officer present. Some exceptions are:*

     (a) a supervising officer who attends or assists at the scene of a premises search may appoint an officer of lower rank as officer in charge of the search if that officer is:
- *more conversant with the facts;*
- *a more appropriate officer to be in charge of the search;*

     (b) when all officers in a premises search are the same rank. The supervising officer if available must make sure one of them is appointed officer in charge of the search, otherwise the officers themselves must nominate one of their number as the officer in charge;

     (c) a senior officer assisting in a specialist role. This officer need not be regarded as having a general supervisory role over the conduct of the search or be appointed or expected to act as the officer in charge of the search.

   Except in (c), nothing in this Note diminishes the role and responsibilities of a supervisory officer who is present at the search or knows of a search taking place.

2G   *An officer of the rank of inspector or above may direct a designated investigating officer not to wear a uniform for the purposes of a specific operation.*

3 Search Warrants and Production Orders

(a) Before making an application

3.1 When information appears to justify an application, the officer must take reasonable steps to check the information is accurate, recent and not provided maliciously or irresponsibly. An application may not be made on the basis of information from an anonymous source if corroboration has not been sought. See *Note 3A*

3.2 The officer shall ascertain as specifically as possible the nature of the articles concerned and their location.

3.3 The officer shall make reasonable enquiries to:

     (i) establish if:
- anything is known about the likely occupier of the premises and the nature of the premises themselves;
- the premises have been searched previously and how recently;

     (ii) obtain any other relevant information.

3.4 An application:
  (a) to a justice of the peace for a search warrant or to a Circuit judge for a search warrant or production order under PACE, Schedule 1 must be supported by a signed written authority from an officer of inspector rank or above:
  Note: If the case is an urgent application to a justice of the peace and an inspector or above is not readily available, the next most senior officer on duty can give the written authority.
  (b) to a circuit judge under the Terrorism Act 2000, Schedule 5 for
    • a production order;
    • search warrant; or
    • an order requiring an explanation of material seized or produced under such a warrant or production order
    • must be supported by a signed written authority from an officer of super-intendent rank or above.

3.5 Except in a case of urgency, if there is reason to believe a search might have an adverse effect on relations between the police and the community, the officer in charge shall consult the local police/community liaison officer:
  • before the search; or
  • in urgent cases, as soon as practicable after the search

(b) Making an application

3.6 A search warrant application must be supported in writing, specifying:
  (a) the enactment under which the application is made, see *Note 2A*;
  (b) (i) whether the warrant is to authorise entry and search of:
      • one set of premises; or
      • if the application is under PACE section 8, or Schedule 1, paragraph 12, more than one set of specified premises or all premises occupied or controlled by a specified person, and
    (ii) the premises to be searched;
  (c) the object of the search, see *Note 3B*;
  (d) the grounds for the application, including, when the purpose of the proposed search is to find evidence of an alleged offence, an indication of how the evidence relates to the investigation;
  (da) Where the application is under PACE section 8, or Schedule 1, paragraph 12 for a single warrant to enter and search:
    (i) more than one set of specified premises, the officer must specify each set of premises which it is desired to enter and search
    (ii) all premises occupied or controlled by a specified person, the officer must specify;
      • as many sets of premises which it is desired to enter and search as it is reasonably practicable to specify
      • the person who is in occupation or control of those premises and any others which it is desired to search
      • why it is necessary to search more premises than those which can be specified
      • why it is not reasonably practicable to specify all the premises which it is desired to enter and search

Code **B**

(db) Whether an application under PACE section 8 is for a warrant authorising entry and search on more than one occasion, and if so, the officer must state the grounds for this and whether the desired number of entries authorised is unlimited or a specified maximum.

(e) there are no reasonable grounds to believe the material to be sought, when making application to a:

(i) justice of the peace or a Circuit judge consists of or includes items subject to legal privilege;

(ii) justice of the peace, consists of or includes excluded material or special procedure material;

Note: this does not affect the additional powers of seizure in the Criminal Justice and Police Act 2001, Part 2 covered in *paragraph 7.7*, see *Note 3B*;

(f) if applicable, a request for the warrant to authorise a person or persons to accompany the officer who executes the warrant, see *Note 3C*.

3.7 A search warrant application under PACE, Schedule 1, paragraph 12(a), shall if appropriate indicate why it is believed service of notice of an application for a production order may seriously prejudice the investigation. Applications for search warrants under the Terrorism Act 2000, Schedule 5, paragraph 11 must indicate why a production order would not be appropriate.

3.8 If a search warrant application is refused, a further application may not be made for those premises unless supported by additional grounds.

Notes for guidance

3A The identity of an informant need not be disclosed when making an application, but the officer should be prepared to answer any questions the magistrate or judge may have about:

- *the accuracy of previous information from that source*
- *any other related matters*

3B The information supporting a search warrant application should be as specific as possible, particularly in relation to the articles or persons being sought and where in the premises it is suspected they may be found. The meaning of 'items subject to legal privilege', 'excluded material' and 'special procedure material' are defined by PACE, sections 10, 11 and 14 respectively.

3C Under PACE, section 16(2), a search warrant may authorise persons other than police officers to accompany the constable who executes the warrant. This includes, e.g. any suitably qualified or skilled person or an expert in a particular field whose presence is needed to help accurately identify the material sought or to advise where certain evidence is most likely to be found and how it should be dealt with. It does not give them any right to force entry, but it gives them the right to be on the premises during the search and to search for or seize property without the occupier's permission.

4 ENTRY WITHOUT WARRANT—PARTICULAR POWERS

(a) Making an arrest etc

4.1 The conditions under which an officer may enter and search premises without a warrant are set out in PACE, section 17. It should be noted that this section does not create or confer any powers of arrest. See other powers in *Note 2B(a)*.

(b) Search of premises where arrest takes place or the arrested person was immediately before arrest

4.2 When a person has been arrested for an indictable offence, a police officer has power under PACE, section 32 to search the premises where the person was arrested or where the person was immediately before being arrested.

(c) Search of premises occupied or controlled by the arrested person

4.3 The specific powers to search premises which <u>are</u> occupied or controlled by a person arrested for an indictable offence are set out in PACE, section 18. They may not be exercised, except if section 18(5) applies, unless an officer of inspector rank or above has given written authority. That authority should only be given when the authorising officer is satisfied that the premises <u>are</u> occupied or controlled by the arrested person and that the necessary grounds exist. If possible the authorising officer should record the authority on the Notice of Powers and Rights and, subject to *paragraph 2.9*, sign the Notice. The record of the grounds for the search and the nature of the evidence sought as required by section 18(7) of the Act should be made in:
- the custody record if there is one, otherwise
- the officer's pocket book, or
- the search record

Code **B**

5 SEARCH WITH CONSENT

5.1 Subject to *paragraph 5.4*, if it is proposed to search premises with the consent of a person entitled to grant entry the consent must, if practicable, be given in writing on the Notice of Powers and Rights before the search. The officer must make any necessary enquiries to be satisfied the person is in a position to give such consent. See *Notes 5A* and *5B*

5.2 Before seeking consent the officer in charge of the search shall state the purpose of the proposed search and its extent. This information must be as specific as possible, particularly regarding the articles or persons being sought and the parts of the premises to be searched. The person concerned must be clearly informed they are not obliged to consent, that any consent given can be withdrawn at any time, including before the search starts or while it is underway and anything seized may be produced in evidence. If at the time the person is not suspected of an offence, the officer shall say this when stating the purpose of the search.

5.3 An officer cannot enter and search or continue to search premises under *paragraph 5.1* if consent is given under duress or withdrawn before the search is completed.

5.4 It is unnecessary to seek consent under *paragraphs 5.1* and *5.2* if this would cause disproportionate inconvenience to the person concerned. See *Note 5C*

Notes for guidance

5A In a lodging house, hostel or similar accommodation, every reasonable effort should be made to obtain the consent of the tenant, lodger or occupier. A search should not be made solely on the basis of the landlord's consent.

5B If the intention is to search premises under the authority of a warrant or a power of entry and search without warrant, and the occupier of the premises co-operates in accordance with paragraph 6.4, there is no need to obtain written consent.

419

5C Paragraph 5.4 is intended to apply when it is reasonable to assume innocent occupiers would agree to, and expect, police to take the proposed action, e.g. if:

- *a suspect has fled the scene of a crime or to evade arrest and it is necessary quickly to check surrounding gardens and readily accessible places to see if the suspect is hiding*
- *police have arrested someone in the night after a pursuit and it is necessary to make a brief check of gardens along the pursuit route to see if stolen or incriminating articles have been discarded*

6 Searching premises—general considerations

(a) Time of searches

6.1   Searches made under warrant must be made within three calendar months of the date of the warrant's issue.

6.2   Searches must be made at a reasonable hour unless this might frustrate the purpose of the search.

6.3   When the extent or complexity of a search mean it is likely to take a long time, the officer in charge of the search may consider using the seize and sift powers referred to in *section 7*.

6.3A A warrant under PACE, section 8 may authorise entry to and search of premises on more than one occasion if, on the application, the justice of the peace is satisfied that it is necessary to authorise multiple entries in order to achieve the purpose for which the warrant is issued. No premises may be entered or searched on any subsequent occasions without the prior written authority of an officer of the rank of inspector who is not involved in the investigation. All other warrants authorise entry on one occasion only.

6.3B Where a warrant under PACE section 8, or Schedule 1, paragraph 12 authorises entry to and search of all premises occupied or controlled by a specified person, no premises which are not specified in the warrant may be entered and searched without the prior written authority of an officer of the rank of inspector who is not involved in the investigation.

(b) Entry other than with consent

6.4 The officer in charge of the search shall first try to communicate with the occupier, or any other person entitled to grant access to the premises, explain the authority under which entry is sought and ask the occupier to allow entry, unless:

    (i)   the search premises are unoccupied;

    (ii) the occupier and any other person entitled to grant access are absent;

    (iii) there are reasonable grounds for believing that alerting the occupier or any other person entitled to grant access would frustrate the object of the search or endanger officers or other people.

6.5 Unless *sub-paragraph 6.4(iii)* applies, if the premises are occupied the officer, subject to *paragraph 2.9*, shall, before the search begins:

    (i)   identify him or herself, show their warrant card (if not in uniform) and state the purpose of and grounds for the search;

    (ii) identify and introduce any person accompanying the officer on the search (such persons should carry identification for production on request) and briefly describe that person's role in the process.

6.6 Reasonable and proportionate force may be used if necessary to enter premises if the officer in charge of the search is satisfied the premises are those specified in any warrant, or in exercise of the powers described in *paragraphs 4.1 to 4.3*, and if:
  (i) the occupier or any other person entitled to grant access has refused entry;
  (ii) it is impossible to communicate with the occupier or any other person entitled to grant access; or
  (iii) any of the provisions of *paragraph 6.4* apply.

(c) **Notice of Powers and Rights**

6.7 If an officer conducts a search to which this Code applies the officer shall, unless it is impracticable to do so, provide the occupier with a copy of a Notice in a standard format:

Code **B**

  (i) specifying if the search is made under warrant, with consent, or in the exercise of the powers described in *paragraphs 4.1 to 4.3*. Note: the notice format shall provide for authority or consent to be indicated, see *paragraphs 4.3 and 5.1*;
  (ii) summarising the extent of the powers of search and seizure conferred by PACE and other relevant legislation as appropriate;
  (ii) explaining the rights of the occupier, and the owner of the property seized;
  (iv) explaining compensation may be payable in appropriate cases for damages caused entering and searching premises, and giving the address to send a compensation application, see *Note 6A*;
  (v) stating this Code is available at any police station.
6.8 If the occupier is:
  • present, copies of the Notice and warrant shall, if practicable, be given to them before the search begins, unless the officer in charge of the search reasonably believes this would frustrate the object of the search or endanger officers or other people
  • not present, copies of the Notice and warrant shall be left in a prominent place on the premises or appropriate part of the premises and endorsed, subject to *paragraph 2.9* with the name of the officer in charge of the search, the date and time of the search
  The warrant shall be endorsed to show this has been done.

(d) **Conduct of searches**

6.9   Premises may be searched only to the extent necessary to achieve the purpose of the search, having regard to the size and nature of whatever is sought.
6.9A A search may not continue under:
  • a warrant's authority once all the things specified in that warrant have been found
  • any other power once the object of that search has been achieved
6.9B No search may continue once the officer in charge of the search is satisfied whatever is being sought is not on the premises. See *Note 6B*. This does not prevent a further search of the same premises if additional grounds come to light supporting a further application for a search warrant or exercise or further exercise of another power. For example, when, as a result of new information, it is believed articles previously not found or additional articles are on the premises.

6.10   Searches must be conducted with due consideration for the property and privacy of the occupier and with no more disturbance than necessary. Reasonable force may be used only when necessary and proportionate because the co-operation of the occupier cannot be obtained or is insufficient for the purpose. See *Note 6C*

6.11   A friend, neighbour or other person must be allowed to witness the search if the occupier wishes unless the officer in charge of the search has reasonable grounds for believing the presence of the person asked for would seriously hinder the investigation or endanger officers or other people. A search need not be unreasonably delayed for this purpose. A record of the action taken should be made on the premises search record including the grounds for refusing the occupier's request.

6.12   A person is not required to be cautioned prior to being asked questions that are solely necessary for the purpose of furthering the proper and effective conduct of a search, see Code C, *paragraph 10.1(c)*. For example, questions to discover the occupier of specified premises, to find a key to open a locked drawer or cupboard or to otherwise seek co-operation during the search or to determine if a particular item is liable to be seized.

6.12A If questioning goes beyond what is necessary for the purpose of the exemption in Code C, the exchange is likely to constitute an interview as defined by Code C, *paragraph 11.1A* and would require the associated safeguards included in Code C, *section 10*.

(e) Leaving premises

6.13   If premises have been entered by force, before leaving the officer in charge of the search must make sure they are secure by:
   • arranging for the occupier or their agent to be present
   • any other appropriate means

(f) Searches under PACE Schedule 1 or the Terrorism Act 2000, Schedule 5

6.14   An officer shall be appointed as the officer in charge of the search, see *paragraph 2.10*, in respect of any search made under a warrant issued under PACE Act 1984, Schedule 1 or the Terrorism Act 2000, Schedule 5. They are responsible for making sure the search is conducted with discretion and in a manner that causes the least possible disruption to any business or other activities carried out on the premises.

6.15   Once the officer in charge of the search is satisfied material may not be taken from the premises without their knowledge, they shall ask for the documents or other records concerned. The officer in charge of the search may also ask to see the index to files held on the premises, and the officers conducting the search may inspect any files which, according to the index, appear to contain the material sought. A more extensive search of the premises may be made only if:
   • the person responsible for them refuses to:
     — produce the material sought, or
     — allow access to the index
   • it appears the index is:
     — inaccurate, or
     — incomplete

— for any other reason the officer in charge of the search has reasonable grounds for believing such a search is necessary in order to find the material sought

Notes for guidance

6A *Whether compensation is appropriate depends on the circumstances in each case. Compensation for damage caused when effecting entry is unlikely to be appropriate if the search was lawful, and the force used can be shown to be reasonable, proportionate and necessary to effect entry. If the wrong premises are searched by mistake everything possible should be done at the earliest opportunity to allay any sense of grievance and there should normally be a strong presumption in favour of paying compensation.*

6B *It is important that, when possible, all those involved in a search are fully briefed about any powers to be exercised and the extent and limits within which it should be conducted.*

6C *In all cases the number of officers and other persons involved in executing the warrant should be determined by what is reasonable and necessary according to the particular circumstances.*

Code **B**

7 SEIZURE AND RETENTION OF PROPERTY

(a) Seizure

7.1 Subject to *paragraph 7.2*, an officer who is searching any person or premises under any statutory power or with the consent of the occupier may seize anything:
   (a) covered by a warrant
   (b) the officer has reasonable grounds for believing is evidence of an offence or has been obtained in consequence of the commission of an offence but only if seizure is necessary to prevent the items being concealed, lost, disposed of, altered, damaged, destroyed or tampered with
   (c) covered by the powers in the Criminal Justice and Police Act 2001, Part 2 allowing an officer to seize property from persons or premises and retain it for sifting or examination elsewhere
   See *Note 7B*

7.2 No item may be seized which an officer has reasonable grounds for believing to be subject to legal privilege, as defined in PACE, section 10, other than under the Criminal Justice and Police Act 2001, Part 2.

7.3 Officers must be aware of the provisions in the Criminal Justice and Police Act 2001, section 59, allowing for applications to a judicial authority for the return of property seized and the subsequent duty to secure in section 60, see *paragraph 7.12(iii)*.

7.4 An officer may decide it is not appropriate to seize property because of an explanation from the person holding it but may nevertheless have reasonable grounds for believing it was obtained in consequence of an offence by some person. In these circumstances, the officer should identify the property to the holder, inform the holder of their suspicions and explain the holder may be liable to civil or criminal proceedings if they dispose of, alter or destroy the property.

7.5 An officer may arrange to photograph, image or copy, any document or other article they have the power to seize in accordance with *paragraph 7.1*. This is subject to specific restrictions on the examination, imaging or copying of certain property seized under the Criminal Justice and Police Act 2001, Part 2. An officer

423

must have regard to their statutory obligation to retain an original document or other article only when a photograph or copy is not sufficient.

7.6 If an officer considers information stored in any electronic form and accessible from the premises could be used in evidence, they may require the information to be produced in a form:

- which can be taken away and in which it is visible and legible; or
- from which it can readily be produced in a visible and legible form

(b) Criminal Justice and Police Act 2001: Specific procedures for seize and sift powers

7.7 The Criminal Justice and Police Act 2001, Part 2 gives officers limited powers to seize property from premises or persons so they can sift or examine it else-where. Officers must be careful they only exercise these powers when it is essential and they do not remove any more material than necessary. The removal of large volumes of material, much of which may not ultimately be retainable, may have serious implications for the owners, particularly when they are involved in business or activities such as journalism or the provision of medical services. Officers must carefully consider if removing copies or images of relevant material or data would be a satisfactory alternative to removing originals. When originals are taken, officers must be prepared to facilitate the provision of copies or images for the owners when reasonably practicable. See *Note 7C*

7.8 Property seized under the Criminal Justice and Police Act 2001, sections 50 or 51 must be kept securely and separately from any material seized under other powers. An examination under section 53 to determine which elements may be retained must be carried out at the earliest practicable time, having due regard to the desirability of allowing the person from whom the property was seized, or a person with an interest in the property, an opportunity of being present or represented at the examination.

7.8A All reasonable steps should be taken to accommodate an interested person's request to be present, provided the request is reasonable and subject to the need to prevent harm to, interference with, or unreasonable delay to the investigatory process. If an examination proceeds in the absence of an inter-ested person who asked to attend or their representative, the officer who exer-cised the relevant seizure power must give that person a written notice of why the examination was carried out in those circumstances. If it is necessary for security reasons or to maintain confidentiality officers may exclude interested persons from decryption or other processes which facilitate the examination but do not form part of it. See *Note 7D*

7.9 It is the responsibility of the officer in charge of the investigation to make sure property is returned in accordance with sections 53 to 55. Material which there is no power to retain must be:

- separated from the rest of the seized property
- returned as soon as reasonably practicable after examination of all the seized property

7.9A Delay is only warranted if very clear and compelling reasons exist, e.g. the:

- unavailability of the person to whom the material is to be returned
- need to agree a convenient time to return a large volume of material

7.9B Legally privileged, excluded or special procedure material which cannot be retained must be returned:
- as soon as reasonably practicable
- without waiting for the whole examination

7.9C As set out in section 58, material must be returned to the person from whom it was seized, except when it is clear some other person has a better right to it. See *Note 7E*

7.10 When an officer involved in the investigation has reasonable grounds to believe a person with a relevant interest in property seized under section 50 or 51 intends to make an application under section 59 for the return of any legally privileged, special procedure or excluded material, the officer in charge of the investigation should be informed as soon as practicable and the material seized should be kept secure in accordance with section 61. See *Note 7C*

Code B

7.11 The officer in charge of the investigation is responsible for making sure property is properly secured. Securing involves making sure the property is not examined, copied, imaged or put to any other use except at the request, or with the consent, of the applicant or in accordance with the directions of the appropriate judicial authority. Any request, consent or directions must be recorded in writing and signed by both the initiator and the officer in charge of the investigation. See *Notes 7F* and *7G*

7.12 When an officer exercises a power of seizure conferred by sections 50 or 51 they shall provide the occupier of the premises or the person from whom the property is being seized with a written notice:
(i) specifying what has been seized under the powers conferred by that section;
(ii) specifying the grounds for those powers;
(iii) setting out the effect of sections 59 to 61 covering the grounds for a person with a relevant interest in seized property to apply to a judicial authority for its return and the duty of officers to secure property in certain circumstances when an application is made;
(iv) specifying the name and address of the person to whom:
- notice of an application to the appropriate judicial authority in respect of any of the seized property must be given;
- an application may be made to allow attendance at the initial examination of the property.

7.13 If the occupier is not present but there is someone in charge of the premises, the notice shall be given to them. If no suitable person is available, so the notice will easily be found it should either be:
- left in a prominent place on the premises
- attached to the exterior of the premises

(c) **Retention**

7.14 Subject to *paragraph 7.15*, anything seized in accordance with the above provisions may be retained only for as long as is necessary. It may be retained, among other purposes:
(i) for use as evidence at a trial for an offence;

    (ii) to facilitate the use in any investigation or proceedings of anything to which it is inextricably linked, see *Note 7H*;

    (iii) for forensic examination or other investigation in connection with an offence;

    (iv) in order to establish its lawful owner when there are reasonable grounds for believing it has been stolen or obtained by the commission of an offence.

7.15 Property shall not be retained under *paragraph 7.14(i), (ii)* or *(iii)* if a copy or image would be sufficient.

(d) Rights of owners etc

7.16 If property is retained, the person who had custody or control of it immediately before seizure must, on request, be provided with a list or description of the property within a reasonable time.

7.17 That person or their representative must be allowed supervised access to the property to examine it or have it photographed or copied, or must be provided with a photograph or copy, in either case within a reasonable time of any request and at their own expense, unless the officer in charge of an investigation has reasonable grounds for believing this would:

    (i) prejudice the investigation of any offence or criminal proceedings; or

    (ii) lead to the commission of an offence by providing access to unlawful material such as pornography;

A record of the grounds shall be made when access is denied.

Notes for guidance

7A *Any person claiming property seized by the police may apply to a magistrates' court under the Police (Property) Act 1897 for its possession and should, if appropriate, be advised of this procedure.*

7B *The powers of seizure conferred by PACE, sections 18(2) and 19(3) extend to the seizure of the whole premises when it is physically possible to seize and retain the premises in their totality and practical considerations make seizure desirable. For example, police may remove premises such as tents, vehicles or caravans to a police station for the purpose of preserving evidence.*

7C *Officers should consider reaching agreement with owners and/or other interested parties on the procedures for examining a specific set of property, rather than awaiting the judicial authority's determination. Agreement can sometimes give a quicker and more satisfactory route for all concerned and minimise costs and legal complexities.*

7D *What constitutes a relevant interest in specific material may depend on the nature of that material and the circumstances in which it is seized. Anyone with a reasonable claim to ownership of the material and anyone entrusted with its safe keeping by the owner should be considered.*

7E *Requirements to secure and return property apply equally to all copies, images or other material created because of seizure of the original property.*

7F *The mechanics of securing property vary according to the circumstances; "bagging up", i.e. placing material in sealed bags or containers and strict subsequent control of access is the appropriate procedure in many cases.*

7G *When material is seized under the powers of seizure conferred by PACE, the duty to retain it under the Code of Practice issued under the Criminal Procedure and*

Investigations Act 1996 is subject to the provisions on retention of seized material in PACE, section 22.

7H Paragraph 7.14(ii) applies if inextricably linked material is seized under the Criminal Justice and Police Act 2001, sections 50 or 51. Inextricably linked material is material it is not reasonably practicable to separate from other linked material without prejudicing the use of that other material in any investigation or proceedings. For example, it may not be possible to separate items of data held on computer disk without damaging their evidential integrity. Inextricably linked material must not be examined, imaged, copied or used for any purpose other than for proving the source and/or integrity of the linked material.

8 ACTION AFTER SEARCHES

Code B

8.1 If premises are searched in circumstances where this Code applies, unless the exceptions in *paragraph 2.3(a)* apply, on arrival at a police station the officer in charge of the search shall make or have made a record of the search, to include:

(i)   the address of the searched premises;

(ii) the date, time and duration of the search;

(iii) the authority used for the search:
- if the search was made in exercise of a statutory power to search premises without warrant, the power which was used for the search:
- if the search was made under a warrant or with written consent;
  — a copy of the warrant and the written authority to apply for it, *see paragraph 3.4*; or
  — the written consent;
  shall be appended to the record or the record shall show the location of the copy warrant or consent.

(iv) subject to *paragraph 2.9*, the names of:
- the officer(s) in charge of the search;
- all other officers and authorised persons who conducted the search;

(v)   the names of any people on the premises if they are known;

(vi) any grounds for refusing the occupier's request to have someone present during the search, see *paragraph 6.11*;

(vii) a list of any articles seized or the location of a list and, if not covered by a warrant, the grounds for their seizure;

(viii) whether force was used, and the reason;

(ix) details of any damage caused during the search, and the circumstances;

(x)   if applicable, the reason it was not practicable:
- (a) to give the occupier a copy of the Notice of Powers and Rights, see *paragraph 6.7*;
- (b) before the search to give the occupier a copy of the Notice, see *paragraph 6.8*;

(xi) when the occupier was not present, the place where copies of the Notice of Powers and Rights and search warrant were left on the premises, see *paragraph 6.8*.

8.2 On each occasion when premises are searched under warrant, the warrant authorising the search on that occasion shall be endorsed to show:

(i) if any articles specified in the warrant were found and the address where found;

(ii) if any other articles were seized;

(iii) the date and time it was executed and if present, the name of the occupier or if the occupier is not present the name of the person in charge of the premises;

(iv) subject to *paragraph 2.9*, the names of the officers who executed it and any authorised persons who accompanied them;

(v) if a copy, together with a copy of the Notice of Powers and Rights was:
  • handed to the occupier; or
  • endorsed as required by *paragraph 6.8*; and left on the premises and where.

8.3 Any warrant shall be returned within three calendar months of its issue or sooner on completion of the search(es) authorised by that warrant, if it was issued by a:
  • justice of the peace, to the designated officer for the local justice area in which the justice was acting when issuing the warrant; or
  • judge, to the appropriate officer of the court concerned,

9 SEARCH REGISTERS

9.1 A search register will be maintained at each sub-divisional or equivalent police station. All search records required under *paragraph 8.1* shall be made, copied, or referred to in the register. See *Note 9A*

Note for guidance

9A Paragraph 9.1 also applies to search records made by immigration officers. In these cases, a search register must also be maintained at an immigration office. See also Note 2D

10 Searches under sections 7A, 7B and 7C of the Prevention of Terrorism Act 2005 in connection with control orders.

10.1 This Code applies to the powers under sections 7A, 7B and 7C of the Prevention of Terrorism Act 2005 to enter and search premises subject to the modifications in the following paragraphs.

10.2 In paragraph 2.3(d), the reference to the investigation into an alleged or suspected offence includes the enforcement of obligations imposed by or under a control order made under the Prevention of Terrorism Act 2005.

10.3 References to the purpose and object of the search, the nature of articles sought and what may be seized and retained include (as appropriate):
  • in relation to section 7A (absconding), determining whether the controlled person has absconded and if it appears so, any material or information that may assist in the pursuit and arrest of the controlled person.
  • in relation to section 7B (failure to grant access to premises), determining whether any control order obligations have been contravened and if it appears so, any material or information that may assist in determining whether the controlled person is complying with the obligations imposed by the control order or in investigating any apparent contravention of those obligations.

- in relation to section 7C (monitoring compliance), determining whether the controlled person is complying with their control order obligations, and any material that may assist in that determination.
- evidence in relation to an offence under section 9 of the Prevention of Terrorism Act 2005 (offences relating to control orders).

Code **B**

Appendix 4

Code C: PACE Code of Practice for the Detention, Treatment and Questioning of Persons by Police Officers

This Code applies to people in police detention after midnight on 10 July 2012, notwithstanding that their period of detention may have commenced before that time.

1 GENERAL

1.0 The powers and procedures in this Code must be used fairly, responsibly, with respect for the people to whom they apply and without unlawful discrimination. The Equality Act 2010 makes it unlawful for police officers to discriminate against, harass or victimise any person on the grounds of the 'protected characteristics' of age, disability, gender reassignment, race, religion or belief, sex and sexual orientation, marriage and civil partnership, pregnancy and maternity when using their powers. When police forces are carrying out their functions, they also have a duty to have regard to the need to eliminate unlawful discrimination, harassment and victimisation and to take steps to foster good relations.

1.1 All persons in custody must be dealt with expeditiously, and released as soon as the need for detention no longer applies.

1.1A A custody officer must perform the functions in this Code as soon as practicable. A custody officer will not be in breach of this Code if delay is justifiable and reasonable steps are taken to prevent unnecessary delay. The custody record shall show when a delay has occurred and the reason. See *Note 1H*.

1.2 This Code of Practice must be readily available at all police stations for consultation by:
- police officers;
- police staff;
- detained persons;
- members of the public.

1.3 The provisions of this Code:
- include the *Annexes*
- do not include the *Notes for Guidance*.

1.4 If an officer has any suspicion, or is told in good faith, that a person of any age may be mentally disordered or otherwise mentally vulnerable, in the absence of clear evidence to dispel that suspicion, the person shall be treated as such for the purposes of this Code. See *Note 1G*.

1.5   If anyone appears to be under 17, they shall be treated as a juvenile for the purposes of this Code in the absence of clear evidence that they are older.

1.6   If a person appears to be blind, seriously visually impaired, deaf, unable to read or speak or has difficulty orally because of a speech impediment, they shall be treated as such for the purposes of this Code in the absence of clear evidence to the contrary.

1.7   'The appropriate adult' means, in the case of a:

    (a) juvenile:

       (i)   the parent, guardian or, if the juvenile is in the care of a local authority or voluntary organisation, a person representing that authority or organisation;

       (ii) a social worker of a local authority;

       (iii) failing these, some other responsible adult aged 18 or over who is not a police officer or employed by the police.

    (b) person who is mentally disordered or mentally vulnerable: See Note 1D.

       (i)   a relative, guardian or other person responsible for their care or custody;

       (ii) someone experienced in dealing with mentally disordered or mentally vulnerable people but who is not a police officer or employed by the police;

       (iii) failing these, some other responsible adult aged 18 or over who is not a police officer or employed by the police.

Code C

1.8   If this Code requires a person be given certain information, they do not have to be given it if at the time they are incapable of understanding what is said, are violent or may become violent or in urgent need of medical attention, but they must be given it as soon as practicable.

1.9   References to a custody officer include any police officer who for the time being, is performing the functions of a custody officer.

1.9A   When this Code requires the prior authority or agreement of an officer of at least inspector or superintendent rank, that authority may be given by a sergeant or chief inspector authorised to perform the functions of the higher rank under the Police and Criminal Evidence Act 1984 (PACE), section 107.

1.10   Subject to *paragraph 1.12*, this Code applies to people in custody at police stations in England and Wales, whether or not they have been arrested, and to those removed to a police station as a place of safety under the Mental Health Act 1983, sections 135 and 136, as a last resort (see paragraph 3.16). *Section 15* applies solely to people in police detention, e.g. those brought to a police station under arrest or arrested at a police station for an offence after going there voluntarily.

1.11   No part of this Code applies to a detained person:

    (a) to whom PACE Code H applies because:

      • they are detained following arrest under section 41 of the Terrorism Act 2000 (TACT) and not charged; or

      • an authorisation has been given under section 22 of the Counter-Terrorism Act 2008 (CTACT) (post-charge questioning of terrorist suspects) to interview them.

    (b) to whom the Code of Practice issued under paragraph 6 of Schedule 14 to TACT applies because they are detained for examination under Schedule 7 to TACT.

1.12   This Code does not apply to people in custody:
  (i)   arrested on warrants issued in Scotland by officers under the Criminal Justice and Public Order Act 1994, section 136(2), or arrested or detained without warrant by officers from a police force in Scotland under section 137(2). In these cases, police powers and duties and the person's rights and entitlements whilst at a police station in England or Wales are the same as those in Scotland;
  (ii) arrested under the Immigration and Asylum Act 1999, section 142(3) in order to have their fingerprints taken;
  (iii) whose detention is authorised by an immigration officer under the Immigration Act 1971;
  (iv) who are convicted or remanded prisoners held in police cells on behalf of the Prison Service under the Imprisonment (Temporary Provisions) Act 1980;
  (v)   *Not used*
  (vi) detained for searches under stop and search powers except as required by Code A.

  The provisions on conditions of detention and treatment in *sections 8* and *9* must be considered as the minimum standards of treatment for such detainees.

1.13   In this Code:
  (a)   'designated person' means a person other than a police officer, designated under the Police Reform Act 2002, Part 4 who has specified powers and duties of police officers conferred or imposed on them;
  (b)   reference to a police officer includes a designated person acting in the exercise or performance of the powers and duties conferred or imposed on them by their designation.
  (c)   where a search or other procedure to which this Code applies may only be carried out or observed by a person of the same sex as the detainee, the gender of the detainee and other parties present should be established and recorded in line with Annex L of this Code.

1.14   Designated persons are entitled to use reasonable force as follows:
  (a)   when exercising a power conferred on them which allows a police officer exercising that power to use reasonable force, a designated person has the same entitlement to use force; and
  (b)   at other times when carrying out duties conferred or imposed on them that also entitle them to use reasonable force, for example:
    • when at a police station carrying out the duty to keep detainees for whom they are responsible under control and to assist any other police officer or designated person to keep any detainee under control and to prevent their escape.
    • when securing, or assisting any other police officer or designated person in securing, the detention of a person at a police station.
    • when escorting, or assisting any other police officer or designated person in escorting, a detainee within a police station.
    • for the purpose of saving life or limb; or
    • preventing serious damage to property.

1.15   Nothing in this Code prevents the custody officer, or other officer given custody of the detainee, from allowing police staff who are not designated persons to carry out individual procedures or tasks at the police station if the law allows. However, the officer remains responsible for making sure the procedures and tasks are carried out correctly in accordance with the Codes of Practice. (see *Note 3F*). Any such person must be:
   (a) a person employed by a police force and under the direction and control of the Chief Officer of that force; or
   (b) employed by a person with whom a police force has a contract for the provision of services relating to persons arrested or otherwise in custody.
1.16   Designated persons and other police staff must have regard to any relevant provisions of the Codes of Practice.
1.17   References to pocket books include any official report book issued to police officers or other police staff.

Notes for Guidance

Code **C**

1A   Although certain sections of this Code apply specifically to people in custody at police stations, those there voluntarily to assist with an investigation should be treated with no less consideration, e.g. offered refreshments at appropriate times, and enjoy an absolute right to obtain legal advice or communicate with anyone outside the police station.

1B   A person, including a parent or guardian, should not be an appropriate adult if they:
   • *are*
      ~ *suspected of involvement in the offence*
      ~ *the victim*
      ~ *a witness*
      ~ *involved in the investigation*
   • received admissions prior to attending to act as the appropriate adult.
   Note: If a juvenile's parent is estranged from the juvenile, they should not be asked to act as the appropriate adult if the juvenile expressly and specifically objects to their presence.

1C   If a juvenile admits an offence to, or in the presence of, a social worker or member of a youth offending team other than during the time that person is acting as the juvenile's appropriate adult, another appropriate adult should be appointed in the interest of fairness.

1D   In the case of people who are mentally disordered or otherwise mentally vulnerable, it may be more satisfactory if the appropriate adult is someone experienced or trained in their care rather than a relative lacking such qualifications. But if the detainee prefers a relative to a better qualified stranger or objects to a particular person their wishes should, if practicable, be respected.

1E   A detainee should always be given an opportunity, when an appropriate adult is called to the police station, to consult privately with a solicitor in the appropriate adult's absence if they want. An appropriate adult is not subject to legal privilege.

1F   A solicitor or independent custody visitor (formerly a lay visitor) present at the police station in that capacity may not be the appropriate adult.

1G   'Mentally vulnerable' applies to any detainee who, because of their mental state or capacity, may not understand the significance of what is said, of questions or of their replies. 'Mental disorder' is defined in the Mental Health Act 1983, section 1(2) as 'any disorder or disability of mind'. When the custody officer has any doubt about the mental state or capacity of a detainee, that detainee should be treated as mentally vulnerable and an appropriate adult called.

1H   *Paragraph 1.1A is intended to cover delays which may occur in processing detainees e.g. if:*

- *a large number of suspects are brought into the station simultaneously to be placed in custody;*
- *interview rooms are all being used;*
- *there are difficulties contacting an appropriate adult, solicitor or interpreter.*

1I   *The custody officer must remind the appropriate adult and detainee about the right to legal advice and record any reasons for waiving it in accordance with section 6.*

1J   *Not used*

1K   *This Code does not affect the principle that all citizens have a duty to help police officers to prevent crime and discover offenders. This is a civic rather than a legal duty; but when police officers are trying to discover whether, or by whom, offences have been committed they are entitled to question any person from whom they think useful information can be obtained, subject to the restrictions imposed by this Code. A person's declaration that they are unwilling to reply does not alter this entitlement.*

2 Custody records

2.1A When a person is brought to a police station:

- under arrest;
- is arrested at the police station having attended there voluntarily; or
- attends a police station to answer bail.

they must be brought before the custody officer as soon as practicable after their arrival at the station or if applicable, following their arrest after attending the police station voluntarily. This applies to designated and non-designated police stations. A person is deemed to be "at a police station" for these purposes if they are within the boundary of any building or enclosed yard which forms part of that police station.

2.1   A separate custody record must be opened as soon as practicable for each person brought to a police station under arrest or arrested at the station having gone there voluntarily or attending a police station in answer to street bail. All information recorded under this Code must be recorded as soon as practicable in the custody record unless otherwise specified. Any audio or video recording made in the custody area is not part of the custody record.

2.2   If any action requires the authority of an officer of a specified rank, subject to *paragraph 2.6A*, their name and rank must be noted in the custody record.

2.3   The custody officer is responsible for the custody record's accuracy and completeness and for making sure the record or copy of the record accompanies a detainee if they are transferred to another police station. The record shall show the:

- time and reason for transfer;
- time a person is released from detention.

2.3A If a person is arrested and taken to a police station as a result of a search in the exercise of any stop and search power to which PACE Code A (Stop and search) or the 'search powers code' issued under TACT applies, the officer carrying out the search is responsible for ensuring that the record of that stop and search, is made as part of the person's custody record. The custody officer must then ensure that the person is asked if they want a copy of the search record and if they do, that they are given a copy as soon as practicable. The person's entitle-ment to a copy of the search record which is made as part of their custody record is in addition to, and does not affect, their entitlement to a copy of their custody record or any other provisions of section 2 (Custody records) of this Code. (See Code A *paragraph 4.2B* and the TACT search powers code *paragraph 5.3.5*).

2.4   A solicitor or appropriate adult must be permitted to inspect a detainee's cus-tody record as soon as practicable after their arrival at the station and at any other time whilst the person is detained. Arrangements for this access must be agreed with the custody officer and may not unreasonably interfere with the custody officer's duties.

2.4A   When a detainee leaves police detention or is taken before a court they, their legal representative or appropriate adult shall be given, on request, a copy of the custody record as soon as practicable. This entitlement lasts for 12 months after release.

2.5   The detainee, appropriate adult or legal representative shall be permitted to inspect the original custody record after the detainee has left police detention provided they give reasonable notice of their request. Any such inspection shall be noted in the custody record.

2.6   Subject to *paragraph 2.6A*, all entries in custody records must be timed and signed by the maker. Records entered on computer shall be timed and contain the operator's identification.

2.6A   Nothing in this Code requires the identity of officers or other police staff to be recorded or disclosed:

(a) *Not used;*

(b) if the officer or police staff reasonably believe recording or disclosing their name might put them in danger.

In these cases, they shall use their warrant or other identification numbers and the name of their police station. See *Note 2A*

2.7   The fact and time of any detainee's refusal to sign a custody record, when asked in accordance with this Code, must be recorded.

Note for Guidance

2A   *The purpose of paragraph 2.6A(b) is to protect those involved in serious organised crime investigations or arrests of particularly violent suspects when there is reliable information that those arrested or their associates may threaten or cause harm to those involved. In cases of doubt, an officer of inspector rank or above should be consulted.*

3 INITIAL ACTION

(a) Detained persons—normal procedure

3.1   When a person is brought to a police station under arrest or arrested at the station having gone there voluntarily, the custody officer must make sure the

Code **C**

person is told clearly about the following continuing rights which may be exercised at any stage during the period in custody:

(i)   the right to have someone informed of their arrest as in *section 5*;

(ii)   the right to consult privately with a solicitor and that free independent legal advice is available;

(iii) the right to consult these Codes of Practice. See *Note 3D*

3.2   The detainee must also be given:

- a written notice setting out:
  - ˜ the above three rights;
  - ˜ the arrangements for obtaining legal advice;
  - ˜ the right to a copy of the custody record as in *paragraph 2.4A*;
  - ˜ the caution in the terms prescribed in *section 10*.
- an additional written notice briefly setting out their entitlements while in custody, see *Notes 3A* and *3B*.

Note: The detainee shall be asked to sign the custody record to acknowledge receipt of these notices. Any refusal must be recorded on the custody record.

3.3   A citizen of an independent Commonwealth country or a national of a foreign country, including the Republic of Ireland, must be informed as soon as practicable about their rights of communication with their High Commission, Embassy or Consulate. See *section 7*

3.4   The custody officer shall:

- record the offence(s) that the detainee has been arrested for and the reason(s) for the arrest on the custody record. See *paragraph 10.3* and *Code G paragraphs 2.2* and *4.3*.
- note on the custody record any comment the detainee makes in relation to the arresting officer's account but shall not invite comment. If the arresting officer is not physically present when the detainee is brought to a police station, the arresting officer's account must be made available to the custody officer remotely or by a third party on the arresting officer's behalf. If the custody officer authorises a person's detention, subject to paragraph 1.8, that officer must record the grounds for detention in the detainee's presence and at the same time, inform them of the grounds. The detainee must be informed of the grounds for their detention before they are questioned about any offence;
- note any comment the detainee makes in respect of the decision to detain them but shall not invite comment;
- not put specific questions to the detainee regarding their involvement in any offence, nor in respect of any comments they may make in response to the arresting officer's account or the decision to place them in detention. Such an exchange is likely to constitute an interview as in *paragraph 11.1A* and require the associated safeguards in *section 11*.

See *paragraph 11.13* in respect of unsolicited comments.

3.5   The custody officer or other custody staff as directed by the custody officer shall:

(a) ask the detainee, whether at this time, they:

(i)   would like legal advice, see *paragraph 6.5*;

(ii)   want someone informed of their detention, see *section 5*;

(b) ask the detainee to sign the custody record to confirm their decisions in respect of (a);

(c) determine whether the detainee:
   (i) is, or might be, in need of medical treatment or attention, see *section 9*;
   (ii) requires:
- an appropriate adult;
- help to check documentation;
- an interpreter;

(d) record the decision in respect of (c).

Where any duties under this paragraph have been carried out by custody staff at the direction of the custody officer, the outcomes shall, as soon as practicable, be reported to the custody officer who retains overall responsibility for the detainee's care and treatment and ensuring that it complies with this Code. See *Note 3F*.

3.6 When these needs are determined, the custody officer is responsible for initiating an assessment to consider whether the detainee is likely to present specific risks to custody staff or themselves. Such assessments should always include a check on the Police National Computer, to be carried out as soon as practicable, to identify any risks highlighted in relation to the detainee. Although such assessments are primarily the custody officer's responsibility, it may be necessary for them to consult and involve others, e.g. the arresting officer or an appropriate healthcare professional, see *paragraph 9.13*. Reasons for delaying the initiation or completion of the assessment must be recorded.

Code **C**

3.7 Chief Officers should ensure that arrangements for proper and effective risk assessments required by *paragraph 3.6* are implemented in respect of all detainees at police stations in their area.

3.8 Risk assessments must follow a structured process which clearly defines the categories of risk to be considered and the results must be incorporated in the detainee's custody record. The custody officer is responsible for making sure those responsible for the detainee's custody are appropriately briefed about the risks. If no specific risks are identified by the assessment, that should be noted in the custody record. See *Note 3E* and *paragraph 9.14*.

3.8A The content of any risk assessment and any analysis of the level of risk relating to the person's detention is not required to be shown or provided to the detainee or any person acting on behalf of the detainee. But information should not be withheld from any person acting on the detainee's behalf, for example, an appropriate adult, solicitor or interpreter, if to do so might put that person at risk.

3.9 The custody officer is responsible for implementing the response to any specific risk assessment, e.g.:
- reducing opportunities for self harm;
- calling an appropriate healthcare professional;
- increasing levels of monitoring or observation;
- reducing the risk to those who come into contact with the detainee. See *Note 3E*.

3.10 Risk assessment is an ongoing process and assessments must always be subject to review if circumstances change.

3.11 If video cameras are installed in the custody area, notices shall be prominently displayed showing cameras are in use. Any request to have video cameras switched off shall be refused.

(b) Detained persons—special groups

3.12 If the detainee appears deaf or there is doubt about their hearing or speaking ability or ability to understand English, and the custody officer cannot establish effective communication, the custody officer must, as soon as practicable, call an interpreter for assistance in the action under *paragraphs 3.1–3.5*. See *section 13*.

3.13 If the detainee is a juvenile, the custody officer must, if it is practicable, ascertain the identity of a person responsible for their welfare. That person:
- may be:
  - ~ the parent or guardian;
  - ~ if the juvenile is in local authority or voluntary organisation care, or is otherwise being looked after under the Children Act 1989, a person appointed by that authority or organisation to have responsibility for the juvenile's welfare;
  - ~ any other person who has, for the time being, assumed responsibility for the juvenile's welfare.
- must be informed as soon as practicable that the juvenile has been arrested, why they have been arrested and where they are detained. This right is in addition to the juvenile's right in *section 5* not to be held incommunicado. See *Note 3C*

3.14 If a juvenile is known to be subject to a court order under which a person or organisation is given any degree of statutory responsibility to supervise or otherwise monitor them, reasonable steps must also be taken to notify that person or organisation (the 'responsible officer'). The responsible officer will normally be a member of a Youth Offending Team, except for a curfew order which involves electronic monitoring when the contractor providing the monitoring will normally be the responsible officer.

3.15 If the detainee is a juvenile, mentally disordered or otherwise mentally vulnerable, the custody officer must, as soon as practicable:
- inform the appropriate adult, who in the case of a juvenile may or may not be a person responsible for their welfare, as in *paragraph 3.13*, of:
  - ˜ the grounds for their detention;
  - ˜ their whereabouts.
- ask the adult to come to the police station to see the detainee.

3.16 It is imperative that a mentally disordered or otherwise mentally vulnerable person, detained under the Mental Health Act 1983, section 136, be assessed as soon as possible. A police station should only be used as a place of safety as a last resort but if that assessment is to take place at the police station, an approved mental health professional and a registered medical practitioner shall be called to the station as soon as possible to carry it out. See *Note 9D*. The appropriate adult has no role in the assessment process and their presence is not required. Once the detainee has been assessed and suitable arrangements made for their treatment or care, they can no longer be detained under section 136. A detainee must be immediately discharged from detention under section 136 if a registered medical practitioner, having examined them, concludes they are not mentally disordered within the meaning of the Act.

3.17 If the appropriate adult is:
- already at the police station, the provisions of *paragraphs 3.1* to *3.5* must be complied with in the appropriate adult's presence;
- not at the station when these provisions are complied with, they must be complied with again in the presence of the appropriate adult when they arrive.

3.18 The detainee shall be advised that:
- the duties of the appropriate adult include giving advice and assistance;
- they can consult privately with the appropriate adult at any time.

3.19 If the detainee, or appropriate adult on the detainee's behalf, asks for a solicitor to be called to give legal advice, the provisions of *section 6* apply.

3.20 If the detainee is blind, seriously visually impaired or unable to read, the custody officer shall make sure their solicitor, relative, appropriate adult or some other person likely to take an interest in them and not involved in the investigation is available to help check any documentation. When this Code requires written consent or signing the person assisting may be asked to sign instead, if the detainee prefers. This paragraph does not require an appropriate adult to be called solely to assist in checking and signing documentation for a person who is not a juvenile, or mentally disordered or otherwise mentally vulnerable (see *paragraph 3.15*).

(c) Persons attending a police station or elsewhere voluntarily

3.21 Anybody attending a police station or other location (see *paragraph 3.22*) voluntarily to assist police with the investigation of an offence may leave at will unless arrested. See *Note 1K*. The person may only be prevented from leaving at will if their arrest on suspicion of committing the offence is necessary in accordance with Code G. See *Code G Note 2G*.

If during an interview it is decided that their arrest is necessary, they must:
- be informed at once that they are under arrest and of the grounds and reasons as required by Code G, and
- be brought before the custody officer at the police station where they are arrested or, as the case may be, at the police station to which they are taken after being arrested elsewhere. The custody officer is then responsible for making sure that a custody record is opened and that they are notified of their rights in the same way as other detainees as required by this Code.

If they are not arrested but are cautioned as in *section 10*, the person who gives the caution must, at the same time, inform them they are not under arrest, they are not obliged to remain at the station or other location but if they agree to remain, they may obtain free and independent legal advice if they want. They shall also be given a copy of the notice explaining the arrangements for obtaining legal advice and told that the right to legal advice includes the right to speak with a solicitor on the telephone and be asked if they want advice. If advice is requested, the interviewer is responsible for securing its provision without delay by contacting the Defence Solicitor Call Centre and for ensuring that the provisions of this Code and Codes E and F concerning the conduct and recording of interviews of suspects are followed insofar as they can be applied to suspects who are not under arrest. See paragraph 3.2 and *Note 6B*.

Code **C**

3.22 If the other location mentioned in paragraph 3.21 is any place or premises for which the interviewer requires the person's informed consent to remain, for example, the person's home, then the references that the person is 'not obliged to remain' and that they 'may leave at will' mean that the person may also withdraw their consent and require the interviewer to leave.

(d) Documentation

3.23 The grounds for a person's detention shall be recorded, in the person's presence if practicable. See *paragraph 1.8.*

3.24 Action taken under *paragraphs 3.12* to *3.20* shall be recorded.

(e) Persons answering street bail

3.25 When a person is answering street bail, the custody officer should link any documentation held in relation to arrest with the custody record. Any further action shall be recorded on the custody record in accordance with paragraphs 3.23 and 3.24 above.

Notes for Guidance

3A   *The notice of entitlements should:*
   - *list the entitlements in this Code, including:*
     - ~ *visits and contact with outside parties, including special provisions for Commonwealth citizens and foreign nationals;*
     - ~ *reasonable standards of physical comfort;*
     - ~ *adequate food and drink;*
     - ~ *access to toilets and washing facilities, clothing, medical attention, and exercise when practicable.*
   - *mention the:*
     - ~ *provisions relating to the conduct of interviews;*
     - ~ *circumstances in which an appropriate adult should be available to assist the detainee and their statutory rights to make representation whenever the period of their detention is reviewed.*

3B   *In addition to notices in English, translations should be available in Welsh, the main mi-nority ethnic languages and the principal European languages, whenever they are likely to be helpful. Audio versions of the notice should also be made available. Access to 'easy read' illustrated versions should also be provided if they are available.*

3C   *If the juvenile is in local authority or voluntary organisation care but living with their parents or other adults responsible for their welfare, although there is no legal obligation to inform them, they should normally be contacted, as well as the authority or organisation unless suspected of involvement in the offence concerned. Even if the juvenile is not living with their parents, consideration should be given to informing them.*

3D   *The right to consult the Codes of Practice does not entitle the person concerned to delay unreasonably any necessary investigative or administrative action whilst they do so. Examples of action which need not be delayed unreasonably include:*
   - *procedures requiring the provision of breath, blood or urine specimens under the Road Traffic Act 1988 or the Transport and Works Act 1992;*
   - *searching detainees at the police station;*

- *taking fingerprints, footwear impressions or non-intimate samples without consent for evidential purposes.*

3E *Home Office Circular 32/2000 and the Guidance on the Safer Detention and Handling of Persons in Police Custody Second Edition (2012) produced on behalf of the Association of Chief Police Officers provide more detailed guidance on risk assessments and identify key risk areas which should always be considered.*

3F *A custody officer or other officer who, in accordance with this Code, allows or directs the carrying out of any task or action relating to a detainee's care, treatment, rights and entitlements to another officer or any police staff must be satisfied that the officer or police staff concerned are suitable, trained and competent to carry out the task or action in question.*

4 DETAINEE'S PROPERTY

(a) Action

4.1 The custody officer is responsible for:
  (a) ascertaining what property a detainee:
    (i) has with them when they come to the police station, whether on:
      - arrest or re-detention on answering to bail;
      - commitment to prison custody on the order or sentence of a court;
      - lodgement at the police station with a view to their production in court from prison custody;
      - transfer from detention at another station or hospital;
      - detention under the Mental Health Act 1983, section 135 or 136;
      - remand into police custody on the authority of a court.
    (ii) might have acquired for an unlawful or harmful purpose while in custody;
  (b) the safekeeping of any property taken from a detainee which remains at the police station.

The custody officer may search the detainee or authorise their being searched to the extent they consider necessary, provided a search of intimate parts of the body or involving the removal of more than outer clothing is only made as in *Annex A*. A search may only be carried out by an officer of the same sex as the detainee. See *Note 4A* and *Annex L.*

4.2 Detainees may retain clothing and personal effects at their own risk unless the custody officer considers they may use them to cause harm to themselves or others, interfere with evidence, damage property, effect an escape or they are needed as evidence. In this event the custody officer may withhold such articles as they consider necessary and must tell the detainee why.

4.3 Personal effects are those items a detainee may lawfully need, use or refer to while in detention but do not include cash and other items of value.

(b) Documentation

4.4 It is a matter for the custody officer to determine whether a record should be made of the property a detained person has with him or had taken from him on arrest. Any record made is not required to be kept as part of the custody record but the custody record should be noted as to where such a record exists. Whenever a record is made the detainee shall be allowed to check and sign the record of property as correct. Any refusal to sign shall be recorded.

Code **C**

4.5 If a detainee is not allowed to keep any article of clothing or personal effects, the reason must be recorded.

Notes for Guidance

4A PACE, Section 54(1) and paragraph 4.1 require a detainee to be searched when it is clear the custody officer will have continuing duties in relation to that detainee or when that detainee's behaviour or offence makes an inventory appropriate. They do not require every detainee to be searched, e.g. if it is clear a person will only be detained for a short period and is not to be placed in a cell, the custody officer may decide not to search them. In such a case the custody record will be endorsed 'not searched', paragraph 4.4 will not apply, and the detainee will be invited to sign the entry. If the detainee refuses, the custody officer will be obliged to ascertain what property they have in accordance with paragraph 4.1.

4B Paragraph 4.4 does not require the custody officer to record on the custody record property in the detainee's possession on arrest if, by virtue of its nature, quantity or size, it is not practicable to remove it to the police station.

4C Paragraph 4.4 does not require items of clothing worn by the person be recorded unless withheld by the custody officer as in paragraph 4.2.

5 RIGHT NOT TO BE HELD INCOMMUNICADO

(a) Action

5.1 Subject to paragraph 5.7B, any person arrested and held in custody at a police station or other premises may, on request, have one person known to them or likely to take an interest in their welfare informed at public expense of their whereabouts as soon as practicable. If the person cannot be contacted the detainee may choose up to two alternatives. If they cannot be contacted, the person in charge of detention or the investigation has discretion to allow further attempts until the information has been conveyed. See *Notes 5C* and *5D*

5.2 The exercise of the above right in respect of each person nominated may be delayed only in accordance with *Annex B.*

5.3 The above right may be exercised each time a detainee is taken to another police station.

5.4 If the detainee agrees, they may at the custody officer's discretion, receive visits from friends, family or others likely to take an interest in their welfare, or in whose welfare the detainee has an interest. See *Note 5B.*

5.5 If a friend, relative or person with an interest in the detainee's welfare enquires about their whereabouts, this information shall be given if the suspect agrees and *Annex B* does not apply. See *Note 5D*

5.6 The detainee shall be given writing materials, on request, and allowed to telephone one person for a reasonable time, see *Notes 5A* and *5E*. Either or both these privileges may be denied or delayed if an officer of inspector rank or above considers sending a letter or making a telephone call may result in any of the consequences in:

(a) *Annex B paragraphs 1* and *2* and the person is detained in connection with an indictable offence.

(b) *Not used.*

Nothing in this paragraph permits the restriction or denial of the rights in *paragraphs 5.1* and *6.1.*

5.7   Before any letter or message is sent, or telephone call made, the detainee shall be informed that what they say in any letter, call or message (other than in a communication to a solicitor) may be read or listened to and may be given in evidence. A telephone call may be terminated if it is being abused. The costs can be at public expense at the custody officer's discretion.

5.7A Any delay or denial of the rights in this section should be proportionate and should last no longer than necessary.

5.7B In the case of a person in police custody for specific purposes and periods in accordance with a direction under the Crime (Sentences) Act 1997, Schedule 1 (productions from prison etc.), the exercise of the rights in this section shall be subject to any additional conditions specified in the direction for the purpose of regulating the detainee's contact and communication with others whilst in police custody. See *Note 5F*.

(b) Documentation

Code **C**

5.8   A record must be kept of any:
   (a) request made under this section and the action taken;
   (b) letters, messages or telephone calls made or received or visit received;
   (c) refusal by the detainee to have information about them given to an outside enquirer. The detainee must be asked to countersign the record accordingly and any refusal recorded.

Notes for Guidance

5A   *A person may request an interpreter to interpret a telephone call or translate a letter.*

5B   *At the custody officer's discretion and subject to the detainee's consent, visits should be allowed when possible, subject to having sufficient personnel to supervise a visit and any possible hindrance to the investigation.*

5C   *If the detainee does not know anyone to contact for advice or support or cannot contact a friend or relative, the custody officer should bear in mind any local voluntary bodies or other organisations who might be able to help. Paragraph 6.1 applies if legal advice is required.*

5D   *In some circumstances it may not be appropriate to use the telephone to disclose information under paragraphs 5.1 and 5.5.*

5E   *The telephone call at paragraph 5.6 is in addition to any communication under paragraphs 5.1 and 6.1.*

5F   *Prison Service Order 1801 (Production of Prisoners at the Request of Police) provides detailed guidance and instructions for police officers and Governors and Directors of Prisons regarding applications for prisoners to be transferred to police custody and their safe custody and treatment while in police custody.*

6 Right to legal advice

(a) Action

6.1   Unless *Annex B* applies, all detainees must be informed that they may at any time consult and communicate privately with a solicitor, whether in person, in writing or by telephone, and that free independent legal advice is available. See *paragraph 3.1, Notes 1J, 6B and 6J*

6.2   *Not used*

6.3 A poster advertising the right to legal advice must be prominently displayed in the charging area of every police station. See *Note 6H*.

6.4 No police officer should, at any time, do or say anything with the intention of dissuading any person who is entitled to legal advice in accordance with this Code, whether or not they have been arrested and are detained, from obtaining legal advice. See *Note 6ZA*.

6.5 The exercise of the right of access to legal advice may be delayed only as in *Annex B*. Whenever legal advice is requested, and unless *Annex B* applies, the custody officer must act without delay to secure the provision of such advice. If the detainee has the right to speak to a solicitor in person but declines to exercise the right the officer should point out that the right includes the right to speak with a solicitor on the telephone. If the detainee continues to waive this right, or a detainee whose right to free legal advice is limited to telephone advice from the Criminal Defence Service (CDS) Direct (see *Note 6B*) declines to exercise that right, the officer should ask them why and any reasons should be recorded on the custody record or the interview record as appropriate. Reminders of the right to legal advice must be given as in *paragraphs 3.5, 11.2, 15.4, 16.4, 2B of Annex A, 3 of Annex K* and *16.5* of this Code and Code D, *paragraphs 3.17(ii)* and *6.3*. Once it is clear a detainee does not want to speak to a solicitor in person or by telephone they should cease to be asked their reasons. See *Note 6K*.

6.5A In the case of a person who is a juvenile or is mentally disordered or otherwise mentally vulnerable, an appropriate adult should consider whether legal advice from a solicitor is required. If the person indicates that they do not want legal advice, the appropriate adult has the right to ask for a solicitor to attend if this would be in the best interests of the person. However, the person cannot be forced to see the solicitor if they are adamant that they do not wish to do so.

6.6 A detainee who wants legal advice may not be interviewed or continue to be interviewed until they have received such advice unless:

    (a) *Annex B* applies, when the restriction on drawing adverse inferences from silence in *Annex C* will apply because the detainee is not allowed an opportunity to consult a solicitor; or

    (b) an officer of superintendent rank or above has reasonable grounds for believing that:

       (i) the consequent delay might:
- lead to interference with, or harm to, evidence connected with an offence;
- lead to interference with, or physical harm to, other people;
- lead to serious loss of, or damage to, property;
- lead to alerting other people suspected of having committed an offence but not yet arrested for it;
- hinder the recovery of property obtained in consequence of the commission of an offence.

        See *Note 6A*

       (ii) when a solicitor, including a duty solicitor, has been contacted and has agreed to attend, awaiting their arrival would cause unreasonable delay to the process of investigation.

Note: In these cases the restriction on drawing adverse inferences from silence in *Annex C* will apply because the detainee is not allowed an opportunity to consult a solicitor.

(c) the solicitor the detainee has nominated or selected from a list:

    (i) cannot be contacted;

    (ii) has previously indicated they do not wish to be contacted; or

    (iii) having been contacted, has declined to attend; and

        • the detainee has been advised of the Duty Solicitor Scheme but has declined to ask for the duty solicitor;

        • in these circumstances the interview may be started or continued without further delay provided an officer of inspector rank or above has agreed to the interview proceeding.

Note: The restriction on drawing adverse inferences from silence in *Annex C* will not apply because the detainee is allowed an opportunity to consult the duty solicitor;

(d) the detainee changes their mind about wanting legal advice or (as the case may be) about wanting a solicitor present at the interview and states that they no longer wish to speak to a solicitor. In these circumstances, the interview may be started or continued without delay provided that:

    (i) an officer of inspector rank or above:

        • speaks to the detainee to enquire about the reasons for their change of mind (see *Note 6K*), and

        • makes, or directs the making of, reasonable efforts to ascertain the solicitor's expected time of arrival and to inform the solicitor that the suspect has stated that they wish to change their mind and the reason (if given);

    (ii) the detainee's reason for their change of mind (if given) and the outcome of the action in (i) are recorded in the custody record;

    (iii) the detainee, after being informed of the outcome of the action in (i) above, confirms in writing that they want the interview to proceed without speaking or further speaking to a solicitor or (as the case may be) without a solicitor being present and do not wish to wait for a solicitor by signing an entry to this effect in the custody record;

    (iv) an officer of inspector rank or above is satisfied that it is proper for the interview to proceed in these circumstances and:

        • gives authority in writing for the interview to proceed and if the authority is not recorded in the custody record, the officer must ensure that the custody record shows the date and time of the authority and where it is recorded, and

        • takes or directs the taking of, reasonable steps to inform the solicitor that the authority has been given and the time when the interview is expected to commence, and records or causes to be recorded, the outcome of this action in the custody record.

    (v) When the interview starts and the interviewer reminds the suspect of their right to legal advice (see *paragraph 11.2*, Code E *paragraph 4.5* and Code F *paragraph 4.5*), the interviewer shall then ensure that the fol-

Code **C**

lowing is recorded in the written interview record or the interview record made in accordance with Code E or F:

- confirmation that the detainee has changed their mind about wanting legal advice or (as the case may be) about wanting a solicitor present and the reasons for it if given;
- the fact that authority for the interview to proceed has been given and, subject to *paragraph 2.6A*, the name of the authorising officer;
- that if the solicitor arrives at the station before the interview is completed, the detainee will be so informed without delay and a *break will be taken* to allow them to speak to the solicitor if they wish, unless *paragraph 6.6(a)* applies, and
- that at any time during the interview, the detainee may again ask for legal advice and that if they do, a break will be taken to allow them to speak to the solicitor, unless *paragraph 6.6(a), (b),* or *(c)* applies.

Note: In these circumstances, the restriction on drawing adverse inferences from silence in *Annex C* will not apply because the detainee is allowed an opportunity to consult a solicitor if they wish.

6.7 If *paragraph 6.6(a)* applies, where the reason for authorising the delay ceases to apply, there may be no further delay in permitting the exercise of the right in the absence of a further authorisation unless *paragraph 6.6(b), (c)* or *(d)* applies. If *paragraph 6.6(b)(i)* applies, once sufficient information has been obtained to avert the risk, questioning must cease until the detainee has received legal advice unless *paragraph 6.6(a), (b)(ii), (c)* or *(d)* applies.

6.8 A detainee who has been permitted to consult a solicitor shall be entitled on request to have the solicitor present when they are interviewed unless one of the exceptions in *paragraph 6.6* applies.

6.9 The solicitor may only be required to leave the interview if their conduct is such that the interviewer is unable properly to put questions to the suspect. See *Notes 6D and 6E*.

6.10 If the interviewer considers a solicitor is acting in such a way, they will stop the interview and consult an officer not below superintendent rank, if one is readily available, and otherwise an officer not below inspector rank not connected with the investigation. After speaking to the solicitor, the officer consulted will decide if the interview should continue in the presence of that solicitor. If they decide it should not, the suspect will be given the opportunity to consult another solicitor before the interview continues and that solicitor given an opportunity to be present at the interview. See *Note 6E*.

6.11 The removal of a solicitor from an interview is a serious step and, if it occurs, the officer of superintendent rank or above who took the decision will consider if the incident should be reported to the Solicitors Regulation Authority. If the decision to remove the solicitor has been taken by an officer below superintendent rank, the facts must be reported to an officer of superintendent rank or above who will similarly consider whether a report to the Solicitors Regulation Authority would be appropriate. When the solicitor concerned is a duty solicitor, the report should be both to the Solicitors Regulation Authority and to the Legal Services Commission.

6.12 'Solicitor' in this Code means:

- a solicitor who holds a current practising certificate;

- an accredited or probationary representative included on the register of representatives maintained by the Legal Services Commission.

6.12A An accredited or probationary representative sent to provide advice by, and on behalf of, a solicitor shall be admitted to the police station for this purpose unless an officer of inspector rank or above considers such a visit will hinder the investigation and directs otherwise. Hindering the investigation does not include giving proper legal advice to a detainee as in *Note 6D*. Once admitted to the police station, *paragraphs 6.6* to *6.10* apply.

6.13 In exercising their discretion under *paragraph 6.12A*, the officer should take into account in particular:
- whether:
  - ˜ the identity and status of an accredited or probationary representative have been satisfactorily established;
  - ˜ they are of suitable character to provide legal advice, e.g. a person with a criminal record is unlikely to be suitable unless the conviction was for a minor offence and not recent.
- any other matters in any written letter of authorisation provided by the solicitor on whose behalf the person is attending the police station. See *Note 6F*.

6.14 If the inspector refuses access to an accredited or probationary representative or a decision is taken that such a person should not be permitted to remain at an interview, the inspector must notify the solicitor on whose behalf the representative was acting and give them an opportunity to make alternative arrangements. The detainee must be informed and the custody record noted.

6.15 If a solicitor arrives at the station to see a particular person, that person must, unless *Annex B* applies, be so informed whether or not they are being interviewed and asked if they would like to see the solicitor. This applies even if the detainee has declined legal advice or, having requested it, subsequently agreed to be interviewed without receiving advice. The solicitor's attendance and the detainee's decision must be noted in the custody record.

(b) Documentation

6.16 Any request for legal advice and the action taken shall be recorded.

6.17 A record shall be made in the interview record if a detainee asks for legal advice and an interview is begun either in the absence of a solicitor or their representative, or they have been required to leave an interview.

Notes for Guidance

6ZA *No police officer or police staff shall indicate to any suspect, except to answer a direct question, that the period for which they are liable to be detained, or if not detained, the time taken to complete the interview, might be reduced:*
- *if they do not ask for legal advice or do not want a solicitor present when they are interviewed; or*
- *if they have asked for legal advice or (as the case may be) asked for a solicitor to be present when they are interviewed but change their mind and agree to be interviewed without waiting for a solicitor.*

Code C

6A *In considering if paragraph 6.6(b) applies, the officer should, if practicable, ask the solicitor for an estimate of how long it will take to come to the station and relate this to the time detention is permitted, the time of day (i.e. whether the rest period under paragraph 12.2 is imminent) and the requirements of other investigations. If the solicitor is on their way or is to set off immediately, it will not normally be appropriate to begin an interview before they arrive. If it appears necessary to begin an interview before the solicitor's arrival, they should be given an indication of how long the police would be able to wait before 6.6(b) applies so there is an opportunity to make arrangements for someone else to provide legal advice.*

6B *A detainee has a right to free legal advice and to be represented by a solicitor. This Note for Guidance explains the arrangements which enable detainees to obtain legal advice. An outline of these arrangements is also included in the Notice of Rights and Entitlements given to detainees in accordance with paragraph 3.2. The arrangements also apply, with appropriate modifications, to persons attending a police station or other location voluntarily who are cautioned prior to being interviewed. See paragraph 3.21.*

When a detainee asks for free legal advice, the Defence Solicitor Call Centre (DSCC) must be informed of the request.

Free legal advice will be limited to telephone advice provided by CDS Direct if a detainee is:

- *detained for a non-imprisonable offence;*
- *arrested on a bench warrant for failing to appear and being held for production at court (except where the solicitor has clear documentary evidence available that would result in the client being released from custody);*
- *arrested for drink driving (driving/in charge with excess alcohol, failing to provide a specimen, driving/in charge whilst unfit through drink), or*
- *detained in relation to breach of police or court bail conditions*

unless one or more exceptions apply, in which case the DSCC should arrange for advice to be given by a solicitor at the police station, for example:

- *the police want to interview the detainee or carry out an eye-witness identification procedure;*
- *the detainee needs an appropriate adult;*
- *the detainee is unable to communicate over the telephone;*
- *the detainee alleges serious misconduct by the police;*
- *the investigation includes another offence not included in the list,*
- *the solicitor to be assigned is already at the police station.*

When free advice is not limited to telephone advice, a detainee can ask for free advice from a solicitor they know or if they do not know a solicitor or the solicitor they know cannot be contacted, from the duty solicitor.

To arrange free legal advice, the police should telephone the DSCC. The call centre will decide whether legal advice should be limited to telephone advice from CDS Direct, or whether a solicitor known to the detainee or the duty solicitor should speak to the detainee.

When a detainee wants to pay for legal advice themselves:

- *the DSCC will contact a solicitor of their choice on their behalf;*
- *they may, when free advice is only available by telephone from CDS Direct, still speak to a solicitor of their choice on the telephone for advice, but the solicitor would not be paid by legal aid and may ask the person to pay for the advice;*

- *they should be given an opportunity to consult a specific solicitor or another solicitor from that solicitor's firm. If this solicitor is not available, they may choose up to two alternatives. If these alternatives are not available, the custody officer has discretion to allow further attempts until a solicitor has been contacted and agreed to provide advice;*
- *they are entitled to a private consultation with their chosen solicitor on the telephone or the solicitor may decide to come to the police station;*
- *If their chosen solicitor cannot be contacted, the DSCC may still be called to arrange free legal advice.*

Apart from carrying out duties necessary to implement these arrangements, an officer must not advise the suspect about any particular firm of solicitors.

6B1   *Not used*

6B2   *Not used*

6C   *Not used*

6D   *The solicitor's only role in the police station is to protect and advance the legal rights of their client. On occasions this may require the solicitor to give advice which has the effect of the client avoiding giving evidence which strengthens a prosecution case. The solicitor may intervene in order to seek clarification, challenge an improper question to their client or the manner in which it is put, advise their client not to reply to particular questions, or if they wish to give their client further legal advice. Paragraph 6.9 only applies if the solicitor's approach or conduct prevents or unreasonably obstructs proper questions being put to the suspect or the suspect's response being recorded. Examples of unacceptable conduct include answering questions on a suspect's behalf or providing written replies for the suspect to quote.*

6E   *An officer who takes the decision to exclude a solicitor must be in a position to satisfy the court the decision was properly made. In order to do this they may need to witness what is happening.*

6F   *If an officer of at least inspector rank considers a particular solicitor or firm of solicitors is persistently sending probationary representatives who are unsuited to provide legal advice, they should inform an officer of at least superintendent rank, who may wish to take the matter up with the Solicitors Regulation Authority.*

6G   *Subject to the constraints of Annex B, a solicitor may advise more than one client in an investigation if they wish. Any question of a conflict of interest is for the solicitor under their professional code of conduct. If, however, waiting for a solicitor to give advice to one client may lead to unreasonable delay to the interview with another, the provisions of paragraph 6.6(b) may apply.*

6H   *In addition to a poster in English, a poster or posters containing translations into Welsh, the main minority ethnic languages and the principal European languages should be displayed wherever they are likely to be helpful and it is practicable to do so.*

6I   *Not used*

6J   *Whenever a detainee exercises their right to legal advice by consulting or communicating with a solicitor, they must be allowed to do so in private. This right to consult or communicate in private is fundamental. If the requirement for privacy is compromised because what is said or written by the detainee or solicitor for the purpose of giving and receiving legal advice is overheard, listened to, or read by others without the informed consent of the detainee, the right will effectively have been denied. When a detainee speaks to a solicitor on the telephone, they should be allowed to do so in*

Code **C**

private unless this is impractical because of the design and layout of the custody area or the location of telephones. However, the normal expectation should be that facilities will be available, unless they are being used, at all police stations to enable detainees to speak in private to a solicitor either face to face or over the telephone.

6K   *A detainee is not obliged to give reasons for declining legal advice and should not be pressed to do so.*

7 CITIZENS OF INDEPENDENT COMMONWEALTH COUNTRIES OR FOREIGN NATIONALS

(a) Action

7.1   A detainee who is a citizen of an independent Commonwealth country or a national of a foreign country, including the Republic of Ireland, has the right, upon request, to communicate at any time with the appropriate High Commission, Embassy or Consulate. That detainee must be informed as soon as practicable of this right and asked if they want to have their High Commission, Embassy or Consulate told of their whereabouts and the grounds for their detention. Such a request should be acted upon as soon as practicable. See *Note 7A*.

7.2   A detainee who is a citizen of a country with which a bilateral consular convention or agreement is in force requiring notification of arrest, must also be informed that subject to *paragraph 7.4*, notification of their arrest will be sent to the appropriate High Commission, Embassy or Consulate as soon as practicable, whether or not they request it. Details of the countries to which this requirement currently applies are available from:
http://www.fco.gov.uk/en/publications-and-documents/treaties/treaty-texts/prisoner-transfer-agreements

7.3   Consular officers may, if the detainee agrees, visit one of their nationals in police detention to talk to them and, if required, to arrange for legal advice. Such visits shall take place out of the hearing of a police officer.

7.4   Notwithstanding the provisions of consular conventions, if the detainee claims that they are a refugee or have applied or intend to apply for asylum, the custody officer must ensure that the UK Border Agency (UKBA) is informed as soon as practicable of the claim. UKBA will then determine whether compliance with relevant international obligations requires notification of the arrest to be sent and will inform the custody officer as to what action police need to take.

(b) Documentation

7.5   A record shall be made:
- when a detainee is informed of their rights under this section and of any requirement in paragraph 7.2;
- of any communications with a High Commission, Embassy or Consulate, and
- of any communications with UKBA about a detainee's claim to be a refugee or to be seeking asylum and the resulting action taken by police.

Note for Guidance

7A   *The exercise of the rights in this section may not be interfered with even though Annex B applies.*

8 Conditions of detention

(a) Action

8.1 So far as it is practicable, not more than one detainee should be detained in each cell. See *Note 8C*.

8.2 Cells in use must be adequately heated, cleaned and ventilated. They must be adequately lit, subject to such dimming as is compatible with safety and security to allow people detained overnight to sleep. No additional restraints shall be used within a locked cell unless absolutely necessary and then only restraint equipment, approved for use in that force by the Chief Officer, which is reasonable and necessary in the circumstances having regard to the detainee's demeanour and with a view to ensuring their safety and the safety of others. If a detainee is deaf, mentally disordered or otherwise mentally vulnerable, particular care must be taken when deciding whether to use any form of approved restraints.

Code **C**

8.3 Blankets, mattresses, pillows and other bedding supplied shall be of a reasonable standard and in a clean and sanitary condition. See *Note 8A*.

8.4 Access to toilet and washing facilities must be provided.

8.5 If it is necessary to remove a detainee's clothes for the purposes of investigation, for hygiene, health reasons or cleaning, replacement clothing of a reasonable standard of comfort and cleanliness shall be provided. A detainee may not be interviewed unless adequate clothing has been offered.

8.6 At least two light meals and one main meal should be offered in any 24 hour period. See *Note 8B*. Drinks should be provided at meal times and upon reasonable request between meals. Whenever necessary, advice shall be sought from the appropriate healthcare professional, see *Note 9A*, on medical and dietary matters. As far as practicable, meals provided shall offer a varied diet and meet any specific dietary needs or religious beliefs the detainee may have. The detainee may, at the custody officer's discretion, have meals supplied by their family or friends at their expense. See *Note 8A*.

8.7 Brief outdoor exercise shall be offered daily if practicable.

8.8 A juvenile shall not be placed in a police cell unless no other secure accommodation is available and the custody officer considers it is not practicable to supervise them if they are not placed in a cell or that a cell provides more comfortable accommodation than other secure accommodation in the station. A juvenile may not be placed in a cell with a detained adult.

(b) Documentation

8.9 A record must be kept of replacement clothing and meals offered.

8.10 If a juvenile is placed in a cell, the reason must be recorded.

8.11 The use of any restraints on a detainee whilst in a cell, the reasons for it and, if appropriate, the arrangements for enhanced supervision of the detainee whilst so restrained, shall be recorded. See *paragraph 3.9*

Notes for Guidance

8A   The provisions in paragraph 8.3 and 8.6 respectively are of particular importance in the case of a person likely to be detained for an extended period. In deciding whether to allow meals to be supplied by family or friends, the custody officer is entitled to take

451

account of the risk of items being concealed in any food or package and the officer's duties and responsibilities under food handling legislation.

8B   *Meals should, so far as practicable, be offered at recognised meal times, or at other times that take account of when the detainee last had a meal.*

8C   *Guidance on the Safer Detention and Handling of Persons in Police Custody Second Edition (2012) produced on behalf of the Association of Chief Police Officers provides more detailed guidance on matters concerning detainee healthcare and treatment and associated forensic issues which should be read in conjunction with sections 8 and 9 of this Code.*

9 CARE AND TREATMENT OF DETAINED PERSONS

(a) General

9.1   Nothing in this section prevents the police from calling an appropriate health-care professional to examine a detainee for the purposes of obtaining evidence relating to any offence in which the detainee is suspected of being involved. See *Notes 9A* and *8C.*

9.2   If a complaint is made by, or on behalf of, a detainee about their treatment since their arrest, or it comes to notice that a detainee may have been treated improperly, a report must be made as soon as practicable to an officer of inspector rank or above not connected with the investigation. If the matter concerns a possible assault or the possibility of the unnecessary or unreasonable use of force, an appropriate healthcare professional must also be called as soon as practicable.

9.3   Detainees should be visited at least every hour. If no reasonably foreseeable risk was identified in a risk assessment, see *paragraphs 3.6–3.10*, there is no need to wake a sleeping detainee. Those suspected of being under the influence of drink or drugs or both or of having swallowed drugs, see *Note 9CA*, or whose level of consciousness causes concern must, subject to any clinical directions given by the appropriate healthcare professional, see *paragraph 9.13*:
- be visited and roused at least every half hour;
- have their condition assessed as in *Annex H*;
- and clinical treatment arranged if appropriate

See *Notes 9B, 9C* and *9H*

9.4   When arrangements are made to secure clinical attention for a detainee, the custody officer must make sure all relevant information which might assist in the treatment of the detainee's condition is made available to the responsible healthcare professional. This applies whether or not the healthcare professional asks for such information. Any officer or police staff with relevant information must inform the custody officer as soon as practicable.

(b) Clinical treatment and attention

9.5   The custody officer must make sure a detainee receives appropriate clinical attention as soon as reasonably practicable if the person:
(a) appears to be suffering from physical illness; or
(b) is injured; or
(c) appears to be suffering from a mental disorder; or
(d) appears to need clinical attention.

9.5A This applies even if the detainee makes no request for clinical attention and whether or not they have already received clinical attention elsewhere. If the need for attention appears urgent, e.g. when indicated as in *Annex H*, the nearest available healthcare professional or an ambulance must be called immediately.

9.5B The custody officer must also consider the need for clinical attention as set out in *Note 9C* in relation to those suffering the effects of alcohol or drugs.

9.6 *Paragraph 9.5* is not meant to prevent or delay the transfer to a hospital if necessary of a person detained under the Mental Health Act 1983, section 136. See *Note 9D*. When an assessment under that Act is to take place at a police station, see *paragraph 3.16*, the custody officer must consider whether an appropriate healthcare professional should be called to conduct an initial clinical check on the detainee. This applies particularly when there is likely to be any significant delay in the arrival of a suitably qualified medical practitioner.

9.7 If it appears to the custody officer, or they are told, that a person brought to a station under arrest may be suffering from an infectious disease or condition, the custody officer must take reasonable steps to safeguard the health of the detainee and others at the station. In deciding what action to take, advice must be sought from an appropriate healthcare professional. See *Note 9E*. The custody officer has discretion to isolate the person and their property until clinical directions have been obtained.

9.8 If a detainee requests a clinical examination, an appropriate healthcare professional must be called as soon as practicable to assess the detainee's clinical needs. If a safe and appropriate care plan cannot be provided, the appropriate healthcare professional's advice must be sought. The detainee may also be examined by a medical practitioner of their choice at their expense.

9.9 If a detainee is required to take or apply any medication in compliance with clinical directions prescribed before their detention, the custody officer must consult the appropriate healthcare professional before the use of the medication. Subject to the restrictions in *paragraph 9.10*, the custody officer is responsible for the safekeeping of any medication and for making sure the detainee is given the opportunity to take or apply prescribed or approved medication. Any such consultation and its outcome shall be noted in the custody record.

9.10 No police officer may administer or supervise the self-administration of medically prescribed controlled drugs of the types and forms listed in the Misuse of Drugs Regulations 2001, Schedule 2 or 3. A detainee may only self-administer such drugs under the personal supervision of the registered medical practitioner authorising their use or other appropriate healthcare professional. The custody officer may supervise the self-administration of, or authorise other custody staff to supervise the self-administration of drugs listed in Schedule 4 or 5 if the officer has consulted the appropriate healthcare professional authorising their use and both are satisfied self-administration will not expose the detainee, police officers or anyone else to the risk of harm or injury.

9.11 When appropriate healthcare professionals administer drugs or authorise the use of other medications, supervise their self-administration or consult with the custody officer about allowing self administration of drugs listed in Schedule 4 or 5, it must be within current medicines legislation and the scope of practice as determined by their relevant statutory regulatory body.

Code **C**

9.12 If a detainee has in their possession, or claims to need, medication relating to a heart condition, diabetes, epilepsy or a condition of comparable potential seriousness then, even though *paragraph 9.5* may not apply, the advice of the appropriate healthcare professional must be obtained.

9.13 Whenever the appropriate healthcare professional is called in accordance with this section to examine or treat a detainee, the custody officer shall ask for their opinion about:
- any risks or problems which police need to take into account when making decisions about the detainee's continued detention;
- when to carry out an interview if applicable; and
- the need for safeguards.

9.14 When clinical directions are given by the appropriate healthcare professional, whether orally or in writing, and the custody officer has any doubts or is in any way uncertain about any aspect of the directions, the custody officer shall ask for clarification. It is particularly important that directions concerning the frequency of visits are clear, precise and capable of being implemented. See *Note 9F*.

(c) Documentation

9.15 A record must be made in the custody record of:
(a) the arrangements made for an examination by an appropriate healthcare professional under *paragraph 9.2* and of any complaint reported under that paragraph together with any relevant remarks by the custody officer;
(b) any arrangements made in accordance with *paragraph 9.5*;
(c) any request for a clinical examination under *paragraph 9.8* and any arrangements made in response;
(d) the injury, ailment, condition or other reason which made it necessary to make the arrangements in (a) to (c); See *Note 9G*.
(e) any clinical directions and advice, including any further clarifications, given to police by a healthcare professional concerning the care and treatment of the detainee in connection with any of the arrangements made in (a) to (c); See *Notes 9E* and *9F*.
(f) if applicable, the responses received when attempting to rouse a person using the procedure in *Annex H*. See *Note 9H*.

9.16 If a healthcare professional does not record their clinical findings in the custody record, the record must show where they are recorded. See *Note 9G*. However, information which is necessary to custody staff to ensure the effective ongoing care and well being of the detainee must be recorded openly in the custody record, see *paragraph 3.8* and *Annex G, paragraph 7*.

9.17 Subject to the requirements of *Section 4*, the custody record shall include:
- a record of all medication a detainee has in their possession on arrival at the police station;
- a note of any such medication they claim to need but do not have with them.

Notes for Guidance

9A   A 'healthcare professional' means a clinically qualified person working within the scope of practice as determined by their relevant statutory regulatory body. Whether a healthcare professional is 'appropriate' depends on the circumstances of the duties they carry out at the time.

9B   Whenever possible juveniles and mentally vulnerable detainees should be visited more frequently.

9C   A detainee who appears drunk or behaves abnormally may be suffering from illness, the effects of drugs or may have sustained injury, particularly a head injury which is not apparent. A detainee needing or dependent on certain drugs, including alcohol, may experience harmful effects within a short time of being deprived of their supply. In these circumstances, when there is any doubt, police should always act urgently to call an appropriate healthcare professional or an ambulance. Paragraph 9.5 does not apply to minor ailments or injuries which do not need attention. However, all such ailments or injuries must be recorded in the custody record and any doubt must be resolved in favour of calling the appropriate healthcare professional.

9CA Paragraph 9.3 would apply to a person in police custody by order of a magistrates' court under the Criminal Justice Act 1988, section 152 (as amended by the Drugs Act 2005, section 8) to facilitate the recovery of evidence after being charged with drug possession or drug trafficking and suspected of having swallowed drugs. In the case of the healthcare needs of a person who has swallowed drugs, the custody officer subject to any clinical directions, should consider the necessity for rousing every half hour. This does not negate the need for regular visiting of the suspect in the cell.

Code **C**

9D   Whenever practicable, arrangements should be made for persons detained for assessment under the Mental Health Act 1983, section 136 to be taken to a hospital. Chapter 10 of the Mental Health Act 1983 Code of Practice (as revised) provides more detailed guidance about arranging assessments under section 136 and transferring detainees from police stations to other places of safety.

9E   It is important to respect a person's right to privacy and information about their health must be kept confidential and only disclosed with their consent or in accordance with clinical advice when it is necessary to protect the detainee's health or that of others who come into contact with them.

9F   The custody officer should always seek to clarify directions that the detainee requires constant observation or supervision and should ask the appropriate healthcare professional to explain precisely what action needs to be taken to implement such directions.

9G   Paragraphs 9.15 and 9.16 do not require any information about the cause of any injury, ailment or condition to be recorded on the custody record if it appears capable of providing evidence of an offence.

9H   The purpose of recording a person's responses when attempting to rouse them using the procedure in Annex H is to enable any change in the individual's consciousness level to be noted and clinical treatment arranged if appropriate.

10 CAUTIONS

(a) When a caution must be given

10.1 A person whom there are grounds to suspect of an offence, see Note 10A, must be cautioned before any questions about an offence, or further questions if the answers provide the grounds for suspicion, are put to them if either the suspect's answers or silence, (i.e. failure or refusal to answer or answer satisfactorily) may be given in evidence to a court in a prosecution. A person need not be cautioned if questions are for other necessary purposes, e.g.:
(a) solely to establish their identity or ownership of any vehicle;

    (b) to obtain information in accordance with any relevant statutory require-
ment, see *paragraph 10.9*;

    (c) in furtherance of the proper and effective conduct of a search, e.g. to deter-
mine the need to search in the exercise of powers of stop and search or to
seek co-operation while carrying out a search;

    (d) to seek verification of a written record as in *paragraph 11.13*.

    (e) *Not used*

10.2 Whenever a person not under arrest is initially cautioned, or reminded they are
under caution, that person must at the same time be told they are not under
arrest and informed of the provisions of *paragraph 3.21* which explain how
they may obtain legal advice according to whether they are at a police station
or elsewhere. See *Note 10C*.

10.3 A person who is arrested, or further arrested, must be informed at the time if
practicable, or if not, as soon as it becomes practicable thereafter, that they are
under arrest and of the grounds and reasons for their arrest, see paragraph 3.4,
Note 10B and *Code G, paragraphs 2.2 and 4.3*.

10.4 As required by *Code G, section 3*, a person who is arrested, or further arrested,
must also be cautioned unless:

    (a) it is impracticable to do so by reason of their condition or behaviour at the
time;

    (b) they have already been cautioned immediately prior to arrest as in *para-
graph 10.1*.

(b) Terms of the cautions

10.5 The caution which must be given on:

    (a) arrest;

    (b) all other occasions before a person is charged or informed they may be
prosecuted; see *section 16*,

should, unless the restriction on drawing adverse inferences from silence
applies, see *Annex C*, be in the following terms:

"You do not have to say anything. But it may harm your defence if you do not
mention when questioned something which you later rely on in Court.
Anything you do say may be given in evidence."

Where the use of the Welsh Language is appropriate, a constable may provide
the caution directly in Welsh in the following terms:

"Does dim rhaid i chi ddweud dim byd. Ond gall niweidio eich amddiffyniad
os na fyddwch chi'n sôn, wrth gael eich holi, am rywbeth y byddwch chi'n
dibynnu arno nes ymlaen yn y Llys. Gall unrhyw beth yr ydych yn ei ddweud
gael ei roi fel tystiolaeth."

See *Note 10G*

10.6 *Annex C, paragraph 2* sets out the alternative terms of the caution to be used
when the restriction on drawing adverse inferences from silence applies.

10.7 Minor deviations from the words of any caution given in accordance with this
Code do not constitute a breach of this Code, provided the sense of the relevant caution is preserved. See *Note 10D*.

10.8 After any break in questioning under caution, the person being questioned must
be made aware they remain under caution. If there is any doubt the relevant caution should be given again in full when the interview resumes. See *Note 10E*.

10.9   When, despite being cautioned, a person fails to co-operate or to answer par-
       ticular questions which may affect their immediate treatment, the person
       should be informed of any relevant consequences and that those conse-
       quences are not affected by the caution. Examples are when a person's refusal
       to provide:
       • their name and address when charged may make them liable to detention;
       • particulars and information in accordance with a statutory requirement,
         e.g. under the Road Traffic Act 1988, may amount to an offence or may
         make the person liable to a further arrest.

(c) Special warnings under the Criminal Justice and Public Order Act 1994, sections 36 and 37

10.10 When a suspect interviewed at a police station or authorised place of deten-
       tion after arrest fails or refuses to answer certain questions, or to answer satis-
       factorily, after due warning, see *Note 10F*, a court or jury may draw such
       inferences as appear proper under the Criminal Justice and Public Order Act
       1994, sections 36 and 37. Such inferences may only be drawn when:
       (a) the restriction on drawing adverse inferences from silence, see *Annex C*,
           does not apply; and
       (b) the suspect is arrested by a constable and fails or refuses to account for any
           objects, marks or substances, or marks on such objects found:
           • on their person;
           • in or on their clothing or footwear;
           • otherwise in their possession; or
           • in the place they were arrested;
       (c) the arrested suspect was found by a constable at a place at or about the
           time the offence for which that officer has arrested them is alleged to have
           been committed, and the suspect fails or refuses to account for their pres-
           ence there.
       When the restriction on drawing adverse inferences from silence applies, the sus-
       pect may still be asked to account for any of the matters in (*b*) or (*c*) but the spe-
       cial warning described in *paragraph 10.11* will not apply and must not be given.

10.11 For an inference to be drawn when a suspect fails or refuses to answer a ques-
       tion about one of these matters or to answer it satisfactorily, the suspect must
       first be told in ordinary language:
       (a) what offence is being investigated;
       (b) what fact they are being asked to account for;
       (c) this fact may be due to them taking part in the commission of the offence;
       (d) a court may draw a proper inference if they fail or refuse to account for
           this fact;
       (e) a record is being made of the interview and it may be given in evidence if
           they are brought to trial.

(d) Juveniles and persons who are mentally disordered or otherwise mentally vulnerable

10.11A The information required in paragraph 10.11 must not be given to a suspect
       who is a juvenile or who is mentally disordered or otherwise mentally vul-
       nerable unless the appropriate adult is present.

Code C

10.12   If a juvenile or a person who is mentally disordered or otherwise mentally vulnerable is cautioned in the absence of the appropriate adult, the caution must be repeated in the adult's presence.

(e) Documentation

10.13   A record shall be made when a caution is given under this section, either in the interviewer's pocket book or in the interview record.

Notes for Guidance

10A   *There must be some reasonable, objective grounds for the suspicion, based on known facts or information which are relevant to the likelihood the offence has been committed and the person to be questioned committed it.*

10B   *An arrested person must be given sufficient information to enable them to understand that they have been deprived of their liberty and the reason they have been arrested, e.g. when a person is arrested on suspicion of committing an offence they must be informed of the suspected offence's nature, when and where it was committed. The suspect must also be informed of the reason or reasons why the arrest is considered necessary. Vague or technical language should be avoided.*

10C   *The restriction on drawing inferences from silence, see* Annex C, paragraph 1, *does not apply to a person who has not been detained and who therefore cannot be prevented from seeking legal advice if they want, see paragraph 3.21.*

10D   *If it appears a person does not understand the caution, the person giving it should explain it in their own words.*

10E   *It may be necessary to show to the court that nothing occurred during an interview break or between interviews which influenced the suspect's recorded evidence. After a break in an interview or at the beginning of a subsequent interview, the interviewing officer should summarise the reason for the break and confirm this with the suspect.*

10F   *The Criminal Justice and Public Order Act 1994, sections 36 and 37 apply only to suspects who have been arrested by a constable or an officer of Revenue and Customs and are given the relevant warning by the police or Revenue and Customs officer who made the arrest or who is investigating the offence. They do not apply to any interviews with suspects who have not been arrested.*

10G   *Nothing in this Code requires a caution to be given or repeated when informing a person not under arrest they may be prosecuted for an offence. However, a court will not be able to draw any inferences under the Criminal Justice and Public Order Act 1994, section 34, if the person was not cautioned.*

11 Interviews—General

(a) Action

11.1A   An interview is the questioning of a person regarding their involvement or suspected involvement in a criminal offence or offences which, under *paragraph 10.1*, must be carried out under caution. Whenever a person is interviewed they must be informed of the nature of the offence, or further offence. Procedures under the Road Traffic Act 1988, section 7 or the Transport and Works Act 1992, section 31 do not constitute interviewing for the purpose of this Code.

11.1   Following a decision to arrest a suspect, they must not be interviewed about the relevant offence except at a police station or other authorised place of detention, unless the consequent delay would be likely to:

(a) lead to:
- interference with, or harm to, evidence connected with an offence;
- interference with, or physical harm to, other people; or
- serious loss of, or damage to, property;

(b) lead to alerting other people suspected of committing an offence but not yet arrested for it; or

(c) hinder the recovery of property obtained in consequence of the commission of an offence.

Interviewing in any of these circumstances shall cease once the relevant risk has been averted or the necessary questions have been put in order to attempt to avert that risk.

11.2   Immediately prior to the commencement or re-commencement of any interview at a police station or other authorised place of detention, the interviewer should remind the suspect of their entitlement to free legal advice and that the interview can be delayed for legal advice to be obtained, unless one of the exceptions in *paragraph 6.6* applies. It is the interviewer's responsibility to make sure all reminders are recorded in the interview record.

11.3   *Not used*

11.4   At the beginning of an interview the interviewer, after cautioning the suspect, see *section 10*, shall put to them any significant statement or silence which occurred in the presence and hearing of a police officer or other police staff before the start of the interview and which have not been put to the suspect in the course of a previous interview. See *Note 11A*. The interviewer shall ask the suspect whether they confirm or deny that earlier statement or silence and if they want to add anything.

11.4A A significant statement is one which appears capable of being used in evidence against the suspect, in particular a direct admission of guilt. A significant silence is a failure or refusal to answer a question or answer satisfactorily when under caution, which might, allowing for the restriction on drawing adverse inferences from silence, see *Annex C*, give rise to an inference under the Criminal Justice and Public Order Act 1994, Part III.

11.5   No interviewer may try to obtain answers or elicit a statement by the use of oppression. Except as in *paragraph 10.9*, no interviewer shall indicate, except to answer a direct question, what action will be taken by the police if the person being questioned answers questions, makes a statement or refuses to do either. If the person asks directly what action will be taken if they answer questions, make a statement or refuse to do either, the interviewer may inform them what action the police propose to take provided that action is itself proper and warranted.

11.6   The interview or further interview of a person about an offence with which that person has not been charged or for which they have not been informed they may be prosecuted, must cease when:

(a) the officer in charge of the investigation is satisfied all the questions they consider relevant to obtaining accurate and reliable information about the offence have been put to the suspect, this includes allowing the suspect

Code **C**

an opportunity to give an innocent explanation and asking questions to test if the explanation is accurate and reliable, e.g. to clear up ambiguities or clarify what the suspect said;

(b) the officer in charge of the investigation has taken account of any other available evidence; and

(c) the officer in charge of the investigation, or in the case of a detained suspect, the custody officer, see *paragraph 16.1*, reasonably believes there is sufficient evidence to provide a realistic prospect of conviction for that offence. See *Note 11B*.

This paragraph does not prevent officers in revenue cases or acting under the confiscation provisions of the Criminal Justice Act 1988 or the Drug Trafficking Act 1994 from inviting suspects to complete a formal question and answer record after the interview is concluded.

(b) Interview records

11.7 (a) An accurate record must be made of each interview, whether or not the interview takes place at a police station.

(b) The record must state the place of interview, the time it begins and ends, any interview breaks and, subject to *paragraph 2.6A*, the names of all those present; and must be made on the forms provided for this purpose or in the interviewer's pocket book or in accordance with the Codes of Practice E or F.

(c) Any written record must be made and completed during the interview, unless this would not be practicable or would interfere with the conduct of the interview, and must constitute either a verbatim record of what has been said or, failing this, an account of the interview which adequately and accurately summarises it.

11.8 If a written record is not made during the interview it must be made as soon as practicable after its completion.

11.9 Written interview records must be timed and signed by the maker.

11.10 If a written record is not completed during the interview the reason must be recorded in the interview record.

11.11 Unless it is impracticable, the person interviewed shall be given the opportunity to read the interview record and to sign it as correct or to indicate how they consider it inaccurate. If the person interviewed cannot read or refuses to read the record or sign it, the senior interviewer present shall read it to them and ask whether they would like to sign it as correct or make their mark or to indicate how they consider it inaccurate. The interviewer shall certify on the interview record itself what has occurred. See *Note 11E*.

11.12 If the appropriate adult or the person's solicitor is present during the interview, they should also be given an opportunity to read and sign the interview record or any written statement taken down during the interview.

11.13 A written record shall be made of any comments made by a suspect, including unsolicited comments, which are outside the context of an interview but which might be relevant to the offence. Any such record must be timed and signed by the maker. When practicable the suspect shall be given the opportunity to read that record and to sign it as correct or to indicate how they consider it inaccurate. See *Note 11E*.

11.14 Any refusal by a person to sign an interview record when asked in accordance with this Code must itself be recorded.

(c) Juveniles and mentally disordered or otherwise mentally vulnerable people

11.15 A juvenile or person who is mentally disordered or otherwise mentally vulnerable must not be interviewed regarding their involvement or suspected involvement in a criminal offence or offences, or asked to provide or sign a written statement under caution or record of interview, in the absence of the appropriate adult unless *paragraphs 11.1, 11.18 to 11.20* apply. See *Note 11C*.

11.16 Juveniles may only be interviewed at their place of education in exceptional circumstances and only when the principal or their nominee agrees. Every effort should be made to notify the parent(s) or other person responsible for the juvenile's welfare and the appropriate adult, if this is a different person, that the police want to interview the juvenile and reasonable time should be allowed to enable the appropriate adult to be present at the interview. If awaiting the appropriate adult would cause unreasonable delay, and unless the juvenile is suspected of an offence against the educational establishment, the principal or their nominee can act as the appropriate adult for the purposes of the interview.

Code **C**

11.17 If an appropriate adult is present at an interview, they shall be informed:
- they are not expected to act simply as an observer; and
- the purpose of their presence is to:
    - ˜ advise the person being interviewed;
    - ˜ observe whether the interview is being conducted properly and fairly;
    - ˜ facilitate communication with the person being interviewed.

(d) Vulnerable suspects—urgent interviews at police stations

11.18 The following persons may not be interviewed unless an officer of superintendent rank or above considers delay will lead to the consequences in *paragraph 11.1(a)* to *(c)*, and is satisfied the interview would not significantly harm the person's physical or mental state (see Annex G):
   (a) a juvenile or person who is mentally disordered or otherwise mentally vulnerable if at the time of the interview the appropriate adult is not present;
   (b) anyone other than in (*a*) who at the time of the interview appears unable to:
      - appreciate the significance of questions and their answers; or
      - understand what is happening because of the effects of drink, drugs or any illness, ailment or condition;
   (c) a person who has difficulty understanding English or has a hearing disability, if at the time of the interview an interpreter is not present.

11.19 These interviews may not continue once sufficient information has been obtained to avert the consequences in *paragraph 11.1(a)* to *(c)*.

11.20 A record shall be made of the grounds for any decision to interview a person under *paragraph 11.18*.

Notes for Guidance

11A   *Paragraph 11.4 does not prevent the interviewer from putting significant statements and silences to a suspect again at a later stage or a further interview.*

11B   *The Criminal Procedure and Investigations Act 1996 Code of Practice, paragraph 3.5 states 'In conducting an investigation, the investigator should pursue all reasonable lines of enquiry, whether these point towards or away from the suspect. What is reasonable will depend on the particular circumstances.' Interviewers should keep this in mind when deciding what questions to ask in an interview.*

11C   *Although juveniles or people who are mentally disordered or otherwise mentally vulnerable are often capable of providing reliable evidence, they may, without knowing or wishing to do so, be particularly prone in certain circumstances to provide information that may be unreliable, misleading or self-incriminating. Special care should always be taken when questioning such a person, and the appropriate adult should be involved if there is any doubt about a person's age, mental state or capacity. Because of the risk of unreliable evidence it is also important to obtain corroboration of any facts admitted whenever possible.*

11D   *Juveniles should not be arrested at their place of education unless this is unavoidable. When a juvenile is arrested at their place of education, the principal or their nominee must be informed.*

11E   *Significant statements described in paragraph 11.4 will always be relevant to the offence and must be recorded. When a suspect agrees to read records of interviews and other comments and sign them as correct, they should be asked to endorse the record with, e.g. 'I agree that this is a correct record of what was said' and add their signature. If the suspect does not agree with the record, the interviewer should record the details of any disagreement and ask the suspect to read these details and sign them to the effect that they accurately reflect their disagreement. Any refusal to sign should be recorded.*

12 Interviews in police stations

(a) **Action**

12.1 If a police officer wants to interview or conduct enquiries which require the presence of a detainee, the custody officer is responsible for deciding whether to deliver the detainee into the officer's custody. An investigating officer who is given custody of a detainee takes over responsibility for the detainee's care and safe custody for the purposes of this Code until they return the detainee to the custody officer when they must report the manner in which they complied with the Code whilst having custody of the detainee.

12.2 Except as below, in any period of 24 hours a detainee must be allowed a continuous period of at least 8 hours for rest, free from questioning, travel or any interruption in connection with the investigation concerned. This period should normally be at night or other appropriate time which takes account of when the detainee last slept or rested. If a detainee is arrested at a police station after going there voluntarily, the period of 24 hours runs from the time of their arrest and not the time of arrival at the police station. The period may not be interrupted or delayed, except:

(a) when there are reasonable grounds for believing not delaying or interrupting the period would:

(i)   involve a risk of harm to people or serious loss of, or damage to, property;

(ii) delay unnecessarily the person's release from custody;

(iii) otherwise prejudice the outcome of the investigation;

(b) at the request of the detainee, their appropriate adult or legal representative;

(c) when a delay or interruption is necessary in order to:

    (i) comply with the legal obligations and duties arising under *section 15*;

    (ii) to take action required under *section 9* or in accordance with medical advice.

If the period is interrupted in accordance with *(a)*, a fresh period must be allowed. Interruptions under *(b)* and *(c)*, do not require a fresh period to be allowed.

12.3 Before a detainee is interviewed the custody officer, in consultation with the officer in charge of the investigation and appropriate healthcare professionals as necessary, shall assess whether the detainee is fit enough to be interviewed. This means determining and considering the risks to the detainee's physical and mental state if the interview took place and determining what safeguards are needed to allow the interview to take place. See *Annex G*. The custody officer shall not allow a detainee to be interviewed if the custody officer considers it would cause significant harm to the detainee's physical or mental state. Vulnerable suspects listed at *paragraph 11.18* shall be treated as always being at some risk during an interview and these persons may not be interviewed except in accordance with *paragraphs 11.18 to 11.20*.

12.4 As far as practicable interviews shall take place in interview rooms which are adequately heated, lit and ventilated.

12.5 A suspect whose detention without charge has been authorised under PACE, because the detention is necessary for an interview to obtain evidence of the offence for which they have been arrested, may choose not to answer questions but police do not require the suspect's consent or agreement to interview them for this purpose. If a suspect takes steps to prevent themselves being questioned or further questioned, e.g. by refusing to leave their cell to go to a suitable interview room or by trying to leave the interview room, they shall be advised their consent or agreement to interview is not required. The suspect shall be cautioned as in *section 10*, and informed if they fail or refuse to co-operate, the interview may take place in the cell and that their failure or refusal to co-operate may be given in evidence. The suspect shall then be invited to co-operate and go into the interview room.

12.6 People being questioned or making statements shall not be required to stand.

12.7 Before the interview commences each interviewer shall, subject to *paragraph 2.6A*, identify themselves and any other persons present to the interviewee.

12.8 Breaks from interviewing should be made at recognised meal times or at other times that take account of when an interviewee last had a meal. Short refreshment breaks shall be provided at approximately two hour intervals, subject to the interviewer's discretion to delay a break if there are reasonable grounds for believing it would:

    (i) involve a:

      • risk of harm to people;

      • serious loss of, or damage to, property;

    (ii) unnecessarily delay the detainee's release;

    (iii) otherwise prejudice the outcome of the investigation.

Code **C**

See *Note 12B*

12.9 If during the interview a complaint is made by or on behalf of the interviewee concerning the provisions of any of the Codes, or it comes to the interviewer's notice that the interviewee may have been treated improperly, the interviewer should:

(i) record the matter in the interview record;

(ii) inform the custody officer, who is then responsible for dealing with it as in *section 9*.

(b) Documentation

12.10 A record must be made of the:

- time a detainee is not in the custody of the custody officer, and why
- reason for any refusal to deliver the detainee out of that custody.

12.11 A record shall be made of:

(a) the reasons it was not practicable to use an interview room; and

(b) any action taken as in *paragraph 12.5*.

The record shall be made on the custody record or in the interview record for action taken whilst an interview record is being kept, with a brief reference to this effect in the custody record.

12.12 Any decision to delay a break in an interview must be recorded, with reasons, in the interview record.

12.13 All written statements made at police stations under caution shall be written on forms provided for the purpose.

12.14 All written statements made under caution shall be taken in accordance with *Annex D*. Before a person makes a written statement under caution at a police station they shall be reminded about the right to legal advice. See *Note 12A*.

Notes for Guidance

12A It is not normally necessary to ask for a written statement if the interview was recorded in writing and the record signed in accordance with paragraph 11.11 or audibly or visually recorded in accordance with Code E or F. Statements under caution should normally be taken in these circumstances only at the person's express wish. A person may however be asked if they want to make such a statement.

12B Meal breaks should normally last at least 45 minutes and shorter breaks after two hours should last at least 15 minutes. If the interviewer delays a break in accordance with paragraph 12.8 and prolongs the interview, a longer break should be provided. If there is a short interview, and another short interview is contemplated, the length of the break may be reduced if there are reasonable grounds to believe this is necessary to avoid any of the consequences in paragraph 12.8(i) to (iii).

13 INTERPRETERS

(a) General

13.1 Chief officers are responsible for making sure appropriate arrangements are in place for provision of suitably qualified interpreters for people who:

- are deaf;
- do not understand English. See *Note 13A*

(b) Foreign languages

13.2   Unless *paragraphs 11.1, 11.18* to *11.20* apply, a person must not be interviewed in the absence of a person capable of interpreting if:
  (a) they have difficulty understanding English;
  (b) the interviewer cannot speak the person's own language;
  (c) the person wants an interpreter present.

13.3   The interviewer shall make sure the interpreter makes a note of the interview at the time in the person's language for use in the event of the interpreter being called to give evidence, and certifies its accuracy. The interviewer should allow sufficient time for the interpreter to note each question and answer after each is put, given and interpreted. The person should be allowed to read the record or have it read to them and sign it as correct or indicate the respects in which they consider it inaccurate. If the interview is audibly recorded or visually recorded, the arrangements in Code E or F apply.

13.4   In the case of a person making a statement to a police officer or other police staff other than in English:
  (a) the interpreter shall record the statement in the language it is made;
  (b) the person shall be invited to sign it;
  (c) an official English translation shall be made in due course.

Code C

(c) Deaf people and people with speech difficulties

13.5   If a person appears to be deaf or there is doubt about their hearing or speaking ability, they must not be interviewed in the absence of an interpreter unless they agree in writing to being interviewed without one or *paragraphs 11.1, 11.18* to *11.20* apply.

13.6   An interpreter should also be called if a juvenile is interviewed and the parent or guardian present as the appropriate adult appears to be deaf or there is doubt about their hearing or speaking ability, unless they agree in writing to the interview proceeding without one or *paragraphs 11.1, 11.18* to *11.20* apply.

13.7   The interviewer shall make sure the interpreter is allowed to read the interview record and certify its accuracy in the event of the interpreter being called to give evidence. If the interview is audibly recorded or visually recorded, the arrangements in Code E or F apply.

(d) Additional rules for detained persons

13.8   All reasonable attempts should be made to make the detainee understand that interpreters will be provided at public expense.

13.9   If *paragraph 6.1* applies and the detainee cannot communicate with the solicitor because of language, hearing or speech difficulties, an interpreter must be called. The interpreter may not be a police officer or any other police staff when interpretation is needed for the purposes of obtaining legal advice. In all other cases a police officer or other police staff may only interpret if the detainee and the appropriate adult, if applicable, give their agreement in writing or if the interview is audibly recorded or visually recorded as in Code E or F.

13.10 When the custody officer cannot establish effective communication with a person charged with an offence who appears deaf or there is doubt about their ability to hear, speak or to understand English, arrangements must be made as soon as practicable for an interpreter to explain the offence and any other information given by the custody officer.

(e) Documentation

13.11 Action taken to call an interpreter under this section and any agreement to be interviewed in the absence of an interpreter must be recorded.

Note for Guidance

13A   Whenever possible, interpreters should be provided in accordance with national arrangements approved or prescribed by the Secretary of State.

14 QUESTIONING—SPECIAL RESTRICTIONS

14.1   If a person is arrested by one police force on behalf of another and the lawful period of detention in respect of that offence has not yet commenced in accordance with PACE, section 41 no questions may be put to them about the offence while they are in transit between the forces except to clarify any voluntary statement they make.

14.2   If a person is in police detention at a hospital they may not be questioned without the agreement of a responsible doctor. See *Note 14A*.

Note for Guidance

14A   If questioning takes place at a hospital under paragraph 14.2, or on the way to or from a hospital, the period of questioning concerned counts towards the total period of detention permitted.

15 REVIEWS AND EXTENSIONS OF DETENTION

(a) Persons detained under PACE

15.1   The review officer is responsible under PACE, section 40 for periodically determining if a person's detention, before or after charge, continues to be necessary. This requirement continues throughout the detention period and except as in *paragraph 15.10*, the review officer must be present at the police station holding the detainee. See *Notes 15A* and *15B*.

15.2   Under PACE, section 42, an officer of superintendent rank or above who is responsible for the station holding the detainee may give authority any time after the second review to extend the maximum period the person may be detained without charge by up to 12 hours. Further detention without charge may be authorised only by a magistrates' court in accordance with PACE, sections 43 and 44. See *Notes 15C, 15D* and *15E*.

15.2A An authorisation under section 42(1) of PACE extends the maximum period of detention permitted before charge for indictable offences from 24 hours to 36 hours. Detaining a juvenile or mentally vulnerable person for longer than 24 hours will be dependent on the circumstances of the case and with regard to the person's:

(a) special vulnerability;

(b) the legal obligation to provide an opportunity for representations to be made prior to a decision about extending detention;

(c) the need to consult and consider the views of any appropriate adult; and

(d) any alternatives to police custody.

15.3   Before deciding whether to authorise continued detention the officer responsible under *paragraph 15.1* or *15.2* shall give an opportunity to make representations about the detention to:

(a) the detainee, unless in the case of a review as in *paragraph 15.1*, the detainee is asleep;

(b) the detainee's solicitor if available at the time; and

(c) the appropriate adult if available at the time.

See *Note 15CA*

15.3A Other people having an interest in the detainee's welfare may also make representations at the authorising officer's discretion.

15.3B Subject to *paragraph 15.10*, the representations may be made orally in person or by telephone or in writing. The authorising officer may, however, refuse to hear oral representations from the detainee if the officer considers them unfit to make representations because of their condition or behaviour. See *Note 15C*.

15.3C The decision on whether the review takes place in person or by telephone or by video conferencing (see *Note 15G*) is a matter for the review officer. In determining the form the review may take, the review officer must always take full account of the needs of the person in custody. The benefits of carrying out a review in person should always be considered, based on the individual circumstances of each case with specific additional consideration if the person is:

(a) a juvenile (and the age of the juvenile); or

(b) suspected of being mentally vulnerable; or

(c) in need of medical attention for other than routine minor ailments; or

(d) subject to presentational or community issues around their detention.

15.4   Before conducting a review or determining whether to extend the maximum period of detention without charge, the officer responsible must make sure the detainee is reminded of their entitlement to free legal advice, see *paragraph 6.5*, unless in the case of a review the person is asleep.

15.5   If, after considering any representations, the review officer under *paragraph 15.1* decides to keep the detainee in detention or the superintendent under *paragraph 15.2* extends the maximum period for which they may be detained without charge, then any comment made by the detainee shall be recorded. If applicable, the officer shall be informed of the comment as soon as practicable. See also *paragraphs 11.4* and *11.13*.

15.6   No officer shall put specific questions to the detainee:

• regarding their involvement in any offence; or

• in respect of any comments they may make:

˜ when given the opportunity to make representations; or

˜ in response to a decision to keep them in detention or extend the maximum period of detention.

Code C

Such an exchange could constitute an interview as in *paragraph 11.1A* and would be subject to the associated safeguards in *section 11* and, in respect of a person who has been charged, *paragraph 16.5*. See also *paragraph 11.13*.

15.7 A detainee who is asleep at a review, see *paragraph 15.1,* and whose continued detention is authorised must be informed about the decision and reason as soon as practicable after waking.

15.8 *Not used*

(b) Review of detention by telephone and video conferencing facilities

15.9 PACE, section 40A provides that the officer responsible under section 40 for reviewing the detention of a person who has not been charged, need not attend the police station holding the detainee and may carry out the review by telephone.

15.9A PACE, section 45A(2) provides that the officer responsible under section 40 for reviewing the detention of a person who has not been charged, need not attend the police station holding the detainee and may carry out the review by video conferencing facilities. See *Note 15G*.

15.9B A telephone review is not permitted where facilities for review by video conferencing exist and it is practicable to use them.

15.9C The review officer can decide at any stage that a telephone review or review by video conferencing should be terminated and that the review will be conducted in person. The reasons for doing so should be noted in the custody record.

See *Note 15F*

15.10 When a review is carried out by telephone or by video conferencing facilities, an officer at the station holding the detainee shall be required by the review officer to fulfil that officer's obligations under PACE section 40 and this Code by:

(a) making any record connected with the review in the detainee's custody record;

(b) if applicable, making the record in (a) in the presence of the detainee; and

(c) for a review by telephone, giving the detainee information about the review.

15.11 When a review is carried out by telephone or by video conferencing facilities, the requirement in *paragraph 15.3* will be satisfied:

(a) if facilities exist for the immediate transmission of written representations to the review officer, e.g. fax or email message, by allowing those who are given the opportunity to make representations, to make their representations:

(i) orally by telephone or (as the case may be) by means of the video conferencing facilities; or

(ii) in writing using the facilities for the immediate transmission of written representations; and

(b) in all other cases, by allowing those who are given the opportunity to make representations, to make their representations orally by telephone or by means of the video conferencing facilities.

(c) Documentation

15.12 It is the officer's responsibility to make sure all reminders given under *paragraph 15.4* are noted in the custody record.

15.13 The grounds for, and extent of, any delay in conducting a review shall be recorded.

15.14 When a review is carried out by telephone or video conferencing facilities, a record shall be made of:

(a) the reason the review officer did not attend the station holding the detainee;

(b) the place the review officer was;

(c) the method representations, oral or written, were made to the review officer, see *paragraph 15.11*.

15.15 Any written representations shall be retained.

15.16 A record shall be made as soon as practicable of:

(a) the outcome of each review of detention before or after charge, and if *paragraph 15.7* applies, of when the person was informed and by whom;

(b) the outcome of any determination under PACE, section 42 by a superintendent whether to extend the maximum period of detention without charge beyond 24 hours from the relevant time. If an authorisation is given, the record shall state the number of hours and minutes by which the detention period is extended or further extended.

(c) the outcome of each application under PACE, section 43, for a warrant of further detention or under section 44, for an extension or further extension of that warrant. If a warrant for further detention is granted under section 43 or extended or further extended under 44, the record shall state the detention period authorised by the warrant and the date and time it was granted or (as the case may be) the period by which the warrant is extended or further extended.

Note: Any period during which a person is released on bail does not count towards the maximum period of detention without charge allowed under PACE, sections 41 to 44.

Notes for Guidance

15A *Review officer for the purposes of:*
- *PACE, sections 40, 40A and 45A means, in the case of a person arrested but not charged, an officer of at least inspector rank not directly involved in the investigation and, if a person has been arrested and charged, the custody officer.*

15B *The detention of persons in police custody not subject to the statutory review requirement in paragraph 15.1 should still be reviewed periodically as a matter of good practice. Such reviews can be carried out by an officer of the rank of sergeant or above. The purpose of such reviews is to check the particular power under which a detainee is held continues to apply, any associated conditions are complied with and to make sure appropriate action is taken to deal with any changes. This includes the detainee's prompt release when the power no longer applies, or their transfer if the power requires the detainee be taken elsewhere as soon as the necessary arrangements are made. Examples include persons:*

(a) arrested on warrant because they failed to answer bail to appear at court;

Code C

    (b) *arrested under the Bail Act 1976, section 7(3) for breaching a condition of bail granted after charge;*

    (c) *in police custody for specific purposes and periods under the Crime (Sentences) Act 1997, Schedule 1;*

    (d) *convicted, or remand prisoners, held in police stations on behalf of the Prison Service under the Imprisonment (Temporary Provisions) Act 1980, section 6;*

    (e) *being detained to prevent them causing a breach of the peace;*

    (f) *detained at police stations on behalf of the Immigration Service;*

    (g) *detained by order of a magistrates' court under the Criminal Justice Act 1988, section 152 (as amended by the Drugs Act 2005, section 8) to facilitate the recovery of evidence after being charged with drug possession or drug trafficking and suspected of having swallowed drugs.*

The detention of persons remanded into police detention by order of a court under the Magistrates' Courts Act 1980, section 128 is subject to a statutory requirement to review that detention. This is to make sure the detainee is taken back to court no later than the end of the period authorised by the court or when the need for their detention by police ceases, whichever is the sooner.

15C   *In the case of a review of detention, but not an extension, the detainee need not be woken for the review. However, if the detainee is likely to be asleep, e.g. during a period of rest allowed as in paragraph 12.2, at the latest time a review or authorisation to extend detention may take place, the officer should, if the legal obligations and time constraints permit, bring forward the procedure to allow the detainee to make representations. A detainee not asleep during the review must be present when the grounds for their continued detention are recorded and must at the same time be informed of those grounds unless the review officer considers the person is incapable of understanding what is said, violent or likely to become violent or in urgent need of medical attention.*

15CA *In paragraph 15.3(b) and (c), 'available' includes being contactable in time to enable them to make representations remotely by telephone or other electronic means or in person by attending the station. Reasonable efforts should therefore be made to give the solicitor and appropriate adult sufficient notice of the time the decision is expected to be made so that they can make themselves available.*

15D   *An application to a Magistrates' Court under PACE, sections 43 or 44 for a warrant of further detention or its extension should be made between 10am and 9pm, and if possible during normal court hours. It will not usually be practicable to arrange for a court to sit specially outside the hours of 10am to 9pm. If it appears a special sitting may be needed outside normal court hours but between 10am and 9pm, the clerk to the justices should be given notice and informed of this possibility, while the court is sitting if possible.*

15E   *In paragraph 15.2, the officer responsible for the station holding the detainee includes a superintendent or above who, in accordance with their force operational policy or police regulations, is given that responsibility on a temporary basis whilst the appointed long-term holder is off duty or otherwise unavailable.*

15F   *The provisions of PACE, section 40A allowing telephone reviews do not apply to reviews of detention after charge by the custody officer. When video conferencing is not required, they allow the use of a telephone to carry out a review of detention before charge. The procedure under PACE, section 42 must be done in person.*

15G   *Video conferencing facilities means any facilities (whether a live television link or
       other facilities) by means of which the review can be carried out with the review
       officer, the detainee concerned and the detainee's solicitor all being able to both see
       and to hear each other. The use of video conferencing facilities for decisions about
       detention under section 45A of PACE is subject to regulations made by the Secretary
       of State being in force.*

16 CHARGING DETAINED PERSONS

(a) Action

16.1   When the officer in charge of the investigation reasonably believes there is
       sufficient evidence to provide a realistic prospect of conviction for the offence
       (see *paragraph 11.6*), they shall without delay, and subject to the following
       qualification, inform the custody officer who will be responsible for consider-
       ing whether the detainee should be charged. See *Notes 11B and 16A*. When a
       person is detained in respect of more than one offence it is permissible to
       delay informing the custody officer until the above conditions are satisfied in
       respect of all the offences, but see *paragraph 11.6*. If the detainee is a juvenile,
       mentally disordered or otherwise mentally vulnerable, any resulting action
       shall be taken in the presence of the appropriate adult if they are present at
       the time. See *Notes 16B* and *16C*.

Code **C**

16.1A Where guidance issued by the Director of Public Prosecutions under PACE,
       section 37A is in force the custody officer must comply with that Guidance
       in deciding how to act in dealing with the detainee. See *Notes 16AA* and
       16AB.

16.1B Where in compliance with the DPP's Guidance the custody officer decides
       that the case should be immediately referred to the CPS to make the charging
       decision, consultation should take place with a Crown Prosecutor as soon as
       is reasonably practicable. Where the Crown Prosecutor is unable to make the
       charging decision on the information available at that time, the detainee may
       be released without charge and on bail (with conditions if necessary) under
       section 37(7)(a). In such circumstances, the detainee should be informed that
       they are being released to enable the Director of Public Prosecutions to make
       a decision under section 37B.

16.2   When a detainee is charged with or informed they may be prosecuted for an
       offence, see *Note 16B*, they shall, unless the restriction on drawing adverse
       inferences from silence applies, see *Annex C*, be cautioned as follows:
           'You do not have to say anything. But it may harm your defence if you do not
           mention now something which you later rely on in court. Anything you do say
           may be given in evidence.'
       Where the use of the Welsh Language is appropriate, a constable may provide
       the caution directly in Welsh in the following terms:
           'Does dim rhaid i chi ddweud dim byd. Ond gall niweidio eich amddiffyniad os na
           fyddwch chi'n sôn, yn awr, am rywbeth y byddwch chi'n dibynnu arno nes ymlaen
           yn y llys. Gall unrhyw beth yr ydych yn ei ddweud gael ei roi fel tystiolaeth.'
       Annex C, paragraph 2 sets out the alternative terms of the caution to be used
       when the restriction on drawing adverse inferences from silence applies.

16.3 When a detainee is charged they shall be given a written notice showing particulars of the offence and, subject to *paragraph 2.6A*, the officer's name and the case reference number. As far as possible the particulars of the charge shall be stated in simple terms, but they shall also show the precise offence in law with which the detainee is charged. The notice shall begin:
'*You are charged with the offence(s) shown below.*' Followed by the caution.
If the detainee is a juvenile, mentally disordered or otherwise mentally vulnerable, a copy of the notice should also be given to the appropriate adult.

16.4 If, after a detainee has been charged with or informed they may be prosecuted for an offence, an officer wants to tell them about any written statement or interview with another person relating to such an offence, the detainee shall either be handed a true copy of the written statement or the content of the interview record brought to their attention. Nothing shall be done to invite any reply or comment except to:
(a) caution the detainee, '*You do not have to say anything, but anything you do say may be given in evidence.*';
Where the use of the Welsh Language is appropriate, caution the detainee in the following terms:
'*Does dim rhaid i chi ddweud dim byd, ond gall unrhyw beth yr ydych yn ei ddweud gael ei roi fel tystiolaeth.*'
and
(b) remind the detainee about their right to legal advice.

16.4A If the detainee:
• cannot read, the document may be read to them
• is a juvenile, mentally disordered or otherwise mentally vulnerable, the appropriate adult shall also be given a copy, or the interview record shall be brought to their attention

16.5 A detainee may not be interviewed about an offence after they have been charged with, or informed they may be prosecuted for it, unless the interview is necessary:
• to prevent or minimise harm or loss to some other person, or the public
• to clear up an ambiguity in a previous answer or statement
• in the interests of justice for the detainee to have put to them, and have an opportunity to comment on, information concerning the offence which has come to light since they were charged or informed they might be prosecuted
Before any such interview, the interviewer shall:
(a) caution the detainee, '*You do not have to say anything, but anything you do say may be given in evidence.*'
Where the use of the Welsh Language is appropriate, the interviewer shall caution the detainee: '*Does dim rhaid i chi ddweud dim byd, ond gall unrhyw beth yr ydych yn ei ddweud gael ei roi fel tystiolaeth.*'
(b) remind the detainee about their right to legal advice.
See *Note 16B*

16.6 The provisions of *paragraphs 16.2* to *16.5* must be complied with in the appropriate adult's presence if they are already at the police station. If they are not at the police station then these provisions must be complied with again in their presence when they arrive unless the detainee has been released. See *Note 16C*.

16.7   When a juvenile is charged with an offence and the custody officer authorises their continued detention after charge, the custody officer must make arrangements for the juvenile to be taken into the care of a local authority to be detained pending appearance in court unless the custody officer certifies in accordance with PACE, section 38(6), that:

(a) for any juvenile; it is impracticable to do so; or,

(b) in the case of a juvenile of at least 12 years old, no secure accommodation is available and other accommodation would not be adequate to protect the public from serious harm from that juvenile. See *Note 16D*.

(b) Documentation

16.8   A record shall be made of anything a detainee says when charged.

16.9   Any questions put in an interview after charge and answers given relating to the offence shall be recorded in full during the interview on forms for that purpose and the record signed by the detainee or, if they refuse, by the interviewer and any third parties present. If the questions are audibly recorded or visually recorded the arrangements in Code E or F apply.

16.10   If arrangements for a juvenile's transfer into local authority care as *in paragraph 16.7* are not made, the custody officer must record the reasons in a certificate which must be produced before the court with the juvenile. See *Note 16D*.

Code **C**

Notes for Guidance

16A   *The custody officer must take into account alternatives to prosecution under the Crime and Disorder Act 1998, reprimands and warnings applicable to persons under 18, and in national guidance on the cautioning of offenders, for persons aged 18 and over.*

16AA   *When a person is arrested under the provisions of the Criminal Justice Act 2003 which allow a person to be re-tried after being acquitted of a serious offence which is a qualifying offence specified in Schedule 5 to that Act and not precluded from further prosecution by virtue of section 75(3) of that Act the detention provisions of PACE are modified and make an officer of the rank of superintendent or above who has not been directly involved in the investigation responsible for determining whether the evidence is sufficient to charge.*

16AB   *Where Guidance issued by the Director of Public Prosecutions under section 37B is in force, a custody officer who determines in accordance with that Guidance that there is sufficient evidence to charge the detainee, may detain that person for no longer than is reasonably necessary to decide how that person is to be dealt with under PACE, section 37(7)(a) to (d), including, where appropriate, consultation with the Duty Prosecutor. The period is subject to the maximum period of detention before charge determined by PACE, sections 41 to 44. Where in accordance with the Guidance the case is referred to the CPS for decision, the custody officer should ensure that an officer involved in the investigation sends to the CPS such information as is specified in the Guidance.*

16B   *The giving of a warning or the service of the Notice of Intended Prosecution required by the Road Traffic Offenders Act 1988, section 1 does not amount to informing a detainee they may be prosecuted for an offence and so does not preclude further questioning in relation to that offence.*

16C *There is no power under PACE to detain a person and delay action under paragraphs 16.2 to 16.5 solely to await the arrival of the appropriate adult. Reasonable efforts should therefore be made to give the appropriate adult sufficient notice of the time the decision (charge etc.) is to be implemented so that they can be present. If the appropriate adult is not, or cannot be, present at that time, the detainee should be released on bail to return for the decision to be implemented when the adult is present, unless the custody officer determines that the absence of the appropriate adult makes the detainee unsuitable for bail for this purpose. After charge, bail cannot be refused, or release on bail delayed, simply because an appropriate adult is not available, unless the absence of that adult provides the custody officer with the necessary grounds to authorise detention after charge under PACE, section 38.*

16D *Except as in paragraph 16.7, neither a juvenile's behaviour nor the nature of the offence provides grounds for the custody officer to decide it is impracticable to arrange the juvenile's transfer to local authority care. Impracticability concerns the transport and travel requirements and the lack of secure accommodation which is provided for the purposes of restricting liberty does not make it impracticable to transfer the juvenile. The availability of secure accommodation is only a factor in relation to a juvenile aged 12 or over when other local authority accommodation would not be adequate to protect the public from serious harm from them. The obligation to transfer a juvenile to local authority accommodation applies as much to a juvenile charged during the daytime as to a juvenile to be held overnight, subject to a requirement to bring the juvenile before a court under PACE, section 46.*

17 TESTING PERSONS FOR THE PRESENCE OF SPECIFIED CLASS A DRUGS

(a) Action

17.1 This section of Code C applies only in selected police stations in police areas where the provisions for drug testing under section 63B of PACE (as amended by section 5 of the Criminal Justice Act 2003 and section 7 of the Drugs Act 2005) are in force and in respect of which the Secretary of State has given a notification to the relevant chief officer of police that arrangements for the taking of samples have been made. Such a notification will cover either a police area as a whole or particular stations within a police area. The notification indicates whether the testing applies to those arrested or charged or under the age of 18 as the case may be and testing can only take place in respect of the persons so indicated in the notification. Testing cannot be carried out unless the relevant notification has been given and has not been withdrawn. See *Note 17F.*

17.2 A sample of urine or a non-intimate sample may be taken from a person in police detention for the purpose of ascertaining whether they have any specified Class A drug in their body only where they have been brought before the custody officer and:

   (a) either the arrest condition, see *paragraph 17.3*, or the charge condition, see *paragraph 17.4* is met;
   (b) the age condition see *paragraph 17.5*, is met;
   (c) the notification condition is met in relation to the arrest condition, the charge condition, or the age condition, as the case may be. (Testing on charge and/or arrest must be specifically provided for in the notification for

the power to apply. In addition, the fact that testing of under 18s is authorised must be expressly provided for in the notification before the power to test such persons applies.) See *paragraph 17.1*; and

    (d) a police officer has requested the person concerned to give the sample (the request condition).

17.3 The arrest condition is met where the detainee:

    (a) has been arrested for a trigger offence, see *Note 17E*, but not charged with that offence; or

    (b) has been arrested for any other offence but not charged with that offence and a police officer of inspector rank or above, who has reasonable grounds for suspecting that their misuse of any specified Class A drug caused or contributed to the offence, has authorised the sample to be taken.

17.4 The charge condition is met where the detainee:

    (a) has been charged with a trigger offence, or

    (b) has been charged with any other offence and a police officer of inspector rank or above, who has reasonable grounds for suspecting that the detainee's misuse of any specified Class A drug caused or contributed to the offence, has authorised the sample to be taken.

17.5 The age condition is met where:

    (a) in the case of a detainee who has been arrested but not charged as in *paragraph 17.3*, they are aged 18 or over;

    (b) in the case of a detainee who has been charged as in *paragraph 17.4*, they are aged 14 or over.

17.6 Before requesting a sample from the person concerned, an officer must:

    (a) inform them that the purpose of taking the sample is for drug testing under PACE. This is to ascertain whether they have a specified Class A drug present in their body;

    (b) warn them that if, when so requested, they fail without good cause to provide a sample they may be liable to prosecution;

    (c) where the taking of the sample has been authorised by an inspector or above in accordance with *paragraph 17.3(b)* or *17.4(b)* above, inform them that the authorisation has been given and the grounds for giving it;

    (d) remind them of the following rights, which may be exercised at any stage during the period in custody:

        (i) the right to have someone informed of their arrest [see section 5];

        (ii) the right to consult privately with a solicitor and that free independent legal advice is available [see section 6]; and

        (iii) the right to consult these Codes of Practice [see section 3].

17.7 In the case of a person who has not attained the age of 17—

    (a) the making of the request for a sample under *paragraph 17.2(d)* above;

    (b) the giving of the warning and the information under *paragraph 17.6* above; and

    (c) the taking of the sample,

may not take place except in the presence of an appropriate adult. See *Note 17G*.

17.8 Authorisation by an officer of the rank of inspector or above within *paragraph 17.3(b)* or *17.4(b)* may be given orally or in writing but, if it is given orally, it must be confirmed in writing as soon as practicable.

Code **C**

17.9　If a sample is taken from a detainee who has been arrested for an offence but not charged with that offence as in *paragraph 17.3*, no further sample may be taken during the same continuous period of detention. If during that same period the charge condition is also met in respect of that detainee, the sample which has been taken shall be treated as being taken by virtue of the charge condition, see *paragraph 17.4*, being met.

17.10　A detainee from whom a sample may be taken may be detained for up to six hours from the time of charge if the custody officer reasonably believes the detention is necessary to enable a sample to be taken. Where the arrest condition is met, a detainee whom the custody officer has decided to release on bail without charge may continue to be detained, but not beyond 24 hours from the relevant time (as defined in section 41(2) of PACE), to enable a sample to be taken.

17.11　A detainee in respect of whom the arrest condition is met, but not the charge condition, see *paragraphs 17.3* and *17.4*, and whose release would be required before a sample can be taken had they not continued to be detained as a result of being arrested for a further offence which does not satisfy the arrest condition, may have a sample taken at any time within 24 hours after the arrest for the offence that satisfies the arrest condition.

(b) Documentation

17.12　The following must be recorded in the custody record:
    (a) if a sample is taken following authorisation by an officer of the rank of inspector or above, the authorisation and the grounds for suspicion;
    (b) the giving of a warning of the consequences of failure to provide a sample;
    (c) the time at which the sample was given; and
    (d) the time of charge or, where the arrest condition is being relied upon, the time of arrest and, where applicable, the fact that a sample taken after arrest but before charge is to be treated as being taken by virtue of the charge condition, where that is met in the same period of continuous detention. See *paragraph 17.9*.

(c) General

17.13　A sample may only be taken by a prescribed person. See *Note 17C*.

17.14　Force may not be used to take any sample for the purpose of drug testing.

17.15　The terms "Class A drug" and "misuse" have the same meanings as in the Misuse of Drugs Act 1971. "Specified" (in relation to a Class A drug) and "trigger offence" have the same meanings as in Part III of the Criminal Justice and Court Services Act 2000.

17.16　Any sample taken:
    (a) may not be used for any purpose other than to ascertain whether the person concerned has a specified Class A drug present in his body; and
    (b) can be disposed of as clinical waste unless it is to be sent for further analysis in cases where the test result is disputed at the point when the result is known, including on the basis that medication has been taken, or for quality assurance purposes.

(d) Assessment of misuse of drugs

17.17 Under the provisions of Part 3 of the Drugs Act 2005, where a detainee has tested positive for a specified Class A drug under section 63B of PACE a police officer may, at any time before the person's release from the police station, impose a requirement on the detainee to attend an initial assessment of their drug misuse by a suitably qualified person and to remain for its duration. Where such a requirement is imposed, the officer must, at the same time, impose a second requirement on the detainee to attend and remain for a follow-up assessment. The officer must inform the detainee that the second requirement will cease to have effect if, at the initial assessment they are informed that a follow-up assessment is not necessary. These requirements may only be imposed on a person if:

    (a) they have reached the age of 18

    (b) notification has been given by the Secretary of State to the relevant chief officer of police that arrangements for conducting initial and follow-up assessments have been made for those from whom samples for testing have been taken at the police station where the detainee is in custody.

17.18 When imposing a requirement to attend an initial assessment and a follow-up assessment the police officer must:

    (a) inform the person of the time and place at which the initial assessment is to take place;

    (b) explain that this information will be confirmed in writing; and

    (c) warn the person that they may be liable to prosecution if they fail without good cause to attend the initial assessment and remain for its duration and if they fail to attend the follow-up assessment and remain for its duration (if so required).

17.19 Where a police officer has imposed a requirement to attend an initial assessment and a follow-up assessment in accordance with paragraph 17.17, he must, before the person is released from detention, give the person notice in writing which:

    (a) confirms their requirement to attend and remain for the duration of the assessments; and

    (b) confirms the information and repeats the warning referred to in paragraph 17.18.

17.20 The following must be recorded in the custody record:

    (a) that the requirement to attend an initial assessment and a follow-up assessment has been imposed; and

    (b) the information, explanation, warning and notice given in accordance with paragraphs 17.17 and 17.19.

17.21 Where a notice is given in accordance with paragraph 17.19, a police officer can give the person a further notice in writing which informs the person of any change to the time or place at which the initial assessment is to take place and which repeats the warning referred to in paragraph 17.18(c).

17.22 Part 3 of the Drugs Act 2005 also requires police officers to have regard to any guidance issued by the Secretary of State in respect of the assessment provisions.

Code C

Notes for Guidance

17A   When warning a person who is asked to provide a urine or non-intimate sample in accordance with paragraph 17.6(b), the following form of words may be used:
"You do not have to provide a sample, but I must warn you that if you fail or refuse without good cause to do so, you will commit an offence for which you may be imprisoned, or fined, or both".
Where the Welsh language is appropriate, the following form of words may be used:
"Does dim rhaid i chi roi sampl, ond mae'n rhaid i mi eich rhybuddio y byddwch chi'n cyflawni trosedd os byddwch chi'n methu neu yn gwrthod gwneud hynny heb reswm da, ac y gellir, oherwydd hynny, eich carcharu, eich dirwyo, neu'r ddau."

17B   A sample has to be sufficient and suitable. A sufficient sample is sufficient in quantity and quality to enable drug-testing analysis to take place. A suitable sample is one which by its nature, is suitable for a particular form of drug analysis.

17C   A prescribed person in paragraph 17.13 is one who is prescribed in regulations made by the Secretary of State under section 63B(6) of the Police and Criminal Evidence Act 1984. [The regulations are currently contained in regulation SI 2001 No. 2645, the Police and Criminal Evidence Act 1984 (Drug Testing Persons in Police Detention) (Prescribed Persons) Regulations 2001.]

17D   Samples, and the information derived from them, may not be subsequently used in the investigation of any offence or in evidence against the persons from whom they were taken.

17E   Trigger offences are:

1.   *Offences under the following provisions of the Theft Act 1968:*
     section 1   *(theft)*
     section 8   *(robbery)*
     section 9   *(burglary)*
     section 10   *(aggravated burglary)*
     section 12   *(taking a motor vehicle or other conveyance without authority)*
     section 12A   *(aggravated vehicle-taking)*
     section 22   *(handling stolen goods)*
     section 25   *(going equipped for stealing etc.)*

2.   *Offences under the following provisions of the Misuse of Drugs Act 1971, if committed in respect of a specified Class A drug:–*
     section 4   *(restriction on production and supply of controlled drugs)*
     section 5(2)   *(possession of a controlled drug)*
     section 5(3)   *(possession of a controlled drug with intent to supply)*

3.   *Offences under the following provisions of the Fraud Act 2006:*
     section 1   *(fraud)*
     section 6   *(possession etc. of articles for use in frauds)*
     section 7   *(making or supplying articles for use in frauds)*

3A. *An offence under section 1(1) of the Criminal Attempts Act 1981 if committed in respect of an offence under*
     (a) any of the following provisions of the Theft Act 1968:
     section 1   *(theft)*
     section 8   *(robbery)*
     section 9   *(burglary)*
     section 22   *(handling stolen goods)*
     (b) section 1 of the Fraud Act 2006 (fraud)

4.   *Offences under the following provisions of the Vagrancy Act 1824:*
     section 3   *(begging)*
     section 4   *(persistent begging)*

17F *The power to take samples is subject to notification by the Secretary of State that appropriate arrangements for the taking of samples have been made for the police area as a whole or for the particular police station concerned for whichever of the following is specified in the notification:*
- *(a) persons in respect of whom the arrest condition is met;*
- *(b) persons in respect of whom the charge condition is met;*
- *(c) persons who have not attained the age of 18.*

Note: Notification is treated as having been given for the purposes of the charge condition in relation to a police area, if testing (on charge) under section 63B(2) of PACE was in force immediately before section 7 of the Drugs Act 2005 was brought into force; and for the purposes of the age condition, in relation to a police area or police station, if immediately before that day, notification that arrangements had been made for the taking of samples from persons under the age of 18 (those aged 14–17) had been given and had not been withdrawn.

17G *Appropriate adult in paragraph 17.7 means the person's –*

Code **C**

- *(a) parent or guardian or, if they are in the care of a local authority or voluntary organisation, a person representing that authority or organisation; or*
- *(b) a social worker of a local authority; or*
- *(c) if no person falling within (a) or (b) above is available, any responsible person aged 18 or over who is not a police officer or a person employed by the police.*

Annex A—intimate and strip searches

A Intimate search

1. An intimate search consists of the physical examination of a person's body orifices other than the mouth. The intrusive nature of such searches means the actual and potential risks associated with intimate searches must never be underestimated.

(a) Action

2. Body orifices other than the mouth may be searched only:
   - (a) if authorised by an officer of inspector rank or above who has reasonable grounds for believing that the person may have concealed on themselves:
      - (i) anything which they could and might use to cause physical injury to themselves or others at the station; or
      - (ii) a Class A drug which they intended to supply to another or to export; and the officer has reasonable grounds for believing that an intimate search is the only means of removing those items; and
   - (b) if the search is under *paragraph 2(a)(ii)* (a drug offence search), the detainee's appropriate consent has been given in writing.

2A. Before the search begins, a police officer or designated detention officer, must tell the detainee:-
   - (a) that the authority to carry out the search has been given;
   - (b) the grounds for giving the authorisation and for believing that the article cannot be removed without an intimate search.

2B. Before a detainee is asked to give appropriate consent to a search under *paragraph 2(a)(ii)* (a drug offence search) they must be warned that if they refuse without good cause their refusal may harm their case if it comes to trial, see

Note A6. This warning may be given by a police officer or member of police staff. In the case of juveniles, mentally vulnerable or mentally disordered suspects the seeking and giving of consent must take place in the presence of the appropriate adult. A juvenile's consent is only valid if their parent's or guardian's consent is also obtained unless the juvenile is under 14, when their parent's or guardian's consent is sufficient in its own right. A detainee who is not legally represented must be reminded of their entitlement to have free legal advice, see Code C, *paragraph 6.5*, and the reminder noted in the custody record.

3.   An intimate search may only be carried out by a registered medical practitioner or registered nurse, unless an officer of at least inspector rank considers this is not practicable and the search is to take place under *paragraph 2(a)(i)*, in which case a police officer may carry out the search. See *Notes A1 to A5*.

3A.   Any proposal for a search under *paragraph 2(a)(i)* to be carried out by someone other than a registered medical practitioner or registered nurse must only be considered as a last resort and when the authorising officer is satisfied the risks associated with allowing the item to remain with the detainee outweigh the risks associated with removing it. See *Notes A1 to A5*.

4.   An intimate search under:
- *paragraph 2(a)(i)* may take place only at a hospital, surgery, other medical premises or police station;
- *paragraph 2(a)(ii)* may take place only at a hospital, surgery or other medical premises and must be carried out by a registered medical practitioner or a registered nurse.

5.   An intimate search at a police station of a juvenile or mentally disordered or otherwise mentally vulnerable person may take place only in the presence of an appropriate adult of the same sex (see *Annex L*), unless the detainee specifically requests a particular adult of the opposite sex who is readily available. In the case of a juvenile the search may take place in the absence of the appropriate adult only if the juvenile signifies in the presence of the appropriate adult they do not want the adult present during the search and the adult agrees. A record shall be made of the juvenile's decision and signed by the appropriate adult.

6.   When an intimate search under *paragraph 2(a)(i)* is carried out by a police officer, the officer must be of the same sex as the detainee (see *Annex L*). A minimum of two people, other than the detainee, must be present during the search. Subject to *paragraph 5*, no person of the opposite sex who is not a medical practitioner or nurse shall be present, nor shall anyone whose presence is unnecessary. The search shall be conducted with proper regard to the sensitivity and vulnerability of the detainee.

(b) Documentation

7.   In the case of an intimate search, the following shall be recorded as soon as practicable, in the detainee's custody record:
(a) for searches under paragraphs 2(a)(i) and (ii);
- the authorisation to carry out the search;
- the grounds for giving the authorisation;
- the grounds for believing the article could not be removed without an intimate search;
- which parts of the detainee's body were searched;

- who carried out the search;
- who was present;
- the result.

(b) for searches under paragraph 2(a)(ii):
- the giving of the warning required by *paragraph 2B*;
- the fact that the appropriate consent was given or (as the case may be) refused, and if refused, the reason given for the refusal (if any).

8. If an intimate search is carried out by a police officer, the reason why it was impracticable for a registered medical practitioner or registered nurse to conduct it must be recorded.

B Strip search

9. A strip search is a search involving the removal of more than outer clothing. In this Code, outer clothing includes shoes and socks.

(a) Action

10. A strip search may take place only if it is considered necessary to remove an article which a detainee would not be allowed to keep, and the officer reasonably considers the detainee might have concealed such an article. Strip searches shall not be routinely carried out if there is no reason to consider that articles are concealed.

The conduct of strip searches

11. When strip searches are conducted:

(a) a police officer carrying out a strip search must be the same sex as the detainee (see *Annex L*);

(b) the search shall take place in an area where the detainee cannot be seen by anyone who does not need to be present, nor by a member of the opposite sex (see *Annex L*) except an appropriate adult who has been specifically requested by the detainee;

(c) except in cases of urgency, where there is risk of serious harm to the detainee or to others, whenever a strip search involves exposure of intimate body parts, there must be at least two people present other than the detainee, and if the search is of a juvenile or mentally disordered or otherwise mentally vulnerable person, one of the people must be the appropriate adult. Except in urgent cases as above, a search of a juvenile may take place in the absence of the appropriate adult only if the juvenile signifies in the presence of the appropriate adult that they do not want the adult to be present during the search and the adult agrees. A record shall be made of the juvenile's decision and signed by the appropriate adult. The presence of more than two people, other than an appropriate adult, shall be permitted only in the most exceptional circumstances;

(d) the search shall be conducted with proper regard to the sensitivity and vulnerability of the detainee in these circumstances and every reasonable effort shall be made to secure the detainee's co-operation and minimise embarrassment. Detainees who are searched shall not normally be required to remove all their clothes at the same time, e.g. a person should be allowed to remove clothing above the waist and redress before removing further clothing;

Code **C**

(e) if necessary to assist the search, the detainee may be required to hold their arms in the air or to stand with their legs apart and bend forward so a visual examination may be made of the genital and anal areas provided no physical contact is made with any body orifice;

(f) if articles are found, the detainee shall be asked to hand them over. If articles are found within any body orifice other than the mouth, and the detainee refuses to hand them over, their removal would constitute an intimate search, which must be carried out as in *Part A*;

(g) a strip search shall be conducted as quickly as possible, and the detainee allowed to dress as soon as the procedure is complete.

(b) Documentation

12. A record shall be made on the custody record of a strip search including the reason it was considered necessary, those present and any result.

Notes for Guidance

A1 *Before authorising any intimate search, the authorising officer must make every reasonable effort to persuade the detainee to hand the article over without a search. If the detainee agrees, a registered medical practitioner or registered nurse should whenever possible be asked to assess the risks involved and, if necessary, attend to assist the detainee.*

A2 *If the detainee does not agree to hand the article over without a search, the authorising officer must carefully review all the relevant factors before authorising an intimate search. In particular, the officer must consider whether the grounds for believing an article may be concealed are reasonable.*

A3 *If authority is given for a search under paragraph 2(a)(i), a registered medical practitioner or registered nurse shall be consulted whenever possible. The presumption should be that the search will be conducted by the registered medical practitioner or registered nurse and the authorising officer must make every reasonable effort to persuade the detainee to allow the medical practitioner or nurse to conduct the search.*

A4 *A constable should only be authorised to carry out a search as a last resort and when all other approaches have failed. In these circumstances, the authorising officer must be satisfied the detainee might use the article for one or more of the purposes in paragraph 2(a)(i) and the physical injury likely to be caused is sufficiently severe to justify authorising a constable to carry out the search.*

A5 *If an officer has any doubts whether to authorise an intimate search by a constable, the officer should seek advice from an officer of superintendent rank or above.*

A6 *In warning a detainee who is asked to consent to an intimate drug offence search, as in paragraph 2B, the following form of words may be used:*
"You do not have to allow yourself to be searched, but I must warn you that if you refuse without good cause, your refusal may harm your case if it comes to trial."
Where the use of the Welsh Language is appropriate, the following form of words may be used:
"Nid oes rhaid i chi roi caniatâd i gael eich archwilio, ond mae'n rhaid i mi eich rhybud dio os gwrthodwch heb reswm da, y gallai eich penderfyniad i wrthod wneud niwed i'ch achos pe bai'n dod gerbron llys."

ANNEX B—DELAY IN NOTIFYING ARREST OR ALLOWING ACCESS
TO LEGAL ADVICE

A Persons detained under PACE

1. The exercise of the rights in *Section 5* or *Section 6*, or both, may be delayed if the person is in police detention, as in PACE, section 118(2), in connection with an indictable offence, has not yet been charged with an offence and an officer of superintendent rank or above, or inspector rank or above only for the rights in *Section 5*, has reasonable grounds for believing their exercise will:
   (i) lead to:
      • interference with, or harm to, evidence connected with an indictable offence; or
      • interference with, or physical harm to, other people; or
   (ii) lead to alerting other people suspected of having committed an indictable offence but not yet arrested for it; or
   (iii) hinder the recovery of property obtained in consequence of the commission of such an offence.

2. These rights may also be delayed if the officer has reasonable grounds to believe that:
   (i) the person detained for an indictable offence has benefited from their criminal conduct (decided in accordance with Part 2 of the Proceeds of Crime Act 2002); and
   (ii) the recovery of the value of the property constituting that benefit will be hindered by the exercise of either right.

3. Authority to delay a detainee's right to consult privately with a solicitor may be given only if the authorising officer has reasonable grounds to believe the solicitor the detainee wants to consult will, inadvertently or otherwise, pass on a message from the detainee or act in some other way which will have any of the consequences specified under *paragraphs 1* or *2*. In these circumstances the detainee must be allowed to choose another solicitor. See *Note B3*.

4. If the detainee wishes to see a solicitor, access to that solicitor may not be delayed on the grounds they might advise the detainee not to answer questions or the solicitor was initially asked to attend the police station by someone else. In the latter case the detainee must be told the solicitor has come to the police station at another person's request, and must be asked to sign the custody record to signify whether they want to see the solicitor.

5. The fact the grounds for delaying notification of arrest may be satisfied does not automatically mean the grounds for delaying access to legal advice will also be satisfied.

6. These rights may be delayed only for as long as grounds exist and in no case beyond 36 hours after the relevant time as in PACE, section 41. If the grounds cease to apply within this time, the detainee must, as soon as practicable, be asked if they want to exercise either right, the custody record must be noted accordingly, and action taken in accordance with the relevant section of the Code.

7. A detained person must be permitted to consult a solicitor for a reasonable time before any court hearing.

Code **C**

B Not used

C Documentation

13. The grounds for action under this Annex shall be recorded and the detainee informed of them as soon as practicable.
14. Any reply given by a detainee under *paragraphs 6* or *11* must be recorded and the detainee asked to endorse the record in relation to whether they want to receive legal advice at this point.

D Cautions and special warnings

15. When a suspect detained at a police station is interviewed during any period for which access to legal advice has been delayed under this Annex, the court or jury may not draw adverse inferences from their silence.

Notes for Guidance

B1 Even if Annex B applies in the case of a juvenile, or a person who is mentally disordered or otherwise mentally vulnerable, action to inform the appropriate adult and the person responsible for a juvenile's welfare if that is a different person, must nevertheless be taken as in paragraph 3.13 and 3.15.

B2 In the case of Commonwealth citizens and foreign nationals, see Note 7A.

B3 A decision to delay access to a specific solicitor is likely to be a rare occurrence and only when it can be shown the suspect is capable of misleading that particular solicitor and there is more than a substantial risk that the suspect will succeed in causing information to be conveyed which will lead to one or more of the specified consequences.

ANNEX C—RESTRICTION ON DRAWING ADVERSE INFERENCES FROM SILENCE AND TERMS OF THE CAUTION WHEN THE RESTRICTION APPLIES

(a) The restriction on drawing adverse inferences from silence

1. The Criminal Justice and Public Order Act 1994, sections 34, 36 and 37 as amended by the Youth Justice and Criminal Evidence Act 1999, section 58 describe the conditions under which adverse inferences may be drawn from a person's failure or refusal to say anything about their involvement in the offence when interviewed, after being charged or informed they may be prosecuted. These provisions are subject to an overriding restriction on the ability of a court or jury to draw adverse inferences from a person's silence. This restriction applies:

    (a) to any detainee at a police station, see *Note 10C* who, before being interviewed, see *section 11* or being charged or informed they may be prosecuted, see *section 16*, has:

    (i) asked for legal advice, see *section 6, paragraph 6.1*;

    (ii) not been allowed an opportunity to consult a solicitor, including the duty solicitor, as in this Code; and

    (iii) not changed their mind about wanting legal advice, see *section 6, paragraph 6.6(d)*.

    Note the condition in (ii) will:

    ˜ apply when a detainee who has asked for legal advice is interviewed before speaking to a solicitor as in *section 6, paragraph 6.6(a)* or *(b)*;

    ˜ not apply if the detained person declines to ask for the duty solicitor, see *section 6, paragraphs 6.6(c)* and *(d)*.

   (b) to any person charged with, or informed they may be prosecuted for, an offence who:

     (i) has had brought to their notice a written statement made by another person or the content of an interview with another person which relates to that offence, see *section 16, paragraph 16.4*;

     (ii) is interviewed about that offence, see *section 16, paragraph 16.5*; or

     (iii) makes a written statement about that offence, see *Annex D paragraphs 4 and 9.*

(b) Terms of the caution when the restriction applies

2. When a requirement to caution arises at a time when the restriction on drawing adverse inferences from silence applies, the caution shall be:

   'You do not have to say anything, but anything you do say may be given in evidence.'

   Where the use of the Welsh Language is appropriate, the caution may be used directly in Welsh in the following terms:

   'Does dim rhaid i chi ddweud dim byd, ond gall unrhyw beth yr ydych chi'n ei ddweud gael ei roi fel tystiolaeth.'

3. Whenever the restriction either begins to apply or ceases to apply after a caution has already been given, the person shall be re-cautioned in the appropriate terms. The changed position on drawing inferences and that the previous caution no longer applies shall also be explained to the detainee in ordinary language. See *Note C2*.

Notes for Guidance

C1 The restriction on drawing inferences from silence does not apply to a person who has not been detained and who therefore cannot be prevented from seeking legal advice if they want to, see paragraphs 10.2 and 3.21.

C2 The following is suggested as a framework to help explain changes in the position on drawing adverse inferences if the restriction on drawing adverse inferences from silence:

(a) begins to apply:

'The caution you were previously given no longer applies. This is because after that caution:

   (i) you asked to speak to a solicitor but have not yet been allowed an opportunity to speak to a solicitor. See paragraph 1(a); or

   (ii) you have been charged with/informed you may be prosecuted. See paragraph 1(b).
'This means that from now on, adverse inferences cannot be drawn at court and your defence will not be harmed just because you choose to say nothing. Please listen carefully to the caution I am about to give you because it will apply from now on. You will see that it does not say anything about your defence being harmed.'

(b) ceases to apply before or at the time the person is charged or informed they may be prosecuted, see paragraph 1(a);

'The caution you were previously given no longer applies. This is because after that caution you have been allowed an opportunity to speak to a solicitor. Please listen carefully to the caution I am about to give you because it will apply from now on. It explains how your defence at court may be affected if you choose to say nothing.'

Code **C**

ANNEX D—WRITTEN STATEMENTS UNDER CAUTION

(a) Written by a person under caution

1. A person shall always be invited to write down what they want to say.

2. A person who has not been charged with, or informed they may be prosecuted for, any offence to which the statement they want to write relates, shall:

    (a) unless the statement is made at a time when the restriction on drawing adverse inferences from silence applies, see Annex C, be asked to write out and sign the following before writing what they want to say:

    'I make this statement of my own free will. I understand that I do not have to say anything but that it may harm my defence if I do not mention when questioned something which I later rely on in court. This statement may be given in evidence.';

    (b) if the statement is made at a time when the restriction on drawing adverse inferences from silence applies, be asked to write out and sign the following before writing what they want to say;

    'I make this statement of my own free will. I understand that I do not have to say anything. This statement may be given in evidence.'

3. When a person, on the occasion of being charged with or informed they may be prosecuted for any offence, asks to make a statement which relates to any such offence and wants to write it they shall:

    (a) unless the restriction on drawing adverse inferences from silence, see *Annex C*, applied when they were so charged or informed they may be prosecuted, be asked to write out and sign the following before writing what they want to say:

    'I make this statement of my own free will. I understand that I do not have to say anything but that it may harm my defence if I do not mention when questioned something which I later rely on in court. This statement may be given in evidence.';

    (b) if the restriction on drawing adverse inferences from silence applied when they were so charged or informed they may be prosecuted, be asked to write out and sign the following before writing what they want to say:

    'I make this statement of my own free will. I understand that I do not have to say anything. This statement may be given in evidence.'

4. When a person, who has already been charged with or informed they may be prosecuted for any offence, asks to make a statement which relates to any such offence and wants to write it they shall be asked to write out and sign the following before writing what they want to say:

    'I make this statement of my own free will. I understand that I do not have to say anything. This statement may be given in evidence.';

5. Any person writing their own statement shall be allowed to do so without any prompting except a police officer or other police staff may indicate to them which matters are material or question any ambiguity in the statement.

(b) Written by a police officer or other police staff

6. If a person says they would like someone to write the statement for them, a police officer, or other police staff shall write the statement.

7. If the person has not been charged with, or informed they may be prosecuted for, any offence to which the statement they want to make relates they shall, before starting, be asked to sign, or make their mark, to the following:

(a) unless the statement is made at a time when the restriction on drawing adverse inferences from silence applies, see *Annex C*:
'I, ..., wish to make a statement. I want someone to write down what I say. I understand that I do not have to say anything but that it may harm my defence if I do not mention when questioned something which I later rely on in court. This statement may be given in evidence.';

(b) if the statement is made at a time when the restriction on drawing adverse inferences from silence applies:
'I, ..., wish to make a statement. I want someone to write down what I say. I understand that I do not have to say anything. This statement may be given in evidence.'

8. If, on the occasion of being charged with or informed they may be prosecuted for any offence, the person asks to make a statement which relates to any such offence they shall before starting be asked to sign, or make their mark to, the following:

Code **C**

(a) unless the restriction on drawing adverse inferences from silence applied, see *Annex C*, when they were so charged or informed they may be prosecuted:
'I, ..., wish to make a statement. I want someone to write down what I say. I understand that I do not have to say anything but that it may harm my defence if I do not mention when questioned something which I later rely on in court. This statement may be given in evidence.';

(b) if the restriction on drawing adverse inferences from silence applied when they were so charged or informed they may be prosecuted:
'I, ..., wish to make a statement. I want someone to write down what I say. I understand that I do not have to say anything. This statement may be given in evidence.'

9. If, having already been charged with or informed they may be prosecuted for any offence, a person asks to make a statement which relates to any such offence they shall before starting, be asked to sign, or make their mark to:
'I, ..., wish to make a statement. I want someone to write down what I say. I understand that I do not have to say anything. This statement may be given in evidence.'

10. The person writing the statement must take down the exact words spoken by the person making it and must not edit or paraphrase it. Any questions that are necessary, e.g. to make it more intelligible, and the answers given must be recorded at the same time on the statement form.

11. When the writing of a statement is finished the person making it shall be asked to read it and to make any corrections, alterations or additions they want. When they have finished reading they shall be asked to write and sign or make their mark on the following certificate at the end of the statement:
'I have read the above statement, and I have been able to correct, alter or add anything I wish. This statement is true. I have made it of my own free will.'

12. If the person making the statement cannot read, or refuses to read it, or to write the above mentioned certificate at the end of it or to sign it, the person taking the statement shall read it to them and ask them if they would like to correct, alter or add anything and to put their signature or make their mark at the end. The person taking the statement shall certify on the statement itself what has occurred.

Annex E—Summary of provisions relating to mentally disordered and otherwise mentally vulnerable people

1. If an officer has any suspicion, or is told in good faith, that a person of any age may be mentally disordered or otherwise mentally vulnerable, or mentally incapable of understanding the significance of questions or their replies that person shall be treated as mentally disordered or otherwise mentally vulnerable for the purposes of this Code. See *paragraph 1.4* and *Note E4*

2. In the case of a person who is mentally disordered or otherwise mentally vulnerable, 'the appropriate adult' means:
   (a) a relative, guardian or other person responsible for their care or custody;
   (b) someone experienced in dealing with mentally disordered or mentally vulnerable people but who is not a police officer or employed by the police;
   (c) failing these, some other responsible adult aged 18 or over who is not a police officer or employed by the police.
   See *paragraph 1.7(b)* and *Note 1D*

3. If the custody officer authorises the detention of a person who is mentally vulnerable or appears to be suffering from a mental disorder, the custody officer must as soon as practicable inform the appropriate adult of the grounds for detention and the person's whereabouts, and ask the adult to come to the police station to see them. If the appropriate adult:
   • is already at the station when information is given as in *paragraphs 3.1* to *3.5* the information must be given in their presence;
   • is not at the station when the provisions of *paragraph 3.1* to *3.5* are complied with these provisions must be complied with again in their presence once they arrive. See *paragraphs 3.15* to *3.17*

4. If the appropriate adult, having been informed of the right to legal advice, considers legal advice should be taken, the provisions of *section 6* apply as if the mentally disordered or otherwise mentally vulnerable person had requested access to legal advice. See *paragraph 3.19* and *Note E1*

5. The custody officer must make sure a person receives appropriate clinical attention as soon as reasonably practicable if the person appears to be suffering from a mental disorder or in urgent cases immediately call the nearest appropriate healthcare professional or an ambulance. It is not intended these provisions delay the transfer of a detainee to a place of safety under the Mental Health Act 1983, section 136 if that is applicable. If an assessment under that Act is to take place at a police station, the custody officer must consider whether an appropriate healthcare professional should be called to conduct an initial clinical check on the detainee. See *paragraph 9.5* and *9.6*

6. It is imperative a mentally disordered or otherwise mentally vulnerable person detained under the Mental Health Act 1983, section 136 be assessed as soon as possible. A police station should only be used as a place of safety as a last resort but if that assessment is to take place at the police station, an approved social worker and registered medical practitioner shall be called to the station as soon as possible to carry it out. Once the detainee has been assessed and suitable arrangements been made for their treatment or care, they can no longer be detained under section 136. A detainee should be immediately discharged from detention if a registered medical practitioner having examined them, concludes they are not mentally disordered within the meaning of the Act. See *paragraph 3.16*

7. If a mentally disordered or otherwise mentally vulnerable person is cautioned in the absence of the appropriate adult, the caution must be repeated in the appropriate adult's presence. See *paragraph 10.12*

8. A mentally disordered or otherwise mentally vulnerable person must not be interviewed or asked to provide or sign a written statement in the absence of the appropriate adult unless the provisions of *paragraphs 11.1* or *11.18* to *11.20* apply. Questioning in these circumstances may not continue in the absence of the appropriate adult once sufficient information to avert the risk has been obtained. A record shall be made of the grounds for any decision to begin an interview in these circumstances. See *paragraphs 11.1, 11.15* and *11.18* to *11.20*

9. If the appropriate adult is present at an interview, they shall be informed they are not expected to act simply as an observer and the purposes of their presence are to:
    - advise the interviewee;
    - observe whether or not the interview is being conducted properly and fairly;
    - facilitate communication with the interviewee See *paragraph 11.17*

10. If the detention of a mentally disordered or otherwise mentally vulnerable person is reviewed by a review officer or a superintendent, the appropriate adult must, if available at the time, be given an opportunity to make representations to the officer about the need for continuing detention. See *paragraph 15.3*

11. If the custody officer charges a mentally disordered or otherwise mentally vulnerable person with an offence or takes such other action as is appropriate when there is sufficient evidence for a prosecution this must be carried out in the presence of the appropriate adult if they are at the police station. A copy of the written notice embodying any charge must also be given to the appropriate adult. See *paragraphs 16.1* to *16.4A*

12. An intimate or strip search of a mentally disordered or otherwise mentally vulnerable person may take place only in the presence of the appropriate adult of the same sex, unless the detainee specifically requests the presence of a particular adult of the opposite sex. A strip search may take place in the absence of an appropriate adult only in cases of urgency when there is a risk of serious harm to the detainee or others. See *Annex A, paragraphs 5* and *11(c)*

13. Particular care must be taken when deciding whether to use any form of approved restraints on a mentally disordered or otherwise mentally vulnerable person in a locked cell. See *paragraph 8.2*

Code **C**

Notes for Guidance

E1 *The purpose of the provision at paragraph 3.19 is to protect the rights of a mentally disordered or otherwise mentally vulnerable detained person who does not understand the significance of what is said to them. If the detained person wants to exercise the right to legal advice, the appropriate action should be taken and not delayed until the appropriate adult arrives. A mentally disordered or otherwise mentally vulnerable detained person should always be given an opportunity, when an appropriate adult is called to the police station, to consult privately with a solicitor in the absence of the appropriate adult if they want.*

E2 *Although people who are mentally disordered or otherwise mentally vulnerable are often capable of providing reliable evidence, they may, without knowing or wanting to do so,*

be particularly prone in certain circumstances to provide information that may be unre-
liable, misleading or self-incriminating. Special care should always be taken when ques-
tioning such a person, and the appropriate adult should be involved if there is any doubt
about a person's mental state or capacity. Because of the risk of unreliable evidence, it is
important to obtain corroboration of any facts admitted whenever possible.

E3 *Because of the risks referred to in Note E2, which the presence of the appropriate adult*
is intended to minimise, officers of superintendent rank or above should exercise their
discretion to authorise the commencement of an interview in the appropriate adult's
absence only in exceptional cases, if it is necessary to avert an immediate risk of serious
harm. See paragraphs 11.1, 11.18 to 11.20.

E4 *There is no requirement for an appropriate adult to be present if a person is detained*
under section 136 of the Mental Health Act 1983 for assessment.

ANNEX F—NOT USED

ANNEX G—FITNESS TO BE INTERVIEWED

1. This Annex contains general guidance to help police officers and healthcare professionals assess whether a detainee might be at risk in an interview.
2. A detainee may be at risk in a interview if it is considered that:
   (a) conducting the interview could significantly harm the detainee's physical or mental state;
   (b) anything the detainee says in the interview about their involvement or suspected involvement in the offence about which they are being interviewed **might** be considered unreliable in subsequent court proceedings because of their physical or mental state.
3. In assessing whether the detainee should be interviewed, the following must be considered:
   (a) how the detainee's physical or mental state might affect their ability to understand the nature and purpose of the interview, to comprehend what is being asked and to appreciate the significance of any answers given and make rational decisions about whether they want to say anything;
   (b) the extent to which the detainee's replies may be affected by their physical or mental condition rather than representing a rational and accurate explanation of their involvement in the offence;
   (c) how the nature of the interview, which could include particularly probing questions, might affect the detainee.
4. It is essential healthcare professionals who are consulted consider the functional ability of the detainee rather than simply relying on a medical diagnosis, e.g. it is possible for a person with severe mental illness to be fit for interview.
5. Healthcare professionals should advise on the need for an appropriate adult to be present, whether reassessment of the person's fitness for interview may be necessary if the interview lasts beyond a specified time, and whether a further specialist opinion may be required.
6. When healthcare professionals identify risks they should be asked to quantify the risks. They should inform the custody officer:
   • whether the person's condition:
     ˜ is likely to improve;

~ will require or be amenable to treatment; and
- indicate how long it may take for such improvement to take effect.

7. The role of the healthcare professional is to consider the risks and advise the custody officer of the outcome of that consideration. The healthcare professional's determination and any advice or recommendations should be made in writing and form part of the custody record.

8. Once the healthcare professional has provided that information, it is a matter for the custody officer to decide whether or not to allow the interview to go ahead and if the interview is to proceed, to determine what safeguards are needed. Nothing prevents safeguards being provided in addition to those required under the Code. An example might be to have an appropriate healthcare professional present during the interview, in addition to an appropriate adult, in order constantly to monitor the person's condition and how it is being affected by the interview.

Annex H—Detained person: observation list

Code **C**

1. If any detainee fails to meet any of the following criteria, an appropriate healthcare professional or an ambulance must be called.

2. When assessing the level of rousability, consider:
Rousability – can they be woken?
- go into the cell
- call their name
- shake gently

Response to questions - can they give appropriate answers to questions such as:
- What's your name?
- Where do you live?
- Where do you think you are?

Response to commands - can they respond appropriately to commands such as:
- Open your eyes!
- Lift one arm, now the other arm!

3. Remember to take into account the possibility or presence of other illnesses, injury, or mental condition, a person who is drowsy and smells of alcohol may also have the following:
- Diabetes
- Epilepsy
- Head injury
- Drug intoxication or overdose
- Stroke

Annex I—Not used

Annex J—Not used

Annex K—X-rays and ultrasound scans

(a) Action

1. PACE, section 55A allows a person who has been arrested and is in police detention to have an X-ray taken of them or an ultrasound scan to be carried out on them (or both) if:

(a) authorised by an officer of inspector rank or above who has reasonable grounds for believing that the detainee:

(i) may have swallowed a Class A drug; and

(ii) was in possession of that Class A drug with the intention of supplying it to another or to export; and

(b) the detainee's appropriate consent has been given in writing.

2. Before an x-ray is taken or an ultrasound scan carried out, a police officer, designated detention officer or staff custody officer must tell the detainee:-

(a) that the authority has been given; and

(b) the grounds for giving the authorisation.

3. Before a detainee is asked to give appropriate consent to an x-ray or an ultrasound scan, they must be warned that if they refuse without good cause their refusal may harm their case if it comes to trial, see *Notes K1* and *K2*. This warning may be given by a police officer or member of police staff. In the case of juveniles, mentally vulnerable or mentally disordered suspects the seeking and giving of consent must take place in the presence of the appropriate adult. A juvenile's consent is only valid if their parent's or guardian's consent is also obtained unless the juvenile is under 14, when their parent's or guardian's consent is sufficient in its own right. A detainee who is not legally represented must be reminded of their entitlement to have free legal advice, see Code C, *paragraph 6.5*, and the reminder noted in the custody record.

4. An x-ray may be taken, or an ultrasound scan may be carried out, only by a registered medical practitioner or registered nurse, and only at a hospital, surgery or other medical premises.

(b) Documentation

5. The following shall be recorded as soon as practicable in the detainee's custody record:

(a) the authorisation to take the x-ray or carry out the ultrasound scan (or both);

(b) the grounds for giving the authorisation;

(c) the giving of the warning required by *paragraph 3*; and

(d) the fact that the appropriate consent was given or (as the case may be) refused, and if refused, the reason given for the refusal (if any); and

(e) if an x-ray is taken or an ultrasound scan carried out:
- where it was taken or carried out;
- who took it or carried it out;
- who was present;
- the result.

6. Paragraphs 1.4–1.7 of this Code apply and an appropriate adult should be present when consent is sought to any procedure under this Annex.

Notes for Guidance

K1 If authority is given for an x-ray to be taken or an ultrasound scan to be carried out (or both), consideration should be given to asking a registered medical practitioner or registered nurse to explain to the detainee what is involved and to allay any concerns the detainee might have about the effect which taking an x-ray or carrying out an ultrasound scan might have on them. If appropriate consent is not given, evidence of the explanation may, if the case comes to trial, be relevant to determining whether the detainee had a good cause for refusing.

K2 *In warning a detainee who is asked to consent to an X-ray being taken or an ultrasound scan being carried out (or both), as in paragraph 3, the following form of words may be used:*

"You do not have to allow an x-ray of you to be taken or an ultrasound scan to be carried out on you, but I must warn you that if you refuse without good cause, your refusal may harm your case if it comes to trial."

Where the use of the Welsh Language is appropriate, the following form of words may be provided in Welsh:

"Does dim rhaid i chi ganiatáu cymryd sgan uwchsain neu belydr-x (neu'r ddau) arnoch, ond mae'n rhaid i mi eich rhybuddio os byddwch chi'n gwrthod gwneud hynny heb reswm da, fe allai hynny niweidio eich achos pe bai'n dod gerbron llys."

ANNEX L—ESTABLISHING GENDER OF PERSONS FOR THE PURPOSE OF SEARCHING

Code **C**

1. Certain provisions of this and other PACE Codes explicitly state that searches and other procedures may only be carried out by, or in the presence of, persons of the same sex as the person subject to the search or other procedure. See *Note L1*.

2. All searches and procedures must be carried out with courtesy, consideration and respect for the person concerned. Police officers should show particular sensitivity when dealing with transgender individuals (including transsexual persons) and transvestite persons (see *Notes L2, L3* and *L4*).

(a) Consideration

3. In law, the gender (and accordingly the sex) of an individual is their gender as registered at birth unless they have been issued with a Gender Recognition Certificate (GRC) under the Gender Recognition Act 2004 (GRA), in which case the person's gender is their acquired gender. This means that if the acquired gender is the male gender, the person's sex becomes that of a man and, if it is the female gender, the person's sex becomes that of a woman and they must be treated as their acquired gender.

4. When establishing whether the person concerned should be treated as being male or female for the purposes of these searches and procedures, the following approach which is designed to minimise embarrassment and secure the person's co-operation should be followed:

   (a) The person must not be asked whether they have a GRC (see *paragraph 8*);

   (b) If there is no doubt as to as to whether the person concerned should be treated as being male or female, they should be dealt with as being of that sex.

   (c) If at any time (including during the search or carrying out the procedure) there is doubt as to whether the person should be treated, or continue to be treated, as being male or female:

      (i) the person should be asked what gender they consider themselves to be. If they express a preference to be dealt with as a particular gender, they should be asked to indicate and confirm their preference by signing the custody record or, if a custody record has not been opened, the search record or the officer's notebook. Subject to (ii) below, the person should be treated according to their preference;

    (ii) if there are grounds to doubt that the preference in (i) accurately reflects the person's predominant lifestyle, for example, if they ask to be treated as a woman but documents and other information make it clear that they live predominantly as a man, or vice versa, they should be treated according to what appears to be their predominant lifestyle and not their stated preference;

    (iii) If the person is unwilling to express a preference as in (i) above, efforts should be made to determine their predominant lifestyle and they should be treated as such. For example, if they appear to live predominantly as a woman, they should be treated as being female; or

    (iv) if none of the above apply, the person should be dealt with according to what reasonably appears to have been their sex as registered at birth.

5. Once a decision has been made about which gender an individual is to be treated as, each officer responsible for the search or procedure should where possible be advised before the search or procedure starts of any doubts as to the person's gender and the person informed that the doubts have been disclosed. This is important so as to maintain the dignity of the person and any officers concerned.

(b) Documentation

6. The person's gender as established under *paragraph 4(c)(i) to (iv)* above must be recorded in the person's custody record, or if a custody record has not been opened, on the search record or in the officer's notebook.

7. Where the person elects which gender they consider themselves to be under *paragraph 4(b)(i)* but following *4(b)(ii)* is not treated in accordance with their preference, the reason must be recorded in the search record, in the officer's notebook or, if applicable, in the person's custody record.

(c) Disclosure of information

8. Section 22 of the GRA defines any information relating to a person's application for a GRC or to a successful applicant's gender before it became their acquired gender as 'protected information'. Nothing in this Annex is to be read as authorising or permitting any police officer or any police staff who has acquired such information when acting in their official capacity to disclose that information to any other person in contravention of the GRA. Disclosure includes making a record of 'protected information' which is read by others.

Note for Guidance

L1 *Provisions to which paragraph 1 applies include:*
- *In Code C; paragraph 4.1 and Annex A paragraphs 5, 6, and 11 (searches, strip and intimate searches of detainees under sections 54 and 55 of PACE);*
- *In Code A; paragraphs 2.8 and 3.6 and Note 4;*
- *In Code D; paragraph 5.5 and Note 5F (searches, examinations and photographing of detainees under section 54A of PACE) and paragraph 6.9 (taking samples);*
- *In Code H; paragraph 4.1 and Annex A paragraphs 6, 7 and 12 (searches, strip and intimate searches under sections 54 and 55 of PACE of persons arrested under section 41 of the Terrorism Act 2000).*

L2 *While there is no agreed definition of transgender (or trans), it is generally used as an umbrella term to describe people whose gender identity (self-identification as being a woman, man, neither or both) differs from the sex they were registered as at birth. The term includes, but is not limited to, transsexual people.*

L3 *Transsexual means a person who is proposing to undergo, is undergoing or has undergone a process (or part of a process) for the purpose of gender reassignment which is a protected characteristic under the Equality Act 2010 (see paragraph 1.0) by changing physiological or other attributes of their sex. This includes aspects of gender such as dress and title. It would apply to a woman making the transition to being a man and a man making the transition to being a woman as well as to a person who has only just started out on the process of gender reassignment and to a person who has completed the process. Both would share the characteristic of gender reassignment with each having the characteristics of one sex, but with certain characteristics of the other sex.*

L4 *Transvestite means a person of one gender who dresses in the clothes of a person of the opposite gender. However, a transvestite does not live permanently in the gender opposite to their birth sex.*

Code **C**

L5 *Chief officers are responsible for providing corresponding operational guidance and instructions for the deployment of transgender officers and staff under their direction and control to duties which involve carrying out, or being present at, any of the searches and procedures described in paragraph 1. The guidance and instructions must comply with the Equality Act 2010 and should therefore complement the approach in this Annex.*

Appendix 5
Code D: PACE Code of Practice for the Identification of Persons by Police Officers

This code has effect in relation to any identification procedure carried out after midnight on 06 March 2011.

1 INTRODUCTION

1.1 This Code of Practice concerns the principal methods used by police to identify people in connection with the investigation of offences and the keeping of accurate and reliable criminal records. The powers and procedures in this code must be used fairly, responsibly, with respect for the people to whom they apply and without unlawful discrimination. The Equality Act 2010 makes it unlawful for police officers to discriminate against, harass or victimise any person on the grounds of the 'protected characteristics' of age, disability, gender reassignment, race, religion or belief, sex and sexual orientation, marriage and civil partnership, pregnancy and maternity when using their powers. When police forces are carrying out their functions they also have a duty to have regard to the need to eliminate unlawful discrimination, harassment and victimisation and to take steps to foster good relations.

1.2 In this code, identification by an eye-witness arises when a witness who has seen the offender committing the crime and is given an opportunity to identify a person suspected of involvement in the offence in a video identification, identification parade or similar procedure. These eye-witness identification procedures (see Part A of section 3 below) are designed to:
   • test the witness's ability to identify the suspect as the person they saw on a previous occasion
   • provide safeguards against mistaken identification.
While this Code concentrates on visual identification procedures, it does not preclude the police making use of aural identification procedures such as a "voice identification parade", where they judge that appropriate.

1.2A In this code, separate provisions in Part B of section 3 below apply when any person, including a police officer, is asked if they recognise anyone they see in an image as being someone they know and to test their claim that they recognise that person as someone who is known to them. Except where stated, these separate provisions are not subject to the eye-witnesses identification procedures described in paragraph 1.2.

1.3 Identification by fingerprints applies when a person's fingerprints are taken to:
   • compare with fingerprints found at the scene of a crime
   • check and prove convictions
   • help to ascertain a person's identity.

1.3A Identification using footwear impressions applies when a person's footwear impressions are taken to compare with impressions found at the scene of a crime.

1.4 Identification by body samples and impressions includes taking samples such as blood or hair to generate a DNA profile for comparison with material obtained from the scene of a crime, or a victim.

1.5 Taking photographs of arrested people applies to recording and checking identity and locating and tracing persons who:
- are wanted for offences
- fail to answer their bail.

1.6 Another method of identification involves searching and examining detained suspects to find, e.g., marks such as tattoos or scars which may help establish their identity or whether they have been involved in committing an offence.

1.7 The provisions of the Police and Criminal Evidence Act 1984 (PACE) and this Code are designed to make sure fingerprints, samples, impressions and photographs are taken, used and retained, and identification procedures carried out, only when justified and necessary for preventing, detecting or investigating crime. If these provisions are not observed, the application of the relevant procedures in particular cases may be open to question.

Code D

2 General

2.1 This Code must be readily available at all police stations for consultation by:
- police officers and police staff
- detained persons
- members of the public

2.2 The provisions of this Code:
- include the *Annexes*
- do not include the *Notes for guidance*.

2.3 Code C, paragraph 1.4, regarding a person who may be mentally disordered or otherwise mentally vulnerable and the *Notes for guidance* applicable to those provisions apply to this Code.

2.4 Code C, paragraph 1.5, regarding a person who appears to be under the age of 17 applies to this Code.

2.5 Code C, paragraph 1.6, regarding a person who appears to be blind, seriously visually impaired, deaf, unable to read or speak or has difficulty communicating orally because of a speech impediment applies to this Code.

2.6 In this Code:
- 'appropriate adult' means the same as in Code C, paragraph 1.7
- 'solicitor' means the same as in Code C, paragraph 6.12
- and the *Notes for guidance* applicable to those provisions apply to this Code.
- where a search or other procedure under this code may only be carried out or observed by a person of the same sex as the person to whom the search or procedure applies, the gender of the detainee and other persons present should be established and recorded in line with Annex F of Code A.

2.7 References to custody officers include those performing the functions of custody officer, see *paragraph 1.9* of Code C.

2.8   When a record of any action requiring the authority of an officer of a speci-
        fied rank is made under this Code, subject to *paragraph 2.18*, the officer's
        name and rank must be recorded.

2.9   When this Code requires the prior authority or agreement of an officer of at
        least inspector or superintendent rank, that authority may be given by a ser-
        geant or chief inspector who has been authorised to perform the functions of
        the higher rank under PACE, section 107.

2.10   Subject to *paragraph 2.18*, all records must be timed and signed by the
        maker.

2.11   Records must be made in the custody record, unless otherwise specified.
        References to 'pocket book' include any official report book issued to police
        officers or police staff.

2.12   If any procedure in this Code requires a person's consent, the consent of a:
        • mentally disordered or otherwise mentally vulnerable person is only valid
          if given in the presence of the appropriate adult
        • juvenile is only valid if their parent's or guardian's consent is also obtained
          unless the juvenile is under 14, when their parent's or guardian's consent
          is sufficient in its own right. If the only obstacle to an identification pro-
          cedure in *section 3* is that a juvenile's parent or guardian refuses consent
          or reasonable efforts to obtain it have failed, the identification officer may
          apply the provisions of *paragraph 3.21*. See *Note 2A*

2.13   If a person is blind, seriously visually impaired or unable to read, the custody
        officer or identification officer shall make sure their solicitor, relative, appro-
        priate adult or some other person likely to take an interest in them and not
        involved in the investigation is available to help check any documentation.
        When this Code requires written consent or signing, the person assisting may
        be asked to sign instead, if the detainee prefers. This paragraph does not
        require an appropriate adult to be called solely to assist in checking and sign-
        ing documentation for a person who is not a juvenile, or mentally disordered
        or otherwise mentally vulnerable (see *Note 2B* and Code C *paragraph 3.15*).

2.14   If any procedure in this Code requires information to be given to or sought
        from a suspect, it must be given or sought in the appropriate adult's presence
        if the suspect is mentally disordered, otherwise mentally vulnerable or a juve-
        nile. If the appropriate adult is not present when the information is first
        given or sought, the procedure must be repeated in the presence of the appro-
        priate adult when they arrive. If the suspect appears deaf or there is doubt
        about their hearing or speaking ability or ability to understand English, and
        effective communication cannot be established, the information must be
        given or sought through an interpreter.

2.15   Any procedure in this Code involving the participation of a suspect who is
        mentally disordered, otherwise mentally vulnerable or a juvenile must take
        place in the presence of the appropriate adult. See Code C paragraph 1.4.

2.15A   Any procedure in this Code involving the participation of a witness who is or
        appears to be mentally disordered, otherwise mentally vulnerable or a juve-
        nile should take place in the presence of a pre-trial support person unless the
        witness states that they do not want a support person to be present. A support
        person must not be allowed to prompt any identification of a suspect by a
        witness. See *Note 2AB*.

2.16 References to:
- 'taking a photograph', include the use of any process to produce a single, still or moving, visual image
- 'photographing a person', should be construed accordingly
- 'photographs', 'films', 'negatives' and 'copies' include relevant visual images recorded, stored, or reproduced through any medium
- 'destruction' includes the deletion of computer data relating to such images or making access to that data impossible

2.17 Except as described, nothing in this Code affects the powers and procedures:
  (i)   for requiring and taking samples of breath, blood and urine in relation to driving offences, etc, when under the influence of drink, drugs or excess alcohol under the:
    - Road Traffic Act 1988, sections 4 to 11
    - Road Traffic Offenders Act 1988, sections 15 and 16
    - Transport and Works Act 1992, sections 26 to 38;
  (ii) under the Immigration Act 1971, Schedule 2, paragraph 18, for taking photographs and fingerprints from persons detained under that Act, Schedule 2, paragraph 16 (Administrative Controls as to Control on Entry etc); for taking fingerprints in accordance with the Immigration and Asylum Act 1999; sections 141 and 142(3), or other methods for collecting information about a person's external physical characteristics provided for by regulations made under that Act, section 144;

Code D

  (iii) under the Terrorism Act 2000, Schedule 8, for taking photographs, fingerprints, skin impressions, body samples or impressions from people:
    - arrested under that Act, section 41,
    - detained for the purposes of examination under that Act, Schedule 7, and to whom the Code of Practice issued under that Act, Schedule 14, paragraph 6, applies ('the terrorism provisions')
    See *Note 2C*;
  (iv) for taking photographs, fingerprints, skin impressions, body samples or impressions from people who have been:
    - arrested on warrants issued in Scotland, by officers exercising powers under the Criminal Justice and Public Order Act 1994, section 136(2)
    - arrested or detained without warrant by officers from a police force in Scotland exercising their powers of arrest or detention under the Criminal Justice and Public Order Act 1994, section 137(2), (Cross Border powers of arrest etc.).
Note: In these cases, police powers and duties and the person's rights and entitlements whilst at a police station in England and Wales are the same as if the person had been arrested in Scotland by a Scottish police officer.

2.18 Nothing in this Code requires the identity of officers or police staff to be recorded or disclosed:
  (a) in the case of enquiries linked to the investigation of terrorism;
  (b) if the officers or police staff reasonably believe recording or disclosing their names might put them in danger.
In these cases, they shall use warrant or other identification numbers and the name of their police station. See *Note 2D*

2.19 In this Code:
- (a) 'designated person' means a person other than a police officer, designated under the Police Reform Act 2002, Part 4, who has specified powers and duties of police officers conferred or imposed on them;
- (b) any reference to a police officer includes a designated person acting in the exercise or performance of the powers and duties conferred or imposed on them by their designation.

2.20 If a power conferred on a designated person:
- (a) allows reasonable force to be used when exercised by a police officer, a designated person exercising that power has the same entitlement to use force;
- (b) includes power to use force to enter any premises, that power is not exercisable by that designated person except:
  - (i) in the company, and under the supervision, of a police officer; or
  - (ii) for the purpose of:
    - saving life or limb; or
    - preventing serious damage to property.

2.21 Nothing in this Code prevents the custody officer, or other officer given custody of the detainee, from allowing police staff who are not designated persons to carry out individual procedures or tasks at the police station if the law allows. However, the officer remains responsible for making sure the procedures and tasks are carried out correctly in accordance with the Codes of Practice. Any such person must be:
- (a) a person employed by a police authority maintaining a police force and under the control and direction of the Chief Officer of that force;
- (b) employed by a person with whom a police authority has a contract for the provision of services relating to persons arrested or otherwise in custody.

2.22 Designated persons and other police staff must have regard to any relevant provisions of the Codes of Practice.

Notes for guidance

2A *For the purposes of paragraph 2.12, the consent required from a parent or guardian may, for a juvenile in the care of a local authority or voluntary organisation, be given by that authority or organisation. In the case of a juvenile, nothing in paragraph 2.12 requires the parent, guardian or representative of a local authority or voluntary organisation to be present to give their consent, unless they are acting as the appropriate adult under paragraphs 2.14 or 2.15. However, it is important that a parent or guardian not present is fully informed before being asked to consent. They must be given the same information about the procedure and the juvenile's suspected involvement in the offence as the juvenile and appropriate adult. The parent or guardian must also be allowed to speak to the juvenile and the appropriate adult if they wish. Provided the consent is fully informed and is not withdrawn, it may be obtained at any time before the procedure takes place.*

2AB *The Youth Justice and Criminal Evidence Act 1999 guidance "Achieving Best Evidence in Criminal Proceedings" indicates that a pre-trial support person should accompany a vulnerable witness during any identification procedure unless the witness states that they do not want a support person to be present. It states that this support person should not be (or not be likely to be) a witness in the investigation.*

2B People who are seriously visually impaired or unable to read may be unwilling to sign police documents. The alternative, i.e. their representative signing on their behalf, seeks to protect the interests of both police and suspects.

2C Photographs, fingerprints, samples and impressions may be taken from a person detained under the terrorism provisions to help determine whether they are, or have been, involved in terrorism, as well as when there are reasonable grounds for suspecting their involvement in a particular offence.

2D The purpose of paragraph 2.18(b) is to protect those involved in serious organised crime investigations or arrests of particularly violent suspects when there is reliable information that those arrested or their associates may threaten or cause harm to the officers. In cases of doubt, an officer of inspector rank or above should be consulted.

3 IDENTIFICATION AND RECOGNITION OF SUSPECTS

(A) Identification of a suspect by an eye-witness

3.0 This part applies when an eye-witness has seen the offender committing the crime or in any other circumstances which tend to prove or disprove the involvement of the person they saw in the crime, for example, close to the scene of the crime, immediately before or immediately after it was committed. It sets out the procedures to be used to test the ability of that eye-witness to identify a person suspected of involvement in the offence as the person they saw on the previous occasion. Except where stated, this part does not apply to the procedures described in Part B and *Note 3AA*.

3.1 A record shall be made of the suspect's description as first given by a potential witness. This record must:

    (a) be made and kept in a form which enables details of that description to be accurately produced from it, in a visible and legible form, which can be given to the suspect or the suspect's solicitor in accordance with this Code; and

    (b) unless otherwise specified, be made before the witness takes part in any identification procedures under *paragraphs 3.5 to 3.10, 3.21* or *3.23.*

A copy of the record shall where practicable, be given to the suspect or their solicitor before any procedures under *paragraphs 3.5 to 3.10, 3.21* or *3.23* are carried out. See *Note 3E*

(a) Cases when the suspect's identity is not known

3.2 In cases when the suspect's identity is not known, a witness may be taken to a particular neighbourhood or place to see whether they can identify the person they saw on a previous occasion. Although the number, age, sex, race, general description and style of clothing of other people present at the location and the way in which any identification is made cannot be controlled, the principles applicable to the formal procedures under *paragraphs 3.5 to 3.10* shall be followed as far as practicable. For example:

    (a) where it is practicable to do so, a record should be made of the witness's description of the suspect, as in paragraph 3.1(a), before asking the witness to make an identification;

    (b) care must be taken not to direct the witness' attention to any individual unless, taking into account all the circumstances, this cannot be avoided. However, this does not prevent a witness being asked to look carefully at the

Code D

people around at the time or to look towards a group or in a particular direction, if this appears necessary to make sure that the witness does not overlook a possible suspect simply because the witness is looking in the opposite direction and also to enable the witness to make comparisons between any suspect and others who are in the area; See *Note 3F*

(c) where there is more than one witness, every effort should be made to keep them separate and witnesses should be taken to see whether they can identify a person independently;

(d) once there is sufficient information to justify the arrest of a particular individual for suspected involvement in the offence, e.g., after a witness makes a positive identification, the provisions set out from paragraph 3.4 onwards shall apply for any other witnesses in relation to that individual;

(e) the officer or police staff accompanying the witness must record, in their pocket book, the action taken as soon as, and in as much detail, as possible. The record should include: the date, time and place of the relevant occasion the witness claims to have previously seen the suspect; where any identification was made; how it was made and the conditions at the time (e.g., the distance the witness was from the suspect, the weather and light); if the witness's attention was drawn to the suspect; the reason for this; and anything said by the witness or the suspect about the identification or the conduct of the procedure.

3.3 A witness must not be shown photographs, computerised or artist's composite likenesses or similar likenesses or pictures (including 'E-fit' images) if the identity of the suspect is known to the police and the suspect is available to take part in a video identification, an identification parade or a group identification. If the suspect's identity is not known, the showing of such images to a witness to obtain identification evidence must be done in accordance with *Annex E*.

(b) Cases when the suspect is known and available

3.4 If the suspect's identity is known to the police and they are available, the identification procedures set out in paragraphs 3.5 to 3.10 may be used. References in this section to a suspect being 'known' mean there is sufficient information known to the police to justify the arrest of a particular person for suspected involvement in the offence. A suspect being 'available' means they are immediately available or will be within a reasonably short time and willing to take an effective part in at least one of the following which it is practicable to arrange:

• video identification;
• identification parade; or
• group identification.

Video identification

3.5 A 'video identification' is when the witness is shown moving images of a known suspect, together with similar images of others who resemble the suspect. Moving images must be used unless:

• the suspect is known but not available (see paragraph 3.21 of this Code); or
in accordance with paragraph 2A of Annex A of this Code, the identification officer does not consider that replication of a physical feature can be achieved

or that it is not possible to conceal the location of the feature on the image of the suspect.

The identification officer may then decide to make use of video identification but using still images.

3.6 Video identifications must be carried out in accordance with *Annex A*.

Identification parade

3.7 An 'identification parade' is when the witness sees the suspect in a line of others who resemble the suspect.

3.8 Identification parades must be carried out in accordance with *Annex B*.

Group identification

3.9 A 'group identification' is when the witness sees the suspect in an informal group of people.

3.10 Group identifications must be carried out in accordance with *Annex C*.

Arranging eye-witness identification procedures

3.11 Except for the provisions in *paragraph 3.19*, the arrangements for, and conduct of, the identification procedures in paragraphs 3.5 to 3.10 and circumstances in which an identification procedure must be held shall be the responsibility of an officer not below inspector rank who is not involved with the investigation, 'the identification officer'. Unless otherwise specified, the identification officer may allow another officer or police staff, see *paragraph 2.21*, to make arrangements for, and conduct, any of these identification procedures. In delegating these procedures, the identification officer must be able to supervise effectively and either intervene or be contacted for advice. No officer or any other person involved with the investigation of the case against the suspect, beyond the extent required by these procedures, may take any part in these procedures or act as the identification officer. This does not prevent the identification officer from consulting the officer in charge of the investigation to determine which procedure to use. When an identification procedure is required, in the interest of fairness to suspects and witnesses, it must be held as soon as practicable.

Code D

Circumstances in which an eye-witness identification procedure must be held

3.12 Whenever:
(i) an eye witness has identified a suspect or purported to have identified them prior to any identification procedure set out in paragraphs 3.5 to 3.10 having been held; or
(ii) there is a witness available who expresses an ability to identify the suspect, or where there is a reasonable chance of the witness being able to do so, and they have not been given an opportunity to identify the suspect in any of the procedures set out in paragraphs 3.5 to 3.10,

and the suspect disputes being the person the witness claims to have seen, an identification procedure shall be held unless it is not practicable or it would serve no useful purpose in proving or disproving whether the suspect was involved in committing the offence, for example:

- where the suspect admits being at the scene of the crime and gives an account of what took place and the eye-witness does not see anything which contradicts that.
- when it is not disputed that the suspect is already known to the witness who claims to have recognised them when seeing them commit the crime.

3.13 An eye-witness identification procedure may also be held if the officer in charge of the investigation considers it would be useful.

Selecting an eye-witness identification procedure

3.14 If, because of paragraph 3.12, an identification procedure is to be held, the suspect shall initially be offered a video identification unless:
  (a) a video identification is not practicable; or
  (b) an identification parade is both practicable and more suitable than a video identification; or
  (c) paragraph 3.16 applies.

The identification officer and the officer in charge of the investigation shall consult each other to determine which option is to be offered. An identification parade may not be practicable because of factors relating to the witnesses, such as their number, state of health, availability and travelling requirements. A video identification would normally be more suitable if it could be arranged and completed sooner than an identification parade. Before an option is offered the suspect must also be reminded of their entitlement to have free legal advice, see Code C, *paragraph 6.5.*

3.15 A suspect who refuses the identification procedure first offered shall be asked to state their reason for refusing and may get advice from their solicitor and/or if present, their appropriate adult. The suspect, solicitor and/or appropriate adult shall be allowed to make representations about why another procedure should be used. A record should be made of the reasons for refusal and any representations made. After considering any reasons given, and representations made, the identification officer shall, if appropriate, arrange for the suspect to be offered an alternative which the officer considers suitable and practicable. If the officer decides it is not suitable and practicable to offer an alternative identification procedure, the reasons for that decision shall be recorded.

3.16 A group identification may initially be offered if the officer in charge of the investigation considers it is more suitable than a video identification or an identification parade and the identification officer considers it practicable to arrange.

Notice to suspect

3.17 Unless *paragraph 3.20* applies, before a video identification, an identification parade or group identification is arranged, the following shall be explained to the suspect:
  (i) the purposes of the video identification, identification parade or group identification;
  (ii) their entitlement to free legal advice; see Code C, paragraph 6.5;
  (iii) the procedures for holding it, including their right to have a solicitor or friend present;
  (iv) that they do not have to consent to or co-operate in a video identification, identification parade or group identification;

(v)   that if they do not consent to, and co-operate in, a video identification, identification parade or group identification, their refusal may be given in evidence in any subsequent trial and police may proceed covertly without their consent or make other arrangements to test whether a witness can identify them, see *paragraph 3.21*;

(vi)   whether, for the purposes of the video identification procedure, images of them have previously been obtained, see *paragraph 3.20*, and if so, that they may co-operate in providing further, suitable images to be used instead;

(vii)   if appropriate, the special arrangements for juveniles;

(viii)   if appropriate, the special arrangements for mentally disordered or otherwise mentally vulnerable people;

(ix)   that if they significantly alter their appearance between being offered an identification procedure and any attempt to hold an identification procedure, this may be given in evidence if the case comes to trial, and the identification officer may then consider other forms of identification, see *paragraph 3.21* and *Note 3C*;

(x)   that a moving image or photograph may be taken of them when they attend for any identification procedure;

(xi)   whether, before their identity became known, the witness was shown photographs, a computerised or artist's composite likeness or similar likeness or image by the police, see *Note 3B*;

(xii)   that if they change their appearance before an identification parade, it may not be practicable to arrange one on the day or subsequently and, because of the appearance change, the identification officer may consider alternative methods of identification, see *Note 3C*;

(xiii)   that they or their solicitor will be provided with details of the description of the suspect as first given by any witnesses who are to attend the video identification, identification parade, group identification or confrontation, see paragraph 3.1.

3.18   This information must also be recorded in a written notice handed to the suspect. The suspect must be given a reasonable opportunity to read the notice, after which, they should be asked to sign a second copy to indicate if they are willing to co-operate with the making of a video or take part in the identification parade or group identification. The signed copy shall be retained by the identification officer.

3.19   The duties of the identification officer under *paragraphs 3.17* and *3.18* may be performed by the custody officer or other officer not involved in the investigation if:

(a)   it is proposed to release the suspect in order that an identification procedure can be arranged and carried out and an inspector is not available to act as the identification officer, see *paragraph 3.11*, before the suspect leaves the station; or

(b)   it is proposed to keep the suspect in police detention whilst the procedure is arranged and carried out and waiting for an inspector to act as the identification officer, see *paragraph 3.11*, would cause unreasonable delay to the investigation.

Code D

The officer concerned shall inform the identification officer of the action taken and give them the signed copy of the notice. See *Note 3C*

3.20 If the identification officer and officer in charge of the investigation suspect, on reasonable grounds that if the suspect was given the information and notice as in *paragraphs 3.17* and *3.18*, they would then take steps to avoid being seen by a witness in any identification procedure, the identification officer may arrange for images of the suspect suitable for use in a video identification procedure to be obtained before giving the information and notice. If suspect's images are obtained in these circumstances, the suspect may, for the purposes of a video identification procedure, co-operate in providing new images which if suitable, would be used instead, see *paragraph 3.17(vi)*.

(c) Cases when the suspect is known but not available

3.21 When a known suspect is not available or has ceased to be available, see *paragraph 3.4*, the identification officer may make arrangements for a video identification (see Annex A). If necessary, the identification officer may follow the video identification procedures but using still images. Any suitable moving or still images may be used and these may be obtained covertly if necessary. Alternatively, the identification officer may make arrangements for a group identification. See *Note 3D*. These provisions may also be applied to juveniles where the consent of their parent or guardian is either refused or reasonable efforts to obtain that consent have failed. (see *paragraph 2.12*).

3.22 Any covert activity should be strictly limited to that necessary to test the ability of the witness to identify the suspect.

3.23 The identification officer may arrange for the suspect to be confronted by the witness if none of the options referred to in paragraphs 3.5 to 3.10 or 3.21 are practicable. A "confrontation" is when the suspect is directly confronted by the witness. A confrontation does not require the suspect's consent. Confrontations must be carried out in accordance with Annex D.

3.24 Requirements for information to be given to, or sought from, a suspect or for the suspect to be given an opportunity to view images before they are shown to a witness, do not apply if the suspect's lack of co-operation prevents the necessary action.

(d) Documentation

3.25 A record shall be made of the video identification, identification parade, group identification or confrontation on forms provided for the purpose.

3.26 If the identification officer considers it is not practicable to hold a video identification or identification parade requested by the suspect, the reasons shall be recorded and explained to the suspect.

3.27 A record shall be made of a person's failure or refusal to co-operate in a video identification, identification parade or group identification and, if applicable, of the grounds for obtaining images in accordance with *paragraph 3.20*.

(e) Showing films and photographs of incidents and information released to the media

3.28 Nothing in this Code inhibits showing films, photographs or other images to the public through the national or local media, or to police officers for the purposes of recognition and tracing suspects. However, when such material is shown to obtain evidence of recognition, the procedures in Part B will apply. See *Note 3AA*.

3.29 When a broadcast or publication is made, see *paragraph 3.28*, a copy of the relevant material released to the media for the purposes of recognising or tracing the suspect, shall be kept. The suspect or their solicitor shall be allowed to view such material before any eye-witness identification procedures under *paragraphs 3.5 to 3.10, 3.21 or 3.23* of Part A are carried out, provided it is practicable and would not unreasonably delay the investigation. Each eye-witness involved in the procedure shall be asked, after they have taken part, whether they have seen any film, photograph or image relating to the offence or any description of the suspect which has been broadcast or published in any national or local media or on any social networking site and if they have, they should be asked to give details of the circumstances, such as the date and place as relevant. Their replies shall be recorded. This paragraph does not affect any separate requirement under the Criminal Procedure and Investigations Act 1996 to retain material in connection with criminal investigations.

Code D

(f) Destruction and retention of photographs taken or used in eye-witness identification procedures

3.30 PACE, section 64A, see *paragraph 5.12*, provides powers to take photographs of suspects and allows these photographs to be used or disclosed only for purposes related to the prevention or detection of crime, the investigation of offences or the conduct of prosecutions by, or on behalf of, police or other law enforcement and prosecuting authorities inside and outside the United Kingdom or the enforcement of a sentence. After being so used or disclosed, they may be retained but can only be used or disclosed for the same purposes.

3.31 Subject to *paragraph 3.33*, the photographs (and all negatives and copies), of suspects not taken in accordance with the provisions in *paragraph 5.12* which are taken for the purposes of, or in connection with, the identification procedures in *paragraphs 3.5 to 3.10, 3.21 or 3.23* must be destroyed unless the suspect:

(a) is charged with, or informed they may be prosecuted for, a recordable offence;

(b) is prosecuted for a recordable offence;

(c) is cautioned for a recordable offence or given a warning or reprimand in accordance with the Crime and Disorder Act 1998 for a recordable offence; or

(d) gives informed consent, in writing, for the photograph or images to be retained for purposes described in *paragraph 3.30*.

3.32 When *paragraph 3.31* requires the destruction of any photograph, the person must be given an opportunity to witness the destruction or to have a certificate confirming the destruction if they request one within five days of being informed that the destruction is required.

3.33 Nothing in *paragraph 3.31* affects any separate requirement under the Criminal Procedure and Investigations Act 1996 to retain material in connection with criminal investigations.

(B) Evidence of recognition by showing films, photographs and other images

3.34 This Part of this section applies when, for the purposes of obtaining evidence of recognition, any person, including a police officer:
   (a) views the image of an individual in a film, photograph or any other visual medium; and
   (b) is asked whether they recognise that individual as someone who is known to them.

See *Notes 3AA* and *3G*

3.35 The films, photographs and other images shall be shown on an individual basis to avoid any possibility of collusion and to provide safeguards against mistaken recognition (see *Note 3G*), the showing shall as far as possible follow the principles for video identification if the suspect is known, see *Annex A*, or identification by photographs if the suspect is not known, see *Annex E*.

3.36 A record of the circumstances and conditions under which the person is given an opportunity to recognise the individual must be made and the record must include:
   (a) Whether the person knew or was given information concerning the name or identity of any suspect.
   (b) What the person has been told before the viewing about the offence, the person(s) depicted in the images or the offender and by whom.
   (c) How and by whom the witness was asked to view the image or look at the individual.
   (d) Whether the viewing was alone or with others and if with others, the reason for it.
   (e) The arrangements under which the person viewed the film or saw the individual and by whom those arrangements were made.
   (f) Whether the viewing of any images was arranged as part of a mass circulation to police and the public or for selected persons.
   (g) The date time and place images were viewed or further viewed or the individual was seen.
   (h) The times between which the images were viewed or the individual was seen.
   (i) How the viewing of images or sighting of the individual was controlled and by whom.
   (j) Whether the person was familiar with the location shown in any images or the place where they saw the individual and if so, why.
   (k) Whether or not on this occasion, the person claims to recognise any image shown, or any individual seen, as being someone known to them, and if they do:
      (i) the reason
      (ii) the words of recognition
      (iii) any expressions of doubt
      (iv) what features of the image or the individual triggered the recognition.

3.37 The record under paragraph 3.36 may be made by:
- the person who views the image or sees the individual and makes the recognition.
- the officer or police staff in charge of showing the images to the person or in charge of the conditions under which the person sees the individual.

Notes for guidance

3AA *The eye-witness identification procedures in Part A should not be used to test whether a witness can recognise a person as someone they know and would be able to give evidence of recognition along the lines that "On (describe date, time location) I saw an image of an individual who I recognised as AB." In these cases, the procedures in Part B shall apply.*

3A *Except for the provisions of Annex E, paragraph 1, a police officer who is a witness for the purposes of this part of the Code is subject to the same principles and procedures as a civilian witness.*

3B *When a witness attending an identification procedure has previously been shown photographs, or been shown or provided with computerised or artist's composite likenesses, or similar likenesses or pictures, it is the officer in charge of the investigation's responsibility to make the identification officer aware of this.*

3C *The purpose of paragraph 3.19 is to avoid or reduce delay in arranging identification procedures by enabling the required information and warnings, see sub-paragraphs 3.17(ix) and 3.17(xii), to be given at the earliest opportunity.*

3D *Paragraph 3.21 would apply when a known suspect deliberately makes themselves 'unavailable' in order to delay or frustrate arrangements for obtaining identification evidence. It also applies when a suspect refuses or fails to take part in a video identification, an identification parade or a group identification, or refuses or fails to take part in the only practicable options from that list. It enables any suitable images of the suspect, moving or still, which are available or can be obtained, to be used in an identification procedure. Examples include images from custody and other CCTV systems and from visually recorded interview records, see Code F Note for Guidance 2D.*

3E *When it is proposed to show photographs to a witness in accordance with Annex E, it is the responsibility of the officer in charge of the investigation to confirm to the officer responsible for supervising and directing the showing, that the first description of the suspect given by that witness has been recorded. If this description has not been recorded, the procedure under Annex E must be postponed. See Annex E paragraph 2*

3F *The admissibility and value of identification evidence obtained when carrying out the procedure under paragraph 3.2 may be compromised if:*
  (a) *before a person is identified, the witness's attention is specifically drawn to that person; or*
  (b) *the suspect's identity becomes known before the procedure.*

3G *The admissibility and value of evidence of recognition obtained when carrying out the procedures in Part B may be compromised if before the person is recognised, the witness who has claimed to know them is given or is made, or becomes aware of, information about the person which was not previously known to them personally but which they have purported to rely on to support their claim that the person is in fact known to them.*

Code D

4 IDENTIFICATION BY FINGERPRINTS AND FOOTWEAR IMPRESSIONS

(A) Taking fingerprints in connection with a criminal investigation

(a) General

4.1   References to 'fingerprints' means any record, produced by any method, of the skin pattern and other physical characteristics or features of a person's:
(i) fingers; or
(ii) palms.

(b) Action

4.2   A person's fingerprints may be taken in connection with the investigation of an offence only with their consent or if *paragraph 4.3* applies. If the person is at a police station consent must be in writing.

4.3   PACE, section 61, provides powers to take fingerprints without consent from any person over the age of ten years:

(a)   under section 61(3), from a person detained at a police station in consequence of being arrested for a recordable offence, see Note 4A, if they have not had their fingerprints taken in the course of the investigation of the offence unless those previously taken fingerprints are not a complete set or some or all of those fingerprints are not of sufficient quality to allow satisfactory analysis, comparison or matching.

(b)   under section 61(4), from a person detained at a police station who has been charged with a recordable offence, see *Note 4A*, or informed they will be reported for such an offence if they have not had their fingerprints taken in the course of the investigation of the offence unless those previously taken fingerprints are not a complete set or some or all of those fingerprints are not of sufficient quality to allow satisfactory analysis, comparison or matching.

(c)   under section 61(4A), from a person who has been bailed to appear at a court or police station if the person:
(i) has answered to bail for a person whose fingerprints were taken previously and there are reasonable grounds for believing they are not the same person; or
(ii) who has answered to bail claims to be a different person from a person whose fingerprints were previously taken;
and in either case, the court or an officer of inspector rank or above, authorises the fingerprints to be taken at the court or police station (an inspector's authority may be given in writing or orally and confirmed in writing, as soon as practicable);

(ca)   under section 61(5A) from a person who has been arrested for a recordable offence and released if the person:
(i) is on bail and has not had their fingerprints taken in the course of the investigation of the offence, or;
(ii) has had their fingerprints taken in the course of the investigation of the offence, but they do not constitute a complete set or some, or all, of the fingerprints are not of sufficient quality to allow satisfactory analysis, comparison or matching.

(cb) under section 61(5B) from a person not detained at a police station who has been charged with a recordable offence or informed they will be reported for such an offence if they have not had their fingerprints taken in the course of the investigation or their fingerprints have been taken in the course of the investigation of the offence, but they do not constitute a complete set or some, or all, of the fingerprints are not of sufficient quality to allow satisfactory analysis, comparison or matching.

(d) under section 61(6), from a person who has been:
   (i) convicted of a recordable offence;
   (ii) given a caution in respect of a recordable offence which, at the time of the caution, the person admitted; or
   (iii) warned or reprimanded under the Crime and Disorder Act 1998, section 65, for a recordable offence,

   if, since their conviction, caution, warning or reprimand their fingerprints have not been taken or their fingerprints which have been taken since then do not constitute a complete set or some, or all, of the fingerprints are not of sufficient quality to allow satisfactory analysis, comparison or matching, and in either case, an officer of inspector rank or above, is satisfied that taking the fingerprints is necessary to assist in the prevention or detection of crime and authorises the taking;

Code D

(e) under section 61(6A) from a person a constable reasonably suspects is committing or attempting to commit, or has committed or attempted to commit, any offence if either:
   • the person's name is unknown and cannot be readily ascertained by the constable; or
   • the constable has reasonable grounds for doubting whether a name given by the person is their real name.
   Note: fingerprints taken under this power are not regarded as having been taken in the course of the investigation of an offence.
   [See *Note 4C*]

(f) under section 61(6D) from a person who has been convicted outside England and Wales of an offence which if committed in England and Wales would be a qualifying offence as defined by PACE, section 65A (see *Note 4AB*) if:
   (i) the person's fingerprints have not been taken previously under this power or their fingerprints have been so taken on a previous occasion but they do not constitute a complete set or some, or all, of the fingerprints are not of sufficient quality to allow satisfactory analysis, comparison or matching; and
   (ii) a police officer of inspector rank or above is satisfied that taking fingerprints is necessary to assist in the prevention or detection of crime and authorises them to be taken.

4.4 PACE, section 63A(4) and Schedule 2A provide powers to:
(a) make a requirement (in accordance with Annex G) for a person to attend a police station to have their fingerprints taken in the exercise of certain powers in paragraph 4.3 above when that power applies at the time the fingerprints would be taken in accordance with the requirement. Those powers are:

    (i) section 61(5A) – Persons arrested for a recordable offence and released, see paragraph 4.3(ca): The requirement may not be made more than six months from the day the investigating officer was informed that the fingerprints previously taken were incomplete or below standard.

   (ii) section 61(5B) – Persons charged etc. with a recordable offence, see paragraph 4.3(cb): The requirement may not be made more than six months from:

- the day the person was charged or reported if fingerprints have not been taken since then; or
- the day the investigating officer was informed that the fingerprints previously taken were incomplete or below standard.

 (iii) section 61(6) – Person convicted, cautioned, warned or reprimanded for a recordable offence in England and Wales, see paragraph 4.3(d): Where the offence for which the person was convicted etc is also a qualifying offence (see *Note 4AB*), there is no time limit for the exercise of this power. Where the conviction etc. is for a recordable offence which is <u>not</u> a qualifying offence, the requirement may not be made more than two years from:

- the day the person was convicted, cautioned, warned or reprimanded, or the day Schedule 2A comes into force (if later), if fingerprints have not been taken since then; or
- the day an officer from the force investigating the offence was informed that the fingerprints previously taken were incomplete or below standard or the day Schedule 2A comes into force (if later).

   (v) section 61(6D) – A person who has been convicted of a qualifying offence (see *Note 4AB*) outside England and Wales, see paragraph 4.3(g): There is no time limit for making the requirement.

Note: A person who has had their fingerprints taken under any of the powers in section 61 mentioned in paragraph 4.3 on two occasions in relation to any offence may not be required under Schedule 2A to attend a police station for their fingerprints to be taken again under section 61 in relation to that offence, unless authorised by an officer of inspector rank or above. The fact of the authorisation and the reasons for giving it must be recorded as soon as practicable.

   (b) arrest, without warrant, a person who fails to comply with the requirement.

4.5 A person's fingerprints may be taken, as above, electronically.

4.6 Reasonable force may be used, if necessary, to take a person's fingerprints without their consent under the powers as in *paragraphs 4.3* and *4.4*.

4.7 Before any fingerprints are taken:

  (a) without consent under any power mentioned in *paragraphs 4.3* and *4.4* above, the person must be informed of:

     (i) the reason their fingerprints are to be taken;

    (ii) the power under which they are to be taken; and

   (iii) the fact that the relevant authority has been given if any power mentioned in *paragraph 4.3 (c), (d)* or *(f)* applies

  (b) with or without consent at a police station or elsewhere, the person must be informed:

(i) that their fingerprints may be subject of a speculative search against other fingerprints, see *Note 4B*; and

(ii) that their fingerprints may be retained in accordance with *Annex F, Part (a)* unless they were taken under the power mentioned in paragraph 4.3(e) when they must be destroyed after they have been checked (See *Note 4C*).

(c) Documentation

4.8A A record must be made as soon as practicable after the fingerprints are taken, of:

- the matters in paragraph 4.7(a)(i) to (iii) and the fact that the person has been informed of those matters; and
- the fact that the person has been informed of the matters in paragraph 4.7(b) (i) and (ii).

The record must be made in the person's custody record if they are detained at a police station when the fingerprints are taken.

4.8 If force is used, a record shall be made of the circumstances and those present.

4.9 Not used

(B) Taking fingerprints in connection with immigration enquiries

Action

4.10 A person's fingerprints may be taken and retained for the purposes of immigration law enforcement and control in accordance with powers and procedures other than under PACE and for which the UK Border Agency (not the police) are responsible. Details of these powers and procedures which are under the Immigration Act 1971, Schedule 2 and Immigration and Asylum Act 1999, section 141, including modifications to the PACE Codes of Practice are contained in Chapter 24 of the Operational Instructions and Guidance manual which is published by the UK Border Agency (See *Note 4D*).

4.11 *Not used*
4.12 *Not used*
4.13 *Not used*
4.14 *Not used*
4.15 *Not used*

(C) Taking footwear impressions in connection with a criminal investigation

(a) Action

4.16 Impressions of a person's footwear may be taken in connection with the investigation of an offence only with their consent or if *paragraph 4.17* applies. If the person is at a police station consent must be in writing.

4.17 PACE, section 61A, provides power for a police officer to take footwear impressions without consent from any person over the age of ten years who is detained at a police station:

(a) in consequence of being arrested for a recordable offence, see *Note 4A*; or if the detainee has been charged with a recordable offence, or informed they will be reported for such an offence; and

(b) the detainee has not had an impression of their footwear taken in the course of the investigation of the offence unless the previously taken

Code D

impression is not complete or is not of sufficient quality to allow satisfactory analysis, comparison or matching (whether in the case in question or generally).

4.18 Reasonable force may be used, if necessary, to take a footwear impression from a detainee without consent under the power in *paragraph 4.17*.

4.19 Before any footwear impression is taken with, or without, consent as above, the person must be informed:

(a) of the reason the impression is to be taken;

(b) that the impression may be retained and may be subject of a speculative search against other impressions, see *Note 4B*, unless destruction of the impression is required in accordance with *Annex F, Part (a)*; and

(c) that if their footwear impressions are required to be destroyed, they may witness their destruction as provided for in *Annex F, Part (a)*.

(b) Documentation

4.20 A record must be made as soon as possible, of the reason for taking a person's footwear impressions without consent. If force is used, a record shall be made of the circumstances and those present.

4.21 A record shall be made when a person has been informed under the terms of *paragraph 4.19(b)*, of the possibility that their footwear impressions may be subject of a speculative search.

Notes for guidance

4A   *References to 'recordable offences' in this Code relate to those offences for which convictions, cautions, reprimands and warnings may be recorded in national police records. See PACE, section 27(4). The recordable offences current at the time when this Code was prepared, are any offences which carry a sentence of imprisonment on conviction (irrespective of the period, or the age of the offender or actual sentence passed) as well as the non-imprisonable offences under the Vagrancy Act 1824 sections 3 and 4 (begging and persistent begging), the Street Offences Act 1959, section 1 (loitering or soliciting for purposes of prostitution), the Road Traffic Act 1988, section 25 (tampering with motor vehicles), the Criminal Justice and Public Order Act 1994, section 167 (touting for hire car services) and others listed in the National Police Records (Recordable Offences) Regulations 2000 as amended.*

4AB *A qualifying offence is one of the offences specified in PACE, section 65A. These indictable offences which concern the use or threat of violence or unlawful force against persons, sexual offences and offences against children include, for example, murder, manslaughter, false imprisonment, kidnapping and other offences such as:*

• *sections 4, 16, 18, 20 to 24 or 47 of the Offences Against the Person Act 1861;*

• *sections 16 to 18 of the Firearms Act 1968;*

• *sections 9 or 10 of the Theft Act 1968 or under section 12A of that Act involving an accident which caused a person's death;*

• *section 1 of the Criminal Damage Act 1971 required to be charged as arson;*

• *section 1 of the Protection of Children Act 1978 and;*

• *sections 1 to 19, 25, 26, 30 to 41, 47 to 50, 52, 53, 57 to 59, 61 to 67, 69 and 70 of the Sexual Offences Act 2003.*

4B   *Fingerprints, footwear impressions or a DNA sample (and the information derived from it) taken from a person arrested on suspicion of being involved in a recordable offence, or charged with such an offence, or informed they will be reported for such an offence, may be subject of a speculative search. This means the fingerprints, footwear impressions or DNA sample may be checked against other fingerprints, footwear impressions and DNA records held by, or on behalf of, the police and other law enforcement authorities in, or outside, the UK, or held in connection with, or as a result of, an investigation of an offence inside or outside the UK. Fingerprints, footwear impressions and samples taken from a person suspected of committing a recordable offence but not arrested, charged or informed they will be reported for it, may be subject to a speculative search only if the person consents in writing. The following is an example of a basic form of words:*

> *"I consent to my fingerprints, footwear impressions and DNA sample and information derived from it being retained and used only for purposes related to the prevention and detection of a crime, the investigation of an offence or the conduct of a prosecution either nationally or internationally.*
>
> *I understand that my fingerprints, footwear impressions or DNA sample may be checked against other fingerprint, footwear impressions and DNA records held by or on behalf of relevant law enforcement authorities, either nationally or internationally.*
>
> *I understand that once I have given my consent for my fingerprints, footwear impressions or DNA sample to be retained and used I cannot withdraw this consent."*

Code **D**

See Annex F regarding the retention and use of fingerprints and footwear impressions taken with consent for elimination purposes.

4C   *The power under section 61(6A) of PACE described in paragraph 4.3(e) allows fingerprints of a suspect who has not been arrested to be taken in connection with any offence (whether recordable or not) using a mobile device and then checked on the street against the database containing the national fingerprint collection. Fingerprints taken under this power cannot be retained after they have been checked. The results may make an arrest for the suspected offence based on the name condition unnecessary (See Code G paragraph 2.9(a)) and enable the offence to be disposed of without arrest, for example, by summons/charging by post, penalty notice or words of advice. If arrest for a non-recordable offence is necessary for any other reasons, this power may also be exercised at the station. Before the power is exercised, the officer should:*

- *inform the person of the nature of the suspected offence and why they are suspected of committing it.*
- *give them a reasonable opportunity to establish their real name before deciding that their name is unknown and cannot be readily ascertained or that there are reasonable grounds to doubt that a name they have given is their real name.*
- *as applicable, inform the person of the reason why their name is not known and cannot be readily ascertained or of the grounds for doubting that a name they have given is their real name, including, for example, the reason why a particular document the person has produced to verify their real name, is not sufficient.*

4D   *Powers to take fingerprints without consent for immigration purposes are given to police and immigration officers under the:*

(a) *Immigration Act 1971, Schedule 2, paragraph 18(2), when it is reasonably necessary for the purposes of identifying a person detained under the Immigration Act*

1971, Schedule 2, paragraph 16 (Detention of person liable to examination or removal), and

(b) *Immigration and Asylum Act 1999, section 141(7) when a person:*
   - *fails without reasonable excuse to produce, on arrival, a valid passport with a photograph or some other document satisfactorily establishing their identity and nationality;*
   - *is refused entry to the UK but is temporarily admitted if an immigration officer reasonably suspects the person might break a residence or reporting condition;*
   - *is subject to directions for removal from the UK;*
   - *has been arrested under the Immigration Act 1971, Schedule 2, paragraph 17;*
   - *has made a claim for asylum*
   - *is a dependant of any of the above.*

The Immigration and Asylum Act 1999, section 142(3), also gives police and immigration officers power to arrest without warrant, a person who fails to comply with a requirement imposed by the Secretary of State to attend a specified place for fingerprinting.

5 EXAMINATIONS TO ESTABLISH IDENTITY AND THE TAKING OF PHOTOGRAPHS

(A) Detainees at police stations

(a) Searching or examination of detainees at police stations

5.1 PACE, section 54A (1), allows a detainee at a police station to be searched or examined or both, to establish:
   (a) whether they have any marks, features or injuries that would tend to identify them as a person involved in the commission of an offence and to photograph any identifying marks, see *paragraph 5.5*; or
   (b) their identity, see *Note 5A*.
   A person detained at a police station to be searched under a stop and search power, see Code A, is not a detainee for the purposes of these powers.

5.2 A search and/or examination to find marks under section 54A (1) (a) may be carried out without the detainee's consent, see *paragraph 2.12*, only if authorised by an officer of at least inspector rank when consent has been withheld or it is not practicable to obtain consent, see *Note 5D*.

5.3 A search or examination to establish a suspect's identity under section 54A (1) (b) may be carried out without the detainee's consent, see *paragraph 2.12*, only if authorised by an officer of at least inspector rank when the detainee has refused to identify themselves or the authorising officer has reasonable grounds for suspecting the person is not who they claim to be.

5.4 Any marks that assist in establishing the detainee's identity, or their identification as a person involved in the commission of an offence, are identifying marks. Such marks may be photographed with the detainee's consent, see *paragraph 2.12*; or without their consent if it is withheld or it is not practicable to obtain it, see *Note 5D*.

5.5 A detainee may only be searched, examined and photographed under section 54A, by a police officer of the same sex.

5.6 Any photographs of identifying marks, taken under section 54A, may be used or disclosed only for purposes related to the prevention or detection of crime, the investigation of offences or the conduct of prosecutions by, or on behalf of, police or other law enforcement and prosecuting authorities inside, and outside, the UK. After being so used or disclosed, the photograph may be retained but must not be used or disclosed except for these purposes, see *Note 5B*.

5.7   The powers, as in *paragraph 5.1*, do not affect any separate requirement under the Criminal Procedure and Investigations Act 1996 to retain material in connection with criminal investigations.

5.8   Authority for the search and/or examination for the purposes of *paragraphs 5.2 and 5.3* may be given orally or in writing. If given orally, the authorising officer must confirm it in writing as soon as practicable. A separate authority is required for each purpose which applies.

5.9   If it is established a person is unwilling to co-operate sufficiently to enable a search and/or examination to take place or a suitable photograph to be taken, an officer may use reasonable force to:
(a) search and/or examine a detainee without their consent; and
(b) photograph any identifying marks without their consent.

5.10 The thoroughness and extent of any search or examination carried out in accordance with the powers in section 54A must be no more than the officer considers necessary to achieve the required purpose. Any search or examination which involves the removal of more than the person's outer clothing shall be conducted in accordance with Code C, Annex A, paragraph 11.

5.11 An intimate search may not be carried out under the powers in section 54A.

(b) Photographing detainees at police stations and other persons elsewhere than at a police station

5.12 Under PACE, section 64A, an officer may photograph:
(a) any person whilst they are detained at a police station; and
(b) any person who is elsewhere than at a police station and who has been:
   (i)   arrested by a constable for an offence;
   (ii)   taken into custody by a constable after being arrested for an offence by a person other than a constable;
   (iii) made subject to a requirement to wait with a community support officer under paragraph 2(3) or (3B) of Schedule 4 to the Police Reform Act 2002;
   (iiia) given a direction by a constable under section 27 of the Violent Crime Reduction Act 2006.
   (iv)   given a penalty notice by a constable in uniform under Chapter 1 of Part 1 of the Criminal Justice and Police Act 2001, a penalty notice by a constable under section 444A of the Education Act 1996, or a fixed penalty notice by a constable in uniform under section 54 of the Road Traffic Offenders Act 1988;
   (v)   given a notice in relation to a relevant fixed penalty offence (within the meaning of paragraph 1 of Schedule 4 to the Police Reform Act 2002) by a community support officer by virtue of a designation applying that paragraph to him;
   (vi)   given a notice in relation to a relevant fixed penalty offence (within the meaning of paragraph 1 of Schedule 5 to the Police Reform Act

Code **D**

2002) by an accredited person by virtue of accreditation specifying that that paragraph applies to him; or

(vii)   given a direction to leave and not return to a specified location for up to 48 hours by a police constable (under section 27 of the Violent Crime Reduction Act 2006).

5.12A Photographs taken under PACE, section 64A:

(a) may be taken with the person's consent, or without their consent if consent is withheld or it is not practicable to obtain their consent, see *Note 5E*; and

(b) may be used or disclosed only for purposes related to the prevention or detection of crime, the investigation of offences or the conduct of prosecutions by, or on behalf of, police or other law enforcement and prosecuting authorities inside and outside the United Kingdom or the enforcement of any sentence or order made by a court when dealing with an offence. After being so used or disclosed, they may be retained but can only be used or disclosed for the same purposes. See *Note 5B*.

5.13   The officer proposing to take a detainee's photograph may, for this purpose, require the person to remove any item or substance worn on, or over, all, or any part of, their head or face. If they do not comply with such a requirement, the officer may remove the item or substance.

5.14   If it is established the detainee is unwilling to co-operate sufficiently to enable a suitable photograph to be taken and it is not reasonably practicable to take the photograph covertly, an officer may use reasonable force, see *Note 5F*.

(a) to take their photograph without their consent; and

(b) for the purpose of taking the photograph, remove any item or substance worn on, or over, all, or any part of, the person's head or face which they have failed to remove when asked.

5.15   For the purposes of this Code, a photograph may be obtained without the person's consent by making a copy of an image of them taken at any time on a camera system installed anywhere in the police station.

(c) Information to be given

5.16   When a person is searched, examined or photographed under the provisions as in *paragraph 5.1* and *5.12*, or their photograph obtained as in *paragraph 5.15*, they must be informed of the:

(a) purpose of the search, examination or photograph;

(b) grounds on which the relevant authority, if applicable, has been given; and

(c) purposes for which the photograph may be used, disclosed or retained.

This information must be given before the search or examination commences or the photograph is taken, except if the photograph is:

(i)   to be taken covertly;

(ii)   obtained as in *paragraph 5.15*, in which case the person must be informed as soon as practicable after the photograph is taken or obtained.

(d) Documentation

5.17   A record must be made when a detainee is searched, examined, or a photograph of the person, or any identifying marks found on them, are taken. The record must include the:

(a) identity, subject to paragraph 2.18, of the officer carrying out the search, examination or taking the photograph;

(b) purpose of the search, examination or photograph and the outcome;

(c) detainee's consent to the search, examination or photograph, or the reason the person was searched, examined or photographed without consent;

(d) giving of any authority as in *paragraphs 5.2* and *5.3*, the grounds for giving it and the authorising officer.

5.18   If force is used when searching, examining or taking a photograph in accordance with this section, a record shall be made of the circumstances and those present.

(B) Persons at police stations not detained

5.19   When there are reasonable grounds for suspecting the involvement of a person in a criminal offence, but that person is at a police station **voluntarily** and not detained, the provisions of *paragraphs 5.1* to *5.18* should apply, subject to the modifications in the following paragraphs.

5.20   References to the 'person being detained' and to the powers mentioned in *paragraph 5.1* which apply only to detainees at police stations shall be omitted.

Code D

5.21   Force may not be used to:

(a) search and/or examine the person to:

(i) discover whether they have any marks that would tend to identify them as a person involved in the commission of an offence; or

(ii) establish their identity, see *Note 5A*;

(b) take photographs of any identifying marks, see *paragraph 5.4*; or

(c) take a photograph of the person.

5.22   Subject to *paragraph 5.24*, the photographs of persons or of their identifying marks which are not taken in accordance with the provisions mentioned in *paragraphs 5.1* or *5.12*, must be destroyed (together with any negatives and copies) unless the person:

(a) is charged with, or informed they may be prosecuted for, a recordable offence;

(b) is prosecuted for a recordable offence;

(c) is cautioned for a recordable offence or given a warning or reprimand in accordance with the Crime and Disorder Act 1998 for a recordable offence; or

(d) gives informed consent, in writing, for the photograph or image to be retained as in *paragraph 5.6*.

5.23   When *paragraph 5.22* requires the destruction of any photograph, the person must be given an opportunity to witness the destruction or to have a certificate confirming the destruction provided they so request the certificate within five days of being informed the destruction is required.

5.24   Nothing in *paragraph 5.22* affects any separate requirement under the Criminal Procedure and Investigations Act 1996 to retain material in connection with criminal investigations.

Notes for guidance

5A The conditions under which fingerprints may be taken to assist in establishing a person's identity, are described in Section 4.

5B Examples of purposes related to the prevention or detection of crime, the investigation of offences or the conduct of prosecutions include:

(a) checking the photograph against other photographs held in records or in connection with, or as a result of, an investigation of an offence to establish whether the person is liable to arrest for other offences;

(b) when the person is arrested at the same time as other people, or at a time when it is likely that other people will be arrested, using the photograph to help establish who was arrested, at what time and where;

(c) when the real identity of the person is not known and cannot be readily ascertained or there are reasonable grounds for doubting a name and other personal details given by the person, are their real name and personal details. In these circumstances, using or disclosing the photograph to help to establish or verify their real identity or determine whether they are liable to arrest for some other offence, e.g. by checking it against other photographs held in records or in connection with, or as a result of, an investigation of an offence;

(d) when it appears any identification procedure in section 3 may need to be arranged for which the person's photograph would assist;

(e) when the person's release without charge may be required, and if the release is:

(i) on bail to appear at a police station, using the photograph to help verify the person's identity when they answer their bail and if the person does not answer their bail, to assist in arresting them; or

(ii) without bail, using the photograph to help verify their identity or assist in locating them for the purposes of serving them with a summons to appear at court in criminal proceedings;

(f) when the person has answered to bail at a police station and there are reasonable grounds for doubting they are the person who was previously granted bail, using the photograph to help establish or verify their identity;

(g) when the person arrested on a warrant claims to be a different person from the person named on the warrant and a photograph would help to confirm or disprove their claim;

(h) when the person has been charged with, reported for, or convicted of, a recordable offence and their photograph is not already on record as a result of (a) to (f) or their photograph is on record but their appearance has changed since it was taken and the person has not yet been released or brought before a court.

5C There is no power to arrest a person convicted of a recordable offence solely to take their photograph. The power to take photographs in this section applies only where the person is in custody as a result of the exercise of another power, e.g. arrest for fingerprinting under PACE, section 27.

5D Examples of when it would not be practicable to obtain a detainee's consent, see paragraph 2.12, to a search, examination or the taking of a photograph of an identifying mark include:

(a) when the person is drunk or otherwise unfit to give consent;

(b) when there are reasonable grounds to suspect that if the person became aware a search or examination was to take place or an identifying mark was to be photographed, they would take steps to prevent this happening, e.g. by violently resisting, covering or concealing the mark etc and it would not otherwise be possible to carry out the search or examination or to photograph any identifying mark;

    (c) in the case of a juvenile, if the parent or guardian cannot be contacted in sufficient time to allow the search or examination to be carried out or the photograph to be taken.

5E Examples of when it would not be practicable to obtain the person's consent, see paragraph 2.12, to a photograph being taken include:

    (a) when the person is drunk or otherwise unfit to give consent;

    (b) when there are reasonable grounds to suspect that if the person became aware a photograph, suitable to be used or disclosed for the use and disclosure described in paragraph 5.6, was to be taken, they would take steps to prevent it being taken, e.g. by violently resisting, covering or distorting their face etc, and it would not otherwise be possible to take a suitable photograph;

    (c) when, in order to obtain a suitable photograph, it is necessary to take it covertly; and

    (d) in the case of a juvenile, if the parent or guardian cannot be contacted in sufficient time to allow the photograph to be taken.

5F The use of reasonable force to take the photograph of a suspect elsewhere than at a police station must be carefully considered. In order to obtain a suspect's consent and co-operation to remove an item of religious headwear to take their photograph, a constable should consider whether in the circumstances of the situation the removal of the headwear and the taking of the photograph should be by an officer of the same sex as the person. It would be appropriate for these actions to be conducted out of public view.

Code D

6 Identification by body samples and impressions

(A) General

6.1 References to:

    (a) an 'intimate sample' mean a dental impression or sample of blood, semen or any other tissue fluid, urine, or pubic hair, or a swab taken from any part of a person's genitals or from a person's body orifice other than the mouth;

    (b) a 'non-intimate sample' means:

       (i)   a sample of hair, other than pubic hair, which includes hair plucked with the root, see Note 6A;

       (ii) a sample taken from a nail or from under a nail;

      (iii) a swab taken from any part of a person's body other than a part from which a swab taken would be an intimate sample;

      (iv) saliva;

       (v) a skin impression which means any record, other than a fingerprint, which is a record, in any form and produced by any method, of the skin pattern and other physical characteristics or features of the whole, or any part of, a person's foot or of any other part of their body.

(B) Action

(a) Intimate samples

6.2 PACE, section 62, provides that intimate samples may be taken under:

   (a) section 62(1), from a person in police detention only:

     (i) if a police officer of inspector rank or above has reasonable grounds to believe such an impression or sample will tend to confirm or disprove the suspect's involvement in a recordable offence, see *Note 4A*, and gives authorisation for a sample to be taken; and

     (ii) with the suspect's written consent;

   (b) section 62(1A), from a person not in police detention but from whom two or more non-intimate samples have been taken in the course of an investigation of an offence and the samples, though suitable, have proved insufficient if:

     (i) a police officer of inspector rank or above authorises it to be taken; and

     (ii) the person concerned gives their written consent. See *Notes 6B* and *6C*

   (c) section 62(2A), from a person convicted outside England and Wales of an offence which if committed in England and Wales would be qualifying offence as defined by PACE, section 65A (see *Note 4AB*) from whom two or more non-intimate samples taken under section 63(3E) (see paragraph 6.6(h) have proved insufficient if:

     (i) a police officer of inspector rank or above is satisfied that taking the sample is necessary to assist in the prevention or detection of crime and authorises it to be taken; and

     (ii) the person concerned gives their written consent.

6.2A PACE, section 63A(4) and Schedule 2A provide powers to:

   (a) make a requirement (in accordance with Annex G) for a person to attend a police station to have an intimate sample taken in the exercise of one of the following powers in paragraph 6.2 when that power applies at the time the sample is to be taken in accordance with the requirement or after the person's arrest if they fail to comply with the requirement:

     (i) section 62(1A) – Persons from whom two or more non-intimate samples have been taken and proved to be insufficient, see paragraph 6.2(b): There is no time limit for making the requirement.

     (ii) section 62(2A) – Persons convicted outside England and Wales from whom two or more non-intimate samples taken under section 63(3E) (see paragraph 6.6(h)) have proved insufficient, see *paragraph 6.2(c)*: There is no time limit for making the requirement.

6.3 Before a suspect is asked to provide an intimate sample, they must be:

   (a) informed:

     (i) of the reason, including the nature of the suspected offence (except if taken under *paragraph 6.2(c)* from a person convicted outside England and Wales).

     (ii) that authorisation has been given and the provisions under which given;

     (iii) that a sample taken at a police station may be subject of a speculative search;

   (b) warned that if they refuse without good cause their refusal may harm their case if it comes to trial, see *Note 6D*. If the suspect is in police detention and not legally represented, they must also be reminded of their entitlement to have free legal advice, see Code C, *paragraph 6.5*, and the reminder noted in the custody record. If *paragraph 6.2(b)* applies and the person is attending a station voluntarily, their entitlement to free legal advice as in Code C, *paragraph 3.21* shall be explained to them.

6.4 Dental impressions may only be taken by a registered dentist. Other intimate samples, except for samples of urine, may only be taken by a registered medical practitioner or registered nurse or registered paramedic.

(b) Non-intimate samples

6.5 A non-intimate sample may be taken from a detainee only with their written consent or if *paragraph 6.6* applies.

6.6 a non-intimate sample may be taken from a person without the appropriate consent in the following circumstances:

(a) under section 63(2A) from a person who is in police detention as a consequence of being arrested for a recordable offence and who has not had a non-intimate sample of the same type and from the same part of the body taken in the course of the investigation of the offence by the police or they have had such a sample taken but it proved insufficient.

(b) Under section 63(3) from a person who is being held in custody by the police on the authority of a court if an officer of at least the rank of inspector authorises it to be taken. An authorisation may be given:

(i) if the authorising officer has reasonable grounds for suspecting the person of involvement in a recordable offence and for believing that the sample will tend to confirm or disprove that involvement, and

(ii) in writing or orally and confirmed in writing, as soon as practicable;

but an authorisation may not be given to take from the same part of the body a further non-intimate sample consisting of a skin impression unless the previously taken impression proved insufficient

(c) under section 63(3ZA) from a person who has been arrested for a recordable offence and released if the person:

(i) is on bail and has not had a sample of the same type and from the same part of the body taken in the course of the investigation of the offence, or;

(ii) has had such a sample taken in the course of the investigation of the offence, but it proved unsuitable or insufficient.

(d) under section 63(3A), from a person (whether or not in police detention or held in custody by the police on the authority of a court) who has been charged with a recordable offence or informed they will be reported for such an offence if the person:

(i) has not had a non-intimate sample taken from them in the course of the investigation of the offence;

(ii) has had a sample so taken, but it proved unsuitable or insufficient, see *Note 6B*; or

(iii) has had a sample taken in the course of the investigation of the offence and the sample has been destroyed and in proceedings relating to that offence there is a dispute as to whether a DNA profile relevant to the proceedings was derived from the destroyed sample.

(e) under section 63(3B), from a person who has been:

(i) convicted of a recordable offence;

    (ii) given a caution in respect of a recordable offence which, at the time of the caution, the person admitted; or

    (iii) warned or reprimanded under the Crime and Disorder Act 1998, section 65, for a recordable offence,

if, since their conviction, caution, warning or reprimand a non-intimate sample has not been taken from them or a sample which has been taken since then has proved to be unsuitable or insufficient and in either case, an officer of inspector rank or above, is satisfied that taking the fingerprints is necessary to assist in the prevention or detection of crime and authorises the taking;

(f) under section 63(3C) from a person to whom section 2 of the Criminal Evidence (Amendment) Act 1997 applies (persons detained following acquittal on grounds of insanity or finding of unfitness to plead).

(g) under section 63(3E) from a person who has been convicted outside England and Wales of an offence which if committed in England and Wales would be a qualifying offence as defined by PACE, section 65A (see *Note 4AB*) if:

    (i) a non-intimate sample has not been taken previously under this power or unless a sample was so taken but was unsuitable or insufficient; and

    (ii) a police officer of inspector rank or above is satisfied that taking a sample is necessary to assist in the prevention or detection of crime and authorises it to be taken.

6.6A PACE, section 63A(4) and Schedule 2A provide powers to:

(a) make a requirement (in accordance with Annex G) for a person to attend a police station to have a non-intimate sample taken in the exercise of one of the following powers in paragraph 6.6 when that power applies at the time the sample would be taken in accordance with the requirement:

    (i) section 63(3ZA) – Persons arrested for a recordable offence and released, see paragraph 6.6(c): The requirement may not be made more than six months from the day the investigating officer was informed that the sample previously taken was unsuitable or insufficient.

    (ii) section 63(3A) – Persons charged etc. with a recordable offence, see paragraph 6.6(d): The requirement may not be made more than six months from:

      • the day the person was charged or reported if a sample has not been taken since then; or

      • the day the investigating officer was informed that the sample previously taken was unsuitable or insufficient.

    (iii) section 63(3B) – Person convicted, cautioned, warned or reprimanded for a recordable offence in England and Wales, see paragraph 6.6(e): Where the offence for which the person was convicted etc is also a qualifying offence (see *Note 4AB*), there is no time limit for the exercise of this power. Where the conviction etc was for a recordable offence that is <u>not</u> a qualifying offence, the requirement may not be made more than two years from:

- the day the person was convicted, cautioned, warned or reprimanded, or the day Schedule 2A comes into force (if later), if a sample has not been taken since then; or
- the day an officer from the force investigating the offence was informed that the sample previously taken was unsuitable or insufficient or the day Schedule 2A comes into force (if later).

    (iv) section 63(3E) – A person who has been convicted of a qualifying offence (see *Note 4AB*) outside England and Wales, see paragraph 6.6(h): There is no time limit for making the requirement.

Note: A person who has had a non-intimate sample taken under any of the powers in section 63 mentioned in paragraph 6.6 on two occasions in relation to any offence may not be required under Schedule 2A to attend a police station for a sample to be taken again under section 63 in relation to that offence, unless authorised by an officer of inspector rank or above. The fact of the authorisation and the reasons for giving it must be recorded as soon as practicable.

    (b) arrest, without warrant, a person who fails to comply with the requirement.

Code D

6.7   Reasonable force may be used, if necessary, to take a non-intimate sample from a person without their consent under the powers mentioned in *paragraph 6.6*.

6.8   Before any non-intimate sample is taken:

    (a) without consent under any power mentioned in paragraphs 6.6 and 6.6A, the person must be informed of:

        (i)   the reason for taking the sample;

        (ii) the power under which the sample is to be taken;

        (iii) the fact that the relevant authority has been given if any power mentioned in *paragraph 6.6(b), (e)* or *(h)* applies;

    (b) with or without consent at a police station or elsewhere, the person must be informed:

        (i)   that their sample or information derived from it may be subject of a speculative search against other samples and information derived from them, see *Note 6E* and

        (ii) that their sample and the information derived from it may be retained in accordance with *Annex F*, Part (a).

(c) Removal of clothing

6.9   When clothing needs to be removed in circumstances likely to cause embarrassment to the person, no person of the opposite sex who is not a registered medical practitioner or registered health care professional shall be present, (unless in the case of a juvenile, mentally disordered or mentally vulnerable person, that person specifically requests the presence of an appropriate adult of the opposite sex who is readily available) nor shall anyone whose presence is unnecessary. However, in the case of a juvenile, this is subject to the overriding proviso that such a removal of clothing may take place in the absence of the appropriate adult only if the juvenile signifies in their presence, that they prefer the adult's absence and they agree.

(c) Documentation

6.10   A record must be made as soon as practicable after the sample is taken of:
- The matters in paragraph 6.8(a)(i) to (iii) and the fact that the person has been informed of those matters; and
- The fact that the person has been informed of the matters in paragraph 6.8(b) (i) and (ii).

6.10A If force is used, a record shall be made of the circumstances and those present.

6.11   A record must be made of a warning given as required by *paragraph 6.3.*

6.12   *Not used*

Notes for guidance

6A *When hair samples are taken for the purpose of DNA analysis (rather than for other purposes such as making a visual match), the suspect should be permitted a reasonable choice as to what part of the body the hairs are taken from. When hairs are plucked, they should be plucked individually, unless the suspect prefers otherwise and no more should be plucked than the person taking them reasonably considers necessary for a sufficient sample.*

6B *(a) An insufficient sample is one which is not sufficient either in quantity or quality to provide information for a particular form of analysis, such as DNA analysis. A sample may also be insufficient if enough information cannot be obtained from it by analysis because of loss, destruction, damage or contamination of the sample or as a result of an earlier, unsuccessful attempt at analysis.*
   (b) An unsuitable sample is one which, by its nature, is not suitable for a particular form of analysis.

6C *Nothing in paragraph 6.2 prevents intimate samples being taken for elimination purposes with the consent of the person concerned but the provisions of paragraph 2.12 relating to the role of the appropriate adult, should be applied. Paragraph 6.2(b) does not, however, apply where the non-intimate samples were previously taken under the Terrorism Act 2000, Schedule 8, paragraph 10.*

6D *In warning a person who is asked to provide an intimate sample as in paragraph 6.3, the following form of words may be used:*
   'You do not have to provide this sample/allow this swab or impression to be taken, but I must warn you that if you refuse without good cause, your refusal may harm your case if it comes to trial.'

6E *Fingerprints or a DNA sample and the information derived from it taken from a person arrested on suspicion of being involved in a recordable offence, or charged with such an offence, or informed they will be reported for such an offence, may be subject of a speculative search. This means they may be checked against other fingerprints and DNA records held by, or on behalf of, the police and other law enforcement authorities in or outside the UK or held in connection with, or as a result of, an investigation of an offence inside or outside the UK. Fingerprints and samples taken from any other person, e.g. a person suspected of committing a recordable offence but who has not been arrested, charged or informed they will be reported for it, may be subject to a speculative search only if the person consents in writing to their fingerprints being subject of such a search. The following is an example of a basic form of words:*

"I consent to my fingerprints/DNA sample and information derived from it being retained and used only for purposes related to the prevention and detection of a crime, the investigation of an offence or the conduct of a prosecution either nationally or internationally.

I understand that this sample may be checked against other fingerprint/DNA records held by or on behalf of relevant law enforcement authorities, either nationally or internationally.

I understand that once I have given my consent for the sample to be retained and used I cannot withdraw this consent."

See Annex F regarding the retention and use of fingerprints and samples taken with consent for elimination purposes.

6F *Samples of urine and non-intimate samples taken in accordance with sections 63B and 63C of PACE may not be used for identification purposes in accordance with this Code. See Code C note for guidance 17D.*

Annex A—Video Identification

(a) General

1. The arrangements for obtaining and ensuring the availability of a suitable set of images to be used in a video identification must be the responsibility of an identification officer, who has no direct involvement with the case.

2. The set of images must include the suspect and at least eight other people who, so far as possible, resemble the suspect in age, general appearance and position in life. Only one suspect shall appear in any set unless there are two suspects of roughly similar appearance, in which case they may be shown together with at least twelve other people.

2A If the suspect has an unusual physical feature, e.g., a facial scar, tattoo or distinctive hairstyle or hair colour which does not appear on the images of the other people that are available to be used, steps may be taken to:

    (a) conceal the location of the feature on the images of the suspect and the other people; or

    (b) replicate that feature on the images of the other people.

    For these purposes, the feature may be concealed or replicated electronically or by any other method which it is practicable to use to ensure that the images of the suspect and other people resemble each other. The identification officer has discretion to choose whether to conceal or replicate the feature and the method to be used. If an unusual physical feature has been described by the witness, the identification officer should, if practicable, have that feature replicated. If it has not been described, concealment may be more appropriate.

2B If the identification officer decides that a feature should be concealed or replicated, the reason for the decision and whether the feature was concealed or replicated in the images shown to any witness shall be recorded.

2C If the witness requests to view an image where an unusual physical feature has been concealed or replicated without the feature being concealed or replicated, the witness may be allowed to do so.

Code D

3. The images used to conduct a video identification shall, as far as possible, show the suspect and other people in the same positions or carrying out the same sequence of movements. They shall also show the suspect and other people under identical conditions unless the identification officer reasonably believes:

   (a) because of the suspect's failure or refusal to co-operate or other reasons, it is not practicable for the conditions to be identical; and
   (b) any difference in the conditions would not direct a witness's attention to any individual image.

4. The reasons identical conditions are not practicable shall be recorded on forms provided for the purpose.

5. Provision must be made for each person shown to be identified by number.

6. If police officers are shown, any numerals or other identifying badges must be concealed. If a prison inmate is shown, either as a suspect or not, then either all, or none of, the people shown should be in prison clothing.

7. The suspect or their solicitor, friend, or appropriate adult must be given a reasonable opportunity to see the complete set of images before it is shown to any witness. If the suspect has a reasonable objection to the set of images or any of the participants, the suspect shall be asked to state the reasons for the objection. Steps shall, if practicable, be taken to remove the grounds for objection. If this is not practicable, the suspect and/or their representative shall be told why their objections cannot be met and the objection, the reason given for it and why it cannot be met shall be recorded on forms provided for the purpose.

8. Before the images are shown in accordance with *paragraph 7*, the suspect or their solicitor shall be provided with details of the first description of the suspect by any witnesses who are to attend the video identification. When a broadcast or publication is made, as in *paragraph 3.28*, the suspect or their solicitor must also be allowed to view any material released to the media by the police for the purpose of recognising or tracing the suspect, provided it is practicable and would not unreasonably delay the investigation.

9. The suspect's solicitor, if practicable, shall be given reasonable notification of the time and place the video identification is to be conducted so a representative may attend on behalf of the suspect. The suspect may not be present when the images are shown to the witness(es). In the absence of the suspect's solicitor, the viewing itself shall be recorded on video. No unauthorised people may be present.

(b) Conducting the video identification

10. The identification officer is responsible for making the appropriate arrangements to make sure, before they see the set of images, witnesses are not able to communicate with each other about the case, see any of the images which are to be shown, see, or be reminded of, any photograph or description of the suspect or be given any other indication as to the suspect's identity, or overhear a witness who has already seen the material. There must be no discussion with the witness about the composition of the set of images and they must not be told whether a previous witness has made any identification.

11. Only one witness may see the set of images at a time. Immediately before the images are shown, the witness shall be told that the person they saw on a specified earlier occasion may, or may not, appear in the images they are shown and

that if they cannot make a positive identification, they should say so. The witness shall be advised that at any point, they may ask to see a particular part of the set of images or to have a particular image frozen for them to study. Furthermore, it should be pointed out to the witness that there is no limit on how many times they can view the whole set of images or any part of them. However, they should be asked not to make any decision as to whether the person they saw is on the set of images until they have seen the whole set at least twice.

12. Once the witness has seen the whole set of images at least twice and has indicated that they do not want to view the images, or any part of them, again, the witness shall be asked to say whether the individual they saw in person on a specified earlier occasion has been shown and, if so, to identify them by number of the image. The witness will then be shown that image to confirm the identification, see *paragraph 17*.

13. Care must be taken not to direct the witness's attention to any one individual image or give any indication of the suspect's identity. Where a witness has previously made an identification by photographs, or a computerised or artist's composite or similar likeness, the witness must not be reminded of such a photograph or composite likeness once a suspect is available for identification by other means in accordance with this Code. Nor must the witness be reminded of any description of the suspect.

Code D

14. After the procedure, each witness shall be asked whether they have seen any broadcast or published films or photographs, or any descriptions of suspects relating to the offence and their reply shall be recorded.

(c) Image security and destruction

15. Arrangements shall be made for all relevant material containing sets of images used for specific identification procedures to be kept securely and their movements accounted for. In particular, no-one involved in the investigation shall be permitted to view the material prior to it being shown to any witness.

16. As appropriate, *paragraph 3.30* or *3.31* applies to the destruction or retention of relevant sets of images.

(d) Documentation

17. A record must be made of all those participating in, or seeing, the set of images whose names are known to the police.

18. A record of the conduct of the video identification must be made on forms provided for the purpose. This shall include anything said by the witness about any identifications or the conduct of the procedure and any reasons it was not practicable to comply with any of the provisions of this Code governing the conduct of video identifications.

ANNEX B—IDENTIFICATION PARADES

(a) General

1. A suspect must be given a reasonable opportunity to have a solicitor or friend present, and the suspect shall be asked to indicate on a second copy of the notice whether or not they wish to do so.

2. An identification parade may take place either in a normal room or one equipped with a screen permitting witnesses to see members of the identification parade without being seen. The procedures for the composition and conduct of the identification parade are the same in both cases, subject to *paragraph 8* (except that an identification parade involving a screen may take place only when the suspect's solicitor, friend or appropriate adult is present or the identification parade is recorded on video).

3. Before the identification parade takes place, the suspect or their solicitor shall be provided with details of the first description of the suspect by any witnesses who are attending the identification parade. When a broadcast or publication is made as in *paragraph 3.28*, the suspect or their solicitor should also be allowed to view any material released to the media by the police for the purpose of recognising or tracing the suspect, provided it is practicable to do so and would not unreasonably delay the investigation.

(b) Identification parades involving prison inmates

4. If a prison inmate is required for identification, and there are no security problems about the person leaving the establishment, they may be asked to participate in an identification parade or video identification.

5. An identification parade may be held in a Prison Department establishment but shall be conducted, as far as practicable under normal identification parade rules. Members of the public shall make up the identification parade unless there are serious security, or control, objections to their admission to the establishment. In such cases, or if a group or video identification is arranged within the establishment, other inmates may participate. If an inmate is the suspect, they are not required to wear prison clothing for the identification parade unless the other people taking part are other inmates in similar clothing, or are members of the public who are prepared to wear prison clothing for the occasion.

(c) Conduct of the identification parade

6. Immediately before the identification parade, the suspect must be reminded of the procedures governing its conduct and cautioned in the terms of Code C, paragraphs 10.5 or 10.6, as appropriate.

7. All unauthorised people must be excluded from the place where the identification parade is held.

8. Once the identification parade has been formed, everything afterwards, in respect of it, shall take place in the presence and hearing of the suspect and any interpreter, solicitor, friend or appropriate adult who is present (unless the identification parade involves a screen, in which case everything said to, or by, any witness at the place where the identification parade is held, must be said in the hearing and presence of the suspect's solicitor, friend or appropriate adult or be recorded on video).

9. The identification parade shall consist of at least eight people (in addition to the suspect) who, so far as possible, resemble the suspect in age, height, general appearance and position in life. Only one suspect shall be included in an identification parade unless there are two suspects of roughly similar appearance, in which case they may be paraded together with at least twelve other people. In no circumstances shall more than two suspects be included in one identification

parade and where there are separate identification parades, they shall be made up of different people.

10. If the suspect has an unusual physical feature, e.g., a facial scar, tattoo or distinctive hairstyle or hair colour which cannot be replicated on other members of the identification parade, steps may be taken to conceal the location of that feature on the suspect and the other members of the identification parade if the suspect and their solicitor, or appropriate adult, agree. For example, by use of a plaster or a hat, so that all members of the identification parade resemble each other in general appearance.

11. When all members of a similar group are possible suspects, separate identification parades shall be held for each unless there are two suspects of similar appearance when they may appear on the same identification parade with at least twelve other members of the group who are not suspects. When police officers in uniform form an identification parade any numerals or other identifying badges shall be concealed.

12. When the suspect is brought to the place where the identification parade is to be held, they shall be asked if they have any objection to the arrangements for the identification parade or to any of the other participants in it and to state the reasons for the objection. The suspect may obtain advice from their solicitor or friend, if present, before the identification parade proceeds. If the suspect has a reasonable objection to the arrangements or any of the participants, steps shall, if practicable, be taken to remove the grounds for objection. When it is not practicable to do so, the suspect shall be told why their objections cannot be met and the objection, the reason given for it and why it cannot be met, shall be recorded on forms provided for the purpose.

Code D

13. The suspect may select their own position in the line, but may not otherwise interfere with the order of the people forming the line. When there is more than one witness, the suspect must be told, after each witness has left the room, that they can, if they wish, change position in the line. Each position in the line must be clearly numbered, whether by means of a number laid on the floor in front of each identification parade member or by other means.

14. Appropriate arrangements must be made to make sure, before witnesses attend the identification parade, they are not able to:
    (i)   communicate with each other about the case or overhear a witness who has already seen the identification parade;
    (ii) see any member of the identification parade;
    (iii) see, or be reminded of, any photograph or description of the suspect or be given any other indication as to the suspect's identity; or
    (iv) see the suspect before or after the identification parade.

15. The person conducting a witness to an identification parade must not discuss with them the composition of the identification parade and, in particular, must not disclose whether a previous witness has made any identification.

16. Witnesses shall be brought in one at a time. Immediately before the witness inspects the identification parade, they shall be told the person they saw on a specified earlier occasion may, or may not, be present and if they cannot make a positive identification, they should say so. The witness must also be told they

should not make any decision about whether the person they saw is on the identification parade until they have looked at each member at least twice.

17. When the officer or police staff (see paragraph 3.11) conducting the identification procedure is satisfied the witness has properly looked at each member of the identification parade, they shall ask the witness whether the person they saw on a specified earlier occasion is on the identification parade and, if so, to indicate the number of the person concerned, see *paragraph 28.*

18. If the witness wishes to hear any identification parade member speak, adopt any specified posture or move, they shall first be asked whether they can identify any person(s) on the identification parade on the basis of appearance only. When the request is to hear members of the identification parade speak, the witness shall be reminded that the participants in the identification parade have been chosen on the basis of physical appearance only. Members of the identification parade may then be asked to comply with the witness' request to hear them speak, see them move or adopt any specified posture.

19. If the witness requests that the person they have indicated remove anything used for the purposes of *paragraph 10* to conceal the location of an unusual physical feature, that person may be asked to remove it.

20. If the witness makes an identification after the identification parade has ended, the suspect and, if present, their solicitor, interpreter or friend shall be informed. When this occurs, consideration should be given to allowing the witness a second opportunity to identify the suspect.

21 After the procedure, each witness shall be asked whether they have seen any broadcast or published films or photographs or any descriptions of suspects relating to the offence and their reply shall be recorded.

22. When the last witness has left, the suspect shall be asked whether they wish to make any comments on the conduct of the identification parade.

(d) Documentation

23. A video recording must normally be taken of the identification parade. If that is impracticable, a colour photograph must be taken. A copy of the video recording or photograph shall be supplied, on request, to the suspect or their solicitor within a reasonable time.

24. As appropriate, *paragraph 3.30* or *3.31*, should apply to any photograph or video taken as in *paragraph 23.*

25. If any person is asked to leave an identification parade because they are interfering with its conduct, the circumstances shall be recorded.

26. A record must be made of all those present at an identification parade whose names are known to the police.

27. If prison inmates make up an identification parade, the circumstances must be recorded.

28. A record of the conduct of any identification parade must be made on forms provided for the purpose. This shall include anything said by the witness or the suspect about any identifications or the conduct of the procedure, and any reasons it was not practicable to comply with any of this Code's provisions.

ANNEX C—GROUP IDENTIFICATION

(a) General

1. The purpose of this Annex is to make sure, as far as possible, group identifications follow the principles and procedures for identification parades so the conditions are fair to the suspect in the way they test the witness' ability to make an identification.

2. Group identifications may take place either with the suspect's consent and co-operation or covertly without their consent.

3. The location of the group identification is a matter for the identification officer, although the officer may take into account any representations made by the suspect, appropriate adult, their solicitor or friend.

4. The place where the group identification is held should be one where other people are either passing by or waiting around informally, in groups such that the suspect is able to join them and be capable of being seen by the witness at the same time as others in the group. For example people leaving an escalator, pedestrians walking through a shopping centre, passengers on railway and bus stations, waiting in queues or groups or where people are standing or sitting in groups in other public places.

5. If the group identification is to be held covertly, the choice of locations will be limited by the places where the suspect can be found and the number of other people present at that time. In these cases, suitable locations might be along regular routes travelled by the suspect, including buses or trains or public places frequented by the suspect.

6. Although the number, age, sex, race and general description and style of clothing of other people present at the location cannot be controlled by the identification officer, in selecting the location the officer must consider the general appearance and numbers of people likely to be present. In particular, the officer must reasonably expect that over the period the witness observes the group, they will be able to see, from time to time, a number of others whose appearance is broadly similar to that of the suspect.

7. A group identification need not be held if the identification officer believes, because of the unusual appearance of the suspect, none of the locations it would be practicable to use, satisfy the requirements of *paragraph 6* necessary to make the identification fair.

8. Immediately after a group identification procedure has taken place (with or without the suspect's consent), a colour photograph or video should be taken of the general scene, if practicable, to give a general impression of the scene and the number of people present. Alternatively, if it is practicable, the group identification may be video recorded.

9. If it is not practicable to take the photograph or video in accordance with *paragraph 8*, a photograph or film of the scene should be taken later at a time determined by the identification officer if the officer considers it practicable to do so.

10. An identification carried out in accordance with this Code remains a group identification even though, at the time of being seen by the witness, the suspect was on their own rather than in a group.

Code **D**

11. Before the group identification takes place, the suspect or their solicitor shall be provided with details of the first description of the suspect by any witnesses who are to attend the identification. When a broadcast or publication is made, as in *paragraph 3.28*, the suspect or their solicitor should also be allowed to view any material released by the police to the media for the purposes of recognising or tracing the suspect, provided that it is practicable and would not unreasonably delay the investigation.

12. After the procedure, each witness shall be asked whether they have seen any broadcast or published films or photographs or any descriptions of suspects relating to the offence and their reply recorded.

(b) Identification with the consent of the suspect

13. A suspect must be given a reasonable opportunity to have a solicitor or friend present. They shall be asked to indicate on a second copy of the notice whether or not they wish to do so.

14. The witness, the person carrying out the procedure and the suspect's solicitor, appropriate adult, friend or any interpreter for the witness, may be concealed from the sight of the individuals in the group they are observing, if the person carrying out the procedure considers this assists the conduct of the identification.

15. The person conducting a witness to a group identification must not discuss with them the forthcoming group identification and, in particular, must not disclose whether a previous witness has made any identification.

16. Anything said to, or by, the witness during the procedure about the identification should be said in the presence and hearing of those present at the procedure.

17. Appropriate arrangements must be made to make sure, before witnesses attend the group identification, they are not able to:
    (i) communicate with each other about the case or overhear a witness who has already been given an opportunity to see the suspect in the group;
    (ii) see the suspect; or
    (iii) see, or be reminded of, any photographs or description of the suspect or be given any other indication of the suspect's identity.

18. Witnesses shall be brought one at a time to the place where they are to observe the group. Immediately before the witness is asked to look at the group, the person conducting the procedure shall tell them that the person they saw may, or may not, be in the group and that if they cannot make a positive identification, they should say so. The witness shall be asked to observe the group in which the suspect is to appear. The way in which the witness should do this will depend on whether the group is moving or stationary.

Moving group

19. When the group in which the suspect is to appear is moving, e.g. leaving an escalator, the provisions of *paragraphs 20 to 24* should be followed.

20. If two or more suspects consent to a group identification, each should be the subject of separate identification procedures. These may be conducted consecutively on the same occasion.

21. The person conducting the procedure shall tell the witness to observe the group and ask them to point out any person they think they saw on the specified earlier occasion.

22. Once the witness has been informed as in *paragraph 21* the suspect should be allowed to take whatever position in the group they wish.

23. When the witness points out a person as in *paragraph 21* they shall, if practicable, be asked to take a closer look at the person to confirm the identification. If this is not practicable, or they cannot confirm the identification, they shall be asked how sure they are that the person they have indicated is the relevant person.

24. The witness should continue to observe the group for the period which the person conducting the procedure reasonably believes is necessary in the circumstances for them to be able to make comparisons between the suspect and other individuals of broadly similar appearance to the suspect as in *paragraph 6*.

Stationary groups

25. When the group in which the suspect is to appear is stationary, e.g. people waiting in a queue, the provisions of *paragraphs 26 to 29* should be followed.

26. If two or more suspects consent to a group identification, each should be subject to separate identification procedures unless they are of broadly similar appearance when they may appear in the same group. When separate group identifications are held, the groups must be made up of different people.

27. The suspect may take whatever position in the group they wish. If there is more than one witness, the suspect must be told, out of the sight and hearing of any witness, that they can, if they wish, change their position in the group.

28. The witness shall be asked to pass along, or amongst, the group and to look at each person in the group at least twice, taking as much care and time as possible according to the circumstances, before making an identification. Once the witness has done this, they shall be asked whether the person they saw on the specified earlier occasion is in the group and to indicate any such person by whatever means the person conducting the procedure considers appropriate in the circumstances. If this is not practicable, the witness shall be asked to point out any person they think they saw on the earlier occasion.

29. When the witness makes an indication as in *paragraph 28*, arrangements shall be made, if practicable, for the witness to take a closer look at the person to confirm the identification. If this is not practicable, or the witness is unable to confirm the identification, they shall be asked how sure they are that the person they have indicated is the relevant person.

All cases

30. If the suspect unreasonably delays joining the group, or having joined the group, deliberately conceals themselves from the sight of the witness, this may be treated as a refusal to co-operate in a group identification.

31. If the witness identifies a person other than the suspect, that person should be informed what has happened and asked if they are prepared to give their name and address. There is no obligation upon any member of the public to give

Code D

535

these details. There shall be no duty to record any details of any other member of the public present in the group or at the place where the procedure is conducted.

32. When the group identification has been completed, the suspect shall be asked whether they wish to make any comments on the conduct of the procedure.

33. If the suspect has not been previously informed, they shall be told of any identifications made by the witnesses.

(c) Identification without the suspect's consent

34. Group identifications held covertly without the suspect's consent should, as far as practicable, follow the rules for conduct of group identification by consent.

35. A suspect has no right to have a solicitor, appropriate adult or friend present as the identification will take place without the knowledge of the suspect.

36. Any number of suspects may be identified at the same time.

(d) Identifications in police stations

37. Group identifications should only take place in police stations for reasons of safety, security or because it is not practicable to hold them elsewhere.

38. The group identification may take place either in a room equipped with a screen permitting witnesses to see members of the group without being seen, or anywhere else in the police station that the identification officer considers appropriate.

39. Any of the additional safeguards applicable to identification parades should be followed if the identification officer considers it is practicable to do so in the circumstances.

(e) Identifications involving prison inmates

40. A group identification involving a prison inmate may only be arranged in the prison or at a police station.

41. When a group identification takes place involving a prison inmate, whether in a prison or in a police station, the arrangements should follow those in *paragraphs 37 to 39*. If a group identification takes place within a prison, other inmates may participate. If an inmate is the suspect, they do not have to wear prison clothing for the group identification unless the other participants are wearing the same clothing.

(f) Documentation

42. When a photograph or video is taken as in *paragraph 8* or *9*, a copy of the photograph or video shall be supplied on request to the suspect or their solicitor within a reasonable time.

43. *Paragraph 3.30* or *3.31*, as appropriate, shall apply when the photograph or film taken in accordance with *paragraph 8* or *9* includes the suspect.

44. A record of the conduct of any group identification must be made on forms provided for the purpose. This shall include anything said by the witness or suspect about any identifications or the conduct of the procedure and any reasons why it was not practicable to comply with any of the provisions of this Code governing the conduct of group identifications.

ANNEX D—CONFRONTATION BY A WITNESS

1. Before the confrontation takes place, the witness must be told that the person they saw may, or may not, be the person they are to confront and that if they are not that person, then the witness should say so.
2. Before the confrontation takes place the suspect or their solicitor shall be provided with details of the first description of the suspect given by any witness who is to attend. When a broadcast or publication is made, as in *paragraph 3.28*, the suspect or their solicitor should also be allowed to view any material released to the media for the purposes of recognising or tracing the suspect, provided it is practicable to do so and would not unreasonably delay the investigation.
3. Force may not be used to make the suspect's face visible to the witness.
4. Confrontation must take place in the presence of the suspect's solicitor, interpreter or friend unless this would cause unreasonable delay.
5. The suspect shall be confronted independently by each witness, who shall be asked "Is this the person?" If the witness identifies the person but is unable to confirm the identification, they shall be asked how sure they are that the person is the one they saw on the earlier occasion.
6. The confrontation should normally take place in the police station, either in a normal room or one equipped with a screen permitting a witness to see the suspect without being seen. In both cases, the procedures are the same except that a room equipped with a screen may be used only when the suspect's solicitor, friend or appropriate adult is present or the confrontation is recorded on video.
7. After the procedure, each witness shall be asked whether they have seen any broadcast or published films or photographs or any descriptions of suspects relating to the offence and their reply shall be recorded.

ANNEX E—SHOWING PHOTOGRAPHS

(a) Action

1. An officer of sergeant rank or above shall be responsible for supervising and directing the showing of photographs. The actual showing may be done by another officer or police staff, see *paragraph 3.11*.
2. The supervising officer must confirm the first description of the suspect given by the witness has been recorded before they are shown the photographs. If the supervising officer is unable to confirm the description has been recorded they shall postpone showing the photographs.
3. Only one witness shall be shown photographs at any one time. Each witness shall be given as much privacy as practicable and shall not be allowed to communicate with any other witness in the case.
4. The witness shall be shown not less than twelve photographs at a time, which shall, as far as possible, all be of a similar type.
5. When the witness is shown the photographs, they shall be told the photograph of the person they saw may, or may not, be amongst them and if they cannot make a positive identification, they should say so. The witness shall also be told they should not make a decision until they have viewed at least twelve photo-

Code **D**

graphs. The witness shall not be prompted or guided in any way but shall be left to make any selection without help.

6. If a witness makes a positive identification from photographs, unless the person identified is otherwise eliminated from enquiries or is not available, other witnesses shall not be shown photographs. But both they, and the witness who has made the identification, shall be asked to attend a video identification, an identification parade or group identification unless there is no dispute about the suspect's identification.

7. If the witness makes a selection but is unable to confirm the identification, the person showing the photographs shall ask them how sure they are that the photograph they have indicated is the person they saw on the specified earlier occasion.

8. When the use of a computerised or artist's composite or similar likeness has led to there being a known suspect who can be asked to participate in a video identification, appear on an identification parade or participate in a group identification, that likeness shall not be shown to other potential witnesses.

9. When a witness attending a video identification, an identification parade or group identification has previously been shown photographs or computerised or artist's composite or similar likeness (and it is the responsibility of the officer in charge of the investigation to make the identification officer aware that this is the case), the suspect and their solicitor must be informed of this fact before the identification procedure takes place.

10. None of the photographs shown shall be destroyed, whether or not an identification is made, since they may be required for production in court. The photographs shall be numbered and a separate photograph taken of the frame or part of the album from which the witness made an identification as an aid to reconstituting it.

(b) Documentation

11. Whether or not an identification is made, a record shall be kept of the showing of photographs on forms provided for the purpose. This shall include anything said by the witness about any identification or the conduct of the procedure, any reasons it was not practicable to comply with any of the provisions of this Code governing the showing of photographs and the name and rank of the supervising officer.

12. The supervising officer shall inspect and sign the record as soon as practicable.

ANNEX F—FINGERPRINTS, FOOTWEAR IMPRESSIONS AND SAMPLES—
DESTRUCTION AND SPECULATIVE SEARCHES

(a) Fingerprints, footwear impressions and samples taken in connection with a criminal investigation from a person suspected of committing the offence under investigation

1. The retention and destruction of fingerprints, footwear impressions and samples taken in connection with a criminal investigation from a person suspected of committing the offence under investigation is subject to PACE, section 64.

(b) Fingerprints, footwear impressions and samples taken in connection with a criminal investigation from a person not suspected of committing the offence under investigation.

2. When fingerprints, footwear impressions or DNA samples are taken from a person in connection with an investigation and the person is not suspected of having committed the offence, see *Note F1*, they must be destroyed as soon as they have fulfilled the purpose for which they were taken unless:

   (a) they were taken for the purposes of an investigation of an offence for which a person has been convicted; and

   (b) fingerprints, footwear impressions or samples were also taken from the convicted person for the purposes of that investigation.

   However, subject to *paragraph 2*, the fingerprints, footwear impressions and samples, and the information derived from samples, may not be used in the investigation of any offence or in evidence against the person who is, or would be, entitled to the destruction of the fingerprints, footwear impressions and samples, see *Note F2*.

3. The requirement to destroy fingerprints, footwear impressions and DNA samples, and information derived from samples, and restrictions on their retention and use in *paragraph 1* do not apply if the person gives their written consent for their fingerprints, footwear impressions or sample to be retained and used after they have fulfilled the purpose for which they were taken, see *Note F1*.

4. When a person's fingerprints, footwear impressions or sample are to be destroyed:

   (a) any copies of the fingerprints and footwear impressions must also be destroyed;

   (b) the person may witness the destruction of their fingerprints, footwear impressions or copies if they ask to do so within five days of being informed destruction is required;

   (c) access to relevant computer fingerprint data shall be made impossible as soon as it is practicable to do so and the person shall be given a certificate to this effect within three months of asking; and

   (d) neither the fingerprints, footwear impressions, the sample, or any information derived from the sample, may be used in the investigation of any offence or in evidence against the person who is, or would be, entitled to its destruction.

5. Fingerprints, footwear impressions or samples, and the information derived from samples, taken in connection with the investigation of an offence which are not required to be destroyed, may be retained after they have fulfilled the purposes for which they were taken but may be used only for purposes related to the prevention or detection of crime, the investigation of an offence or the conduct of a prosecution in, as well as outside, the UK and may also be subject to a speculative search. This includes checking them against other fingerprints, footwear impressions and DNA records held by, or on behalf of, the police and other law enforcement authorities in, as well as outside, the UK.

(b) Fingerprints taken in connection with Immigration Service enquiries

6. See paragraph 4.10.

Code D

Notes for guidance

F1   Fingerprints, footwear impressions and samples given voluntarily for the purposes of elimination play an important part in many police investigations. It is, therefore, important to make sure innocent volunteers are not deterred from participating and their consent to their fingerprints, footwear impressions and DNA being used for the purposes of a specific investigation is fully informed and voluntary. If the police or volunteer seek to have the fingerprints, footwear impressions or samples retained for use after the specific investigation ends, it is important the volunteer's consent to this is also fully informed and voluntary.

Examples of consent for:

- *DNA/fingerprints/footwear impressions - to be used only for the purposes of a specific investigation;*
- *DNA/fingerprints/footwear impressions - to be used in the specific investigation and retained by the police for future use.*

*To minimise the risk of confusion, each consent should be physically separate and the volunteer should be asked to sign **each consent.***

(a) DNA:

    (i)   DNA sample taken for the purposes of elimination or as part of an intelligence-led screening and to be used only for the purposes of that investigation and destroyed afterwards:

    "I consent to my DNA/mouth swab being taken for forensic analysis. I understand that the sample will be destroyed at the end of the case and that my profile will only be compared to the crime stain profile from this enquiry. I have been advised that the person taking the sample may be required to give evidence and/or provide a written statement to the police in relation to the taking of it".

    (ii) DNA sample to be retained on the National DNA database and used in the future:

    "I consent to my DNA sample and information derived from it being retained and used only for purposes related to the prevention and detection of a crime, the investigation of an offence or the conduct of a prosecution either nationally or internationally."

    "I understand that this sample may be checked against other DNA records held by, or on behalf of, relevant law enforcement authorities, either nationally or internationally".

    "I understand that once I have given my consent for the sample to be retained and used I cannot withdraw this consent."

(b) Fingerprints:

    (i)   Fingerprints taken for the purposes of elimination or as part of an intelligence-led screening and to be used only for the purposes of that investigation and destroyed afterwards:

    "I consent to my fingerprints being taken for elimination purposes. I understand that the fingerprints will be destroyed at the end of the case and that my fingerprints will only be compared to the fingerprints from this enquiry. I have been advised that the person taking the fingerprints may be required to give

evidence and/or provide a written statement to the police in relation to the taking of it."

   (ii) *Fingerprints to be retained for future use:*

"*I consent to my fingerprints being retained and used only for purposes related to the prevention and detection of a crime, the investigation of an offence or the conduct of a prosecution either nationally or internationally*".

"*I understand that my fingerprints may be checked against other records held by, or on behalf of, relevant law enforcement authorities, either nationally or internationally.*"

"*I understand that once I have given my consent for my fingerprints to be retained and used I cannot withdraw this consent.*"

  (c) *Footwear impressions:*

   (i) *Footwear impressions taken for the purposes of elimination or as part of an intelligence-led screening and to be used only for the purposes of that investigation and destroyed afterwards:*

"*I consent to my footwear impressions being taken for elimination purposes. I understand that the footwear impressions will be destroyed at the end of the case and that my footwear impressions will only be compared to the footwear impressions from this enquiry. I have been advised that the person taking the footwear impressions may be required to give evidence and/or provide a written statement to the police in relation to the taking of it.*"

   (ii) *Footwear impressions to be retained for future use:*

"*I consent to my footwear impressions being retained and used only for purposes related to the prevention and detection of a crime, the investigation of an offence or the conduct of a prosecution, either nationally or internationally*".

"*I understand that my footwear impressions may be checked against other records held by, or on behalf of, relevant law enforcement authorities, either nationally or internationally.*"

"*I understand that once I have given my consent for my footwear impressions to be retained and used I cannot withdraw this consent.*"

F2 *The provisions for the retention of fingerprints, footwear impressions and samples in paragraph 1 allow for all fingerprints, footwear impressions and samples in a case to be available for any subsequent miscarriage of justice investigation.*

ANNEX G—REQUIREMENT FOR A PERSON TO ATTEND A POLICE STATION FOR FINGERPRINTS AND SAMPLES.

1. A requirement under Schedule 2A for a person to attend a police station to have fingerprints or samples taken:

  (a) must give the person a period of at least seven days within which to attend the police station; and

  (b) may direct them to attend at a specified time of day or between specified times of day.

2. When specifying the period and times of attendance, the officer making the requirements must consider whether the fingerprints or samples could reasonably be taken at a time when the person is required to attend the police station for any other reason. See Note G1.

3. An officer of the rank of inspector or above may authorise a period shorter than 7 days if there is an urgent need for person's fingerprints or sample for the purposes of the investigation of an offence. The fact of the authorisation and the reasons for giving it must be recorded as soon as practicable.
4. The constable making a requirement and the person to whom it applies may agree to vary it so as to specify any period within which, or date or time at which, the person is to attend. However, variation shall not have effect for the purposes of enforcement, unless it is confirmed by the constable in writing.

Notes for Guidance

G1 *The specified period within which the person is to attend need not fall within the period allowed (if applicable) for making the requirement.*

G2 *To justify the arrest without warrant of a person who fails to comply with a requirement, (see paragraph 4.4(b) above), the officer making the requirement, or confirming a variation, should be prepared to explain how, when and where the requirement was made or the variation was confirmed and what steps were taken to ensure the person understood what to do and the consequences of not complying with the requirement.*

Appendix 6
Code E: PACE Code of Practice on Audio Recording Interviews with Suspects

This code applies to interviews carried out after midnight on 1 May 2010, notwithstanding that the interview may have commenced before that time.

1 GENERAL

1.1 This Code of Practice must be readily available for consultation by:
- police officers
- police staff
- detained persons
- members of the public.

1.2 The *Notes for Guidance* included are not provisions of this Code.

1.3 Nothing in this Code shall detract from the requirements of Code C, the Code of Practice for the detention, treatment and questioning of persons by police officers.

1.4 This Code does not apply to those people listed in Code C, *paragraph 1.12.*

1.5 The term:
- 'appropriate adult' has the same meaning as in Code C, *paragraph 1.7.*
- 'solicitor' has the same meaning as in Code C, *paragraph 6.12.*

1.5A Recording of interviews shall be carried out openly to instil confidence in its reliability as an impartial and accurate record of the interview.

1.6 In this Code:
- (aa) 'recording media' means any removable, physical audio recording medium (such as magnetic tape, optical disc or solid state memory) which can be played and copied.
- (a) 'designated person' means a person other than a police officer, designated under the Police Reform Act 2002, Part 4 who has specified powers and duties of police officers conferred or imposed on them;
- (b) any reference to a police officer includes a designated person acting in the exercise or performance of the powers and duties conferred or imposed on them by their designation.
- (c) 'secure digital network' is a computer network system which enables an original interview recording to be stored as a digital multi media file or a series of such files, on a secure file server which is accredited by the National Accreditor for Police Information Systems in the National Police Improvement Agency (NPIA) in accordance with the UK Government Protective Marking Scheme. (see section 7 of this Code).

1.7   Sections 2 to 6 of this code set out the procedures and requirements which apply to all interviews together with the provisions which apply only to interviews recorded using removable media. *Section 7* sets out the provisions which apply to interviews recorded using a secure digital network and specifies the provisions in sections 2 to 6 which do not apply to secure digital network recording.

1.8   Nothing in this Code prevents the custody officer, or other officer given custody of the detainee, from allowing police staff who are not designated persons to carry out individual procedures or tasks at the police station if the law allows. However, the officer remains responsible for making sure the procedures and tasks are carried out correctly in accordance with this Code. Any such police staff must be:

(a) a person employed by a police authority maintaining a police force and under the control and direction of the Chief Officer of that force; or

(b) employed by a person with whom a police authority has a contract for the provision of services relating to persons arrested or otherwise in custody.

1.9   Designated persons and other police staff must have regard to any relevant provisions of the Codes of Practice.

1.10   References to pocket book include any official report book issued to police officers or police staff.

1.11   References to a custody officer include those performing the functions of a custody officer as in *paragraph 1.9* of Code C.

2 RECORDING AND SEALING MASTER RECORDINGS

2.1 Not used.

2.2 One recording, the master recording, will be sealed in the suspect's presence. A second recording will be used as a working copy. The master recording is either of the two recordings used in a twin deck/drive machine or the only recording in a single deck/drive machine. The working copy is either the second/third recording used in a twin/triple deck/drive machine or a copy of the master recording made by a single deck/drive machine. See *Notes 2A* and *2B* [*This paragraph does not apply to interviews recorded using a secure digital network, see paragraphs 7.4 to 7.6*]

2.3 Nothing in this Code requires the identity of officers or police staff conducting interviews to be recorded or disclosed:

(a) in the case of enquiries linked to the investigation of terrorism (see *paragraph 3.2)*; or

(b) if the interviewer reasonably believes recording or disclosing their name might put them in danger.

In these cases interviewers should use warrant or other identification numbers and the name of their police station. See *Note 2C*

Notes for guidance

2A *The purpose of sealing the master recording in the suspect's presence is to show the recording's integrity is preserved. If a single deck/drive machine is used the working copy of the master recording must be made in the suspect's presence and without the master recording leaving their sight. The working copy shall be used for making further copies if needed.*

2B Not used.

2C The purpose of paragraph 2.3(b) is to protect those involved in serious organised crime investigations or arrests of particularly violent suspects when there is reliable informa- tion that those arrested or their associates may threaten or cause harm to those involved. In cases of doubt, an officer of inspector rank or above should be consulted.

3 INTERVIEWS TO BE AUDIO RECORDED

3.1 Subject to *paragraphs 3.3* and *3.4*, audio recording shall be used at police stations for any interview:
    (a) with a person cautioned under Code C, *section 10* in respect of any indictable offence, including an offence triable either way, see *Note 3A*
    (b) which takes place as a result of an interviewer exceptionally putting further questions to a suspect about an offence described in *paragraph 3.1(a)* after they have been charged with, or told they may be prosecuted for, that offence, see Code C, *paragraph 16.5*
    (c) when an interviewer wants to tell a person, after they have been charged with, or informed they may be prosecuted for, an offence described in *para- graph 3.1(a)*, about any written statement or interview with another person, see Code C, *paragraph 16.4*.

3.2 The Terrorism Act 2000 makes separate provision for a Code of Practice for the audio recording of interviews of those arrested under Section 41 of, or Schedule 7 to, the 2000 Act. The provisions of this Code do not apply to such interviews. [See *Note 3C*].

Code **E**

3.3 The custody officer may authorise the interviewer not to audio record the inter- view when it is:
    (a) not reasonably practicable because of equipment failure or the unavailabil- ity of a suitable interview room or recording equipment and the authorising officer considers, on reasonable grounds, that the interview should not be delayed; or
    (b) clear from the outset there will not be a prosecution.
    Note: In these cases the interview should be recorded in writing in accordance with Code C, *section 11*. In all cases the custody officer shall record the specific reasons for not audio recording. See *Note 3B*

3.4 If a person refuses to go into or remain in a suitable interview room, see Code C, *paragraph 12.5*, and the custody officer considers, on reasonable grounds, that the interview should not be delayed the interview may, at the custody officer's discretion, be conducted in a cell using portable recording equipment or, if none is available, recorded in writing as in Code C, *section 11*. The reasons for this shall be recorded.

3.5 The whole of each interview shall be audio recorded, including the taking and reading back of any statement.

3.6 A sign or indicator which is visible to the suspect must show when the recording equipment is recording.

Notes for guidance

3A Nothing in this Code is intended to preclude audio recording at police discretion of interviews at police stations with people cautioned in respect of offences not covered by paragraph 3.1, or responses made by persons after they have been charged with, or told they may be prosecuted for, an offence, provided this Code is complied with.

3B *A decision not to audio record an interview for any reason may be the subject of comment in court. The authorising officer should be prepared to justify that decision.*

3C *If, during the course of an interview under this Code, it becomes apparent that the interview should be conducted under one of the terrorism codes for recording of interviews the interview should only continue in accordance with the relevant code.*

4 THE INTERVIEW

(a) General

4.1 The provisions of Code C:
- *sections 10 and 11*, and the applicable *Notes for Guidance* apply to the conduct of interviews to which this Code applies
- *paragraphs 11.7 to 11.14* apply only when a written record is needed.

4.2 Code C, *paragraphs 10.10, 10.11* and Annex C describe the restriction on drawing adverse inferences from a suspect's failure or refusal to say anything about their involvement in the offence when interviewed or after being charged or informed they may be prosecuted, and how it affects the terms of the caution and determines if and by whom a special warning under sections 36 and 37 of the Criminal Justice and Public Order Act 1994 can be given.

(b) Commencement of interviews

4.3 When the suspect is brought into the interview room the interviewer shall, without delay but in the suspect's sight, load the recorder with new recording media and set it to record. The recording media must be unwrapped or opened in the suspect's presence. [*This paragraph does not apply to interviews recorded using a secure digital network, see paragraphs 7.4 and 7.5*].

4.4 The interviewer should tell the suspect about the recording process and point out the sign or indicator which shows that the recording equipment is activated and recording. See *paragraph 3.6*. The interviewer shall:
- (a) say the interview is being audibly recorded
- (b) subject to *paragraph 2.3*, give their name and rank and that of any other interviewer present
- (c) ask the suspect and any other party present, e.g. a solicitor, to identify themselves
- (d) state the date, time of commencement and place of the interview
- (e) state the suspect will be given a notice about what will happen to the copies of the recording. [*This sub-paragraph does not apply to interviews recorded using a secure digital network, see paragraphs 7.4 and 7.6 to 7.7*]

See *Note 4A*

4.5 The interviewer shall:
- caution the suspect, see Code C, *section 10*
- remind the suspect of their entitlement to free legal advice, see Code C, *paragraph 11.2*.

4.6 The interviewer shall put to the suspect any significant statement or silence, see Code C, *paragraph 11.4*.

(c) Interviews with deaf persons

4.7 If the suspect is deaf or is suspected of having impaired hearing, the interviewer shall make a written note of the interview in accordance with Code C, at the same time as audio recording it in accordance with this Code. See *Notes 4B and 4C*

(d) Objections and complaints by the suspect

4.8 If the suspect objects to the interview being audibly recorded at the outset, during the interview or during a break, the interviewer shall explain that the interview is being audibly recorded and that this Code requires the suspect's objections to be recorded on the audio recording. When any objections have been audibly recorded or the suspect has refused to have their objections recorded, the interviewer shall say they are turning off the recorder, give their reasons and turn it off. The interviewer shall then make a written record of the interview as in Code C, *section 11*. If, however, the interviewer reasonably considers they may proceed to question the suspect with the audio recording still on, the interviewer may do so. This procedure also applies in cases where the suspect has previously objected to the interview being visually recorded, see *Code F 4.8*, and the investigating officer has decided to audibly record the interview. See *Note 4D*

4.9 If in the course of an interview a complaint is made by or on behalf of the person being questioned concerning the provisions of this Code or Code C, the interviewer shall act as in Code C, *paragraph 12.9*. See *Notes 4E* and *4F*

4.10 If the suspect indicates they want to tell the interviewer about matters not directly connected with the offence and they are unwilling for these matters to be audio recorded, the suspect should be given the opportunity to tell the interviewer at the end of the formal interview.

(e) Changing recording media

4.11 When the recorder shows the recording media only has a short time left, the interviewer shall tell the suspect the recording media are coming to an end and round off that part of the interview. If the interviewer leaves the room for a second set of recording media, the suspect shall not be left unattended. The interviewer will remove the recording media from the recorder and insert the new recording media which shall be unwrapped or opened in the suspect's presence. The recorder should be set to record on the new media. To avoid confusion between the recording media, the interviewer shall mark the media with an identification number immediately after they are removed from the recorder. [*This paragraph does not apply to interviews recorded using a secure digital network as this does not use removable media, see paragraphs 1.6 (c), 7.4 and 7.14 to 7.15.*]

(f) Taking a break during interview

4.12 When a break is taken, the fact that a break is to be taken, the reason for it and the time shall be recorded on the audio recording.

Code **E**

547

4.12A When the break is taken and the interview room vacated by the suspect, the recording media shall be removed from the recorder and the procedures for the conclusion of an interview followed, see *paragraph 4.18*.

4.13 When a break is a short one and both the suspect and an interviewer remain in the interview room, the recording may be stopped. There is no need to remove the recording media and when the interview recommences the recording should continue on the same recording media. The time the interview recommences shall be recorded on the audio recording.

4.14 After any break in the interview the interviewer must, before resuming the interview, remind the person being questioned that they remain under caution or, if there is any doubt, give the caution in full again. See *Note 4G*.
[*Paragraphs 4.12 to 4.14 do not apply to interviews recorded using a secure digital network, see paragraphs 7.4 and 7.8 to 7.10*]

(g) Failure of recording equipment

4.15 If there is an equipment failure which can be rectified quickly, e.g. by inserting new recording media, the interviewer shall follow the appropriate procedures as in *paragraph 4.11*. When the recording is resumed the interviewer shall explain what happened and record the time the interview recommences. If, however, it will not be possible to continue recording on that recorder and no replacement recorder is readily available, the interview may continue without being audibly recorded. If this happens, the interviewer shall seek the custody officer's authority as in *paragraph 3.3*. See *Note 4H*. [*This paragraph does not apply to interviews recorded using a secure digital network, see paragraphs 7.4 and 7.11*]

(h) Removing recording media from the recorder

4.16 When recording media is removed from the recorder during the interview, they shall be retained and the procedures in *paragraph 4.18* followed. [*This paragraph does not apply to interviews recorded using a secure digital network as this does not use removable media, see 1.6 (c), 7.4 and 7.14 to 7.15.*]

(i) Conclusion of interview

4.17 At the conclusion of the interview, the suspect shall be offered the opportunity to clarify anything he or she has said and asked if there is anything they want to add.

4.18 At the conclusion of the interview, including the taking and reading back of any written statement, the time shall be recorded and the recording shall be stopped. The interviewer shall seal the master recording with a master recording label and treat it as an exhibit in accordance with force standing orders. The interviewer shall sign the label and ask the suspect and any third party present during the interview to sign it. If the suspect or third party refuse to sign the label an officer of at least inspector rank, or if not available the custody officer, shall be called into the interview room and asked, subject to *paragraph 2.3*, to sign it.

4.19 The suspect shall be handed a notice which explains:
- how the audio recording will be used
- the arrangements for access to it

- that if the person is charged or informed they will be prosecuted, a copy of the audio recording will be supplied as soon as practicable or as otherwise agreed between the suspect and the police or on the order of a court.

[*Paragraphs 4.17 to 4.19 do not apply to interviews recorded using a secure digital network, see paragraphs 7.4 and 7.12 to 7.13*]

Notes for guidance

4A For the purpose of voice identification the interviewer should ask the suspect and any other people present to identify themselves.

4B This provision is to give a person who is deaf or has impaired hearing equivalent rights of access to the full interview record as far as this is possible using audio recording.

4C The provisions of Code C, section 13 on interpreters for deaf persons or for interviews with suspects who have difficulty understanding English continue to apply.

4D The interviewer should remember that a decision to continue recording against the wishes of the suspect may be the subject of comment in court.

4E If the custody officer is called to deal with the complaint, the recorder should, if possible, be left on until the custody officer has entered the room and spoken to the person being interviewed. Continuation or termination of the interview should be at the interviewer's discretion pending action by an inspector under Code C, paragraph 9.2.

4F If the complaint is about a matter not connected with this Code or Code C, the decision to continue is at the interviewer's discretion. When the interviewer decides to continue the interview, they shall tell the suspect the complaint will be brought to the custody officer's attention at the conclusion of the interview. When the interview is concluded the interviewer must, as soon as practicable, inform the custody officer about the existence and nature of the complaint made.

4G The interviewer should remember that it may be necessary to show to the court that nothing occurred during a break or between interviews which influenced the suspect's recorded evidence. After a break or at the beginning of a subsequent interview, the interviewer should consider summarising on the record the reason for the break and confirming this with the suspect.

4H Where the interview is being recorded and the media or the recording equipment fails the officer conducting the interview should stop the interview immediately. Where part of the interview is unaffected by the error and is still accessible on the media, that media shall be copied and sealed in the suspect's presence and the interview recommenced using new equipment/media as required. Where the content of the interview has been lost in its entirety the media should be sealed in the suspect's presence and the interview begun again. If the recording equipment cannot be fixed or no replacement is immediately available the interview should be recorded in accordance with Code C, section 11.

5 After the interview

5.1 The interviewer shall make a note in their pocket book that the interview has taken place, was audibly recorded, its time, duration and date and the master recording's identification number.

5.2 If no proceedings follow in respect of the person whose interview was recorded, the recording media must be kept securely as in *paragraph 6.1* and *Note 6A*.

Code **E**

[This section (paragraphs 5.1, 5.2 and Note 5A) does not apply to interviews recorded using a secure digital network, see paragraphs 7.4 and 7.14 to 7.15]

Note for guidance

5A *Any written record of an audibly recorded interview should be made in accordance with national guidelines approved by the Secretary of State, and with regard to the advice contained in the Manual of Guidance for the preparation, processing and submission of prosecution files.*

6 MEDIA SECURITY

6.1 The officer in charge of each police station at which interviews with suspects are recorded shall make arrangements for master recordings to be kept securely and their movements accounted for on the same basis as material which may be used for evidential purposes, in accordance with force standing orders. See *Note 6A*

6.2 A police officer has no authority to break the seal on a master recording required for criminal trial or appeal proceedings. If it is necessary to gain access to the master recording, the police officer shall arrange for its seal to be broken in the presence of a representative of the Crown Prosecution Service. The defendant or their legal adviser should be informed and given a reasonable opportunity to be present. If the defendant or their legal representative is present they shall be invited to reseal and sign the master recording. If either refuses or neither is present this should be done by the representative of the Crown Prosecution Service. See *Notes 6B* and *6C*

6.3 If no criminal proceedings result or the criminal trial and, if applicable, appeal proceedings to which the interview relates have been concluded, the chief officer of police is responsible for establishing arrangements for breaking the seal on the master recording, if necessary.

6.4 When the master recording seal is broken, a record must be made of the procedure followed, including the date, time, place and persons present.
[This section (paragraphs 6.1 to 6.4 and Notes 6A to 6C) does not apply to interviews recorded using a secure digital network, see paragraphs 7.4 and 7.14 to 7.15]

Notes for guidance

6A *This section is concerned with the security of the master recording sealed at the conclusion of the interview. Care must be taken of working copies of recordings because their loss or destruction may lead to the need to access master recordings.*

6B *If the recording has been delivered to the crown court for their keeping after committal for trial the crown prosecutor will apply to the chief clerk of the crown court centre for the release of the recording for unsealing by the crown prosecutor.*

6C *Reference to the Crown Prosecution Service or to the crown prosecutor in this part of the Code should be taken to include any other body or person with a statutory responsibility for prosecution for whom the police conduct any audibly recorded interviews.*

7 RECORDING OF INTERVIEWS BY SECURE DIGITAL NETWORK

7.1 A secure digital network does not use removable media and this section specifies the provisions which will apply when a secure digital network is used.

7.2 *Not used.*

7.3 The following requirements are solely applicable to the use of a secure digital network for the recording of interviews.

(a) Application of sections 1 to 6 of Code E

7.4 Sections 1 to 6 of Code E above apply except for the following paragraphs:
- Paragraph 2.2 under "Recording and sealing of master recordings"
- Paragraph 4.3 under "(b) Commencement of interviews"
- Paragraph 4.4(e) under "(b) Commencement of interviews"
- Paragraphs 4.11–4.19 under "(e) Changing recording media", "(f) Taking a break during interview", "(g) Failure of recording equipment", "(h) Removing recording media from the recorder" and "(i) Conclusion of interview"
- Paragraphs 6.1–6.4 and Notes 6A to 6C under "Media security"

(b) Commencement of Interview

7.5 When the suspect is brought into the interview room, the interviewer shall without delay and in the sight of the suspect, switch on the recording equipment and enter the information necessary to log on to the secure network and start recording.

7.6 The interviewer must then inform the suspect that the interview is being recorded using a secure digital network and that recording has commenced.

7.7 In addition to the requirements of paragraph 4.4 (a–d) above, the interviewer must inform the person that:
- they will be given access to the recording of the interview in the event that they are charged or informed that they will be prosecuted but if they are not charged or informed that they will be prosecuted they will only be given access as agreed with the police or on the order of a court; and
- they will be given a written notice at the end of the interview setting out their rights to access the recording and what will happen to the recording.

Code E

(c) Taking a break during interview

7.8 When a break is taken, the fact that a break is to be taken, the reason for it and the time shall be recorded on the audio recording. The recording shall be stopped and the procedures in paragraphs 7.12 and 7.13 for the conclusion of an interview followed.

7.9 When the interview recommences the procedures in paragraphs 7.5 to 7.7 for commencing an interview shall be followed to create a new file to record the continuation of the interview. The time the interview recommences shall be recorded on the audio recording.

7.10 After any break in the interview the interviewer must, before resuming the interview, remind the person being questioned that they remain under caution or, if there is any doubt, give the caution in full again. See *Note 4G*

(d) Failure of recording equipment

7.11 If there is an equipment failure which can be rectified quickly, e.g. by commencing a new secure digital network recording, the interviewer shall follow the appropriate procedures as in *paragraphs 7.8 to 7.10*. When the recording is resumed the interviewer shall explain what happened and record the time the interview recommences. If, however, it is not possible to continue recording on the secure digital network the interview should be recorded on removable media as in *paragraph 4.3* unless the necessary equipment is not available.

If this happens the interview may continue without being audibly recorded and the interviewer shall seek the custody officer's authority as in *paragraph 3.3*. See *Note 4H*.

(e) Conclusion of interview

7.12 At the conclusion of the interview, the suspect shall be offered the opportunity to clarify anything he or she has said and asked if there is anything they want to add.

7.13 At the conclusion of the interview, including the taking and reading back of any written statement:
    (a) the time shall be orally recorded
    (b) the suspect shall be handed a notice which explains:
      • how the audio recording will be used
      • the arrangements for access to it
      • that if they are charged or informed that they will be prosecuted, they will be given access to the recording of the interview either electronically or by being given a copy on removable recording media, but if they are not charged or informed that they will prosecuted, they will only be given access as agreed with the police or on the order of a court.
      See *Note 7A*.
    (c) the suspect must be asked to confirm that he or she has received a copy of the notice at *paragraph 7.13(b)* above. If the suspect fails to accept or to acknowledge receipt of the notice, the interviewer will state for the recording that a copy of the notice has been provided to the suspect and that he or she has refused to take a copy of the notice or has refused to acknowledge receipt.
    (d) the time shall be recorded and the interviewer shall notify the suspect that the recording is being saved to the secure network. The interviewer must save the recording in the presence of the suspect. The suspect should then be informed that the interview is terminated.

(f) After the interview

7.14 The interviewer shall make a note in their pocket book that the interview has taken place, was audibly recorded, its time, duration and date and the original recording's identification number.

7.15 If no proceedings follow in respect of the person whose interview was recorded, the recordings must be kept securely as in *paragraphs 7.16* and *7.17*.
    See *Note 5A*

(g) Security of secure digital network interview records

7.16 Interview record files are stored in read only format on non-removable storage devices, for example, hard disk drives, to ensure their integrity. The recordings are first saved locally to a secure non-removable device before being transferred to the remote network device. If for any reason the network connection fails, the recording remains on the local device and will be transferred when the network connections are restored.

7.17 Access to interview recordings, including copying to removable media, must be strictly controlled and monitored to ensure that access is restricted to those who have been given specific permission to access for specified purposes when this is necessary. For example, police officers and CPS lawyers involved in the preparation of any prosecution case, persons interviewed if they have been charged or informed they may be prosecuted and their legal representatives.

Note for Guidance

7A *The notice at paragraph 7.13 above should provide a brief explanation of the secure digital network and how access to the recording is strictly limited. The notice should also explain the access rights of the suspect, his or her legal representative, the police and the prosecutor to the recording of the interview. Space should be provided on the form to insert the date and the file reference number for the interview.*

Code **E**

Appendix 7
Code F: PACE Code of Practice on Visual Recording with Sound of Interviews with Suspects

The contents of this code should be considered if an interviewing officer decides to make a visual recording with sound of an interview with a suspect after midnight on 1 May 2010.

There is no statutory requirement under PACE to visually record interviews.

1 GENERAL

1.1 This code of practice must be readily available for consultation by police officers and other police staff, detained persons and members of the public.

1.2 The notes for guidance included are not provisions of this code. They form guidance to police officers and others about its application and interpretation.

1.3 Nothing in this code shall be taken as detracting in any way from the requirements of the Code of Practice for the Detention, Treatment and Questioning of Persons by Police Officers (Code C). [See *Note 1A*].

1.4 The interviews to which this Code applies are set out in paragraphs 3.1–3.3.

1.5 In this code, the term "appropriate adult", "solicitor" and "interview" have the same meaning as those set out in Code C. The corresponding provisions and Notes for Guidance in Code C applicable to those terms shall also apply where appropriate.

1.5A The visual recording of interviews shall be carried out openly to instil confidence in its reliability as an impartial and accurate record of the interview.

1.6 Any reference in this code to visual recording shall be taken to mean visual recording with sound and in this code:

(aa) 'recording media' means any removable, physical audio recording medium (such as magnetic tape, optical disc or solid state memory) which can be played and copied.

(a) 'designated person' means a person other than a police officer, designated under the Police Reform Act 2002, Part 4 who has specified powers and duties of police officers conferred or imposed on them;

(b) any reference to a police officer includes a designated person acting in the exercise or performance of the powers and duties conferred or imposed on them by their designation.

(c) 'secure digital network' is a computer network system which enables an original interview recording to be stored as a digital multi media file or a series of such files, on a secure file server which is accredited by the

National Accreditor for Police Information Systems in the National Police Improvement Agency (NPIA) in accordance with the UK Government Protective Marking Scheme. (see section 7 of this Code).

1.7   References to "pocket book" in this Code include any official report book issued to police officers.

Note for Guidance

1A   *As in paragraph 1.9 of Code C, references to custody officers include those carrying out the functions of a custody officer.*

2 RECORDING AND SEALING OF MASTER RECORDINGS

2.1 Not used

2.2 The camera(s) shall be placed in the interview room so as to ensure coverage of as much of the room as is practicably possible whilst the interviews are taking place. [See *Note 2A*].

2.3 The certified recording medium will be of a high quality, new and previously unused. When the certified recording medium is placed in the recorder and switched on to record, the correct date and time, in hours, minutes and seconds, will be superimposed automatically, second by second, during the whole recording. [See *Note 2B*]. See section 7 regarding the use of a secure digital network to record the interview.

2.4 One copy of the certified recording medium, referred to in this code as the master copy, will be sealed before it leaves the presence of the suspect. A second copy will be used as a working copy. [See *Note 2C* and *2D*].

2.5 Nothing in this code requires the identity of an officer to be recorded or disclosed if:

(a)   the interview or record relates to a person detained under the Terrorism Act 2000 (see paragraph 3.2); or

(b)   otherwise where the officer reasonably believes that recording or disclosing their name might put them in danger.

2.6 In these cases, the officer will have their back to the camera and shall use their warrant or other identification number and the name of the police station to which they are attached. Such instances and the reasons for them shall be recorded in the custody record. [See *Note 2E*.]

Code **F**

Notes for Guidance

2A   *Interviewing officers will wish to arrange that, as far as possible, visual recording arrangements are unobtrusive. It must be clear to the suspect, however, that there is no opportunity to interfere with the recording equipment or the recording media.*

2B   *In this context, the certified recording media should be capable of having an image of the date and time superimposed upon them as they record the interview.*

2C   *The purpose of sealing the master copy before it leaves the presence of the suspect is to establish their confidence that the integrity of the copy is preserved.*

2D   *The recording of the interview may be used for identification procedures in accordance with paragraph 3.21 or Annex E of Code D.*

2E   *The purpose of the paragraph 2.5(b) is to protect police officers and others involved in the investigation of serious organised crime or the arrest of particularly violent suspects when there is reliable information that those arrested or their associates may threaten or cause harm to the officers, their families or their personal property.*

3 INTERVIEWS TO BE VISUALLY RECORDED

3.1 Subject to paragraph 3.2 below, if an interviewing officer decides to make a visual recording these are the areas where it might be appropriate:

(a) with a suspect in respect of an indictable offence (including an offence triable either way) [see *Notes 3A* and *3B*];

(b) which takes place as a result of an interviewer exceptionally putting further questions to a suspect about an offence described in sub-paragraph (a) above after they have been charged with, or informed they may be prosecuted for, that offence [see *Note 3C*];

(c) in which an interviewer wishes to bring to the notice of a person, after that person has been charged with, or informed they may be prosecuted for an offence described in sub-paragraph (a) above, any written statement made by another person, or the content of an interview with another person [see *Note 3D*]

(d) with, or in the presence of, a deaf or deaf/blind or speech impaired person who uses sign language to communicate;

(e) with, or in the presence of anyone who requires an "appropriate adult"; or

(f) in any case where the suspect or their representative requests that the interview be recorded visually.

3.2 The Terrorism Act 2000 makes separate provision for a code of practice for the video recording of interviews in a police station of those detained under Schedule 7 or section 41 of the Act. The provisions of this code do not therefore apply to such interviews [see *Note 3E*].

3.3 The custody officer may authorise the interviewing officer not to record the interview visually:

(a) where it is not reasonably practicable to do so because of failure of the equipment, or the non-availability of a suitable interview room, or recorder, and the authorising officer considers on reasonable grounds that the interview should not be delayed until the failure has been rectified or a suitable room or recorder becomes available. In such cases the custody officer may authorise the interviewing officer to audio record the interview in accordance with the guidance set out in Code E;

(b) where it is clear from the outset that no prosecution will ensue; or

(c) where it is not practicable to do so because at the time the person resists being taken to a suitable interview room or other location which would enable the interview to be recorded, or otherwise fails or refuses to go into such a room or location, and the authorising officer considers on reasonable grounds that the interview should not be delayed until these conditions cease to apply.

In all cases the custody officer shall make a note in the custody records of the reasons for not taking a visual record. [See *Note 3F*].

3.4 When a person who is voluntarily attending the police station is required to be cautioned in accordance with Code C prior to being interviewed, the subsequent interview shall be recorded, unless the custody officer gives authority in accordance with the provisions of paragraph 3.3 above for the interview not to be so recorded.

3.5 The whole of each interview shall be recorded visually, including the taking and reading back of any statement.

3.6 A sign or indicator which is visible to the suspect must show when the visual recording equipment is recording.

Notes for Guidance

3A *Nothing in the code is intended to preclude visual recording at police discretion of interviews at police stations with people cautioned in respect of offences not covered by paragraph 3.1, or responses made by interviewees after they have been charged with, or informed they may be prosecuted for, an offence, provided that this code is complied with.*

3B *Attention is drawn to the provisions set out in Code C about the matters to be considered when deciding whether a detained person is fit to be interviewed.*

3C *Code C sets out the circumstances in which a suspect may be questioned about an offence after being charged with it.*

3D *Code C sets out the procedures to be followed when a person's attention is drawn after charge, to a statement made by another person. One method of bringing the content of an interview with another person to the notice of a suspect may be to play him a recording of that interview.*

3E *If, during the course of an interview under this Code, it becomes apparent that the interview should be conducted under one of the terrorism codes for video recording of interviews the interview should only continue in accordance with the relevant code.*

3F *A decision not to record an interview visually for any reason may be the subject of comment in court. The authorising officer should therefore be prepared to justify their decision in each case.*

Code **F**

4 THE INTERVIEW

(a) General

4.1 The provisions of Code C in relation to cautions and interviews and the Notes for Guidance applicable to those provisions shall apply to the conduct of interviews to which this Code applies.

4.2 Particular attention is drawn to those parts of Code C that describe the restrictions on drawing adverse inferences from a suspect's failure or refusal to say anything about their involvement in the offence when interviewed, or after being charged or informed they may be prosecuted and how those restrictions affect the terms of the caution and determine whether a special warning under Sections 36 and 37 of the Criminal Justice and Public Order Act 1994 can be given.

(b) Commencement of interviews

4.3 When the suspect is brought into the interview room the interviewer shall without delay, but in sight of the suspect, load the recording equipment and set it to record. The recording media must be unwrapped or otherwise opened in the presence of the suspect. [See *Note 4A*]

4.4 The interviewer shall then tell the suspect formally about the visual recording and point out the sign or indicator which shows that the recording equipment is activated and recording. *See paragraph 3.6.* The interviewer shall:

(a) explain the interview is being visually recorded;

(b) subject to paragraph 2.5, give his or her name and rank, and that of any other interviewer present;

(c) ask the suspect and any other party present (e.g. his solicitor) to identify themselves;

(d) state the date, time of commencement and place of the interview; and

(e) state that the suspect will be given a notice about what will happen to the recording.

4.5 The interviewer shall then caution the suspect, which should follow that set out in Code C, and remind the suspect of their entitlement to free and independent legal advice and that they can speak to a solicitor on the telephone.

4.6 The interviewer shall then put to the suspect any significant statement or silence (i.e. failure or refusal to answer a question or to answer it satisfactorily) which occurred before the start of the interview, and shall ask the suspect whether they wish to confirm or deny that earlier statement or silence or whether they wish to add anything. The definition of a "significant" statement or silence is the same as that set out in Code C.

(c) Interviews with the deaf

4.7 If the suspect is deaf or there is doubt about their hearing ability, the provisions of Code C on interpreters for the deaf or for interviews with suspects who have difficulty in understanding English continue to apply.

(d) Objections and complaints by the suspect

4.8 If the suspect raises objections to the interview being visually recorded either at the outset or during the interview or during a break in the interview, the interviewer shall explain the fact that the interview is being visually recorded and that the provisions of this code require that the suspect's objections shall be recorded on the visual recording. When any objections have been visually recorded or the suspect has refused to have their objections recorded, the interviewer shall say that they are turning off the recording equipment, give their reasons and turn it off. If a separate audio recording is being maintained, the officer shall ask the person to record the reasons for refusing to agree to visual recording of the interview. Paragraph 4.8 of Code E will apply if the person objects to audio recording of the interview. The officer shall then make a written record of the interview. If the interviewer reasonably considers they may proceed to question the suspect with the visual recording still on, the interviewer may do so. See *Note 4G.*

4.9 If in the course of an interview a complaint is made by the person being questioned, or on their behalf, concerning the provisions of this code or of Code C, then the interviewer shall act in accordance with Code C, record it in the interview record and inform the custody officer. [See *Notes 4B* and *4C*].

4.10 If the suspect indicates that they wish to tell the interviewer about matters not directly connected with the offence of which they are suspected and that they are unwilling for these matters to be recorded, the suspect shall be given the opportunity to tell the interviewer about these matters after the conclusion of the formal interview.

(e) Changing the recording media

4.11 In instances where the recording medium is not of sufficient length to record all of the interview with the suspect, further certified recording medium will be used. When the recording equipment indicates that the recording medium has only a short time left to run, the interviewer shall advise the suspect and round off that part of the interview. If the interviewer wishes to continue the interview but does not already have further certified recording media with him, they shall obtain a set. The suspect should not be left unattended in the interview room. The interviewer will remove the recording media from the recording equipment and insert the new ones which have been unwrapped or otherwise opened in the suspect's presence. The recording equipment shall then be set to record. Care must be taken, particularly when a number of sets of recording media have been used, to ensure that there is no confusion between them. This could be achieved by marking the sets of recording media with consecutive identification numbers.

(f) Taking a break during the interview

4.12 When a break is to be taken during the course of an interview and the interview room is to be vacated by the suspect, the fact that a break is to be taken, the reason for it and the time shall be recorded. The recording equipment must be turned off and the recording media removed. The procedures for the conclusion of an interview set out in paragraph 4.19, below, should be followed.

4.13 When a break is to be a short one, and both the suspect and a police officer are to remain in the interview room, the fact that a break is to be taken, the reasons for it and the time shall be recorded on the recording media. The recording equipment may be turned off, but there is no need to remove the recording media. When the interview is recommenced the recording shall continue on the same recording media and the time at which the interview recommences shall be recorded.

4.14 When there is a break in questioning under caution, the interviewing officer must ensure that the person being questioned is aware that they remain under caution. If there is any doubt, the caution must be given again in full when the interview resumes. [See *Note 4D* and *4E*].

(g) Failure of recording equipment

4.15 If there is a failure of equipment which can be rectified quickly, the appropriate procedures set out in paragraph 4.12 shall be followed. When the recording is resumed the interviewer shall explain what has happened and record the time the interview recommences. If, however, it is not possible to continue recording on that particular recorder and no alternative equipment is readily available, the interview may continue without being recorded visually. In such circumstances, the procedures set out in paragraph 3.3 of this code for seeking the authority of the custody officer will be followed. [See *Note 4F*].

Code **F**

559

(h) Removing used recording media from recording equipment

4.16 Where used recording media are removed from the recording equipment during the course of an interview, they shall be retained and the procedures set out in paragraph 4.18 below followed.

(i) Conclusion of interview

4.17 Before the conclusion of the interview, the suspect shall be offered the opportunity to clarify anything he or she has said and asked if there is anything that they wish to add.

4.18 At the conclusion of the interview, including the taking and reading back of any written statement, the time shall be recorded and the recording equipment switched off. The master recording shall be removed from the recording equipment, sealed with a master recording label and treated as an exhibit in accordance with the force standing orders. The interviewer shall sign the label and also ask the suspect and any third party present during the interview to sign it. If the suspect or third party refuses to sign the label, an officer of at least the rank of inspector, or if one is not available, the custody officer, shall be called into the interview room and asked, subject to *paragraph 2.5*, to sign it.

4.19 The suspect shall be handed a notice which explains the use which will be made of the recording and the arrangements for access to it. The notice will also advise the suspect that a copy of the tape shall be supplied as soon as practicable if the person is charged or informed that he will be prosecuted.

Notes for Guidance

4A The interviewer should attempt to estimate the likely length of the interview and ensure that an appropriate quantity of certified recording media and labels with which to seal the master copies are available in the interview room.

4B Where the custody officer is called immediately to deal with the complaint, wherever possible the recording equipment should be left to run until the custody officer has entered the interview room and spoken to the person being interviewed. Continuation or termination of the interview should be at the discretion of the interviewing officer pending action by an inspector as set out in Code C.

4C Where the complaint is about a matter not connected with this code of practice or Code C, the decision to continue with the interview is at the discretion of the interviewing officer. Where the interviewing officer decides to continue with the interview, the person being interviewed shall be told that the complaint will be brought to the attention of the custody officer at the conclusion of the interview. When the interview is concluded, the interviewing officer must, as soon as practicable, inform the custody officer of the existence and nature of the complaint made.

4D In considering whether to caution again after a break, the officer should bear in mind that he may have to satisfy a court that the person understood that he was still under caution when the interview resumed.

4E The officer should bear in mind that it may be necessary to satisfy the court that nothing occurred during a break in an interview or between interviews which influenced the suspect's recorded evidence. On the re-commencement of an interview, the officer should consider summarising on the record the reason for the break and confirming this with the suspect.

4F   *If any part of the recording media breaks or is otherwise damaged during the interview, it should be sealed as a master copy in the presence of the suspect and the interview resumed where it left off. The undamaged part should be copied and the original sealed as a master tape in the suspect's presence, if necessary after the interview. If equipment for copying is not readily available, both parts should be sealed in the suspect's presence and the interview begun again.*

4G   *The interviewer should be aware that a decision to continue recording against the wishes of the suspect may be the subject of comment in court.*

5 AFTER THE INTERVIEW

5.1   The interviewer shall make a note in his or her pocket book of the fact that the interview has taken place and has been recorded, its time, duration and date and the identification number of the master copy of the recording media.

5.2   Where no proceedings follow in respect of the person whose interview was recorded, the recording media must nevertheless be kept securely in accordance with paragraph 6.1 and Note 6A.

Note for Guidance

5A   *Any written record of a recorded interview shall be made in accordance with national guidelines approved by the Secretary of State, and with regard to the advice contained in the Manual of Guidance for the preparation, processing and submission of files.*

6 MASTER COPY SECURITY

(a) General

6.1   The officer in charge of the police station at which interviews with suspects are recorded shall make arrangements for the master copies to be kept securely and their movements accounted for on the same basis as other material which may be used for evidential purposes, in accordance with force standing orders. [See Note 6A].

Code **F**

(b) Breaking master copy seal for criminal proceedings

6.2   A police officer has no authority to break the seal on a master copy which is required for criminal trial or appeal proceedings. If it is necessary to gain access to the master copy, the police officer shall arrange for its seal to be broken in the presence of a representative of the Crown Prosecution Service. The defendant or their legal adviser shall be informed and given a reasonable opportunity to be present. If the defendant or their legal representative is present they shall be invited to reseal and sign the master copy. If either refuses or neither is present, this shall be done by the representative of the Crown Prosecution Service. [See Notes 6B and 6C].

(c) Breaking master copy seal: other cases

6.3   The chief officer of police is responsible for establishing arrangements for breaking the seal of the master copy where no criminal proceedings result, or the criminal proceedings, to which the interview relates, have been concluded and it becomes necessary to break the seal. These arrangements should be those which the chief officer considers are reasonably necessary to demonstrate to the person interviewed and any other party who may wish to use or refer to the interview record that the master copy has not been tampered with and that the interview record remains accurate. [See *Note 6D*]

6.4 Subject to paragraph 6.6, a representative of each party must be given a reasonable opportunity to be present when the seal is broken, the master copy copied and re-sealed.

6.5 If one or more of the parties is not present when the master copy seal is broken because they cannot be contacted or refuse to attend or paragraph 6.6 applies, arrangements should be made for an independent person such as a custody visitor, to be present. Alternatively, or as an additional safeguard, arrangement should be made for a film or photographs to be taken of the procedure.

6.6 Paragraph 6.5 does not require a person to be given an opportunity to be present when:

(a) it is necessary to break the master copy seal for the proper and effective further investigation of the original offence or the investigation of some other offence; and

(b) the officer in charge of the investigation has reasonable grounds to suspect that allowing an opportunity might prejudice any such an investigation or criminal proceedings which may be brought as a result or endanger any person. [See *Note 6E*]

(d) Documentation

6.7 When the master copy seal is broken, copied and re-sealed, a record must be made of the procedure followed, including the date time and place and persons present.

Notes for Guidance

6A This section is concerned with the security of the master copy which will have been sealed at the conclusion of the interview. Care should, however, be taken of working copies since their loss or destruction may lead unnecessarily to the need to have access to master copies.

6B If the master copy has been delivered to the Crown Court for their keeping after committal for trial the Crown Prosecutor will apply to the Chief Clerk of the Crown Court Centre for its release for unsealing by the Crown Prosecutor.

6C Reference to the Crown Prosecution Service or to the Crown Prosecutor in this part of the code shall be taken to include any other body or person with a statutory responsibility for prosecution for whom the police conduct any recorded interviews.

6D The most common reasons for needing access to master copies that are not required for criminal proceedings arise from civil actions and complaints against police and civil actions between individuals arising out of allegations of crime investigated by police.

6E Paragraph 6.6 could apply, for example, when one or more of the outcomes or likely outcomes of the investigation might be; (i) the prosecution of one or more of the original suspects, (ii) the prosecution of someone previously not suspected, including someone who was originally a witness; and (iii) any original suspect being treated as a prosecution witness and when premature disclosure of any police action, particularly through contact with any parties involved, could lead to a real risk of compromising the investigation and endangering witnesses.

7 VISUAL RECORDING OF INTERVIEWS BY SECURE DIGITAL NETWORK

7.1 This section applies if an officer wishes to make a visual recording with sound of an interview mentioned in section 3 of this Code using a secure digital network which does not use removable media (see *paragraph 1.6(c)* above).

7.3 The provisions of sections 1 to 6 of this Code which relate or apply only to removable media will not apply to a secure digital network recording.

7.4 The statutory requirement and provisions for the audio recording of interviews using a secure digital network set out in section 7 of Code E should be applied to the visual recording with sound of interviews mentioned in section 3 of this code as if references to audio recordings of interviews include visual recordings with sound.

Code **F**

Appendix 8
Code G: PACE Code of Practice for the Statutory Power of Arrest by Police Officers

This Code applies to any arrest made by a police officer after midnight on 12 November 2012

1 INTRODUCTION

1.1 This Code of Practice deals with the statutory power of police to arrest a person who is involved, or suspected of being involved, in a criminal offence. The power of arrest must be used fairly, responsibly, with respect for people suspected of committing offences and without unlawful discrimination. The Equality Act 2010 makes it unlawful for police officers to discriminate against, harass or victimise any person on the grounds of the 'protected characteristics' of age, disability, gender reassignment, race, religion or belief, sex and sexual orientation, marriage and civil partnership, pregnancy and maternity when using their powers. When police forces are carrying out their functions they also have a duty to have regard to the need to eliminate unlawful discrimination, harassment and victimisation and to take steps to foster good relations.

1.2 The exercise of the power of arrest represents an obvious and significant interference with the Right to Liberty and Security under Article 5 of the European Convention on Human Rights set out in Part I of Schedule 1 to the Human Rights Act 1998.

1.3 The use of the power must be fully justified and officers exercising the power should consider if the necessary objectives can be met by other, less intrusive means. Absence of justification for exercising the power of arrest may lead to challenges should the case proceed to court. It could also lead to civil claims against police for unlawful arrest and false imprisonment. When the power of arrest is exercised it is essential that it is exercised in a non-discriminatory and proportionate manner which is compatible with the Right to Liberty under Article 5. See *Note 1B*.

1.4 Section 24 of the Police and Criminal Evidence Act 1984 (as substituted by section 110 of the Serious Organised Crime and Police Act 2005) provides the statutory power for a constable to arrest without warrant for all offences. If the provisions of the Act and this Code are not observed, both the arrest and the conduct of any subsequent investigation may be open to question.

1.5 This Code of Practice must be readily available at all police stations for consultation by police officers and police staff, detained persons and members of the public.

1.6 The *Notes for Guidance* are not provisions of this code.

2. Elements of Arrest under Section 24 PACE

2.1   A lawful arrest requires two elements:

A person's involvement or suspected involvement or attempted involvement in the commission of a criminal offence;

AND

Reasonable grounds for believing that the person's arrest is necessary.

- both elements must be satisfied, and
- it can never be necessary to arrest a person unless there are reasonable grounds to suspect them of committing an offence.

2.2   The arrested person must be informed that they have been arrested, even if this fact is obvious, and of the relevant circumstances of the arrest in relation to both the above elements. The custody officer must be informed of these matters on arrival at the police station. See *paragraphs 2.9, 3.3* and *Note 3* and *Code C paragraph 3.4.*

(a) 'Involvement in the commission of an offence'

2.3   A constable may arrest without warrant in relation to any offence (see *Notes 1* and *1A*) anyone:

- who is about to commit an offence or is in the act of committing an offence;
- whom the officer has reasonable grounds for suspecting is about to commit an offence or to be committing an offence;
- whom the officer has reasonable grounds to suspect of being guilty of an offence which he or she has reasonable grounds for suspecting has been committed;
- anyone who is guilty of an offence which has been committed or anyone whom the officer has reasonable grounds for suspecting to be guilty of that offence.

2.3A There must be some reasonable, objective grounds for the suspicion, based on known facts and information which are relevant to the likelihood the offence has been committed and the person liable to arrest committed it. See *Notes 2* and *2A*.

(b) Necessity criteria

2.4   The power of arrest is <u>only</u> exercisable if the constable has reasonable grounds for *believing* that it is necessary to arrest the person. The statutory criteria for what may constitute necessity are set out in paragraph 2.9 and it remains an operational decision at the discretion of the constable to decide:

- which one or more of the necessity criteria (if any) applies to the individual; and
- if any of the criteria do apply, whether to arrest, grant street bail after arrest, report for summons or for charging by post, issue a penalty notice or take any other action that is open to the officer.

2.5   In applying the criteria, the arresting officer has to be satisfied that at least one of the reasons supporting the need for arrest is satisfied.

2.6   Extending the power of arrest to all offences provides a constable with the ability to use that power to deal with any situation. However applying the necessity

Code **G**

criteria requires the constable to examine and justify the reason or reasons why a person needs to be arrested or (as the case may be) further arrested, for an offence for the custody officer to decide whether to authorise their detention for that offence. See *Note 2C*

2.7 The criteria in paragraph 2.9 below which are set out in section 24 of PACE as substituted by section 110 of the Serious Organised Crime and Police Act 2005 are exhaustive. However, the circumstances that may satisfy those criteria remain a matter for the operational discretion of individual officers. Some examples are given to illustrate what those circumstances might be and what officers might consider when deciding whether arrest is necessary.

2.8 In considering the individual circumstances, the constable must take into account the situation of the victim, the nature of the offence, the circumstances of the suspect and the needs of the investigative process.

2.9 When it is practicable to tell a person why their arrest is necessary (as required by paragraphs 2.2, 3.3 and *Note 3*), the constable should outline the facts, information and other circumstances which provide the grounds for believing that their arrest is necessary and which the officer considers satisfy one or more of the statutory criteria in sub-paragraphs (a) to (f), namely:

(a) to enable the name of the person in question to be ascertained (in the case where the constable does not know, and cannot readily ascertain, the person's name, or has reasonable grounds for doubting whether a name given by the person as his name is his real name):

An officer might decide that a person's name cannot be readily ascertained if they fail or refuse to give it when asked, particularly after being warned that failure or refusal is likely to make their arrest necessary (see *Note 2D*). Grounds to doubt a name given may arise if the person appears reluctant or hesitant when asked to give their name or to verify the name they have given.

Where mobile fingerprinting is available and the suspect's name cannot be ascertained or is doubted, the officer should consider using the power under section 61(6A) of PACE (see *Code D paragraph 4.3(e)*) to take and check the fingerprints of a suspect as this may avoid the need to arrest solely to enable their name to be ascertained.

(b) correspondingly as regards the person's address:

An officer might decide that a person's address cannot be readily ascertained if they fail or refuse to give it when asked, particularly after being warned that such a failure or refusal is likely to make their arrest necessary. See *Note 2D*. Grounds to doubt an address given may arise if the person appears reluctant or hesitant when asked to give their address or is unable to provide verifiable details of the locality they claim to live in.

When considering reporting to consider summons or charging by post as alternatives to arrest, an address would be satisfactory if the person will be at it for a sufficiently long period for it to be possible to serve them with the summons or requisition and charge; or, that some other person at that address specified by the person will accept service on their behalf. When considering issuing a penalty notice, the address should be one where the person will be in the event of enforcement action if the person does not pay the penalty or is convicted and fined after a court hearing.

(c) to prevent the person in question:
    (i) causing physical injury to himself or any other person;
This might apply where the suspect has already used or threatened violence against others and it is thought likely that they may assault others if they are not arrested. See *Note 2D*
    (ii) suffering physical injury;
This might apply where the suspect's behaviour and actions are believed likely to provoke, or have provoked, others to want to assault the suspect unless the suspect is arrested for their own protection. See *Note 2D*
    (iii) causing loss or damage to property;
This might apply where the suspect is a known persistent offender with a history of serial offending against property (theft and criminal damage) and it is thought likely that they may continue offending if they are not arrested.
    (iv) committing an offence against public decency (only applies where members of the public going about their normal business cannot reasonably be expected to avoid the person in question);
This might apply when an offence against public decency is being committed in a place to which the public have access and is likely to be repeated in that or some other public place at a time when the public are likely to encounter the suspect. See *Note 2D*
    (v) causing an unlawful obstruction of the highway;
This might apply to any offence where its commission causes an unlawful obstruction which it is believed may continue or be repeated if the person is not arrested, particularly if the person has been warned that they are causing an obstruction. See *Note 2D*
(d) to protect a child or other vulnerable person from the person in question.
This might apply when the health (physical or mental) or welfare of a child or vulnerable person is likely to be harmed or is at risk of being harmed, if the person is not arrested in cases where it is not practicable and appropriate to make alternative arrangements to prevent the suspect from having any harmful or potentially harmful contact with the child or vulnerable person.

Code **G**

(e) to allow the prompt and effective investigation of the offence or of the conduct of the person in question. See *Note 2E*
This may arise when it is thought likely that unless the person is arrested and then either taken in custody to the police station or granted 'street bail' to attend the station later, see *Note 2J*, further action considered necessary to properly investigate their involvement in the offence would be frustrated, unreasonably delayed or otherwise hindered and therefore be impracticable. Examples of such actions include:
    (i) interviewing the suspect on occasions when the person's voluntary attendance is not considered to be a practicable alternative to arrest, because for example:
      • it is thought unlikely that the person would attend the police station voluntarily to be interviewed.
      • it is necessary to interview the suspect about the outcome of other investigative action for which their arrest is necessary, see (ii) to (v) below.

- arrest would enable the special warning to be given in accordance with Code C paragraphs 10.10 and 10.11 when the suspect is found:
  - ˜ in possession of incriminating objects, or at a place where such objects are found;
  - ˜ at or near the scene of the crime at or about the time it was committed.
- the person has made false statements and/or presented false evidence;
- it is thought likely that the person:
  - ˜ may steal or destroy evidence;
  - ˜ may collude or make contact with, co-suspects or conspirators;
  - ˜ may intimidate or threaten or make contact with, witnesses. See *Notes 2F and 2G*

(ii) when considering arrest in connection with the investigation of an indictable offence (see *Note 6*), there is a need:
  - to enter and search without a search warrant any premises occupied or controlled by the arrested person or where the person was when arrested or immediately before arrest;
  - to prevent the arrested person from having contact with others;
  - to detain the arrested person for more than 24 hours before charge.

(iii) when considering arrest in connection with any *recordable offence* and it is necessary to secure or preserve evidence of that offence by taking fingerprints, footwear impressions or samples from the suspect for evidential comparison or matching with other material relating to that offence, for example, from the crime scene. See *Note 2H*

(iv) when considering arrest in connection with any offence and it is necessary to search, examine or photograph the person to obtain evidence. See *Note 2H*

(v) when considering arrest in connection with an offence to which the statutory Class A drug testing requirements in Code C section 17 apply, to enable testing when it is thought that drug misuse might have caused or contributed to the offence. See *Note 2I*.

(f) to prevent any prosecution for the offence from being hindered by the disappearance of the person in question.
This may arise when it is thought that:
  - if the person is not arrested they are unlikely to attend court if they are prosecuted;
  - the address given is not a satisfactory address for service of a summons or a written charge and requisition to appear at court because the person will not be at it for a sufficiently long period for the summons or charge and requisition to be served and no other person at that specified address will accept service on their behalf.

3 Information to be given on arrest

(a) Cautions—when a caution must be given

3.1 Code C paragraphs 10.1 and 10.2 set out the requirement for a person whom there are grounds to suspect of an offence (see *Note 2*) to be cautioned before being questioned or further questioned about an offence.

3.2 *Not used.*

3.3 A person who is arrested, or further arrested, must be informed at the time if practicable, or if not, as soon as it becomes practicable thereafter, that they are under arrest and of the grounds and reasons for their arrest, see paragraphs 2.2 and *Note 3*.

3.4 A person who is arrested, or further arrested, must be cautioned unless:
  (a) it is impracticable to do so by reason of their condition or behaviour at the time;
  (b) they have already been cautioned immediately prior to arrest as in *paragraph 3.1.*

(b) Terms of the caution (Taken from Code C section 10)

3.5 The caution, which must be given on arrest, should be in the following terms:
"You do not have to say anything. But it may harm your defence if you do not mention when questioned something which you later rely on in Court. Anything you do say may be given in evidence."
Where the use of the Welsh Language is appropriate, a constable may provide the caution directly in Welsh in the following terms:
"Does dim rhaid i chi ddweud dim byd. Ond gall niweidio eich amddiffyniad os na fyddwch chi'n sôn, wrth gael eich holi, am rywbeth y byddwch chi'n dibynnu arno nes ymlaen yn y Llys. Gall unrhyw beth yr ydych yn ei ddweud gael ei roi fel tystiolaeth."
See *Note 4*

3.6 Minor deviations from the words of any caution given in accordance with this Code do not constitute a breach of this Code, provided the sense of the relevant caution is preserved. See *Note 5*

3.7 *Not used.*

4 RECORDS OF ARREST

(a) General

4.1 The arresting officer is required to record in his pocket book or by other methods used for recording information:
  • the nature and circumstances of the offence leading to the arrest;
  • the reason or reasons why arrest was necessary;
  • the giving of the caution; and
  • anything said by the person at the time of arrest.

4.2 Such a record should be made at the time of the arrest unless impracticable to do. If not made at that time, the record should then be completed as soon as possible thereafter.

4.3 On arrival at the police station or after being first arrested at the police station, the arrested person must be brought before the custody officer as soon as practicable and a custody record must be opened in accordance with section 2 of Code C. The information given by the arresting officer on the circumstances and reason or reasons for arrest shall be recorded as part of the custody record. Alternatively, a copy of the record made by the officer in accordance with paragraph 4.1 above shall be attached as part of the custody record. See *paragraph 2.2* and *Code C paragraphs 3.4 and 10.3.*

Code **G**

4.4 The custody record will serve as a record of the arrest. Copies of the custody record will be provided in accordance with paragraphs 2.4 and 2.4A of Code C and access for inspection of the original record in accordance with paragraph 2.5 of Code C.

(b) Interviews and arrests

4.5 Records of interview, significant statements or silences will be treated in the same way as set out in sections 10 and 11 of Code C and in Codes E and F (audio and visual recording of interviews).

Notes for Guidance

1   *For the purposes of this Code, 'offence' means any statutory or common law offence for which a person may be tried by a magistrates' court or the Crown court and punished if convicted. Statutory offences include assault, rape, criminal damage, theft, robbery, burglary, fraud, possession of controlled drugs and offences under road traffic, liquor licensing, gambling and immigration legislation and local government byelaws. Common law offences include murder, manslaughter, kidnapping, false imprisonment, perverting the course of justice and escape from lawful custody.*

1A   *This code does not apply to powers of arrest conferred on constables under any arrest warrant, for example, a warrant issued under the Magistrates' Courts Act 1980, sections 1 or 13, or the Bail Act 1976, section 7(1), or to the powers of constables to arrest without warrant other than under section 24 of PACE for an offence. These other powers to arrest without warrant do not depend on the arrested person committing any specific offence and include:*

- *PACE, section 46A, arrest of person who fails to answer police bail to attend police station or is suspected of breaching any condition of that bail for the custody officer to decide whether they should be kept in police detention which applies whether or not the person commits an offence under section 6 of the Bail Act 1976 (e.g. failing without reasonable cause to surrender to custody);*
- *Bail Act 1976, section 7(3), arrest of person bailed to attend court who is suspected of breaching, or is believed likely to breach, any condition of bail to take them to court for bail to be re-considered;*
- *Children & Young Persons Act 1969, section 32(1A) (absconding)—arrest to return the person to the place where they are required to reside;*
- *Immigration Act 1971, Schedule 2 to arrest a person liable to examination to determine their right to remain in the UK;*
- *Mental Health Act 1983, section 136 to remove person suffering from mental disorder to place of safety for assessment;*
- *Prison Act 1952, section 49, arrest to return person unlawfully at large to the prison etc. where they are liable to be detained;*
- *Road Traffic Act 1988, section 6D arrest of driver following the outcome of a preliminary roadside test requirement to enable the driver to be required to provide an evidential sample;*
- *Common law power to stop or prevent a Breach of the Peace—after arrest a person aged 18 or over may be brought before a justice of the peace court to show cause why they should not be bound over to keep the peace—not criminal proceedings.*

1B   *Juveniles should not be arrested at their place of education unless this is unavoidable. When a juvenile is arrested at their place of education, the principal or their nominee must be informed. (From Code C Note 11D)*

2   Facts and information relevant to a person's suspected involvement in an offence should not be confined to those which tend to indicate the person has committed or attempted to commit the offence. Before making a decision to arrest, a constable should take account of any facts and information that are available, including claims of innocence made by the person, that might dispel the suspicion.

2A   Particular examples of facts and information which might point to a person's innocence and may tend to dispel suspicion include those which relate to the statutory defence provided by the Criminal Law Act 1967, section 3(1) which allows the use of reasonable force in the prevention of crime or making an arrest and the common law of self-defence. This may be relevant when a person appears, or claims, to have been acting reasonably in defence of themselves or others or to prevent their property or the property of others from being stolen, destroyed or damaged, particularly if the offence alleged is based on the use of unlawful force, e.g. a criminal assault. When investigating allegations involving the use of force by school staff, the power given to all school staff under the Education and Inspections Act 2006, section 93, to use reasonable force to prevent their pupils from committing any offence, injuring persons, damaging property or prejudicing the maintenance of good order and discipline may be similarly relevant. The Association of Chief Police Officers and the Crown Prosecution Service have published joint guidance to help the public understand the meaning of reasonable force and what to expect from the police and CPS in cases which involve claims of self defence. Separate advice for school staff on their powers to use reasonable force is available from the Department for Education.

2B   If a constable who is dealing with an allegation of crime and considering the need to arrest becomes an investigator for the purposes of the Code of Practice under the Criminal Procedure and Investigations Act 1996, the officer should, in accordance with paragraph 3.5 of that Code, "pursue all reasonable lines of inquiry, whether these point towards or away from the suspect. What is reasonable in each case will depend on the particular circumstances."

2C   For a constable to have reasonable grounds for believing it necessary to arrest, he or she is not required to be satisfied that there is no viable alternative to arrest. However, it does mean that in all cases, the officer should consider that arrest is the practical, sensible and proportionate option in all the circumstances at the time the decision is made. This applies equally to a person in police detention after being arrested for an offence who is suspected of involvement in a further offence and the necessity to arrest them for that further offence is being considered.

Code G

2D   Although a warning is not expressly required, officers should if practicable, consider whether a warning which points out their offending behaviour, and explains why, if they do not stop, the resulting consequences may make their arrest necessary. Such a warning might:
• if heeded, avoid the need to arrest, or
• if it is ignored, support the need to arrest and also help prove the mental element of certain offences, for example, the person's intent or awareness, or help to rebut a defence that they were acting reasonably.

A person who is warned that they may be liable to arrest if their real name and address cannot be ascertained, should be given a reasonable opportunity to establish their real name and address before deciding that either or both are unknown and cannot be readily ascertained or that there are reasonable grounds to doubt that a name and

address they have given is their real name and address. They should be told why their
name is not known and cannot be readily ascertained and (as the case may be) of the
grounds for doubting that a name and address they have given is their real name and
address, including, for example, the reason why a particular document the person has
produced to verify their real name and/or address, is not sufficient.

2E The meaning of "prompt" should be considered on a case by case basis taking account
of all the circumstances. It indicates that the progress of the investigation should not be
delayed to the extent that it would adversely affect the effectiveness of the investigation.
The arresting officer also has discretion to release the arrested person on 'street bail' as
an alternative to taking the person directly to the station. See Note 2J.

2F An officer who believes that it is necessary to interview the person suspected of committing the offence must then consider whether their arrest is necessary in order to carry out
the interview. The officer is not required to interrogate the suspect to determine whether
they will attend a police station voluntarily to be interviewed but they must consider
whether the suspect's voluntary attendance is a practicable alternative for carrying out
the interview. If it is, then arrest would not be necessary. Conversely, an officer who
considers this option but is not satisfied that it is a practicable alternative, may have
reasonable grounds for deciding that the arrest is necessary at the outset 'on the street'.
Without such considerations, the officer would not be able to establish that arrest was
necessary in order to interview.

Circumstances which suggest that a person's arrest 'on the street' would not be necessary to interview them might be where the officer:

- is satisfied as to their identity and address and that they will attend the police station voluntarily to be interviewed, either immediately or by arrangement at a future
  date and time; and
- is not aware of any other circumstances which indicate that voluntary attendance
  would not be a practicable alternative. See paragraph 2.9(e)(i) to (v).

When making arrangements for the person's voluntary attendance, the officer should
tell the person:

- that to properly investigate their suspected involvement in the offence they must be
  interviewed under caution at the police station, but in the circumstances their arrest
  for this purpose will not be necessary if they attend the police station voluntarily to
  be interviewed;
- that if they attend voluntarily, they will be entitled to free legal advice before, and to
  have a solicitor present at, the interview;
- that the date and time of the interview will take account of their circumstances and
  the needs of the investigation; and
- that if they do not agree to attend voluntarily at a time which meets the needs of the
  investigation, or having so agreed, fail to attend, or having attended, fail to remain
  for the interview to be completed, their arrest will be necessary to enable them to be
  interviewed.

2G When the person attends the police station voluntarily for interview by arrangement as
in Note 2F above, their arrest on arrival at the station prior to interview would only be
justified if:

- new information coming to light after the arrangements were made indicates that
  from that time, voluntary attendance ceased to be a practicable alternative and the
  person's arrest became necessary; and

- it was not reasonably practicable for the person to be arrested before they attended the station.

  If a person who attends the police station voluntarily to be interviewed decides to leave before the interview is complete, the police would at that point be entitled to consider whether their arrest was necessary to carry out the interview. The possibility that the person might decide to leave during the interview is therefore not a valid reason for arresting them before the interview has commenced. See Code C paragraph 3.21.

2H The necessity criteria do not permit arrest solely to enable the routine taking, checking (speculative searching) and retention of fingerprints, samples, footwear impressions and photographs when there are no prior grounds to believe that checking and comparing the fingerprints etc. or taking a photograph would provide relevant evidence of the person's involvement in the offence concerned or would help to ascertain or verify their real identity.

2I The necessity criteria do not permit arrest for an offence solely because it happens to be one of the statutory drug testing "trigger offences" (see Code C Note 17E) when there is no suspicion that Class A drug misuse might have caused or contributed to the offence.

2J Having determined that the necessity criteria have been met and having made the arrest, the officer can then consider the use of street bail on the basis of the effective and efficient progress of the investigation of the offence in question. It gives the officer discretion to compel the person to attend a police station at a date/time that best suits the overall needs of the particular investigation. Its use is not confined to dealing with child care issues or allowing officers to attend to more urgent operational duties and granting street bail does not retrospectively negate the need to arrest.

3 An arrested person must be given sufficient information to enable them to understand they have been deprived of their liberty and the reason they have been arrested, as soon as practicable after the arrest, e.g. when a person is arrested on suspicion of committing an offence they must be informed of the nature of the suspected offence and when and where it was committed. The suspect must also be informed of the reason or reasons why arrest is considered necessary. Vague or technical language should be avoided. When explaining why one or more of the arrest criteria apply, it is not necessary to disclose any specific details that might undermine or otherwise adversely affect any investigative processes. An example might be the conduct of a formal interview when prior disclosure of such details might give the suspect an opportunity to fabricate an innocent explanation or to otherwise conceal lies from the interviewer.

4 Nothing in this Code requires a caution to be given or repeated when informing a person not under arrest they may be prosecuted for an offence. However, a court will not be able to draw any inferences under the Criminal Justice and Public Order Act 1994, section 34, if the person was not cautioned.

5 If it appears a person does not understand the caution, the person giving it should explain it in their own words.

6 Certain powers available as the result of an arrest—for example, entry and search of premises, detention without charge beyond 24 hours, holding a person incommunicado and delaying access to legal advice—only apply in respect of indictable offences _and_ are subject to the specific requirements on authorisation as set out in PACE and the relevant Code of Practice.

Code G

Appendix 9

Code H: PACE Code of Practice in connection with the Detention, Treatment and Questioning by Police Officers of Persons in Police Detention under Section 41 of, and Schedule 8 to, The Terrorism Act 2000

The Treatment and Questioning by Police Officers of Detained Persons in respect of whom an Authorisation to Question after Charge has been given under Section 22 of the Counter-Terrorism Act 2008

(Summary)

This new Code H, brought into force at midnight on 10 July 2012, applies to all people in police detention following their arrest under section 41 of the Terrorism Act 2000 (TACT) as well as persons in respect of whom an authorization under section 22 of the Counter-Terrorism Act 2008 has been given after that date. It should be noted that it applies *only* to such detainees. Code C will continue to apply in respect of all other categories of detainee.

Many of the provisions mirror those to be found in Code C. For reasons of space therefore, Code H has not been reproduced in full here; rather, the table below sets out the equivalent Code C provisions. Where there is a minor difference, the effect of that difference has been commented upon. Where however there is a significant difference between the Codes, the relevant provision of Code H is set out in full. Direct quotes from Code H are shown italicized.

The full text of Code H can be found on at: http://police.homeoffice.gov.uk/operational-policing/powers-pace-codes/pace-code-intro/

Code H	Code C	Text and Commentary
1 General		
1.0	10.	
1.1		*This Code of Practice applies to, and only to: (a) persons in police detention after being arrested under section 41 of the Terrorism Act 2000 (TACT) and detained under section 41 of, or Schedule 8 to that Act and not charged, and (b) detained persons in respect of whom an authorisation has been given under section 22 of the Counter-Terrorism Act 2008 (post-charge questioning of terrorist suspects) to interview them in which case, section 15 of this Code will apply.*
1.2		*The provisions in PACE Code C apply when a person:* *(a) is in custody otherwise than as a result of being arrested section 41 of TACT or detained for examination under Schedule 7 to TACT;* *(b) is charged with an offence, or* *(c) is being questioned about any offence after being charged with that offence without an authorisation being given under section 22 of the Counter-Terrorism Act 2008.*
1.3		*In this Code references to an offence and to a person's involvement or suspected involvement in an offence where the person has not been charged with an offence, include being concerned, or suspected of being concerned in the commission, preparation or instigation of acts of terrorism.*
1.4		*The Code of Practice issued under paragraph 6 of Schedule 14 to TACT applies to persons detained for examination under Schedule 7 to TACT.*
1.5	1.1	
1.6		Commentary: There is no provision for bail under TACT prior to charge.
1.7	1.1A	
1.8	1.2	

Code **H**

1.9	1.3	
1.10	1.4	
1.11	1.5	
1.12	1.6	
1.13	1.7	
1.14	1.8	
1.15	1.9	
1.16	1.9A	
1.17	1.13	
1.18	1.14	
1.19	1.15	
1.20	1.16	
1.21	1.17	
Note 1A	Note 1A	
Note 1B	Note 1B	Commentary: Code H adds that a person should not be an appropriate adult if they are suspected of involvement in the offence or involvement in the commission, preparation or instigation of acts of terrorism.
Note 1C	Note 1C	
Note 1D	Note 1D	
Note 1E	Note 1E	
Note 1F	Note 1F	
Note 1G	Note 1G	
Note 1H	Note 1H	
Note 1I	Note 1I	

Code H	Code C	Text and Commentary
Note 1J	Note 1J	
Note 1K	Note 1K	
Note 1L		*If a person is moved from a police station to receive medical treatment, or for any other reason, the period of detention is still calculated from the time of arrest under section 41 of TACT (or, if a person was being detained under TACT Schedule 7 when arrested, from the time at which the examination under Schedule 7 began).*
Note 1M		*Under paragraph 1 of Schedule 8 to TACT, all police stations are designated for detention of persons arrested under section 41 of TACT. Paragraph 4 of Schedule 8 requires that the constable who arrests a person under section 41 takes them as soon as practicable to the police station which the officer considers is 'most appropriate'.*
Note 1N		*The powers under Part IV of PACE to detain and release on bail (before or after charge) a person arrested under section 24 of PACE for any offence (see PACE Code G (Arrest)) do not apply to persons whilst they are detained under the terrorism powers following their arrest/ detention under section 41 of, or Schedule 7 to, TACT. If when the grounds for detention under these powers cease the person is arrested under section 24 of PACE for a specific offence, the detention and bail provisions of PACE will apply and must be considered from the time of that arrest.*
2 Custody Records		
2.1	2.1A	Commentary: The two Codes are the same save that Code H applies to those persons brought to a police station following arrest under TACT section 41; who are arrested at a police station under that provision having gone there voluntarily; or who are detained for post-charge questioning under section 22 of the Counter-Terrorism Act 2008.
2.2	2.1	
2.3	2.2	
2.3A	2.3A	
2.4	2.3	
2.5	2.4	Commentary: Code H adds that arrangements for access must not unreasonably interfere with the custody officer's duties or the justifiable needs of the investigation.
2.6	2.4A	
2.7	2.5	Commentary: Code C permits the detainee, appropriate adult or legal representative to inspect the custody record after the detainee has left the police station. Code H permits such an inspection, once the detained person is no longer being held under the provisions of TACT section 41 and Schedule 8 or being questioned after charge as authorized under section 22 of the Counter-Terrorism Act 2008.

Code H

2.8	2.6, 2.6A	Commentary: Code H does not require the identities of officers or other police staff to be recorded or disclosed in the case of enquiries linked to the investigation of terrorism; warrant or other identification numbers should be used instead. See *Note 2A*
2.9	2.7	
Note 2A	Note 2A	*The purpose of paragraph 2.8 is to protect those involved in terrorist investigations or arrests of terrorist suspects from the possibility that those arrested, their associates or other individuals or groups may threaten or cause harm to those involved.*
3 Initial Action		
3.1	3.1	
3.2	3.2	
3.3	3.3	
3.4	3.4	Commentary: Under Code H, the custody officer must record that the person was arrested under s 41 of the Terrorism Act 2000 rather than recording a specific offence as under the equivalent provision in Code C. Code C requires the custody officer to record the grounds for detention and to notify the detainee of those grounds; there is no equivalent provision in this part of Code H.
3.5	3.5	
3.6	3.6	Commentary: Under Code H 3.6, in carrying out a risk assessment, the custody officer has to consider whether the detainee is likely to present a specific risk not only to the custody staff, but to any individual who may have contact with the detainee (*e.g. legal advisers, medical staff*) or themselves. In making this judgment it *will be necessary* (as opposed to Code C *may be necessary*) for the custody officer to obtain information from other sources, especially the investigation team.
3.7	3.7	
3.8	3.8	Commentary: Code H and Code C are substantially the same, but Code H adds that *The content of any risk assessment and any analysis of the level of risk relating to the person's detention is not required to be shown or provided to the detainee or any person acting on behalf of the detainee.*
3.8A	3.8A	
3.9	3.9	
3.10	3.10	
3.11	3.11	

Code H	Code C	Text and Commentary
3.12		*A constable, prison officer or other person authorised by the Secretary of State may take any steps which are reasonably necessary for:* *(a) photographing the detained person;* *(b) measuring him; or* *(c) identifying him.*
3.13		*Paragraph 3.12 concerns the power in TACT Schedule 8 paragraph 2. The power in TACT Schedule 8 paragraph 2 does not cover the taking of fingerprints, intimate samples or non-intimate samples, which is covered in TACT Schedule 8 paragraphs 10–15.*
3.14	3.12	
3.15	3.13	
3.16	3.14	
3.17	3.15	
3.18	3.17	
3.19	3.18	
3.20	3.19	
3.21	3.20	
3.22	3.23	
3.23	3.24	
Note 3A	Note 3A	
Note 3B	Note 3B	
Note 3C	Note 3C	
Note 3D	Note 3D	Commentary: There is no reference to footwear impressions in Code H.
Note 3E		*The investigation team will include any officer involved in questioning a suspect, gathering or analysing evidence in relation to the offences of which the detainee is suspected of having committed. Should a custody officer require information from the investigation team, the first point of contact should be the officer in charge of the investigation.*

Code **H**

Note 3F	Commentary: Code C additionally draws attention to the Guidance on Safer Detention & Handling of Persons in Police Custody.
Note 3G	*Arrests under TACT section 41 can only be made where an officer has reasonable grounds to suspect that the individual concerned is a 'terrorist'. This differs from the PACE power of arrest in that it need not be linked to a specific offence. There may also be circumstances where an arrest under TACT is made on the grounds of sensitive information which can not be disclosed. In such circumstances, the grounds for arrest may be given in terms of the interpretation of a 'terrorist' set out in TACT sections 40(1)(a) or 40(1)(b).*
Note 3H	*For the purpose of arrests under TACT section 41, the review officer is responsible for authorising detention (see paragraphs 14.1 and 14.2, and Notes for Guidance 14A and 14B). The review officer's role is explained in TACT Schedule 8 Part II. A person may be detained after arrest pending the first review, which must take place as soon as practicable after the person's arrest.*
Note 3I	

4 Detainee's Property

4.1	Commentary: Code H adds that the custody officer has responsibility for ascertaining what property a detainee has with them *either on first arrival at the police station or on any subsequent arrivals at a police station in connection with that detention.*
4.2	
4.3	
4.4	Commentary: This should be read with Note 4D in Code C
4.5	
Note 4A	
Note 4B	
Note 4C	
Note 4D	*Section 43(2) of TACT allows a constable to search a person who has been arrested under section 41 to discover whether he has anything in his possession that may constitute evidence that he is a terrorist.*

5 Right not to be Held Incommunicado

5.1	Commentary: Code H slightly alters the mirror provision in Code C. Code C permits the detainee to request that a person 'known to them' be informed of his arrest; Code H refers to a *named person who is a friend, relative or a person known to them.*
5.2	

Code H	Code C	Text and Commentary
5.3	5.3	Commentary: Code H adds that the right to have someone informed of the person's whereabouts, *does not afford such a right to a person on transfer to prison, where a detainee's rights will be governed by Prison Rules.*
5.4	5.4	*Custody Officers should liaise closely with the investigation team (see Note 3E) to allow risk assessments to be made where particular visitors have been requested by the detainee or identified themselves to police. In circumstances where the nature of the investigation means that such requests cannot be met, consideration should be given, in conjunction with a representative of the relevant scheme, to increasing the frequency of visits from independent visitor schemes. See Notes 5B and 5C*
5.5	5.5	
5.6	5.6	Commentary: Code H 5.6 together with Note 5G draws attention to the possibility that a detainee might seek to pass information detrimental to public safety or the investigation, and the need to carefully consider whether the detainee should be permitted to make a telephone call where that call is made in a language that cannot be readily understood.
5.7	5.7	
5.7A	5.7A	
5.8	5.8	
Note 5A	Note 5A	
Note 5B	Note 5B	*Custody Officers should bear in mind the exceptional nature of prolonged TACT detention and consider the potential benefits that visits may bring to the health and welfare of detainees who are held for extended periods.*
Note 5C		*Official visitors should be given access following consultation with the officer who has overall responsibility for the investigation provided the detainee consents, and they do not compromise safety or security or unduly delay or interfere with the progress of an investigation. Official visitors should still be required to provide appropriate identification and subject to any screening process in place at the place of detention.* *Official visitors may include:* • *An accredited faith representative* • *Members of either House of Parliament* • *Public officials needing to interview the prisoner in the course of their duties* • *Other persons visiting with the approval of the officer who has overall responsibility for the investigation* • *Consular officials visiting a detainee who is a national of the country they represent subject to Annex F* *Visits from appropriate members of the Independent Custody Visitors Scheme should be dealt with in accordance with the separate Code of Practice on Independent Custody Visiting.*
Note 5D	Note 5C	

Code **H**

Note 5E	Note 5D	
Note 5F	Note 5E	Commentary: Code H permits further calls to be made at the custody officer's discretion.
Note 5G		*The nature of terrorism investigations means that officers should have particular regard to the possibility of suspects attempting to pass information which may be detrimental to public safety, or to an investigation.*
6 Right to Legal Advice		
6.1	6.1	Commentary: Under Code H an appropriate adult if present must be told of the right to legal advice (from the duty solicitor) as well as the detainee.
6.2	6.3	
6.3	6.4	
6.4	6.5	
6.5		*An officer of the rank of Commander or Assistant Chief Constable may give a direction under TACT Schedule 8 paragraph 9 that a detainee may only consult a solicitor within the sight and hearing of a qualified officer. Such a direction may only be given if the officer has reasonable grounds to believe that if it were not, it may result in one of the consequences set out in TACT Schedule 8 paragraphs 8(4) or 8(5)(c). See Annex B paragraph 3 and Note 6I. A 'qualified officer' means a police officer who:* *(a) is at least the rank of inspector;* *(b) is of the uniformed branch of the force of which the officer giving the direction is a member; and* *(c) in the opinion of the officer giving the direction, has no connection with the detained person's case.* *Officers considering the use of this power should first refer to Home Office Circular 40/2003.*
6.6	6.5A	
6.7	6.6	
6.8	6.7	
6.9	6.8	
6.10	6.9	
6.11	6.10	
6.12	6.11	
6.13	6.12	

Code H	Code C	Text and Commentary
6.14	6.12A	
6.15	6.13	
6.16	6.14	
6.17	6.15	
6.18	6.16	
6.19	6.17	
Note 6ZA	Note 6ZA	
Note 6A	Note 6A	Commentary: At the end of Note 6A, Code H adds that *Nothing within this section is intended to prevent police from ascertaining immediately after the arrest of an individual whether a threat to public safety exists.*
Note 6B	Note 6B	Commentary: Note 6B in each Code sets out the applicable procedure for obtaining legal advice.
Note 6C	Note 6D	
Note 6D	Note 6E	
Note 6E	Note 6F	
Note 6F	Note 6G	
Note 6G	Note 6H	
Note 6H	Note 6I	
Note 6I	Note 6J	Commentary: Code H reiterates that even for detainees arrested under s 41 TACT, the right to consult privately with a solicitor is fundamental, unless a direction has been given under Schedule 8, paragraph 9 of the Terrorism Act 2000.
Note 6J	Note 6K	

7 Citizens of Independent Commonwealth Countries or Foreign Nationals

7.1	7.1	
7.2	7.2	
7.3	7.3	
7.4	7.4	

Code **H**

7.5	7.5	
Note 7A	Note 7A	
8 Conditions of Detention		
8.1	8.1	
8.2	8.2	
8.3	8.3	
8.4	8.4	
8.5	8.5	
8.6	8.6	Commentary: Not only should meals meet the dietary and religious needs of the detainee, but, adds Code H, *detainees should also be made aware that the meals offered meet such needs.*
8.7	8.7	Commentary: Code H adds that *Where facilities exist, indoor exercise shall be offered as an alternative if outside conditions are such that a detainee can not be reasonably expected to take outdoor exercise (e.g. in cold or wet weather) or if requested by the detainee for reasons of security.*
	8.8	*Where practicable, provision should be made for detainees to practice religious observance. Consideration should be given to providing a separate room which can be used as a prayer room. The supply of appropriate food and clothing, and suitable provision for prayer facilities, such as uncontaminated copies of religious books, should also be considered. See Note 8D*
8.9	8.9	
8.10		*Police stations should keep a reasonable supply of reading material available for detainees, including but not limited to, the main religious texts. See Note 8D. Detainees should be made aware that such material is available and reasonable requests for such material should be met as soon as practicable unless to do so would:* *(i) interfere with the investigation; or* *(ii) prevent or delay an officer from discharging his statutory duties, or those in this Code.* *If such a request is refused on the grounds of (i) or (ii) above, this should be noted in the custody record and met as soon as possible after those grounds cease to apply.*
8.11	8.9	
8.12	8.11	
Note 8A	Note 8A	Commentary: Code H adds that *If an officer needs to examine food or other items supplied by family and friends before deciding whether they can be given to the detainee, he should inform the person who has brought the item to the police station of this and the reasons for doing so.*

Code H	Code C	Text and Commentary
Note 8B	Note 8B	
Note 8C		*In light of the potential for detaining individuals for extended periods of time, the overriding principle should be to accommodate a period of exercise, except where to do so would hinder the investigation, delay the detainee's release or charge, or it is declined by the detainee.*
Note 8D		*Police forces should consult with representatives of the main religious communities to ensure the provision for religious observance is adequate, and to seek advice on the appropriate storage and handling of religious texts or other religious items.*

9 Care and Treatment of Detained Persons

Code H	Code C	Text and Commentary
9.1	9.1	*Notwithstanding other requirements for medical attention as set out in this section, detainees who are held for more than 96 hours must be visited by an appropriate healthcare professional at least once every 24 hours.*
9.2	9.2	
9.3	9.3	
9.4	9.4	
9.5	9.5	
9.6	9.5A	
9.7	9.5B	
9.8	9.7	
9.9	9.8	
9.10	9.9	
9.11	9.10	
9.12	9.11	
9.13	9.12	
9.14	9.13	
9.15	9.14	
9.16		

Code **H**

9.17	9.15	
9.18	9.16	
9.19	9.17	
Note 9A	Note 9A	
Note 9B	Note 9B	
Note 9C	Note 9C	
Note 9D	Note 9E	
Note 9E	Note 9F	
Note 9F	Note 9G	
Note 9G	Note 9H	
10 Cautions	10.1	Commentary: The examples given in Code C 10.1 of when a person need not be cautioned are not included in the mirror provision in Code H.
10.2	10.3	
10.3	10.4	
10.4	10.5	Commentary: The caution must also be given before post-charge questioning under section 22 of the Counter-Terrorism Act 2008.
10.5	10.6	
10.6	10.7	
10.7	10.8	
10.8	10.9	
10.9	10.10	
10.10	10.11	
10.10A	10.11A	

Code H	Code C	Text and Commentary
10.11	10.12	
10.12	10.13	
Note 10A	Note 10A	
Note 10B	Note 10B	
Note 10C	Note 10D	
Note 10D	Note 10E	
Note 10E	Note 10F	
Note 10F	Note 10G	
11 Interviews		
11.1	11.1A	*An interview in this Code is the questioning of a person arrested on suspicion of being a terrorist which, under paragraph 10.1, must be carried out under caution. Whenever a person is interviewed they must be informed of the grounds for arrest; see Note 3G*
11.2	11.1	*Commentary: Under Code H, a suspect arrested under s 41 TACT must not be interviewed except at a place designated for detention under Schedule 8 paragraph 1 of the Terrorism Act 2000 unless it is an urgent interview as in Code C.*
11.3	11.2	
11.4	11.4	
11.5	11.4A	
11.6	11.5	
11.7	11.6	
11.8		*Interviews of a person detained under section 41 of, or Schedule 8 to, TACT must be video recorded with sound in accordance with the Code of Practice issued under paragraph 3 of Schedule 8 to the Terrorism Act 2000, or in the case of post-charge questioning authorised under section 22 of the Counter-Terrorism Act 2008, the Code of Practice issued under section 25 of that Act.*
11.9	11.15	

Code **H**

11.10	11.17	Commentary: Code H adds that *The appropriate adult may be required to leave the interview if their conduct is such that the interviewer is unable properly to put questions to the suspect. This will include situations where the appropriate adult's approach or conduct prevents or unreasonably obstructs proper questions being put to the suspect or the suspect's responses being recorded. If the interviewer considers an appropriate adult is acting in such a way, they will stop the interview and consult an officer not below superintendent rank, if one is readily available, and otherwise an officer not below inspector rank not connected with the investigation. After speaking to the appropriate adult, the officer consulted will decide if the interview should continue without the attendance of that appropriate adult. If they decide it should not, another appropriate adult should be obtained before the interview continues, unless the provisions of paragraph 11.11 below apply.*
11.11	11.18	
11.12	11.19	
11.13	11.20	
Note 11A	Note 11A	
Note 11B	Note 11B	
Note 11C	Note 11C	
Note 11D		*Consideration should be given to the effect of extended detention on a detainee and any subsequent information they provide, especially if it relates to information on matters that they have failed to provide previously in response to similar questioning; see Annex G*
Note 11E	Note 11E	
12 Interviews in Police Stations		
12.1	12.1	
12.2	12.2	Commentary: In Code H the 24 hour time period runs from the time of their arrest or, if a person is detained under TACT Schedule 7, the time at which the examination under Schedule 7 began.
12.3	12.3	
12.4	12.4	
12.5	12.5	
12.6	12.6	
12.7	12.7	
12.8	12.8	

Code H	Code C	Text and Commentary
12.9		*During extended periods where no interviews take place, because of the need to gather further evidence or analyse existing evidence, detainees and their legal representative shall be informed that the investigation into the relevant offence remains ongoing. If practicable, the detainee and legal representative should also be made aware in general terms of any reasons for long gaps between interviews. Consideration should be given to allowing visits, more frequent exercise, or for reading and writing materials to be offered; see paragraph 5.4, section 8 and Note 12C.*
12.10	12.9	
12.11	12.10	
12.12	12.11	
12.13	12.12	
12.14	12.13	
12.15	12.14	
Note 12A	Note 12A	
Note 12B	Note 12B	
Note 12C		*Consideration should be given to the matters referred to in paragraph 12.9 after a period of over 24 hours without questioning. This is to ensure that extended periods of detention without an indication that the investigation remains ongoing do not contribute to a deterioration of the detainee's well-being.*
13 Interpreters		
13.1	13.1	
13.2	13.2	
13.3		Not used
13.4	13.4	
13.5	13.5	
13.6	13.6	
13.7		Not used
13.8	13.8	

Code **H**

13.9	13.9
13.10	13.10
13.11	13.11
Note 13A	Note 13A

14 Reviews and Extensions of Detention

14.1 The powers and duties of the review officer are in the Terrorism Act 2000, Schedule B, Part II. See Notes 14A and 14B. A review officer should carry out his duties at the police station where the detainee is held, and be allowed such access to the detainee as is necessary for him to exercise those duties.

14.2 For the purposes of reviewing a person's detention, no officer shall put specific questions to the detainee:

- regarding their involvement in any offence; or
- in respect of any comments they may make:
  - when given the opportunity to make representations; or
  - in response to a decision to keep them in detention or extend the maximum period of detention.

Such an exchange could constitute an interview as in paragraph 11.1 and would be subject to the associated safeguards in section 11 and, in respect of a person who has been charged see PACE Code C Section 16.8.

14.3 If detention is necessary for longer than 48 hours from the time of arrest (or if a person was being detained under TACT Schedule 7, from the time at which the examination under Schedule 7 began), a police officer of at least superintendent rank, or a Crown Prosecutor may apply for a warrant of further detention or for an extension or further extension of such a warrant under paragraph 29 or (as the case may be) 36 of Part III of Schedule 8 to the Terrorism Act 2000. See Note 14C.

14.4 When an application is made for a warrant as described in paragraph 14.3, the detained person and their representative must be informed of their rights in respect of the application. These include:

i) the right to a written notice of the application; See Note 14G.
ii) the right to make oral or written representations to the judicial authority/High Court judge about the application;
iii) the right to be present and legally represented at the hearing of the application, unless specifically excluded by the judicial authority/High Court judge;
iv) their right to free legal advice (see section 6 of this Code).

14.5 If the Detention of Terrorists Suspects (Temporary Extension) Bill is enacted and in force, a High Court judge may extend or further extend a warrant of further detention to authorise a person to be detained beyond a period of 14 days from the time of their arrest (or if they were being detained under TACT Schedule 7, from the time at which their examination under Schedule 7 began). The provisions of Annex J will apply when a warrant of further detention is so extended or further extended.

Code H	Code C	Text and Commentary
14.6		Not used
14.7		Not used
14.8		Not used
14.9		Not used
14.10		Not used
14.11	15.12	It is the responsibility of the officer who gives any reminders as at paragraph 14.4 to ensure that these are noted in the custody record, as well as any comments made by the detained person upon being told of those rights.
14.12	15.13	
14.13	15.15	
14.14	15.16	Commentary: Code H simply states that a record shall be made as soon as practicable about the outcome of each review, determination or application.
14.15		Not used
Note 14A		TACT Schedule 8 Part II sets out the procedures for review of detention up to 48 hours from the time of arrest under TACT section 41 (or if a person was being detained under TACT Schedule 7, from the time at which the examination under Schedule 7 began). These include provisions for the requirement to review detention, postponing a review, grounds for continued detention, designating a review officer, representations, rights of the detained person and keeping a record. The review officer's role ends after a warrant has been issued for extension of detention under Part III of Schedule 8.
Note 14B		A review officer may authorise a person's continued detention if satisfied that detention is necessary: a) to obtain relevant evidence whether by questioning the person or otherwise; b) to preserve relevant evidence; c) while awaiting the result of an examination or analysis of relevant evidence; d) for the examination or analysis of anything with a view to obtaining relevant evidence; e) pending a decision to apply to the Secretary of State for a deportation notice to be served on the detainee, the making of any such application, or the consideration of any such application by the Secretary of State; f) pending a decision to charge the detainee with an offence.

Code **H**

Note 14C	Applications for warrants to extend detention beyond 48 hours may be made for periods of 7 days at a time (initially under TACT Schedule 8 paragraph 29, and extensions thereafter under TACT Schedule 8, paragraph 36), up to a maximum period of 14 days (or 28 days if the Detention of Terrorists Suspects (Temporary Extension) Bill is enacted and in force) from the time of their arrest (or if they were being detained under TACT Schedule 7, from the time at which their examination under Schedule 7 began). Applications may be made for shorter periods than 7 days, which must be specified. The judicial authority or High Court judge may also substitute a shorter period if they feel a period of 7 days is inappropriate.
Note 14D	Unless Note 14F applies, applications for warrants that would take the total period of detention up to 14 days or less should be made to a judicial authority, meaning a District Judge (Magistrates' Court) designated by the Lord Chief Justice to hear such applications.
Note 14E	If by virtue of the relevant provisions described in Note 14C being enacted the maximum period of detention is extended to 28 days, any application for a warrant which would take the period of detention beyond 14 days from the time of arrest (or if a person was being detained under TACT Schedule 7, from the time at which the examination under Schedule 7 began), must be made to a High Court Judge.
Note 14F	If, when the Detention of Terrorists Suspects (Temporary Extension) Bill is enacted and in force, an application is made to a High Court Judge for a warrant which would take detention beyond 14 days and the High Court judge instead issues a warrant for a period of time which would not take detention beyond 14 days, further applications for extension of detention must also be made to a High Court judge, regardless of the period of time to which they refer.
Note 14G	TACT Schedule 8 Paragraph 31 requires a notice to be given to the detained person if a warrant is sought for further detention. This must be provided before the judicial hearing of the application for that warrant and must include: a) notification that the application for a warrant has been made b) the time at which the application was made c) the time at which the application is to be heard d) the grounds on which further detention is sought. A notice must also be provided each time an application is made to extend an existing warrant.
Note 14H	An officer applying for an order under TACT Schedule 8 Paragraph 34 to withhold specified information on which they intend to rely when applying for a warrant of further detention or the extension or further extension of such a warrant, may make the application for the order orally or in writing. The most appropriate method of application will depend on the circumstances of the case and the need to ensure fairness to the detainee.
Note 14I	After hearing any representations by or on behalf of the detainee and the applicant, the judicial authority or High Court judge may direct that the hearing relating to the extension of detention under Part III of Schedule 8 is to take place using video conferencing facilities. However, if the judicial authority requires the detained person to be physically present at any hearing, this should be complied with as soon as practicable. Paragraph 33(4) to (9) of TACT Schedule 8 govern the hearing of applications via video-link or other means.

Code H	Code C	Text and Commentary
Note 14J		Not used
Note 14K		Not used
15 Charging and post-charge questioning in terrorism cases		
15.1		*Charging of detained persons is covered by PACE and guidance issued under PACE by the Director of Public Prosecutions. Decisions to charge persons to whom this Code (H) applies, the charging process and related matters are subject to section 16 of PACE Code C.*
15.2		*Under section 22 of the Counter-Terrorism Act 2008, a judge of the Crown Court may authorise the questioning of a person about an offence for which they have been charged, informed that they may be prosecuted or sent for trial, if the offence:* • *is a terrorism offence as set out in section 27 of the Counter-Terrorism Act 2008; or* • *is an offence which appears to the judge to have a terrorist connection. See Note 15C. The decision on whether to apply for such questioning will be based on the needs of the investigation. There is no power to detain a person solely for the purposes of post-charge questioning. A person can only be detained whilst being so questioned (whether at a police station or in prison) if they are already there in lawful custody under some existing power. If at a police station the contents of sections 8 and 9 of this Code must be considered the minimum standards of treatment for such detainees.*
15.3		*The Crown Court judge may authorise the questioning if they are satisfied that:* • *further questioning is necessary in the interests of justice;* • *the investigation for the purposes of which the further questioning is being proposed is being conducted diligently and expeditiously; and* • *the questioning would not interfere unduly with the preparation of the person's defence to the charge or any other criminal charge that they may be facing.* *See Note 15E*
15.4		*The judge authorising questioning may specify the location of the questioning*
15.5		*The judge may only authorise a period up to a maximum of 48 hours before further authorisation must be sought. The 48-hour period would run continuously from the commencement of questioning. This period must include breaks in questioning in accordance with paragraphs 8.6 and 12.2 of this Code (see Note 15B).*
15.6		*Nothing in this Code shall be taken to prevent a suspect seeking a voluntary interview with the police at any time.*

Code **H**

15.7	For the purposes of this section, any reference in sections 6, 10, 11, 12 and 13 of this Code to: • 'suspect' means the person in respect of whom an authorisation has been given under section 22 of the Counter-Terrorism Act 2008 (post-charge questioning of terrorist suspects) to interview them; • 'interview' means post-charge questioning authorised under section 22 of the Counter-Terrorism Act 2008; • 'offence' means an offence for which the person has been charged, informed that they may be prosecuted or sent for trial and about which the person is being questioned; and • 'place of detention' means the location of the questioning specified by the judge (see paragraph 15.4), and the provisions of those sections apply (as appropriate), to such questioning (whether at a police station or in prison) subject to the further modifications in the following paragraphs:
15.8	In section 6 of this Code, for the purposes of post-charge questioning: • access to a solicitor may not be delayed under Annex B; and • paragraph 6.5 (direction that a detainee may only consult a solicitor within the sight and hearing of a qualified officer) does not apply.
15.9	In section 10 of this Code, unless the restriction on drawing adverse inferences from silence applies (see paragraph 15.10), for the purposes of post-charge questioning, the caution must be given in the following terms before any such questions are asked: "You do not have to say anything. But it may harm your defence if you do not mention when questioned something which you later rely on in Court. Anything you do say may be given in evidence." Where the use of the Welsh Language is appropriate, a constable may provide the caution directly in Welsh in the following terms: "Does dim rhaid i chi ddweud dim byd. Ond gall niweidio eich amddiffyniad os na fyddwch chi'n sôn, wrth gael eich holi, am rywbeth y byddwch chi'n dibynnu arno nes ymlaen yn y Llys. Gall unrhyw beth yr ydych yn ei ddweud gael ei roi fel tystiolaeth."
15.10	The only restriction on drawing adverse inferences from silence, see Annex C, applies in those situations where a person has asked for legal advice and is questioned before receiving such advice in accordance with paragraph 6.7(b).
15.11	In section 11, for the purposes of post-charge questioning, whenever a person is questioned, they must be informed of the offence for which they have been charged or informed that they may be prosecuted, or that they have been sent for trial and about which they are being questioned.
15.12	Paragraph 11.2 (place where questioning may take place) does not apply to post-charge questioning.
15.13	All interviews must be video recorded with sound in accordance with the separate Code of Practice issued under section 25 of the Counter-Terrorism Act 2008 for the video recording with sound of post-charge questioning authorised under section 22 of the Counter-Terrorism Act 2008 (see paragraph 11.8).
Note 15A	If a person is detained at a police station for the purposes of post-charge questioning, a custody record must be opened in accordance with section 2 of this Code. The custody record must note the power under which the person is being detained, the time at which the person was transferred into police custody, their time of arrival at the police station and their time of being presented to the custody officer.

Code H	Code C	Text and Commentary
Note 15B		*The custody record must note the time at which the interview process commences. This shall be regarded as the relevant time for any period of questioning in accordance with paragraph 15.5 of this Code.*
Note 15C		*Where reference is made to 'terrorist connection' in paragraph 15.2, this is determined in accordance with section 30 of the Counter-Terrorism Act 2008. Under section 30 of that Act a court must in certain circumstances determine whether an offence has a terrorist connection. These are offences under general criminal law which may be prosecuted in terrorism cases (for example explosives-related offences and conspiracy to murder). An offence has a terrorist connection (section 98 of the Act). Normally the court will make the determination during the sentencing process, however for the purposes of terrorism (section 98 of the Act). Normally the court will make the determination during the sentencing process, however for the purposes of post-charge questioning, a Crown Court Judge must determine whether the offence could have a terrorist connection.*
Note 15D		*The powers under section 22 of the Counter-Terrorism Act 2008 are separate from and additional to the normal questioning procedures within this code. Their overall purpose is to enable the further questioning of a terrorist suspect after charge. They should not therefore be used to replace or circumvent the normal powers for dealing with routine questioning.*
Note 15E		*Post-charge questioning has been created because it is acknowledged that terrorist investigations can be large and complex and that a great deal of evidence can come to light following the charge of a terrorism suspect. This can occur, for instance, from the translation of material or as the result of additional investigation. When considering an application for post-charge questioning, the police must 'satisfy' the judge on all three points under paragraph 15.3 are all met. It is important therefore, when making the application, to consider the following questions:* • *What further evidence is the questioning expected to provide?* • *Why was it not possible to obtain this evidence before charge?* • *How and why was the need to question after charge first recognised?* • *How is the questioning expected to contribute further to the case?* • *To what extent could the time and place for further questioning interfere with the preparation of the person's defence (for example if authorisation is sought close to the time of a trial)?* • *What steps will be taken to minimise any risk that questioning might interfere with the preparation of the person's defence?* *This list is not exhaustive but outlines the type of questions that could be relevant to any asked by a judge in considering an application.*

16 Testing Persons for the Presence of Specified Class A Drugs

16.1		*The provisions for drug testing under section 63B of PACE (as amended by section 5 of the Criminal Justice Act 2003 and section 7 of the Drugs Act 2005), do not apply to persons to whom this Code applies. Guidance on these provisions can be found in section 17 of PACE Code C.*

Annex A—Intimate and Strip Searches

1	1	

Code H

		Commentary
2	2	Commentary: The difference between Annex A 2 in Codes C and H is that under Code H, an intimate search can only be authorized where there are reasonable grounds for believing that the detainee may have something concealed upon them that could be used to cause physical injury, whereas under Code C, an intimate search can additionally be authorized in respect of Class A drugs.
3	2A	
4	3	
5	3A	
6	5	
7	6	
8	7	
9	8	
10	9	
11	10	
12	11	
13	12	
Note A1	Note A1	
Note A2	Note A2	
Note A3	Note A3	
Note A4	Note A4	
Note A5	Note A5	

Annex B—Delay in Notifying Arrest or Allowing Access to Legal Advice for Persons Detained Under the Terrorism Act 2000

1	1	Commentary: Note that Code H refers to a 'serious offence' rather than an indictable offence. Code H adds further possible grounds for delaying notification or access to legal advice, namely the possibility of: *(e) interference with the gathering of information about the commission, preparation or instigation of acts of terrorism, (f) the alerting of a person and thereby making it more difficult to prevent an act of terrorism, or (g) the alerting of a person and thereby making it more difficult to secure a person's apprehension, prosecution or conviction in connection with the commission, preparation or instigation of an act of terrorism.*

Code H	Code C	Text and Commentary
2	2	
3	3	
4	4	
5	5	
6	6	Commentary: The length of time for which rights can be delayed under Code H is 48 hours from the time of arrest or the time at which an examination under Schedule 7 began.
7	7	
8	13	
9	14	
10	15	
Note B1	Note B1	
Note B2	Note B2	
Note B3	Note B3	
Annex C—Restriction on Drawing Adverse Inferences from Silence and the Terms of the Caution when the Restriction Applies		
1	1	Commentary: Code H adds a proviso to 1(b); that being, unless post-charge questioning has been authorised in accordance with section 22 of the Counter-Terrorism Act 2008, in which case the restriction will apply only if the person has asked for legal advice, see section 6, paragraph 6.1, and is questioned before receiving such advice in accordance with paragraph 6.7(b). See paragraph 15.11
2	2	
3	3	
Note C1	Note C2	
Annex D—Written Statements Under Caution		
1	1	
2	2	

Code **H**

Annex E—Summary of Provisions Relating to Mentally Disordered and Otherwise Mentally Vulnerable People

3	3
4	4
5	5
6	6
7	7
8	8
9	9
10	10
11	11
12	12
1	1
2	2
3	3
4	4
5	5
6	7
7	8
8	9
9	11
10	12
11	13
Note E1	Note E1

Code H	Code C	Text and Commentary
Note E2	Note E2	
Note E3	Note E3	
Annex F—Not used		
Annex G—Fitness to be Interviewed		
1	1	
2	2	
3	3	
4	4	
5	5	
6	6	
7	7	
8	8	
Annex H—Detained Person: Observation List		
1	1	
2	2	
3	3	
Annex I	Annex L	Establishing Gender of Persons for the Purpose of Searching
Annex J		Transfer of Persons Detained for More than 14 Days to Prison

Code **H**

1	When a warrant of further detention is extended or further extended by a High Court judge to authorise a person's detention beyond a period of 14 days from the time of their arrest (or if they were being detained under TACT Schedule 7, from the time at which their examination under Schedule 7 began), the person must be transferred from detention in a police station to detention in a designated prison as soon as is practicable after the warrant is issued, unless: (a) the detainee specifically requests to remain in detention at a police station and that request can be accommodated, or (b) there are reasonable grounds to believe that transferring the detainee to a prison would: (i) significantly hinder a terrorism investigation; (ii) delay charging of the detainee or their release from custody, or (iii) otherwise prevent the investigation from being conducted diligently and expeditiously. Any grounds in (b)(i) to (iii) above which are relied upon for not transferring the detainee to prison must be presented to the senior judge as part of the application for the extension or further extension of the warrant. See Note J1.
2	If at any time during which a person remains in detention at a police station under the warrant, the grounds at (b)(i) to (iii) cease to apply, the person must be transferred to a prison as soon as practicable.
3	Police should maintain an agreement with the National Offender Management Service (NOMS) that stipulates named prisons to which individuals may be transferred under this paragraph. This should be made with regard to ensuring detainees are moved to the most suitable prison for the purposes of the investigation and their welfare, and should include provision for the transfer of male, female and juvenile detainees. Police should ensure that the Governor of a prison to which they intend to transfer a detainee is given reasonable notice of this. Where practicable, this should be no later than the point at which a warrant is applied for that would take the period of detention beyond 14 days.
4	Following a detainee's transfer to a designated prison, their detention will be governed by the terms of Schedule 8 to TACT 2000 and the Prison Rules and this Code of Practice will not apply during any period that the person remains in prison detention. The Code will once more apply if the person is transferred back from prison detention to police detention. In order to enable the Governor to arrange for the production of the detainee back into police custody, police should give notice to the Governor of the relevant prison as soon as possible of any decision to transfer a detainee from prison back to a police station. Any transfer between a prison and a police station should be conducted by police and this Code will be applicable during the period of transit. See Note 2]. A detainee should only remain in police custody having been transferred back from a prison, for as long as is necessary for the purpose of the investigation.
5	The investigating team and custody officer should provide as much information as necessary to enable the relevant prison authorities to provide appropriate facilities to detain an individual. This should include, but not be limited to: (i) medical assessments (ii) security and risk assessments (iii) details of the detained person's legal representatives (iv) details of any individuals from whom the detained person has requested visits, or who have requested to visit the detained person.

Code H	Code C	Text and Commentary
6		Where a detainee is to be transferred to prison, the custody officer should inform the detainee's legal adviser beforehand that the transfer is to take place (including the name of the prison). The custody officer should also make all reasonable attempts to inform: • family or friends who have been informed previously of the detainee's detention; and • the person who was initially informed of the detainee's detention in accordance with paragraph 5.1.
7		Any decision not to transfer a detained person to a designated prison under paragraph 1 must be recorded, along with the reasons for this decision. If a request under paragraph 1(a) is not accommodated, the reasons for this should also be recorded.
Note J1		Transfer to prison is intended to ensure that individuals who are detained for extended periods of time are held in a place designed for longer periods of detention than police stations. Prison will provide detainees with a greater range of facilities more appropriate to longer detention periods.
Note J2		This Code will only apply as is appropriate to the conditions of detention during the period of transit. There is obviously no requirement to provide such things as bed linen or reading materials for the journey between prison and police station.

Code **H**

Index